SECOND EDITION

Strategies for College Writing

A Rhetorical Reader

◆ ◆ ◆ ◆ ◆

ROBERT FUNK
Eastern Illinois University

LINDA S. COLEMAN
Eastern Illinois University

SUSAN X DAY
Iowa State University

Prentice
Hall

Upper Saddle River, New Jersey 07458

Library of Congress Cataloging-in-Publication Data

Strategies for college writing / [compiled by] Robert Funk, Linda S. Coleman, Susan X
Day.—2nd ed.
  p. cm.
  Includes index.
  ISBN 0-13-098255-5
  1. College readers. 2. English language—Rhetoric—Problems, exercises, etc. 3. Report
writing—Problems, exercises, etc. I. Funk, Robert. II. Coleman, Linda S. III. Day, Susan.

PE1417 .S7654 2003
808'.0427—dc21   2002017689

Editor-in-Chief: Leah Jewell
Senior Acquisitions Editor: Corey Good
Editorial Assistant: John Ragozzine
Executive Managing Editor: Ann Marie McCarthy
Production Liaison: Fran Russello
Project Manager: Linda B. Pawelchak
Asst. Manufacturing Manager: Mary Ann Gloridande
Cover Director: Jayne Conte
Cover Design: Bruce Kenselaar
Cover Image: Nina Frenkel/Getty Images, Inc./Artville LLC
Sr. Marketing Manager: Brandy Dawson
Copy Editing: Kathleen Lafferty/Roaring Mountain Editorial Services

Acknowledgments begin on page 554, which constitutes
a continuation of this copyright page.

This book was set in 10/12 Times Ten by Clarinda Company
and was printed and bound by RR Donnelley & Sons, Inc.
The cover was printed by Phoenix Color Corp.

©2003, 2000 by Pearson Education, Inc.
Upper Saddle River, New Jersey 07458

Printed in the United States of America
10 9 8 7 6 5 4 3 2 1

ISBN 0-13-098255-5

Pearson Education LTD, *London*
Pearson Education Australia PTY. Limited, *Sydney*
Pearson Education Singapore, Pte. Ltd
Pearson Education North Asia Ltd, *Hong Kong*
Pearson Education Canada, Ltd, *Toronto*
Pearson Educación de Mexico, S.A. de C.V.
Pearson Education—Japan, *Tokyo*
Pearson Education Malaysia, Pte. Ltd
Pearson Education, *Upper Saddle River, New Jersey*

Contents

◆ ◆ ◆ ◆ ◆

◆ CHAPTER **3**
Strategies for Discovering and Relating Experiences: Narration 33

◆ CHAPTER **4**
Strategies for Appealing to the Senses: Description   79

◆ CHAPTER **5**
Strategies for Making a Point: Exemplification   122

◆ CHAPTER **6**
Strategies for Explaining How Things Work: Process Analysis   177

◆ CHAPTER **7**
Strategies for Clarifying Meaning: Definition   223

◆ CHAPTER **8**
Strategies for Organizing Ideas and Experience: Division and Classification   268

◆ CHAPTER **9**

Strategies for Examining Connections: Comparison and Contrast   325

◆ CHAPTER **10**
Strategies for Interpreting Meaning: Cause and Effect 376

◆ CHAPTER 11
Strategies for Influencing Opinion: Argument   421

◆ CHAPTER 12
Further Readings: Two Thematic Clusters   492

APPENDIX
Using and Documenting Sources   517

Preface

◆ ◆ ◆ ◆ ◆

Strategies for College Writing, second edition, emphasizes the interconnectedness of reading and writing by teaching students to read with a writer's eye and to write with a reader's expectations. The book employs a set of innovative and coordinated activities that enable students to understand their roles as readers and to connect their reading experiences to their own writing. The numerous readings, pedagogical features, and writing topics give instructors the freedom to select from a broad range of assignments and approaches.

A Writer's Approach to Analytical Reading.   The opening chapter, "Engaged Reading," presents an effective and easy-to-use procedure for reading nonfiction from a writer's perspective. The chapter applies the familiar journalists' questions—*Who? What? Why? How?*—to the process of reading and analyzing essays. This approach shows students how to evaluate their roles as readers and how to respond to the rhetorical contexts of their reading assignments. To illustrate the procedure, the chapter contains a professional essay, along with the responses of a student using the *Who, What, Why,* and *How* questions to analyze that essay.

A Concise Survey of the Writing Process.   Chapter 2, "Writing from Reading," offers practical guidance on the primary tasks of the writing process: discovering, organizing, drafting, revising, and editing. This chapter also explains how students can connect their reading experiences to their own writing. A sample student essay—based on the *Who, What, Why,* and *How* analysis from Chapter 1—illustrates these connections.

A Contextual Study of Rhetorical Strategies.   Chapters 3 through 11 explain and illustrate the strategies that students use to organize and develop their college writing assignments: narration, description, exemplification, process analysis, definition, division and classification, comparison and contrast, cause and effect, and argument. The discussions of the individual strategies include these important pedagogical features:

♦ A **chapter introduction** presents each major rhetorical strategy in the context of a sample professional selection and a student essay written in response to that selection. The accompanying analysis points out how the student's thinking and writing have been influenced by the reading. These introductions provide advice on how to get started, how to organize and develop content, how to open and close the essay, and how to use the professional model.

♦ Brief **Writer's Workshop** activities, which can be done collaboratively, help students review the key rhetorical points for the two essays in the introduction.

♦ A **Checklist for Reading and Writing** at the end of each introduction sums up the major issues for understanding and applying each strategy.

♦ A detailed **Writing from Reading Assignment** follows the second professional selection in each chapter. Students are given step-by-step directions for designing an essay written in response to the professional selection.

♦ **Additional professional readings** provide further examples of each major strategy.

Interactive, Integrated Apparatus.   The connection between reading and writing is stressed in the apparatus that accompanies each of the professional selections:

♦ The **prereading apparatus** consists of a "preparing to read" question (which can be used as a journal prompt) and an introductory headnote.

♦ The **postreading apparatus** follows the *Who, What, Why,* and *How* approach established in the opening chapter. It includes "First Responses" (which could also be used for journal writing) and questions that explore voice and tone (*Who*), content and meaning (*What*), purpose (*Why*), and style and structure (*How*).

♦ Several **Ideas for Writing** direct students to try their hand at writing a short essay using the ideas and strategies they have examined in the professional selection.

◆ Each chapter ends with **Further Ideas for Using** the strategy. These topics include suggestions for **collaborative writing** and for **combining strategies.**

◆ **Internet activities,** part of the postreading apparatus, include suggestions for using the resources of the Internet to answer questions about the professional essays and to gather ideas and information for writing essays. A brief article on Internet use, "Twelve Tips to Search the Internet Successfully," appears at the end of Chapter 2.

This extensive apparatus gives teachers and students a wide variety of choices for exploring the reading-writing connection.

Varied, Thought-Provoking Readings.   The sixty-six professional selections have been chosen to illustrate the major rhetorical strategies used in nonfiction writing. They include essays and excerpts of various lengths and cover a wide range of styles and viewpoints. Each chapter begins with two relatively brief readings and then offers longer, more demanding selections for analysis and writing. The topics and issues are intended to engage students and stimulate their thinking. A special effort has been made to appeal to a cross section of readers by including a number of essays by women and multicultural writers. There is a mix of standard works and new selections.

The ten **student essays** are an important component of the book's pedagogy. They were written by college freshmen and sophomores employing the reading-writing approach that this book teaches. These essays demonstrate how student writers are able to use the ideas and strategies they encounter in professional readings by applying and adapting them to their own writing.

Other Features.   For instructors who want to correlate reading assignments or organize their course around issue-centered units, the **Thematic Table of Contents** groups the readings according to several common themes. Each group includes a pair of essays that can be studied together for the way they complement or challenge each other with their individual takes on a specific theme. The text also contains a **glossary** of useful rhetorical terms.

◆ WHAT'S NEW IN THE SECOND EDITION

New Readings.   Twenty-six new readings—more than a third of the selections—address a variety of current topics, from the ordinary (French fries, shopping) to the controversial (immigration, the Internet). Many of these new essays include proven favorites by Langston Hughes, Gary Soto, Joan Didion, Alice Walker, Diane Ackerman, Amy Tan, Lewis Thomas, John Holt, Stephanie Ericsson, Scott Russell Sanders, Barbara Ehrenreich, and

Bharati Mukherjee, whereas others introduce newer pieces by Malcolm Gladwell, William Finnegan, Phyllis Rose, Stephen King, Amy Wu, Steve Silberman, Claudia Dreifus, Ian Frazier, and Thad Williamson. Four of the ten student essays are also new to this edition.

Three Pro-Con Debates on New Topics in the Argument Chapter.   To meet the changing interests and concerns of both students and instructors, the chapter on argument now includes three debates: on the pros and cons of young people on the Internet, on daytime TV talk shows, and on the death penalty.

Appendix on Using and Documenting Sources.   The appendix offers concise but complete guidance on the use of secondary sources: using and incorporating quotations, avoiding plagiarism, and citing and documenting sources (including electronic sources) in the latest MLA style. The appendix also includes a sample documented student essay that uses nonfiction sources, the kind of research paper that undergraduates are frequently asked to write.

Two Thematic Clusters in Chapter 12.   This chapter presents a cluster of three essays on two provocative topics of current interest: immigration and sports.

Increased Instruction on Revision and Attention to Audience.   Chapter 2 (on the writing process) contains expanded coverage of the revising and editing stages, including suggestions for getting peer feedback and working in writing groups. The focus on audience has been augmented throughout the book.

Additional Suggestions for Using Computers and the Internet.   There are a number of new ideas for using the Internet to benefit both reading and writing, and advice on using the word processor is now included in Chapter 2.

Acknowledgments.   We want to extend our thanks to the many people who have helped to develop and produce this book, especially to our editors at Prentice Hall, Corey Good and his assistant John Ragozzine, and the production editor, Linda Pawelchak. We are also grateful for the perceptive criticisms and useful suggestions provided by our reviewers: Scott E. Alt, Goldey Beacom College; Dan Baldwin, Eastern Iowa Community College; Sandra Barnhill, South Plains College; Joy Barnes, J. Sargeant Reynolds Community College; Stephen Drinane, Rockland Community College;

Kathy Griffith Fish, Cumberland College; Tom Fish, Cumberland College; Bob Graham, Skagit Valley College; Mahbub Jamal, Prince George's Community College; Judy S. Kaplow, William Rainey Harper College; Ellen Lindeen, Waubonsee Community College; Timothy C. Miller, Millersville University; Lucille B. Motley, J. Sargeant Reynolds Community College; Zelda Provenzano, Drexel University; Gretchen Ronnow, Wayne State College; Debra Shein, Idaho State University; Derek Soles, Wichita State University; Bonnie L. Tensen, Seminole Community College; and Jackie Walsh, McNeese State University. Finally, we want to thank Bill, Casey, and Brian for their forbearance and loving support.

Robert Funk
Linda S. Coleman
Susan X Day

Thematic Table of Contents

♦ ♦ ♦ ♦ ♦

◆ BUILDING COMMUNITY

◆ RACE AND ETHNICITY

◆ SCIENCE, HEALTH, AND ECOLOGY

◆ GETTING AN EDUCATION

◆ THE WORKING LIFE

◆ PERSONAL SPACES

◆ WRITING AND SPEAKING

◆ RITUALS AND TRADITIONS

Engaged Reading

◆ ◆ ◆ ◆ ◆

Like a good conversation, successful reading or writing is a dynamic process, requiring both an articulate speaker and an active listener. The experience of being talked down to or of being listened to without being heard is all too common. These conversations are the ones people resent or, at best, forget as quickly as possible. By contrast, to enjoy the experience and to learn from it, both the reader and the writer must be aware of each other's needs, abilities, and motives. This chapter will explore the reader-writer relationship from the reader's point of view, outlining the goals of and steps to **engaged reading.** As a more aware reader, you will in turn improve the style and substance of your own writing.

◆ GETTING STARTED

Being open and staying focused are essential to a good first reading. Physical surroundings have much to do with these states of mind. Some people demand perfect silence in the early morning, a favorite chair, a carton of milk. Others seek out late-night, crowded coffee shops, enjoying the excitement of the busy world around them while being free to shut it out at will. The key is finding a time and place when the reading gets the attention it deserves and needs. Sometimes, of course, favorite settings may not be available, and focus will simply demand greater discipline, for example, if an article must be read off the Internet and the only computer available is in a crowded lab.

Travelers often feel more comfortable about and well prepared for trips to unfamiliar places if they study maps and read guidebooks. Looking ahead at reading selections will provide similar results. An essay's or Web site's **title** can sometimes offer immediate access to the writer's **subject,** goals, and attitudes. Other clues may be gained from notes about the author: what he or she does for a living, other things written by that author, or comments that he or she might have made about the essay you are about to read.

Where the **essay** was originally published can tell you the kind of reader the author most wanted to reach or can help you decide the reliability of the author's views. On the Internet, the Web address tells whether the site has an education connection (ends in "edu") or is sponsored by the government (ends in "gov"). Looking out for road signs and roadblocks is a good idea, too. Subheadings, charts, illustrations, footnotes, and definitions of unfamiliar terms may all be included in a reading, and it is useful to know where the help is and when the problems may arise.

Marking the Text

With printed texts, beginning with pen or pencil in hand is among the best ways to avoid passive reading. Whether you make comments in the margins of a book you plan to keep, stick Post-its in texts you plan to sell back, or take notes in a reading journal, you will remember more and understand more fully if you respond as you read. A simple "I disagree!" "Why did she do that?" "thesis?" "This reminds me of that Madonna song" can lead you back to the problem areas and can help you to outline the arguments the author is offering and your responses to them. Quick reminders might include placing question marks next to passages that cause confusion, circling words to look up in the dictionary, and underlining phrases and sentences that identify major ideas or examples. In particularly difficult or complex readings, making brief notes at the end of paragraphs or subsections is a good way to ensure that you understand a main point before moving on to the next. With electronic texts, whether e-books or Internet sources, you can either print out sections for note taking or save them to a file and make notes on the computer. It is a good idea to take your computer notes in a different font or to bold your comments for quick access.

◆ READING WITH A PLAN: *WHO? WHAT? WHY?* AND *HOW?*

Like the journalist always digging to completely understand a story and ever on the lookout for a story to tell, engaged readers ask questions of the things they read as well as of themselves as they read. The *Who, What, Why,* and *How* of both the writer and the reader can become a quick and simple way to understand a reading and use it as a springboard to your own writing. The following more specific questions, which focus on both the writer and the reader of an essay, will enable you to develop the habits of an engaged reader. After studying the questions, you will have the opportunity to practice their effectiveness while reading an essay by Deborah Tannen and then to compare your reactions with a fellow student's in-depth responses to the same essay.

EXPLORING *WHO?*

Writer: Who is the writer or speaker in the reading?
Reader: Who am I as I read this piece?

EXPLORING *WHAT?*

Writer: What primary and secondary ideas does the writer want to convey to me?
Reader: What connection do I have to these ideas?

EXPLORING *WHY?*

Writer: Why has the author decided to write on this subject?
Reader: Why do I respond the way I do to this reading? Why might others respond differently?

EXPLORING *HOW?*

Writer: How is the essay organized and developed?
Reader: How might I adapt these strategies to my own immediate writing goals?

To discover how this approach to reading works, read the following essay and then record your responses to the *Who, What, Why,* and *How* questions. As you read, notice the way an active reader has marked the essay to emphasize major points, remind herself of words to look up, and respond to Tannen's ideas.

Gender Gap in Cyberspace

DEBORAH TANNEN

Deborah Tannen, professor of linguistics at Georgetown University, writes academic and popular articles on how men and women communicate with one another. In this essay, which appeared in *Newsweek* in 1994, Tannen focuses attention on the ways in which cyberspace helps to reveal our everyday gender differences to us.

I was a computer pioneer, but I'm still something of a novice. That paradox is telling.

Starts with a "mystery"

I was the second person on my block to get a computer. The first was my colleague Ralph. He helped me get started and went on to become a maven, reading computer magazines, hungering for the new technology he read about, and buying and mastering it as quickly as he could afford. I hung on to old equipment far too long because I dislike giving up what I'm used to, fear making the wrong decision about what to buy, and resent the time it takes to install and learn a new system.

a comparison & contrast?

me too!

My first Apple came with videogames; I gave them away. Playing games on the computer didn't interest me. If I had free time I'd spend it talking on the telephone to friends.

Shows her priorities

Ralph got hooked. His wife was often annoyed by the hours he spent at his computer and the money he spent upgrading it. My marriage had no such strains—until I discovered e-mail. Then I got hooked. E-mail draws me the same way the phone does: it's a souped-up conversation.

Now a man's point of view?

nice phrase

E-mail deepened my friendship with Ralph. Though his office was next to mine, we rarely had extended conversations because he is shy. Face to face he mumbled so, I could barely tell he was speaking. But when we both got on e-mail, I started receiving long, self-revealing messages; we poured our hearts out to each other. A friend discovered that e-mail opened up that kind of communication with her father. He would never talk much on the phone (as her mother would), but they have become close since they both got on line.

Why, I wondered, would some men find it easier to open up on e-mail? It's a combination of the technology (which they enjoy) and the (obliqueness) of the written word, just as many men will reveal feelings in dribs and drabs while riding in the car or doing something, which they'd never talk about sitting face to face. It's too intense, too bearing-down on them, and once you start you have to keep going. With a computer in between, it's safer.

Good question

This sounds familiar!

It was on e-mail, in fact, that I described to Ralph how boys in groups often struggle to get the upper hand whereas girls tend to maintain an appearance of cooperation. And he pointed out that this explained why boys are more likely to be captivated by computers than girls are. Boys are typically motivated by a social structure that says if you don't dominate you will be dominated. Computers, by their nature, balk; you type a perfectly appropriate command and it refuses to do what it should. Many boys and men are incited by this defiance: "I'm

All boys & girls?

going to whip this into line and teach it who's boss! I'll get *Uses dialogue for both sides* it to do what I say!" (and if they work hard enough, they always can). Girls and women are more likely to respond, "This thing won't cooperate. Get it away from me!"

Although no one wants to think of herself as "typ- *Yes!* ical"—how much nicer to be (*sui generis*)—my relationship to my computer is—gulp—fairly typical for a

Main idea? { woman. Most women (with plenty of exceptions) aren't excited by tinkering with the technology, grappling with the challenge of eliminating bugs or getting the biggest and best computer. These dynamics appeal to many men's interest in making sure they're on the top side of the inevitable who's-up-who's-down struggle that life is for them. E-mail appeals to my view of life as a contest *"You Have Mail"* for connections to others. When I see that I have fifteen messages, I feel loved.

I once posted a technical question on a computer network for linguists and was flooded with long dispositions, some pages long. I was staggered by the generosity and the expertise, but wondered where these guys found the time—and why all the answers I got were from men.

Like coed classrooms and meetings, discussions on e-mail networks tend to be dominated by male voices, unless they're specifically women-only, like single-sex schools. On line, women don't have to worry about getting the floor (you just send a message when you feel like

Calls on other linguists { it), but, according to linguists Susan Herring and Laurel Sutton, who have studied this, they have the usual problems of having their messages ignored or attacked.

The anonymity of public networks frees a small number of men to send long, (vituperative) sarcastic messages that many other men either can tolerate or actually enjoy, but that turn most women off.   *Why?*

The anonymity of networks leads to another sad part of the e-mail story: there are men who (deluge) women with questions about their appearance and invitations to sex. On college campuses, as soon as women students log on, they are bombarded by references to sex, like going to work and finding pornographic posters adorning the walls.   *Sexual harassment?*

Most women want one thing from a computer—to work. This is significant counterevidence to the claim that men want to focus on information while women are interested in rapport. That claim I found was often true in casual conversation, in which there is no particular information to be conveyed. But with computers, it is often women who are more focused on information, because they don't respond to the challenge of getting equipment to submit.

Once I had learned the basics, my interest in computers waned. I use it to write books (though I never mastered having it do bibliographies or tables of contents) and write checks (but not balance my checkbook). Much as I'd like to use it to do more, I begrudge the time it would take to learn.   *Time use— another main idea*

Ralph's computer expertise costs him a lot of time. Chivalry requires that he rescue (novices) in need, and he is called upon by damsel novices far more often than   *?*

(knaves.) More men would rather study the instruction booklet than ask directions, as it were, from another person. "When I do help men," Ralph wrote (on e-mail, of course), "they want to be more involved. I once installed a hard drive for a guy, and he wanted to be there with me, wielding the screwdriver and giving his own advice where he could." Women, he finds, usually are not interested in what he's doing; they just want him to get the computer to the point where they can do what they want.

Nice sense of humor

Is that true for me?

Which pretty much explains how I managed to be a pioneer without becoming an expert.

Circles back to Intro

◆ ◆ ◆

◆ USING *WHO? WHAT? WHY?* AND *HOW?*

We asked Jennifer Hoff, a freshman student, to use the *Who, What, Why,* and *How* questions to better understand Tannen as a writer and herself as a reader, digging deeper into her own initial understanding and extending what she learned from her reading into practical lessons for her own writing. Her responses are spontaneous and unedited, meant for her own use rather than to communicate final thoughts to someone else. As you read, compare your responses to Jennifer's.

Exploring Who?

Writer

Who is the writer or speaker in the reading?

The writer or speaker is a married woman, writing in first person, and telling of her experiences with computers and men. The speaker is real, not just a made up character. She seems to be sociable, understanding, inquisitive, and capable of a sense of humor. She is projecting a voice she feels is "typical" of many women in the battle of miscommunication between men and women. She is not trying to say that women are better than men at communicating; they just like to engage in it more. She also has a humorous side to her essay which makes it easier to agree with and relate to in some way.

Reader

Who am I as I read this piece?

I am a female, freshman college student who is eighteen years old. Personally, I am drawn in by this voice. I can relate to her because I like to talk everything out and have that "souped-up conversation." I too have that feeling of being loved when I have new e-mail. I am also that "typical" woman who is happy knowing just enough to get my personal tasks done and I have no problem with asking for help.

I would like to use her voice and style in my own writing. She tries not to alienate anyone. She accepts Ralph for who he is and she includes Ralph in her essay as an example for men. As I am writing, I could pretend that I am simply talking to someone else, sort of like if someone only heard one side of a conversation.

Exploring **What?**

Writer

What primary and secondary ideas does the writer want to convey to me?

The writer wants me to understand that men and women communicate differently in style, length, and other ways. Her secondary ideas revolve around her primary ones; they include many examples of how men and women communicate differently. For example, most women enjoy long talks, either face to face or on the phone, where they can unleash their feelings, dreams, or maybe just gossip. Most men fear intimate conversations that involve emotions. However, a secondary idea that the writer also conveys is that not all people fall under the category of these typical men and women.

Reader

What connection do I have to these ideas?

I am also a very open person and would rather talk everything out. I have experienced listening to unemotional, tough guy voices on the phone or in person but then reading e-mail that is full of feeling, excitement, and sincerity from that same person. Since I started college, I only use the computer for writing papers and using e-mail.

Tannen writes for both a male and female audience but there may be different consequences for different readers. For me, the consequences are going away entertained and being able to relate to another woman. I also can accept that men and women communicate differently and you have to roll with it instead of trying to change who people are.

In my writing, I like to elaborate on my thoughts and emotions but I also don't want to offend anyone. I guess I try to make everyone happy or to make sure I've covered everything, sometimes giving too much information. I think that if I wrote about the difficulty of communicating between men and women I would want feedback to hear how different people handled different communication problems. Just like Tannen, I would attempt to find answers or finally be willing to accept the differences between men and women.

Exploring **Why?**

Writer

Why has the author decided to write on this subject?
Her specialty is in sociolinguistics. Therefore, she likes to dwell on the different ways men and women communicate and ways to better those communication lines. The writer's purpose seems to be in combining a simple, entertaining story about a woman's experience with computers with an underlying lesson of how men and women communicate differently and ways they can understand each other better. The writer is not trying to have her essay be a battle between the stereotypical man and woman.

Reader

Why do I respond the way I do to this reading? Why might others respond differently?
I was entertained. I definitely could relate to her ideas. I want to be able to understand both men and women better. I also want to be able to express my ideas to other people better. My next step would be to try to accept that men and women just are the way they are and not let that make or break my day.

Exploring **How?**

Writer

How is the essay organized and developed?
The essay is organized as one side of a conversation. She is telling the readers how she sees the communication world. She also brings in experts in linguistics to back up her ideas. She is descriptive and full of examples to back up her views. She uses parentheses for little additions that tell the reader what she is thinking, to create humor or to clarify that some people are exceptions to the so-called typical. She tries to not be sexist by bringing in Ralph. She uses writing techniques such as changing the words "men and women" to "boys and girls," possibly to indicate that communication problems occur throughout life. Many times the writer will start off a section of her essay with a question and then elaborate on an answer through personal examples. Some of her

questions remain unanswered as if she is hoping that guys might get back to her with answers to some of her questions.

Reader

How might I adapt these strategies to my own immediate writing goals?
I can adapt these strategies by providing a medium for all readers to relate to. I should try to focus on a specific supporting point but I can also include other ideas around the main idea to make my writing more entertaining and intriguing.

◆ MAKING THE READING-WRITING CONNECTION

How did your reactions to Tannen's essay compare to Jennifer's? As you followed Jennifer's responses, did you notice how she elaborates on her answers, not just stopping with her first thoughts but explaining and looking for concrete examples and additional ideas? You see this in the "Who am I as I read this piece" section, for example. Jennifer begins by noting that she relates to Tannen because they are both female, but then zeros in on specifics, such as how good she feels when she gets e-mail. Note also that Jennifer's thinking builds on itself as she moves from question to question, with ideas such as the one about the "typical" woman becoming unifying devices or touchstones for her reactions. By the time she asks herself if she can use the kind of voice Tannen has used, Jennifer is really ready to apply what she has learned to how she might achieve her own best writing voice.

Notice, too, that the questions not only require Jennifer to look closely at her own responses, but also prompt her to see how others would respond to Tannen. This exploration leads her to conclude that she might test her thoughts by talking with others, for example, a male friend or fellow student. She might also want to talk with someone not familiar with e-mail. This informal research would expand her understanding of male/female communication and help her to think about her own future writing on the topic and her readers' responses to it. In fact, by the end of the *What?* questions, Jennifer has staked out her own territory on the topic and is ready to look at the *Why?* and *How?* for a more precise sense of purpose and organization.

In the *How?* section of her discovery writing, Jennifer very successfully captures Tannen's tone and the overall shape of her essay when she characterizes it as being "one side of a conversation." She also pays close attention to Tannen's use of questions as part of this strategy and to the importance of using personal examples to answer at least some of her questions. By reading Tannen's essay so closely, Jennifer has added to her own bag of writing tricks.

In all but one case, Jennifer attempts to answer questions even when they might at first seem to overlap with other questions or answers already given. Asking questions from several different directions is like looking through a prism—the center is the same, but it becomes slightly different when viewed from each unique angle. By answering these diverse and comprehensive questions, Jennifer has discovered how personal this topic has become and is able to see that the bottom line for her is not wanting "to follow along that line of having miscommunication make or break my day," a clever use of the Clint Eastwood movie line, but also a very specific and important goal.

Developing the Habit

Using the *Who, What, Why,* and *How* questions is one of many ways to better understand what you read and in turn to communicate more effectively with others. It is important at the start to write out your full responses, as Jennifer did, which will make this reading style a habit of mind, so that in future readings you will find yourself asking the questions *as* you read, making the reading process more interesting because you are having active and informed conversation with the author. In the remaining chapters of this book, at the conclusion of each essay, you will find specific *Who, What, Why,* and *How* questions to help you practice this reading technique and develop in-depth responses. Your answers will be valuable for reviewing essays before class as well as for setting your mind to work on similar topics and strategies for achieving your personal writing goals. In short, engaging in active reading provides a solid foundation for successful writing, as the next chapter will explain.

◆ USING THE CORE STRATEGIES

Strategies for College Writing will also introduce you to professional and student models of the nine modes of organization that are the building blocks of most writing you will undertake in your personal, civic, and professional lives. Once familiar with these strategies, you can identify the method an author is employing to help you understand more quickly and fully the *Who, What, Why,* and *How* of an essay. As a writer, you can call on one or more of the strategies to solve the organizational challenges of particular writing assignments or to accomplish specific goals with individual topics and tasks. Here is a brief description of the purpose or purposes each strategy can achieve and some specific applications:

- *Narration:* Tells what happens over time; for example, a letter home from college after the first week of the first semester or a recounting of a Civil War battle for American History 101

- *Description:* Tells how something looks, acts, sounds, feels, smells, or tastes; for example, a travel journal kept while visiting Alaska or a lab report on a visit to a local swamp for an ecology class

- *Exemplification:* Explains and clarifies a generalization through illustration; for example, a feature story on athletes who work with local charities or an essay on the role of tourism in the Delta states

- *Process analysis:* Tells how to do something or how something functions; for example, a brochure on how to run a successful restaurant or a set of instructions for setting up an e-mail account

- *Definition:* Explains the meanings of words, concepts, objects, or phenomena; for example, a chapter on good parenting in a high school consumer studies textbook or a job description of what a marketing specialist does

- *Division and classification:* Imposes or reveals order and makes ideas more understandable; for example, a movie guide on types of American films or an educational Web site on kinds of learning disabilities

- *Comparison and contrast:* Purposefully directs a reader's attention to similarities and differences; for example, an architect's analysis of possible sites for a new mall or a sociology project on the immigration experiences of Asians and Hispanics

- *Cause and effect:* Traces the *why* to reveal the root of a problem or to illuminate the consequence of an action; for example, a museum guide to an exhibit on the environmental impact of a volcano or a research paper on why so few female students major in math or certain types of science

- *Argument:* Seeks to persuade readers to think and act in agreement with the writer's opinion; for example, a book arguing for the need for international cooperation on global warming or a letter to the school paper requesting increased coverage of nontraditional sports

▪️ *Internet Activity.* Deborah Tannen has given several interviews that are available online. To learn more about Tannen's research on the relationship between gender and communication, locate some of these interviews and read them. Links to several online chats and audio interviews are listed on Tannen's Web site at www.georgetown.edu/faculty/tannend/interviews.htm. Your instructor might ask you to report back to the class with information and insights you gathered about Tannen's work.

◆ ◆ ◆ ◆ ◆ ◆ ◆ ◆ C H A P T E R 2 ◆ ◆ ◆ ◆ ◆ ◆ ◆ ◆

Writing from Reading

◆ ◆ ◆ ◆ ◆

The connections between reading and writing are strong: in both activities you use language to create meaning. In Chapter 1, you explored the reader-writer relationship from the reader's point of view and saw how writing can help you to understand and remember what you read. In this chapter, you will see how reading can help you to improve your writing.

◆ DEVELOPING YOUR WRITING SKILLS

As you read the essays in this book, you will be shaping and developing your writing skills. Reading can supply you with content for your own writing; you will discover new ideas and new ways of thinking about the world. Even when you already have a topic in mind, reading can help you come up with the materials to enlarge and support that topic.

As you read, you will also encounter a wide range of writing styles, ways to approach a topic, and methods for organizing and presenting ideas. Most of the time, you don't pay much attention to these features: they just seep into your mind with the rest of the material. In this textbook, however, you will examine the reading-writing connection more consciously than you have probably ever done before. By asking questions about the texts you read (Why did the author begin this way? What is the point of this comparison? How does this example work?), you will see how a writer puts an essay together, and that knowledge will help you to plan and develop your own essays.

◆ CONSTRUCTING AN ESSAY

Writing an **essay** is a lot like building a house. A writer fits separate pieces of meaning together to make an understandable statement. If you want to write well, you need to learn the basic skills of constructing an essay.

Despite differences in education and personality, most writers follow a remarkably similar process of *discovering, organizing, drafting, revising,* and *editing.* Whether building a single paragraph or a ten-page article, successful writers usually follow a series of steps that go roughly like this:

1. Find a topic, generate ideas, and collect information. (Discovering)
2. Focus on a central idea and map out an approach. (Organizing)
3. Write a first draft. (Drafting)
4. Rework and improve the draft. (Revising)
5. Proofread and correct mechanical errors. (Editing)

If you follow these steps, you will be able to write more productively and more easily. The process will give you a sense of direction for producing a well-written essay. But keep in mind that this sequence is only a general guide. The steps often overlap and loop around. For example, you might begin by reading and gathering information, then skip ahead to drafting, stop to check the organization, add more examples, then do some more planning and edit some sentences before continuing with the draft. The important point to remember is that writing is done in stages; successful writers take the time to construct their essays step by step and to polish and finish their work.

Generating Ideas

One of the most difficult challenges of writing is coming up with a topic. Even when you are responding to a reading, you still have to decide what to say about it. As you saw in Chapter 1, the *Who, What, Why,* and *How* questions not only help you gain a better understanding of what you read, but they also unlock your own thinking about a topic and lead you to discover ideas and viewpoints to write about. Writing out your responses to the *Who, What, Why,* and *How* questions will produce a wide range of thoughts and impressions that you can draw on for your own essays. These questions will also lead you to examine and perhaps adopt a writer's strategies and techniques. Thinking about **audience, purpose, tone,** organization, and use of language will help you make important decisions about the style and approach you want to use in your writing.

As you review your responses to the *Who, What, Why,* and *How* questions, try to identify a **subject** area that appeals to you. Many writers begin with a general topic, which they narrow and refine as they work. For example, you might start out writing about tennis, shift to recent improvements in equipment, and end up focusing on the way metal racquets have changed the game. One good way to sift through a broad topic is to do some brainstorming about it.

Brainstorming involves making a list of everything you can think of about a topic. You might list feelings, ideas, facts, examples, personal experiences, problems—anything that comes to mind. There is no need to write in sentences; just jot down words and phrases. Don't try to organize your thoughts; just list them as they occur to you. If you give yourself a time limit, you'll find that ideas come faster that way. You can also brainstorm with classmates or friends. You'll discover that their ideas help to trigger more of yours. When you've finished brainstorming, reread your list and mark promising ideas.

Having read "Gender Gap in Cyberspace" in Chapter 1, Jennifer Hoff wanted to write about the differences in the way males and females go about performing some activity, so she used brainstorming to look for a specific area to focus on.

what do men and women talk about?

how do they behave differently in some situations?

at parties

on dates

at concerts

at sports events

when talking to members of the opposite sex

when talking to members of the same sex

one-on-one vs. in groups

with their parents and families

on the telephone

in classes and in the dorm

at church or at weddings or funerals

do men have heart-to-heart talks?

gossip, small talk

jokes and pranks—any differences?

Making this list helped Jennifer identify several specific situations she could use. The brainstorming also stirred up memories of some observations she had made at the time of her grandmother's death. She now had an idea she could focus on for her essay: the different ways that men and women behave at funerals.

If brainstorming doesn't help you settle on a topic, you can try other strategies: talking into a tape recorder, discussing ideas with your instructor or classmates, interviewing someone with expertise in the subject, surfing the Internet, or rereading your answers to the *Who, What, Why,* and *How* questions. You can also try shifting the **focus** of your topic or coming up with a different one. The point is to keep working until you can find something that you'd like to write about and that fits your assignment.

Making a Plan

Once you have reviewed your responses to the *Who, What, Why,* and *How* questions and have done some brainstorming to find a topic, you need to decide on a specific focus for your paper. One way to find direction for your writing is to ask yourself, "What point do I want to make?" The answer to this question will lead you to your main idea, or **thesis.** After you decide what point you want to make, you can then sort through your notes and decide which details to use and which ones to toss.

A thesis says something *about* the subject of an essay. As a reader, your job is to discover the writer's thesis. The answers to the *What* and *Why* questions will direct you to a writer's main ideas. As a writer, your job is to provide a clear thesis for your readers. Look at the difference between a subject and a thesis in these examples:

Subject: Differences in the ways men and women use computers
Thesis: Men want to master a computer's technology; women just want the thing to work.

Subject: Communication styles of males and females
Thesis: Males often struggle to get the upper hand in a conversation, while women tend to maintain an appearance of cooperation.

You can, of course, change or refine your thesis as the paper develops, but having an idea of what you want to say makes the actual writing considerably easier.

Organizing Your Ideas

Having a plan or scratch outline to follow makes you less likely to wander from your main idea and allows you to concentrate on one idea at a time as you write. You can begin by making a list of all the points you want to cover in your essay. Review the list and cross off any ideas that don't fit or points that are too similar to other points. Then revise your list, putting the ideas in the order you plan to cover them. Specific organizational strategies will be discussed in later chapters; but, in general, if there is no chronology (time order) involved or there are no steps that belong in a certain order, begin with a fairly important and interesting point to get your readers' attention and end with your strongest point to leave your audience feeling that you have said something worthwhile. The following brief outline is based on the thesis that Jennifer devised after reviewing her brainstorming ideas:

> *Thesis:* Because people respond to death in the same way they cope with life, men and women handle it differently.

1. Opening--grandma's death

   Phone calls from friends:

   Jim's was short and disappointing to me

   Jane was more interested and supporting (over the phone)

2. My friends at the wake

   Jim showed up but didn't say much, but joked with my dad

   Jane didn't show--said she couldn't handle "that sort of thing"

3. My realization: men and women react to death in different ways

   Differing reactions depend on how they deal with life

4. Men and women at the wake

   Actions: women hugged and kissed; men shook hands, nodded

   Conversation: men talked about sports, jobs; women talked about other people

5. At the funeral

   People continued their roles

   Men were strong and silent

   Women held on to others, cried openly

6. Each gender has specific traits
      Women: treat life like a soap opera
         Interested in other people's business (gossip)
         Ruled by emotions but provide comfort
      Men: less social and outgoing
         Put others at ease--helps put themselves at ease
         Want to keep emotions in check but helps them to
         do what needs to be done
7. Conclusion--both ways of dealing with life and death
   are effective

Writing a Draft

If you have an outline or plan to work from, you shouldn't have any trouble producing the first **draft** of your paper. Getting started is probably the hardest part. Don't worry about writing a perfect **introduction** at this point. Remember that you are writing a *draft:* you can revise it later when you have a clearer, stronger sense of where the paper is headed. The main goal is to get your ideas down on paper in a reasonably complete form.

One good reason for giving yourself plenty of time to write an essay is that you may get stuck or think you are running out of ideas. When that happens, try rereading what you have already written. Writing is a back-and-forth process; writers frequently read through what they've already written to find clues about what to write next. You can also return to the discovery step in the process to explore the topic further and gather more ideas. Start by reviewing your responses to the *Who, What, Why,* and *How* questions; this material may provide the inspiration you are looking for. If you still need help, consider using one or more of these methods for generating additional material for your draft:

1. *Freewriting.* Start with the idea or point you are stuck on. Put it at the top of the page or computer screen. Then, write nonstop for a limited period of time, usually five to ten minutes. Don't worry about grammar, punctuation, or spelling; focus on recording your thoughts as they come to you. The most important thing is to keep writing as fast as you can without stopping. After you finish, reread what you have written and underline anything you might be able to use. If you want to pursue an idea that surfaces in the **freewriting,** copy the key sentence on another sheet of paper or computer screen and take off from there for another five or ten minutes. You can

repeat this step as many times as you need to, as long as you think it's productive and helps you to advance the topic you're writing about.

2. *Clustering.* **Clustering** is a visual way of generating ideas. Because it's nonlinear, you may find that it frees you from conventional patterns of thinking and enables you to probe ideas more deeply and creatively. Choose a single word or phrase that seems to be the focus of what you want to explore, write it in the center of a full sheet of paper, and draw a circle around it. Surround that focus idea with related words and phrases that you connect to it with lines (like spokes in a wheel). If some of the satellite ideas lead to more specific clusters, write them down as well. Figure 2–1 shows how Jennifer used clustering to develop the last section of her essay.

3. *Questioning.* Try to look at your essay from the readers' point of view by using some of the *Who, What, Why,* and *How* questions. Ask yourself

Figure 2–1 Sample Clustering

questions such as "Who is my main audience?" "What readers do I want to reach?" "What specific purpose do I have in regard to those readers?" "What primary and secondary points do I want to make?" "What explanations and information do my readers need to understand my points?" "How do I want my readers to perceive me?" Returning to these basic issues should stimulate your thinking and put you back on track with your draft.

◆ REVISING AND EDITING

When you have finished the first draft, set it aside, at least overnight, so that you can look at it in a new light. This process of looking at your draft again is called **revising,** which literally means "re-seeing." You want to try to see your work now with different eyes—the eyes of a reader.

A common myth about writing is that good writers get it right the first time. The truth is that good writers almost never say what they want to on the first try; they nearly always plan on revising. Teacher and writer Anne Lamott says that every piece of writing should go through at least three drafts (see pp. 140–44). The first draft she calls "the down draft—you just get it down"; the second draft is "the up draft—you fix it up"; and the last draft is "the dental draft, where you check every tooth, to see if it's loose or cramped or decayed, or even, God help us, healthy." We agree that these drafts are essential, but we call them the rough draft, the revision draft, and the editing draft. If you don't work through those last two, you won't achieve the best results, no matter how good you think your first draft is.

Revising from the Top Down

Not all revising is the same. One kind of revision involves large-scale changes, ones that significantly affect the content and **structure** of your paper. Such changes might include enlarging or narrowing your thesis, adding more examples or cutting irrelevant ones, and reorganizing points to improve logic or gain **emphasis.** A second kind of revision focuses on improving style: checking paragraph unity, strengthening transitions, combining and refining sentences, finding more effective words. It's usually more productive to focus on the major issues first. As you revise the content and organization, you may eliminate some minor problems at the same time or change the way you approach them. If you try to do the fine-tuning and polishing first, you can burn up valuable time and energy by reworking sections that you later cut and never get around to the major revisions.

The following checklist will help you revise your first draft; it focuses on general questions first and takes up smaller matters later.

◆ ◆ ◆ *Checklist for Revising* ◆ ◆ ◆

1. Will my purpose be clear to readers? Did I make the point I set out to make?
2. Is the thesis clear and intelligent? Is it useful and relevant to my readers?
3. Is the essay unified and logically organized? Do all the parts relate to the thesis?
4. Have I given enough reasons, examples, and details to support my ideas and keep readers interested?
5. Will readers be able to follow my thinking? Do I use transitions to signal connections, additions, and qualifications?
6. Have I used the strategies for organization to full advantage?
7. Are the sentences clear and effectively structured?
8. Does the introduction capture the readers' attention and make the main point of the paper clear?
9. Does the conclusion provide appropriate closure for the paper?

Getting Feedback: Peer Review

Writers routinely seek the help of potential readers to find out what is working and what is not working in their drafts. Even professional writers ask for suggestions from editors, reviewers, teachers, and friends. Someone else can often see places where you *thought* you were being clear but were actually filling in details in your head, not on the page.

You can help people who are reviewing your paper by assuring them that you want honest, critical responses. Here are some guidelines to follow when asking for help with your revision:

1. *Specify the kind of help you want.* If you already know that the spelling needs to be checked, then ask your readers to ignore those errors and focus on other elements in the draft. If you want suggestions about the thesis or the introduction or the examples, then ask questions about those specific features.

2. *Ask productive questions.* Be sure to pose questions that require more than a yes or no answer. Ask readers to tell you in detail what *they* see. You can use the questions in the "Checklist for Revising" at the top of this page to help you solicit feedback.

3. *Don't get defensive.* Listen carefully to what your reviewers have to say. Above all, don't argue with them. If something confused them, it confused them. You want to see the writing through *their* eyes, not browbeat them into seeing it the way you do.

4. *Make your own decisions.* This is your paper; you're responsible for accepting or rejecting the feedback you get. If you don't agree with a suggestion, then don't follow it. But also keep in mind that your peer reviewers are likely to be more objective about your writing than you are.

Revising in Peer Groups

In many writing classes, students work together on their papers. Meeting in small groups, they read photocopies of one another's drafts and respond to them. Sometimes students post their drafts on a class Web site or submit them electronically on a networked computer system. If your instructor doesn't arrange for peer review, try to get several readers' reactions to your drafts. You can meet together outside of class or use an Internet mailing list.

Working in peer review groups gives you a chance to write for readers other than the teacher. You increase your audience awareness, get immediate feedback on your drafts, and have a chance to discuss them with someone who doesn't have the power of a grade over you. Yet it takes skill to be an honest and critical reader of someone else's writing. When giving feedback, whether in groups or one on one, you should observe certain ground rules to ensure that your responses are productive and helpful:

- Remember that drafts are works in progress which writers intend to develop and improve. You are acting as an informed, interested reader who has questions and suggestions for improvement.
- Pay attention to *what* the other writers are saying, just as you hope they'll pay attention to what you're saying. In other words, focus on content first.
- Avoid saying that everything is wonderful or finding fault with small details. Instead, give thoughtful, sympathetic responses—the kind of feedback you would like to receive.
- Talk about the writing, not about the writer. If you notice errors, feel free to mention them, but concentrate on responding and suggesting rather than correcting the writer.

Once you've gathered reactions and suggestions from your peer reviewers—and perhaps from your instructor, too—you are ready to begin rewriting.

Rewriting on a Word Processor

A word processor helps you to see that writing is *changeable.* You can consider every word, sentence, or paragraph as just one possible choice among many. Because you can delete, move, and save the text in different files, the word processor invites you to explore alternatives. You can try a change and see how it reads; if the revision flops, you can easily restore the original draft. Some word-processing programs have a "document compare" or "compare versions" feature that will let you look closely at the changes you have made between files (for example, draft1 and draft2). If your word processor doesn't have this feature, you can open both files at the same time in two windows and track the changes you've made from one draft to the next.

Editing the Final Draft

When you are satisfied with the changes you've made to improve content and organization, you can move on to sentence structure, spelling, word choice, punctuation, capitalization, and mechanics. This part of the process is called **editing,** and you can't skip it. The appearance of your paper is important: it says a lot about you as a writer and about your relationship with your readers. If you expect them to take your writing seriously, you don't want to distract them with errors or insult them with a sloppy presentation. The following checklist identifies key points to keep in mind as you edit.

◆ ◆ ◆ *Checklist for Editing* ◆ ◆ ◆

- *Sentences.* Does each sentence include a subject and verb and make complete sense by itself? Are the sentences smooth and concise? Do the predicates logically complete the subjects?
- *Sentence boundaries.* Did you run any independent clauses together without a conjunction or a semicolon? Did you put commas before coordinating conjunctions (such as *and* or *but*) that join independent clauses? Did you use semicolons (and not just commas) between independent clauses joined by *indeed, moreover, however, nevertheless, thus,* and *hence?*
- *Pronouns.* Does each pronoun refer clearly to a specific noun? Do you need to revise any sentences to avoid using the generic pronoun *he* when referring to all human beings?
- *Subject-verb agreement.* Do singular subjects have singular verbs? Do plural subjects, including compound subjects, have plural verbs?

◆ *Commonly confused words.* Did you mix up any of these easily confused words: *its/it's, their/they're/there, your/you're, to/too/two, our/are, effect/affect, who's/whose, use/used, then/than, woman/women, cite/site/ sight?*

◆ *Shifts.* Did you shift from the present tense to the past tense for no reason? Did you shift from first person (*I, we*) to third person (*he, she, they*) without noticing?

◆ *Modifiers.* Did you place modifying phrases and clauses close to the words they modify?

◆ *Spelling and typos.* Did you leave out any words or carelessly repeat any? Did you run your computer spell checker?

◆ *Readability.* Did you use headings and paragraph breaks to improve the clarity and appearance of your text? Is your essay neat and clearly printed?

◆ *Manuscript form.* Did you double space throughout? Did you include an appropriate heading? Did you give your essay a title and capitalize it correctly? Did you leave margins of at least one inch on all four sides (top, bottom, left, and right)?

Editing on a Word Processor

Computer software can help with sentence-level revisions. You can use the spell checker to identify questionable spellings and suggest possible alternatives. Of course, a spell checker does not understand your text and can't determine if its suggestions are appropriate or even plausible, but it can focus your attention on words that you may need to change. Other programs, called text analyzers or style checkers, will give you information about word choice, sentence length, and other features of style. These programs point out *possible* problems, such as a long sentence or a weak verb, but you have to decide whether the verb is effective or the sentence really is too long. The responsibility for the final choices is yours.

You can also use the word processor to search your essay for troublesome words, overused terms, or problematic punctuation marks (such as apostrophes in possessives or commas between sentences). As the computer moves to each case, you can decide whether or not to change it. When proofreading on screen, you can use the cursor to scroll down one line at a time, which forces you to consider each line carefully before moving on. You might also read the text aloud from the screen.

◆ SAMPLE STUDENT ESSAY WITH AUTHOR'S COMMENTS

Here is the final draft of the essay that Jennifer Hoff wrote about the differences in male and female behavior at her grandmother's funeral. Jennifer's comments in the margin call attention to some of the strategies she used in presenting her ideas.

Jennifer Hoff
English 1092, Section 2
20 April 2000

Dealing with Death, Coping with Life

My Grandma's death came as something of a shock to my family. I was pretty shaken up by this unfortunate event. My friend Jim called right after I got the news. He seemed to sense that something was wrong, but he didn't come right out and ask what the problem was. I told him about my grandma, expecting a comforting response, but he simply said, "I'm sorry. I'll let you go. If there is anything I can do just let me know, okay?" Shortly afterwards my friend Jane called. She also sensed that something was wrong, but she was quick to ask what the matter was. After I told her my grandma had passed away, her immediate response was, "Are you okay? I'll be right over." She wanted to know everything that happened and how all my family members were coping.

A few days later, sitting at the funeral home greeting people I knew and people I had never seen before, I was longing to see the face of a friend. I didn't really expect my friends to attend the wake, but I was hoping someone might come to raise my spirits. Finally, a friend did show up. It was

I start with the examples of my two friends.

In this ¶, I want to show the differences in Jane's reactions.

This ¶ shifts to the funeral home and how my friends behaved.

Jim, who came with his mom. At first he didn't say much, talking only when his mom or I said something first. But when my dad joined in our conversation, he and Jim took turns telling jokes. Like most of the guys at the wake, my dad and Jim acted as sources of comic relief, trying to create an atmosphere of humor and lightheartedness. Their behavior told people, "Hey, no matter what has happened, everything is fine." As for my female friends, I'm sure they would have given me endless empathy, if any of them had shown up. I wondered how Jane could seem so concerned about my family but then never bother to attend the wake and give her support. She later explained to me that she wanted to come and was all ready to walk out the door, but she just could not handle "that sort of thing."

As I continued to observe those people behind the signatures on the guest list, I noted their behavior as they engaged in conversation. I also thought about my friends' reactions, and I began to realize that the way people react to death seems to mirror the way they cope with life. And men and women respond quite differently.

All the guests approached my grieving family with the usual "sorry about your loss" speech. Most of the women offered a hug and sometimes even a kiss on the cheek. Most of the men seemed to feel that a handshake or a simple nod of the head would suffice. After these initial greetings, the conversations continued to differ. The men sneaked away to corners of the room and talked about sports or their jobs. I heard my dad and his co-workers discussing the chances of their favorite football teams; my older brother and his

Margin notes:

I start to focus on gender differences here.

In this ¶ I am ready to state my thesis.

In this ¶ I provide support by directly comparing the two styles of conversation.

friend challenged each other to some
sort of athletic contest. By contrast,
the women stayed together in the middle
of the room and discussed which family
members turned out to be losers and
which ones had not bothered to show up.
I heard my aunt say, "Did you see how
all of Uncle Ed's kids showed up in
jeans?" My mom commented on my grandma's
appearance: "Doesn't her make-up look
nice? The undertaker did a wonderful job
on her." Other women agreed and also
discussed her clothes and the floral
arrangements in the funeral home.

At the funeral the next day,
everyone fulfilled their expected duties.
A few selected men, looking strong and
steady, were pallbearers, wearing white
gloves as they carried the heavy casket.
The rest of the congregation followed
behind, some—mostly women—clutching the
arms of another person for comfort. Most
of these women were crying openly.
However, I did not see any men shed
tears, although some man must have cried
secretly because I heard someone in the
distance say, "I never saw him cry
before."

This ¶ offers more support by comparing behavior at the funeral.

I guess each gender has its own
specific characteristics or tendencies.
Both sexes put restrictions on what they
can or want to do emotionally in life.
Most women treat life as a soap opera.
Every aspect of life is a big deal and
something to talk about. The women at
the wake seemed to be concerned with
everyone else but themselves; basically,
they were gossiping. They were also
dominated by their emotions. For many
women, tears are a natural reaction to
both good and bad circumstances. Even my
friend Jane let her feelings control
her: she could not handle how she feels

In the next two ¶s I discuss the pros and cons of the differences.

at wakes and funerals, so she stayed at home. Being ruled by emotions, however, is not always a bad thing. Women's open expressions of feeling can be a major source of comfort. Most women at the wake did not think twice about giving a hug to anyone, man or woman. These women may have also gossiped about the people they hugged, but only because they are prone to dwell on every aspect of life, especially the social parts.

Men tend to approach life a little differently. They take a back seat during the social transactions that women feed on. They would rather be the heroes who rescue the women from their emotions by making them laugh, as my dad and Jim did, or by carrying the heavy casket and taking the burden off others. By supplying comic relief, men also help put themselves at ease, suppressing the emotions on the verge of being unleashed. Most men are not being insincere when they don't ask what is wrong or when they give a handshake instead of a hug. They just seem to have a hands-off approach to the emotions mixed in with life. But a man's choice not to let his emotions rule him is not altogether unfortunate. By containing their emotions, men gain the control they need to carry out the difficult jobs that need to be done in difficult situations.

My observations are far from conclusive. People are more complicated than they appear to be. But I saw human beings facing the death of a loved one in the same way they handle life. Women follow their emotions; men rein them in. Both reactions seem to work.

In my conclusion I acknowledge the limits of my ideas and sum up my main point.

◆ ◆ ◆ ▇ Internet Sources for Writers ◆ ◆ ◆

You can find advice on the **writing process** at a hundred or more Web sites and online services. Some are hypertext guides that allow you to follow links to various topics as you make your way through the stages of writing. These materials vary widely in quality, presentation, and amount of detail. The following are some of the most helpful and usable sites:

- ◆ *The University of Victoria's Hypertext Writer's Guide* (http://web.uvic. ca/wguide/) will help you through the basics of the writing process and answer questions about essays, paragraphs, sentences, words, and documentation.
- ◆ *Paradigm Online Writing Assistant* (http://www.powa.org/) offers useful advice on writing various types of papers. It contains sections on discovery, organization, editing, and other topics.
- ◆ *Writer's Web* (http://www.urich.edu/~writing/wweb.html), from the University of Richmond, contains sections on generating ideas, drafting and organizing, focusing and connecting ideas, creating and supporting an argument, editing a draft, punctuation, sentence structure and mechanics, editing for clarity and style, documentation, and using sources effectively.
- ◆ *Purdue University's Online Writing Lab* (http://owl.english.purdue.edu/) has over seventy-five handouts about the process and mechanics of writing. It is one of the most extensive collections of advice about writing on the Web.

◆ ◆ ◆ ▇ Using Internet Resources ◆ ◆ ◆

Throughout this book, you will find suggestions for using sources from the Internet to help you with your reading and your writing. The following article gives you some practical advice on how to make your Internet searches more efficient and more productive.

Twelve Tips to Search the Internet Successfully

BRUCE MAXWELL

Bruce Maxwell is the author of *How to Find Health Information on the Internet* and *How to Access the Federal Government on the Internet*. This article appeared in the November 6–8, 1998, edition of *USA Weekend*.

Trying to navigate the World Wide Web without help is like trying to do research in a library that has no librarians, a jumble of card catalogs listing just a fraction of the collection, and 320 million books.

To flounder less and learn more in your maiden voyages on the Web, follow these tips.

ONE: If your subject is broad (cancer, archaeology, politics), start with a directory—such as Yahoo! (http://www.yahoo.com)—that categorizes Web sites by subject. Just pick the most likely subject, then drill down through layers of subcategories until you find what you want.

TWO: If your subject is narrow (such as a particular bed-and-breakfast you want to try), choose a search engine: AltaVista (http://altavista.com), HotBot (http://hotbot.lycos.com), Excite (http://www.excite.com), Infoseek (http://infoseek.go.com) or Northern Light (http://www.nlsearch.com).

THREE: For comprehensive research, use several search engines or try a meta-search engine such as MetaCrawler (http://www.metacrawler.com) that simultaneously queries numerous engines.

FOUR: Before using a search engine, read any instructions it offers. Yes, these documents can be snoozers. But each engine has its quirks, and knowing them will help you craft a more accurate search.

FIVE: When choosing keywords for a search engine, select six to eight words to help narrow your search. If you type just one or two words, you'll likely get thousands or even millions of documents. Use nouns whenever possible, and put the most important words first. Put a "+" before any word you want to include, and a "−" before any word you want to exclude (this works with most engines).

SIX: To increase your search's accuracy, use phrases instead of single words. Put quotation marks around the phrase.

SEVEN: Many search engines will let you refine the results of your initial query. Do it.

EIGHT: When you find a good Web site about your topic, check whether it provides links to similar sites.

NINE: You may be able to guess the address of specific sites. Many are "www," a period, the name or acronym of the site's operator, a period and three letters denoting the site's type. Thus: www.microsoft.com (commercial), www.fbi.gov (federal government) and www.harvard.edu (education).

TEN: Double-check your spelling. You'd be amazed at how many people misspell words in their queries.

ELEVEN: Keep in mind that even if you type a precise query, many of the documents returned won't be applicable. Computers (and search engines) aren't perfect.

TWELVE: Remember: The Internet does not contain the sum of all knowledge. You may still need to hit the library.

Where to Get Searching Help

Many excellent searching guides and sites are available on the Internet. Among the best:

Tutorial: Guide to Effective Searching of the Internet. ⟨http://www.brightplanet.com/deepcontent/tutorials/search/index.asp⟩

Search Engine Watch. ⟨http://searchenginewatch.com⟩

How to Search the World Wide Web: A Tutorial for Beginners and Non-Experts. ⟨http://204.17.98.73/midlib/tutor.htm⟩

The Spider's Apprentice: A Helpful Guide to Web Search Engines. ⟨http://www.monash.com/spidap.html⟩

Learn about the Internet. ⟨http://www1.sympatico.ca/help/Learn/⟩

◆ ◆ ◆

CHAPTER 3

Strategies for Discovering and Relating Experiences

Narration

◆ ◆ ◆ ◆ ◆

Narrative writing tells what happens over time.

◆ Writers use narrative to bring ideas and experiences to life.
◆ Effective narrations are organized according to time or logic.
◆ Writers must decide when to summarize events and when to narrate them in detail.

Among the oldest and most powerful ways people come to understand their own lives and to communicate with one another is through the sharing of stories. This chapter introduces you to two types of storytelling: informal **discovery** writing and formal **narration.**

◆ INFORMAL DISCOVERY WRITING

Discovery writing is a method of recording thoughts and experiences for your own enjoyment and use. Novelist Virginia Woolf called the ideas generated in her writer's diary "the diamonds of the dustheap." Like most good writers, she recognized the importance of having a place to think regularly about her life and the world around her. In the diary, she was free to let her mind wander in its own way and time. In addition to the everyday pleasure of writing without worrying about a reader's feelings or judgments, it was in this diary that many of her stories were born and took shape.

A diary is one of the many forms of discovery writing. Like **freewriting** and **brainstorming,** keeping a diary is an unstructured process by which writers are able to explore past or present experience for its value to them and, possibly, to others later. Among the most famous of diaries is holocaust victim Anne Frank's, which she began before she went, at age thirteen, into hiding with her family to escape Nazi persecution. Here is her first entry, written on June 14, 1942:

> I'll begin from the moment I got you [her diary], the moment I saw you lying on the table among my other birthday presents. (I went along when you were bought, but that didn't count.)
>
> On Friday, June 12, I was awake at six o'clock, which isn't surprising, since it was my birthday. But I'm not allowed to get up at that hour, so I had to control my curiosity until quarter to seven. When I couldn't wait any longer, I went to the dining room, where Moortje (the cat) welcomed me by rubbing against my legs.
>
> A little after seven I went to Daddy and Mama and then to the living room to open my presents, and *you* were the first thing I saw, maybe one of my nicest presents.

Throughout the three years before her death in the Nazi concentration camps, Anne turned to her diary, and through it to an imagined friend, Kitty, to reflect on and shape her adolescent self-image:

> I hope I will be able to confide everything to you, as I have never been able to confide to anyone, and I hope you will be a great source of comfort and support.

And later she added:

> So far you truly have been a great source of comfort to me, and so has Kitty, whom I now write to regularly. This way of keeping a diary is much nicer, and now I can hardly wait for those moments when I'm able to write in you.
>
> Oh, I'm so glad I brought you along!

Anne's diary was often the place where she tried to work out her relationship with her mother. Here is a longer entry, from January 2, 1944, a year and a half after she went into hiding:

This morning, when I had nothing to do, I leafed through the pages of my diary and came across so many letters dealing with the subject of "Mother" in such strong terms that I was shocked. I said to myself, "Anne, is that really you talking about hate? Oh, Anne, how could you?"

I continued to sit with the open book in my hand and wonder why I was filled with so much anger and hate that I had to confide it all to you. I tried to understand the Anne of last year and make apologies for her, because as long as I leave you with these accusations and don't attempt to explain what prompted them, my conscience won't be clear. I was suffering then (and still do) from moods that kept my head under water (figuratively speaking) and allowed me to see things only from my own perspective, without calmly considering what the others—those whom I, with my mercurial temperament, had hurt or offended—had said, and then acting as they would have done.

I hid inside myself, thought of no one but myself and calmly wrote down all my joy, sarcasm and sorrow in my diary. Because this diary has become a kind of memory book, it means a great deal to me, but I could easily write "over and done with" on many of its pages.

I was furious at Mother (and still am a lot of the time). It's true, she didn't understand me, but I didn't understand her either. Because she loved me, she was tender and affectionate, but because of the difficult situations I put her in, and the sad circumstances in which she found herself, she was nervous and irritable, so I can understand why she was often short with me.

I was offended, took it far too much to heart and was insolent and beastly to her, which, in turn, made her unhappy. We were caught in a vicious circle of unpleasantness and sorrow. Not a very happy period for either of us, but at least it's coming to an end. I didn't want to see what was going on, and I felt very sorry for myself, but that's understandable too.

Those violent outbursts on paper are simply expressions of anger that, in normal life, I could have worked off by locking myself in my room and stamping my foot a few times or calling Mother names behind her back.

The period of tearfully passing judgment on Mother is over. I've grown wiser and Mother's nerves are a bit steadier. Most of the time I manage to hold my tongue when I'm annoyed, and she does too; so on the surface, we seem to be getting along better. But there's one thing I can't do, and that's to love Mother with the devotion of a child.

I soothe my conscience with the thought that it's better for unkind words to be down on paper than for Mother to have to carry them around in her heart.

Although Anne Frank was never able to grow into adulthood and complete her goal of becoming a writer, she kept her diary with that future in mind. Clearly, there were many diamonds she might have polished later.

◆ FROM DISCOVERY TO NARRATION

In preparation for exploring and later narrating a relationship of her own, Tara Coburn, a first-year student, was asked to read these selections from Anne's diary. Although she might simply have used the ideas in the diary to do some brainstorming or freewriting of her own, Tara instead used a few simple *Who, What,* and *Why* questions to take a closer, more systematic look at Anne's diary and to better understand her own responses to Anne's ideas. Such writing remains **informal,** meant primarily for the writer's own use, but because it is more directed, it helps a writer progress toward fuller understanding of the topic as well as to more focused attention on how and why that topic might be of interest to others.

Starting with *Who,* Tara found Anne to be "caring, sincere, and natural," someone she "would like to be friends with." Of Anne's tone, she concluded that it "reminds me of the tone I have used when I write letters or e-mail to friends, especially if I have exciting news." Based on this comfort and familiarity, Tara also found herself drawn to the use of a diary for working out personal problems, especially the challenge of a daughter sorting out her feelings about her mother. More specifically, in Anne's movement back and forth between self-criticism and feeling "wiser and more mature," Tara found a comforting model for handling her own relationship with her mother:

> Even though most teenagers are not as isolated as Anne was, some still do not have supportive friends to whom they can tell their problems. A majority of teens would identify with Anne's feelings about her mother. I feel the same way, sometimes. I regret some things that I said and did now that I am older, in the same way Anne looked upon her past.

She also identified in the diary an important purpose for doing discovery writing:

> Anne is challenging herself to become a better person. She is disturbed by the ways she has acted in the past, and she wants to behave differently. Anne realizes that she has been unfair, vicious, and unloving at times. At the time that she is writing the third passage, Anne is a very different person from the person she was before. She wants to continue to change for the better.

◆ FORMAL NARRATION: RELATING DISCOVERIES TO READERS

Narration is the challenge of plucking an uncut or rough diamond out of the dustheap of our personal experiences and turning it into an essay that others will find entertaining and meaningful. After reading Anne Frank's diary for the *Who, What,* and *Why,* Tara took a close look at the *How,* and using Anne as a model, she did her own discovery writing. Finally, she decided to write the following essay about her own mother. As you read her essay, be sure to underline major ideas and note your responses or observations about her writing style in the margins.

Tara Coburn
English 1091, Section 7
November 9, 1998

A Better Place

The phrase "be careful what you wish for" really   1
started to make sense to me when I was sixteen. I had
always wished that my parents would stop fighting. When
they announced that they were getting a divorce,
though, I regretted ever hoping for it. Later that
year, when my mother moved into an apartment, the
relationship between us began to change drastically.
During the first few weeks that she was gone, I handled
these changes very badly. I thought that my
relationship with my mother was doomed. Gradually,

however, my expectations became more realistic and my perspective broadened. I now realize that the divorce has actually brought my mother and me to a better place.

Before my parents even began considering divorce,   2
my ties with my mother were not as strong as I wanted them to be. We tried to become close, but our relationship always took a backseat to the relationship between my parents. Near the end of their marriage, not a day went by that they did not have a major fight. The constant turmoil and distractions in the house kept both of us from becoming close with each other. Because of the stress and unhappiness in our lives, our relationship was never more than a shallow bond.

Even though the situation between us was not what   3
I wanted, the changes after the divorce hit me very hard. For a while, I thought that I was dealing with it well. It was not until the night that my mother moved out that I panicked. I remember standing outside where she had dropped me off when I suddenly realized that I was going into a house where my mother did not live. Feelings of betrayal and abandonment that I had kept hidden began to overwhelm me. As I began to cry, I turned to her and started screaming. I told her that she did not love me and she was going to forget about me. I knew that I did not mean what I said, but I could not help myself. The pain of that loss really deafened me from hearing how awful I sounded, and I said a lot that I wish I had not.

Because I have had time to reflect on that night, I   4
have come to realize that I reacted very irrationally. It was my own stubborn selfishness that prevented me from realizing that our new situation was a chance to become closer. This opportunity became clear to me one day when I was visiting my mother's apartment. My father called to talk to her, and soon after, the distantly familiar sounds of shouting started coming from the other room. I was shocked. It had been a pleasantly long time since I had heard them fight. That was a major turning point in my view of my mother because I could see how calmer, friendlier environments made both of our lives better. I see now

that my mother was trying to help both of us while I was busy feeling sorry for myself. In the end, a lot of the hurt subsided from both of us, and I was able to see that she really made a wise choice.

Seeing my relationship with my mother from both of   5
our perspectives not only made me feel better, but it also changed how I treat my mother. Before I judge her actions, I try to remind myself that she has gone through a lot. She and I are very different people, and I have accepted that I will not always agree with her. This was probably one of the most valuable things that I have discovered. I never really knew her before the divorce because our lives were so hectic. Communicating with her is much easier now, so I have gotten to know her better. We are different people, but I really like the person that she is. We have fun together. Our relationship is how I had always wanted it to be; it just needed space.

◆ ◆ ◆ *Writer's Workshop* ◆ ◆ ◆
Responding to a Narrative

Before looking more closely at Tara's essay as an example of narration, analyze your responses to her story using the *Who, What, Why,* and *How* questions in Chapter 1 (p. 3). You might want to compare your answers with those of your classmates by discussing them in small groups, by posting responses on a class Web page or electronic bulletin board, or by passing your answers around to two or three other students.

◆ GETTING STARTED ON A NARRATIVE

Most narratives are lively stories that bring experience to life through vivid language and concrete detail. After doing either discovery writing or focused prewriting, a writer seeks a more specific purpose for turning a memory into a narrative and identifies an audience that might be interested in or benefit from the story. Or, in reverse, a writer may want to explain an idea to a certain audience, and the narration becomes a method for illustrating that idea to those readers. In both cases, narratives offer insights that have been gained from experience and that in turn might be of value to particular readers. For Tara, the memory of her evolving relationship with her mother made her realize how much closer they have become, an insight that gives her a valuable thesis to share with others her age who are in the process of establishing mature relationships with their parents. For columnist Mike Royko, a childhood memory of the day Jackie Robinson integrated major league baseball in Chicago becomes an opportunity to make the abstract idea of prejudice very human and real.

◆ ORGANIZING A NARRATIVE

Who are the best storytellers you know? Which ones put you to sleep? Narratives are often thought to be especially easy because events can simply be retold as they happened, in **chronological order.** From experience, though, we know that a good narrative writer often improves on real life by adding to, deleting from, or reordering events. Such changes make the stories clearer in our minds and give them greater drama and energy.

Having a definite **purpose** helps a writer organize a narrative according to time (for example, from morning to night) or in a logical sequence of events. Choosing the right framework for the story and the right events is key to success. Tara decided to describe her evolving relationship with her mother by stages: before, during, and after the divorce. This approach organizes her changing feelings toward her mother and thus unifies the story and her purpose for recounting it. Writer George Orwell uses the events surrounding his shooting of an elephant—and within the events the distinctly different responses of various people to these scenes—to underscore his complex thesis: "it gave me a better glimpse than I had had before of the real nature of imperialism—the real motives for which despotic governments act."

Writers also have the option to rearrange events and time, using **flashbacks** or digressions, for example, to provide contrast between then and now or to fill in information a reader needs to understand an event. Tara's memory of the shouting matches between her parents provides a vivid contrast to the "calmer, friendlier" postdivorce reality.

◆ DEVELOPING A NARRATIVE

Developing a narrative involves careful decision making. Depending on the writer's purpose and audience, some parts of the story might be summarized to capture only the important elements, while others might be drawn in very specific detail for **emphasis.** Because Tara's readers are unfamiliar with her family and her past, she provides in each section of her essay an overview of her feelings during that time and concretely explains the experiences that led to these feelings. In some cases, though, she recalls a very specific interaction with her mother to drive her point home. It is in these scenes—for example, walking alone into the house for the first time—that Tara rises to the challenge of bringing ideas to life through careful phrasing and precise detail. She wasn't simply afraid; she "panicked." Showing us her tears and her screams helps us to sympathize with her conclusion that "I said a lot that I wish I had not."

Another very effective way to develop a narrative is to use carefully selected **dialogue** that captures the tone of a conversation or perhaps the personality of a person in the story. In telling his story "Street Scene: Minor Heroism in a Major Metropolitan Area," Ian Frazier writes the following lines from a conversation he had with a police officer:

> The cop sat in his car. The window was down. I walked over and asked, "Excuse me—did they ever get a pulse?" He winced slightly at the nakedness of my question. A pause. Then he shook his head. "Nahhh. Not really."

This brief dialogue captures the tension between routine and crisis that Frazier stresses throughout the story.

◆ OPENING AND CLOSING A NARRATIVE

Before writing, narrative writers must determine whether to state their thesis directly or let their story speak for itself. Some writers, such as Maxine Hong Kingston, prefer to begin and end their essays with the start and close of the events, implying their purpose in the way they select scenes and phrase their descriptions:

> "You must not tell anyone," my mother said, "what I am about to tell you. In China your father had a sister who killed herself. She jumped into the family well. We say that your father has all brothers because it is as if she had never been born."

This dramatic opening brings the reader immediately into the story, leaving the specific purpose for telling this story open-ended. Others, such as Tara, use the introduction to establish their thesis and provide the reader with a reason for being interested in their personal story.

Conclusions in these essays can pose a challenge. At the end of "Salvation," writer Langston Hughes chooses to explain the explicit results of his disappointing conversion experience: "But I was really crying because I couldn't bear to tell her [his aunt] that I had lied, that I had deceived everybody in the church, and that I hadn't seen Jesus, and that now I didn't believe there was a Jesus any more, since he didn't come to help me." In her original draft, Tara tried a similar approach, including this paragraph as a conclusion:

```
    Unfortunately, for my mother and I to find
balance in our relationship, we first had to
separate. More families like mine are splitting
up, and I am sure that I am not the only teenager
to react badly, at first. Divorce is always
unfortunate, but does not have to be an ending,
like I first thought. It can be an opportunity for
members of a family to build on their
relationships and improve themselves, like my
mother and I have. Though I said and did some
things that I regret, we have come closer.
Although making mistakes is not pleasant, I am
glad that I have learned from the ones I have
made.
```

When she reread the draft, though, Tara realized that these ideas had already been conveyed in the story and in her paragraph-by-paragraph analysis of her feelings, so she cut what had become a second conclusion.

◆ USING THE MODEL

As a result of reading Anne Frank's diary and then answering several questions about it, Tara ended up writing an essay with a topic and purpose very similar to Anne's. Both young women write about their pasts from the perspective of their presents. Their greater maturity allows both to see events from their own as well as their mothers' points of view. Having read both Anne's and Tara's stories, you might want to use this same multiple perspective to examine other topics or relationships that might be shared with others. For example, you could write about forming a sympathetic relationship with a friend or coach or teacher you used to find difficult to like or understand—as an illustration to others who would miss valuable opportunities by resisting changes in their lives.

◆ ◆ ◆ *Checklist for Reading and Writing* ◆ ◆ ◆ *Narrative Essays*

1. Is the purpose for telling this story made clear? Has it been achieved?
2. Has a conscious decision been made about which events to include or exclude and how best to organize them? Are connections between scenes or paragraphs made clear?
3. Do the intended readers have enough information about people, places, and times to understand the scenes included and the ideas communicated?
4. Are the scenes made lively through language appealing to the reader's senses of smell, touch, sight, and sound?
5. Would any additional concrete details add clarity to a scene or support to an idea within the essay?

◆ ◆ ◆ PREPARING TO READ

Have you ever experienced a single event that significantly changed an opinion you had about a person or a group of people? Did you realize the importance of the event at the time?

◆ ◆ ◆

Jackie's Debut: A Unique Day

MIKE ROYKO

When Chicago native Mike Royko, a lifelong newspaper journalist, died in 1997, he was a columnist for the *Chicago Tribune*. Throughout his career, his sharp-tongued observations about everyday urban life brought him national recognition, including a Pulitzer Prize. On October 15, 1972, writing for the *Chicago Daily News* on the death of major league baseball great Jackie Robinson, Royko dug into his childhood memories and recorded a snapshot of the complex reality of American race relations.

All that Saturday, the wise men of the neighborhood, who sat in chairs 1 on the sidewalk outside the tavern, had talked about what it would do to baseball.

I hung around and listened because baseball was about the most im- 2 portant thing in the world, and if anything was going to ruin it, I was worried.

Most of the things they said, I didn't understand, although it sounded 3 terrible. But could one man bring such ruin?

They said he could and would. And the next day he was going to be in 4 Wrigley Field for the first time, on the same diamond as Hack, Nicholson, Cavarretta, Schmidt, Pafko, and all my other idols.

I had to see Jackie Robinson, the man who was going to somehow 5 wreck everything. So the next day, another kid and I started walking to the ball park early.

We always walked to save the streetcar fare. It was five or six miles, but 6 I felt about baseball the way Abe Lincoln felt about education.

Usually, we could get there just at noon, find a seat in the grandstands 7 and watch some batting practice. But not that Sunday, May 18, 1947.

By noon, Wrigley Field was almost filled. The crowd outside spilled off 8 the sidewalk and into the streets. Scalpers were asking top dollar for box seats and getting it.

I had never seen anything like it. Not just the size, although it was   9
a new record, more than 47,000. But this was 25 years ago, and in 1947 few
blacks were seen in the Loop, much less up on the white North Side at a
Cub game.

That day, they came by the thousands, pouring off the northbound Ls   10
and out of their cars.

They didn't wear baseball-game clothes. They had on church clothes   11
and funeral clothes—suits, white shirts, ties, gleaming shoes, and straw hats.
I've never seen so many straw hats.

Big as it was, the crowd was orderly. Almost unnaturally so. People   12
didn't jostle each other.

The whites tried to look as if nothing unusual was happening, while the   13
blacks tried to look casual and dignified. So everybody looked slightly ill
at ease.

For most, it was probably the first time they had been that close to each   14
other in such great numbers.

We managed to get in, scramble up a ramp and find a place to stand be-   15
hind the last row of grandstand seats. Then they shut the gates. No place remained to stand.

Robinson came up in the first inning. I remember the sound. It wasn't   16
the shrill, teen-age cry you now hear, or an excited gut roar. They applauded,
long, rolling applause. A tall middle-aged black man stood next to me, a smile
of almost painful joy on his face, beating his palms together so hard they
must have hurt.

When Robinson stepped into the batter's box, it was as if someone had   17
flicked a switch. The place went silent.

He swung at the first pitch and they erupted as if he had knocked it   18
over the wall. But it was only a high foul that dropped into the box seats. I
remember thinking it was strange that a foul could make that many people
happy. When he struck out, the low moan was genuine.

I've forgotten most of the details of the game, other than that the   19
Dodgers won and Robinson didn't get a hit or do anything special, although
he was cheered on every swing and every routine play.

But two things happened I'll never forget. Robinson played first, and   20
early in the game a Cub star hit a grounder and it was a close play.

Just before the Cub reached first, he swerved to his left. And as he got   21
to the bag, he seemed to slam his foot down hard at Robinson's foot.

It was obvious to everyone that he was trying to run into him or spike   22
him. Robinson took the throw and got clear at the last instant.

I was shocked. That Cub, a home-town boy, was my biggest hero. It was   23
not only an unheroic stunt, but it seemed a rude thing to do in front of people who would cheer for a foul ball. I didn't understand why he had done it.
It wasn't at all big league.

I didn't know that while the white fans were relatively polite, the   24
Cubs and most other teams kept up a steady stream of racial abuse from
the dugout. I thought all they did down there was talk about how good
Wheaties are.

Later in the game, Robinson was up again and he hit another foul ball.   25
This time it came into the stands low and fast, in our direction. Somebody in
the seats grabbed for it, but it caromed off his hand and kept coming. There
was a flurry of arms as the ball kept bouncing, and suddenly it was between
me and my pal. We both grabbed. I had a baseball.

The two of us stood there examining it and chortling. A genuine, major-   26
league baseball that had actually been gripped and thrown by a Cub pitcher,
hit by a Dodger batter. What a possession.

Then I heard a voice say: "Would you consider selling that?"   27

It was the black man who had applauded so fiercely.   28

I mumbled something. I didn't want to sell it.   29

"I'll give you $10 for it," he said.   30

Ten dollars. I couldn't believe it. I didn't know what $10 could buy be-   31
cause I'd never had that much money. But I knew that a lot of men in the
neighborhood considered $60 a week to be good pay.

I handed it to him, and he paid me with ten $1 bills.   32

When I left the ball park, with that much money in my pocket, I was   33
sure that Jackie Robinson wasn't bad for the game.

Since then, I've regretted a few times that I didn't keep the ball. Or   34
that I hadn't given it to him free. I didn't know, then, how hard he probably
had to work for that $10.

But Tuesday I was glad I had sold it to him. And if that man is still   35
around, and has that baseball, I'm sure he thinks it was worth every cent.

FIRST RESPONSES

How might you have responded to being in the stands at this game?
What would you have done with the caught baseball? Have you been called
on to make any similar decisions in your life?

TAKING A CLOSER LOOK

Exploring *Who:* Voice and Tone

1. How did the young boy's feelings about his baseball heroes change in
   the course of this baseball game? How does the adult Royko view his

boyhood attitudes? Identify two or three places where he makes these two different points of view most clear.

2. What tone of voice does Royko use when he opens with the warnings of "the wise men of the neighborhood"? When do you realize his current feelings about these elders? Are there other attitudes expressed in the early paragraphs that can be read differently after you have finished the essay?

3. What reactions does Royko hope you will have toward his boyhood ideas and actions? What does he expect of you as you read? How did you respond, for example, when the boy thinks, "I had to see Jackie Robinson, the man who was going to somehow wreck everything"?

Exploring *What:* Content and Meaning

1. What did you learn about the game of baseball in 1947 from reading this essay? About Chicago? Was this new information for you? Why or why not?

2. What did you learn about black and white interaction at that time? Did any of the behaviors of the white or black players or spectators surprise you? Is race still an issue in sports? For the players? For the crowds?

3. How well did the essay prepare you for understanding the two major events during the game, the slide and the foul ball? How did you feel when the Cub player slid into Robinson? Did you understand why the boy sold the ball to the black man?

Exploring *Why:* Purpose

1. Royko is generally known for his critical attitude toward human frailties. Remembering that the essay was written the day Robinson died, how do you think Royko hoped readers would respond to his experience? Has remembering the event been valuable for Royko himself? How does paragraph 34 help to answer that question?

2. If the black man to whom he sold the ball read Royko's essay, would he agree with Royko's conclusion? Can you name a few ways in which this black fan would remember things differently about this day?

3. ▣ *Using the Internet.* Visit the Negro League Baseball Online Archives (www.nc5.infi.net/moxie/nlb/nlb.html) or the Negro League's Web site (www.blackbaseball.com/). What did you know about this league before visiting the Web site? How does this additional information add to your reading of Royko's essay?

Exploring *How:* Style and Strategy

1. You have looked closely at many of the **details** Royko includes in his essay. What did he exclude? Why? Why does the essay begin and end where it does? For example, how would the essay be different if it began with the Cub player's slide into Robinson?

2. Why did the author give so many details about how the black spectators were dressed? Which of your senses does Royko appeal to in paragraphs 16 to 18? What is the effect on your feelings about the game that day?

3. Why does Royko tell us that he "felt about baseball the way Abe Lincoln felt about education"?

◆ WRITING FROM READING ASSIGNMENT

Mike Royko's narrative captures a pivotal moment in his own and the nation's growth toward maturity. Lack of experience with people who are different from us is one of our many youthful limitations. Its consequence is often prejudice, which affects how we think and act. The following assignment uses Royko's essay as a model and assists you in writing a narrative about a specific and direct experience you had with someone or something you were unfamiliar with, perhaps even prejudiced against. You might, for example, consider a time you had to play on the same basketball team with a student from a different school, went on a field trip with a person from another country, or worked with a critically ill or elderly person while volunteering at a hospital.

A. Begin by doing some freewriting or brainstorming to discover a topic. Explore what you felt at the time of the experience as well as what you are feeling as you remember the scenes. Did you realize at the time that your attitudes were changing? What do you think you learned from the experience?

B. After you have identified the story you wish to recount and one or two specific insights you gained from the interaction, reread the Royko essay to look carefully at how he narrates his story and when and where he makes clear his reasons for writing about this experience. Go back to your topic and make a list of all the events or scenes in your story, and then do some additional brainstorming to recall all the details you can associate with each scene. Jot them down. Now write a working thesis for your essay.

C. Royko sets a context for the story he is about to tell by revealing his naive understanding of the racist attitudes of the day. He also invites the readers to come along with him as he finds out "what it would do to baseball." Do you need to provide a similar introduction for your readers? How else might you arouse readers' interest in your story and help them focus on what you believe is important about the change you are about to narrate? Write a draft introduction.

D. Royko has organized his essay in chronological order, from the day before the game until he leaves the park. Like Tara Coburn's essay, Royko's reveals a progression in his attitudes: before, during, and after the game. Find a logical pattern for the sequence of events in your narrative. Decide if you want to present all the events in order or if you need flashbacks or digressions to help clarify an idea or provide essential information. Write an outline or list of scenes for your essay. Think carefully about what you are including as well as what you are leaving out.

E. Royko's point of view is largely that of a fifteen-year-old boy, but his adult voice sometimes intervenes. In paragraph 24, for example, he shares with us what he now knows was going on in the dugout that he couldn't have known as a boy. Decide what point of view you will use and when and if you will vary that point of view. Now write a draft of your essay.

F. As you discovered in question 2 under "Exploring *How*," Royko uses sounds to draw his readers into the scene. Use specific detail and description to bring your scenes to life. You might use analogy, such as Royko's to Abe Lincoln, to help your readers understand more fully the ideas behind your story.

G. Take a close look at your conclusion before writing your final draft. Have you avoided the pitfall Tara fell into when she wrote her double conclusion? Be sure that insights you gained from your experience are clear to your readers.

◆ ◆ ◆ PREPARING TO READ

Can you remember a particular childhood experience that dramatically changed your feelings about an institution you were connected to, such as a school, a club, or a church? What were your feelings or attitudes before the experience, and how did they change?

◆ ◆ ◆

Salvation

LANGSTON HUGHES

Langston Hughes (1902–1967) was born in Joplin, Missouri, and spent his childhood in the Midwest as well as in Mexico. As a young man, he moved to New York to see Harlem and quickly became a significant figure in the Harlem Renaissance, a major literary movement of the 1920s and 30s. His life-long commitment to exploring and representing African American experience is reflected in his large body of poetry, fiction, plays, and nonfiction, including *The Weary Blues* (1926), poems written out of the African American blues tradition; *Not Without Laughter* (1930), an autobiographical novel set in the Kansas of his boyhood; and *The Big Sea* (1940), an autobiography from which "Salvation" is drawn.

I was saved from sin when I was going on thirteen. But not really saved.   1
It happened like this. There was a big revival at my Auntie Reed's church. Every night for weeks there had been much preaching, singing, praying, and shouting, and some very hardened sinners had been brought to Christ, and the membership of the church had grown by leaps and bounds. Then just before the revival ended, they held a special meeting for children, "to bring the young lambs to the fold." My aunt spoke of it for days ahead. That night I was escorted to the front row and placed on the mourners' bench with all the other young sinners, who had not yet been brought to Jesus.

My aunt told me that when you were saved you saw a light, and some-   2
thing happened to you inside! And Jesus came into your life! And God was with you from then on! She said you could see and hear and feel Jesus in your soul. I believed her. I had heard a great many old people say the same thing and it seemed to me they ought to know. So I sat there calmly in the hot crowded church, waiting for Jesus to come to me.

The preacher preached a wonderful rhythmical sermon, all moans and 3
shouts and lonely cries and dire pictures of hell, and then he sang a song
about the ninety and nine safe in the fold, but one little lamb was left in the
cold. Then he said, "Won't you come? Won't you come to Jesus? Young lambs,
won't you come?" And he held out his arms to all us young sinners there on
the mourners' bench. And the little girls cried. And some of them jumped up
and went to Jesus right away. But most of us just sat there.

A great many old people came and knelt around us and prayed, old 4
women with jet-black faces and braided hair, old men with work-gnarled
hands. And the church sang a song about the lower lights are burning, some
poor sinners to be saved. And the whole building rocked with prayer
and song.

Still I kept waiting to see Jesus. 5

Finally all the young people had gone to the altar and were saved, but 6
one boy and me. He was a rounder's son named Westley. Westley and I were
surrounded by sisters and deacons praying. It was very hot in the church,
and getting late now. Finally Westley said to me in a whisper: "Goddamn!
I'm tired o' sitting here. Let's get up and be saved." So he got up and was
saved.

Then I was left all alone on the mourners' bench. My aunt came and 7
knelt at my knees and cried, while prayers and songs swirled all around me
in the little church. The whole congregation prayed for me alone, in a mighty
wail of moans and voices. And I kept waiting serenely for Jesus, waiting, waiting—but he didn't come. I wanted to see him, but nothing happened to me.
Nothing! I wanted something to happen to me, but nothing happened.

I heard the songs and the minister saying: "Why don't you come? My 8
dear child, why don't you come to Jesus? Jesus is waiting for you. He wants
you. Why don't you come? Sister Reed, what is this child's name?"

"Langston," my aunt sobbed. 9

"Langston, why don't you come? Why don't you come and be saved? 10
Oh, Lamb of God! Why don't you come?"

Now it was really getting late. I began to be ashamed of myself, hold- 11
ing everything up so long. I began to wonder what God thought about Westley, who certainly hadn't seen Jesus either, but who was now sitting proudly
on the platform, swinging his knickerbockered legs and grinning down at
me, surrounded by deacons and old women on their knees praying. God had
not struck Westley dead for taking his name in vain or for lying in the tem-
ple. So I decided that maybe to save further trouble, I'd better lie, too, and say
that Jesus had come, and get up and be saved.

So I got up. 12

Suddenly the whole room broke into a sea of shouting, as they saw me 13
rise. Waves of rejoicing swept the place. Women leaped into the air. My aunt

threw her arms around me. The minister took me by the hand and led me to the platform.

When things quieted down, in a hushed silence, punctuated by a few ec-   14
static "Amens," all the new young lambs were blessed in the name of God. Then joyous singing filled the room.

That night, for the last time in my life but one—for I was a big boy   15
twelve years old—I cried. I cried, in bed alone, and couldn't stop. I buried my head under the quilts, but my aunt heard me. She woke up and told my uncle I was crying because the Holy Ghost had come into my life, and because I had seen Jesus. But I was really crying because I couldn't bear to tell her that I had lied, that I had deceived everybody in the church, and I hadn't seen Jesus, and that now I didn't believe there was a Jesus any more, since he didn't come to help me.

◆ ◆ ◆

FIRST RESPONSES

Have you ever lied to escape a confusing or embarrassing situation? How did it make you feel? Do you now believe you were correct to act as you did?

TAKING A CLOSER LOOK

Exploring *Who:* Voice and Tone

1. List the emotions the young Langston feels toward his experience of being saved. How many different emotions does it create in the adult Hughes who is telling the story?

2. How does your childhood religious experience compare with Langston's? Does the similarity or difference affect your response to the essay?

3. ▉▐ *Using the Internet.* Visit the Web site at www.nku.edu/~diesmanj/ hughes.html#dreamdeferred, and read Hughes's poem "Dream Deferred." Then surf the site to read about Hughes's work as a whole and the Harlem Renaissance. How does this information add to your insight into Hughes's feelings about social and religious practices in his African American community?

Exploring *What:* Content and Meaning

1. Why is Langston confused by his aunt's description of salvation in paragraph 2? Did you experience any similar problems with language as a child?
2. What in the description of the sermon (para. 3) might explain why the young girls "jumped up and went to Jesus right away"?
3. Why does Langston finally get up?
4. How would you explain the difference between how his aunt explains Langston's crying and the real reasons?

Exploring *Why:* Purpose

1. How does the **paradox** presented in the first two sentences of the essay set up your feelings for the story that follows?
2. Why is Hughes so direct in explaining his reactions to the experience? What does his conclusion tell you about what he wants his readers to feel and think about?

Exploring *How:* Style and Strategy

1. Why did Hughes include **dialogue** in some places and not in others? For example, how effective is the dialogue that ends paragraph 6? Would paraphrase have achieved the same purpose?
2. Why does Hughes use repetition in the closing sentences of paragraph 7?
3. What is the effect of making paragraphs 5 and 12 one-sentence paragraphs?

IDEAS FOR WRITING A NARRATIVE

1. Narrate an experience when someone you cared about pressured you, directly or indirectly, to act in a way you didn't wish to act. Use dialogue and other concrete details to show the pressure you felt and the actions you took.
2. Hughes narrates his childhood experience to help define the word *salvation*. Think of an experience that has helped you to define a similarly significant concept, such as *friendship, commitment, discipline,* or *obsession*. Tell the story in a way that reflects your understanding of the term both before and after the experience.
3. Write an essay about an incident from your childhood using your point of view as a child and your point of view today.

◆ ◆ ◆ PREPARING TO READ

Have you ever witnessed a dramatic or startling public event, such as an accident or a fire? How did the people around you react? How did you react?

◆ ◆ ◆

Street Scene: Minor Heroism in a Major Metropolitan Area

IAN FRAZIER

Journalist Ian Frazier (born in 1951 in Cleveland, Ohio) writes fre-quently for both *The Atlantic Monthly* and *The New Yorker.* He is perhaps best known for his biting humor in books such as *Coyote v. Acme* (1996), for which he received the first Thurber House Award for American Humor in 1997. At the core of all his writing, however, is a connection of particular people to particular places, from an assembled cast of varied characters who evoke the complex spirit of the *Great Plains* (1989) to his own *Family* (1994), pieced together in a memory book to create "a meaning that would defeat death," to the Oglala Indians of Pine Ridge, South Dakota, in *On the Rez* (2000). The following essay first appeared in *The Atlantic Monthly* in Febru-ary 1995.

On a Saturday morning I left my Brooklyn apartment to shop for a 1 dinner party and saw a crowd—baseball caps, legs straddling bicycles, an arm holding a lamp stand with a dangling price tag—around a person on the side-walk. I was almost at my doorstep; I went closer, and saw a woman lying on her back with her lips turned into her mouth and her eyes neither open nor closed. Her hair was gray, her face the same color as the pavement. A slight, brown-haired woman was giving her mouth-to-mouth resuscitation, while a well-built brown-skinned man with hair close-cropped like a skullcap was performing chest massage. He and the woman giving mouth-to-mouth were counting, "One, two, three, four, five." Then he would pause and she would breathe into the woman's mouth.

A police car drove up and a young Hispanic cop got out. He went over 2 to the woman and talked to the pair trying to revive her. Someone pointed out to him the woman's son, a tall, gangly man who stood nearby, kind of bobbing up and down and nodding to himself. The cop patted the son on the arm and spoke to him. A large, lumpy-faced man with his pants high on his waist said to me, "The ambulance will never come. They never come when you call anymore. They don't care. In New York nobody cares. People are so arrogant on the street in Manhattan. I call New York a lost city. Used to be a great city, now it's a lost city. People are nicer out west or upstate. I went to Methodist Hospital and the nurse wouldn't talk to me. I told her right to her face . . ." After a minute I realized it made no difference if I listened to him or not. The pair at work on the woman paused for a moment while the man asked if anyone had a razor so he could cut the woman's shirt. Someone found a pocket knife. He bent over his work again. Minutes passed. The cop asked if he was getting tired and he said he wasn't. Sirens rose in the distance, faded. Then one rose and didn't fade, and in the next second an Emergency Medical Service truck from Long Island College Hospital pulled up. The chest-massage guy didn't quit until the EMS paramedic took over; then he straightened up, looked at the truck, and said, "Long *Island*? Fuckin' Methodist is only three blocks away."

The EMS guys put the woman on a stretcher and lifted her into the   3 back of the truck. Hands gathered up a few items the woman had dropped on the sidewalk; someone pointed out her false teeth. The woman who had been giving mouth-to-mouth bent over and picked up the teeth. She paused just a second before touching them. I thought this was from squeamishness; then I saw it was from care. Gently she handed the teeth to one of the paramedics. Then she and the chest-massage guy parted without a word, or none that I saw. The guy walked toward his car, a two-tone Pontiac. Apparently he had just been driving by; its door was still open. I went up to him and thanked him for what he had done. I shook his hand. His strength went right up my arm like a warm current. I ran after the woman, who was now well down the block. I tapped her shoulder and she turned around and I said thank you. Her eyes were full of what had just happened. There were tears on her upper cheeks. She said something like, "Oh, of course, don't mention it." She was a thin-faced white woman with Prince Valiant hair and a green windbreaker— an ordinary-looking person, but glowingly beautiful.

The EMS guys and the cop worked on the woman in the back of the   4 truck with the doors open. The crowd dispersed. The son crouched inside the truck holding the IV bottle for a while; then he stood outside again. Eventually the cop got out of the back of the truck. The son climbed in, the EMS guys closed the doors, and the truck drove off with sirens going. The cop sat in his car. The window was down. I walked over and asked, "Excuse me—did they ever get a pulse?" He winced slightly at the nakedness of my question. A pause. Then he shook his head. "Nahhh. Not really."

I went to the park across the street. A bunch of kids were hanging   5 around the entrance jawing back and forth at each other. In my neighborhood there is a gang called NAB, or Ninth Avenue Boys. Newspaper stories say they've done a lot of beatings and robberies nearby. From a few feet away I heard one kid say to another, "You shut your stupid fuckin' chicken-breath mouth." I felt as strong as the strangers I had just talked to. I walked through the kids without fear.

◆ ◆ ◆

FIRST RESPONSES

Would you have stopped to help this woman? What motivates good Samaritans? What causes others not to act?

TAKING A CLOSER LOOK

Exploring *Who:* Voice and Tone

1. What were Frazier's feelings about the people and events he witnessed? At what point in the essay did you discover his attitudes? Why does he wait so long to reveal them? Did they change as a result of his experience?

2. In paragraph 3, when the woman who has been helping grasps the victim's false teeth, Frazier remarks: "She paused just a second before touching them. I thought this was from squeamishness; then I saw it was from care." What effect does this observation have on your understanding of Frazier's thinking about this woman?

3. How does Frazier expect you to respond when he concludes, "I walked through the kids without fear"? What in your experience or in the essay led to your feelings about his own minor act of heroism?

Exploring *What:* Content and Meaning

1. What is Frazier's definition of heroism? How many other responses to the victim does Frazier describe? What human strengths and weaknesses are suggested by these responses?

2. What impressions of the police, the paramedics, and the city does the essay create?

3. Were you surprised when Frazier went up and thanked the man and woman who had tried to save the victim? What was his motive, and what did he gain from his spontaneous act?

Exploring *Why:* Purpose

1. Why would Frazier believe that this personal experience and insight would be valuable to his readers?

2. ▉▛ *Using the Internet.* With one of the Internet search engines, use the keyword "heroism" to find other articles on acts of heroism, and compare the definitions. Based on these examples, how would you define the term? Has this reading changed how you might react in a crisis?

Exploring *How:* Style and Strategy

1. How directly does Frazier define heroism? How would the essay have changed if he had decided instead to include a direct thesis in his introduction and an analytical conclusion?

2. Look closely at paragraph 1 for the ways that people and actions are described. How well can you picture the crowd around the woman receiving CPR? Which of your senses does Frazier appeal to? Why?

3. Did you notice Frazier's occasional use of very brief sentences? Look, for example, at the line "Minutes passed" toward the end of paragraph 2. What are the effects of this sentence at this point in the action? Can you find other such sentences in paragraph 4?

4. Frazier intentionally included only a few bits and pieces of dialogue. Why? With what effect?

IDEAS FOR WRITING A NARRATIVE

1. Narrate a crisis that you experienced, either as a direct participant or as an observer. Use concrete detail and dialogue to support the actions you recount.

2. Recall a time when you had to overcome a fear in order to accomplish a goal, such as conquering a fear of heights to go on a hiking trip with friends. As you tell this story, concentrate on your changing feelings through the course of the experience.

3. Tell the story of a time when you witnessed (or displayed) courage.

◆ ◆ ◆ PREPARING TO READ

Did one of your parents or grandparents ever tell you a story about his or her own life to teach you a lesson or help you make a decision in your own life? Did the story have the desired effect on you?

◆ ◆ ◆

No Name Woman

MAXINE HONG KINGSTON

Maxine Hong Kingston's fiction and essays have brought the unique experiences of West Coast Chinese American subculture into national view. Born in 1940 in Stockton, California, to first-generation Chinese immigrant parents, Kingston earned a degree in English literature from the University of California, Berkeley. Her autobiographical novel *The Woman Warrior,* from which "No Name Woman" is drawn, won a National Book Critics Circle Award in 1976. *China Men* (1980), a work of historical fiction, won the American Book Award, and her contemporary novel *Tripmaster Monkey* (1990) won the PEN West Award.

"You must not tell anyone," my mother said, "what I am about to tell 1 you. In China your father had a sister who killed herself. She jumped into the family well. We say that your father has all brothers because it is as if she had never been born.

"In 1924 just a few days after our village celebrated seventeen hurry- 2 up weddings—to make sure that every young man who went 'out on the road' would responsibly come home—your father and his brothers and your grandfather and his brothers and your aunt's new husband sailed for America, the Gold Mountain. It was your grandfather's last trip. Those lucky enough to get contracts waved good-bye from the decks. They fed and guarded the stowaways and helped them off in Cuba, New York, Bali, Hawaii. 'We'll meet in California next year,' they said. All of them sent money home.

"I remember looking at your aunt one day when she and I were dress- 3 ing; I had not noticed before that she had such a protruding melon of a stomach. But I did not think, 'She's pregnant,' until she began to look like other pregnant women, her shirt pulling and the white tops of her black pants showing. She could not have been pregnant, you see, because her husband had been gone for years. No one said anything. We did not discuss it. In early summer she was ready to have the child, long after the time when it could have been possible.

"The village had also been counting. On the night the baby was to be   4
born the villagers raided our house. Some were crying. Like a great saw, teeth strung with lights, files of people walked zigzag across our land, tearing the rice. Their lanterns doubled in the disturbed black water, which drained away through the broken bunds. As the villagers closed in, we could see that some of them, probably men and women we knew well, wore white masks. The people with long hair hung it over their faces. Women with short hair made it stand up on end. Some had tied white bands around their foreheads, arms, and legs.

"At first they threw mud and rocks at the house. Then they threw eggs   5
and began slaughtering our stock. We could hear the animals scream their deaths—the roosters, the pigs, a last great roar from the ox. Familiar wild heads flared in our night windows; the villagers encircled us. Some of the faces stopped to peer at us, their eyes rushing like searchlights. The hands flattened against the panes, framed heads, and left red prints.

"The villagers broke in the front and the back doors at the same time,   6
even though we had not locked the doors against them. Their knives dripped with the blood of our animals. They smeared blood on the doors and walls. One woman swung a chicken, whose throat she had slit, splattering blood in red arcs about her. We stood together in the middle of our house, in the family hall with the pictures and tables of the ancestors around us, and looked straight ahead.

"At that time the house had only two wings. When the men came back   7
we would build two more to enclose our courtyard and a third one to begin a second courtyard. The villagers pushed through both wings, even your grandparents' rooms, to find your aunt's, which was also mine until the men returned. From this room a new wing for one of the younger families would grow. They ripped up her clothes and shoes and broke her combs, grinding them underfoot. They tore her work from the loom. They scattered the cooking fire and rolled the new weaving in it. We could hear them in the kitchen breaking our bowls and banging the pots. They overturned the great waist-high earthenware jugs; duck eggs, pickled fruits, vegetables burst out and mixed in acrid torrents. The old woman from the next field swept a broom through the air and loosed the spirits-of-the-broom over our heads. 'Pig.' 'Ghost.' 'Pig,' they sobbed and scolded while they ruined our house.

"When they left, they took sugar and oranges to bless themselves. They   8
cut pieces from the dead animals. Some of them took bowls that were not broken and clothes that were not torn. Afterward we swept up the rice and sewed it back up into sacks. But the smells from the spilled preserves lasted. Your aunt gave birth in the pigsty that night. The next morning when I went up for the water, I found her and the baby plugging up the family well.

"Don't let your father know that I told you. He denies her. Now that   9
you have started to menstruate, what happened to her could happen to you.
Don't humiliate us. You wouldn't like to be forgotten as if you had never
been born. The villagers are watchful."

Whenever she had to warn us about life, my mother told stories that ran   10
like this one, a story to grow up on. She tested our strength to establish realities. Those in the emigrant generations who could not reassert brute
survival died young and far from home. Those of us in the first American
generations have had to figure out how the invisible world the emigrants
built around our childhoods fit in solid America.

The emigrants confused the gods by diverting their curses, misleading   11
them with crooked streets and false names. They must try to confuse their offspring as well, who, I suppose, threaten them in similar ways—always trying
to get things straight, always trying to name the unspeakable. The Chinese I
know hide their names; sojourners take new names when their lives change
and guard their real names with silence.

Chinese-Americans, when you try to understand what things in you are   12
Chinese, how do you separate what is peculiar to childhood, to poverty, in-
sanities, one family, your mother who marked your growing with stories, from
what is Chinese? What is Chinese tradition and what is the movies?

If I want to learn what clothes my aunt wore, whether flashy or ordinary,   13
I would have to begin, "Remember Father's drowned-in-the-well sister?" I
cannot ask that. My mother has told me once and for all the useful parts. She
will add nothing unless powered by Necessity, a riverbank that guides her
life. She plants vegetable gardens rather than lawns; she carries the odd-
shaped tomatoes home from the fields and eats food left for the gods.

Whenever we did frivolous things, we used up energy; we flew high   14
kites. We children came up off the ground over the melting cones our parents
brought home from work and the American movie on New Years' Day—
Oh, You Beautiful Doll with Betty Grable one year, and *She Wore a Yellow
Ribbon* with John Wayne another year. After the one carnival ride each, we
paid in guilt; our tired father counted his change on the dark walk home.

Adultery is extravagance. Could people who hatch their own chicks   15
and eat the embryos and the heads for delicacies and boil the feet in vinegar
for party food, leaving only the gravel, eating even the gizzard lining—could
such people engender a prodigal aunt? To be a woman, to have a daughter
in starvation time was a waste enough. My aunt could not have been the lone
romantic who gave up everything for sex. Women in the old China did not
choose. Some man had commanded her to lie with him and be his secret evil.
I wonder whether he masked himself when he joined the raid on her family.

Perhaps she encountered him in the fields or on the mountain where the   16
daughters-in-law collected fuel. Or perhaps he first noticed her in the mar-
ketplace. He was not a stranger because the village housed no strangers. She

had to have dealings with him other than sex. Perhaps he worked an adjoining field, or he sold her the cloth for the dress she sewed and wore. His demand must have surprised, then terrified her. She obeyed him; she always did as she was told.

When the family found a young man in the next village to be her husband, she stood tractably beside the best rooster, his proxy, and promised before they met that she would be his forever. She was lucky that he was her age and she would be the first wife, an advantage secure now. The night she first saw him, he had sex with her. Then he left for America. She had almost forgotten what he looked like. When she tried to envision him, she only saw the black and white face in the group photograph the men had had taken before leaving. 17

The other man was not, after all, much different from her husband. They both gave orders: she followed. "If you tell your family, I'll beat you. I'll kill you. Be here again next week." No one talked sex, ever. And she might have separated the rapes from the rest of living if only she did not have to buy her oil from him or gather wood in the same forest. I want her fear to have lasted just as long as rape lasted so that the fear could have been contained. No drawn-out fear. But women at sex hazarded birth and hence lifetimes. The fear did not stop but permeated everywhere. She told the man, "I think I'm pregnant." He organized the raid against her. 18

On nights when my mother and father talked about their life back home, sometimes they mentioned an "outcast table" whose business they still seemed to be settling, their voices tight. In a commensal tradition, where food is precious, the powerful older people made wrongdoers eat alone. Instead of letting them start separate new lives like the Japanese, who could become samurais and geishas, the Chinese family, faces averted but eyes glowering sideways, hung on to the offenders and fed them leftovers. My aunt must have lived in the same house as my parents and eaten at an outcast table. My mother spoke about the raid as if she had seen it, when she and my aunt, a daughter-in-law to a different household, should not have been living together at all. Daughters-in-law lived with their husbands' parents, not their own; a synonym for marriage in Chinese is "taking a daughter-in-law." Her husband's parents could have sold her, mortgaged her, stoned her. But they had sent her back to her own mother and father, a mysterious act hinting at disgraces not told me. Perhaps they had thrown her out to deflect the avengers. 19

She was the only daughter; her four brothers went with her father, husband, and uncles "out on the road" and for some years became western men. When the goods were divided among the family, three of the brothers took land, and the youngest, my father, chose an education. After my grandparents gave their daughter away to her husband's family, they had dispensed all the adventure and all the property. They expected her alone to keep the 20 traditional ways, which her brothers, now among the barbarians, could fumble without detection. The heavy, deep-rooted women were to maintain the past against the flood, safe for returning. But the rare urge west had fixed upon our family, and so my aunt crossed boundaries not delineated in space.

The work of preservation demands that the feelings playing about in   21
one's guts not be turned into action. Just watch their passing like cherry blossoms. But perhaps my aunt, my forerunner, caught in a slow life, let dreams grow and fade and after some months or years went toward what persisted. Fear at the enormities of the forbidden kept her desires delicate, wire and bone. She looked at a man because she liked the way the hair was tucked behind his ears, or she liked the question-mark line of a long torso curving at the shoulder and straight at the hip. For warm eyes or a soft voice or a slow walk—that's all—a few hairs, a line, a brightness, a sound, a pace, she gave up family. She offered us up for a charm that vanished with tiredness, a pigtail that didn't toss when the wind died. Why, the wrong lighting could erase the dearest thing about him.

It could very well have been, however, that my aunt did not take sub-   22
tle enjoyment of her friend, but, a wild woman, kept rollicking company. Imagining her free with sex doesn't fit, though. I don't know any women like that, or men either. Unless I see her life branching into mine, she gives me no ancestral help.

To sustain her being in love, she often worked at herself in the mirror,   23
guessing at the colors and shapes that would interest him, changing them frequently in order to hit on the right combination. She wanted him to look back.

On a farm near the sea, a woman who tended her appearance reaped   24
a reputation for eccentricity. All the married women blunt-cut their hair in flaps about their ears or pulled it back in tight buns. No nonsense. Neither style blew easily into heart-catching tangles. And at their weddings they displayed themselves in their long hair for the last time. "It brushed the backs of my knees," my mother tells me. "It was braided, and even so, it brushed the backs of my knees."

At the mirror my aunt combed individuality into her bob. A bun could   25
have been contrived to escape into black streamers blowing in the wind or in quiet wisps about her face, but only the older women in our picture album wear buns. She brushed her hair back from her forehead, tucking the flaps behind her ears. She looped a piece of thread, knotted into a circle between her index fingers and thumbs, and ran the double strand across her forehead. When she closed her fingers as if she were making a pair of shadow geese bite, the string twisted together catching the little hairs. Then she pulled the thread away from her skin, ripping the hairs out neatly, her eyes watering from the needles of pain. Opening her fingers, she cleaned the thread, then rolled it along her hairline and the tops of the eyebrows. My mother did the same to

me and my sisters and herself. I used to believe that the expression "caught by the short hairs" meant a captive held with a depilatory string. It especially hurt at the temples, but my mother said we were lucky we didn't have to have our feet bound when we were seven. Sisters used to sit on their beds and cry together, she said, as their mothers or their slave removed the bandages for a few minutes each night and let the blood gush back into their veins. I hope that the man my aunt loved appreciated a smooth brow, that he wasn't just a tits-and-ass man.

Once my aunt found a freckle on her chin, at a spot that the almanac 26
said predestined her for unhappiness. She dug it out with a hot needle and washed the wound with peroxide.

More attention to her looks than these pullings of hairs and pickings at 27
spots would have caused gossip among the villagers. They owned work clothes and good clothes, and they wore good clothes for feasting the new seasons. But since a woman combing her hair hexes beginnings, my aunt rarely found an occasion to look her best. Women looked like great sea snails—the corded wood, babies, and laundry they carried were the whorls on their backs. The Chinese did not admire a bent back; goddesses and warriors stood straight. Still there must have been a marvelous freeing of beauty when a worker laid down her burden and stretched and arched.

Such commonplace loveliness, however, was not enough for my aunt. 28
She dreamed of a lover for the fifteen days of New Year's, the time for families to exchange visits, money, and food. She plied her secret comb. And sure enough she cursed the year, the family, the village, and herself.

Even as her hair lured her imminent lover, many other men looked at 29
her. Uncles, cousins, nephews, brothers would have looked, too, had they been home between journeys. Perhaps they had already been restraining their curiosity, and they left, fearful that their glances, like a field of nesting birds, might be startled and caught. Poverty hurt, and that was their first reason for leaving. But another, final reason for leaving the crowded house was the never-said.

She may have been unusually beloved, the precious only daughter, 30
spoiled and mirror-gazing because of the affection the family lavished on her. When her husband left, they welcomed the chance to take her back from the in-laws; she could live like the little daughter for just a while longer. There are stories that my grandfather was different from other people, "crazy ever since the little Jap bayoneted him in the head." He used to put his naked penis on the dinner table, laughing. And one day he brought home a baby girl, wrapped up inside his brown western-style greatcoat. He had traded one of his sons, probably my father, the youngest, for her. My grandmother made him trade back. When he finally got a daughter of his own, he doted on her. They must have all loved her, except perhaps my father, the only brother who never went back to China, having once been traded for a girl.

Brothers and sisters, newly men and women, had to efface their sexual   31
color and present plain miens. Disturbing hair and eyes, a smile like no other,
threatened the ideal of five generations living under one roof. To focus blurs,
people shouted face to face and yelled from room to room. The immigrants
I know have loud voices, unmodulated to American tones even after years
away from the village where they called their friendships out across the fields.
I have not been able to stop my mother's screams in public libraries or over
telephones. Walking erect (knees straight, toes pointed forward, not pigeon-
toed, which is Chinese-feminine) and speaking in an inaudible voice, I have
tried to turn myself American-feminine. Chinese communication was loud,
public. Only sick people had to whisper. But at the dinner table, where the
family members came nearest one another, no one could talk, not the outcasts
nor any eaters. Every word that falls from the mouth is a coin lost. Silently
they gave and accepted food with both hands. A preoccupied child who took
his bowl with one hand got a sideways glare. A complete moment of total
attention is due everyone alike. Children and lovers have no singularity here,
but my aunt used a secret voice, a separate attentiveness.

She kept the man's name to herself throughout her labor and dying; she   32
did not accuse him that he be punished with her. To save her inseminator's
name she gave silent birth.

He may have been somebody in her own household, but intercourse   33
with a man outside the family would have been no less abhorrent. All the
village were kinsmen, and the titles shouted in loud country voices never let
kinship be forgotten. Any man within visiting distance would have been neu-
tralized as a lover—"brother," "younger brother," "older brother"—one hundred and fifteen relationship titles. Parents researched birth charts probably
not so much to assure good fortune as to circumvent incest in a population
that has but one hundred surnames. Everybody has eight million relatives.
How useless then sexual mannerisms, how dangerous.

As if it came from an atavism deeper than fear, I used to add "brother"   34
silently to boys' names. It hexed the boys, who would or would not ask me
to dance, and made them less scary and as familiar and deserving of benev-
olence as girls.

But, of course, I hexed myself also—no dates. I should have stood up,   35
both arms waving, and shouted out across libraries, "Hey, you! Love me
back." I had no idea, though, how to make attraction selective, how to control its direction and magnitude. If I made myself American-pretty so that the
five or six Chinese boys in the class fell in love with me, everyone else—the
Caucasian, Negro, and Japanese boys—would too. Sisterliness, dignified and
honorable, made much more sense.

Attraction eludes control so stubbornly that whole societies designed to   36
organize relationships among people cannot keep order, not even when they
bind people to one another from childhood and raise them together. Among
the very poor and the wealthy, brothers married their adopted sisters, like

doves. Our family allowed some romance, paying adult brides prices and providing dowries so that their sons and daughters could marry strangers. Marriage promises to turn strangers into friendly relatives—a nation of siblings.

In the village structure, spirits shimmered among the live creatures, balanced and held in equilibrium by time and land. But one human being flaring up into violence could open up a black hole, a maelstrom that pulled in the sky. The frightened villagers, who depended on one another to maintain the real, went to my aunt to show her a personal, physical representation of the break she made in the "roundness." Misallying couples snapped off the future, which was to be embodied in true offspring. The villagers punished her for acting as if she could have a private life, secret and apart from them. 37

If my aunt had betrayed the family at a time of large grain yields and peace, when many boys were born, and wings were being built on many houses, perhaps she might have escaped such severe punishment. But the men—hungry, greedy, tired of planting in dry soil, cuckolded—had been forced to leave the village in order to send food-money home. There were ghost plagues, bandit plagues, wars with the Japanese, floods. My Chinese brother and sister had died of an unknown sickness. Adultery, perhaps only a mistake during good times, became a crime when the village needed food. 38

The round moon cakes and round doorways, the round tables of graduated size that fit one roundness inside another, round windows and rice bowls—these talismans had lost their power to warn this family of the law: A family must be whole, faithfully keeping the descent line by having sons to feed the old and the dead who in turn look after the family. The villagers came to show my aunt and lover-in-hiding a broken house. The villagers were speeding up the circling of events because she was too shortsighted to see that her infidelity had already harmed the village, that waves of consequences would return unpredictably, sometimes in disguise, as now, to hurt her. This roundness had to be made coin-sized so that she would see its circumference: Punish her at the birth of her baby. Awaken her to the inexorable. People who refused fatalism because they could invent small resources insisted on culpability. Deny accidents and wrest fault from the stars. 39

After the villagers left, their lanterns now scattering in various directions toward home, the family broke their silence and cursed her. "Aiaa, we're going to die. Death is coming. Death is coming. Look what you've done. You've killed us. Ghost! Dead Ghost! Ghost! You've never been born." She ran out into the fields, far enough from the house so that she could no longer hear their voices, and pressed herself against the earth, her own land no more. When she felt the birth coming, she thought that she had been hurt. Her body seized together. "They've hurt me too much," she thought. "This is gall, and it will kill me." With forehead and knees against the earth, her body convulsed and then relaxed. She turned on her back, lay on the ground. The black well of sky and stars went out and out forever; her body and her 40 complexity seemed to disappear. She was one of the stars, a bright dot in blackness, without home, without a companion, in eternal cold and silence. An agoraphobia rose in her, speeding higher and higher, bigger and bigger; she would not be able to contain it; there would be no end to fear.

Flayed, unprotected against space, she felt pain return, focusing her body. 41 This pain chilled her—a cold, steady kind of surface pain. Inside, spasmodically, the other pain, the pain of the child, heated her. For hours she lay on the ground, alternately body and space. Sometimes a vision of normal comfort obliterated reality: She saw the family in the evening gambling at the dinner table, the young people massaging their elders' backs. She saw them congratulating one another, high joy on the mornings the rice shoots came up. When these pictures burst, the stars drew yet further apart. Black space opened.

She got to her feet to fight better and remembered that old-fashioned 42 women gave birth in their pigsties to fool the jealous, pain-dealing gods, who do not snatch piglets. Before the next spasms could stop her, she ran to the pigsty, each step a rushing out into emptiness. She climbed over the fence and knelt in the dirt. It was good to have a fence enclosing her, a tribal person alone.

Laboring, this woman who had carried her child as a foreign growth 43 that sickened her every day, expelled it at last. She reached down to touch the hot, wet, moving mass, surely smaller than anything human, and could feel that it was human after all—fingers, toes, nails, nose. She pulled it up on to her belly, and it lay curled there, butt in the air, feet precisely tucked one under the other. She opened her loose shirt and buttoned the child inside. After resting, it squirmed and thrashed and she pushed it up to her breast. It turned its head this way and that until it found her nipple. There, it made little snuffling noises. She clenched her teeth at its preciousness, lovely as a young calf, a piglet, a little dog.

She may have gone to the pigsty as a last act of responsibility: She would 44 protect this child as she had protected its father. It would look after her soul, leaving supplies on her grave. But how would this tiny child without family find her grave when there would be no marker for her anywhere, neither in the earth nor the family hall? No one would give her a family hall name. She had taken the child with her into the wastes. At its birth the two of them had felt the same raw pain of separation, a wound that only the family pressing tight could close. A child with no descent line would not soften her life but only trail after her, ghostlike, begging her to give it purpose. At dawn the villagers on their way to the fields would stand around the fence and look.

Full of milk, the little ghost slept. When it awoke, she hardened her 45 breasts against the milk that crying loosens. Toward morning she picked up the baby and walked to the well.

Carrying the baby to the well shows loving. Otherwise abandon it. Turn 46 its face into the mud. Mothers who love their children take them along. It was probably a girl; there is some hope of forgiveness for boys.

"Don't tell anyone you had an aunt. Your father does not want to hear   47
her name. She has never been born." I have believed that sex was unspeakable and words so strong and fathers so frail that "aunt" would do my father mysterious harm. I have thought that my family, having settled among immigrants who had also been their neighbors in the ancestral land, needed to clean their name, and a wrong word would incite the kinspeople even here. But there is more to this silence: They want me to participate in her punishment. And I have.

In the twenty years since I heard this story I have not asked for details   48
nor said my aunt's name; I do not know it. People who comfort the dead can also chase after them to hurt them further—a reverse ancestor worship. The real punishment was not the raid swiftly inflicted by the villagers, but the family's deliberately forgetting her. Her betrayal so maddened them, they saw to it that she would suffer forever, even after death. Always hungry, always needing, she would have to beg food from other ghosts, snatch and steal it from those whose living descendants give them gifts. She would have to fight the ghosts massed at crossroads for the buns a few thoughtful citizens leave to decoy her away from village and home so that the ancestral spirits could feast unharassed. At peace, they could act like gods, not ghosts, their descent lines providing them with paper suits and dresses, spirit money, paper houses, paper automobiles, chicken, meat, and rice into eternity—essences delivered up in smoke and flames, steam and incense rising from each rice bowl. In an attempt to make the Chinese care for people outside the family, Chairman Mao encourages us now to give our paper replicas to the spirits of outstanding soldiers and workers, no matter whose ancestors they may be. My aunt remains forever hungry. Goods are not distributed evenly among the dead.

My aunt haunts me—her ghost drawn to me because now, after fifty   49
years of neglect, I alone devote pages of paper to her, though not origamied into houses and clothes. I do not think she always means me well. I am telling on her, and she was a spite suicide, drowning herself in the drinking water. The Chinese are always very frightened of the drowned one, whose weeping ghost, wet hair hanging and skin bloated, waits silently by the water to pull down a substitute.

◆ ◆ ◆

FIRST RESPONSES

Which story about the aunt's relationship with her baby's father do you most want to believe? Why? Does that choice affect your response to the aunt's death?

TAKING A CLOSER LOOK

Exploring *Who:* Voice and Tone

1. How does Kingston feel about her aunt? About her mother? About being both Chinese and American? Why does she believe that narrating the events which led to her attitudes and feelings will be valuable to her readers, too?

2. What tone of voice does Kingston use when she writes in paragraph 25, "I hope that the man my aunt loved appreciated a smooth brow, that he wasn't just a tits-and-ass man"? What does the sentence tell you about Kingston?

3. How much does the author expect readers to know about the Chinese culture? Does she include experiences or feelings that anyone, regardless of nationality, can relate to?

4. ▆ *Using the Internet.* The University of Minnesota has established a Maxine Hong Kingston Web site at http://voices.cla.umn.edu/authors/ MaxineHongKingston.html. Does the information provided there add to your understanding of Kingston's perspective in "No Name Woman"? If so, how?

Exploring *What:* Content and Meaning

1. Why did the villagers attack Kingston's family's home? Reread paragraph 39 to see if it gives you additional insight into their reasons. Find evidence that Kingston has some sympathy for their motives.

2. Could this essay have been written by a man? Why or why not? How would it be different if one of Kingston's brothers tried to retell the mother's story about the aunt?

3. What does Kingston mean when she says, "Carrying the baby to the well shows loving"? How has Kingston prepared you to understand her point?

Exploring *Why:* Purpose

1. Kingston directly reveals her mother's reason for narrating her aunt's story: "Now that you have started to menstruate, what happened to her could happen to you." How did you respond to this warning? What are Kingston's reasons for telling us this same story?

2. What does the author mean when she says in the conclusion, "I do not think she [her aunt] always means me well"? What risks does Kingston

face in telling us this story? Have you ever repeated a story that you were asked not to share with anyone?

Exploring *How:* Style and Strategy

1. Kingston writes, "Unless I see her life [her aunt's] branching into mine, she gives me no ancestral help." Does this statement explain why she writes multiple versions of her aunt's story? What sources does Kingston use to piece together the interpretations she creates? Paragraph 19 might offer you some answers to this question.

2. Read paragraphs 4 and 5 and identify the **similes** (comparisons using *like* or *as*). How do these comparisons add to your understanding of the scene Kingston is describing?

3. Kingston uses vivid, descriptive language to bring her scenes to life. Look at one of the major scenes, either the villagers' attack or the childbirth, and identify Kingston's use of concrete detail and appeal to the senses to achieve her desired affect on the reader.

IDEAS FOR WRITING A NARRATIVE

1. Write a narrative in which you tell the story of an important moment in your life from your own point of view. Then rewrite the story from the point of view of someone else involved in the story.

2. Narrate a story that reveals a time you felt torn between two roles that you hold, such as daughter versus sister, employee versus friend, or student versus friend.

3. Tell the story of a time when you were happy or unhappy with your family life.

Did you ever have to perform an extremely difficult or distasteful task? Why did you believe that you had to do it? How did you feel afterward?

◆ ◆ ◆

Shooting an Elephant

GEORGE ORWELL

Novelist, essayist, and critic, George Orwell (pen name of Eric Blair, 1903–1950) was born in India, where his father was in the civil service. He was educated at Eton but was financially unable to go on to Oxford or Cambridge. Instead, he spent five years with the Imperial Police in Burma. Orwell is widely regarded as one of the finest satirists of the twentieth century. His most famous novels are *Animal Farm,* a scathing attack on communism, and *1984,* a chilling depiction of a totalitarian society. Several of his best essays, including this one, draw upon his experiences in Burma.

In Moulmein, in Lower Burma, I was hated by large numbers of people—the only time in my life that I have been important enough for this to happen to me. I was subdivisional police officer of the town, and in an aimless, petty kind of way anti-European feeling was very bitter. No one had the guts to raise a riot, but if a European woman went through the bazaars alone somebody would probably spit betel juice over her dress. As a police officer I was an obvious target and was baited whenever it seemed safe to do so. When a nimble Burman tripped me up on the football field and the referee (another Burman) looked the other way, the crowd yelled with hideous laughter. This happened more than once. In the end the sneering yellow faces of young men that met me everywhere, the insults hooted after me when I was at a safe distance, got badly on my nerves. The young Buddhist priests were the worst of all. There were several thousands of them in the town and none of them seemed to have anything to do except stand on street corners and jeer at Europeans.   1

All this was perplexing and upsetting. For at that time I had already made up my mind that imperialism was an evil thing and the sooner I chucked up my job and got out of it the better. Theoretically—and secretly, of course—I was all for the Burmese and all against the oppressors, the British. As for the job I was doing, I hated it more bitterly than I can perhaps make clear.   2

In a job like that you see the dirty work of Empire at close quarters. The wretched prisoners huddling in the stinking cages of the lockups, the grey, cowed faces of the long-term convicts, the scarred buttocks of the men who had been flogged with bamboos—all these oppressed me with an intolerable sense of guilt. But I could get nothing into perspective. I was young and ill-educated and I had had to think out my problems in the utter silence that is imposed on every Englishman in the East. I did not even know that the British Empire is dying, still less did I know that it is a great deal better than the younger empires that are going to supplant it. All I knew was that I was stuck between my hatred of the empire I served and my rage against the evil-spirited little beasts who tried to make my job impossible. With one part of my mind I thought of the British Rajas as an unbreakable tyranny, as something clamped down, in *saecula saeculorum,* upon the will of prostrate peoples; with another part I thought that the greatest joy in the world would be to drive a bayonet into a Buddhist priest's guts. Feelings like these are the normal by-products of imperialism; ask any Anglo-Indian official, if you can catch him off duty.

One day something happened which in a roundabout way was en-   3
lightening. It was a tiny incident in itself, but it gave me a better glimpse than I had had before of the real nature of imperialism—the real motives for which despotic governments act. Early one morning the sub-inspector at a police station at the other end of town rang me up on the phone and said that an elephant was ravaging the bazaar. Would I please come and do something about it? I did not know what I could do, but I wanted to see what was happening and I got on to a pony and started out. I took my rifle, an old .44 Winchester and much too small to kill an elephant, but I thought the noise might be useful *in terrorem.* Various Burmans stopped me on the way and told me about the elephant's doings. It was not, of course, a wild elephant, but a tame one which had gone "must." It had been chained up, as tame elephants always are when their attack of "must" is due, but on the previous night it had broken its chain and escaped. Its mahout, the only person who could manage it when it was in that state, had set out in pursuit, but had taken the wrong direction and was now twelve hours' journey away, and in the morning the elephant had suddenly reappeared in the town. The Burmese population had no weapons and were quite helpless against it. It had already destroyed somebody's bamboo hut, killed a cow, and raided some fruit stalls and devoured the stock; also it had met the municipal rubbish van and, when the driver jumped out and took to his heels, had turned the van over and inflicted violences upon it.

The Burmese sub-inspector and some Indian constables were waiting   4
for me in the quarter where the elephant had been seen. It was a very poor quarter, a labyrinth of squalid bamboo huts, thatched with palm-leaf, winding all over a steep hillside. I remember that it was a cloudy, stuffy morning

at the beginning of the rains. We began questioning the people as to where the elephant had gone and, as usual, failed to get any definite information. That is invariably the case in the East; a story always sounds clear enough at a distance, but the nearer you get to the scene of events the vaguer it becomes. Some of the people said that the elephant had gone in one direction, some said that he had gone in another, some professed not even to have heard of any elephant. I had almost made up my mind that the whole story was a pack of lies, when we heard yells a little distance away. There was a loud, scandalized cry of "Go away, child! Go away this instant!" and an old woman with a switch in her hand came round the corner of a hut, violently shooing away a crowd of naked children. Some more women followed, clicking their tongues and exclaiming; evidently there was something that the children ought not to have seen. I rounded the hut and saw a man's dead body sprawling in the mud. He was an Indian, a black Dravidian coolie, almost naked, and he could not have been dead many minutes. The people said that the elephant had come suddenly upon him round the corner of the hut, caught him with its trunk, put its foot on his back, and ground him into the earth. This was the rainy season and the ground was soft, and his face had scored a trench a foot deep and a couple of yards long. He was lying on his belly with arms crucified and head sharply twisted to one side. His face was coated with mud, the eyes wide open, the teeth bared and grinning with an expression of unendurable agony. (Never tell me, by the way, that the dead look peaceful. Most of the corpses I have seen looked devilish.) The friction of the great beast's foot had stripped the skin from his back as neatly as one skins a rabbit. As soon as I saw the dead man I sent an orderly to a friend's house nearby to borrow an elephant rifle. I had already sent back the pony, not wanting it to go mad with fright and throw me if it smelled the elephant.

The orderly came back in a few minutes with a rifle and five cartridges,   5 and meanwhile some Burmans had arrived and told us that the elephant was in the paddy fields below, only a few hundred yards away. As I started forward practically the whole population of the quarter flocked out of the houses and followed me. They had seen the rifle and were all shouting excitedly that I was going to shoot the elephant. They had not shown much interest in the elephant when he was merely ravaging their homes, but it was different now that he was going to be shot. It was a bit of fun to them, as it would be to an English crowd; besides they wanted the meat. It made me vaguely uneasy. I had no intention of shooting the elephant—I had merely sent for the rifle to defend myself if necessary—and it is always unnerving to have a crowd following you. I marched down the hill, looking and feeling a fool, with the rifle over my shoulder and an ever-growing army of people jostling at my heels. At the bottom, when you got away from the huts, there was a metalled road and beyond that a miry waste of paddy fields a thousand yards across, not yet ploughed but soggy from the first rains and dotted with coarse grass. The elephant was standing eight yards from the road, his left side towards us. He took not the slightest notice of the crowd's approach. He was tearing up bunches of grass, beating them against his knees to clean them and stuffing them into his mouth.

I had halted on the road. As soon as I saw the elephant I knew with per- 6 fect certainty that I ought not to shoot him. It is a serious matter to shoot a working elephant—it is comparable to destroying a huge and costly piece of machinery—and obviously one ought not to do it if it can possibly be avoided. And at that distance, peacefully eating, the elephant looked no more dangerous than a cow. I thought then and I think now that his attack of "must" was already passing off; in which case he would merely wander harmlessly about until the mahout came back and caught him. Moreover, I did not in the least want to shoot him. I decided that I would watch him for a little while to make sure that he did not turn savage again, and then go home.

But at that moment, I glanced round at the crowd that had followed me. 7 It was an immense crowd, two thousand at the least and growing every minute. It blocked the road for a long distance on either side. I looked at the sea of yellow faces above the garish clothes—faces all happy and excited over this bit of fun, all certain that the elephant was going to be shot. They were watching me as they would watch a conjuror about to perform a trick. They did not like me, but with the magical rifle in my hands I was momentarily worth watching. And suddenly I realized that I should have to shoot the elephant after all. The people expected it of me and I had got to do it. I could feel their two thousand wills pressing me forward, irresistibly. And it was at this moment, as I stood there with the rifle in my hands, that I first grasped the hollowness, the futility of the white man's dominion in the East. Here was I, the white man with his gun, standing in front of the unarmed native crowd—seemingly the leading actor of the piece; but in reality I was only an absurd puppet pushed to and fro by the will of those yellow faces behind. I perceived in this moment that when the white man turns tyrant it is his own freedom that he destroys. He becomes a sort of hollow, posing dummy, the conventionalized figure of a sahib. For it is the condition of his rule that he shall spend his life in trying to impress the "natives," and so in every crisis he has got to do what the "natives" expect of him. He wears a mask, and his face grows to fit it. I had got to shoot the elephant. I had committed myself to doing it when I sent for the rifle. A sahib has got to act like a sahib; he has got to appear resolute, to know his own mind and do definite things. To come all that way, rifle in hand, with two thousand people marching at my heels, and then to trail feebly away, having done nothing—no, that was impossible. The crowd would laugh at me. And my whole life, every white man's life in the East, was one long struggle not to be laughed at.

But I did not want to shoot the elephant. I watched him beating his 8 bunch of grass against his knees, with that preoccupied grandmotherly air that elephants have. It seemed to me that it would be murder to shoot him. At that age I was not squeamish about killing animals, but I had never shot an elephant and never wanted to. (Somehow it always seems worse to kill a large animal.) Besides, there was the beast's owner to be considered. Alive, the elephant was worth at least a hundred pounds; dead, he would only be worth the value of his tusks, five pounds, possibly. But I had got to act quickly. I turned to some experienced-looking Burmans who had been there when we arrived, and asked them how the elephant had been behaving. They all said the same thing: He took no notice of you if you left him alone, but he might charge if you went too close to him.

It was perfectly clear to me what I ought to do. I ought to walk up to   9
within, say, twenty-five yards of the elephant and test his behavior. If he charged, I could shoot; if he took no notice of me, it would be safe to leave him until the mahout came back. But also I knew that I was going to do no such thing. I was a poor shot with a rifle and the ground was soft mud into which one would sink at every step. If the elephant charged and I missed him, I should have about as much chance as a toad under a steamroller. But even then I was not thinking particularly of my own skin, only of the watchful yellow faces behind. For at that moment, with the crowd watching me, I was not afraid in the ordinary sense, as I would have been if I had been alone. A white man mustn't be frightened in front of "natives"; and so, in general, he isn't frightened. The sole thought in my mind was that if anything went wrong those two thousand Burmans would see me pursued, caught, trampled on, and reduced to a grinning corpse like that Indian up the hill. And if that happened it was quite probable that some of them would laugh. That would never do. There was only one alternative. I shoved the cartridges into the magazine and lay down on the road to get a better aim.

The crowd grew very still, and a deep, low, happy sigh, as of people who   10
see the theatre curtain go up at last, breathed from innumerable throats. They were going to have their bit of fun after all. The rifle was a beautiful German thing with cross-hair sights. I did not then know that in shooting an elephant one would shoot to cut an imaginary bar running from ear-hole to ear-hole. I ought, therefore, as the elephant was sideways on, to have aimed straight at his ear-hole; actually I aimed several inches in front of this, thinking the brain would be further forward.

When I pulled the trigger I did not hear the bang or feel the kick—one   11
never does when a shot goes home—but I heard the devilish roar of glee that went up from the crowd. In that instant, in too short a time, one would have thought, even for the bullet to get there, a mysterious, terrible change had come over the elephant. He neither stirred nor fell, but every line of his body had altered. He looked suddenly stricken, shrunken, immensely old, as though the frightful impact of the bullet had paralyzed him without knocking him down. At last, after what seemed a long time—it might have been five seconds, I dare say—he sagged flabbily to his knees. His mouth slobbered. An

enormous senility seemed to have settled upon him. One could have imagined him thousands of years old. I fired again into the same spot. At the second shot he did not collapse but climbed with desperate slowness to his feet and stood weakly upright, with legs sagging and head drooping. I fired a third time. That was the shot that did for him. You could see the agony of it jolt his whole body and knock the last remnant of strength from his legs. But in falling he seemed for a moment to rise, for as his hind legs collapsed beneath him he seemed to tower upward like a huge rock toppling, his trunk reaching skywards like a tree. He trumpeted, for the first and only time. And then down he came, his belly towards me, with a crash that seemed to shake the ground even where I lay.

I got up. The Burmans were already racing past me across the mud. It 12 was obvious that the elephant would never rise again, but he was not dead. He was breathing very rhythmically with long rattling gasps, his great mound of a side painfully rising and falling. His mouth was wide open. I could see far down into caverns of pale pink throat. I waited a long time for him to die, but his breathing did not weaken. Finally, I fired my two remaining shots into the spot where I thought his heart must be. The thick blood welled out of him like red velvet, but still he did not die. His body did not even jerk when the shots hit him, the tortured breathing continued without a pause. He was dying, very slowly and in great agony, but in some world remote from me where not even a bullet could damage him further. I felt I had got to put an end to that dreadful noise. It seemed dreadful to see the great beast lying there, powerless to move and yet powerless to die, and not even to be able to finish him I sent back for my small rifle and poured shot after shot into his heart, and down his throat. They seemed to make no impression. The tortured gasps continued as steadily as the ticking of a clock.

In the end I could not stand it any longer and went away. I heard later 13 that it took him half an hour to die. Burmans were bringing dahs and baskets even before I left, and I was told they had stripped his body almost to the bones by the afternoon.

Afterwards, of course, there were endless discussions about the shoot- 14 ing of the elephant. The owner was furious, but he was only an Indian and could do nothing. Besides, legally I had done the right thing, for a mad elephant has to be killed, like a mad dog, if its owner fails to control it. Among the Europeans opinion was divided. The older men said I was right, the younger men said it was a damn shame to shoot an elephant for killing a coolie, because the elephant was worth more than any damn Coringhee coolie. And afterwards I was very glad that the coolie had been killed; it put me legally in the right and it gave me sufficient pretext for shooting the elephant. I often wondered whether any of the others grasped that I had done it solely to avoid looking a fool.

◆ ◆ ◆

FIRST RESPONSES

Do you think Orwell should have killed the elephant? What other choices did he have? Do you sympathize with him? Do you sympathize with the elephant?

TAKING A CLOSER LOOK

Exploring *Who:* Voice and Tone

1. What attitude does Orwell have toward the Burmese people? How do they feel about him? How might the incident have ended if he had had other Europeans with him when he encountered the elephant?
2. How does Orwell want to present himself in paragraphs 6 through 9? How did you respond to this section of the essay?
3. Orwell says he shot the elephant "solely to avoid looking a fool." What do you think of this admission? Have you ever felt you had to go against your instincts to avoid looking foolish?

Exploring *What:* Content and Meaning

1. Where is Burma, and what was Orwell doing there?
2. What is Orwell's thesis? Where does he state it?
3. ■ *Using the Internet.* Orwell uses the word *imperialism* several times. What does it mean? Using an Internet search engine, do a keyword search for *imperialism,* and see if you can find any current or recent events where the term is applicable.
4. List the reasons Orwell considers when he tries to decide what to do. Do any of these reasons seem suspect?
5. Why does Orwell say, "I was very glad that the coolie had been killed" (para. 14)?

Exploring *Why:* Purpose

1. Is Orwell trying to justify his actions? Or does he have a different purpose? To what extent is this essay an exploration of the author's beliefs?
2. A **parable** is defined as "an illustrative story that teaches a lesson." In what ways is this essay a parable?

Exploring *How:* Style and Strategy

1. Where does the narrative begin? Why does Orwell take so long to get to the central incident? How did you react to this long introduction?
2. Why does the author use Latin phrases? What effect did these have on you?
3. Why does Orwell enclose some remarks in parentheses (para. 4 and 8)?
4. Why didn't Orwell use any **dialogue** in this essay? What does he lose by omitting dialogue? What does he gain?
5. What effect do the graphic details of the dead man and the dying elephant have on your reactions to the essay? Could Orwell have accomplished his purpose without including these details?
6. How does Orwell build tension after he shoots the elephant?

IDEAS FOR WRITING A NARRATIVE

1. Narrate an experience that led you to a realization about your place in the world around you (for example, as a white person, as a woman, as a midwesterner, as a youth, or as a college student). Explain what you learned and how it changed your social or political outlook.
2. Write a narrative about a time when you felt isolated or outnumbered. Describe the situation and also your feelings.
3. Write an essay about a time when you resisted group pressure to do something that went against your values.

◆ FURTHER IDEAS FOR USING NARRATION

1. Write a narrative about a time when you surprised yourself—by being more courageous, more fearful, smarter or dumber, more conservative or liberal, or more outgoing or introverted than you usually are, for example. Be sure to establish why you were surprised. Imply rather than state why you behaved (or thought or felt) differently from your ordinary expectations.

2. Situations at school and work, as well as relationships with family and friends, can force us into making difficult ethical choices, such as telling a truth that will help one person but hurt another or feeling forced to share information that was told in confidence. Once made, however, these decisions offer us a foundation for positive future action. Narrate an experience in which, for better or worse, you learned a valuable ethical lesson.

3. Watch a movie with a child of eight or younger. A few hours later, or the next day, ask the child to tell you the story of the movie you saw together, and audiotape the narrative. Write an essay considering the differences between the child's narrative and one you might give (for example, if you were writing a film review). Discuss what you learned about narrating experience from this exercise. (As an alternative, you could do this exercise with someone older than you are or someone from a clearly different cultural background from yours.)

4. Interview someone about his or her immigrant experience, and edit the interview into a narrative essay.

5. COLLABORATIVE WRITING. In a small group, brainstorm and create a set of interview questions that will help you elicit material for writing a vivid narrative based on another person's experience. You might decide to focus on interviewing someone who has gone through a certain era or type of experience, such as a person in a rock and roll band, someone who was a foot soldier in a war, a person who has written a book, someone who witnessed an historic event, or even someone who has gone through a more ordinary life event like giving birth, getting fired, winning or losing an important contest. Then, each group member can use the questions, perform the interview, and write a narrative based on it.

6. ▇▐ *Using the Internet.* There are numerous sites for writers on the Internet. Visit a Web site like the StoryTellers Challenge (www.storytellerschallenge.com/index1.asp), which gives topics in the form of "challenges." On the "Truer Than Fiction" page you will find suggestions for writing nonfiction as well as sample essays from other writers. Another useful site is Storytellernet at www.storyteller.net. The "Story of the Week" page might spark some ideas.

◆ ◆ ◆ ◆ ◆ ◆ ◆ ◆ C H A P T E R 4 ◆ ◆ ◆ ◆ ◆ ◆ ◆ ◆

Strategies for Appealing to the Senses

Description

◆ ◆ ◆ ◆ ◆

Descriptive writing tells how something looks, acts, sounds, feels, smells, or tastes.

◆ Writers use description to present information and express feelings.

◆ Extended descriptions convey a dominant impression of the subject.

◆ Effective descriptions employ specific details, images, and comparisons.

You use **descriptions** all the time. In talking with your friends or writing to your family, you describe where you've been, what you saw, who you went out with. Good descriptions add life and interest to any conversation or piece of writing.

Although you seldom need to make description the basis for an entire essay, virtually everything you write includes descriptive details. They enliven narratives, clarify explanations, perk up examples, sharpen comparisons, and add vigor to arguments. No matter what you have to say, accurate and effective descriptions will help you say it better.

In the following selection, Gary Soto affectionately reveals the habits and attitudes of his grandfather by describing the trees in his backyard. In the essay that follows, a student takes a similar look at his own grandfather by describing his Grandpa's old room. Both pieces are filled with first-rate examples of descriptive writing.

The Grandfather

GARY SOTO

Born in Fresno, California, in 1952, Gary Soto is the author of ten books of poetry, most notably *New and Selected Poems*, a 1995 finalist for the National Book Award. Soto's honors include the Andrew Carnegie Medal and the Literature Award from the Hispanic Heritage Foundation. The following essay comes from his memoir, *Living Up the Street* (1985).

Grandfather believed a well-rooted tree was the color of money. His money he kept hidden behind portraits of sons and daughters or taped behind the calendar of an Aztec warrior. He tucked it into the sofa, his shoes and slippers, and into the tight-lipped pockets of his suits. He kept it in his soft brown wallet that was machine tooled with "MEXICO" and a campesino and donkey climbing a hill. He had climbed, too, out of Mexico, settled in Fresno, and worked thirty years at Sun Maid Raisin, first as a packer and later, when he was old, as a watchman with a large clock on his belt.   1

After work, he sat in the backyard under the arbor, watching the water gurgle in the rose bushes that ran along the fence. A lemon tree hovered over the clothesline. Two orange trees stood near the alley. His favorite tree, the avocado, which had started in a jam jar from a seed and three toothpicks lanced in its sides, rarely bore fruit. He said it was the wind's fault, and the mayor's, who allowed office buildings so high that the haze of pollen from the countryside could never find its way into the city. He sulked about this. He said that in Mexico buildings only grew so tall. You could see the moon at night, and the stars were clear points all the way to the horizon. And wind reached all the way from the sea, which was blue and clean, unlike the oily water sloshing against a San Francisco pier.   2

During its early years, I could leap over that tree, kick my bicycling legs over the top branch, and scream my fool head off because I thought for sure I was flying. I ate fruit to keep my strength up, fuzzy peaches and branch-scuffed plums cooled in the refrigerator. From the kitchen chair he brought out in the evening, Grandpa would scold, "Hijo, what's the matta with you? You gonna break it."   3

By the third year, the tree was as tall as I, its branches casting a mea- 4
ger shadow on the ground. I sat beneath the shade, scratching the words in
the hard dirt with a stick. I had learned "Nile" in summer school and a dirty
word from my brother who wore granny sunglasses. The red ants tumbled into
my letters, and I buried them, knowing that they would dig themselves back
into fresh air.

A tree was money. If a lemon cost seven cents at Hanoian's Market, 5
then Grandfather saved fistfuls of change and more because in winter the
branches of his lemon tree hung heavy yellow fruit. And winter brought oranges, juicy and large as softballs. Apricots he got by the bagfuls from a son,
who himself was wise for planting young. Peaches he got from a neighbor,
who worked the night shift at Sun Maid Raisin. The chile plants, which also
saved him from giving up his hot, sweaty quarters, were propped up with
sticks to support an abundance of red fruit.

But his favorite tree was the avocado because it offered hope and the 6
promise of more years. After work, Grandpa sat in the back yard, shirtless,
tired of flagging trucks loaded with crates of raisins, and sipped glasses of ice
water. His yard was neat: five trees, seven rose bushes, whose fruit were the
red and white flowers he floated in bowls, and a statue of St. Francis that stood
in a circle of crushed rocks, arms spread out to welcome hungry sparrows.

After ten years, the first avocado hung on a branch, but the meat was 7
flecked with black, an omen, Grandfather thought, a warning to keep an eye
on the living. Five years later, another avocado hung on a branch, larger than
the first and edible when crushed with a fork into a heated tortilla. Grandfather sprinkled it with salt and laced it with a river of chile.

"It's good," he said, and let me taste. 8

I took a big bite, waved a hand over my tongue, and ran for the garden 9
hose gurgling in the rose bushes. I drank long and deep, and later ate the
smile from an ice cold watermelon.

Birds nested in the tree, quarreling jays with liquid eyes and cool, pul- 10
sating throats. Wasps wove a horn-shaped hive one year, but we smoked them
away with swords of rolled up newspapers lit with matches. By then, the tree
was tall enough for me to climb to look into the neighbor's yard. But by then
I was too old for that kind of thing and went about with my brother, hair
slicked back and our shades dark as oil.

After twenty years, the tree began to bear. Although Grandfather com- 11
plained about how much he lost because pollen never reached the poor part
of town, because at the market he had to haggle over the price of avocados,
he loved that tree. It grew, as did his family, and when he died, all his sons
standing on each other's shoulders, oldest to youngest, could not reach the
highest branches. The wind could move the branches, but the trunk, thicker
than any waist, hugged the ground.

◆ ◆ ◆ *Writer's Workshop I* ◆ ◆ ◆
Responding to a Description

Use the *Who, What, Why,* and *How* questions (see p. 3) to explore your own understanding of the ideas and writing strategies employed by Gary Soto in "The Grandfather." Your instructor may ask you to record these responses in a journal, post them to an electronic bulletin board, or bring them to class to use in small group discussions.

◆ WRITING FROM READING

After reading "The Grandfather," freshman Kevin McNeal explored his reactions to Soto's description, using the *Who, What, Why,* and *How* questions. Impressed with the way Soto brought his subject to life, Kevin wondered if he could do the same with someone he knew. He decided to write about his own grandfather and began to brainstorm for ideas. This is the essay he eventually produced.

```
Kevin McNeal
English 1092
February 14, 2001


                    Last Visit

    The curtains were closed. They made light and dust  1
into a fog that played with some leftover tobacco
smell. The stuff tricked me into thinking it was pipe
smoke, just for a minute, until I remembered no one
had smoked a pipe there for months. Just like no one
had worn the soft felt hats hanging on the rack, no
one had used the pipe cleaners lying on the desk, and
no one had slept in the flannel pajamas lying
lifelessly across the twin bed. I was the first in
months to look at the pictures on my Grandpa's dresser
through that smoky haze of sunlight. I had seen them
before when I came into Grandpa's room to look at his
jars full of pennies or to steal some candy he had
hidden to save my teeth. The pictures looked strange
and solemn now.
```

Until I stepped on a crumpled paper on grandpa's 2
floor and jumped at the loudness of the rustle, I
hadn't noticed how silent the room was. My steps
echoed as I walked to his bed over the hardwood floor.
My eyes ran over a hundred different familiar things:
the earth-colored hats, the massive typewriter that
sat like a lead weight on his desk, rows of brown
leather shoes, and the ancient pipe-cleaner animals I
made him to trade for the candy. They looked so soft
and dear in the strange light that I almost forgot
they were just things which didn't mean very much when
he had worn them or used them.

Everything was different, and his room looked like 3
a dream or a church or a shrine full of treasures that
seem aloof through the clouds of incense. Nothing
really moves in those places; real people only pass
through to feel time stop, to feel outside their real
world. I wanted to stay and nap on the bed like I did
when Grandpa was gone to work, but his bedroom didn't
feel like it belonged to the real world anymore
either. It felt like a place to stop and remember but
not to stay and disturb. I sat on his bed and hugged
his old pajamas; they smelled like a forgotten teddy
bear pulled from an attic. I lay my head on his pillow
and watched the dust roll through the sunlight.

It rolled down and rested on grandpa's bedside 4
table and onto his alarm clock. It was an old-style
clock, made of yellow metal with bells on the top.
Through the haze it looked like an ancient relic. I
could remember the sound of it ticking in my head, but
I had never heard it ring; Grandpa was always up
cooking bacon in his pajamas long before I dressed for
grade school. I wanted to wind it and hear it again,
maybe even set it to ring. But it didn't seem like I
should change it or anything else there. When it was
Grandpa's it had always been my favorite room, but
everything that was warm and messy and comfortable was
frozen into a frame like a picture.

I wanted to stay, but I also felt like I'd been 5
playing in some place where playing is forbidden. I
took a last look at the pictures and hats and wondered
who would clear the room; I wondered who would take

the penny jars. My feet clacked over the hardwood on my way out into the sounds of bacon snapping and the conversation of my mom and sister in the kitchen. When I pulled shut the door of the room, I felt the weight of the old alarm clock swinging in my coat pocket.

◆ GETTING STARTED ON A DESCRIPTION

People write descriptions for two reasons: (1) to present information accurately and clearly and (2) to covey their feelings about the subject. The first kind of description is an *objective* one; the second is *expressive*. Kevin Mc-Neal decided that he wanted to follow Gary Soto's lead and express his feelings about the person he would be describing. Kevin began by reviewing his responses to the *Who, What, Why,* and *How* of Soto's description. Then he put his recollections down on paper, sorting out the emotions he had about his Grandpa. Here are some excerpts from the freewriting Kevin did about his subject:

I always called my grandfather Grandpa, as far back as I can remember and it seems to be the way I thought about him, affectionate, friendly, not formal at all. I wouldn't say we were close. I'd see him a lot but sometimes not for a few days or weeks at a time. He lived with us ever since his wife, my grandmother died. I don't know exactly when that was. He was my mother's father, and I don't remember my grandmother at all.

Grandpa kidded me a lot I remember but not the mean kind of teasing. He spent a lot of time in his room alone and didn't always eat with us or even watch tv or do other things with us. He was just around. And he worked during the day. But I could always talk to him and visit him in his room, never shut me out or told me to go away, I even took naps on his bed when he was at work, even when I was older and out of grade school.

After he stopped working I'd hear him and see him a lot more, I'd hear the radio in his room, he didn't have a tv. We would talk at breakfast, which he made for my sister and me. In thinking back I feel that we were close and comfortable. He wasn't a cranky old man who tried to tell me what to do. When he died his room

```
stayed pretty much the way it was for a long time and
I didn't even want to go back in there. I wonder why,
maybe because I didn't want to break the spell or
upset the calm, or more likely, didn't want to
recognize that he was gone. He died suddenly, a couple
of years, maybe only one year after he quit work. It
was very unexpected, I remember being shocked and
feeling a lot worse than I thought I would. Looking
back I realize how much I miss him and how his room
felt to me, how much it reminded me of him. The last
time I went in that's hard to think about and makes me
sad even now, almost 5 years later. Grandpa was
someone I love a lot, more than I knew when he was
around. I know he cared for me and just let me be
myself, which is what I miss about him. I wish I'd
talked to him more and done stuff with him, but I know
he knew I loved him.
```

After reading over his freewriting, Kevin saw that he had paid a lot of attention to his grandfather's room. This reminded him of the way Soto described the trees in his grandfather's yard and linked those trees to his grandfather's thoughts and feelings.

◆ ORGANIZING A DESCRIPTION

Some descriptions can be arranged spatially—top to bottom, left to right, near to far, back to front, and so on—like the movement of a camera filming a room or scene. But there's no built-in approach (like presenting a narrative in chronological order) that will work for all descriptions. A writer has to tailor the arrangement of **details** to suit the subject.

Kevin thought he could build his description around his grandfather's room, in much the same way that Soto focused on his grandfather's trees. Kevin looked again at his comments about the *Who, What, Why,* and *How* of Soto's essay. This time he noticed how the author uses the avocado tree to unify his description and to show the changes in his grandfather's life. Deciding that he could do something similar, Kevin sat down at his computer to brainstorm a list of details and impressions from his last visit to his grandfather's room:

not much light—hazy, smoky
the light didn't seem real

dust in the air, the smell was musty, also smoky

not a big space, not crowded either

pajamas on the bed—flannel?

it was just a twin bed, had I noticed that before?

pipe cleaners on the dresser and table, the smell of smoke too, or was that real?

lots of small things I saw, ordinary things, hadn't paid them much attention

jars of pennies, pictures, hats and shoes, a big typewriter

pipe cleaner animals—why where they there?

where was the candy?

things seemed frozen, unreal, also like a church

silence, loud noise of walking on the hardwood floors

mixed feeling, uncomfortable but wanting to stay

didn't seem like his room anymore

big alarm clock, an old one—reminds me of his cooking bacon in the morning

same thing going on in the kitchen now, with mom and my sister

With this material to draw on, Kevin was ready to write his first draft.

◆ DEVELOPING A DESCRIPTION

Effective descriptions depend on language that appeals to the readers' senses. Because readers are seldom familiar with the people or places being described, a writer has to present a vivid picture and create a sense of intimacy. As Kevin was working on his draft, he re-examined Gary Soto's description and noted that the author relies heavily on **images,** words and phrases that prompt the reader to see, hear, smell, taste, and feel what he's describing: a "lemon tree hovered over the clothesline," "oily water sloshing against a San Francisco pier," "fuzzy peaches and branch-scuffed plums cooled in the refrigerator," "a horn-shaped hive," "the trunk, thicker than any waist." Soto also describes movements and actions with precise, vivid verbs: tucked, gurgle, sulked, leap, propped up, tumbled, sipped, floated, flecked, crushed, hugged the ground. Kevin observed, too, that Soto uses comparisons, describing one thing in terms of another. Some of them are **similes,** which use *like* or *as:* "oranges, juicy and large as softballs," "our shades dark as oil." But some are **metaphors,** which don't use *like* or *as* but imply a comparison by talking about one item as if it were another: "a river of chile," "bicycling legs," "quarreling jays with liquid eyes and cool, pulsating throats," "swords of rolled up newspapers lit with matches."

Kevin also liked the way Soto uses ordinary objects to reflect the grandfather's moods and reveal his thoughts: "But his favorite tree was the avocado because it offered hope and the promise of more years"; "After ten years, the first avocado hung on a branch, but the meat was flecked with black, an omen, Grandfather thought, a warning to keep an eye on the living." Kevin thought that he would try to use this strategy in developing his own description.

◆ USING THE MODEL

As you have seen, Gary Soto's essay helped Kevin in several ways: it encouraged him to try writing a description of his own grandfather, it suggested how he might focus his material, and it showed him how to use descriptive language effectively. But Kevin didn't just copy Soto's approach. For one thing, instead of writing about the changes in his grandfather's life, Kevin chose to focus his attention on his final memories of Grandpa. He also decided not to quote his grandfather, the way Soto does, and he ended his essay with a glimpse of his own actions, a technique that Soto uses but in a different way. In other words, Kevin used Soto's essay as a model, but he also retained his independence as a writer.

The selections in the rest of this chapter illustrate how description can be used to shape and develop an essay. If you work with them the way that Kevin worked with Soto's example, you will discover many first-rate ideas and strategies for writing your own descriptions.

◆ ◆ ◆ *Writer's Workshop II* ◆ ◆ ◆
Analyzing a Description

Working individually or with a small group of classmates, read through Kevin McNeal's essay "Last Visit," and respond to the following questions:

1. Identify as many images, similes, and metaphors as you can. Which ones are most effective? Are there any that don't work for you?
2. Does Kevin use precise, vivid verbs? Find several examples. Are there any places he could improve his verb choices?
3. What feelings do the descriptions convey? What is Kevin's attitude toward his subject? Is that attitude clear and consistent? What could he do to improve his depiction of Grandpa?

4. Why doesn't Kevin use any dialogue or quotations? Do you think his description might have been improved if he had? Where could he have placed it?

5. Do you think Kevin's conclusion is effective? What other kind of ending could he have written?

◆ ◆ ◆ Checklist for Reading and Writing ◆ ◆ ◆
Descriptive Essays

1. What is the purpose of the description? Is that purpose spelled out for readers, or do they have to reach their own conclusions? Has the author supplied enough detail to help them form their inferences?

2. Is the description objective or expressive? If objective, are the details accurate and complete? If expressive, what feelings does it convey?

3. Is the material arranged appropriately? Do the parts of the description work together?

4. Is the language concrete and vivid? Does the description contain images that appeal to the readers' senses? Are the comparisons fresh and effective?

◆ ◆ ◆ **PREPARING TO READ**

Have you ever visited a place (like a school, a neighborhood, a vacation spot) that you hadn't seen for a while and noticed that it looked very different from the way you remembered it? Had the place changed or had you?

◆ ◆ ◆

Two Views of the Mississippi

MARK TWAIN

Before becoming Mark Twain, America's most beloved humorist, Samuel Clemens (1830–1910) was a riverboat pilot, a journalist, and an unsuccessful gold miner. He said late in his life that those days on the river were the happiest he ever spent. In *Life on the Mississippi,* he explains how he became a pilot and learned to "read" the river. In the following passage, Twain tells of one drawback to that otherwise rewarding experience.

The face of the water, in time, became a wonderful book—a book that　1 was a dead language to the uneducated passenger but which told its mind to me without reserve, delivering its most cherished secrets as clearly as if it uttered them with a voice. And it was not a book to be read once and thrown aside, for it had a new story to tell every day. Throughout the long twelve hundred miles there was never a page that was void of interest, never one that you could leave unread without loss, never one that you would want to skip, thinking you could find higher enjoyment in some other thing. There never was so wonderful a book written by man, never one whose interest was so absorbing, so unflagging, so sparklingly renewed with every reperusal. The passenger who could not read it was charmed with a peculiar sort of faint dimple on its surface (on the rare occasions when he did not overlook it altogether) but to the pilot that was an *italicized* passage; indeed it was more than that, it was a legend of the largest capitals with a string of shouting exclamation-points at the end of it, for it meant that a wreck or a rock was buried there that could tear the life out of the strongest vessel that ever floated. It is the faintest and simplest expression the water ever makes, and the most hideous to a pilot's eye. In truth, the passenger who could not read this book saw nothing but all manner of pretty pictures in it, painted by the sun and shaded by the clouds, whereas to the trained eye these were not pictures at all, but the grimmest and most dead-earnest of reading matter.

Now when I had mastered the language of this water, and had come to   2
know every trifling feature that bordered the great river as familiarly as I
knew the letters of the alphabet, I had made a valuable acquisition. But I
had lost something, too. I had lost something which could never be restored
to me while I lived. All the grace, the beauty, the poetry, had gone out of the
majestic river! I still keep in mind a certain wonderful sunset which I witnessed when steamboating was new to me. A broad expanse of the river was
turned to blood; in the middle distance the red hue brightened into gold,
through which a solitary log came floating black and conspicuous; in one
place a long, slanting mark lay sparkling upon the water; in another the surface was broken by boiling, tumbling rings, that were as many-tinted as an
opal; where the ruddy flush was faintest was a smooth spot that was covered
with graceful circles and radiating lines, ever so delicately traced; the shore
on our left was densely wooded, and the somber shadow that fell from this
forest was broken in one place by a long, ruffled trail that shone like silver;
and high above the forest wall a clean-stemmed dead tree waved a single
leafy bough that glowed like a flame in the unobstructed splendor that was
flowing in the sun. There were graceful curves, reflected images, woody
heights, soft distances; and over the whole scene, far and near, the dissolving
lights drifted steadily, enriching it every passing moment with new marvels
of coloring.

I stood like one bewitched. I drank it in, in a speechless rapture. The   3
world was new to me, and I had never seen anything like this at home. But
as I have said, a day came when I began to cease from noting the glories and
charms which the moon and sun and the twilight wrought upon the river's
face; another day came when I ceased altogether to note them. Then, if that
sunset scene had been repeated, I should have looked upon it without rapture, and should have commented upon it, inwardly, after this fashion: "This
sun means that we are going to have wind to-morrow; that floating log means
that the river is rising, small thanks to it; that slanting mark on the water
refers to a bluff reef which is going to kill somebody's steamboat one of these
nights, if it keeps on stretching out like that; those tumbling 'boils' show a
dissolving bar and a changing channel there; the lines and circles in the slick
water over yonder are a warning that that troublesome place is shoaling up
dangerously; that silver streak in the shadow of the forest is the 'break' from
a new snag, and he has located himself in the very best place he could have
found to fish for steamboats; that tall dead tree, with a single living branch,
is not going to last long, and then how is a body ever going to get through this
blind place at night without the friendly old landmark?"

No, the romance and beauty were all gone from the river. All the value   4
any feature of it had for me now was the amount of usefulness it could fur-
nish toward compassing the safe piloting of a steamboat. Since those days, I
have pitied doctors from my heart. What does the lovely flush in a beauty's

cheek mean to a doctor but a "break" that ripples above some deadly disease? Are not all her visible charms sown thick with what are to him the signs and symbols of hidden decay? Does he ever see her beauty at all, or doesn't he simply view her professionally and comment upon her unwholesome condition all to himself? And doesn't he sometimes wonder whether he has gained most or lost most by learning his trade?

◆ ◆ ◆

FIRST RESPONSES

Do you agree that gaining knowledge takes away the appreciation of beauty? Have you ever had a learning experience that robbed you of a childhood illusion? Have you had the opposite experience, when learning increased your appreciation of something?

TAKING A CLOSER LOOK

Exploring *Who:* Voice and Tone

1. Have you read any books and stories by Mark Twain? How does this selection compare with his other works?
2. What does Twain think about passengers? How do you respond to the way he talks about passengers?
3. What attitude toward the river does Twain have? What attitude does he expect his readers to have?

Exploring *What:* Content and Meaning

1. How is the Mississippi River like a book? What is the "language" of the river?
2. What did Twain lose by learning to be a riverboat pilot? What did he gain?
3. Why does Twain feel sorry for doctors? Can you think of other professionals who might lose as much as they gain by learning their trades?
4. *Using the Internet.* Have you ever been on a riverboat? Do you understand all the terms and details about the river that Twain uses? For information about this subject, search the Internet using "riverboat pilots" as the keywords, or visit the Mississippi River Home Page (www.greatriver.com/) for an interview with a modern riverboat pilot.

Exploring *Why:* Purpose

1. Is Twain writing primarily for passengers, or is he writing for other pilots?
2. What is the main point of this selection? Is Twain providing you with information, or is he trying to persuade you of something?
3. Why does Twain include the detailed description of the sunset in paragraph 2? What feelings does the description evoke? Do you think your feelings are the same as Twain's?

Exploring *How:* Style and Strategy

1. Why does Twain compare the river to a book? How does he extend that description throughout the selection? Find words and phrases that continue the book metaphor.
2. Point out other comparisons that Twain uses to develop his description. Are these **similes** (comparisons that use *like* or *as*), or are they **metaphors** (implied comparisons that declare one thing to be another)?
3. Twain also personifies the river; that is, he gives it human characteristics. Find phrases and sentences that involve **personification.** Why does the author use this figure of speech?
4. What transitional phrases and sentences match up the parts of the description?
5. Why does Twain conclude with comments about doctors? Why do you think he decided to end this way? Would you have written a different conclusion?

◆ WRITING FROM READING ASSIGNMENT

People often feel warm and sentimental about the past. Do you have any fond memories of the "good old days"? The main point of this writing assignment is to develop an expressive description of something or someone from your past that has been replaced, but not necessarily by something better.

A. First, reread "Two Views of the Mississippi," paying special attention to the feelings the descriptions convey. Also review your responses to the previous *Who, What, Why,* and *How* questions.
B. Then think of a person, place, or thing that you miss. Brainstorm a list of details and examples that you might use to describe your subject;

freewrite about your feelings for the subject and the impression you want to present to your audience.

C. Begin your draft by letting your readers know that you have a fine, new whatever—best friend, favorite restaurant, music teacher, TV series, racing bike, sports car, designer jeans, neighborhood bakery—but that the new model doesn't measure up to what you had before.

D. Then describe your former favorite. Use plenty of precise details, vivid images, and **figurative** comparisons, as Mark Twain does in his second paragraph, to appeal to your readers' senses. Show your readers what makes you feel the way you do about this past treasure.

E. Next, make a transition similar to Twain's: "But as I have said [. . .]." Or write your own: "After Lauren moved to California, I began to hang out with Megan; and although we've become really close, I still miss my former best buddy."

F. Now describe your replacement, focusing on its shortcomings, on all the ways in which it doesn't live up to the item you miss. Follow the same order in presenting the failings as you did in describing the virtues. (Look at how Twain uses exactly the same order in telling the two ways he saw the river. In his third paragraph, he begins with the sunset, then mentions the log, then the slanting mark on the water, then the "tumbling boils," then the lines and circles, then the streak in the shadow, and finally the dead tree, just as he did in his second paragraph.)

G. In your conclusion, express again the way you feel about having to make do with the unsatisfactory replacement and your longing to have the old one back.

You could write this same essay about a person or thing that has been replaced by someone or something a whole lot better.

◆ ◆ ◆ PREPARING TO READ

What is the city of Las Vegas known for? What image and reputation does it have? Do you think it's a good place to get married?

◆ ◆ ◆

Marrying Absurd

JOAN DIDION

Novelist, essayist, and screenwriter, Joan Didion was born in 1934 in Sacramento and educated at the University of California at Berkeley. She worked in New York as an editor at *Vogue* magazine until 1963, the year her first novel, *Run River,* was published. She has since written five more novels, including *Play It As It Lays* (1971) and *The Last Thing He Wanted* (1996), and three collections of essays, *Slouching Towards Bethlehem* (1969), *The White Album* (1979), and *After Henry* (1992). *Salvador,* based on a 1983 trip to El Salvador, marked her growing interest in politics, which is also reflected in *Miami* (1987), her study of Cuban exiles in Florida. In many of her works, Didion explores the discrepancy between people's lofty expectations and the reality of their experience.

To be married in Las Vegas, Clark County Nevada, a bride must swear   1
that she is eighteen or has parental permission and a bridegroom that he is twenty-one or has parental permission. Someone must put up five dollars for the license. (On Sundays and holidays, fifteen dollars. The Clark County Courthouse issues marriage licenses at any time of the day or night except between noon and one in the afternoon, between eight and nine in the evening, and between four and five in the morning.) Nothing else is required. The State of Nevada, alone among these United States, demands neither a premarital blood test nor a waiting period before or after the issuance of a marriage license. Driving in across the Mojave from Los Angeles, one sees the signs way out on the desert, looming up from that moonscape of rattlesnakes and mesquite, even before the Las Vegas lights appear like a mirage on the horizon: "GETTING MARRIED? Free License Information First Strip Exit." Perhaps the Las Vegas wedding industry achieved its peak operational efficiency between 9:00 P.M. and midnight of August 26, 1965, an otherwise unremarkable Thursday which happened to be, by Presidential order, the last day on which anyone could improve his draft status merely by getting married. One hundred and seventy-one couples were pronounced

man and wife in the name of Clark County and the State of Nevada that night, sixty-seven of them by a single justice of the peace, Mr. James A. Brennan. Mr. Brennan did one wedding at the Dunes and the other sixty-six in his office, and charged each couple eight dollars. One bride lent her veil to six others. "I got it down from five to three minutes," Mr. Brennan said later of his feat. "I could've married them *en masse,* but they're people, not cattle. People expect more when they get married."

What people who get married in Las Vegas actually do expect—what, 2 in the largest sense, their "expectations" are—strikes one as a curious and self-contradictory business. Las Vegas is the most extreme and allegorical of American settlements, bizarre and beautiful in its venality and in its devotion to immediate gratification, a place the tone of which is set by mobsters and call girls and ladies' room attendants with amyl nitrite poppers in their uniform pockets. Almost everyone notes that there is no "time" in Las Vegas, no night and no day and no past and no future (no Las Vegas casino, however, has taken the obliteration of the ordinary time sense quite so far as Harold's Club in Reno, which for a while issued, at odd intervals in the day and night, mimeographed "bulletins" carrying news from the world outside); neither is there any logical sense of where one is. One is standing on a highway in the middle of a vast hostile desert looking at an eighty-foot sign which blinks "STARDUST" or "CAESAR'S PALACE." Yes, but what does that explain? This geographical implausibility reinforces the sense that what happens there has no connection with "real" life; Nevada cities like Reno and Carson City are ranch towns, Western towns, places behind which there is some historical imperative. But Las Vegas seems to exist only in the eye of the beholder. All of which makes it an extraordinarily stimulating and interesting place, but an odd one in which to want to wear a candlelight satin Priscilla of Boston wedding dress with Chantilly lace insets, tapered sleeves, and a detachable modified train.

And yet the Las Vegas wedding business seems to appeal to precisely 3 that impulse. "Sincere and Dignified Since 1954," one wedding chapel advertises. There are nineteen such wedding chapels in Las Vegas, intensely competitive, each offering better, faster, and, by implication, more sincere services than the next: Our Photos Best Anywhere, Your Wedding on A Phonograph Record, Candlelight with Your Ceremony, Honeymoon Accommodations, Free Transportation from Your Motel to Courthouse to Chapel and Return to Motel, Religious or Civil Ceremonies, Dressing Rooms, Flowers, Rings, Announcements, Witnesses Available, and Ample Parking. All of these services, like most others in Las Vegas (sauna baths, payroll-check cashing, chinchilla coats for sale or rent) are offered twenty-four hours a day, seven days a week, presumably on the premise that marriage, like craps, is a game to be played when the table seems hot.

But what strikes one most about the Strip chapels, with their wishing 4 wells and stained-glass paper windows and their artificial bouvardia, is that so much of their business is by no means a matter of simple convenience, of late-night liaisons between show girls and baby Crosbys. Of course there is some of that. (One night about eleven o'clock in Las Vegas I watched a bride in an orange minidress and masses of flame-colored hair stumble from a Strip chapel on the arm of her bridegroom, who looked the part of the expendable nephew in movies like *Miami Syndicate*. "I gotta get the kids," the bride whimpered. "I gotta pick up the sitter, I gotta get to the midnight show." "What you gotta get," the bridegroom said, opening the door of a Cadillac Coupe de Ville and watching her crumple on the seat, "is sober.") But Las Vegas seems to offer something other than "convenience"; it is merchandising "niceness," the facsimile of proper ritual, to children who do not know how else to find it, how to make the arrangements, how to do it "right." All day and evening long on the Strip, one sees actual wedding parties, waiting under the harsh lights at a crosswalk, standing uneasily in the parking lot of the Frontier while the photographer hired by The Little Church of the West ("Wedding Place of the Stars") certifies the occasion, takes the picture: the bride in a veil and white satin pumps, the bridegroom usually in a white dinner jacket, and even an attendant or two, a sister or a best friend in hot-pink *peau de soie,* a flirtation veil, a carnation nosegay. "When I Fall in Love It Will Be Forever," the organist plays, and then a few bars of Lohengrin. The mother cries; the stepfather, awkward in his role, invites the chapel hostess to join them for a drink at the Sands. The hostess declines with a professional smile; she has already transferred her interest to the group waiting outside. One bride out, another in, and again the sign goes up on the chapel door: "One moment please—Wedding."

I sat next to one such wedding party in a Strip restaurant the last time   5
I was in Las Vegas. The marriage had just taken place; the bride still wore her dress, the mother her corsage. A bored waiter poured out a few swallows of pink champagne ("on the house") for everyone but the bride, who was too young to be served. "You'll need something with more kick than that," the bride's father said with heavy jocularity to his new son-in-law; the ritual jokes about the wedding night had a certain Panglossian character, since the bride was clearly several months pregnant. Another round of pink champagne, this time not on the house, and the bride began to cry. "It was just as nice," she sobbed, "as I hoped and dreamed it would be."

◆ ◆ ◆

FIRST RESPONSES

After reading this essay, do you think people should get married in Las Vegas? Why or why not?

TAKING A CLOSER LOOK

Exploring *Who:* Voice and Tone

1. Is Didion writing for people who might get married in Las Vegas? Does she expect her readers to share her attitude toward Las Vegas weddings? Do you?
2. How would you describe the essay's prevailing tone? Is it playful or serious? Fascinated or critical? How do you react to that tone?
3. Twice Didion uses "I" to refer to herself ("I watched a bride in an orange minidress"); other times she uses the impersonal pronoun "one" ("what strikes one most"). What role does she establish with these pronouns? Why doesn't she acknowledge her personal presence more often?

Exploring *What:* Content and Meaning

1. What does the author find "absurd" about the weddings in Las Vegas? Is her title fair and accurate?
2. Didion says that "there is no 'time' in Las Vegas" and no "logical sense of where one is." How does she illustrate this point? Do you concur with her view?
3. What does Didion mean when she says in paragraph 4 that Las Vegas is "merchandising 'niceness,' the facsimile of proper ritual, to children who do not know how else to find it"?
4. ▆▊ *Using the Internet.* This essay first appeared in the *Saturday Evening Post* in 1967. Do you think the author's observations and conclusions are still valid? How would Didion have to revise her essay to bring it up to date? To answer this question, visit a Web site like the one for the City of Las Vegas (www.ci.las-vegas.nv.us/).

Exploring *Why:* Purpose

1. Is the author making fun of the people and the weddings she describes? If not, what is her intention?
2. One critic said that Didion's essays "promote a moral vision." What moral vision does this essay promote?

Exploring *How:* Style and Strategy

1. Where might you typically find a description like this: "a candlelight satin Priscilla of Boston wedding dress with Chantilly lace insets,

tapered sleeves, and a detachable modified train" (para. 2)? How does this language support Didion's viewpoint?

2. The author uses a wealth of details in her descriptions. Cite five examples that you find particularly vivid, and explain what they add to a reader's understanding of the scene.

3. In paragraph 3, Didion refers to a number of advertising slogans. What is her point? How do these references support her general thesis?

4. How does the author's concluding example emphasize her point of view?

IDEAS FOR WRITING A DESCRIPTION

1. Describe a place that has an unusual or contradictory quality to it. Use sensory details that reveal your feelings about the place, but do not name the emotions themselves.

2. Go to some place (a restaurant, library, mall, park, or laundromat, for example) where you can observe people without being noticed. Make a list of details about several of the people you see there; choose details that appeal to the senses. Then develop those details into a series of descriptive profiles. Use figurative images to create a **dominant impression** of each person you describe.

3. Describe a bus station, airport, or train terminal.

◆ ◆ ◆ PREPARING TO READ

Do you believe that spirits can inhabit a place? Do you know a place that is haunted or has some mystery surrounding it? How do you explain such places and beliefs?

◆ ◆ ◆

White Breast Flats

EMILIE GALLANT

Emilie Gallant is a member of the Piegan tribe of Canada. She was born in Alberta and received a degree from the University of Calgary. This essay first appeared in *A Gathering of Spirits* (1984), an anthology of drawings, poems, stories, and other writings by Native American women. In this selection, Gallant describes a place filled with childhood memories about a way of life that no longer exists.

As one grows older, and the past recedes swiftly as a bird, wings extended in the wind, there are people and places whose contours, caught through the clouds of memory, take on the dimensions of myth. For me, one such place is White Breast Flats on the Piegan Reserve in southwest Alberta where the plains give way to the foothills, the Rockies loom near, and the great obelisk Chief Mountain stands powerfully at the entrance to northern Montana. White Breast Flats is a name known only to a few. My grandfather, Otohkostskaksin (Yellow Dust), was the one who told me that name, and recently, when I read the name in a book, I felt a special joy. Seeing it in print, so many years and miles later, seemed to establish the place as fact, and it opened again the pages of that precious time in my past.

White Breast Flats was occupied solely by my grandparents, and on occasion by my mother. It was located on the first bottomland north of the Old Man River on the west end of the reserve, and the land that rose behind it— the valley wall I suppose you could call it—reached its highest point there, a half-mile from bottom to top, two miles in span. That valley wall was laced with a maze of foot-trails, and there were bushes aplenty of saskatoon, whiteberries, gooseberries, chokecherries, and bullberries. There were also wild turnips and cactusberries there. All of these berries gave nourishment to my sisters, to my brother, and to me as we played or just wandered through.

The bottomland stretched from the base of the hill towards the river for   3
a mile and a half at its farthest point and a quarter of a mile at its closest. The
one-roomed log house my grandparents lived in was situated about a half a
mile from the hill and about two hundred feet from the river. The Old Man
has probably eaten away the spot where the house stood, for the bank crept
a little closer each year. The trees there were of several varieties, but other
than the willows, cottonwoods, chokecherry, saskatoon, and pussy willows, I
am still unable to name the trees that made up the forest. Where there were
no trees, the grasses grew wild and rampant, and I can still see fields of yellow and white sweet clover and the ever-present and venomous purple this-
tles which stabbed at us with their thorns every chance they got.

We were brought up to fear bears; and although I never saw a bear   4
while I was growing up, I was always on the lookout for the one which I was
sure was waiting for me to relax my guard. The most fearsome thing I ever
saw was a snake. I was afraid of water, and the river bank we clambered
down to reach the green, swirling currents was dotted with holes which I
thought were the homes of deadly and poisonous snakes. My sisters were
both strong swimmers and enjoyed swimming across the river, but I would
churn inwardly with fear as I watched them splash and drift away, bantering
and yelling with abandon. And there I would be, standing first on one dirt-
caked rock with a dried-up water spider stuck to it, and moving to another,
sometimes walking in the water up to my knees very cautiously and carefully, for the rocks were slippery. Sometimes a fish would awake and swim off
suddenly, making my heart jump and my throat constrict with a scream I held
in. The river was a malevolent thing to me, never friendly. I watched warily
for the mythical water-being which I was convinced lived somewhere in the
greenest, deepest part. It had to. Otherwise, where did all the foam come
from which flecked the river's surface; it had to be the water-being's spittle.

One particular day, I was standing on the river's edge again, watching   5
my two sisters, whom I resented and admired for their fearlessness, when I
slipped and fell into the water. It was in the evening and the sun's last rays
had turned the river into a golden, glinting, and somehow not so perilous
place. I imagined that the water below the surface where the water-being
lived was illuminated. In a matter of minutes the warmth of the day was exchanged for the coolness of the evening. My skin prickled with goosebumps
from the chill, and I decided to put on my cotton dress until the two mermaids
left the water. I picked up my dress and almost died with fright! A big snake
slithered out of my dress. I screamed, and my mother, who had been washing and rinsing clothes some distance away, came running, and I got to ride
her piggyback all the way home. I even had her throw my dress in the river,
something I always remember, for we were very poor and could ill afford to
throw clothing away.

There were plants that my grandmother would collect for her medici-   6
nal and everyday purposes. She would hang mint to dry in bunches from a line

tied across the length of the room, close to the ceiling. I loved the smell of it, and although I didn't care for mint tea then, I do now. It's not only the taste that I enjoy; it's the remembering of moments of my childhood. Every so often I happen upon a cup of wild mint tea, and the bitterness of it, if the tea is made too strong, brings me back to my mother's house when I was probably five or six years old and deathly ill—or so I remember, because my grandmother was summoned. She was a medicine woman and had in her possession all kinds of herbs and roots with which she brought back to health anyone who was ailing. She came into the house on a cold, winter day, bundled up with shawls and blankets. The snowy wind whipped the log house until chinks of the limestone plaster were peeled off and swept away in the storm. My mother kept plugging up the cracks with rags to keep the snow from being blasted inside. The wet snow that stuck to my grandmother's wraps hissed as it hit the stove. She carried a flour sack, and from this she took out a bag made from fawn hide, spotted and with the little hooves on it. Inside the bag she had wrapped still other small bundles, and she took out something greasy and rubbed my chest. On top of that she placed a layer of dried leaves. Ritually she spat on these, and covered the leaves with a hot cloth. She gave me a drink of an awful-tasting brew, and I wouldn't have drunk it if she hadn't been the one to give it to me. She then chanted holy songs, her voice a little frail and weak at first but gaining strength and fullness until the sound was a soothing prayer. She had a sacred rattle made from rawhide and painted with red ochre; this she shook in time with the cadence of her voice. She closed her eyes as she sang, and as I watched her I saw that she had painted her face with the red ochre, and the hair that framed her face was tinted with it. After her song, she prayed that my health be restored and I be blessed with a long and happy life. From a little buckskin bag rubbed with the sacred red ochre, she took some paint that had the consistency of uncooked pastry but which became oily when she rubbed it in her hand. This she rubbed on my face and then she left, leaving some brew and plants for my mother to administer to me. She also left an orange in plain sight that I could have when I was well enough. Oranges during the Second World War were rare, and not seen unless at a feast.

Sometimes I can detect the smell of sweetgrass when there is none 7 around. I've grown to know that is only my grandparents coming to visit me. Sweetgrass—an appropriate name for a special plant. Sweetgrass is the incense the old Indians used to honor the Creator, and the burning of it was a daily occurrence in my grandparents' home. Each morning my grandfather would get up and make the fire in the stove and as soon as the warmth made getting up comfortable, my grandmother would rise and they would pray together. He would burn incense to greet the Creator, and to give thanks for life and health of family and friends, and to ask for guidance in living the day, as well as for help in some special need. Then they shared a song between them and a smoke on their pipe from chunk tobacco.

A quarter of a mile east of the house and just where the woods began   8
was a spring. This was where my grandfather got our drinking water. He used
a wooden stoneboat to haul it. The stoneboat was constructed of two logs at
the bottom; they were the runners, smooth and heavy. On top of them were
wide planks of board, bolted onto the logs. The planks were so old I used to
sit and scratch them with my fingernails and a papery, powdery substance
would come off the wood. Grandfather would hitch up the team, and we children tagged along, jumping on and off the stoneboat with our dogs barking
happily behind us until we reached the spring. He tied the team to a tree
above the spring and carried two pails to bring the water back to the old
metal-girded wooden barrel. He would make twenty or thirty trips until the
barrel was full, and then he would put a canvas cover over it and tie the cover
on with a rope. Once the water was brought home, my grandmother would
have a drink of it first, then set about to making a pot of tea.

A slow-moving stream which leaked off the river and eased by the   9
spring was a refrigerator for butter, meat, and the seasonal garden vegetables.
The vegetables came from my grandfather's garden at the base of the hill.
Everything grew in abundance there: carrots, rhubarb, turnips, onion, radishes,
lettuce, potatoes, and sugar beets. It was neat and ordered, with its straight
rows and well-tended mounds of earth. It was fascinating to watch the steam
rising from the garden after my grandfather watered it or after a rainfall or
shower. I thought a mysterious creature, perhaps a cousin of the water-being,
inhabited the earth, and the steam was its breath just as the flecks of foam in
the river were the water-being's spittle. I never hung around the garden alone.

The stream that adjoined the spring was the home of a thousand min-   10
nows. We would catch some in a jar and take them home, and although we
fed them flies and bread, they always died. Long-legged water spiders glided
silently around the stream and the little frogs of grey, green, or brown jumped
noiselessly, even when they landed in the water. Only our big, clumsy dogs
would ruin the silent stream with their panting, lolling tongues as they
splashed in, sitting right in the water to have a drink. Then they would shake
their wet bodies mightily until it seemed as though it was raining. Our shouts
of anger and surprise would usually result in their jumping on us with friendly
licks and muddy paws. Surprisingly, of all the dogs we had (it seems they
were all shaggy) the only one I remember is Pete. Pete, the short-haired
hound with long legs, a tail like a whip, and shiny ears, one of which would
sometimes get stuck inside out or underside up, was blacker than the deepest badger hole we dared to peep into, and he had white, laughing teeth and
a rosy, wet tongue.

There was a faded, creaking ghost house on top of the hill. It had two   11
stories and no windows or doors, just openings from which whitemen ghosts
watched passersby. It used to belong to a white man I knew only as Inopikini,
which means Long Nose. We would go to the ghost house in broad daylight,
always in the protective company of my mother and grandmother. The wind

was always blowing through the house, flapping wallpaper, rattling floorboards, shingles, and window casings. It was a wonderful, mysterious, scary place to go poking around in. It had lots of rooms, small ones and big ones. There were old curly shoes, clothing of all kinds, pieces of furniture, bits of toys, stray dishes, cracked cups without handles, and faded pictures still in their frames. We never took anything, because then Inopikini would haunt us until we returned what we had taken, or else, if he was a real mean ghost, he would twist our faces.

There was a trapdoor in one room which we never dared to open because we were sure something stayed down there, but we would stomp across it, each one stomping harder than the last but always with mother or grandmother in the room. After we verbally challenged the ghosts who had the guts to come out and meet us face to face, we would climax our visit by scaring only ourselves and stampede off in hysterical screams, our bodies prickling and our eyes wild with fear, not daring to look back lest we see Inopikini hot on our trail. 12

I always expected to see a tall, emaciated man with hair all over his skin and blood around his nostrils and perhaps little horns growing out of his head. He was always garbed, in my imagination, in the cracked, curly boots he left in his house and his body covered with the rags scattered about through the rooms. 13

Summer reminds me of my grandmother mashing cherries in her tipi, which was erected as soon as it was warm enough to sleep outside. My old grandmother used to herd us up the hill to dig for turnips and pick berries for some upcoming feast, but those were the times we wished berries didn't grow. It was always a hot day when we yearned to be down by the spring and we quarreled amongst ourselves and sneaked away. 14

On hot summer days when I wearied of playing or had nothing to do, I would go and ask my grandmother to check my head because it was itchy. She would put aside whatever she was doing and check my head, all the while telling me stories until I fell asleep. Sometimes when I didn't fall asleep soon enough for her, she would tell me to erase a cloud by rubbing my hands together and concentrating on that cloud. I demolished many a cloud. My grandmother was a tireless old woman who never rested. She was always busy beading, fixing deerskins, fixing berries (drying, mashing, sorting), repairing clothing, cooking, sweeping, washing clothes, and minding us kids. She would gather wood on a big piece of canvas and carry it home on her back or drag it behind her. Then she would sit at the woodpile and chop wood with her hatchet, which she also used for butchering the deer my grandfather killed. 15

I haven't been to White Breast Flats for a long time now, too long. The log house and outer buildings have long been dismantled and carried away for firewood, and the paths and roads are overcome by weeds. Only the descendants of the magpies, gophers, rabbits, and frogs have reclaimed their 16 ancestral grounds. Perhaps a rusted wagon wheel or a skeletal haymower tells a hanging eagle that people once lived here. White Breast Flats will not happen again; it only lives in the longings and hearts of Ippisuwahs, Piiksi Kiipipi Pahtskikaikana, and Itsinakaki, the grandchildren whose voices once rang clear and echoed through its secret places.

◆ ◆ ◆

FIRST RESPONSES

Did reading this essay cause you to recall any childhood memories of your own? If so, what are they, and how do they seem to relate to this essay? If not, can you explain why the essay didn't trigger any memories?

TAKING A CLOSER LOOK

Exploring *Who:* Voice and Tone

1. What is Gallant's attitude toward White Breast Flats and the memories she has of that place? Is her tone what you would expect of someone recalling her childhood? She says she hasn't been back to White Breast Flats for a long time. Why do you suppose that is?
2. Does Gallant change her voice in this essay? Does she maintain the voice of an adult looking back, or does she shift her tone as she moves back into her memories?
3. Is this essay written primarily for Native Americans? Can other readers identify with Gallant's memories? Do you?

Exploring *What:* Content and Meaning

1. The author says that people and places from the past "take on the dimensions of myth." What does she mean? Do you think that your past has taken on mythic dimensions?
2. What rituals of her tribe does Gallant describe? Are there similar rituals in your family or community? Why or why not?
3. What connections between nature and human beings does the author establish?
4. What point does the last paragraph make about White Breast Flats?
5. ◼ *Using the Internet.* Find a Web site that shows this landscape; look for the Chief Mountain or the Piegan Reserve in southwest Alberta, Canada. Did you visualize this place in the same way when you were reading Gallant's essay?

Exploring *Why:* Purpose

1. What is Gallant's reason for writing about the people and places of her past?
2. Is this an informative essay? Does the author want to do more than share information? Why does she make so many references to spirits, ghosts, and supernatural forces?
3. How do you think Gallant wants you to respond to her recollections? Did she succeed?

Exploring *How:* Style and Strategy

1. Gallant opens her essay with two **images:** the past receding "swiftly as a bird, wings extended in the wind," and the "contours" of people and places "caught through the clouds of memory." Why does she begin with these metaphors? What tone do they set for her essay?
2. Find other examples of similes, metaphors, and images. Are they effective? What feelings do they evoke?
3. At several points, the author lists the names of plants, bushes, trees, and vegetables. Why does she enumerate the specific names of these items? What effect is she trying to create?
4. In paragraph 5, Gallant briefly recounts the incident with the snake and her dress. How many other incidents does she narrate in this essay? Do these brief narratives blend in well with the descriptions?

IDEAS FOR WRITING A DESCRIPTION

1. Write a three- or four-paragraph description of a solitary experience you once had, such as being alone with nature, going to the movies by yourself, taking a long trip by yourself, being alone in a crowd, staying home alone for the first time, or taking a long, relaxing bath. Try to convey the dominant feelings of the experience, whether it was positive or negative, tedious or exhilarating, scary or refreshing.
2. Smells and tastes can trigger strong memories. Write an essay that describes some of the distinctive smells and tastes from your past; describe the memories they evoke.
3. Write an essay describing a place or situation in which you feel physically quite uncomfortable or unusually comfortable. Consider, for instance, waiting to see the dentist or relaxing in your room—but you can think of more interesting situations than those. Try to include details that will enable your readers to feel the experience.

◆ ◆ ◆ PREPARING TO READ

Is there any part of your physical appearance that you'd like to change? How far would you go to improve your looks?

◆ ◆ ◆

In the Kitchen

HENRY LOUIS GATES JR.

Henry Louis Gates Jr. was born in 1950 in Keyser, West Virginia. He was educated at Yale University and earned his doctorate from Cambridge University in 1979. Gates is one of the nation's leading scholars in African American studies. He has taught at Yale, Cornell, and Duke universities; since 1991, he has been the chair of the Afro-American Studies program at Harvard. The editor and author of numerous works of literary criticism and cultural theory, Gates has also written a memoir of his youth in West Virginia, *Colored People* (1994). The following selection is the fourth chapter in that book.

We always had a gas stove in the kitchen, though electric cooking became fashionable in Piedmont, like using Crest toothpaste rather than Colgate, or watching Huntley and Brinkley rather than Walter Cronkite. But for us it was gas, Colgate, and good ole Walter Cronkite, come what may. We used gas partly out of loyalty to Big Mom, Mama's mama, because she was mostly blind and still loved to cook, and she could feel her way better with gas than with electric. 1

But the most important thing about our gas-equipped kitchen was that Mama used to do hair there. She had a "hot comb"—a fine-toothed iron instrument with a long wooden handle—and a pair of iron curlers that opened and closed like scissors: Mama would put them into the gas fire until they glowed. You could smell those prongs heating up. 2

I liked what that smell meant for the shape of my day. There was an intimate warmth in the women's tones as they talked with my mama while she did their hair. I knew what the women had been through to get their hair ready to be "done," because I would watch Mama do it to herself. How that scorched kink could be transformed through grease and fire into a magnificent head of wavy hair was a miracle to me. Still is. 3

Mama would wash her hair over the sink, a towel wrapped round her shoulders, wearing just her half-slip and her white bra. (We had no shower 4 until we moved down Rat Tail Road into Doc Wolverton's house, in 1954.) After she had dried it, she would grease her scalp thoroughly with blue Bergamot hair grease, which came in a short, fat jar with a picture of a beautiful colored lady on it. It's important to grease your scalp real good, my mama would explain, to keep from burning yourself.

Of course, her hair would return to its natural kink almost as soon as   5
the hot water and shampoo hit it. To me, it was another miracle how hair so "straight" would so quickly become kinky again once it even approached some water.

My mama had only a few "clients" whose heads she "did"—and did, I   6
think, because she enjoyed it, rather than for the few dollars it brought in. They would sit on one of our red plastic kitchen chairs, the kind with the shiny metal legs, and brace themselves for the process. Mama would stroke that red-hot iron, which by this time had been in the gas fire for half an hour or more, slowly but firmly through their hair, from scalp to strand's end. It made a scorching, crinkly sound, the hot iron did, as it burned its way through damp kink, leaving in its wake the straightest of hair strands, each of them standing up long and tall but drooping at the end, like the top of a heavy willow tree. Slowly, steadily, with deftness and grace, Mama's hands would transform a round mound of Odetta kink into a darkened swamp of everglades. The Bergamot made the hair shiny; the heat of the hot iron gave it a brownish-red cast. Once all the hair was as straight as God allows kink to get, Mama would take the well-heated curling iron and twirl the straightened strands into more or less loosely wrapped curls. She claimed that she owed her strength and skill as a hairdresser to her wrists, and her little finger would poke out the way it did when she sipped tea. Mama was a southpaw, who wrote upside down and backwards to produce the cleanest, roundest letters you've ever seen.

The "kitchen" she would all but remove from sight with a pair of shears   7
bought for this purpose. Now, the *kitchen* was the room in which we were sitting, the room where Mama did hair and washed clothes, and where each of us bathed in a galvanized tub. But the word has another meaning, and the "kitchen" I'm speaking of now is the very kinky bit of hair at the back of the head, where the neck meets the shirt collar. If there ever was one part of our African past that resisted assimilation, it was the kitchen. No matter how hot the iron, no matter how powerful the chemical, no matter how stringent the mashed-potatoes-and-lye formula of a man's "process," neither God nor woman nor Sammy Davis, Jr., could straighten the kitchen. The kitchen was permanent, irredeemable, invincible kink. Unassimilably African. No matter what you did, no matter how hard you tried, nothing could dekink a person's kitchen. So you trimmed it off as best you could.

When hair had begun to "turn," as they'd say, or return to its natural   8
kinky glory, it was the kitchen that turned first. When the kitchen started

creeping up the back of the neck, it was time to get your hair done again. The kitchen around the back, and nappy edges at the temples.

Sometimes, after dark, Mr. Charlie Carroll would come to have his hair   9 done. Mr. Charlie Carroll was very light-complected and had a ruddy nose, the kind of nose that made me think of Edmund Gwenn playing Kris Kringle in *Miracle on 34th Street*. At the beginning, they did it after Rocky and I had gone to sleep. It was only later that we found out he had come to our house so Mama could iron his hair—not with a hot comb and curling iron but with our very own Proctor-Silex steam iron. For some reason, Mr. Charlie would conceal his Frederick Douglass mane under a big white Stetson hat, which I never saw him take off. Except when he came to our house, late at night, to have his hair pressed.

(Later, Daddy would tell us about Mr. Charlie's most prized piece of   10 knowledge, which the man would confide only after his hair had been pressed, as a token of intimacy. "Not many people know this," he'd say in a tone of circumspection, "but George Washington was Abraham Lincoln's daddy." Nodding solemnly, he'd add the clincher: "A white man told me." Though he was in dead earnest, this became a humorous refrain around the house—a "white man told me"—used to punctuate especially preposterous assertions.)

My mother furtively examined my daughters' kitchens whenever we   11 went home for a visit in the early eighties. It became a game between us. I had told her not to do it, because I didn't like the politics it suggested of "good" and "bad" hair. "Good" hair was straight. "Bad" hair was kinky. Even in the late sixties, at the height of Black Power, most people could not bring themselves to say "bad" for "good" and "good" for "bad." They still said that hair like white hair was "good," even if they encapsulated it in a disclaimer like "what we used to call 'good.'"

Maggie would be seated in her high chair, throwing food this way and   12 that, and Mama would be cooing about how cute it all was, remembering how I used to do the same thing, and wondering whether Maggie's flinging her food with her left hand meant that she was going to be a southpaw too. When my daughter was just about covered with Franco-American Spaghettios, Mama would seize the opportunity and wipe her clean, dipping her head, tilted to one side, down under the back of Maggie's neck. Sometimes, if she could get away with it, she'd even rub a curl between her fingers, just to make sure that her bifocals had not deceived her. Then she'd sigh with satisfaction and relief, thankful that her prayers had been answered. No kink . . . yet. "Mama!" I'd shout, pretending to be angry. (Every once in a while, if no one was looking, I'd peek too.)

I say "yet" because most black babies are born with soft, silken hair.   13 Then, sooner or later, it begins to "turn," as inevitably as do the seasons or the leaves on a tree. And if it's meant to turn, it *turns*, no matter how hard you try to stop it. People once thought baby oil would stop it. They were wrong.

Everybody I knew as a child wanted to have good hair. You could be   14
as ugly as homemade sin dipped in misery and still be thought attractive if
you had good hair. Jesus Moss was what the girls at Camp Lee, Virginia, had
called Daddy's hair during World War II. I know he played that thick head
of hair for all it was worth, too. Still would, if he could.

My own hair was "not a bad grade," as barbers would tell me when they   15
cut my head for the first time. It's like a doctor reporting the overall results
of the first full physical that he has given you. "You're in good shape" or
"Blood pressure's kind of high; better cut down on salt."

I spent much of my childhood and adolescence messing with my hair.   16
I definitely wanted straight hair. Like Pop's.

When I was about three, I tried to stick a wad of Bazooka bubble gum   17
to that straight hair of his. I suppose what fixed that memory for me is the
spanking I got for doing so: he turned me upside down, holding me by my
feet, the better to paddle my behind. Little *nigger,* he shouted, walloping
away. I started to laugh about it two days later, when my behind stopped
hurting.

When black people say "straight," of course, they don't usually mean   18
"straight" literally, like, say, the hair of Peggy Lipton (the white girl on The
Mod Squad) or Mary of Peter, Paul, and Mary fame; black people call that
"stringy" hair. No, "straight" just means not kinky, no matter what contours
the curl might take. Because Daddy had straight hair, I would have done *anything* to have straight hair—and I used to try everything to make it straight,
short of getting a process, which only riffraff were dumb enough to do.

Of the wide variety of techniques and methods I came to master in the   19
great and challenging follicle prestidigitation, almost all had two things in
common: a heavy, oil-based grease and evenly applied pressure. It's no accident that many of the biggest black companies in the fifties and sixties made
hair products. Indeed, we do have a vast array of hair grease. And I have
tried it all, in search of that certain silky touch, one that leaves neither the
hand nor the pillow sullied by grease.

I always wondered what Frederick Douglass put on *his* hair, or Phillis   20
Wheatley. Or why Wheatley has that rag on her head in the little engraving
in the frontispiece of her book. One thing is for sure: you can bet that when
Wheatley went to England to see the Countess of Huntington, she did not
stop by the Queen's Coiffeur on the way. So many black people still get their
hair straightened that it's a wonder we don't have a national holiday for
Madame C. J. Walker, who invented the process for straightening kinky hair,
rather than for Dr. King. Jheri-curled or "relaxed"—it's still fried hair.

I used all the greases, from sea-blue Bergamot, to creamy vanilla Duke   21
(in its orange-and-white jar), to the godfather of grease, the formidable Murray's. Now, Murray's was some *serious* grease. Whereas Bergamot was like oily
Jell-O and Duke was viscous and sickly sweet, Murray's was light brown and

hard. Hard as lard and twice as greasy, Daddy used to say whenever the subject of Murray's came up. Murray's came in an orange can with a screw-on top. It was so hard that some people would put a match to the can, just to soften it and make it more manageable. In the late sixties, when Afros came into style, I'd use Afro-Sheen. From Murray's to Duke to Afro-Sheen: that was my progression in black consciousness.

We started putting hot towels or washrags over our greased-down,   22
Murray's-coated heads, in order to melt the wax into the scalp and follicles. Unfortunately, the wax had a curious habit of running down your neck, ears, and forehead. Not to mention your pillowcase.

Another problem was that if you put two palmfuls of Murray's on your   23
head, your hair turned white. Duke did the same thing. It was a challenge: if you got rid of the white stuff, you had a magnificent head of wavy hair. Murray's turned kink into waves. Lots of waves. Frozen waves. A hurricane couldn't have blown those waves around.

That was the beauty of it. Murray's was so hard that it froze your hair   24
into the wavy style you brushed it into. It looked really good if you wore a part. A lot of guys had parts *cut* into their hair by a barber, with clippers or a straight-edge razor. Especially if you had kinky hair—in which case you'd generally wear a short razor cut, or what we called a Quo Vadis.

Being obsessed with our hair, we tried to be as innovative as possible.   25
Everyone knew about using a stocking cap, because your father or your uncle or the older guys wore them whenever something really big was about to happen, secular or sacred, a funeral or a dance, a wedding or a trip in which you confronted official white people, or when you were trying to look really sharp. When it was time to be clean, you wore a stocking cap. If the event was really a big one, you made a new cap for the occasion.

A stocking cap was made by asking your mother for one of her hose,   26
and cutting it with a pair of scissors about six inches or so from the open end, where the elastic goes up to the top of the thigh. Then you'd knot the cut end, and behold—a conical-shaped hat or cap, with an elastic band that you pulled down low on your forehead and down around your neck in the back. A good stocking cap, to work well, had to fit tight and snug, like a press. And it had to fit that tightly because it *was* a press: it pressed your hair with the force of the hose's elastic. If you greased your hair down real good and left the stocking cap on long enough—*voilà:* you got a head of pressed-against-the-scalp waves. If you used Murray's, and if you wore a stocking cap to sleep, you got a *whole lot* of waves. (You also got a ring around your forehead when you woke up, but eventually that disappeared.)

And then you could enjoy your concrete 'do. Swore we were bad, too,   27
with all that grease and those flat heads. My brother and I would brush it out a bit in the morning, so it would look—ahem—"natural."

Grown men still wear stocking caps, especially older men, who gener- 28
ally keep their caps in their top drawer, along with their cuff links and their
see-through silk socks, their Maverick tie, their silk handkerchief, and whatever else they prize most.

A Murrayed-down stocking cap was the respectable version of the 29
process, which, by contrast, was most definitely not a cool thing to have, at
least if you weren't an entertainer by trade.

Zeke and Keith and Poochie and a few other stars of the basketball 30
team all used to get a process once or twice a year. It was expensive, and to
get one you had to go to Pittsburgh or D.C. or Uniontown, someplace where
there were enough colored people to support a business. They'd disappear,
then reappear a day or two later, strutting like peacocks, their hair burned
slightly red from the chemical lye base. They'd also wear "rags" or cloths or
handkerchiefs around it when they slept or played basketball. Do-rags, they
were called. But the result was *straight* hair, with a hint of wave. No curl. Do-
it-yourselfers took their chances at home with a concoction of mashed potatoes and lye.

The most famous process, outside of what Malcolm X describes in his 31
Autobiography and maybe that of Sammy Davis, Jr., was Nat King Cole's. Nat
King Cole had patent-leather hair.

"That man's got the finest process money can buy." That's what Daddy 32
said the night Cole's TV show aired on NBC, November 5, 1956. I remember
the date because everyone came to our house to watch it and to celebrate one
of Daddy's buddies' birthdays. Yeah, Uncle Joe chimed in, they can do shit
to his hair that the average Negro can't even *think* about—secret shit.

Nat King Cole was *clean*. I've had an ongoing argument with a Nige- 33
rian friend about Nat King Cole for twenty years now. Not whether or not
he could sing; any fool knows that he could sing. But whether or not he was
a handkerchief-head for wearing that patent-leather process.

Sammy Davis's process I detested. It didn't look good on him. Worse 34
still, he liked to have a fried strand dangling down the middle of his forehead, shaking it out from the crown when he sang. But Nat King Cole's hair
was a thing unto itself, a beautifully sculpted work of art that he and he alone
should have had the right to wear.

The only difference between a process and a stocking cap, really, was 35
taste; yet Nat King Cole—unlike, say, Michael Jackson—looked *good* in his
process. His head looked like Rudolph Valentino's in the twenties, and some
say it was Valentino that the process imitated. But Nat King Cole wore a
process because it suited his face, his demeanor, his name, his style. He was
as clean as he wanted to be.

I had forgotten all about Nat King Cole and that patent-leather look 36
until the day in 1971 when I was sitting in an Arab restaurant on the island

of Zanzibar, surrounded by men in fezzes and white caftans, trying to learn how to eat curried goat and rice with the fingers of my right hand, feeling two million miles from home, when all of a sudden the old transistor radio sitting on top of a china cupboard stopped blaring out its Swahili music to play "Fly Me to the Moon" by Nat King Cole. The restaurant's din was not affected at all, not even by half a decibel. But in my mind's eye, I saw it: the King's sleek black magnificent tiara. I managed, barely, to blink back the tears.

FIRST RESPONSES

Do you and your friends want to have good hair? Do you agree with Gates that people can be ugly and still be thought attractive if they have good hair? Is hair really that important?

TAKING A CLOSER LOOK

Exploring *Who:* Voice and Tone

1. How does Gates feel about black people getting their hair straightened? He says that in his childhood and adolescence he "definitely wanted straight hair." Do you think he still does?
2. Is Gates writing primarily for African American readers? In what ways is this topic of interest to all audiences?
3. What do you think about people who wear wigs or hairpieces? Do you have the same opinion of the people Gates writes about in this essay?

Exploring *What:* Content and Meaning

1. What is the "kitchen"? What does Gates mean when he says, "If there ever was one part of our African past that resisted assimilation, it was the kitchen"?
2. In paragraph 11, Gates says that in the early 1980s "good" hair was straight and "bad" hair was kinky. Is that distinction still true today?
3. Who are Frederick Douglass and Phillis Wheatley? Why does Gates wonder what they put on their heads (para. 20)?
4. What is a "process"? Why was it not considered "cool" to have one? Why was it all right for entertainers to have one?
5. What does Nat King Cole represent to Gates? Why does he use him as a reference point?

Exploring *Why:* Purpose

1. Why did Gates choose to write about this topic? Is he making some comment about himself? About the African American community? Is it the kind of topic you'd ever write about?

2. Does Gates have a political agenda in writing about this topic? Do you think he wants you to take sides on the straight versus kinky question? What do *you* think about this issue?

3. ■▯ *Using the Internet.* Visit the African American Web Connection (www.aawc.com/aawc.html) or a similar Web site to see if you can find the latest opinions on the topic of kinky hair.

Exploring *How:* Style and Strategy

1. Why does Gates begin by describing the kitchen in his boyhood home? How does he use this setting to move into the main topic of this essay? Is this transition effective?

2. Gates describes several different methods for straightening kinky hair. What details and images does he use to help you visualize these procedures and their effects? Which ones did you find most effective?

3. Where is there humor in this essay? How do you respond to these humorous touches? Do you think they're appropriate?

4. Why does Gates conclude with an anecdote about Nat King Cole? Do you like this ending?

IDEAS FOR WRITING A DESCRIPTION

1. Write a detailed description of someone you know (a friend, classmate, or relative), but don't reveal the person's name or identity. Then show your description to others who also know the person to see if they recognize your subject.

2. Describe some ritual or routine (exercise, diet, grooming methods, beauty practices) that you follow to improve your health or appearance. Use descriptive words and phrases to convey how you feel about this activity.

3. ■▯ *Using the Internet.* People send messages about themselves by the way they wear their hair. Describe several distinctive hairstyles (crewcut, colorful dyes, buns, ponytails, mohawks, lacquered spikes, etc.), and explain why you think people adopt them. Or describe the current favorite in hairdos, and explain why it's popular. Do a search on the Internet (keywords: "hair styles") to see what you can find out about the latest hair fashions.

◆ ◆ ◆ PREPARING TO READ

Did you have a favorite getaway place as a child? Why was this place special? How did it make you feel?

◆ ◆ ◆

Once More to the Lake

E. B. WHITE

For more than fifty years, Elwyn Brooks White (1899–1985) was a regular contributor to *The New Yorker* and *Harper's* magazines. His feature articles, editorials, and commentaries earned him recognition as one of America's most incisive and wittiest essayists. He also wrote two highly acclaimed children's books, *Stuart Little* (1945) and *Charlotte's Web* (1952). The following personal essay first appeared in *Harper's* in 1941.

One summer, along about 1904, my father rented a camp on a lake in Maine and took us all there for the month of August. We all got ringworm from some kittens and had to rub Pond's Extract on our arms and legs night and morning, and my father rolled over in a canoe with all his clothes on; but outside of that the vacation was a success and from then on none of us ever thought there was any place in the world like that lake in Maine. We returned summer after summer—always on August 1st for one month. I have since become a salt-water man, but sometimes in summer there are days when the restlessness of the tides and the fearful cold of the sea water and the incessant wind that blows across the afternoon and into the evening make me wish for the placidity of a lake in the woods. A few weeks ago this feeling got so strong I bought myself a couple of bass hooks and a spinner and returned to the lake where we used to go, for a week's fishing and to revisit old haunts.

I took along my son, who had never had any fresh water up his nose and who had seen lily pads only from train windows. On the journey over to the lake I began to wonder what it would be like. I wondered how time would have marred this unique, this holy spot—the coves and streams, the hills that the sun set behind, the camps and the paths behind the camps. I was sure that the tarred road would have found it out and I wondered in what other ways it would be desolated. It is strange how much you can remember about places like that once you allow your mind to return into the grooves that lead back. You remember one thing, and that suddenly reminds you of another thing. I guess I remembered clearest of all the early mornings, when the lake was cool and motionless, remembered how the bedroom smelled of the lumber it was made of and the wet woods whose scent entered through the screen. The partitions in the camp were thin and did not extend clear to the top of the rooms, and as I was always the first up I would dress softly so as not to wake the others, and sneak out into the sweet outdoors and start out in the canoe, keeping close along the shore in the long shadows of the pines. I remembered being very careful never to rub my paddle against the gunwale for fear of disturbing the stillness of the cathedral.

The lake had never been what you would call a wild lake. There were　3
cottages sprinkled about the shores, and it was in farming country although the shores of the lake were quite heavily wooded. Some of the cottages were owned by nearby farmers, and you would live at the shore and eat your meals at the farmhouse. That's what our family did. But although it wasn't wild, it was a fairly large and undisturbed lake and there were places in it which, to a child at least, seemed infinitely remote and primeval.

I was right about the tar: It led to within half a mile of the shore. But　4
when I got back there, with my boy, and we settled into a camp near a farmhouse and into the kind of summertime I had known, I could tell that it was going to be pretty much the same as it had been before—I knew it, lying in bed the first morning, smelling the bedroom, and hearing the boy sneak quietly out and go off along the shore in a boat. I began to sustain the illusion that he was I, and therefore, by simple transposition, that I was my father. This sensation persisted, kept cropping up all the time we were there. It was not an entirely new feeling, but in this setting it grew much stronger. I seemed to be living a dual existence. I would be in the middle of some simple act, I would be picking up a bait box or laying down a table fork, or I would be saying something, and suddenly it would be not I but my father who was saying the words or making the gesture. It gave me a creepy sensation.

We went fishing the first morning. I felt the same damp moss covering　5
the worms in the bait can, and saw the dragonfly alight on the tip of my rod as it hovered a few inches from the surface of the water. It was the arrival of this fly that convinced me beyond any doubt that everything was as it always had been, that the years were a mirage and there had been no years. The small waves were the same, chucking the rowboat under the chin as we fished at anchor, and the boat was the same boat, the same color green and the ribs broken in the same places, and under the floorboards the same fresh-water leavings and debris—the dead hellgrammite, the wisps of moss, the rusty discarded fishhook, the dried blood from yesterday's catch. We stared silently at the tips of our rods, at the dragonflies that came and went. I lowered the tip of mine into the water, tentatively, pensively dislodging the fly, which darted two feet away, poised, darted two feet back, and came to rest again a

little farther up the rod. There had been no years between the ducking of this dragonfly and the other one—the one that was part of memory. I looked at the boy, who was silently watching his fly, and it was my hands that held his rod, my eyes watching. I felt dizzy and didn't know which rod I was at the end of.

We caught two bass, hauling them in briskly as though they were mack-   6
erel, pulling them over the side of the boat in a businesslike manner without any landing net, and stunning them with a blow on the back of the head. When we got back for a swim before lunch, the lake was exactly where we had left it, the same number of inches from the dock, and there was only the merest suggestion of a breeze. This seemed an utterly enchanted sea, this lake you could leave to its own devices for a few hours and come back to, and find that it had not stirred, this constant and trustworthy body of water. In the shallows, the dark, watersoaked sticks and twigs, smooth and old, were un-dulating in clusters on the bottom against the clean ribbed sand, and the track of the mussel was plain. A school of minnows swam by, each minnow with its small individual shadow, doubling the attendance, so clear and sharp in the sunlight. Some of the other campers were in swimming, along the shore, one of them with a cake of soap, and the water felt thin and clear and un-substantial. Over the years there had been this person with the cake of soap, this cultist, and here he was. There had been no years.

Up to the farmhouse to dinner through the teeming, dusty field, the   7
road under our sneakers was only a two-track road. The middle track was missing, the one with the marks of the hooves and splotches of dried, flaky manure. There had always been three tracks to choose from in choosing which track to walk in; now the choice was narrowed down to two. For a mo-ment I missed terribly the middle alternative. But the way led past the ten-nis court, and something about the way it lay there in the sun reassured me; the tape had loosened along the backline, the alleys were green with plantains and other weeds, and the net (installed in June and removed in September) sagged in the dry noon, and the whole place steamed with midday heat and hunger and emptiness. There was a choice of pie for dessert, and one was blueberry and one was apple, and the waitresses were the same country girls, there having been no passage of time, only the illusion of it as in a dropped curtain—the waitresses were still fifteen; their hair had been washed, that was the only difference—they had been to the movies and seen the pretty girls with the clean hair.

Summertime, oh summertime, pattern of life indelible, the fade-proof   8
lake, the woods unshatterable, the pasture with the sweetfern and the juniper forever and ever, summer without end; this was the background, and the life along the shore was the design, the cottages with their innocent and tranquil design, their tiny docks with the flagpole and the American flag floating against the white clouds in the blue sky, the little paths over the roots of the trees leading from camp to camp and the paths leading back to the outhouses

and the can of lime for sprinkling, and at the souvenir counters at the store the miniature birch-bark canoes and the post cards that showed things looking a little better than they looked. This was the American family at play, escaping the city heat, wondering whether the newcomers in the camp at the head of the cove were "common" or "nice," wondering whether it was true that the people who drove up for Sunday dinner at the farmhouse were turned away because there wasn't enough chicken.

It seemed to me, as I kept remembering all this, that those times and   9
those summers had been infinitely precious and worth saving. There had been jollity and peace and goodness. The arriving (at the beginning of August) had been so big a business in itself, at the railway station the farm wagon drawn up, the first smell of the pine-laden air, the first glimpse of the smiling farmer, and the great importance of the trunks and your father's enormous authority in such matters, and the feel of the wagon under you for the long ten-mile haul, and at the top of the last long hill catching the first view of the lake after eleven months of not seeing this cherished body of water. The shouts and cries of the other campers when they saw you, and the trunks to be unpacked, to give up their rich burden. (Arriving was less exciting nowadays, when you sneaked up in your car and parked it under a tree near the camp and took out the bags and in five minutes it was all over, no fuss, no loud wonderful fuss about trunks.)

Peace and goodness and jollity. The only thing that was wrong now, re-   10
ally, was the sound of the place, an unfamiliar nervous sound of the outboard motors. This was the note that jarred, the one thing that would sometimes break the illusion and set the years moving. In those other summertimes all motors were inboard; and when they were at a little distance, the noise they made was a sedative, an ingredient of summer sleep. They were one-cylinder and two-cylinder engines, and some were make-and-break and some were jump-spark, but they all made a sleepy sound across the lake. The one-lungers throbbed and fluttered, and the twin-cylinder ones purred and purred, and that was a quiet sound too. But now the campers all had outboards. In the daytime, in the hot mornings, these motors made a petulant, irritable sound; at night, in the still evening when the afterglow lit the water, they whined about one's ears like mosquitoes. My boy loved our rented outboard, and his great desire was to achieve singlehanded mastery over it, and authority, and he soon learned the trick of choking it a little (but not too much), and the adjustment of the needle valve. Watching him I would remember the things you could do with the old one-cylinder engines with the heavy flywheel, how you could have it eating out of your hand if you got really close to it spiritually. Motor boats in those days didn't have clutches, and you would make a landing by shutting off the motor at the proper time and coasting in with a dead rudder. But there was a way of reversing them, if you learned the trick, by cutting the switch and putting it on again exactly on the final dying revolution of the flywheel, so that it would kick back against compression and

begin reversing. Approaching a dock in a strong following breeze, it was difficult to slow up sufficiently by the ordinary coasting method, and if a boy felt he had complete mastery over his motor, he was tempted to keep it running beyond its time and then reverse it a few feet from the dock. It took a cool nerve, because if you threw the switch a twentieth of a second too soon you could catch the flywheel when it still had speed enough to go up past center, and the boat would leap ahead, charging bull-fashion at the dock.

We had a good week at the camp. The bass were biting well and the   11
sun shone endlessly, day after day. We would be tired at night and lie down in the accumulated heat of the little bedrooms after the long hot day and the breeze would stir almost imperceptibly outside and the smell of the swamp drift in through the rusty screens. Sleep would come easily and in the morning the red squirrel would be on the roof, tapping out his gay routine. I kept remembering everything, lying in bed in the mornings—the small steamboat that had a long rounded stern like the lip of a Ubangi, and how quietly she ran on the moonlight sails, when the older boys played their mandolins and the girls sang and we ate doughnuts dipped in sugar, and how sweet the music was on the water in the shining night, and what it had felt like to think about girls then. After breakfast we would go up to the store and the things were in the same place—the minnows in a bottle, the plugs and spinners disarranged and pawed over by the youngsters from the boys' camp, the Fig Newtons and the Beeman's gum. Outside, the road was tarred and cars stood in front of the store. Inside, all was just as it had always been, except there was more Coca-Cola and not so much Moxie and root beer and birch beer and sarsaparilla. We would walk out with a bottle of pop apiece and sometimes the pop would backfire up our noses and hurt. We explored the streams, quietly, where the turtles slid off the sunny logs and dug their way into the soft bottom; and we lay on the town wharf and fed worms to the tame bass. Everywhere we went I had trouble making out which was I, the one walking at my side, the one walking in my pants.

One afternoon while we were there at that lake a thunderstorm came   12
up. It was like the revival of an old melodrama that I had seen long ago with childish awe. The second-act climax of the drama of the electrical disturbance over a lake in America had not changed in any important respect. This was the big scene, still the big scene. The whole thing was so familiar, the first feeling of oppression and heat and a general air around camp of not wanting to go very far away. In midafternoon (it was all the same) a curious darkening of the sky, and a lull in everything that had made life tick; and then the way the boats suddenly swung the other way at their moorings with the coming of a breeze out of the new quarter, and the premonitory rumble. Then the kettle drum, then the snare, then the bass drum and cymbals, then crackling light against the dark, and the gods grinning and licking their chops in the hills. Afterward the calm, the rain steadily rustling in the calm lake, the return of light and hope and spirits, and the campers running out in joy and

relief to go swimming in the rain, their bright cries perpetuating the death-less joke about how they were getting simply drenched, and the children screaming with delight at the new sensation of bathing in the rain, and the joke about getting drenched linking the generations in a strong indestructible chain. And the comedian who waded in carrying an umbrella.

When the others went swimming my son said he was going in too. He   13
pulled his dripping trunks from the line where they had hung all through the shower, and wrung them out. Languidly, and with no thought of going in, I watched him, his hard little body, skinny and bare, saw him wince slightly as he pulled up around his vitals the small, soggy, icy garment. As he buckled the swollen belt suddenly my groin felt the chill of death.

◆ ◆ ◆

FIRST RESPONSES

How do you feel about the author and the revelation he makes in the final paragraph? Can you identify with his situation? Explain why you feel the way you do.

TAKING A CLOSER LOOK

Exploring *Who:* Voice and Tone

1. How old was the author when he wrote this essay? How much does his age matter to his attitude and state of mind?
2. How would you describe the author's mood at the beginning of the essay? How has his mood changed in the end? What were you feeling as you read this essay? Did your feelings change?
3. What age group is White addressing in this essay? Are you part of the audience White is writing to? Can people who have never been to the Maine woods relate to this essay?
4. How did White's son feel about the trip to the lake? Can you be sure that White is conveying his son's impressions, or is the author projecting his own memories?

Exploring *What:* Content and Meaning

1. Explain the illusion that White describes in paragraph 4. How does he explain this sensation to himself? Have you ever had a similar sensation?

2. What role does time play in this essay? Find images and references that bring out the theme of time's passing.

3. What is the point of the discussion of inboard and outboard motors (para. 10)?

4. Explain the last sentence. Does it raise an issue that concerns you?

Exploring *Why:* Purpose

1. In what sense is the author writing this essay for himself? What feelings is he trying to come to terms with?

2. ◼️ *Using the Internet.* How would a travel agent's description of the lake be different from White's? Find a travel agency's Web site on the Internet to see what kinds of information it gives. What details and impressions does White include that a travel brochure would not? Why does he include this kind of material?

3. Do you think this essay contains a message or a lesson? What is it? Have you had any experiences that might communicate the same point?

Exploring *How:* Style and Strategy

1. Point out images that re-create the sights, sounds, smells, and tastes of White's childhood visit. How effectively do these images communicate the quality of memory?

2. What do you think of White's reference to the lake as "this holy spot" and a "cathedral" (para. 2)?

3. This essay is both a description and a comparison. How closely related are the two strategies? In what ways does the description contribute to the comparison?

4. Describe the impact of the final paragraph. Is that the way you expected the essay to end? How would you have concluded an essay like this one?

IDEAS FOR WRITING A DESCRIPTION

1. Describe the perfect place to escape to, real or imagined.

2. Describe yourself as you think your parents see you. What qualities do they like? Which ones would they like you to change?

3. Describe a place that has a strong appeal (either positive or negative) to you. Include sensory details that will help reveal your feelings, but do not name the emotions themselves.

◆ ◆ ◆

◆ FURTHER IDEAS FOR USING DESCRIPTION

1. Write a two-part description of the same person, place, or object. In the first part, give an objective description; in the second part, present an expressive (subjective) description by using details and sensory images to convey your feelings about the subject. Choose something or someone you can describe in detail.

2. Think of a setting that is quite familiar to you but probably unknown to your classmates. Write an essay in which you try to convey the experience of being in that setting, as several writers in this chapter do. You might want to consider nature, family, school, and solitary settings in choosing your topic.

3. Attempt to describe, in concrete, sensory terms, a certain feeling such as grief, happiness, hope, boredom, or mistrust. Try to evoke the feeling without labeling it.

4. COLLABORATIVE WRITING. Go to an art exhibit with a small group of classmates. Choose which works each of you will describe for an exhibit catalog. Together, organize your descriptions and revise them for a consistent style and tone. Then collaboratively write a paragraph or two of introduction for the catalog.

5. COMBINING STRATEGIES. Combine narrative and description to write an account of an experience that changed you in some important way. Do not *tell* your readers explicitly what the change was, but let the description-narration clearly *show* how you were changed.

6. ■▯ *Using the Internet.* Describe a memorable vacation you had. Assume that your readers have not visited this place. Use the Internet to refresh your memory and gather more details for your description. If you went to the Black Hills, for instance, you could browse the Black Hills Information Web site at www.blackhills-info.com/.

CHAPTER 5

Strategies for Making a Point

Exemplification

◆ ◆ ◆ ◆ ◆

> **Exemplification writing explains and clarifies a generalization through illustration.**
>
> ◆ Writers use examples that are appropriate, relevant, and sufficiently detailed.
>
> ◆ Effective exemplification is organized to connect examples logically and clearly to the thesis and to one another.

You began using exemplification at a very early age. When your mother or father wouldn't let you ride your bike more than a block from the house, you probably informed them that your best friend had been going two whole blocks safely for at least the last month. Successful writers also make their points, or at least make them clearer and more interesting, by providing **examples.**

Exemplification, like narration and description, may be the focus of an entire essay, or it may be employed to bring other writing strategies to life. A *Sports Illustrated* story on the various community service activities of

Michael Jordan or Mia Hamm reminds us that many athletes can and do provide positive role models for young people. And an in-depth example of a successful project at your current job may very well convince a prospective employer that you are the best candidate. Examples are, in a way, the "show" part of "show and tell." When writers simply tell readers their point, the result can be the kind of dense, dry, confusing essay that needs to be read and reread. Lively, clear, appropriate illustrations, however, ensure that readers will understand a step in a process, remember an essential trait in a definition, distinguish clearly one category from another, or visualize the consequence of an action.

Journalist Brent Staples turned to his own experience as a black man to create the following essay, which exemplifies the look, the feel, and the consequences of racism. After reading about Staples's experience, student writer Robert Lincoln looked at his own life to understand the nature of stereotypes. His essay follows Staples's.

Just Walk On By: A Black Man Ponders His Power to Alter Public Space

BRENT STAPLES

Born in 1951 to a poor and troubled family, Brent Staples earned a Ph.D. in psychology from the University of Chicago and has since established himself as a respected reporter and editorial writer with the *New York Times*. The following selection was originally published in *Ms.* magazine in 1986 and appeared as part of Staples's coming-of-age memoir, *Parallel Time: Growing Up in Black and White* (1994). His current interest is in the power figures behind the nineteenth- and early-twentieth-century black press.

My first victim was a woman—white, well dressed, probably in her early 　1 twenties. I came upon her late one evening on a deserted street in Hyde Park, a relatively affluent neighborhood in an otherwise mean, impoverished section of Chicago. As I swung onto the avenue behind her, there seemed to be a discreet, uninflammatory distance between us. Not so. She cast back a worried glance. To her, the youngish black man—a broad six feet two inches with a beard and billowing hair, both hands shoved into the pockets of a bulky military jacket—seemed menacingly close. After a few more quick glimpses, she picked up her pace and was soon running in earnest. Within seconds she disappeared into a cross street.

That was more than a decade ago. I was 22 years old, a graduate student   2
newly arrived at the University of Chicago. It was in the echo of that terrified woman's footfalls that I first began to know the unwieldy inheritance I'd come into—the ability to alter public space in ugly ways. It was clear that she thought herself the quarry of a mugger, rapist, or worse. Suffering a bout of insomnia, however, I was stalking sleep, not defenseless wayfarers. As a softy who is scarcely able to take a knife to a raw chicken—let alone hold it to a person's throat—I was surprised, embarrassed, and dismayed all at once. Her flight made me feel like an accomplice in tyranny. It also made it clear that I was indistinguishable from the muggers who occasionally seeped into the area from the surrounding ghetto. That first encounter, and those that followed, signified that a vast, unnerving gulf lay between nighttime pedestrians—particularly women—and me. And I soon gathered that being perceived as dangerous is a hazard in itself. I only needed to turn a corner into a dicey situation or crowd some frightened, armed person in a foyer somewhere, or make an errant move after being pulled over by a policeman. Where fear and weapons meet—and they often do in urban America—there is always the possibility of death.

In that first year, my first away from my hometown, I was to become   3
thoroughly familiar with the language of fear. At dark, shadowy intersections in Chicago, I could cross in front of a car stopped at a traffic light and elicit the *thunk, thunk, thunk, thunk* of the driver—black, white, male or female—hammering down the door locks. On less traveled streets after dark, I grew accustomed to but never comfortable with people who crossed to the other side of the street rather than pass me. Then there were the standard unpleasantries with police, doormen, bouncers, cab drivers, and others whose business it is to screen out troublesome individuals *before* there is any nastiness.

I moved to New York nearly two years ago and I have remained an   4
avid night walker. In central Manhattan, the near-constant crowd cover minimizes tense one-on-one street encounters. Elsewhere—visiting friends in SoHo, where sidewalks are narrow and tightly spaced buildings shut out the sky—things can get very taut indeed.

Black men have a firm place in New York mugging literature. Norman   5
Podhoretz in his famed (or infamous) 1963 essay, "My Negro Problem—and Ours," recalls growing up in terror of black males; they "were tougher than we were, more ruthless," he writes—and as an adult on the Upper West Side of Manhattan, he continues, he cannot constrain his nervousness when he meets black men on certain streets. Similarly, a decade later, the essayist and novelist Edward Hoagland extols a New York where once "Negro bitterness bore down mainly on other Negroes." Where some see mere

panhandlers, Hoagland sees "a mugger who is clearly screwing up his nerve to do more than just *ask* for money." But Hoagland has "the New Yorker's quick-hunch posture for broken-field maneuvering," and the bad guy swerves away.

I often witness that "hunch posture," from women after dark on the warrenlike streets of Brooklyn where I live. They seem to set their faces on neutral and, with their purse straps strung across their chests bandolier style, they forge ahead as though bracing themselves against being tackled. I understand, of course, that the danger they perceive is not a hallucination. Women are particularly vulnerable to street violence, and young black males are drastically overrepresented among the perpetrators of that violence. Yet these truths are no solace against the kind of alienation that comes of being ever the suspect, against being set apart, a fearsome entity with whom pedestrians avoid making eye contact.

It is not altogether clear to me how I reached the ripe old age of 22 without being conscious of the lethality nighttime pedestrians attributed to me. Perhaps it was because in Chester, Pennsylvania, the small, angry industrial town where I came of age in the 1960s, I was scarcely noticeable against a backdrop of gang warfare, street knifings, and murders. I grew up one of the good boys, had perhaps a half-dozen fist fights. In retrospect, my shyness of combat has clear sources.

Many things go into the making of a young thug. One of those things is the consummation of the male romance with the power to intimidate. An infant discovers that random flailings send the baby bottle flying out of the crib and crashing to the floor. Delighted, the joyful babe repeats those motions again and again, seeking to duplicate the feat. Just so, I recall the points at which some of my boyhood friends were finally seduced by the perception of themselves as tough guys. When a mark cowered and surrendered his money without resistance, myth and reality merged—and paid off. It is, after all, only manly to embrace the power to frighten and intimidate. We, as men, are not supposed to give an inch of our lane on the highway; we are to seize the fighter's edge in work and in play and even in love; we are to be valiant in the face of hostile forces.

Unfortunately, poor and powerless young men seem to take all this nonsense literally. As a boy, I saw countless tough guys locked away; I have since buried several, too. They were babies, really—a teenage cousin, a brother of 22, a childhood friend in his mid-twenties—all gone down in episodes of bravado played out in the streets. I came to doubt the virtues of intimidation early on. I chose, perhaps even unconsciously, to remain a shadow—timid, but a survivor.

The fearsomeness mistakenly attributed to me in public places often has a perilous flavor. The most frightening of these confusions occurred in the late 1970s and early 1980s when I worked as a journalist in Chicago. One day, rushing into the office of a magazine I was writing for with a deadline story in hand, I was mistaken for a burglar. The office manager called security and, with an ad hoc posse, pursued me through the labyrinthine halls, nearly to my editor's door. I had no way of proving who I was. I could only move briskly toward the company of someone who knew me.

Another time I was on assignment for a local paper and killing time   11
before an interview. I entered a jewelry store on the city's affluent Near North Side. The proprietor excused herself and returned with an enormous red Doberman pinscher straining at the end of a leash. She stood, the dog extended toward me, silent to my questions, her eyes bulging nearly out of her head. I took a cursory look around, nodded, and bade her good night. Relatively speaking, however, I never fared as badly as another black male journalist. He went to nearby Waukegan, Illinois, a couple of summers ago to work on a story about a murderer who was born there. Mistaking the reporter for the killer, police hauled him from his car at gunpoint and but for his press credentials would probably have tried to book him. Such episodes are not uncommon. Black men trade tales like this all the time.

In "My Negro Problem—and Ours," Podhoretz writes that the hatred   12
he feels for blacks makes itself known to him through a variety of avenues—one being his discomfort with that "special brand of paranoid touchiness" to which he says blacks are prone. No doubt he is speaking here of black men. In time, I learned to smother the rage I felt at so often being taken for a criminal. Not to do so would surely have led to madness—via that special "paranoid touchiness" that so annoyed Podhoretz at the time he wrote the essay.

I began to take precautions to make myself less threatening. I move   13
about with care, particularly late in the evening. I give a wide berth to nervous people on subway platforms during the wee hours, particularly when I have exchanged business clothes for jeans. If I happen to be entering a building behind some people who appear skittish, I may walk by, letting them clear the lobby before I return, so as not to seem to be following them. I have been calm and extremely congenial on those rare occasions when I've been pulled over by the police.

And on late-evening constitutionals along streets less traveled by, I em-   14
ploy what has proved to be an excellent tension-reducing measure: I whistle melodies from Beethoven and Vivaldi and the more popular classical composers. Even steely New Yorkers hunching toward nighttime destinations seem to relax, and occasionally they even join in the tune. Virtually everybody seems to sense that a mugger wouldn't be warbling bright, sunny selections from Vivaldi's *Four Seasons*. It is my equivalent of the cowbell that hikers wear when they know they are in bear country.

◆ ◆ ◆

◆ ◆ ◆ *Writer's Workshop I* ◆ ◆ ◆
Responding to an Exemplification Essay

Use the *Who, What, Why,* and *How* questions (see p. 3) to explore your own understanding of the ideas and writing strategies employed by Brent Staples in "Just Walk On By." Your instructor may ask you to record these responses in a journal, post them to an electronic bulletin board, or bring them to class to use in small group discussions.

◆ WRITING FROM READING

The *Who, What, Why,* and *How* questions helped freshman Bobby Lincoln understand Brent Staples's successful strategies for exemplifying what all Americans lose when they act on stereotypes or are victimized by them. Bobby soon recognized that this very difficult and abstract problem, one many people distance themselves from, had been made clear and immediate through Staples's honest and detailed revelation of his specific feelings and concrete actions. As Bobby put it, "By telling stories he doesn't come across as having a specific agenda, and therefore his readers are less likely to dismiss what he has to say." After freewriting to identify a stereotype that affects how other people might see him, Bobby wrote the following essay.

```
Robert Lincoln
English 1090
September 10, 2000
```

Out and About

    For a couple of years in high school I maintained   1
an online journal. I did this because I found it
surprising how many people, friends and strangers
alike, read it on a regular basis. Every now and then
a friend would bring up something in the journal, and
we would talk about it. I enjoyed the benefit of not
having to tell the same story twenty times to twenty
different people: with an online journal I could tell
it once.

    Such was the case with Luke, a guy I went to   2
school with from first grade through high school. He
and his girlfriend were at a mutual friend's house,

and she was reading my most recent ranting. Luke stood behind her and perused the text on the computer screen. "Bob's gay?" he asked all of a sudden. Yes, they told him matter-of-factly, he is. "Bob *Lincoln*?" He could not believe it. He had known me for something like 11 years and hadn't suspected a thing the entire time. "Cool," he said at last. Then they set out to do whatever it was they had planned to do that day.

This reaction was not an isolated one. Many times   3
friends and acquaintances have been genuinely shocked to discover I am homosexual. "But you don't *act* gay," someone once told me. "Duh," I retorted. "I don't need to *act* gay because I *am* gay." Besides, what does it mean to act gay? For the answer I turn to the numerous theories, lies, and misconceptions I have come across over the years. Apparently, all gay men are effeminate, talk with a lisp, wear flashy clothes, dance extremely well, have at least one limp wrist, are promiscuous, and absolutely adore Barbra Streisand, Madonna, Cher, and Bette Midler. Okay, I confess: I love Madonna, Cher, and Bette Midler. Other than that, if we go by the popular definition, I'm as heterosexual as they come. I've neither seen *Yentl* nor do I know what a yentl is.

It probably shouldn't come as any surprise when   4
people react the way they do given the messages society and the media send out on a regular basis. Because of the media's influence, I always thought Australians lived in grass huts and had to chase dingoes off their property--until I met my first real-life Australian. Similarly, very rarely are homosexuals portrayed as the full range of diverse people that they really are. When I went to stay with a friend over Spring Break, her Aunt Eileen invited us over for dinner. It wasn't until afterward that I heard how I was received by Aunt Eileen. Before meeting me, she had never met an openly gay man. In fact, she was expecting me to sashay into the house wearing a pink feather boa and screaming, "Hey, girlfriend!" in my best RuPaul voice. I can imagine her surprise when she discovered that I'm nothing like the person she anticipated and that I can hold a decent conversation about something other than the new fall line at GAP and how sexy football players look in

those tight pants. (Truth be told, we didn't talk about those things only because the subjects never came up.)

There are, however, some benefits that come from not fitting the stereotypes. Some people treat me like an incredible phenomenon, a mystery of biological science. "You mean to tell me," they say in a very British-scientist accent, "you are gay and you can't recite a single line from *Funny Girl*? That's absurd! That's preposterous! That's absolutely divine!" Instantly I am a superhero, the Eighth Wonder of the World. The advantage of their stereotyping includes my being able to check out a guy while he remains completely oblivious that I am doing so. Once you talk sports with guys, they're willing to let you see them naked, because, as everyone knows, there are no gay men who know anything about sports . . . except maybe men's gymnastics.   5

It's probably good that I can laugh about this situation. Right? Why should I be upset by something that hasn't yet affected me directly? I wasn't the kid teased in fifth grade because he couldn't throw a baseball the "right" way. My nicknames never included Nancy or Sally, but only because I played football with the boys not hula-hoop with the girls. And, as a result, I didn't have to avoid going to school some days because my peers never threatened to beat me up if they saw me. In short, I wasn't the victim of one of hundreds of hate crimes committed in recent years against gays and lesbians who fit the perceived stereotypes.   6

I'm not laughing now. It just isn't funny anymore.   7

◆ GETTING STARTED ON EXEMPLIFICATION

When you have an idea to *explain*, a point to *clarify*, or an opinion to *convince* someone of, you need to begin a search for the best examples to support your **generalization.** This central idea, or **thesis,** will probably be a work in progress at this point, too, especially if you have not yet identified a specific audience. Although you should have a **purpose** for writing in mind, its exact scope and phrasing will be made clearer when you know who your readers will be and when you have selected the best illustrations to suit their needs.

At this stage, you must decide how best to "show" the generalization you wish to "tell." The source of your examples will depend on the assignment and your thesis. If your writing will focus on personal experience, then **brainstorming, freewriting,** or one of the more structured discovery systems discussed in Chapter 2 is the best starting point. After he had decided to write about being gay, Bobby made two simple lists, one of popular stereotypes and one of personal examples that either illustrate that such stereotypes exist or that contradict those stereotypes. He then did some brainstorming to come up with examples from popular culture and from his personal experiences.

For both Bobby and Brent Staples, all the necessary examples were right at their fingertips, so the challenge was to take the time to find an *appropriate* number, to ensure that each was *relevant* to the point he wanted to make, and to remember or describe the example in *sufficient detail* to make it clear and convincing for the reader. There are times when one extended, in-depth example will be all that is needed to support the thesis. Staples, however, knew that some readers might be skeptical about his claims, so the single opening incident had to be followed up with similar experiences in different times and places. His instincts also led him to go beyond his own experience and to recall other black men who had been victimized by race stereotyping. Readers might dismiss his experiences as unique, but together with those of other professional black men, they form a persuasive body of evidence.

If the assignment or your thesis requires examples that don't arise from your own experience, getting started may involve doing research at the library or interviewing people with direct experience with or expertise on your topic. Bobby, for example, might have interviewed other gay men about their childhoods or looked for case studies on the subject gathered by psychologists or sociologists. Staples's experiences could have been presented in a slightly different context had he identified writings by white women who describe their reactions to stranger contact with members of a different race. Had he expanded his purpose in this way, his thesis—"It was in the echo of that terrified woman's footfalls that I first began to know the unwieldy inheritance I'd come into—the ability to alter public space in ugly ways"—would need to be expanded to include the two points of view.

◆ ORGANIZING EXEMPLIFICATION

Time and space provide the basic starting points for organizing narrative and descriptive essays. The thesis and purpose direct the plan for an essay developed through examples. Whether you use one extended example or a series of examples to make your point, some intentional and thoughtful sequence, which is revealed through *transitions,* is needed to avoid turning your essay into a loosely strung together list.

Staples's thesis implies a persuasive purpose: to illustrate a problem, to give examples of the consequences, and to provide evidence of the precautions he must take to avoid both the problem and the consequences. His essay therefore divides into three parts, with appropriate examples given in each section. Bobby chose a slightly different strategy, but he has a similarly indirect persuasive purpose. He first clarifies the stereotypes through a series of personal examples, accompanied by references to familiar popular icons associated with gay culture; he then concludes with the real problems such preconceptions can cause.

In the essays that follow, you will see writers employ a number of additional organizing methods. Sue Hubbell, for example, uses geography to organize "On the Interstate: A City of the Mind." Her thesis—"In the early morning there is a city of the mind that stretches from coast to coast, from border to border"—offers a built-in plan for the essay, with each scene of truck stop life coming from a different part of the country. You'll notice when you read her essay that she went a step further in her organization and provided descriptions of similar items and kinds of people at each location.

Extended examples require equally careful planning. If the example is a story, narrative strategies might be used. Or, if the example is a place, descriptive methods are helpful. In the case of Sallie Tisdale's "A Weight That Women Carry," the essay reveals the harmful effects of modern attitudes toward weight through the author's own three stages of personal development: a self-confident child; a guilt-ridden, obsessive young adult; and finally, a self-accepting woman.

◆ DEVELOPING EXEMPLIFICATION

Once the organization is decided upon and you have selected the likely examples to be used and determined where each might best be placed, you must think about the level of specificity and amount of detail to be provided in each section of the paper. There is no magic formula for deciding how fully to develop examples, but giving full consideration to your readers' needs and attitudes can be a big help. Readers familiar with your example may need to be reminded of only a name, a time, or a place to bring the entire experience back to them. Someone with little information about your topic or who is skeptical about your generalization requires more extended information. Staples uses a mixture of approaches to development along a spectrum from the general to the very specific. The introduction is at the most concrete end of the range and brings his topic into vivid **focus.** We see one particular woman, his "first victim," and the setting; we feel her unique fear as she "cast back a worried glance." In paragraph 5, by contrast, Staples generalizes about the typical reactions he encounters in an attempt to convince us that such fears are broadly exhibited.

Bobby decided to move back and forth between specific personal experiences and more generalized examples within each section. For instance, his experience with Aunt Eileen is given broader meaning by his references to the GAP and football players. Both kinds of examples illustrate that people stereotype gay men as fashion conscious and sex-obsessed. Bobby also provides detailed **dialogue,** such as his quip to his friend, "I don't need to *act* gay because I *am gay,*" to cause the reader to laugh but then to see his serious point.

In yet another approach, author Alice Walker uses comparison to organize her examples in "In Search of Our Mothers' Gardens." After defining the role of a certain type of African American woman, the "Saint," she uses Phillis Wheatley as an extended example and then compares this now famous poet to the many less famous women, such as her mother, who illustrate the Saint's creativity.

◆ OPENING AND CLOSING EXEMPLIFICATION

Because exemplification essays are developed around a central generalization, their **introductions** are usually organized to introduce this thesis and provide readers with an immediate sense of this topic's interest or usefulness to them. Another common strategy is to begin with a provocative example, as Staples does. Notice, however, that very early in the second paragraph, Staples provides a thesis to connect this example to a broader purpose. Bobby found Staples's essay especially effective because it "forces the reader to assume the role of one of Staples's victims and he is then better able to prove his point." He uses a similar approach, hoping his readers will experience the same surprise Luke did when he found out that Bobby is gay.

The **conclusion** to an essay developed through examples generally returns the reader to the generalization so as to ensure the success and clarity of the writer's purpose. Staples's closing completes his three-part purpose, leaving readers with the sounds of whistled classical music to challenge racist assumptions about individual personalities and accomplishments. Because he has only implied his thesis throughout the essay, Bobby concludes with explicit examples of the harm caused by stereotypes and calls on his readers to recognize how such thinking deserves a serious response.

Writer Jon D. Hull's conclusion to "Slow Descent into Hell" illustrates another more subtle and indirect approach. The reader's exposure to the real people who live and die homeless in America is framed by an introduction and conclusion that focus on the same man, George. Although the essay begins with some hope for this human being who insists on staying clean and who evades the chronic alcoholism of his peers, in the end, when George returns to the McDonald's washroom, the reader has seen far too many examples of failure to remain as optimistic.

◆ USING THE MODEL

Both Brent Staples and Bobby Lincoln chose to explore the nature of stereotypes. Staples realized that before he could challenge the dangerous effects of racist assumptions, he would first have to convince readers of their continued existence. Examples fulfilled that goal and in turn provided evidence of racism's consequences. Bobby decided on a less serious approach to the topic, but he turned to Staples's essay for its method of carefully examining a personal experience in relation to popularly held views. Is there something about your life that either reinforces or challenges a common notion or assumption? Would it make an interesting essay?

◆ ◆ ◆ *Writer's Workshop II:* ◆ ◆ ◆
Analyzing an Exemplification Essay

Working individually or with a small group of classmates, read through Bobby Lincoln's essay "Out and About" and respond to the following questions.

1. Is Luke an effective opening example? Why? What if Bobby had started with Aunt Eileen instead?
2. In what paragraph does Bobby's thesis become clear? What is his reason for revealing it here?
3. Did you recognize most of the popular culture references in Bobby's essay? Did they fit your understanding of gay stereotypes? How did this affect your response to Bobby's essay?
4. Why does Bobby use two questions at the beginning of the sixth paragraph? How do they affect the tone of his essay?

◆ ◆ ◆ *Checklist for Reading and Writing* ◆ ◆ ◆
Exemplification Essays

1. Is there a clear, unifying thesis? Do all examples explain or clarify that generalization to the intended readers?
2. Does each paragraph have a topic sentence or a clear central focus?
3. Is there a logical order for the body paragraphs? Are the examples within each paragraph arranged coherently? Are there transitions to help direct readers from one example to the next?
4. Are there sufficient examples, and are they appropriate for the paper?
5. Are examples developed in enough detail to be interesting and useful?

◆ ◆ ◆ **PREPARING TO READ**

Sometimes while traveling, we get brief and fascinating glimpses into other people's lives. Is there a particularly interesting stranger or bit of overheard conversation that has stayed with you long after the trip was over? What makes this memory so vivid?

◆ ◆ ◆

On the Interstate:
A City of the Mind

SUE HUBBELL

Whether writing about toothpicks or life on an Ozark farm, journalist and essayist Sue Hubbell (born in 1935) finds natural history in everyday life. Formerly a regular contributor to *The New Yorker,* she now writes for *Natural History, Vogue,* and *Smithsonian.* Hubbell has also written three books on "the invertebrate world," most recently *Waiting for Aphrodite: Journeys into the Time before Bones* (1999). At one time a trucker herself, Hubbell recorded part of her life on the road in "On the Interstate," which appeared in *Time* in 1985. An expanded essay on trucker life appears in her collection *Far Flung Hubbell* (1995), which has been described as "wigged out journeys" written in a "calm, tongue-firmly-in-cheek prose."

In the early morning there is a city of the mind that stretches from coast   1
to coast, from border to border. Its cross streets are the interstate highways, and food, comfort, companionship are served up in its buildings, the truck stops near the exits. Its citizens are all-night drivers, the truckers, and the waitresses at the stops.

In the daylight the city fades and blurs when the transients appear,   2
tourists who merely want a meal and a tank of gas. They file into the carpeted dining rooms away from the professional drivers' side, sit at the Formica tables set off by imitation cloth flowers in bud vases. They eat and are gone, do not return. They are not a part of the city and obscure it.

It is 5 A.M. in a truck stop in West Virginia. Drivers in twos, threes, and   3
fours are eating breakfast and talking routes and schedules.

"Truckers!" growls a manager. "They say they are in a hurry. They com-   4
plain if the service isn't fast. We fix it so they can have their fuel pumped while they are eating and put in telephones on every table so they can check

with their dispatchers at the same time. They could be out of here in half an hour. But what do they do? They sit and talk for two hours."

The truckers are lining up for seconds at the breakfast buffet (all you   5
can eat for $3.99—biscuits with chipped-beef gravy, fruit cup, French toast with syrup, bacon, pancakes, sausage, scrambled eggs, doughnuts, Danish, cereal in little boxes).

The travel store at the truck stop has a machine to measure heartbeat   6
in exchange for a quarter. There are racks of jackets, belts, truck supplies, tape cassettes. On the wall are paintings for sale, simulated wood with likenesses of John Wayne or a stag. The rack by the cash register is stuffed with Twinkies and chocolate Suzy Qs.

It is 5 A.M. in New Mexico. Above the horseshoe-shaped counter on   7
panels where a menu is usually displayed, an overhead slide show is in progress. The pictures change slowly, allowing the viewer to take in all the details. A low shot of a Peterbilt, its chrome fittings sparkling in the sunshine, is followed by one of a bosomy young woman, the same who must pose for those calendars found in autoparts stores. She almost has on clothes, and she is offering to check a trucker's oil. The next slide is a side view of a whole tractor-trailer rig, its 18 wheels gleaming and spoked. It is followed by one of a blond bulging out of a hint of cop clothes writing a naughty trucker a ticket.

The waitress looks too tired and too jaded to be offended. The jaws of   8
the truckers move mechanically as they fork up their eggs-over-easy. They stare at the slides, glassy eyed, as intent on chrome as on flesh.

It is 4 A.M. in Oklahoma. A recycled Stuckey's with blue tile roof calls   9
itself simply Truck Stop. The sign also boasts showers, scales, truck wash and a special on service for $88.50. At a table inside, four truckers have ordered a short stack and three eggs a piece, along with bacon, sausage, and coffee (Trucker's Superbreakfast—$3.79).

They have just started drinking their coffee, and the driver with the   10
Roadway cap calls over the waitress, telling her there is salt in the sugar he put in his coffee. She is pale, thin, young, has dark circles under her eyes. The truckers have been teasing her, and she doesn't trust them. She dabs a bit of sugar from the canister on a finger and tastes it. Salt. She samples sugar from the other canisters. They have salt too, and she gathers them up to replace them. Someone is hazing her, breaking her into her new job. Her eyes shine with tears.

She brings the food and comes back when the truckers are nearly done.   11
She carries a water jug and coffeepot on her tray. The men are ragging her again, and her hands tremble. The tray falls with a crash. The jug breaks. Glass, water, and coffee spread across the floor. She sits down in the booth, tears rolling down her cheeks.

"I'm so tired. My old man . . . he left me," she says, the tears coming   12
faster now. "The judge says he's going to take my kid away if I can't take

care of him, so I stay up all day and just sleep when he takes a nap and the boss yells at me and . . . and . . . the truckers all talk dirty . . . I'm so tired."

She puts her head down on her arms and sobs luxuriantly. The truckers are gone, and I touch her arm and tell her to look at what they have left. There is a $20 bill beside each plate. She looks up, nods, wipes her eyes on her apron, pockets the tips, and goes to get a broom and a mop.

It is 3:30 A.M. in Illinois at a glossy truck stop that offers all mechanical services, motel rooms, showers, Laundromat, game room, TV lounge, truckers' bulletin board, and a stack of newspapers published by the Association of Christian Truckers. Piped-in music fills the air.

The waitress in the professional drivers' section is a big motherly-looking woman with red hair piled in careful curls on top of her head. She correctly sizes up the proper meal for the new customer at the counter. "Don't know what you want, honey? Try the chicken-noodle soup with a hot roll. It will stick to you like you've got something, and you don't have to worry about grease."

She has been waitressing 40 years, 20 of them in this truck stop. As she talks she polishes the stainless steel, fills mustard jars, adds the menu inserts for today's special (hot turkey sandwich, mashed potatoes and gravy, pot of coffee—$2.50).

"The big boss, well, he's a love, but some of the others aren't so hot. But it's a job. Gotta work somewhere. I need a day off though. Been working six, seven days straight lately. Got shopping to do. My lawn needs mowing."

Two truckers are sitting at a booth. Their faces are lined and leathery. One cap says HARLEY-DAVIDSON, the other COORS.

Harley-Davidson calls out, "If you wasn't so mean, Flossie, you'd have a good man to take care of you and you wouldn't have to mow the damn lawn."

She puts down the mustard jar, walks over to Harley-Davidson and Coors, stands in front of them, hands on wide hips. "Now you listen here, Charlie, I'm a good enough woman for any man, but all you guys want are chippies."

Coors turns bright red. She glares at him. "You saw my ex in here last Saturday night with a chippie on his arm. He comes in here all the time with two, three chippies just to prove to me what a high old time he's having. If that's a good time, I'd rather baby-sit my grandkids."

Chippies are not a topic of conversation that Charlie and Coors wish to pursue. Coors breaks a doughnut in two, and Charlie uses his fork to make a spillway for the gravy on the double order of mashed potatoes that accompanies his scrambled eggs.

Flossie comes back to the counter and turns to the new customer in mirror shades at this dark hour, a young trucker with cowboy boots and hat.

"John boy. Where you been? Haven't seen you in weeks. Looks like you need a nice omelet. Cook just made some of those biscuits you like too."

I leave a tip for Flossie and pay my bill. In the men's room, where I am 24 shunted because the ladies' is closed for cleaning, someone has scrawled poignant words: NO TIME TO EAT NOW.

◆ ◆ ◆

FIRST RESPONSES

Have you ever worked a job that brought you into regular contact with people like these waitresses or truckers? How would you handle those truckers' demands, practical jokes, and one-liners if you were a waitress or a manager?

TAKING A CLOSER LOOK

Exploring *Who:* Voice and Tone

1. How directly is Sue Hubbell involved in the events in this essay? How might the essay have changed if she had not been a trucker herself?
2. In paragraph 12, why does the waitress choose to turn to Hubbell to share her complaints?
3. How would you describe Hubbell's responses to the truckers? To the waitresses? Can you find any humor in this essay?
4. Reread paragraph 2. What does the writer mean when she describes the tourists as "transients"? What is she implying about most of her readers here? Have you ever been a truck stop transient?

Exploring *What:* Content and Meaning

1. What do these truck stop scenes tell you about daily life as a trucker? As a waitress? How has it reinforced or changed your attitudes toward these jobs and the people who hold them? You might want to start by looking at the food they eat.
2. What are the differences between the young waitress in Oklahoma and the "motherly-looking" waitress in Illinois? If you look closely, can you also find similarities?
3. Why is the waitress described as sobbing "luxuriantly" in paragraph 13? Do you understand why she feels as she does at such a moment?

4. In paragraphs 18 to 22, what is the effect of referring to the two truckers as Harley-Davidson and Coors? What is a "chippie"? What does the word tell us about Flossie?

Exploring *Why:* Purpose

1. Do Hubbell's examples convince you that there is a "city of the mind" at these truck stops? Do they make you want to spend some time at truck stops? Is that Hubbell's purpose?

2. What does the word *poignant* mean in the concluding paragraph? Why has Hubbell used it to describe the men's room graffiti? Why is this paragraph the final impression Hubbell wishes to leave us with?

3. 🖥 *Using the Internet.* How would the truckers and waitresses described here respond to Hubbell's view of them? Using one of the Internet search engines, locate a trucker's site to analyze the ways in which other writers discuss issues of interest to truckers.

Exploring *How:* Style and Strategy

1. Why does Hubbell describe four different truck stops? What subpoints do the examples have in common?

2. What view of the truckers is suggested by paragraphs 7 and 8? Why is this New Mexico truck stop included as the second example rather than as the third or fourth one?

3. Why is the cowboy trucker in paragraph 23 included in the essay? Don't we already have a pretty clear image of Flossie and this truck stop?

4. Hubbell uses quite a bit of **dialogue.** Why? Select any example, and describe how your feelings about the scene would change without the dialogue.

◆ WRITING FROM READING ASSIGNMENT

"On the Interstate" offers a behind-the-scenes look at a place and a life that many Americans pass by every day. In this writing assignment, gather examples from your experience to reveal a place, job, or person that you know well but that others may know only on the surface or, perhaps, that others misunderstand because of their lack of experience.

A. Begin by brainstorming about places, jobs, and people that you know especially well and would like others to know or understand better, such as camp counselors' bunkhouses, the duties of a golf caddie, grunge music fans.

B. Select a topic, and write a tentative generalization that you would like to offer your readers about this topic. What do you want them to know, and why might they be interested in knowing it?

C. Having settled on a topic, do some additional brainstorming, freewriting, or clustering to come up with as many examples as you can to support your purpose for writing. At this point, you might review the kinds of major examples that make up "On the Interstate." Hubbell uses different examples of the same kind of place in different locations. She might have shown us the same truck stop on different days or even at different times during the day. Consider all your choices. Do you have enough examples to prove your point?

D. After you have a sufficient number of suitable examples, do some freewriting on *each* example to recall as many details as possible. Look at the concrete examples in paragraphs 5 and 6 of "On the Interstate," and also think about your reactions to the dialogue in that essay. How much will your readers already know, and how much information will they need to see the people or places you are exemplifying?

E. Now that you have your examples, turn your working generalization into a thesis and write a draft of an introduction. Reread the first paragraph of "On the Interstate." Do you, too, want to preview the subtopics you will develop? What other approach might grab the readers' interest in your topic and keep them reading?

F. In the previous *How* questions, you considered the order of Hubbell's examples. What sequence will best serve your purpose and your readers' needs?

G. In each of her examples, Hubbell includes the same types of people and descriptions of the settings. What will your examples have in common? How do these points support your thesis?

H. After you complete a draft of your essay, return to the "Checklist for Reading and Writing Exemplification Essays" (p. 133), and evaluate how fully your examples complete the purpose with which you began your project.

◆ ◆ ◆ **PREPARING TO READ**

When you imagine your favorite writer sitting down to begin writing, what do you see him or her doing, feeling, thinking? How does this compare with your experience as a writer?

◆ ◆ ◆

Shitty First Drafts

ANNE LAMOTT

Anne Lamott (born in 1954 in San Francisco) is equally at home as a writer of fiction and nonfiction. Her most recent novel, *Crooked Little Heart* (1997), returns to the young heroine of an earlier novel, *Rosie* (1983), who is a talented young tennis pro. Rosie's athletic ability and privilege add to instead of protecting her from life's challenges. Lamott's alcoholism and struggles as a single mother and professional writer have been the focus of her nonfiction, including her autobiographical book *Operating Instructions: A Journal of My Son's First Year* (1993); *Bird by Bird: Some Instructions on Writing and Life* (1995), from which "Shitty First Drafts" is taken; and *Traveling Mercies: Some Thoughts on Faith* (2000). Lamott has been keeping an electronic journal called "Mothers Who Think," which can be found at www.salon.com.

Shitty first drafts. All good writers write them. This is how they end up   1
with good second drafts and terrific third drafts. People tend to look at successful writers, writers who are getting their books published and maybe even doing well financially, and think that they sit down at their desks every morning feeling like a million dollars, feeling great about who they are and how much talent they have and what a great story they have to tell; that they take in a few deep breaths, push back their sleeves, roll their necks a few times to get all the cricks out, and dive in, typing fully formed passages as fast as a court reporter. But this is just the fantasy of the uninitiated. I know some very great writers, writers you love who write beautifully and have made a great deal of money, and not *one* of them sits down routinely feeling wildly enthusiastic and confident. Not one of them writes elegant first drafts. All right, one of them does, but we do not like her very much. We do not think that she has a rich inner life or that God likes her or can even stand her.

(Although when I mentioned this to my priest friend Tom, he said you can safely assume you've created God in your own image when it turns out that God hates all the same people you do.)

Very few writers really know what they are doing until they've done it. Nor do they go about their business feeling dewy and thrilled. They do not type a few stiff warm-up sentences and then find themselves bounding along like huskies across the snow. One writer I know tells me that he sits down every morning and says to himself nicely, "It's not like you don't have a choice, because you do—you can either type or kill yourself." We all often feel like we are pulling teeth, even those writers whose prose ends up being the most natural and fluid. The right words and sentences just do not come pouring out like ticker tape most of the time. Now, Muriel Spark is said to have felt that she was taking dictation from God every morning—sitting there, one supposes, plugged into a Dictaphone, typing away, humming. But this is a very hostile and aggressive position. One might hope for bad things to rain down on a person like this.

For me and most of the other writers I know, writing is not rapturous. In fact, the only way I can get anything written at all is to write really, really shitty first drafts.

The first draft is the child's draft, where you let it all pour out and then let it romp all over the place, knowing that no one is going to see it and that you can shape it later. You just let this childlike part of you channel whatever voices and visions come through and onto the page. If one of the characters wants to say, "Well, so what, Mr. Poopy Pants?" you let her. No one is going to see it. If the kid wants to get into really sentimental, weepy, emotional territory, you let him. Just get it all down on paper, because there may be something great in those six crazy pages that you would never have gotten to by more rational, grown-up means. There may be something in the very last line of the very last paragraph on page six that you just love, that is so beautiful or wild that you now know what you're supposed to be writing about, more or less, or in what direction you might go—but there was no way to get to this without first getting through the first five and a half pages.

I used to write food reviews for *California* magazine before it folded. (My writing food reviews had nothing to do with the magazine folding, although every single review did cause a couple of canceled subscriptions. Some readers took umbrage at my comparing mounds of vegetable puree with various ex-presidents' brains.) These reviews always took two days to write. First I'd go to a restaurant several times with a few opinionated, articulate friends in tow. I'd sit there writing down everything anyone said that was at all interesting or funny. Then on the following Monday I'd sit down at my desk with my notes, and try to write the review. Even after I'd been doing this for years, panic would set in. I'd try to write a lead, but instead I'd write a couple of dreadful sentences, xx them out, try again, xx everything out, and then feel despair and worry settle on my chest like an x-ray apron. It's over, I'd think, calmly; I'm not going to be able to get the magic to work this time. I'm ruined. I'm through. I'm toast. Maybe, I'd think, I can get my old job back as a clerk-typist. But probably not. I'd get up and study my teeth in the mirror for a while. Then I'd stop, remember to breathe, make a few phone calls, hit the kitchen and chow down. Eventually I'd go back and sit down at my desk, and sigh for the next ten minutes. Finally I would pick up my one-inch picture frame, stare into it as if for the answer, and every time the answer would come: all I had to do was to write a really shitty first draft of, say, the opening paragraph. And no one was going to see it.

So I'd start writing without reining myself in. It was almost just typing, 6 just making my fingers move. And the writing would be *terrible*. I'd write a lead paragraph that was a whole page, even though the entire review could only be three pages long, and then I'd start writing up descriptions of the food, one dish at a time, bird by bird, and the critics would be sitting on my shoulders, commenting like cartoon characters. They'd be pretending to snore, or rolling their eyes at my overwrought descriptions, no matter how hard I tried to tone those descriptions down, no matter how conscious I was of what a friend said to me gently in my early days of restaurant reviewing. "Annie," she said, "it is just a piece of *chicken*. It is just a bit of *cake*."

But because by then I had been writing for so long, I would eventually 7 let myself trust the process—sort of, more or less. I'd write a first draft that was maybe twice as long as it should be, with a self-indulgent and boring beginning, stupefying descriptions of the meal, lots of quotes from my black-humored friends that made them sound more like the Manson girls than food lovers, and no ending to speak of. The whole thing would be so long and incoherent and hideous that for the rest of the day I'd obsess about getting creamed by a car before I could write a decent second draft. I'd worry that people would read what I'd written and believe that the accident had really been a suicide, that I had panicked because my talent was waning and my mind was shot.

The next day, though, I'd sit down, go through it all with a colored pen, 8 take out everything I possibly could, find a new lead somewhere on the second page, figure out a kicky place to end it, and then write a second draft. It always turned out fine, sometimes even funny and weird and helpful. I'd go over it one more time and mail it in.

Then, a month later, when it was time for another review, the whole 9 process would start again, complete with the fears that people would find my first draft before I could rewrite it.

Almost all good writing begins with terrible first efforts. You need to 10 start somewhere. Start by getting something—anything—down on paper. A friend of mine says that the first draft is the down draft—you just get it down. The second draft is the up draft—you fix it up. You try to say what you have to say more accurately. And the third draft is the dental draft, where you check every tooth, to see if it's loose or cramped or decayed, or even, God help us, healthy.

What I've learned to do when I sit down to work on a shitty first draft   11 is to quiet the voices in my head. First there's the vinegar-lipped Reader Lady, who says primly, "Well, *that's* not very interesting, is it?" And there's the emaciated German male who writes these Orwellian memos detailing your thought crimes. And there are your parents, agonizing over your lack of loyalty and discretion; and there's William Burroughs, dozing off or shooting up because he finds you as bold and articulate as a houseplant; and so on. And there are also the dogs: let's not forget the dogs, the dogs in their pen who will surely hurtle and snarl their way out if you ever *stop* writing, because writing is, for some of us, the latch that keeps the door of the pen closed, keeps those crazy ravenous dogs contained.

Quieting these voices is at least half the battle I fight daily. But this is   12 better than it used to be. It used to be 87 percent. Left to its own devices, my mind spends much of its time having conversations with people who aren't there. I walk along defending myself to people, or exchanging repartee with them, or rationalizing my behavior, or seducing them with gossip, or pretending I'm on their TV talk show or whatever. I speed or run an aging yellow light or don't come to a full stop, and one nanosecond later am explaining to imaginary cops exactly why I had to do what I did, or insisting that I did not in fact do it.

I happened to mention this to a hypnotist I saw many years ago, and he   13 looked at me very nicely. At first I thought he was feeling around on the floor for the silent alarm button, but then he gave me the following exercise, which I still use to this day.

Close your eyes and get quiet for a minute, until the chatter starts up.   14 Then isolate one of the voices and imagine the person speaking as a mouse. Pick it up by the tail and drop it into a mason jar. Then isolate another voice, pick it up by the tail, drop it in the jar. And so on. Drop in any high-maintenance parental units, drop in any contractors, lawyers, colleagues, children, anyone who is whining in your head. Then put the lid on, and watch all these mouse people clawing at the glass, jabbering away, trying to make you feel like shit because you won't do what they want—won't give them more money, won't be more successful, won't see them more often. Then imagine that there is a volume-control button on the bottle. Turn it all the way up for a minute, and listen to the stream of angry, neglected, guilt-mongering voices. Then turn it all the way down and watch the frantic mice lunge at the glass, trying to get to you. Leave it down, and get back to your shitty first draft.

A writer friend of mine suggests opening the jar and shooting them all   15
in the head. But I think he's a little angry, and I'm sure nothing like this would
ever occur to you.

◆ ◆ ◆

FIRST RESPONSES

When you write your first drafts, do you hear voices similar to the ones
Lamott describes in paragraph 11? What names might you give your voices?

TAKING A CLOSER LOOK

Exploring *Who:* Voice and Tone

1. Were you surprised by the title of this essay? How did it affect your in-
    terest in reading the rest of the essay? Did Lamott turn out to be the
    kind of person the title led you to expect?
2. Why does Lamott include the parenthetical comments in paragraphs 1
    and 5? What impression of her do they create?
3. Lamott draws examples from her friends and from other professional
    writers. Why not rely on her own opinions and experiences?

Exploring *What:* Content and Meaning

1. What does Lamott mean when she says "writing is not rapturous"?
    Why would anyone think it was? Does the essay convince you that it
    is not?
2. What is involved in writing a "child's draft"? Have you been encour-
    aged to write such drafts before? If not, is it something you think you
    might enjoy and benefit from?
3. Why did Lamott "hit the kitchen" and have to "remember to breathe"
    while she was writing the drafts of her food reviews? Have you ever had
    this experience? How does it make you feel to know that Lamott acts
    in these ways?
4.   *Using the Internet.* The Web site Quotes for Writers can be found
    at www.mtco.com/~lbamber/quotes.htm. Visit the site and click on one
    of the many categories, from "beginnings" to "conquering fear." When
    you have read several quotations, test their insights against the ones
    offered by Lamott.

Exploring *Why:* Purpose

1. The subtitle of the book in which this essay appears is "Some Instructions on Writing and Life." What relationship does Lamott see between "shitty first drafts" and life in general?

2. Are you the "uninitiated" reader Lamott describes in paragraph 1 of the essay? What does that tell you about whom Lamott expects to read her book?

3. What is a Dictaphone? Why does Lamott imagine Muriel Spark using one? And why does she "hope for bad things to rain down on" Spark?

4. What does Lamott mean in paragraph 7 when she says she has learned to "trust the process"? What in your writing process do you count on each time you sit down to write?

Exploring *How:* Style and Strategy

1. Why does Lamott offer readers the extended example of writing her food reviews? What does it add to your understanding of draft writing that had not been learned by that point in her essay? How would the essay change if she had begun with this extended example?

2. How many **similes** (comparisons using *like* or *as*) can you find in paragraph 2? What is Lamott's purpose for using so many in the same paragraph?

3. What feeling is Lamott trying to capture when she uses this series of short sentences in the middle of paragraph 5: "I'm ruined. I'm through. I'm toast"?

IDEAS FOR WRITING AN EXEMPLIFICATION ESSAY

1. Write an essay using examples to show the behind-the-scenes realities of a task that you know especially well, such as preparing for a recital or athletic event, being a volunteer nurse's aid, making Big Macs.

2. Is there a person you know who is exceptional in some way? Write an essay demonstrating how and why this person is an exceptional example. If you know more than one person who is exceptional, you might use multiple examples instead.

3. Write an essay in which you warn speakers, conversationalists, teachers, or writers about a certain practice or usage that bothers you. Give examples to support your point.

◆ ◆ ◆ PREPARING TO READ

Have you ever spent time with a person who you were previously distant from or perhaps afraid of because of a significant difference between your life and the other person's? What similarities did you find as you got to know the person? How did the experience change you?

◆ ◆ ◆

Slow Descent into Hell

JON D. HULL

Like most journalists working for popular magazines, *Time* correspondent and Midwest Bureau Chief Jon D. Hull has written about many of today's most pressing issues: the Middle East, gun control, abortion protests, and inner-city gang rituals. To prepare to write the following essay, Hull lived briefly on the streets of Philadelphia, where he met George, Red, and Gary, people he hoped his readers would also come to know as dramatic examples of the frightening cycle of homelessness.

A smooth bar of soap, wrapped neatly in a white handkerchief and   1
tucked safely in the breast pocket of a faded leather jacket, is all that keeps George from losing himself to the streets. When he wakes each morning from his makeshift bed of newspapers in the subway tunnels of Philadelphia, he heads for the rest room of a nearby bus station or McDonald's and begins an elaborate ritual of washing off the dirt and smells of homelessness: first the hands and forearms, then the face and neck and finally the fingernails and teeth. Twice a week he takes off his worn Converse high tops and socks and washes his feet in the sink, ignoring the cold stares of well-dressed commuters.

George, 28, is a stocky, round-faced former high school basketball star   2
who once made a living as a construction worker. But after he lost his job just over a year ago, his wife kicked him out of the house. For a few weeks he lived on the couches of friends, but the friendships soon wore thin. Since then he has been on the street, starting from scratch and looking for a job. "I got to get my life back," George says after rinsing his face for the fourth time. He begins brushing his teeth with his forefinger. "If I don't stay clean," he mutters, "the world ain't even going to look me in the face. I just couldn't take that."

George lives in a world where time is meaningless and it's possible to   3
go months without being touched by anyone but a thug. Lack of sleep, food
or conversation breeds confusion and depression. He feels himself slipping
but struggles to remember what he once had and to figure out how to get it
back. He rarely drinks alcohol and keeps his light brown corduroy pants and
red-checked shirt meticulously clean. Underneath, he wears two other shirts
to fight off the cold, and he sleeps with his large hands buried deep within his
coat pockets amid old sandwiches and doughnuts from the soup kitchens
and garbage cans.

Last fall he held a job for six weeks at a pizza joint, making $3.65 an   4
hour kneading dough and clearing tables. Before work, he would take off
two of his three shirts and hide them in an alley. It pleases him that no one
knew he was homeless. Says George: "Sure I could have spent that money on
some good drink or food, but you gotta suffer to save. You gotta have money
to get out of here and I gotta get out of here." Some days he was scolded for
eating too much of the food. He often worked without sleep, and with no
alarm clock to wake him from the subways or abandoned tenements, he
missed several days and was finally fired. He observes, "Can't get no job without a home, and you can't get a home without a job. They take one and you
lose both."

George had $64 tucked in his pocket on the evening he was beaten   5
senseless in an alley near the Continental Trailways station. "Those damn
chumps," he says, gritting his teeth, "took every goddam penny. I'm gonna
kill 'em." Violence is a constant threat to the homeless. It's only a matter of
time before newcomers are beaten, robbed, or raped. The young prey on the
old, the big on the small, and groups attack lonely individuals in the back
alleys and subway tunnels. After it's over, there is no one to tell about the
pain, nothing to do but walk away.

Behind a dumpster sits a man who calls himself Red enjoying the last   6
drops of a bottle of wine called Wild Irish Rose. It's 1 A.M., and the ther-
mometer hovers around 20 degrees, with a biting wind. His nickname comes
from a golden retriever his family once had back in Memphis, and a sparkle
comes to his eyes as he recalls examples of the dog's loyalty. One day he
plans to get another dog, and says, "I'm getting to the point where I can't
talk to people. They're always telling me to do something or get out of their
way. But a dog is different."

At 35, he looks 50, and his gaunt face carries discolored scars from the   7
falls and fights of three years on the streets. An upper incisor is missing, and
his lower teeth jut outward against his lower lip, giving the impression that
he can't close his mouth. His baggy pants are about five inches too long and
when he walks, their frayed ends drag on the ground. "You know something?"
he asks, holding up the bottle. "I wasn't stuck to this stuff until the cold got
to me. Now I'll freeze without it. I could go to Florida or someplace, but I

know this town and I know who the creeps are. Besides, it's not too bad in the summer."

Finishing the bottle, and not yet drunk enough to sleep out in the cold, he gathers his blanket around his neck and heads for the subways beneath city hall, where hundreds of the homeless seek warmth. Once inside, the game of cat-and-mouse begins with the police, who patrol the maze of tunnels and stairways and insist that everybody remain off the floor and keep moving. Sitting can be an invitation to trouble, and the choice between sleep and warmth becomes agonizing as the night wears on.   8

For the first hour, Red shuffles through the tunnels, stopping occasionally to urinate against the graffiti-covered walls. Then he picks a spot and stands for half an hour, peering out from the large hood of his coat. In the distance, the barking of German shepherds echoes through the tunnels as a canine unit patrols the darker recesses of the underground. Nearby, a young man in a ragged trench coat stands against the wall, slapping his palms against his sides and muttering, "I've got to get some paperwork done. I've just got to get some paperwork done!" Red shakes his head. "Home sweet home," he says. Finally exhausted, he curls up on the littered floor, lying on his side with his hands in his pockets and his hood pulled all the way over his face to keep the rats away. He is asleep instantly.   9

Whack! A police baton slaps his legs and a voice booms, "Get the hell up, you're outta here. Right now!" Another police officer whacks his nightstick against a metal grating as the twelve men sprawled along the tunnel crawl to their feet. Red pulls himself up and walks slowly up the stairs to the street, never looking back.   10

Pausing at every pay phone to check the coin-return slots, he makes his way to a long steam grate whose warm hiss bears the acrid smell of a dry cleaner's shop. He searches for newspaper and cardboard to block the moisture but retain the heat. With his makeshift bed made, he curls up again, but the rest is short-lived. "This s.o.b. use to give off more heat," he says, staring with disgust at the grate. He gathers the newspapers and moves down the block, all the while muttering about the differences among grates. "Some are good, some are bad. I remember I was getting a beautiful sleep on this one baby and then all this honking starts. I was laying right in a damn driveway and nearly got run over by a garbage truck."   11

Stopping at a small circular vent shooting jets of steam, Red shakes his head and curses: "This one is too wet, and it'll go off sometimes, leaving you to freeze." Shaking now with the cold, he walks four more blocks and finds another grate, where he curls up and fishes a half-spent cigarette from his pocket. The grate is warm, but soon the moisture from the steam has soaked his newspapers and begins to gather on his clothes. Too tired to find another grate, he sets down more newspapers, throws his blanket over his head and sprawls across the grate. By morning he is soaked.   12

At the St. John's Hospice for Men, close to the red neon marquees of   13
the porno shops near city hall, a crowd begins to gather at 4 P.M. Men and
women dressed in ill-fitting clothes stamp their feet to ward off the cold and
keep their arms pressed against their sides. Some are drunk; others simply talk
aloud to nobody in words that none can understand. Most are loners who
stand in silence with the sullen expression of the tired and hungry.

A hospice worker lets in a stream of women and old men. The young   14
men must wait until 5 P.M., and the crowd of more than 200 are asked to form
four rows behind a yellow line and watch their language. It seems an impossible task. A trembling man who goes by the name Carper cries, "What goddam row am I in!" as he pulls his red wool hat down until it covers his eyebrows. Carper has spent five to six years on the streets, and thinks he may be
33. The smell of putrid wine and decaying teeth poisons his breath; the fluid
running from his swollen eyes streaks his dirty cheeks before disappearing
into his beard. "Am I in a goddam row? Who the hell's running the rows?"
he swears. An older man with a thick gray beard informs Carper he is in Row
3 and assures him it is the best of them all. Carper's face softens into a smile;
he stuffs his hands under his armpits and begins rocking his shoulders with
delight.

Beds at the shelters are scarce, and fill up first with the old, the very   15
young, and women. Young men have little hope of getting a bed, and some
have even come to scorn the shelters. Says Michael Brown, 24: "It stinks to
high heaven in those places. They're just packed with people and when the
lights go out, it's everybody for themselves." Michael, a short, self-described
con man, has been living on the streets three years, ever since holding up a
convenience store in Little Rock. He fled, fearing capture, but now misses the
two young children he left behind. He says he is tired of the streets and plans
to turn himself in to serve his time.

Michael refuses to eat at the soup kitchens, preferring to panhandle   16
for a meal: "I don't like to be around those people. It makes you feel like
some sort of crazy. Before you know it, you're one of them." He keeps a tear
in the left seam of his pants, just below the pocket; when he panhandles
among commuters, he tells them that his subway fare fell out of his pants.
When that fails, he wanders past fast-food outlets, waiting for a large group
eating near the door to get up and leave. Then he snatches the remaining
food off the table and heads down the street, smiling all the more if the food
is still warm. At night he sleeps in the subway stations, catnapping between
police rounds amid the thunder of the trains. "Some of these guys sleep right
on the damn floor," he says. "Not me. I always use two newspapers and lay
them out neatly. Then I pray the rats don't get me."

It was the last swig of the bottle, and the cheap red wine contained flot-   17
sam from the mouths of three men gathered in a vacant lot in northeast
Philadelphia. Moments before, a homeless and dying man named Gary had

vomited. The stench and nausea were dulled only by exhaustion and the cold. Gary, wheezing noisily, his lips dripping with puke, was the last to drink from the half-gallon jug of Thunderbird before passing it on, but no one seemed to care. There was no way to avoid the honor of downing the last few drops. It was an offer to share extended by those with nothing, and there was no time to think about the sores on the lips of the previous drinkers or the strange things floating in the bottle or the fact that it was daybreak and time for breakfast. It was better to drink and stay warm and forget about everything.

Though he is now dying on the streets, Gary used to be a respectable   18
citizen. His full name is Gary Shaw, 48, and he is a lifelong resident of Philadelphia and a father of three. He once worked as a precision machinist, making metal dies for casting tools. "I could work with my eyes closed," he says. "I was the best there was." But he lost his job and wife to alcohol. Now his home is an old red couch with the springs exposed in a garbage-strewn clearing amid abandoned tenements. Nearby, wood pulled from buildings burns in a 55-gallon metal drum while the Thunderbird is passed around. When evening falls, Gary has trouble standing, and he believes his liver and kidneys are on the verge of failing. His thighs carry deep burn marks from sleeping on grates, and a severe beating the previous night has left bruises on his lower back and a long scab across his nose. The pain is apparent in his eyes, still brilliant blue, and the handsome features of his face are hidden beneath a layer of grime.

By 3 A.M., Gary's back pains are unbearable, and he begins rocking   19
back and forth while the others try to keep him warm. "Ah, please God help me. I'm f---ing dying, man. I'm dying." Two friends try to wave down a patrol car. After 45 minutes, a suspicious cop rolls up to the curb and listens impatiently to their plea: "It's not drugs, man, I promise. The guy was beat up bad and he's dying. Come on, man, you've got to take us to the hospital." The cop nods and points his thumb toward the car. As Gary screams, his two friends carefully lift him into the back seat for the ride to St. Mary Hospital.

In the emergency room, half an hour passes before a nurse appears   20
with a clipboard. Address: unknown. No insurance. After an X-ray, Gary is told that a bone in his back may be chipped. He is advised to go home, put some ice on it and get some rest. "I don't have a goddam home!" he cries, his face twisted in pain. "Don't you know what I am? I'm a goddam bum, that's what, and I'm dying!" After an awkward moment, he is told to come back tomorrow and see the radiologist. The hospital pays his cab fare back to the couch.

Gary returns in time to share another bottle of Thunderbird, and the   21
warm rush brings his spirits up. "What the hell are we doing in the city?" asks Ray Kelly, 37, who was once a merchant seaman. "I know a place in

Vermont where the fishing's great and you can build a whole damn house in the woods. There's nobody to bother you and plenty of food." Gary interrupts to recall fishing as a boy, and the memories prior to his six years on the street come back with crystal clarity. "You got it, man, we're all getting out of here tomorrow," he says with a grin. In the spirit of celebration, King, a 34-year-old from Puerto Rico, removes a tube of glue from his pocket with the care of a sommelier, sniffs it and passes it around.

When the sun rises, Ray and King are fast asleep under a blanket on the   22
couch. Gary is sitting at the other end, staring straight ahead and breathing heavily in the cold air. Curling his numb and swollen fingers around the arm of the couch, he tries to pull himself up but fails. When another try fails, he sits motionless and closes his eyes. Then the pain hits his back again and he starts to cry. He won't be getting out of here today, and probably not tomorrow either.

Meanwhile, somewhere across town in the washroom of a McDonald's,   23
George braces for another day of job hunting, washing the streets from his face so that nobody knows where he lives.

◆ ◆ ◆

FIRST RESPONSES

What choices has George made about how to live his life on the streets? Did he have other options? What choices might you make in his situation?

TAKING A CLOSER LOOK

Exploring *Who:* Voice and Tone

1. Although Hull spent time with these men, he does not include himself as part of this story. Why? Do you still know something about Hull's attitudes?
2. In paragraph 1, Hull describes George as "ignoring the cold stares of well-dressed commuters." Would you have stared as well? Why has Hull included this detail so early in the essay?
3. In paragraph 16, when Michael says, "I don't like to be around those people," who is he talking about? Hull seems to be providing his readers with a strong sense of the **irony** to be found in street life. Are there other examples of such ironies in the essay?

Exploring *What:* Content and Meaning

1. In paragraph 3, Hull tells his readers that "it's possible to go months without being touched by anyone but a thug." Can you imagine this kind of separation from friends and family? How does it make you feel about these men?

2. George and Red, like many of the men on the streets, "are loners who stand in silence." Find examples of how George, Red, and the others attempt to maintain their individuality. What other survival tactics have these men developed?

3. Would you call Gary and his friends a community? What do these men share? What are the pros and cons of this advanced stage of homelessness?

Exploring *Why:* Purpose

1. What surprised you about these men, and what reinforced the views you already held? How does what you learned make you feel about your own life and future?

2. "Descent into Hell" begins and ends with George. By the time you return to George in the last paragraph, what have you learned to change your expectations for or attitudes toward him?

3. Who is responsible for Gary's health problems? Where else could Red sleep than on the grate? Do you understand why the police and the medical staff responded as they did?

4. ▓▌ *Using the Internet.* A Ph.D. student in philosophy has created a Web site for homeless people called Vagrant Gaze. He provides single-shot disposable cameras to individuals who live on the streets and places their photographs on the Web site. Visit Vagrant Gaze (www.bestweb.net/~vagrant/index.htm), and look at these self-created images. How do they correspond to the images created by Hull? To those in your own mind?

Exploring *How:* Style and Strategy

1. Hull begins with George as his first example rather than with Red or Gary. Why? What differences and similarities do you see among George, Red, and Gary? Is there a clear reason for the order of the three major examples?

2. Why did Hull choose to give three extended examples of homelessness rather than several more short examples?

3. What specific sights, sounds, smells, and feelings do you most remember from the essay? Why does Hull go into such specific sensory detail?

4. Why does Hull include only men as examples in this essay?

5. Gary tells the emergency room nurse, "I don't have a goddam home [. . .]. Don't you know what I am? I'm a goddam bum, that's what, and I'm dying!" Why does Hull take the chance of including such dialogue, which may be objectionable to some people?

IDEAS FOR WRITING AN EXEMPLIFICATION ESSAY

1. Think of a time when you found yourself in a situation you never expected to be in. Write an essay showing how you behaved in this situation. If appropriate, also include how others reacted to you in this situation.

2. Write an essay using examples to explain an incident in which you or someone you know was treated unfairly. Describe both the unfair treatment and the reactions to it. You might choose to analyze the causes or let the situation speak for itself.

3. Think of a situation or circumstance that makes you feel insecure or frightened or tense. Write an essay using examples to describe this situation, and explain its effect on you.

◆ ◆ ◆ **PREPARING TO READ**

Have you ever wished you could be someone else? What kind of person would that be? What keeps you from being that person?

◆ ◆ ◆

In Search of Our Mothers' Gardens

ALICE WALKER

Alice Walker (born in 1944 in Georgia) is most widely known as author of the Pulitzer–Prize winning *The Color Purple* (1982), a novel Steven Spielberg made into a film starring Whoopi Goldberg and Oprah Winfrey. Her early fiction, based in part on her experiences as a civil rights worker in the 1960s, includes *In Love and Trouble: Stories of Black Women* (1973) and *You Can't Keep a Good Woman Down* (1981). More recent books are the essays *Anything We Love Can Be Saved: A Writer's Activism* (1998) and the stories *The Way Forward Is with a Broken Heart* (2000). Walker calls her prose "womanist" in honor of the unique experience of African American women. The term first appeared in the essay collection *In Search of Our Mothers' Gardens* (1983) and continues to serve as an important reminder of the diversity of female experience.

> I described her own nature and temperament. Told how they needed a
> larger life for their expression. . . . I pointed out that in lieu of proper
> channels, her emotions had overflowed into paths that dissipated them.
> I talked, beautifully I thought, about an art that would be born, an art
> that would open the way for women the likes of her. I asked her to
> hope, and build up an inner life against the coming of that day. . . . I
> sang, with a strange quiver in my voice, a promise song.
> —Jean Toomer, *"Avey," Cane*

The poet speaking to a prostitute who falls asleep while he's talking—   1
When the poet Jean Toomer walked through the South in the early   2
twenties, he discovered a curious thing: black women whose spirituality was so intense, so deep, so *unconscious,* that they were themselves unaware of the richness they held. They stumbled blindly through their lives: creatures

so abused and mutilated in body, so dimmed and confused by pain, that they considered themselves unworthy even of hope. In the selfless abstractions their bodies became to the men who used them, they became more than "sexual objects," even more than mere women: they became "Saints." Instead of being perceived as whole persons, their bodies became shrines, what was thought to be their minds became temples suitable for worship. These crazy Saints stared out at the world, wildly, like lunatics—or quietly, like suicides; and the "God" that was in their gaze was as mute as a great stone.

Who were these Saints? These crazy, loony, pitiful women? 3

Some of them, without a doubt, were our mothers and grandmothers. 4

In the still heat of the post-Reconstruction South, this is how they 5 seemed to Jean Toomer: exquisite butterflies trapped in an evil honey, toiling away their lives in an era, a century, that did not acknowledge them, except as "the *mule* of the world." They dreamed dreams that no one knew— not even themselves, in any coherent fashion—and saw visions no one could understand. They wandered or sat about the countryside crooning lullabies to ghosts, and drawing the mother of Christ in charcoal on courthouse walls.

They forced their minds to desert their bodies and their striving spirits 6 sought to rise, like frail whirlwinds from the hard red clay. And when those frail whirlwinds fell, in scattered particles, upon the ground, no one mourned. Instead, men lit candles to celebrate the emptiness that remained, as people do who enter a beautiful but vacant space to resurrect a God.

Our mothers and grandmothers, some of them: moving to music not 7 yet written. And they waited.

They waited for a day when the unknown thing that was in them would 8 be made known; but guessed, somehow in their darkness, that on the day of their revelation they would be long dead. Therefore to Toomer they walked, and even ran, in slow motion. For they were going nowhere immediate, and the future was not yet within their grasp. And men took our mothers and grandmothers, "but got no pleasure from it." So complex was their passion and their calm.

To Toomer, they lay vacant and fallow as autumn fields, with harvest 9 time never in sight: and he saw them enter loveless marriages, without joy; and become prostitutes, without resistance, and become mothers of children, without fulfillment.

For these grandmothers and mothers of ours were not Saints, but Artists; 10 driven to a numb and bleeding madness by the springs of creativity in them for which there was no release. They were Creators, who lived lives of spiritual waste, because they were so rich in spirituality—which is the basis of Art—that the strain of enduring their unused and unwanted talent drove them insane. Throwing away this spirituality was their pathetic attempt to lighten the soul to a weight their work-worn, sexually abused bodies could bear.

What did it mean for a black woman to be an artist in our grandmothers' time? In our great-grandmothers' day? It is a question with an answer cruel enough to stop the blood. 11

Did you have a genius of a great-grandmother who died under some ignorant and depraved white overseer's lash? Or was she required to bake biscuits for a lazy backwater tramp, when she cried out in her soul to paint watercolors of sunsets, or the rain falling on the green and peaceful pasturelands? Or was her body broken and forced to bear children (who were more often than not sold away from her)—eight, ten, fifteen, twenty children—when her one joy was the thought of modeling heroic figures of rebellion, in stone or clay? 12

How was the creativity of the black woman kept alive, year after year and century after century, when for most of the years black people have been in America, it was a punishable crime for a black person to read or write? And the freedom to paint, to sculpt, to expand the mind with an action did not exist. Consider, if you can bear to imagine it, what might have been the result if singing, too, had been forbidden by law. Listen to the voices of Bessie Smith, Billie Holiday, Nina Simone, Roberta Flack, and Aretha Franklin, among others, and imagine those voices muzzled for life. Then you may begin to comprehend the lives of our "crazy," "Sainted" mothers and grandmothers. The agony of the lives of women who might have been Poets, Novelists, Essayists, and Short Story Writers (over a period of centuries), who died with their real gifts stifled within them. 13

And, if this were the end of the story, we would have cause to cry out in my paraphrase of Okot p'Bitek's great poem: 14

O, my clanswomen
Let us all cry together!
Come,
Let us mourn the death of our mother,
The death of a Queen
The ash that was produced
By a great fire!
O, this homestead is utterly dead
Close the gates
With *lacari* thorns,
For our mother
The creator of the Stool is lost!
And all the young women
Have perished in the wilderness!

But this is not the end of the story, for all the young women—our mothers and grandmothers, *ourselves*—have not perished in the wilderness. And 15 if we ask ourselves why, and search for and find the answer, we will know beyond all efforts to erase it from our minds, just exactly who, and of what, we black American women are.

One example, perhaps the most pathetic, most misunderstood one, can   16
provide a backdrop for our mothers' work: Phillis Wheatley, a slave in the 1700s.

Virginia Woolf, in her book *A Room of One's Own,* wrote that in order   17
for a woman to write fiction she must have two things, certainly: a room of her own (the key and lock) and enough money to support herself.

What then are we to make of Phillis Wheatley, a slave, who owned not   18
even herself? This sickly, frail black girl who required a servant of her own at times—her health was so precarious—and who, had she been white, would have been easily considered the intellectual superior of all women and most of the men in the society of her day.

Virginia Woolf wrote further, speaking of course not of our Phillis, that   19
"any woman born with a great gift in the sixteenth century [insert "eigh-teenth century," insert "black woman," insert "born or made a slave"] would certainly have gone crazed, shot herself, or ended her days in some lonely cot-tage outside the village, half witch, half wizard [insert "Saint"], feared and mocked at. For it needs little skill and psychology to be sure that a highly gifted girl who had tried to use her gift for poetry would have been so thwarted and hindered by contrary instincts [add "chains, guns, the lash, the ownership of one's body by someone else, submission to an alien religion"], that she must have lost her health and sanity to a certainty."

The key words, as they relate to Phillis, are "contrary instincts." For   20
when we read the poetry of Phillis Wheatley—and when we read the novels of Nella Larsen or the oddly false-sounding autobiography of that freest of all black women writers, Zora Hurston—evidence of "contrary instincts" is everywhere. Her loyalties were completely divided, as was, without question, her mind.

But how could this be otherwise? Captured at seven, a slave of wealthy,   21
doting whites who instilled in her the "savagery" of the Africa they "rescued" her from . . . one wonders if she was even able to remember her homeland as she had known it, or as it really was.

Yet, because she did not try to use her gift for poetry in a world that   22
made her a slave, she was "so thwarted and hindered by . . . contrary instincts, that she . . . lost her health. . . ." In the last years of brief life, burdened not only with the need to express her gift but also with a penniless, friendless "freedom" and several small children for whom she was forced to do stren-uous work to feed, she lost her health, certainly. Suffering from malnutrition and neglect and who knows what mental agonies, Phillis Wheatley died.

So torn by "contrary instincts" was black, kidnapped, enslaved Phillis   23
that her description of "the Goddess"—as she poetically called the Liberty

she did not have—is ironically, cruelly humorous. And, in fact, has held Phillis up to ridicule for more than a century. It is usually read prior to hanging Phillis's memory as that of a fool. She wrote:

> The Goddess comes, she moves divinely fair,
> Olive and laurel binds her *golden* hair.
> Wherever shines this native of the skies,
> Unnumber'd charms and recent graces rise. [My italics]

It is obvious that Phillis, the slave, combed the "Goddess's" hair every   24
morning; prior, perhaps, to bringing in the milk, or fixing her mistress's lunch. She took her imagery from the one thing she saw elevated above all others.

With the benefit of hindsight we ask, "How could she?"   25

But at last, Phillis, we understand. No more snickering when your stiff,   26
struggling, ambivalent lines are forced on us. We know now that you were not an idiot or a traitor; only a sickly little black girl, snatched from your home and country and made a slave; a woman who still struggled to sing the song that was your gift, although in a land of barbarians who praised you for your bewildered tongue. It is not so much what you sang, as that you kept alive, in so many of our ancestors, *the notion of song.*

Black women are called, in the folklore that so aptly identifies one's   27
status in society, "the *mule* of the world," because we have been handed the burdens that everyone else—*everyone else*—refused to carry. We have also been called "Matriarchs," "Superwomen," and "Mean and Evil Bitches." Not to mention "Castraters" and "Sapphire's Mama." When we have pleaded for understanding, our character has been distorted; when we have asked for simple caring, we have been handed empty inspirational appellations, then stuck in the farthest corner. When we have asked for love, we have been given children. In short, even our plainer gifts, our labors of fidelity and love, have been knocked down our throats. To be an artist and a black woman, even today, lowers our status in many respects, rather than raises it: and yet, artists we will be.

Therefore we must fearlessly pull out of ourselves and look at and iden-   28
tify with our lives the living creativity some of our great-grandmothers were not allowed to know. I stress *some* of them because it is well known that the majority of our great-grandmothers knew, even without "knowing" it, the re-ality of their spirituality, even if they didn't recognize it beyond what hap-pened in the singing at church—and they never had any intention of giving it up.

How they did it—those millions of black women who were not Phillis   29
Wheatley, or Lucy Terry or Frances Harper or Zora Hurston or Nella Larsen

or Bessie Smith; or Elizabeth Catlett, or Katherine Dunham, either—brings me to the title of this essay, "In Search of Our Mothers' Gardens," which is a personal account that is yet shared, in its theme and its meaning, by all of us. I found, while thinking about the far-reaching world of the creative black woman, that often the truest answer to a question that really matters can be found very close.

In the late 1920s my mother ran away from home to marry my fa-   30
ther. Marriage, if not running away, was expected of seventeen-year-old girls. By the time she was twenty, she had two children and was pregnant with a third. Five children later, I was born. And this is how I came to know my mother: she seemed a large, soft, loving-eyed woman who was rarely impatient in our home. Her quick, violent temper was on view only a few times a year; she battled with the white landlord who had the misfortune to suggest to her that her children did not need to go to school.

She made all the clothes we wore, even my brothers' overalls. She   31
made all the towels and sheets we used. She spent the summers canning vegetables and fruits. She spent the winter evenings making quilts enough to cover all our beds.

During the "working" day, she labored beside—not behind—my fa-   32
ther in the fields. Her day began before sunup, and did not end until late at night. There was never a moment for her to sit down, undisturbed, to unravel her own private thoughts; never a time free from interruption—by work or the noisy inquiries of her many children. And yet, it is to my mother—and all our mothers who were not famous—that I went in search of the secrets of what has fed that muzzled and often mutilated, but vibrant, creative spirit that the black woman has inherited, and that pops out in wild and unlikely places to this day.

But when, you will ask, did my overworked mother have time to   33
know or care about feeding the creative spirit?

The answer is so simple that many of us have spent years discover-   34
ing it. We have constantly looked high, when we should have looked high—and low.

For example: in the Smithsonian Institution in Washington, D.C.,   35
there hangs a quilt unlike any other in the world. In fanciful, inspired, and yet simple and identifiable figures, it portrays the story of the Crucifixion. It is considered rare, beyond price. Though it follows no known pattern of quilt-making, and though it is made of bits and pieces of worthless rags, it is obviously the work of a person of powerful imagination and deep spiritual feeling. Below this quilt I saw a note that says it was made by "an anonymous Black woman in Alabama, a hundred years ago."

If we could locate this "anonymous" black woman from Alabama,   36
she would turn out to be one of our grandmothers—an artist who left her

mark in the only materials she could afford, and in the only medium her position in society allowed her to use.

As Virginia Woolf wrote further, in *A Room of One's Own:*   37

> Yet Genius of a sort must have existed among women as it must have existed among the working class. [Change this to "slaves" and "the wives or the daughters of sharecroppers."] Now and again an Emily Bronte or a Robert Bums [change this to "a Zora Hurston or a Richard Wright"] blazes out and proves its presence. But certainly it never got itself on to paper. When, however, one reads of a witch being ducked, of a woman possessed by devils [or "Sainthood"], of a wise woman selling herbs [our root workers], or even a very remarkable man who had a mother, then I think we are on the track of a lost novelist, a suppressed poet, of some mute and inglorious Jane Austen. . . . Indeed, I would venture to guess that Anon, who wrote so many poems without signing them, was often a woman. . . .

And so our mothers and grandmothers have, more often than not   38
anonymously, handed on the creative spark, the seed of the flower they themselves never hoped to see: or like a sealed letter they could not plainly read.

And so it is, certainly, with my own mother. Unlike "Ma" Rainey's songs,   39
which retained their creator's name even while blasting forth from Bessie Smith's mouth, no song or poem will bear my mother's name. Yet so many of the stories that I write, that we all write, are my mother's stories. Only recently did I fully realize this: that through years of listening to my mother's stories of her life, I have absorbed not only the stories themselves, but something of the manner in which she spoke, something of the urgency that involves the knowledge that her stories—like her life—must be recorded. It is probably for this reason that so much of what I have written is about characters whose counterparts in real life are so much older than I am.

But the telling of these stories, which came from my mother's lips as nat-   40
urally as breathing, was not the only way my mother showed herself as an artist. For stories, too, were subject to being distracted, to dying without conclusion. Dinners must be started, and cotton must be gathered before the big rains. The artist that was and is my mother showed itself to me only after many years. This is what I finally noticed:

Like Mem, a character in *The Third Life of Grange Copeland,* my   41
mother adorned with flowers whatever shabby house we were forced to live in. And not just your typical straggly country stand of zinnias, either. She planted ambitious gardens—and still does—with over fifty different varieties of plants that bloom profusely from early March until late November. Before she left home for the fields, she watered her flowers, chopped up the grass, and laid out new beds. When she returned from the fields she might divide clumps

of bulbs, dig a cold pit, uproot and replant roses, or prune branches from her taller bushes or trees—until night came and it was too dark to see.

Whatever she planted grew as if by magic, and her fame as a grower of flowers spread over three counties. Because of her creativity with her flowers, even my memories of poverty are seen through a screen of blooms—sunflowers, petunias, roses, dahlias, forsythia, spirea, delphiniums, verbena . . . and on and on. 42

And I remember people coming to my mother's yard to be given cuttings from her flowers; I hear again the praise showered on her because whatever rocky soil she landed on, she turned into a garden. A garden so brilliant with colors, so original in its design, so magnificent with life and creativity, that to this day people drive by our house in Georgia—perfect strangers and imperfect strangers—and ask to stand or walk in my mother's art. 43

I notice that it is not only when my mother is working in her flowers that she is radiant, almost to the point of being invisible—except as Creator: hand and eye. She is involved in work her soul must have. Ordering the universe in the image of her personal conception of Beauty. 44

Her face, as she prepares the Art that is her gift, is a legacy of respect she leaves to me, for all that illuminates and cherishes life. She has handed down respect for the possibilities—and the will to grasp them. 45

For her, so hindered and intruded upon in so many ways, being an artist has still been a daily part of her life. This ability to hold on, even in very simple ways, is work black women have done for a very long time. 46

This poem is not enough, but it is something, for the woman who literally covered the holes in our walls with sunflowers: 47

They were women then
My mama's generation
Husky of voice—Stout of
Step
With fists as well as
Hands
How they battered down
Doors
And ironed
Starched white
Shirts
How they led
Armies
Headragged Generals
Across mined
Fields
Booby-trapped
Kitchens

To discovery books
Desks
A place for us
How they knew what we
Must know
Without knowing a page
Of it
Themselves.

Guided by my heritage of a love of beauty and a respect for strength—   48
in search of my mother's garden, I found my own.

And perhaps in Africa over two hundred years ago, there was just such   49
a mother; perhaps she painted vivid and daring decorations in oranges and
yellows and greens on the walls of her hut; perhaps she sang—in a voice like
Roberta Flack's—*sweetly* over the compounds of her village; perhaps she
wove the most stunning mats or told the most ingenious stories of all the village storytellers. Perhaps she was herself a poet—though only her daughter's name is signed to the poems that we know.

Perhaps Phillis Wheatley's mother was also an artist.   50

Perhaps in more than Phillis Wheatley's biological life is her mother's   51
signature made clear.

◆ ◆ ◆

FIRST RESPONSES

What comes to mind when you think of the word "artist"? Do you
know any? Do any of your family members or friends have a talent or gift
that you might define as artistic?

TAKING A CLOSER LOOK

Exploring *Who:* Voice and Tone

1. What relationship does Walker see herself as having to the women she
   writes about? What emotions do their experiences create in her? Find
   one or two examples from the essay that support your answer.
2. Why does Walker place the term *Saints* in quotations the first time she
   uses it in paragraph 2? Whose point of view is she representing there?
   How do the point of view and the reader's understanding change when
   she repeats the term in paragraph 10?

3. To whom is Walker speaking in paragraphs 12 and 14 when she uses the pronouns "you" and "we"? How do these pronouns affect your response to the essay?
4. ◼️ *Using the Internet.* Walker names many different famous women in the essay. How many of them do you recognize? Using the Internet, an electronic encyclopedia, or the library, look up two or three of these women and then reread the paragraphs they appear in to see how the information adds to your understanding of Walker's points.

Exploring *What:* Content and Meaning

1. Explain the difference between Walker's definition of Saints and Jean Toomer's. Why does Walker prefer the term *artist?* See paragraph 9, for example.
2. What historical, social, and personal conditions have kept African American women from expressing their creativity? List the specific ways in which Phillis Wheatley and Walker's mother exemplify the challenges met and solutions found.
3. What does Walker mean by "contrary instincts" in paragraph 19? How does Wheatley illustrate this difficulty?
4. Explain the paradox in paragraph 28 when Walker says, "our great-grandmothers knew, even without 'knowing' it, the reality of their spirituality [. . .]."
5. Reread the three poems quoted in the essay. How do the women described in the poems compare and differ?

Exploring *Why:* Purpose

1. What does Walker hope to gain from revisiting the past? How does her poem (para. 47) offer answers to this question?
2. Walker laments the many artists "who died with their real gifts stifled within them." Does she convince you that this is a significant loss to the world, not just for them?
3. Were you familiar with the terms for African American women that Walker lists in paragraph 27? Why does she include them here?
4 Do you agree with Walker that "often the truest answer to a question that really matters can be found very close"?

Exploring *How:* Style and Strategy

1. Are Walker's two major extended examples, Wheatley and Walker's mother, meant as comparisons? As contrasts? Explain.

2. To what literal and what **figurative** gardens does Walker refer in her title?

3. In paragraph 7, Walker introduces music as another primary metaphor and comparison within her essay. Identify the other places music references appear, and discuss her reasons for choosing them.

4. Walker uses several short paragraphs throughout her essay. Why and with what effect?

5. What simile does Walker use in paragraph 6? What point does it help readers to understand?

IDEAS FOR WRITING EXEMPLIFICATION

1. Choose either someone you know personally or a popular figure you know a substantial amount about, and write an essay using this person to exemplify an especially admirable trait. Whomever you select, write with the assumption that your readers are unfamiliar with the person's accomplishments and that you need to convince them through several strong and concrete details.

2. Is there something unique about your local community, high school, friends, family, or other group to which you belong that would make it a valuable model for others? Write an essay built around examples that prove your claim.

◆ ◆ ◆ **PREPARING TO READ**

How often do you weigh yourself? What emotions do you feel when you do? Do you freely share your weight with others?

◆ ◆ ◆

A Weight That Women Carry

SALLIE TISDALE

Journalist and creative writing teacher Sallie Tisdale (born in 1957) writes on nature, travel, and public institutions for a wide range of popular magazines, including *Audubon, Antioch Review, Harper's,* and the *New York Times Magazine.* Calling on her early training as a nurse, Tisdale investigated public health problems in two early books, *The Sorcerer's Apprentice: Tales of a Modern Hospital* (1986) and *Harvest Moon: Portrait of a Nursing Home* (1987). In her most recent books, *Stepping Westward: The Long Search for Home in the Pacific Northwest* (1991), *Talk Dirty to Me: An Intimate Philosophy of Sex* (1994), and *The Best I Ever Tasted: The Secret of Food* (2000), Tisdale focuses on her personal understanding of ecology, sexuality, and food. "The Weight That Women Carry" appeared in 1993 in *Harper's.*

I don't know how much I weigh these days, though I can make a good 1
guess. For years I'd known that number, sometimes within a quarter pound, known how it changed from day to day and hour to hour. I want to weigh myself now; I lean toward the scale in the next room, imagine standing there, lining up the balance. But I don't do it. Going this long, starting to break the scale's spell—it's like waking up suddenly sober.

By the time I was sixteen years old I had reached my adult height of five 2
feet six inches and weighed 164 pounds. I weighed 164 pounds before and after a healthy pregnancy. I assume I weigh about the same now; nothing significant seems to have happened to my body, this same old body I've had all these years. I usually wear a size 14, a common clothing size for American women. On bad days I think my body looks lumpy and misshapen. On my good days, which are more frequent lately, I think I look plush and strong; I think I look like a lot of women whose bodies and lives I admire.

I'm not sure when the word "fat" first sounded pejorative to me, or 3
when I first applied it to myself. My grandmother was a petite woman, the only one in my family. She stole food from other people's plates, and hid the

debris of her own meals so that no one would know how much she ate. My mother was a size 14, like me, all her adult life; we shared clothes. She fretted endlessly over food scales, calorie counters, and diet books. She didn't want to quit smoking because she was afraid she would gain weight, and she worried about her weight until she died of cancer five years ago. Dieting was always in my mother's way, always there in the conversations above my head, the dialogue of stocky women. But I was strong and healthy and didn't pay too much attention to my weight until I was grown.

It probably wouldn't have been possible for me to escape forever. It   4
doesn't matter that whole human epochs have celebrated big men and women, because the brief period in which I live does not; since I was born, even the voluptuous calendar girl has gone. Today's models, the women whose pictures I see constantly, unavoidably, grow more minimal by the day. When I berate myself for not looking like—whomever I think I should look like that day, I don't really care that no one looks like that. I don't care that Michelle Pfeiffer doesn't look like the photographs I see of Michelle Pfeiffer. I want to look—think I should look—like the photographs. I want her little miracles: the makeup artists, photographers, and computer imagers who can add a mole, remove a scar, lift the breasts, widen the eyes, narrow the hips, flatten the curves. The final product is what I see, have seen my whole adult life. And I've seen this: even when big people become celebrities, their weight is constantly remarked upon and scrutinized; their successes seem always to be *in spite of* their weight. I thought my successes must be, too.

I feel myself expand and diminish from day to day, sometimes from   5
hour to hour. If I tell someone my weight, I change in their eyes: I become bigger or smaller, better or worse, depending on what that number, my weight, means to them. I know many men and women, young and old, gay and straight, who look fine, whom I love to see and whose faces and forms I cherish, who despise themselves for their weight. For their ordinary, human bodies. They and I are simply bigger than we think we should be. We always talk about weight in terms of gains and losses, and don't wonder at the strangeness of the words. In trying always to lose weight, we've lost hope of simply being seen for ourselves.

My weight has never actually affected anything—it's never seemed to   6
mean anything one way or the other to how I lived. Yet for the last ten years I've felt quite bad about it. After a time, the number on the scale became my totem, more important than my experience—it was layered, metaphorical, *metaphysical,* and it had bewitching power. I thought if I could change that number I could change my life.

In my mid-twenties I started secretly taking diet pills. They made me   7
feel strange, half-crazed, vaguely nauseated. I lost about twenty-five pounds, dropped two sizes, and bought new clothes. I developed rituals and taboos around food, ate very little, and continued to lose weight. For a long time

afterward I thought it only coincidental that with every passing week I also grew more depressed and irritable.

I could recite the details, but they're remarkable only for being so common. I lost more weight until I was rather thin, and then I gained it all back. It came back slowly, pound by pound, in spite of erratic and melancholy and sometimes frantic dieting, dieting I clung to even though being thin had changed nothing, had meant nothing to my life except that I was thin. Looking back, I remember blinding moments of shame and lightning-bright moments of clearheadedness, which inevitably gave way to rage at the time I'd wasted—rage that eventually would become, once again, self-disgust and the urge to lose weight. So it went, until I weighed exactly what I'd weighed when I began.   8

I used to be attracted to the sharp angles of the chronic dieter—the caffeine-wild, chain-smoking, skinny women I see sometimes. I considered them a pinnacle not of beauty but of will. Even after I gained back my weight, I wanted to be like that, controlled and persevering, live that underfed life so unlike my own rather sensual and disorderly existence. I felt I should always be dieting, for the dieting of it; dieting had become a rule, a given, a constant. Every ordinary value is distorted in this lens. I felt guilty for not being completely absorbed in my diet, for getting distracted, for not caring enough all the time. The fat person's character flaw is a lack of narcissism. She's let herself go.   9

So I would begin again—and at first it would all seem so . . . . easy. Simple arithmetic. After all, 3,500 calories equal one pound of fat—so the books and articles by the thousands say. I would calculate how long it would take to achieve the magic number on the scale, to succeed, to win. All past failures were suppressed. If 3,500 calories equal one pound, all I needed to do was cut 3,500 calories out of my intake every week. The first few days of a new diet would be colored with a sense of control—organization and planning, power over the self. Then the basic futile misery took over.   10

I would weigh myself with foreboding, and my weight would determine how went the rest of my day, my week, my life. When 3,500 calories didn't equal one pound lost after all, I figured it was my body that was flawed, not the theory. One friend, who had tried for years to lose weight following prescribed diets, made what she called "an amazing discovery." The real secret to a diet, she said, was that you had to be willing to be hungry *all the time.* You had to eat even less than the diet allowed.   11

I believed that being thin would make me happy. Such a pernicious, enduring belief. I lost weight and wasn't happy and saw that elusive happiness disappear in a vanishing point, requiring more—more self-disgust, more of the misery of dieting. Knowing all that I know now about the biology and anthropology of weight, knowing that people naturally come in many   12 shapes and sizes, knowing that diets are bad for me and won't make me thin—sometimes none of this matters. I look in the mirror and think: Who am I kidding? *I've got to do something about myself.* Only then will this vague discontent disappear. Then I'll be loved [. . .].

Fat is perceived as an *act* rather than a thing. It is antisocial, and curable 13 through the application of social controls. Even the feminist revisions of dieting, so powerful in themselves, pick up the theme: the hungry, empty heart; the woman seeking release from sexual assault, or the man from the loss of the mother, through food and fat. Fat is now a symbol not of the personality but of the soul—the cluttered, neurotic, immature soul.

Fat people eat for "mere gratification," I read, as though no one else 14 does. Their weight is *intentioned,* they simply eat "too much," their flesh is lazy flesh. Whenever I went on a diet, eating became cheating. One pretzel was cheating. Two apples instead of one was cheating—a large potato instead of a small, carrots instead of broccoli. It didn't matter which diet I was on; diets have failure built in, failure is in the definition. Every substitution—even carrots for broccoli—was a triumph of desire over will. When I dieted, I didn't feel pious just for sticking to the rules. I felt condemned for the act of eating itself, as though my hunger were never normal. My penance was to not eat at all.

My attitude toward food became quite corrupt. I came, in fact, to sub- 15 consciously believe food itself was corrupt. Diet books often distinguish between "real" and "unreal" hunger, so that *correct* eating is hollowed out, unemotional. A friend of mine who thinks of herself as a compulsive eater says she feels bad only when she eats for pleasure. "Why?" I ask, and she says, "Because I'm eating food I don't need." A few years ago I might have admired that. Now I try to imagine a world where we eat only food we need, and it seems inhuman. I imagine a world devoid of holidays and wedding feasts, wakes and reunions, a unique shared joy. "What's wrong with eating a cookie because you like cookies?" I ask her, and she hasn't got an answer. These aren't rational beliefs, any more than the unnecessary pleasure of ice cream is rational. Dieting presumes pleasure to be an insignificant, or at least malleable, human motive.

I felt no joy in being thin—it was just work, something I had to do. But 16 when I began to gain back the weight, I felt despair. I started reading about the "recidivism" of dieting. I wondered if I had myself to blame not only for needing to diet in the first place but for dieting itself, the weight inevitably regained. I joined organized weight-loss programs, spent a lot of money, listened to lectures I didn't believe on quack nutrition, ate awful, processed diet foods. I sat in groups and applauded people who'd lost a half pound, feeling smug because I'd lost a pound and a half. I felt ill much of the time, found exercise increasingly difficult, cried often. And I thought that if I could only lose a little weight, everything would be all right [. . .].

Recently I was talking with a friend who is naturally slender about a mutual acquaintance who is quite large. To my surprise my friend reproached this woman because she had seen her eating a cookie at lunchtime. "How is she going to lose weight that way?" my friend wondered. When you are as fat as our acquaintance is, you are primarily, fundamentally, seen as fat. It is your essential characteristic. There are so many presumptions in my friend's casual, cruel remark. She assumes that this woman should diet all the time—and that she *can*. She pronounces whole categories of food to be denied her. She sees her unwillingness to behave in this externally prescribed way, even for a moment, as an act of rebellion. In his story "A Hunger Artist," Kafka writes that the guards of the fasting man were "usually butchers, strangely enough." Not so strange, I think.

I know that the world, even if it views me as overweight (and I'm not sure it really does), clearly makes a distinction between me and this very big woman. I would rather stand with her and not against her, see her for all she is besides fat. But I know our experiences aren't the same. My thin friend assumes my fat friend is unhappy because she is fat: therefore, if she loses weight she will be happy. My fat friend has a happy marriage and family and a good career, but insofar as her weight is a source of misery, I think she would be much happier if she could eat her cookie in peace, if people would shut up and leave her weight alone. But the world never lets up when you are her size; she cannot walk to the bank without risking insult. Her fat is seen as perverse bad manners. I have no doubt she would be rid of the fat if she could be. If my left-handedness invited the criticism her weight does, I would want to cut that hand off [. . .].

The predominant biological myth of weight is that thin people live longer than fat people. The truth is far more complicated. (Some deaths of fat people attributed to heart disease seem actually to have been the result of radical dieting.) If health were our real concern, it would be dieting we questioned, not weight. The current ideal of thinness has never been held before, except as a religious ideal; the underfed body is the martyr's body. Even if people can lose weight, maintaining an artificially low weight for any period of time requires a kind of starvation. Lots of people are naturally thin, but for those who are not, dieting is an unnatural act; biology rebels. The metabolism of the hungry body can change inalterably, making it ever harder and harder to stay thin. I think chronic dieting made me gain weight—not only pounds, but fat. This equation seemed so strange at first that I couldn't believe it. But the weight I put back on after losing was much more stubborn than the original weight. I had lost it by taking diet pills and not eating much

17

18

19

of anything at all for quite a long time. I haven't touched the pills again, but not eating much of anything no longer works.

When Oprah Winfrey first revealed her lost weight, I didn't envy her. 20 I thought, She's in trouble now. I knew, I was certain, she would gain it back; I believed she was biologically destined to do so. The tabloid headlines blamed it on a cheeseburger or mashed potatoes; they screamed OPRAH PASSES 200 POUNDS, and I cringed at her misery and how the world wouldn't let up, wouldn't leave her alone, wouldn't let her be anything else. How dare the world do this to anyone? I thought, and then realized I did it to myself.

The "Ideal Weight" charts my mother used were at their lowest 21 acceptable-weight ranges in the 1950s, when I was a child. They were based on sketchy and often inaccurate actuarial evidence, using, for the most part, data on northern Europeans and allowing for the most minimal differences in size for a population of less than half a billion people. I never fit those weight charts, I was always just outside the pale. As an adult, when I would join an organized diet program, I accepted their version of my Weight Goal as gospel, knowing it would be virtually impossible to reach. But reach I tried; that's what one does with gospel. Only in the last few years have the weight tables begun to climb back into the world of the average human. The newest ones distinguish by gender, frame, and age. And suddenly I'm not off the charts anymore. I have a place.

A man who is attracted to fat women says, "I actually have less specific 22 physical criteria than most men. I'm attracted to women who weigh 170 or 270 or 370. Most men are only attracted to women who weigh between 100 and 135. So who's got more of a fetish?" We look at fat as a problem of the fat person. Rarely do the tables get turned, rarely do we imagine that it might be the viewer, not the viewed, who is limited. What the hell is wrong with *them*, anyway? Do they believe everything they see on television?

A fashion magazine recently celebrated the return of the "well-fed" 23 body; a particular model was said to be "the archetype of the new womanly woman . . . stately, powerful." She is a size 8. The images of women presented to us, images claiming so maliciously to be the images of women's whole lives, are not merely social fictions. They are *absolute* fictions; they can't exist. How would it feel, I began to wonder, to cultivate my own real womanliness rather than despise it? Because it was my fleshy curves I wanted to be rid of after all. I dreamed of having a boy's body, smooth, hipless, lean. A body rapt with possibility, a receptive body suspended before the storms of maturity. A dear friend of mine, nursing her second child, weeps at her newly voluptuous body. She loves her children and hates her own motherliness, wanting to be unripened again, to be a bud and not a flower.

Recently I've started shopping occasionally at stores for "large women," 24 where the smallest size is a 14. In department stores the size 12 and 14 and

16 clothes are kept in a ghetto called the Women's Department. (And who would want that, to be the size of a woman? We all dream of being "juniors" instead.) In the specialty stores the clerks are usually big women and the customers are big, too, big like a lot of women in my life—friends, my sister, my mother and aunts. Not long ago I bought a pair of jeans at Lane Bryant and then walked through the mall to the Gap, with its shelves of generic clothing. I flicked through the clearance rack and suddenly remembered the Lane Bryant shopping bag in my hand and its enormous weight, the sheer heaviness of that brand name shouting to the world. The shout is that I've let myself go. I still feel like crying out sometimes: Can't I feel satisfied? But I am not supposed to be satisfied, not allowed to be satisfied. My discontent fuels the market; I need to be afraid in order to fully participate [. . .].

The possibility of living another way, living without dieting, began to   25
take root in my mind a few years ago, and finally my second trip through Weight Watchers ended dieting for me. This last time I just couldn't stand the details, the same kind of details I'd seen and despised in other programs, on other diets: the scent of resignation, the weighing-in by the quarter pound, the before and after photographs of group leaders prominently displayed. Jean Nidetch, the founder of Weight Watchers, says, "Most fat people need to be hurt badly before they do something about themselves." She mocks every aspect of our need for food, of a person's sense of entitlement to food, of daring to *eat what we want*. Weight Watchers refuses to release its own weight charts except to say they make no distinction for frame size; neither has the organization ever released statistics on how many people who lose weight on the program eventually gain it back. I hated the endlessness of it, the turning of food into portions and exchanges, everything measured out, permitted, denied. I hated the very idea of "maintenance." Finally I realized I didn't just hate the diet. I was sick of the way I acted on a diet, the way I whined, my niggardly, penny-pinching behavior. What I liked in myself seemed to shrivel and disappear when I dieted. Slowly, slowly I saw these things. I saw that my pain was cut from whole cloth, imaginary, my own invention. I saw how much time I'd spent on something ephemeral, something that simply wasn't important, didn't matter. I saw that the real point of dieting is dieting—to not be done with it, ever.

I looked in the mirror and saw a woman, with flesh, curves, muscles, a   26
few stretch marks, the beginnings of wrinkles, with strength and softness in equal measure. My body is the one part of me that is always, undeniably, here. To like myself means to be, literally, shameless, to be wanton in the pleasures of being inside a body. I feel *loose* this way, a little abandoned, a little dangerous. That first feeling of liking my body—not being resigned to it or despairing of change, but actually *liking* it—was tentative and guilty and frightening. It was alarming, because it was the way I'd felt as a child, before the world had interfered. Because surely I was wrong; I knew, I'd known for

so long, that my body wasn't all right this way. I was afraid even to act as though I were all right: I was afraid that by doing so I'd be acting a fool.

For a time I was thin. I remember—and what I remember is nothing special—strain, a kind of hollowness, the same troubles and fears, and no magic. So I imagine losing weight again. If the world applauded, would this comfort me? Or would it only compromise whatever approval the world gives me now? What else will be required of me besides thinness? What will happen to me if I get sick, or lose the use of a limb, or, God forbid, grow old?   27

By fussing endlessly over my body, I've ceased to inhabit it. I'm trying to reverse this equation now, to trust my body and enter it again with a whole heart. I know more now than I used to about what constitutes "happy" and "unhappy," what the depths and textures of contentment are like. By letting go of dieting, I free up mental and emotional room. I have more space, I can move. The pursuit of another, elusive body, the body someone else says I should have, is a terrible distraction, a sidetracking that might have lasted my whole life long. By letting myself go, I go places.   28

Each of us in this culture, this twisted, inchoate culture, has to choose between battles: one battle is against the cultural ideal, and the other is against ourselves. I've chosen to stop fighting myself. Maybe I'm tilting at windmills; the cultural ideal is ever-changing, out of my control. It's not a cerebral journey, except insofar as I have to remind myself to stop counting, to stop thinking in terms of numbers. I know, even now that I've quit dieting and eat what I want, how many calories I take in every day. If I eat as I please, I eat a lot one day and very little the next; I skip meals and snack at odd times. My nourishment is good—as far as nutrition is concerned, I'm in much better shape than when I was dieting. I know that the small losses and gains in my weight over a period of time aren't simply related to the number of calories I eat. Someone asked me not long ago how I could possibly know my calorie intake if I'm not dieting (the implication being, perhaps, that I'm dieting secretly). I know because calorie counts and grams of fat and fiber are embedded in me. I have to work to not think of them, and I have to learn to not think of them in order to really live without fear [. . .].   29

I repeat with Walt Whitman, "I dote on myself . . . there is that lot of me, and all so luscious." I'm eating better, exercising more, feeling fine—and then I catch myself thinking, *Maybe I'll lose some weight.* But my mood changes or my attention is caught by something else, something deeper, more lingering. Then I can catch a glimpse of myself by accident and think only: That's me. My face, my hips, my hands. Myself.   30

◆ ◆ ◆

FIRST RESPONSES

Do you agree with Tisdale that weight is one of the first things we notice about other people? Does it affect how you judge a stranger? Is it a significant part of your feelings about your friends and family members?

TAKING A CLOSER LOOK

Exploring *Who:* Voice and Tone

1. What addiction is Tisdale comparing her weight obsession to in paragraph 1? What first impression does this comparison give you of Tisdale?
2. Because Tisdale's attitudes have changed over the years, she speaks in a number of different voices in this essay. How many can you identify? What emotions characterize each of these periods of her life, and how do you respond to each of them? For example, what is Tisdale feeling when she says, "Rarely do the tables get turned, rarely do we imagine that it might be the viewer, not the viewed, who is limited. What the hell is wrong with *them?*" How does her tone affect your response to the idea she is presenting?
3. In paragraph 9, when Tisdale says, "The fat person's character flaw is a lack of narcissism. She's let herself go," whose point of view is she expressing?
4. Tisdale ends her essay by claiming Walt Whitman as a role model for her current self-image. Is he a good choice? Why does she quote from him instead of simply mentioning him?

Exploring *What:* Content and Meaning

1. What celebrities besides Oprah have been popular *"in spite of"* their weight? Are they primarily male or female? What limits has weight placed on their career choices?
2. If Tisdale knows that Michelle Pfeiffer's image is created by makeup and photographers, why does she still think she should be able to look like Pfeiffer? How does she know many of her readers share this desire?
3. Do you agree with Tisdale's claim that "My weight has never actually affected anything—it never seemed to mean anything one way or the

other to how I lived." How do food and your weight affect your everyday life?

4. How does the author's current attitude toward weight contrast with her earlier desire for control and order as a dieter? Which Tisdale would you rather have as a friend?

5. ▆ *Using the Internet.* In June 1998, the federal government changed the ideal weight charts. Find the National Heart, Lung, and Blood Institute site (www.nhlbi.nih.gov/guidelines/obesity/bmi_tbl.htm), where this chart can be found. Next, using a database such as InfoTrac or Academic Index, locate at least one popular magazine article (in *Time* or *Newsweek,* for example) on the release of this chart and how it compares with earlier charts. What would Tisdale say about the changes?

Exploring *Why:* Purpose

1. Why does Tisdale describe her process of coming to terms with her weight as a battle? How have the combatants and the sites of the battles changed over the years?

2. Paragraphs 8 and 10 capture Tisdale's dieting cycles. What does she feel are the social and biological causes for these cycles? Had you already heard about the effect of dieting on metabolism? Does this medical fact affect your attitudes toward your own or other people's weight?

3. Why does Tisdale see a friend feeling "bad only when she eats for pleasure" as "inhuman"? Do you agree with her?

4. How has weight affected Tisdale's friendships? How optimistic is she about changing such behaviors?

Exploring *How:* Style and Strategy

1. How does Tisdale justify using primarily only her own experience to prove what she believes is a widespread American problem? How else might she have developed her thesis?

2. Tisdale uses a number of **euphemisms** for the word *fat,* for example, "stocky" and "plump." Why? Can you think of other examples of common words for people we consider overweight?

3. What does "recidivism" mean in paragraph 16? Why does she use such a technical word here?

4. Why does Tisdale hate Weight Watchers' use of the term *maintenance?* In what other contexts do you use that word? How might that use affect your feelings about yourself if you were on a diet?

IDEAS FOR WRITING AN EXEMPLIFICATION ESSAY

1. Write an essay using examples to trace a change in your attitude toward something about yourself or your family. Show each stage of your feelings as clearly and objectively as possible, and provide a clear explanation for the changes that have taken place.

2. Do people make assumptions about you when they first see you because of some aspect of your physical appearance? Write an essay in which you use examples of such responses to analyze the effects of first impressions.

3. Write an essay illustrating that appearances can be deceiving.

◆ ◆ ◆

◆ FURTHER IDEAS FOR USING EXEMPLIFICATION

1. As a child, your parents probably started their sentences with the comment, "When you grow up you'll understand that . . ." Were they right? Write an essay using examples from your experience to explain how you learned the truth or error of one or more of their warnings.

2. ▓▒ *Using the Internet.* Write an essay using your own experiences, as well as those of people you know, to exemplify the pros and cons of family vacations. Use an Internet search engine to visit the sites of typical vacation destinations, such as the Grand Canyon and Disneyland, to gather additional ideas. In your essay, consider both the parents' and the children's points of view.

3. COLLABORATIVE WRITING. Meet with a small group of other students to compare notes on your past experiences with writing. Discuss the attitudes and feelings about writing that have resulted from these experiences. Include personal writing, school assignments, and work-related tasks. After the discussion session, write an essay using past experience to explain your current thoughts and feelings about writing, including any changes you have experienced in these attitudes.

4. COMBINING STRATEGIES. After spending a few hours watching any of the many video TV channels, such as MTV, VH1, BET, or CMT, write an essay explaining what you believe are the most common attitudes toward women in the music videos shown on that channel—pop, rock, rap, or country. As you present your examples, remember that your readers may or may not have seen these videos, so you will need to narrate events and describe lyrics as appropriate.

5. COMBINING STRATEGIES. Narrate one particular interaction you had with someone you know well who is in a position of authority, such as a teacher, a pastor, or a judge. Concentrate on how this particular interaction exemplifies the nature of your relationship with that person.

Strategies for Explaining How Things Work

Process Analysis

◆ ◆ ◆ ◆ ◆

Process writing tells how to do something or how something functions.

◆ Process writing is used to give directions and explain behaviors.

◆ Effective process writing is organized according to time or logic.

◆ Writers must decide what background information is needed, what steps to include, and what pitfalls to mention.

Communicating directions so that almost anyone can understand them is a difficult task, as you know if you've ever tried to do it. Explaining a process is quite similar; after you've performed a certain job over and over, it's hard to explain to someone else exactly how it's done. And when a child asks, "Where does the rain come from?" most people would rather come up with a cute story than grapple with the workings of nature.

But knowing how to provide an orderly, step-by-step explanation of how something is done or how it works is a valuable skill. For instance, if you're a political science major, you might be asked to explain how a bill gets passed in Congress or how the electoral college works. If you're taking a science class, you might have to explain how photosynthesis works or recount the steps followed in an experiment. If you're taking physical education, you might be asked to write out the process for treating a sports injury or for improving a tennis serve. Sometimes the explanation may be just part of a larger essay or on-the-job report. For example, proposing a solution to your company's mail problems should include an account of how the current mail system works before addressing the changes to be made.

Often, **process writing** proceeds step by step: how to wash a dog, how to make English muffins, or how to change a light switch. But another version of process writing describes a process that is not necessarily in **chronological order:** designing a home for Alzheimer's patients or explaining how to keep your brain in top shape to avoid Alzheimer's disease. The second variety doesn't lend itself to easy step-by-step organization, so you have to sort your points and arrange them in a **logical order.** Both kinds of process writing also involve analysis, since you must analyze your material thoroughly before you begin writing about it.

In the following essay, humorist Bud Herron calls upon his own harrowing experience to advise cat owners how to bathe a cat and come out alive. Student writer James R. Bryans read the cat bathing piece and arranged his own more serious essay following Herron's model.

Cat Bathing as a Martial Art

BUD HERRON

Howard "Bud" Herron is the publisher of *The Republic,* Columbus, Indiana's daily newspaper. He wrote the following article as a column in 1983, when he was editor of a newspaper in Franklin, Indiana. "Don't know how it got on the Internet," says Herron, "but it has been floating around for years. It has been in numerous magazines and newspapers and at least two books."

Some people say cats never have to be bathed. They say cats lick themselves clean. They say cats have a special enzyme of some sort in their saliva that works like new, improved Wisk—dislodging the dirt where it hides and whisking it away. 1

I've spent most of my life believing this folklore. Like most blind be- 2
lievers, I've been able to discount all the facts to the contrary: the kitty odors
that lurk in the corners of the garage and dirt smudges that cling to the throw
rug by the fireplace. The time comes, however, when a man must face reality, when he must look squarely in the face of massive public sentiment to the
contrary and announce: "This cat smells like a port-a-potty on a hot day in
Juarez." When that day arrives at your house, as it has at mine, I have some
advice you might consider as you place your feline friend under your arm and
head for the bathtub:

◆ Know that although the cat has the advantage of quickness and lack 3
of concern for human life, you have the advantage of strength. Capitalize on
that advantage by selecting the battlefield. Don't try to bathe him in an open
area where he can force you to chase him. Pick a very small bathroom. If
your bathroom is more than four feet square, I recommend that you get in
the tub with the cat and close the sliding-glass doors as if you were about to
take a shower. (A simple shower curtain will not do. A berserk cat can shred
a three-ply rubber curtain quicker than a politician can shift positions.)

◆ Know that a cat has claws and will not hesitate to remove all the skin 4
from your body. Your advantage here is that you are smart and know how to
dress to protect yourself. I recommend canvas overalls tucked into high-top
construction boots, a pair of steel-mesh gloves, an army helmet, a hockey
face mask, and a long-sleeved flak jacket.

◆ Prepare everything in advance. There is no time to go out for a towel 5
when you have a cat digging a hole in your flak jacket. Draw the water. Make
sure the bottle of kitty shampoo is inside the glass enclosure. Make sure the
towel can be reached, even if you are lying on your back in the water.

◆ Use the element of surprise. Pick up your cat nonchalantly, as if to 6
simply carry him to his supper dish. (Cats will not usually notice your strange
attire. They have little or no interest in fashion as a rule. If he does notice your
garb, calmly explain that you are taking part in a product testing experiment
for J. C. Penney.)

◆ Once you are inside the bathroom, speed is essential to survival. In 7
a single liquid motion, shut the bathroom door, step into the tub enclosure,
slide the glass door shut, dip the cat in the water, and squirt him with shampoo. You have begun one of the wildest 45 seconds of your life.

◆ Cats have no handles. Add the fact that he now has soapy fur, and the 8
problem is radically compounded. Do not expect to hold on to him for more

than two or three seconds at a time. When you have him, however, you must remember to give him another squirt of shampoo and rub like crazy. He'll then spring free and fall back into the water, thereby rinsing himself off. (The national record for cats is three latherings, so don't expect too much.)

◆ Next, the cat must be dried. Novice cat bathers always assume this   9
part will be the most difficult, for humans generally are worn out at this point and the cat is just getting really determined. In fact, the drying is simple compared to what you have just been through. That's because by now the cat is semi-permanently affixed to your right leg. You simply pop the drain plug with your foot, reach for your towel and wait. (Occasionally, however, the cat will end up clinging to the top of your army helmet. If this happens, the best thing you can do is to shake him loose and to encourage him toward your leg.) After all the water is drained from the tub, it is a simple matter to just reach down and dry the cat.

In a few days the cat will relax enough to be removed from your leg. He   10
will usually have nothing to say for about three weeks and will spend a lot of time sitting with his back to you. He might even become psychoceramic and develop the fixed stare of a plaster figurine. You will be tempted to assume he is angry. This isn't usually the case. As a rule he is simply plotting ways to get through your defenses and injure you for life the next time you decide to give him a bath. But at least now he is clean.

◆ ◆ ◆

◆ ◆ ◆ *Writer's Workshop I* ◆ ◆ ◆
Responding to a Process Analysis

Use the *Who, What, Why,* and *How* questions (see p. 3) to explore your own understanding of the ideas and writing strategies employed by Bud Herron in "Cat Bathing as a Martial Art." Your instructor may ask you to record these responses in a journal, post them on an electronic discussion site, or bring them to class to use in small group discussions.

◆ WRITING FROM READING

After applying the *Who, What, Why,* and *How* questions to Herron's essay, freshman James R. Bryans chose to explain a process less dangerous than cat bathing—buying land. Although he adopts a tone more serious than Herron's, he does include some humor in his essay, and he follows essentially the same structure: a two-paragraph introduction giving background material; a step-by-step chronological account of the process; and a one-paragraph conclusion. Here is Jim's essay.

James R. Bryans
English 101
April 17, 1998

Buying Land: Easier Said Than Done

There are times in a man's life when he wants   1
something so badly he can taste it. This obsession may
lead a normally sane man to undertake a course of
action he would not normally take. For me, this
obsession was the desire to own my own piece of
property.

Little did I know, as an 18-year-old prospective   2
land baron, that I would have to go through a tedious,
complicated process to achieve my goal. All I wanted
was 13 acres of woods that my grandfather and his
three siblings owned. I believed that all I would have
to do was say, "Hey, I'd like to buy your land." Then
I'd sign a deed and that would be that.

First of all, I wasn't sure that my Aunt Pauline   3
and my Uncle Virgil would want to sell this land that
had belonged to their grandparents. My grandfather,
and my Uncle Lloyd, I thought, would just give me
their stake in the land for nothing. As it turned out,
the four of them had discussed the matter and decided
to sell the land. I offered to buy it, and they
agreed. This part was what I thought was to be the
hardest, but I was so wrong.

I had to get the papers from Aunt Pauline. These   4
papers included the old "abstract of title," often
referred to as simply an abstract, which is a history
of ownership of a piece of real estate. Also, I was
given an old deed--a document that certifies a person's
legal ownership to a plot of land and includes
information regarding township, section, range, lot
numbers, and so forth--and some other pieces of paper.
Well, this was simple enough so far.

The next order of business was to go to see the lawyer. Unfortunately, a person cannot buy property without going to a lawyer, and this, of course, is a considerable expense. He took my papers and told me that new ones would have to be drawn up. I did not see anything wrong with the old ones, myself, but I still had to wait for a new abstract and a new deed to be prepared.   5

Once the deed was prepared, I had to get the signatures of all the sellers on it. Each of these signatures had to be witnessed by a notary public, a person who can legally certify a document's authenticity, but does not have to be an attorney. So, my father, who has a notary public's license, went to my grandfather and to Aunt Pauline, who lived in our area. But the other two owners, Uncle Virgil and Uncle Lloyd, lived out of state--one in Florida and the other in Missouri. Fortunately, my father decided he wanted to see his kinfolk anyway, so he just went for a visit and took the deed with him. He returned with all of the necessary signatures and notarization.   6

When all of this signing and notarizing was done, there was still a recording fee to pay. Now, what this is, is a similar thing to the Stamp Act that made the American Colonists mad enough to revolt. I had to pay to have my deed stamped, showing that the state would recognize me as the legal owner, and the fee for this stamp made me eligible to pay property taxes. In other words, I had to pay a tax to be able to pay taxes. But if I had neglected to pay the recording fee, I would not officially be the owner of my land, which would have defeated the purpose of owning land, I do believe.   7

In conclusion, my journey to the status of land owner was a long, complex, and expensive one. It took time, patience, and, of course, money. Buying land requires a knowledge of the system that one may truly obtain only by going through the system. A lawyer is usually more than happy to help with the process--for a price. In fact, the only way to buy land legally without a lawyer is to be one. In the end, though, I am very glad that I bought that land. Maybe someday I will be able to buy some more. And, next time, I'll know what to expect.   8

◆ GETTING STARTED ON A PROCESS ANALYSIS

Before beginning to explain a process in writing, you'll want to consider your prospective readers. Sizing up your **audience** is crucial if you are explaining a technical process, such as how to replace a hard drive. You need to judge how much—or how little—your readers already know about the complex insides of a personal computer. If you don't give enough background information, you'll lose the beginners at the outset, and they may remain permanently lost. But if you give too much background, the more experienced users may become impatient, skip along, and maybe miss some vital step. It is probably better to err on the side of providing more background information than some readers need than to risk confusing the novices.

If your process is not complex, figuring out your audience is easier. Bud Herron, for instance, has an easily identifiable audience: cat owners. He may even engage a few readers who don't care for cats but can appreciate the humor anyway, but he's mostly writing for people who know how cats behave; therein lies much of his humor. Similarly, Jim Bryans doesn't have to worry about whether his readers have ever bought land before because, as he complains, you can't do it without a lawyer anyway. So, Jim addresses his advice to anyone who might be interested in buying a piece of land.

◆ ORGANIZING A PROCESS ANALYSIS

The basic organizing principle behind process writing involves time. You are usually involved with relating a series of events, and these events may not float through your mind in the same order they should appear in your written work. Your readers will be frustrated and confused by **flashbacks** or detours to supply information you should have covered earlier. Therefore, the scratch outline takes on great importance in this type of writing. A blank piece of unlined paper will help you get started. On this page, list the steps or stages of the process as you think of them, and be sure to space the items widely apart. In the spaces, you can add points you forgot the first time through. When you get to the end of your process, read through the steps while visualizing the process to pinpoint anything you may have forgotten.

If you'll glance back at Herron's essay, you'll notice that following his two introductory paragraphs establishing the need for cat bathing, his main points (using his own phrasing) go like this:

- ◆ selecting the battlefield
- ◆ dress to protect yourself
- ◆ prepare everything in advance
- ◆ use the element of surprise

- ◆ speed is essential
- ◆ cats have no handles (hard to hold onto)
- ◆ the cat must be dried

As you can see, the essay follows essentially the order in which the contest between cat and cat-bather will take place, in case anyone wants to risk life and limb by following this advice.

If you'll look again at James Bryans's essay, you'll see that he organizes his material in the same way Herron does. After a two-paragraph introduction stating his desire to become a "prospective land baron," Jim presents his main points this way:

- ◆ arranges to buy the land
- ◆ gets deed and abstract
- ◆ hires a lawyer
- ◆ obtains signatures of sellers
- ◆ pays recording fee

There are, of course, other sorts of process papers that do not lend themselves to this easy chronological organization, topics such as "How to choose a personal computer" or "How to live within your means." For such subjects, you must figure out a clear, **logical arrangement** that suits your material.

◆ DEVELOPING A PROCESS ANALYSIS

Developing a process essay simply involves explaining each step fully and clearly while keeping your audience in mind. But here are some guidelines that are especially important if you are giving instructions about a mechanical or technical process.

◆ *Define terms.* In parentheses or in a concise sentence, define any word that would be unfamiliar to most of your readers, like "motherboard" or "gigabyte," in explaining how to upgrade your computer—or any common word you're using in an unfamiliar way, like "rubber" or "vulnerable," in explaining how to keep score in bridge. Just after using the legal term *abstract,* Jim Bryans briefly defines it: "an abstract, which is a history of ownership of a piece of real estate." He later defines *notary public* as "a person who can legally certify a document's authenticity, but does not have to be an attorney."

◆ *Be specific.* Remember that in writing, you must make yourself clear without those gestures you use to make yourself understood when speaking. Instead of saying, "Strip the insulation back *a little bit* on a piece of wire"—and then showing your listener a short space between your thumb and forefinger—you need to write, "Strip the insulation back *one inch* on a piece of wire." Notice that Bud Herron is not content with just telling a prospective cat-bather to wear heavy clothes. He specifically recommends "canvas overalls tucked into high-top construction boots, a pair of steel-mesh gloves, an army helmet, a hockey face mask, and a long-sleeved flak jacket."

◆ *Include reasons.* You can often help your readers better understand the process by explaining the reasons for taking certain steps. Bud Herron, after advising his readers "to prepare everything in advance," explains why: because, "There is no time to go out for a towel when you have a cat digging a hole in your flak jacket."

◆ *Include "don'ts."* If there happens to be a common—or uncommon but disastrous—mistake that people can make in following the process, you need to warn your readers. For instance, "Do not stick your fingers in the fusebox unless you have pulled out the main fuse" is handy advice. Herron cautions, "Don't try to bathe [your cat] in an open area where he can force you to chase him." He later warns, "Do not expect to hold on to him for more than two or three seconds at a time," so that we understand the need to wash rapidly.

◆ *Mention possible pitfalls.* Whenever things are likely to go wrong despite your careful directions, let your readers know about it. When describing the process of making bread, for instance, you should note that if the water is too hot, it will kill the yeast and the dough won't rise. Jim Bryans advises us that although paying the double tax seems unfair, it is absolutely necessary: "If I had neglected to pay the recording fee, I would not officially be the owner of my land." Herron's process is full of pitfalls, some quite dire: "A berserk cat can shred a three-ply rubber curtain quicker than a politician can shift positions"; "Know that a cat has claws and will not hesitate to remove all the skin from your body"; "Make sure the towel can be reached, even if you are lying on your back in the water."

◆ OPENING AND CLOSING A PROCESS ANALYSIS

By the time your readers finish your first paragraph, they should know what process you are going to describe. To open a "how-to" process paper, you may reassure your readers by giving your credentials—telling them why they should listen to *you* on this subject. Jim Bryans begins by telling of his desire to own a piece of land and cites as credentials his experience in land buying.

You might begin by mentioning the advantages of knowing how to perform this process. Bud Herron opens by refuting the accepted wisdom that cats do not need bathing by telling us about his cat, who is desperately dirty. Thus, he convinces us of the value of reading his instructions. We know from the humorous tone that he grossly exaggerates on all counts, but still his advice could be followed by anyone cocky enough to try washing a full-grown cat with claws intact.

Another common element of process introductions is a list of materials involved. In a how-to paper, it is convenient for the readers to have all the necessary items named in one place. If they are going to follow directions for washing the cat, they should be told (as Herron tells his readers) to collect the soap and towels before they collect the cat; otherwise, the beast will bolt while they are gone. If you decide to include such a list, double-check to make sure you do not leave anything out.

A truly impressive closing is hard to come by in process writing, but here are a few ideas that may help. You can enumerate the advantages of knowing the process, as Jim Bryans does in his final paragraph. Be sure, of course, that you are not just repeating the introduction. In his conclusion, Jim takes a parting shot at lawyers, declares that he's glad he bought the land, and says that he hopes to repeat the process again someday. You can speculate on the results of completing the process, as Herron does. He concludes that the cat may be angry about his mistreatment, but usually isn't. "As a rule he is simply plotting ways to get through your defenses and injure you for life the next time you decide to give him a bath." His final short, emphatic sentence provides a word of comfort: "But at least now he is clean."

With some topics, you can mention related or complementary processes that your reader might be interested in. If you have just explained how to design a raised-bed vegetable garden, you could close with the suggestion that your readers might like to try the same technique with a butterfly garden. If all else fails, you can give your readers a few cheery words of encouragement. Just one warning: do not mindlessly insist that a process is "fun and easy" when you know it is not. You might lose your credibility. Try "difficult but rewarding" instead.

◆ USING THE MODEL

Although both Bud Herron and Jim Bryans explain processes, their essays are quite different. Herron writes in a humorous tone giving step-by-step instructions. Bryans, after reading that model, chose a serious approach to a slightly different kind of process. His advice about buying land involves not so much steps as stages that occur over a long period of time, but he follows the same chronological organization that Herron does. Because his topic involves legal **jargon,** Jim also includes several definitions that were not necessary in the model explaining how to bathe a cat.

Have you ever done something unusual for a person your age, such as buying land? Or do you know how to perform well some difficult task, like cat bathing? Or do you know how to do something that others might like to learn how to do, like constructing a picnic table or designing a butterfly garden? Would it make an interesting essay?

◆ ◆ ◆ Writer's Workshop II ◆ ◆ ◆
Analyzing Process Writing

Working individually or with a group of classmates, read through James Bryans's essay "Buying Land: Easier Said Than Done," and respond to the following questions.

1. What do you find out about the topic of the essay in the first two paragraphs? Is the thesis stated or implied?
2. Do you think you would be able to follow this process if you decided to buy a piece of land? Are the steps clear? Are there questions you might like to ask the author?
3. How are transitions made between paragraphs? Are there transitional words or phrases within paragraphs?
4. What strategy does Jim use in his conclusion? Can you think of a more effective one?

◆ ◆ ◆ Checklist for Reading and Writing ◆ ◆ ◆
Process Essays

1. Can you identify the process or the purpose of the essay in the introduction?
2. Is there enough background information so that readers will be able to understand the process? Is there perhaps too much?
3. If the process requires equipment or materials, are they listed at the beginning? Is everything necessary included?
4. Are the steps given in chronological order? Are any steps missing? Are reasons given when understanding the reasons for doing a step would be helpful?
5. Is the process easy to follow, or would more transitional devices help? If there are too many transitions, which ones could be omitted?
6. Are all unfamiliar terms defined? Are all instructions specific enough?
7. If there are any *don'ts* or pitfalls involved in this process, are these mentioned?
8. Does the ending give readers a sense of closure?

◆ ◆ ◆ PREPARING TO READ

Have you ever watched a Laurel and Hardy slapstick comedy in which these two try to perform manual labor, such as building a house or hanging wallpaper? Have you ever tried to hang wallpaper yourself? Was your work satisfactory, or could you imagine yourself signing on as one of the Three Stooges?

◆ ◆ ◆

Wall Covering

DERECK WILLIAMSON

A freelance journalist who writes with humor about life and its ironies, Dereck Williamson lives in New Jersey and publishes articles in many popular magazines. He also writes amusing do-it-yourself books full of useful, tongue-in-cheek advice. The following selection, which first appeared in *The Saturday Review,* is taken from *The Complete Book of Pitfalls: A Victim's Guide to Repairs, Maintenance, and Repairing the Maintenance* (1971).

Over the years, starting even before Adolf Hitler, paperhanging has 1 gotten a million laughs. In the movies, great rolls of paper curl up over people who fall off ladders covered with paste as dogs chase cats around the room. It's what advertising copy writers call "a laff riot."

People who have done their own wallpapering rarely even chuckle at 2 the antics on the silver screen. They remember great rolls of curling paper causing them to fall off ladders on dogs and cats covered with paste. (Never mind what modifies what, you picky grammarians; *everything* was covered with paste.)

In recent years the job of wall decorating has become a little easier, 3 but paperhanging is still nothing to be sneezed at. Especially when you're trying to line up the edges.

The most difficult job is preparing the surface. The very thought makes 4 the brain cringe. So many more jobs would get done around the home if you didn't have to "prepare the surface" first. By the time you get a surface prepared, all enthusiasm for the project at hand has disappeared. Remember Uncle Percy who invited you and all the other kids for a Sunday drive? As you gathered around he said, "First we must wash the car. . . ."

Many people have such severe hang-ups about preliminary work that   5
they flee from place to place all their lives, leaving a trail of unprepared surfaces behind them. Or else they tackle the job without preparing the surface.
That's possible in a paperhanging project, but it's not a good idea. Chances
are you'll run into trouble. Putting new paper on old paper is risky unless
the old paper is still adhering firmly. And you know it isn't. Deep in your
heart you know the old paper is loose and cracked and awful.

Too many layers of wallpaper can give a closed-in feeling. Many city   6
apartments have been papered over so many times that there's no room in
the rooms. A good rule of thumb is that if both elbows touch walls—and
you're standing in the room the long way—you should remove all the old
wallpaper and start all over again. However, if you have unusually long elbows, you might possibly get away with one more layer of paper.

To remove old layers of wallpaper you need old clothes, a wide putty   7
knife, and a compulsive urge to destroy. You loosen up the paper either by
soaking it with hot water or using a wallpaper steamer. You rent the latter at
a paint store, not a shipping office.

Do-it-yourself books say the job is messy, but that it goes fast once you   8
start. Only the first part is true. Have you ever heard of a messy job going fast?
You'll be steaming and soaking and scraping and slopping and slushing and
slogging around that room for days. Only two things will relieve the boredom.
The first is the layer by layer discovery of what hideous taste the previous tenants had. The other is the prospect of finding a million dollar bill or an original Van Gogh between the wall and first layer of paper, a logical hiding place
for money and paintings.

As you wield the scraper, be careful not to gouge the walls. Not only will   9
the Van Gogh be ruined, but you'll have to fill up the holes before you put
on the new paper.

Cracks and holes should be filled with spackling compound and sanded   10
smooth after dry. The next step is to apply a coat of wall size, a gluelike substance which seals the surface and also fills in small depressions. Like your
ears and eyes.

Materials you'll need for papering are a paste brush and bucket, a   11
sponge, a plumb line, chalk, a stepladder, a yardstick, scissors, razor blades, a
smoothing brush, a seam roller, and the same putty knife you used for wall-
gouging.

Instructions that come with the wallpaper tell you that a long, clean, flat   12
work surface is essential for preparing the paper. The illustration shows a
smiling man standing at a banquet table, brushing paste on an endless strip
of paper. He is wearing a necktie. Do you know anybody who wears a necktie when he applies wallpaper paste?

Face the fact that paperhanging is a grubby job, and that you won't   13
have enough space to work in. If you're lucky, you'll find room someplace to

set up a lone card table, and you'll make do with that. Afterward, the table   14
won't be any good for card-playing. Each time you shuffle, the bottom card
will stick to the table. You'll have to play with an incomplete deck, stopping
every few hands to steam and scrape cards.

There are formulas for estimating the amount of paper you'll need, but   15
they don't take into account dog and cat damage. Your best bet is to supply
the dealer with your room dimensions, plus window and door measurements,
and a list of household pets. The dealer will give you enough rolls of paper
to do the room. Make sure he has more of the same pattern on hand.

Start papering next to a door. (Don't paper over the door.) From the   16
door frame, measure out a distance of one inch less than the width of the
paper, and make a mark. Then, using the chalked plumb line, snap a perfectly
vertical line against the wall. Then go to bed. That's quite enough for
one day.

When you return to the room several months later, maybe someone   17
will have already papered it. Or taken away the rolls of paper and applied a
decent coat of whitewash. If not, you've got to start hanging the wallpaper.

Cut off a piece from the roll the distance from floor to ceiling plus about
eight inches to allow trimming on the top and bottom. Then lay the paper face
down on the work table and start brushing paste on the back, as the remainder of the roll falls off the table into the fresh bucket of paste.

After plucking out the roll and flinging it against the wall in a blind   18
rage, finish applying paste to the first strip and then start on exposed parts of
your body. Remove your clothes and cover yourself completely with paste.
Now you are ready to (1) go out in the street and dance, or (2) apply the first
strip of paper to the wall. If you choose to be dull and hang paper, here's the
technique:

Carefully line up the first strip so the edge touches the chalk line, and   19
smooth it out against the wall. It helps if you apply the paste on one half of
the paper's length first, fold it over loosely paste side to paste side, and then
do the same thing with the other half. It also helps if you don't lose your head
as you're trying to hold the paper up against the wall and unfold it at the
same time.

Once the paper is lined up, use a smoothing brush or damp sponge to   20
flatten out the strip and remove bubbles and wrinkles. Then carefully trim off
the top and bottom with a razor blade, and wipe off the excess paste.

Some paper comes with untrimmed edges, and you use a long straight-   21
edge to trim off the selvage. That's done while the paper is on the table. Next
time, get smart and buy paper already trimmed.

Each succeeding layer of paper is applied to the wall just a tiny bit away   22
from the preceding one, and then sort of nudged over in place so it matches
up. Press the edges down with the seam roller. Before you put paste on the
next strip, the books say to hold it up against the wall to make sure it will

match up with the other piece. To do this, just pull the roll apart until one hand is up against the ceiling molding and the other hand is against the baseboard. Then go out in the kitchen and eat a bunch of bananas.

Save leftover strips and use them around windows and doors. Remove   23
wall fixtures and switch plates, paper over them, and then cut out the openings later if you can find them. Some people carefully paper each individual switch plate, making sure it exactly fits in with the wall pattern. This type of person Simonizes the inside of his glove compartment, and fills unused pegboard holes with Plastic Wood.

One kind of paper comes with the paste already applied. You put a   24
water trough on the floor, soak each precut strip in the water for a minute, then slowly pull one end out of the trough, unrolling the paper and climbing the ladder and scratching your nose and lighting a cigarette. The trough gets moved along the floor as you apply successive strips. Try to keep your feet out of it.

When you come to the corner, take the paper around to the next wall   25
about an inch. Before starting on the new wall, make another chalk mark if you can find the plumb bob under all that rubble.

In order to paper ceilings it takes two people, both insane. If you're   26
thinking of papering your ceiling you don't need instructions, you need a doctor.

◆ ◆ ◆

FIRST RESPONSES

Do you think Williamson has ever hung wallpaper? Do you think you could put up wallpaper following his directions? Would you want to?

TAKING A CLOSER LOOK

Exploring *Who:* Voice and Tone

1. Point out some examples of exaggeration that contribute to the essay's humorous tone. What other sources of humor do you find in the essay?
2. Who is the intended audience for this piece?
3. How much knowledge does Williamson presume his readers will have of tools and techniques?
4. Are there any words you think he should have defined, even for this audience?

Exploring *What:* Content and Meaning

1. What is the hardest thing about wallpapering? What happens if you skip that difficult step?
2. In several places Williamson offers good advice for making the job go more smoothly. What are a couple of these tips?
3. What is the problem with the standard formulas for estimating how much paper is needed for a wallpapering job?
4. What are a couple of *don'ts* that Williamson mentions? What are a couple of pitfalls? Where does he include a definition?

Exploring *Why:* Purpose

1. Can you tell from the first three introductory paragraphs what Williamson's purpose is? Does he state his thesis or imply it?
2. Locate a couple of places where the author provides reasons for doing or not doing something. Find one example that is seriously intended to help readers understand the process and one that is included just to add to the humor.
3. Paragraph 21 about trimming off selvages is out of place chronologically. Where does it belong in the step-by-step account? Why did Williamson not put it there? Were you bothered by the lapse in chronology? If not, why not?
4. *Using the Internet.* Could you really put up wallpaper following these directions? What elements resemble the format of serious instructions? What elements do not? Look on an Internet site, such as Wallcoverings Online (www.wallcoverings.org/index2.html), that gives serious advice on hanging wallpaper, and compare the instructions.

Exploring *How:* Style and Strategy

1. How does Williamson attempt to get you interested in reading about wallpapering in his first three paragraphs?
2. In two different places (paragraphs 7 and 11), Williamson gives lists of needed equipment. Why doesn't he follow the standard advice for process writing and provide a single list at the beginning?
3. Find two examples of the kind of precise language customarily used in explaining a process.
4. In paragraph 8, he includes a list of six items in a series separated not by commas, in the usual way, but by *ands*. Try inserting *ands* in place of the commas in the long series in paragraph 11. Does the strategy work

there? Why or why not? Now try inserting *and*s to replace the commas in the short series in the opening sentence of paragraph 12.

5. How do you think the technique works there? Can you generalize about what a writer achieves with this strategy? How often do you think it can be used and still be effective?

◆ WRITING FROM READING ASSIGNMENT

In a decidedly humorous tone, "Wall Covering" provides directions and advice for hanging wallpaper. For this writing assignment, think of some process or procedure that you know well enough to explain to others—either seriously or with tongue in cheek. Perhaps you know how to do something that most people don't, like glass blowing or wind surfing. Or maybe you're especially skillful at doing some familiar task, like simonizing a car or making an omelet. Or maybe you're knowledgeable about a process that will help people save money, like negotiating a good price on a new car.

A. Begin by thinking through the process chronologically, from start to finish, jotting down on a piece of paper the steps you go through. Be sure to leave plenty of space between the steps.

B. Then, go over the process again in your mind, focusing this time on any pitfalls or *don't*s or any bits of advice or reasons that might prove useful. Add these in the open spaces where they belong in the time frame. If your explanation would benefit from examples, like those Williamson uses, brainstorm for ideas and write them in where they belong.

C. Now, check over your list of steps or stages one more time to be sure you haven't left anything out.

D. Begin your essay, as Williamson does, by discussing how people normally respond to your process: finding it too difficult, too boring, too time consuming, too comical, or too puzzling. Then let them know that the task is not impossible if they follow your instructions.

E. Now present your process, step by step, following your plan. Be sure to include sufficient reasons, examples, and advice. And don't forget the *don't*s and pitfalls.

F. Close by offering encouragement or by mentioning the advantages of learning this skill.

G. Read what you've written to see whether you've used any words your readers might not be familiar with. If so, define them briefly. Then consult the "Checklist for Reading and Writing Process Essays" (p. 187) to see how well you have fulfilled the criteria for good process writing.

◆ ◆ ◆ PREPARING TO READ

Have you ever been so curious about a natural process, like the wind, the blue sky, blooming flowers, thunder and lightning, that you explored it in depth? Why or why not? If so, what was it? What secrets of nature would you like to know more about?

◆ ◆ ◆

Why Leaves Turn Color in the Fall

DIANE ACKERMAN

Poet, essayist, and naturalist, Diane Ackerman was born in Waukegan, Illinois, in 1948 and received degrees from Pennsylvania State and Cornell universities. Not content to read about life, Ackerman goes out, experiences it, and then writes about it in ways that break down the traditional barriers between poetry and science. In *The Moon by Whale Light* (1991), she relates her adventures among bats, penguins, crocodiles, and whales; in *On Extended Wings* (1985) she recounts her experience of learning to fly a plane. Her most successful book, *A Natural History of the Senses* (1999), has been described as a "voluptuous and fact-filled literary tour of human perception that explores such puzzles as why human beings crave chocolate and how color affects us." The following essay comes from that book.

1   The stealth of autumn catches one unaware. Was that a goldfinch perching in the early September woods, or just the first turning leaf? A red-winged blackbird or a sugar maple closing up shop for the winter? Keen-eyed as leopards, we stand still and squint hard, looking for signs of movement. Early-morning frost sits heavily on the grass, and turns barbed wire into a string of stars. On a distant hill, a small square of yellow appears to be a lighted stage. At last the truth dawns on us: Fall is staggering in, right on schedule, with its baggage of chilly nights, macabre holidays, and spectacular, heart-stoppingly beautiful leaves. Soon the leaves will start cringing on the trees, and roll up in clenched fists before they actually fall off. Dry seedpods will rattle like tiny gourds. But first there will be weeks of gushing color so bright, so pastel, so confettilike, that people will travel up and down the East Coast just to stare at it—a whole season of leaves.

2   Where do the colors come from? Sunlight rules most living things with its golden edicts. When the days begin to shorten, soon after the summer

solstice on June 21, a tree reconsiders its leaves. All summer it feeds them so they can process sunlight, but in the dog days of summer the tree begins pulling nutrients back into its trunk and roots, pares down, and gradually chokes off its leaves. A corky layer of cells forms at the leaves' slender petioles, then scars over. Undernourished, the leaves stop producing the pigment chlorophyll, and photosynthesis ceases. Animals can migrate, hibernate, or store food to prepare for winter. But where can a tree go? It survives by dropping its leaves, and by the end of autumn only a few fragile threads of fluid-carrying xylem hold leaves to their stems.

A turning leaf stays partly green at first, then reveals splotches of yellow and red as the chlorophyll gradually breaks down. Dark green seems to stay longest in the veins, outlining and defining them. During the summer, chlorophyll dissolves in the heat and light, but it is also being steadily replaced. In the fall, on the other hand, no new pigment is produced, and so we notice the other colors that were always there, right in the leaf, although chlorophyll's shocking green hid them from view. With their camouflage gone, we see these colors for the first time all year, and marvel, but they were always there, hidden like a vivid secret beneath the hot glowing greens of summer.   3

The most spectacular range of fall foliage occurs in the northeastern United States and in eastern China, where the leaves are robustly colored, thanks in part to a rich climate. European maples don't achieve the same flaming reds as their American relatives, which thrive on cold nights and sunny days. In Europe, the warm, humid weather turns the leaves brown or mildly yellow. Anthocyanin, the pigment that gives apples their red and turns leaves red or red-violet, is produced by sugars that remain in the leaf after the supply of nutrients dwindles. Unlike the carotenoids, which color carrots, squash, and corn, and turn leaves orange and yellow, anthocyanin varies from year to year, depending on the temperature and amount of sunlight. The fiercest colors occur in years when the fall sunlight is strongest and the nights are cool and dry (a state of grace scientists find vexing to forecast). This is also why leaves appear dizzyingly bright and clear on a sunny fall day: The anthocyanin flashes like a marquee.   4

Not all leaves turn the same colors. Elms, weeping willows, and the ancient ginkgo all grow radiant yellow, along with hickories, aspens, bottlebrush buckeyes, cottonweeds, and tall, keening poplars. Basswood turns bronze, birches bright gold. Water-loving maples put on a symphonic display of scarlets. Sumacs turn red, too, as do flowering dogwoods, black gums, and sweet gums. Though some oaks yellow, most turn a pinkish brown. The farmlands also change color, as tepees of cornstalks and bales of shredded-wheat-textured hay stand drying in the fields. In some spots, one slope of a hill may be green and the other already in bright color, because the hillside facing south gets more sun and heat than the northern one.   5

An odd feature of the colors is that they don't seem to have any spe-   6
cial purpose. We are predisposed to respond to their beauty, of course. They
shimmer with the colors of sunset, spring flowers, the tawny buff of a colt's
pretty rump, the shuddering pink of a blush. Animals and flowers color for a
reason—adaptation to their environment—but there is no adaptive reason
for leaves to color so beautifully in the fall any more than there is for the
sky or ocean to be blue. It's just one of the haphazard marvels the planet be-
stows every year. We find the sizzling colors thrilling, and in a sense they
dupe us. Colored like living things, they signal death and disintegration. In
time, they will become fragile and, like the body, return to dust. They are as
we hope our own fate will be when we die: Not to vanish, just to sublime
from one beautiful state into another. Though leaves lose their green life,
they bloom with urgent colors, as the woods grow mummified day by day,
and Nature becomes more carnal, mute, and radiant.

We call the season "fall," from the Old English *feallan,* to fall, which   7
leads back through time to the Indo-European *phol,* which also means to
fall. So the word and the idea are both extremely ancient, and haven't really
changed since the first of our kind needed a name for fall's leafy abundance.
As we say the word, we're reminded of that other Fall, in the garden of Eden,
when fig leaves never withered and scales fell from our eyes. Fall is the time
when leaves fall from the trees, just as spring is when flowers spring up, summer is when we simmer, and winter is when we whine from the cold.

Children love to play in piles of leaves, hurling them into the air like   8
confetti, leaping into soft unruly mattresses of them. For children, leaf fall is
just one of the odder figments of Nature, like hailstones or snowflakes. Walk
down a lane overhung with trees in the never-never land of autumn, and you
will forget about time and death, lost in the sheer delicious spill of color.
Adam and Eve concealed their nakedness with leaves, remember? Leaves
have always hidden our awkward secrets.

But how do the colored leaves fall? As a leaf ages, the growth hormone,   9
auxin, fades, and cells at the base of the petiole divide. Two or three rows of
small cells, lying at right angles to the axis of the petiole, react with water, then
come apart, leaving the petioles hanging on by only a few threads of xylem.
A light breeze, and the leaves are airborne. They glide and swoop, rocking in
invisible cradles. They are all wing and may flutter from yard to yard on small
whirlwinds or updrafts, swiveling as they go. Firmly tethered to earth, we
love to see things rise up and fly—soap bubbles, balloons, birds, fall leaves.
They remind us that the end of a season is capricious, as is the end of life. We
especially like the way leaves rock, careen, and swoop as they fall. Everyone
knows the motion. Pilots sometimes do a maneuver called a "falling leaf," in
which the plane loses altitude quickly and on purpose, by slipping first to the
right, then to the left. The machine weighs a ton or more, but in one pilot's
mind it is a weightless thing, a falling leaf. She has seen the motion before, in

the Vermont woods where she played as a child. Below her the trees radiate gold, copper, and red. Leaves are falling, although she can't see them fall, as she falls, swooping down for a closer view.

At last the leaves leave. But first they turn color and thrill us for weeks   10
on end. Then they crunch and crackle underfoot. They *shush,* as children drag their small feet through leaves heaped along the curb. Dark, slimy mats of leaves cling to one's heels after a rain. A damp, stuccolike mortar of semi-decayed leaves protects the tender shoots with a roof until spring, and makes a rich humus. An occasional bulge or ripple in the leafy mounds signals a shrew or a field mouse tunneling out of sight. Sometimes one finds in fossil stones the imprint of a leaf, long since disintegrated, whose outlines remind us how detailed, vibrant, and alive are the things of this earth that perish.

◆ ◆ ◆

FIRST RESPONSES

Has gaining knowledge about why leaves change color affected your appreciation of their beauty? Explain.

TAKING A CLOSER LOOK

Exploring *Who:* Voice and Tone

1. ◼ *Using the Internet.* How does Ackerman's account seem different from what you would expect to read in a science textbook? What audience is Ackerman writing for? Visit a Web site for a children's science museum (for example, the Brigham Young University Earth Science Museum), and compare that approach with Ackerman's.

2. What does Ackerman do in her opening paragraph to draw you into her topic?

3. In what ways does the author communicate her enthusiasm for the natural world?

Exploring *What:* Content and Meaning

1. What causes leaves to change color? Why do trees turn color at different rates? What causes some leaves to be particularly bright some years?

2. Were there any facts about the color changing process that surprised you?

3. What is the purpose of the colors? Why does Ackerman call it "odd"?
4. What other process does the author describe? How are the two processes related?

Exploring *Why:* Purpose

1. What is Ackerman's purpose in this essay? Is it simply to provide information? What other purpose(s) might she have in mind?
2. In an interview, Ackerman once said, "One of the things that all artists have to do is to find the extraordinary in the everyday and the commonplace and familiar in the extraordinary." In what ways has she accomplished those goals in this essay?

Exploring *How:* Style and Structure

1. In paragraph 7, Ackerman discusses the origin and meaning of the word *fall.* Why does she include this definition? How does it relate to the rest of the essay?
2. Ackerman is widely regarded as a gifted poet. Find several examples of **similes, metaphors, images, personification,** and other poetic language in this essay. How do these poetic descriptions contribute to the essay's success and intention?
3. Reread the final sentence. What does the author mean? Why has she chosen to end her essay in this way?

IDEAS FOR WRITING A PROCESS ANALYSIS

1. Research any other natural process, and explain it in a way that almost anyone could understand. Some possibilities: how a tornado forms, why bees swarm, why hair turns gray, what causes lightning, how a caterpillar transforms into a butterfly, why the sky changes color at sunset.
2. ■⌐ *Using the Internet.* Write an essay advising how to avoid some contagious disease, such as the common cold, influenza, tuberculosis, or AIDS. You can gather details from a medical Web site, such as the Mayo Clinic Health Oasis (www.mayohealth.org).
3. Explain for a nonspecialized audience how a tool or mechanical object works or how to get maximum performance from it. Such as: a racing bicycle, a particular exercise machine, a power tool, a kitchen implement, a spreadsheet, a particular computer program, management of a particular small business, an election campaign.

◆ ◆ ◆ PREPARING TO READ

Have you ever attended a funeral at which the body was displayed? What was your reaction? Did you think the deceased looked "lifelike"? Did you notice what the casket looked like? Did you pay any attention to the clothing of the deceased?

◆ ◆ ◆

Embalming Mr. Jones

JESSICA MITFORD

Born in England to a prominent family, Jessica Mitford (1917–1996) spoke of herself as uneducated because, having always been privately tutored by governesses, she had no diplomas. She became a U.S. citizen in 1944 and began an illustrious career as an investigative journalist—a muckraker, as she described her vocation. Mitford never shrank from the controversial or gruesome. *The Trial of Dr. Spock* (1969) describes the trial of pediatrician Benjamin Spock for assisting Vietnam War draft resisters, *Kind and Usual Punishment* (1973) is an indictment of the U.S. penal system, and *The American Way of Birth* (1992) critiques the unnecessary expenses associated with childbirth. In her influential exposé of the funeral industry, *The American Way of Death* (1963), from which the following excerpt is taken, she ridicules the irrational and expensive process of preparing corpses for viewing.

The drama begins to unfold with the arrival of the corpse at the 1 mortuary.

Alas, poor Yorick! How surprised he would be to see how his counter- 2 part of today is whisked off to a funeral parlor and is in short order, sprayed, sliced, pierced, pickled, trussed, trimmed, creamed, waxed, painted, rouged, and neatly dressed—transformed from a common corpse into a Beautiful Memory Picture. This process is known in the trade as embalming and restorative art, and is so universally employed in the United States and Canada that the funeral director does it routinely, without consulting corpse or kin. He regards as eccentric those few who are hardy enough to suggest that it might be dispensed with. Yet no law requires embalming, no religious doctrine commends it, nor is it dictated by considerations of health, sanitation, or even of personal daintiness. In no part of the world but in Northern America is it widely used. The purpose of embalming is to make the corpse presentable for viewing in a suitably costly container; and here too the funeral director routinely, without first consulting the family, prepares the body for public display.

Is all this legal? The processes to which a dead body may be subjected are after all to some extent circumscribed by law. In most states, for instance, the signature of next of kin must be obtained before an autopsy may be performed, before the deceased may be cremated, before the body may be turned over to a medical school for research purposes; or such provision must be made in the decedent's will. In the case of embalming, no such permission is required nor is it ever sought. A textbook, *The Principles and Practices of Embalming,* comments on this: "There is some question regarding the legality of much that is done within the preparation room." The author points out that it would be most unusual for a responsible member of a bereaved family to instruct the mortician, in so many words, to "*embalm*" the body of a deceased relative. The very term *embalming* is so seldom used that the mortician must rely upon custom in the matter. The author concludes that unless the family specifies otherwise, the act of entrusting the body to the care of a funeral establishment carries with it an implied permission to go ahead and embalm.

Embalming is indeed a most extraordinary procedure, and one must wonder at the docility of Americans who each year pay hundreds of millions of dollars for its perpetuation, blissfully ignorant of what it is all about, what is done, how it is done. Not one in ten thousand has any idea of what actually takes place. Books on the subject are extremely hard to come by. They are not to be found in most libraries or bookshops.

In an era when huge television audiences watch surgical operations in the comfort of their living rooms, when, thanks to the animated cartoon, the geography of the digestive system has become familiar territory even to the nursery school set, in a land where the satisfaction of curiosity about all matters is a national pastime, the secrecy surrounding embalming can, surely, hardly be attributed to the inherent gruesomeness of the subject. Custom in this regard has within this century suffered a complete reversal. In the early days of American embalming, when it was performed in the home of the deceased, it was almost mandatory for some relative to stay by the embalmer's side and witness the procedure. Today, family members who might wish to be in attendance would certainly be dissuaded by the funeral director. All others, except apprentices, are excluded by law from the preparation room.

A close look at what does actually take place may explain in large measure the undertaker's intractable reticence concerning a procedure that has become his major *raison d'être.* Is it possible he fears that public information about embalming might lead patrons to wonder if they really want this service? If the funeral men are loath to discuss the subject outside the trade, the reader may, understandably, be equally loath to go on reading at this point. For those who have the stomach for it, let us part the formaldehyde curtain. . . .

The body is first laid out in the undertaker's morgue—or rather, Mr. 7
Jones is reposing in the preparation room—to be readied to bid the world farewell.

The preparation room in any of the better funeral establishments has 8
the tiled and sterile look of a surgery, and indeed the embalmer-restorative artist who does his chores there is beginning to adopt the term "dermasurgeon" (appropriately corrupted by some mortician-writers as "demisurgeon") to describe his calling. His equipment, consisting of scalpels, scissors, augers, forceps, clamps, needles, pumps, tubes, bowls and basins, is crudely imitative of the surgeon's, as is his technique, acquired in a nine- or twelve-month post-high-school course in an embalming school. He is supplied by an advanced chemical industry with a bewildering array of fluids, sprays, pastes, oils, powders, creams, to fix or soften tissue, shrink or distend it as needed, dry it here, restore the moisture there. There are cosmetics, waxes, and paints to fill and cover features, even plaster of Paris to replace entire limbs. There are ingenious aids to prop and stabilize the cadaver: a Van-Pose Head Rest, the Edwards Arm and Hand Positioner, the Repose Block (to support the shoulders during the embalming), and the Throop Foot Positioner, which resembles an old-fashioned stocks.

Mr. John H. Eckels, president of the Eckels College of Mortuary Sci- 9
ence, thus describes the first part of the embalming procedure: "In the hands of a skilled practitioner, this work may be done in a comparatively short time and without mutilating the body other than by slight incision—so slight that it scarcely would cause serious inconvenience if made upon a living person. It is necessary to remove the blood, and doing this not only helps in the disinfecting, but removes the principal cause of disfigurements due to discoloration."

Another textbook discusses the all-important time element: "The ear- 10
lier this is done, the better, for every hour that elapses between death and embalming will add to the problems and complications encountered. . . ." Just how soon should one get going on the embalming? The author tells us, "On the basis of such scanty information made available to this profession through its rudimentary and haphazard system of technical research, we must conclude that the best results are to be obtained if the subject is embalmed before life is completely extinct—that is, before cellular death has occurred. In the average case, this would mean within an hour after somatic death." For those who feel that there is something a little rudimentary, not to say

haphazard, about this advice, a comforting thought is offered by another writer. Speaking of fears entertained in early days of premature burial, he points out, "One of the effects of embalming by chemical injection, however, has been to dispel fears of live burial." How true; once the blood is removed, chances of live burial are indeed remote.

To return to Mr. Jones, the blood is drained out through the veins and   11 replaced by embalming fluid pumped in through the arteries. As noted in *The Principles and Practices of Embalming*, "every operator has a favorite injection and drainage point—a fact which becomes a handicap only if he fails or refuses to forsake his favorites when conditions demand it." Typical favorites are the carotid artery, femoral artery, jugular vein, subclavian vein. There are various choices of embalming fluid. If Flextone is used, it will produce a "mild, flexible rigidity. The skin retains a velvety softness, the tissues are rubbery and pliable. Ideal for women and children." It may be blended with B. and G. Products Company's Lyf-Lyk tint, which is guaranteed to reproduce "nature's own skin texture . . . the velvety appearance of living tissue." Suntone comes in three separate tints: Suntan; Special Cosmetic Tint, a pink shade "especially indicated for young female subjects"; and Regular Cosmetic Tint, moderately pink.

About three to six gallons of a dyed and perfumed solution of formalde-   12 hyde, glycerin, borax, phenol, alcohol, and water is soon circulating through Mr. Jones, whose mouth has been sewn together with a "needle directed upward between the upper lip and gum and brought out through the left nostril," with the corners raised slightly "for a more pleasant expression." If he should be bucktoothed, his teeth are cleaned with Bon Ami and coated with colorless nail polish. His eyes, meanwhile, are closed with flesh-tinted eye caps and eye cement.

The next step is to have at Mr. Jones with a thing called a trocar. This   13 is a long, hollow needle attached to a tube. It is jabbed into the abdomen, poked around the entrails and chest cavity, the contents of which are pumped out and replaced with "cavity fluid." This done, and the hole in the abdomen sewn up, Mr. Jones's face is heavily creamed (to protect the skin from burns which may be caused by leakage of the chemicals), and he is covered with a sheet and left unmolested for a while. But not for long—there is more, much more, in store for him. He has been embalmed, but not yet restored, and the best time to start the restorative work is eight to ten hours after embalming, when the tissues have become firm and dry.

The object of all this attention to the corpse, it must be remembered,   14 is to make it presentable for viewing in an attitude of healthy repose. "Our customs require the presentation of our dead in the semblance of normality . . . unmarred by the ravages of illness, disease or mutilation," says Mr. J. Sheridan Mayer in his *Restorative Art*. This is a rather large order since few people die in the full bloom of health, unravaged by illness and unmarked by some disfigurement. The funeral industry is equal to the challenge: "In some cases the gruesome appearance of a mutilated or disease-ridden subject may be quite discouraging. The task of restoration may seem impossible and shake the confidence of the embalmer. This is the time for intestinal fortitude and determination. Once the formative work is begun and affected tissues are cleaned or removed, all doubts of success vanish. It is surprising and gratifying to discover the results which may be obtained."

The embalmer, having allowed an appropriate interval to elapse, returns to the attack, but now he brings into play the skill and equipment of sculptor and cosmetician. Is a hand missing? Casting one in plaster of Paris is a simple matter. "For replacement purposes, only a cast of the back of the hand is necessary; this is within the ability of the average operator and is quite adequate." If a lip or two, a nose or an ear should be missing, the embalmer has at hand a variety of restorative waxes with which to model replacements. Pores and skin texture are simulated by stippling with a little brush, and over this cosmetics are laid on. Head off? Decapitation cases are rather routinely handled. Ragged edges are trimmed, and head joined to torso with a series of splints, wires and sutures. It is a good idea to have a little something at the neck—a scarf or high collar—when time for viewing comes. Swollen mouth? Cut out tissue as needed from inside the lips. If too much is removed, the surface contour can easily be restored by padding with cotton. Swollen necks and cheeks are reduced by removing tissue through vertical incisions made down each side of the neck. "When the deceased is casketed, the pillow will hide the suture incisions . . . as an extra precaution against leakage, the suture may be painted with liquid sealer." 15

The opposite condition is more likely to present itself—that of emaciation. His hypodermic syringe now loaded with massage cream, the embalmer seeks out and fills the hollowed and sunken areas by injection. In this procedure the backs of the hands and fingers and the under-chin area should not be neglected. 16

Positioning the lips is a problem that recurrently challenges the ingenuity of the embalmer. Closed too tightly they tend to give a stern, even disapproving expression. Ideally, embalmers feel, the lips should give the impression of being ever so slightly parted, the upper lip protruding slightly for a more youthful appearance. This takes some engineering, however, as the lips tend to drift apart. Lip drift can sometimes be remedied by pushing one or two straight pins through the inner margin of the lower lip and then inserting them between the two upper front teeth. If Mr. Jones happens to have no teeth, the pins can just as easily be anchored in his Armstrong Face Former and Denture Replacer. Another method to maintain lip closure is to dislocate the lower jaw, which is then held in its new position by a wire run through holes which have been drilled through the upper and lower jaws at the midline. As the French are fond of saying, *il faut soffrir pour être belle.* 17

If Mr. Jones has died of jaundice, the embalming fluid will very likely   18
turn him green. Does this deter the embalmer? Not if he has intestinal fortitude. Masking pastes and cosmetics are heavily laid on, burial garments and
casket interiors are color-correlated with particular care, and Jones is displayed beneath rose-colored lights. Friends will say, "How *well* he looks."
Death by carbon monoxide, on the other hand, can be rather a good thing
from the embalmer's viewpoint: "One advantage is the fact that this type
of discoloration is an exaggerated form of a natural pink coloration." This
is nice because the healthy glow is already present and needs but little
attention.

The patching and filling completed, Mr. Jones is now shaved, washed,   19
and dressed. Cream-based cosmetic, available in pink, flesh, suntan, brunette,
and blond, is applied to his hands and face, his hair is shampooed and combed
(and, in the case of Mrs. Jones, set), his hands manicured. For the horny-
handed son of toil special care must be taken; cream should be applied to remove ingrained grime, and the nails cleaned. "If he were not in the habit of
having them manicured in life, trimming and shaping is advised for better
appearance—never questioned by kin."

Jones is now ready for casketing (this is the present participle of the   20
verb "to casket"). In this operation his right shoulder should be depressed
slightly "to turn the body a bit to the right and soften the appearance of lying
flat on the back." Positioning the hands is a matter of importance, and special rubber positioning blocks may be used. The hands should be cupped
slightly for a more lifelike, relaxed appearance. Proper placement of the body
requires a delicate sense of balance. It should lie as high as possible in the casket, yet not so high that the lid, when lowered, will hit the nose. On the other
hand, we are cautioned, placing the body too low "creates the impression
that the body is in a box."

Jones is next wheeled into the appointed slumber room where a few last   21
touches may be added—his favorite pipe placed in his hand or, if he was a
great reader, a book propped into position. (In the case of little Master Jones
a Teddy bear may be clutched.) Here he will hold open house for a few days,
visiting hours 10 A.M. to 9 P.M.

◆ ◆ ◆

FIRST RESPONSES

Have you ever been involved in planning a funeral? How rational was
your thinking at the time? Did you or anyone else question the suggestions
of the person "selling" the services? What was the family's reaction when
the bill came? How would you feel about preplanning a funeral?

TAKING A CLOSER LOOK

Exploring *Who:* Voice and Tone

1. Clearly, Mitford is serious in her criticism of the practice of making a corpse "presentable for viewing in an attitude of healthy repose" (para. 14), but most people would not describe her tone as serious. Why not? What adjectives would you choose to describe Mitford's tone, that is, her attitude toward her topic?

2. Most readers find this piece quite funny, despite its grim subject matter. Point out several examples of humor, and explain what makes it funny. For instance, in paragraph 18, Mitford observes that "Death by carbon monoxide, on the other hand, can be rather a good thing from the embalmer's viewpoint." That statement is humorous because of the abrupt contrast between what the reader expects and what the embalmer expects. Death by carbon monoxide is definitely not "rather a good thing" for most of us average readers.

Exploring *What:* Content and Meaning

1. Who was the "poor Yorick" alluded to at the beginning of the second paragraph?

2. What does Mitford say is the purpose of embalming?

3. In paragraph 5, we are told that "All others, except apprentices, are excluded by law from the preparation room." Why do you think a law was passed preventing family members from being present while embalming takes place?

4. Did you learn more about embalming than you really wanted to know? Why do you think Mitford included so many gruesome details?

5. Explain this metaphor at the end of paragraph 6: "let us part the formaldehyde curtain. . . ." What does it mean, and how does it function as a transition?

6. Mitford makes clear that embalming is not required either by law or by religious doctrine. Why, then, do you think people continue to pay exorbitant prices for extravagant funerals that sometimes the family cannot afford?

Exploring *Why:* Purpose

1. Why do you think Mitford wrote this piece? What was she hoping to accomplish?

2. What is her purpose in mentioning and quoting from textbooks like *The Principles and Practices of Embalming?*

3. Do you agree with Mitford when she says that "the secrecy surrounding embalming can, surely, hardly be attributed to the inherent gruesomeness of the subject" (para. 5)? What does Mitford think is the reason for the secrecy? Can you think of anything else that might account for this lack of knowledge by the public?

4. Did you find Mitford's satirical approach effective?

Exploring *How:* Style and Strategy

1. After a fairly long introduction, in which Mitford questions the whole practice of embalming, she begins an explanation of the process involved in preparing a body for public viewing. But several times she departs from her step-by-step account to provide relevant information. Explain why she includes the digression in paragraph 8, for instance.

2. Successful **satire** hinges largely on appropriate word choice. Comment on the effect Mitford achieves with these words and phrases: "whisked off" (para. 2); "sprayed, sliced, pierced, pickled, trussed, trimmed, creamed, waxed, painted, rouged, and neatly dressed" (para. 2); "a suitably costly container" (para. 2); "blissfully ignorant" (para. 4); "to have at Mr. Jones" (para. 13); "returns to the attack" (para. 15); "head off?" (para. 15); "the patching and filling completed" (para. 19).

3. Besides the usual transitional words used in process writing *(first, to return to, the next step is, is now, next),* Mitford uses several rhetorical questions. Find three of these questions, and explain how they function.

4. In paragraph 14, Mitford quotes textbook author J. Sheridan Mayer as saying, "This is the time for intestinal fortitude and determination." In paragraph 18, she repeats his "intestinal fortitude" phrase. What does she achieve with this repetition?

5. How does Mitford subtly echo her introduction in her conclusion? Comment on her verbal strategies in the final paragraph. In other words, how does her word choice make the ending effective?

IDEAS FOR WRITING A PROCESS ANALYSIS

1. With a group of classmates, discuss some social ritual that can make people uncomfortable, such as family reunions, holiday dinners, or class reunions. Jot down details as they come to you during this brainstorming session. Then organize your ideas chronologically, and write a satire similar to Jessica Mitford's in which you criticize or make

fun of the process people typically are expected to go through on these occasions.

2. ■⬛ *Using the Internet.* Mitford's essay was influential in modifying the business practices of the funeral industry and in prompting alternative funeral plans. Locate the Web site of the Funeral Consumers Alliance (www.funerals.org) for information about burial societies and nonprofit funeral groups. Then write an account of the process you might go through today if you were using the help of a burial society to plan the funeral of Mr. Jones.

3. Think of a modern custom or practice that you approve of. Write an essay in which you analyze the way the custom or practice proceeds. Following Mitford's model, explain the process clearly while conveying your attitude toward it at the same time.

◆ ◆ ◆ PREPARING TO READ

How do you feel when you receive a letter? Does anyone regularly write to you? To whom do you write, and why? Do you send your letters through cyberspace, or do you use "snail mail"?

◆ ◆ ◆

How to Write a Personal Letter

GARRISON KEILLOR

Garrison Keillor (born in 1942) is the host of *A Prairie Home Companion* broadcast on National Public Radio. He is famous for his spoken essays reporting the "News from Lake Wobegon," a make-believe Minnesota town where "all the men are strong, all the women are good-looking, and all the children are above average." Listeners are delighted by the charming quirkiness of the everyday lives of Lake Wobegon's citizens. In the following essay, reprinted from his book, *We Are Still Married* (1989), Keillor gives advice and encouragement to letter writers in the same warm, neighborly voice that characterizes his popular radio show.

We shy persons need to write a letter now and then, or else we'll dry up 1 and blow away. It's true. And I speak as one who loves to reach for the phone, dial the number, and talk. The telephone is to shyness what Hawaii is to February; it's a way out of the woods. *And yet:* a letter is better.

Such a sweet gift—a piece of handmade writing, in an envelope that is 2 not a bill, sitting in our friend's path when she trudges home from a long day spent among wahoos and savages, a day our words will help repair. They don't need to be immortal, just sincere. She can read them twice and again tomorrow: *You're someone I care about, Corinne, and think of often, and every time I do, you make me smile.*

We need to write; otherwise nobody will know who we are. They will 3 have only a vague impression of us as A Nice Person, because, frankly, we don't shine at conversation, we lack the confidence to thrust our faces forward and say, "Hi, I'm Heather Hooten; let me tell you about my week." Mostly we say "Uh-huh" and "Oh really." People smile and look over our shoulder, looking for someone else to meet.

So a shy person sits down and writes a letter. To be known by another 4 person—to meet and talk freely on the page—to be close despite distance. To escape from anonymity and be our own sweet selves and express the music of our souls.

Same thing that moves a giant rock star to sing his heart out in front of 123,000 people moves us to take ballpoint in hand and write a few lines to our dear Aunt Eleanor. *We want to be known.* We want her to know that we have fallen in love, that we quit our job, that we're moving to New York, and we want to say a few things that might not get said in casual conversation: *Thank you for what you've meant to me. I am very happy right now.* 5

The first step in writing letters is to get over the guilt of *not* writing. You don't "owe" anybody a letter. Letters are a gift. The burning shame you feel when you see unanswered mail makes it harder to pick up a pen and makes for a cheerless letter when you finally do. *I feel bad about not writing, but I've been so busy,* etc. Skip this. Few letters are obligatory, and they are *Thanks for the wonderful gift* and *I am terribly sorry to hear about George's death* and *Yes, you're welcome to stay with us next month.* Write these promptly if you want to keep your friends. Don't worry about the others, except love letters, of course. When your true love writes *Dear Light of My Life, Joy of My Heart, O Lovely Pulsating Core of My Sensate Life,* some response is called for. 6

Some of the best letters are tossed off in a burst of inspiration, so keep your writing stuff in one place where you can sit down for a few minutes and—*Dear Roy, I am in the middle of an essay but thought I'd drop you a line. Hi to your sweetie too*—dash off a note to a pal. Envelopes, stamps, address book, everything in a drawer so you can write fast when the pen is hot. 7

A blank white 8″ × 11″ sheet can look as big as Montana if the pen's not so hot—try a smaller page and write boldly. Get a pen that makes a sensuous line, get a comfortable typewriter, a friendly word processor—whichever feels easy to the hand. 8

Sit for a few minutes with the blank sheet of paper in front of you, and meditate on the person you will write to, let your friend come to mind until you can almost see her or him in the room with you. Remember the last time you saw each other and how your friend looked and what you said and what perhaps was unsaid between you, and when your friend becomes real to you, start to write. 9

Write the salutation—*Dear* You—and take a deep breath and plunge in. A simple declarative sentence will do, followed by another and another. Tell us what you're doing and tell it like you were talking to us. Don't think about grammar, don't think about style, don't try to write dramatically, just give us your news. Where did you go, who did you see, what did they say, what do you think? 10

If you don't know where to begin, start with the present: *I'm sitting at the kitchen table on a rainy Saturday morning. Everyone is gone and the house is quiet.* Let your simple description of the present moment lead to something else; let the letter drift gently along. 11

The toughest letter to crank out is one that is meant to impress, as we all know from writing job applications; if it's hard work to slip off a letter to 12 a friend, maybe you're trying too hard to be terrific. A letter is only a report to someone who already likes you for reasons other than your brilliance. Take it easy.

Don't worry about form. It's not a term paper. When you come to the end of one episode, just start a new paragraph. You can go from a few lines about the sad state of pro football to the fight with your mother to your fond memories of Mexico to your cat's urinary-tract infection to a few thoughts on personal indebtedness and on to the kitchen sink and what's in it. The more you write, the easier it gets, and when you have a True True Friend to write to, a *compadre,* a soul sibling, then it's like driving a car; you just press on the gas.

Don't tear up the page and start over when you write a bad line—try to write your way out of it. Make mistakes and plunge on. Let the letter cook along and let yourself be bold. Outrage, confusion, love—whatever is in your mind, let it find a way to the page. Writing is a means of discovery, always, and when you come to the end and write *Yours ever* or *Hugs and Kisses,* you'll know something you didn't when you wrote *Dear Pal.*

Probably your friend will put your letter away, and it'll be read again a few years from now—and it will improve with age. And forty years from now, your friend's grandkids will dig it out of the attic and read it, a sweet and precious relic of the ancient Eighties that gives them a sudden clear glimpse of you and her and the world we old-timers knew. You will have then created an object of art. Your simple lines about where you went, who you saw, what they said, will speak to those children, and they will feel in their hearts the humanity of our times.

You can't pick up a phone and call the future and tell them about our times. You have to pick up a piece of paper.

◆ ◆ ◆

FIRST RESPONSES

After reading Keillor's essay, are you encouraged to write a letter to a friend or loved one instead of making a phone call? Explain why or why not.

TAKING A CLOSER LOOK

Exploring *Who:* Voice and Tone

1. In his opening sentence, Keillor adopts the persona (the voice and characteristics) of a shy person. What does he achieve by assuming that role?

2. What three adjectives would you choose to best describe his tone?

3. Did you feel included in Keillor's audience? Explain why or why not.

4. Does this writing style strike you as formal or informal? Point out words and phrases that influenced your decision. Why do you think Keillor made this choice about level of formality?

Exploring *What:* Content and Meaning

1. ▣ *Using the Internet.* Why does Keillor think we should write letters instead of just make phone calls? Do you think he would consider an e-mail message as valuable as a letter written on paper? Take a look at the Web site called A Beginner's Guide to Effective E-mail (www.web-foot.com/advice/email.top.html), and compare the suggestions there with Keillor's. Do you find any common ground?

2. What does Keillor suggest are the main problems people have in getting around to writing letters? Do you think that perhaps e-mail would help avoid some of these problems?

3. After telling his readers in paragraph 6 that "Few letters are obligatory," Keillor names three kinds that are. What are they? Have you ever written any of these kinds of letters? If so, which kind was the hardest to write?

4. In general, his advice in paragraphs 8 through 14 applies to the kind of writing you are doing in this class. If you were going to revise that section as instruction to help a classmate, what would you change or leave out—besides the *Dear Pal* and the *Hugs and Kisses* parts? What two important steps would you need to add at the end to keep your classmate from flunking the course?

Exploring *Why:* Purpose

1. What would you say is Keillor's main point in this essay?

2. Why do you think Keillor cares whether people write letters or not?

3. Do you think his strategy of addressing himself primarily to shy people was a wise choice, given his purpose?

4. If you are not a shy person, did you find the essay convincing?

Exploring *How:* Style and Strategy

1. Keillor mentions several fictitious persons in this essay (*Corinne, Heather Hooten, our dear Aunt Eleanor*). What does he achieve with this strategy?

2. Make a brief list of Keillor's pieces of advice. What is the reasoning behind the order he uses? Explain how this organization suits his purpose.

3. What is the purpose of the lines and phrases printed in italics? Were you confused by them, or do you think it was a clever strategy?

4. Locate five sentences of six words or fewer, and explain what Keillor achieves with each one.

IDEAS FOR WRITING A PROCESS ANALYSIS

1. In the reading, Keillor advocates writing a letter, even when a phone call is possible. Write an essay in which you promote doing something in the old-fashioned way even though new ways are available. Think about writing by hand rather than on a word processor, baking bread, sewing clothes, building furniture, doing math without a calculator, walking to work, mowing the lawn, raking the leaves, or rowing your boat.

2. Try writing a letter to a friend, using Keillor's advice if you want. At the same time, take notes on how you perform the task. Record the thoughts and feelings that you experience along the way as well as the techniques you use. Then write an essay recounting the process of writing the letter. Put direct quotations from the letter in italics to illustrate your points.

3. Keillor asserts that "writing is a means of discovery" (para. 14). Write an essay about a piece of writing you once did (or tried to do) that led you to an unexpected discovery. The discovery could be about yourself, about the writing process, about the subject matter, about the intended audience, about the assignment, or about a combination of things.

◆ ◆ ◆ **PREPARING TO READ**

What are the best French fries you've ever tasted? Why were they so good? Can you explain why some fries taste better than others?

◆ ◆ ◆

The Trouble with French Fries

MALCOLM GLADWELL

Malcolm Galdwell was born in England in 1963 and grew up in Canada. He graduated from the University of Toronto and spent nine years as a reporter for the *Washington Post,* first as a science writer and then as New York City bureau chief. He's been a staff writer for *The New Yorker* since 1996; his work has also appeared in the *New Republic,* the *Spectator,* and *Vogue.* Praised for his ability to explain the complicated in an engaging way, Gladwell has written about such diverse topics as risk theory, retail fashion marketing, early childhood development, health care reform, and the care of the elderly. His book *The Tipping Point* (2000) examines why major changes in society often happen suddenly and unexpectedly. The following article appeared in *The New Yorker* in March 2001.

Ray Kroc was the great visionary of American fast food, the one who   1
brought the lessons of the manufacturing world to the restaurant business. Before the fifties, it was impossible, in most American towns, to buy fries of consistent quality. Ray Kroc was the man who changed that. "The french fry" he once wrote, "would become almost sacrosanct for me, its preparation a ritual to be followed religiously." A potato that has too great a percentage of water—and potatoes, even the standard Idaho russet burbank, vary widely in their water content—will come out soggy at the end of the frying process. It was Kroc, back in the fifties, who sent out field men, armed with hydrometers, to make sure that all his suppliers were producing potatoes in the optimal solids range of twenty to twenty-three per cent. Freshly harvested potatoes, furthermore, are rich in sugars, and if you slice them up and deep-fry them the sugars will caramelize and brown the outside of the fry long before the inside is cooked. To make a crisp French fry, a potato has to be stored at a warm temperature for several weeks in order to convert those sugars to starch. Here Kroc led the way as well, mastering the art of "curing" potatoes by storing them under a giant fan in the basement of his first restaurant, outside Chicago.

Perhaps his most enduring achievement, though, was the so-called 2 potato computer—developed for McDonald's by a former electrical engineer for Motorola named Louis Martino—which precisely calibrated the optimal cooking time for a batch of fries[. . .]. Previously, making high-quality French fries had been an art. The potato computer, the hydrometer, and the curing bins made it a science. By the time Kroc was finished, he had figured out how to turn potatoes into an inexpensive snack that would always be hot, salty, flavorful, and crisp, no matter where or when you bought it.

This was the first fast-food revolution—the mass production of food 3 that had reliable mass appeal. But today as the McDonald's franchise approaches its fiftieth anniversary, it is clear that fast food needs a second revolution. As many Americans now die every year from obesity-related illnesses—heart disease and complications of diabetes—as from smoking, and the fast-food toll grows heavier every year[. . .]. Ray Kroc's French fries are killing us.

Fast-food French fries are made from a baking potato like an Idaho 4 russet, or any other variety that is mealy, or starchy, rather than waxy. The potatoes are harvested, cured, washed, peeled, sliced, and then blanched— cooked enough so that the insides have a fluffy texture but not so much that the fry gets soft and breaks. Blanching is followed by drying, and drying by a thirty-second deep fry, to give the potatoes a crisp shell. Then the fries are frozen until the moment of service, when they are deep-fried again, this time for somewhere around three minutes. Depending on the fast-food chain involved, there are other steps interspersed in this process. McDonald's fries, for example, are briefly dipped in a sugar solution, which gives them their golden-brown color; Burger King fries are dipped in a starch batter, which is what gives those fries their distinctive hard shell and audible crunch. But the result is similar. The potato that is first harvested in the field is roughly eighty per cent water. The process of creating a French fry consists, essentially, of removing as much of that water as possible—through blanching, drying, and deep-frying—and replacing it with fat.

Elisabeth Rozin, in her book *The Primal Cheeseburger,* points out that 5 the idea of enriching carbohydrates with fat is nothing new. It's a standard part of the cuisine of almost every culture. Bread is buttered; macaroni comes with cheese; dumplings are fried; potatoes are scalloped, baked with milk and cheese, cooked in the dripping of roasting meat, mixed with mayonnaise in a salad, or pan-fried in butterfat as latkes. But, as Rozin argues, deep-frying is in many ways the ideal method of adding fat to carbohydrates. If you put butter on a mashed potato, for instance, the result is texturally unexciting: it simply creates a mush. Pan-frying results in uneven browning and crispness. But when a potato is deep-fried, the heat of the oil turns the water inside the potato into steam, which causes the hard granules of starch inside the potato to swell and soften: that's why the inside of the fry is fluffy and light. At the same time, the outward migration of the steam limits the amount of oil that seeps into the interior, preventing the fry from getting greasy and concentrating the oil on the surface, where it turns the outer layer of the potato brown and crisp[. . .].

This is the trouble with the French fry. The fact that it is cooked in fat   6 makes it unhealthy. But the contrast that deep-frying creates between its interior and its exterior—between the golden shell and the pillowy whiteness beneath—is what makes it so irresistible. The average American now eats a staggering thirty pounds of French fries a year, up from four pounds when Ray Kroc was first figuring out how to mass-produce a crisp fry. Meanwhile, fries themselves have become less healthful. Ray Kroc, in the early days of McDonald's, was a fan of a hot-dog stand on the North Side of Chicago called Sam's, which used what was then called the Chicago method of cooking fries. Sam's cooked its fries in animal fat, and Kroc followed suit, prescribing for his franchises a specially formulated beef tallow[. . .]. Among aficionados, there is general agreement that those early McDonald's fries were the finest mass-market fries ever made: the beef tallow gave them an unsurpassed rich, buttery taste. But in 1990, in the face of public concern about the health risks of cholesterol in animal-based cooking oil, McDonald's and the other major fast-food houses switched to vegetable oil. That wasn't an improvement, however. In the course of making vegetable oil suitable for deep-frying, it is subjected to a chemical process called hydrogenation, which creates a new substance called a trans unsaturated fat. In the hierarchy of fats, polyunsaturated fats—the kind found in regular vegetable oils—are the good kind; they lower your cholesterol. Saturated fats are the bad kind. But trans fats are worse: they wreak havoc with the body's ability to regulate cholesterol. According to a recent study involving some eighty thousand women, for every five-per-cent increase in the amount of saturated fats that a woman consumes, her risk of heart disease increases by seventeen per cent. But only a two-per-cent increase in trans fats will increase her heart-disease risk by ninety-three per cent. Walter Willert, an epidemiologist at Harvard—who helped design the study—estimates that the consumption of trans fats in the United States probably causes about thirty thousand premature deaths a year.

The French-fry problem ought to have a simple solution: cook fries in   7 oil that isn't so dangerous. Oils that are rich in monounsaturated fats, like canola oil, aren't nearly as bad for you as saturated fats, and are generally stable enough for deep-frying. It's also possible to "fix" animal fats so that they aren't so problematic. For example, K. C. Hayes, a nutritionist at Brandeis University, has helped develop an oil called Appetize. It's largely beef tallow, which gives it a big taste advantage over vegetable shortening, and makes it stable enough for deep-frying. But it has been processed to remove the cholesterol, and has been blended with pure corn oil, in a combination that Hayes says removes much of the heart-disease risk.

Perhaps the most elegant solution would be for McDonald's and the other chains to cook their fries in something like Olestra, a fat substitute developed by Procter & Gamble. Ordinary fats are built out of a molecular structure known as a triglyceride: it's a microscopic tree, with a trunk made of glycerol and three branches made of fatty acids. Our bodies can't absorb triglycerides, so in the digestive process each of the branches is broken off by enzymes and absorbed separately. In the production of Olestra, the glycerol trunk of a fat is replaced with a sugar, which has room for not three but eight fatty acids. And our enzymes are unable to break down a fat tree with eight branches—so the Olestra molecule can't be absorbed by the body at all. "Olestra" is as much a process as a compound: you can create an "Olestra" version of any given fat. Potato chips, for instance, tend to be fried in cottonseed oil, because of its distinctively clean taste. Frito-Lay's no-fat Wow! chips are made with an Olestra version of cottonseed oil, which behaves just like regular cottonseed oil except that it's never digested. A regular serving of potato chips has a hundred and fifty calories, ninety of which are fat calories from the cooking oil. A serving of Wow! chips has seventy-five calories and no fat. If Procter & Gamble were to seek F.D.A. approval for the use of Olestra in commercial deep-frying (which it has not yet done), it could make an Olestra version of the old McDonald's formula that would deliver every nuance of the old buttery, meaty tallow at a fraction of the calories. 8

Olestra, it must be said, does have some drawbacks—in particular, a reputation for what is delicately called "gastrointestinal distress." The F.D.A. has required all Olestra products to carry a somewhat daunting label saying that they may cause "Cramping and loose stools." Not surprisingly, sales have been disappointing, and Olestra has never won the full acceptance of the nutrition community. Most of this concern, however, appears to be overstated. Procter & Gamble has done randomized, double-blind studies—one of which involved more than three thousand people over six weeks—and found that people eating typical amounts of Olestra-based chips don't have significantly more gastrointestinal problems than people eating normal chips. Diarrhea is such a common problem in America—nearly a third of adults have at least one episode each month—that even F.D.A. regulators now appear to be convinced that in many of the complaints they received Olestra was unfairly blamed for a problem that was probably caused by something else. The agency has promised Procter & Gamble that the warning label will be reviewed. 9

Perhaps the best way to put the Olestra controversy into perspective is to compare it to fibre. Fibre is vegetable matter that goes right through you: it's not absorbed by the gastrointestinal tract. Nutritionists tell us to eat it because it helps us lose weight and it lowers cholesterol—even though if you eat too many baked beans or too many bowls of oat bran you will suffer the 10 consequences. Do we put warning labels on boxes of oat bran? No, because the benefits of fibre clearly outweigh its drawbacks. Research has suggested that Olestra, like fibre, helps people lose weight and lowers cholesterol; too much Olestra, like too much fibre, may cause problems[. . .]. If we had Olestra fries, then, they shouldn't be eaten for breakfast, lunch, and dinner. In fact, fast-food houses probably shouldn't use hundred-per-cent Olestra; they should cook their fries in a blend, using the Olestra to displace the most dangerous trans and saturated fats. But these are minor details. The point is that it is entirely possible, right now, to make a delicious French fry that does not carry with it a death sentence. A French fry can be much more than a delivery vehicle for fat.

Is it really that simple, though? Consider the cautionary tale of the efforts of a group of food scientists at Auburn University, in Alabama, more than a decade ago to come up with a better hamburger. The Auburn team wanted to create a leaner beef that tasted as good as regular ground beef. They couldn't just remove the fat, because that would leave the meat dry and mealy. They wanted to replace the fat. "If you look at ground beef it contains moisture, fat, and protein," says Dale Huffman, one of the scientists who spearheaded the Auburn project. "Protein is relatively constant in all beef at about twenty per cent. The traditional McDonald's ground beef is around twenty per cent fat. The remainder is water. So you have an inverse ratio of water and fat. If you reduce fat, you need to increase water." The goal of the Auburn scientists was to cut about two-thirds of the fat from normal ground beef which meant that they needed to find something to add to the beef that would hold an equivalent amount of water—and continue to retain that water even as the beef was being grilled. Their choice? Seaweed, or, more precisely, carrageenan. "It's been in use for centuries," Huffman explains. "It's the stuff that keeps the suspension in chocolate milk—otherwise the chocolate would settle at the bottom. It has tremendous water-holding ability. There's a loose bond between the carrageenan and the moisture." They also selected some basic flavor enhancers, designed to make up for the lost fat "taste." The result was a beef patty that was roughly three-quarters water, twenty per cent protein, five per cent or so fat, and a quarter of a per cent seaweed. They called it AU Lean.   11

It didn't take the Auburn scientists long to realize that they had created something special. They installed a test kitchen in their laboratory, got hold of a McDonald's grill, and began doing blind taste comparisons of AU Lean burgers and traditional twenty-per-cent-fat burgers. Time after time, the AU Lean burgers won. Next, they took their invention into the field. They recruited a hundred families and supplied them with three kinds of ground beef for home cooking over consecutive three-week intervals—regular "market" ground beef with twenty per cent fat, ground beef with five per cent fat, and AU Lean. The families were asked to rate the different kinds of beef   12 without knowing which was which. Again, the AU Lean won hands down—trumping the other two on "likability," "tenderness," "flavorfulness," and "juiciness."

What the Auburn team showed was that, even though people love the   13
taste and feel of fat—and naturally gravitate toward high-fat food—they can be fooled into thinking that there is a lot of fat in something when there isn't. Adam Drewnowski, a nutritionist at the University of Washington, has found a similar effect with cookies. He did blind taste tests of normal and reduced-calorie brownies, biscotti, and chocolate-chip, oatmeal, and peanut-butter cookies. If you cut the sugar content of any of those cookies by twenty-five per cent, he found, people like the cookies much less. But if you cut the fat by twenty-five per cent they barely notice. "People are very finely attuned to how much sugar there is in a liquid or a solid," Drewnowski says. "For fat, there's no sensory break point. Fat comes in so many guises and so many textures it is very difficult to perceive how much is there." This doesn't mean we are oblivious of fat levels, of course. Huffman says that when his group tried to lower the fat in AU Lean below five per cent, people didn't like it anymore. But, within the relatively broad range of between five and twenty-five per cent, you can add water and some flavoring and most people can't tell the difference.

What's more, people appear to be more sensitive to the volume of food   14
they consume than to its calorie content. Barbara Rolls, a nutritionist at Penn State, has demonstrated this principle with satiety studies. She feeds one group of people a high-volume snack and another group a low-volume snack. Even though the two snacks have the same calorie count, she finds that people who eat the high-volume snack feel more satisfied. "People tend to eat a constant weight or volume of food in a given day, not a constant portion of calories," she says. Eating AU Lean, in short, isn't going to leave you with a craving for more calories; you'll feel just as full.

For anyone looking to improve the quality of fast food, all this is heart-   15
ening news. It means that you should be able to put low-fat cheese and low-fat mayonnaise in a Big Mac without anyone's complaining. It also means that there's no particular reason to use twenty-percent-fat ground beef in a fast-food burger. In 1990, using just this argument, the Auburn team suggested to McDonald's that it make a Big Mac out of AU Lean. Shortly thereafter, McDonald's came out with the McLean Deluxe. Other fast-food houses scrambled to follow suit. Nutritionists were delighted. And fast food appeared on the verge of a revolution.

Only, it wasn't. The McLean was a flop, and four years later it was off   16
the market. What happened? Part of the problem appears to have been that McDonald's rushed the burger to market before many of the production kinks had been worked out. More important, though, was the psychological handicap the burger faced. People liked AU Lean in blind taste tests because they didn't know it was AU Lean; they were fooled into thinking it was reg-

ular ground beef. But nobody was fooled when it came to the McLean Deluxe. It was sold as the healthy choice—and who goes to McDonald's for health food?

Leann Birch, a developmental psychologist at Penn State, has looked   17
at the impact of these sorts of expectations on children. In one experiment, she took a large group of kids and fed them a big lunch. Then she turned them loose in a room with lots of junk food. "What we see is that some kids eat almost nothing," she says. "But other kids really chow down, and one of the things that predicts how much they eat is the extent to which parents have restricted their access to high-fat, high-sugar food in the past: the more the kids have been restricted, the more they eat." Birch explains the results two ways. First, restricting food makes kids think not in terms of their own hunger but in terms of the presence and absence of food. As she puts it, "The kid is essentially saying, 'If the food's here I better get it while I can, whether or not I'm hungry.' We see these five-year-old kids eating as much as four hundred calories." Birch's second finding, though, is more important. Because the children on restricted diets had been told that junk food was bad for them, they clearly thought that it had to taste good. When it comes to junk food, we seem to follow an implicit script that powerfully biases the way we feel about food. We like fries not in spite of the fact that they're unhealthy but because of it.

That is sobering news for those interested in improving the American   18
diet. For years, the nutrition movement in this country has made transparency one of its principal goals: it has assumed that the best way to help people improve their diets is to tell them precisely what's in their food, to label certain foods good and certain foods bad. But transparency can backfire, because sometimes nothing is more deadly for our taste buds than the knowledge that what we are eating is good for us. McDonald's should never have called its new offering the McLean Deluxe, in other words. They should have called it the Burger Supreme or the Monster Burger, and then buried the news about reduced calories and fat in the tiniest type on the remotest corner of their Web site. And if we were to cook fries in some high-tech, healthful cooking oil—whether Olestrized beef tallow or something else with a minimum of trans and saturated fat—the worst thing we could do would be to market them as healthy fries. They will not taste nearly as good if we do.

◆ ◆ ◆

FIRST RESPONSES

Do you think people should stop eating French fries? Why or why not?

TAKING A CLOSER LOOK

Exploring *Who:* Voice and Tone

1. Do you think the author of this article is an expert on making and marketing French fries? How does he convince you that he knows what he's writing about?
2. What audience is Gladwell addressing in this article? Are you part of that audience?
3. Gladwell has been praised for having a "clear style and personable tone." Do you agree with this assessment? Find sentences you think best illustrate Gladwell's voice and tone.

Exploring *What:* Content and Meaning

1. What did Ray Kroc do to improve the making of French fries? Why were the early McDonald's fries "the finest mass-market fries ever made"?
2. What happened when fast-food chains tried to substitute vegetable oil for animal-based cooking oil?
3. What is Olestra? How does it differ from ordinary fats? What are its drawbacks?
4. Why was the McLean Deluxe a flop? What does Galdwell suggest for marketing low-fat, healthy foods in the future?

Exploring *Why:* Purpose

1. Gladwell says that Ray Kroc's French fries are killing us. What evidence does he present to support this claim?
2. What changes in the American diet is Gladwell arguing for? How effective are his arguments? How does his use of process analysis support his arguments?
3. ■ *Using the Internet.* With what general attitude would Gladwell have us approach science-designed changes in food? Go to a Web site about organic food production or to one about genetically altered tomatoes to find other views on this issue.

Exploring *How:* Style and Strategy

1. How many different processes does Galdwell explain or summarize? Find at least four.

2. In paragraph 10, Gladwell compares Olestra to fibre. What's the point of this comparison? What is Gladwell trying to show?

3. How many times does Gladwell refer to studies done by university researchers? What is the effect of these references?

4. Notice how often the author uses short sentences or questions to begin paragraphs. Why do you suppose he uses this technique?

IDEAS FOR WRITING A PROCESS ANALYSIS

1. Write an essay like Gladwell's in which you use process analysis to explain a problem and then suggest a solution. For example, show how obesity contributes to poor health and then offer sensible guidelines for losing weight. Other possible topics are smoking, excessive alcohol consumption, lack of exercise, poor study habits, and chronic lateness.

2. *Using the Internet.* Explain the important steps for achieving success in some role: parent, athlete, coach, teacher, business manager, salesperson, broker, musician, painter, writer, or any profession or occupation of your choice. To gather accurate information on your topic, consult a Web site that deals with careers, such as USA Careers (www.usacareers.opm.gov/).

3. Investigate your school's policy on grade appeals or proficiency exams, and then write a how-to guide for fellow students.

◆ ◆ ◆

◆ FURTHER IDEAS FOR USING PROCESS ANALYSIS

1. Using Dereck Williamson's essay as a model, provide the *real* instructions for some task you have found to be more difficult than the directions or instructions admitted.

2. Write an essay about the process of getting used to some new condition of life: a move, an illness, an office reorganization, marriage, prison, a career change, or additions to the family, for example. Or provide advice for improving relationships, such as how to win the approval of your mate's parents or how to get your mate to help with the housework.

3. ▉▐ *Using the Internet.* Find out about funeral customs in another country by searching the Internet. (Your library's online catalog can also direct you to appropriate articles or books.) Write an essay in which you analyze the process described in your source, and use it as the basis for agreeing or disagreeing with Jessica Mitford's opinion of American funeral practices.

4. COLLABORATIVE WRITING. With a small group of fellow students, think of some established process that could use improvement, such as grading, registration, income tax, courtship, or weddings. Take notes while the group brainstorms to figure out how a preferable arrangement would function. Then, after the discussion, write an essay proposing the new process and explaining how it would work.

5. COMBINING STRATEGIES. Think of some process that can be done several different ways, such as preparing food. Which process is better? Fried, baked, or broiled? Decide which way you think is best. Then write an essay arguing that although there are several ways to fix this food (or perform this process), the way you are about to explain is the best way. Then explain the process, and present your reasons for considering it the best choice.

6. Find a complicated set of instructions, like those for programming a VCR. Study them until you figure them out. Then write a new set of instructions that a novice user would find easy to follow.

Strategies for Clarifying Meaning

Definition

◆ ◆ ◆ ◆ ◆

Definitions explain the meanings of words, concepts, objects, or phenomena.

◆ Writers use definitions to clarify, evaluate, and increase awareness.

◆ Extended definitions explore the nature of complex subjects and controversial terms.

◆ Effective definitions include specific characteristics, examples, analogies, and contrasts.

If Harvey tells you he's going to leave work at 5:30 P.M., mail a package at the post office, stop by the ATM for some cash, go to the liquor store for some wine, pick up a pizza at the Italian Village, and get home in time for dinner at 6:00, you may conclude that he's not very bright. On the other hand, this same person may be the author of three books on molecular biology, a well-known scientist you admire for his mental ability. Do you think Harvey is intelligent or not? The answer to this question is a matter of **definition;** it all depends on what you mean by "intelligent."

Defining exactly what we mean is essential to clear and productive communication. After all, one person's "protest march" might be another person's "street riot." Indeed, many of our national debates about such issues as "affirmative action," "sexual harassment," "political correctness," "free speech," "multiculturalism," and "the right to die" turn on what people mean by these terms.

Writers also use definition to explore ideas and evaluate principles. In the essay that follows, Ellen Goodman explains what it means to be a "workaholic" by focusing on a single individual whose life and behavior define the condition. The detailed description of Phil not only *shows* what a workaholic is, but it also conveys Goodman's reservations about such people.

The Company Man

ELLEN GOODMAN

A syndicated columnist whose writing appears in over four hundred newspapers, Ellen Goodman (born in 1941) began her career in journalism in 1963, the year after she graduated from Radcliffe College. She started as a reporter and feature writer for the *Detroit Free Press* and then moved to the *Boston Globe,* where she has been publishing her weekly syndicated column, "At Large," since 1971. Goodman's strong interest in social changes continues to play the central role in her work. She writes about family, politics, ethics, generation gaps, abortion, and the ever-changing status of women. In 1999, she coauthored *I Know Just What You Mean,* a reflection on friendships between women. Her columns have been praised for their keen observations and incisive wit, and she has won a number of writing awards, including the 1980 Pulitzer Prize for Distinguished Commentary.

He worked himself to death, finally and precisely, at 3:00 A.M. Sunday morning. 1

The obituary didn't say that, of course. It said that he died of a coronary thrombosis—I think that was it—but everyone among his friends and acquaintances knew it instantly. He was a perfect Type A, a workaholic, a classic, they said to each other and shook their heads—and thought for five or ten minutes about the way they lived. 2

This man who worked himself to death finally and precisely at 3:00 A.M. Sunday morning—on his day off—was fifty-one years old and a vice-president. He was, however, one of six vice-presidents, and one of three who might conceivably—if the president died or retired soon enough—have moved to the top spot. Phil knew that. 3

He worked six days a week, five of them until eight or nine at night, dur- 4 ing a time when his own company had begun the four-day week for everyone but the executives. He worked like the Important People. He had no outside "extracurricular interests," unless, of course, you think about a monthly golf game that way. To Phil, it was work. He always ate egg salad sandwiches at his desk. He was, of course, overweight, by 20 or 25 pounds. He thought it was okay, though, because he didn't smoke.

On Saturdays, Phil wore a sports jacket to the office instead of a suit, 5 because it was the weekend.

He had a lot of people working for him, maybe sixty, and most of them 6 liked him most of the time. Three of them will be seriously considered for his job. The obituary didn't mention that.

But it did list his "survivors" quite accurately. He is survived by his wife, 7 Helen, forty-eight years old, a good woman of no particular marketable skills, who worked in an office before marrying and mothering. She had, according to her daughter, given up trying to compete with his work years ago, when the children were small. A company friend said, "I know how much you will miss him." And she answered, "I already have."

"Missing him all these years," she must have given up part of herself 8 which had cared too much for the man. She would be "well taken care of."

His "dearly beloved" eldest of the "dearly beloved" children is a hard- 9 working executive in a manufacturing firm down South. In the day and a half before the funeral, he went around the neighborhood researching his father, asking the neighbors what he was like. They were embarrassed.

His second child is a girl, who is twenty-four and newly married. She 10 lives near her mother and they are close, but whenever she was alone with her father, in a car driving somewhere, they had nothing to say to each other.

The youngest is twenty, a boy, a high-school graduate who has spent 11 the last couple of years, like a lot of his friends, doing enough odd jobs to stay in grass and food. He was the one who tried to grab at his father, and tried to mean enough to him to keep the man at home. He was his father's favorite. Over the last two years, Phil stayed up nights worrying about the boy.

The boy once said, "My father and I only board here." 12

At the funeral, the sixty-year-old company president told the forty- 13 eight-year-old widow that the fifty-one-year-old deceased had meant much to the company and would be missed and would be hard to replace. The widow didn't look him in the eye. She was afraid he would read her bitterness and, after all, she would need him to straighten out the finances—the stock options and all that.

Phil was overweight and nervous and worked too hard. If he wasn't at 14 the office, he was worried about it. Phil was a Type A, a heart-attack natural. You could have picked him out in a minute from a lineup.

So when he finally worked himself to death, at precisely 3:00 A.M. Sun- 15 day morning, no one was really surprised.

By 5:00 P.M. the afternoon of the funeral, the company president had   16
begun, discreetly of course, with care and taste, to make inquiries about his
replacement. One of three men. He asked around: "Who's been working the
hardest?"

◆ ◆ ◆

◆ ◆ ◆ *Writer's Workshop I* ◆ ◆ ◆ *Responding to a Definition*

Use the *Who, What, Why,* and *How* questions (p. 3) to explore your own
understanding of the ideas and writing strategies used by Ellen Goodman in
"The Company Man." Your instructor may ask you to record these responses
in a journal, post them on an electronic bulletin board, or bring them to class
to use in small group discussions.

◆ WRITING FROM READING

After reading "The Company Man," freshman Megan Quick used the
Who, What, Why, and *How* questions to explore her understanding of Goodman's ideas and to develop material for writing a similar essay. Megan asked
herself several questions about a possible topic: "Do I know someone who
stands for a certain quality? Is this someone I dislike or admire? Is it someone I know well enough to write about?" These questions led her to focus on
her high school music teacher, Mr. Woods. The definition essay she wrote
about him follows.

Megan Quick
English 1091
November 8, 1997

In Tune with His Students

He walked into his students' lives in the fall of   1
1994. Though the students could not have known it
then, their new band director would have a profound
effect on their lives in just a few short years. He
would share in their thoughts and feelings, in their
successes and disappointments. He would be the perfect
example of dedication and inspiration.

Derek Woods is an educator and a friend to his students. He is involved in their lives both personally and professionally. Students look to Mr. Woods for advice about friendships, dating, family conflicts, career decisions, college choices, and music. To some, he is a counselor, to others he is a mentor, but mostly he is just a great teacher and friend. When he's feeling sentimental, he calls his students his "kids"--all fifty of them. When he's invited to a student party, he usually comes. Other times Mr. Woods helps to arrange the get-togethers himself. At the end of the marching band season, he takes the section leaders out for lunch as a reward for all their hard work. When students have performed well or achieved a personal success, he will congratulate them publicly. He will also let them know if they are not performing up to their potential. After the senior band members graduate, he tells them he does not want to see them back in their hometown working at dead-end jobs--because they have more potential than that. Mr. Woods believes in his students and knows they can be successful if they try.

Accomplishing goals is important to Mr. Woods. His practices are intense, yet fun. On a regular basis, Mr. Woods puts the band through such unusual activities as group hugs, four-count jumping jacks, and massage lines (where the band stands in single-file lines and the members massage the person standing in front of them). Other favorite activities include march-offs (a drill where Mr. Woods gives marching commands until only the person who has made no mistakes is left) and leprechaun kicks (executed by clicking the ankles together in midair). Leprechaun kicks are performed only on joyous or special occasions. Yet somehow Mr. Woods manages to keep the students focused. Before every competition and after every practice, Mr. Woods gives the entire band a pep talk. He must be doing something right because he has led the marching band to two consecutive state titles.

One of Mr. Woods's goals is to make his students the best they can be. He cares about their well-being, their success in life. Mr. Woods applies several philosophies in his quest for student excellence. He insists that "the band is only as good as its worst player." He also says, "If you are going to play a wrong note, play it with confidence"--but never make the same mistake twice. On the marching field, he is constantly reminding the students to "Give 110% at all times!" He shows them how music unifies people of all races, colors, genders, and ages. Music is a powerful tool, and Mr. Woods instills the desire in his students to use their musical abilities to create positive benefits.

His obvious enthusiasm for his subject and his   5
interest in his students have caused many of them to develop a lifelong interest in music. He has inspired some students, like me, to major in music education; others he has encouraged to become professional musicians. Those students did not know what they were getting into the day they met Derek Woods; but ask any of them, and they will tell you that they are glad he stepped into their lives.

◆ GETTING STARTED ON A DEFINITION

A good definition can be reassuring or troubling: it can focus your readers' thinking and ease their minds, or it can shake up their long-held views and little-considered opinions. Either way, definition concerns meaning and therefore has a place in almost every mode of writing.

The first decision you have to make is what kind of definition you're going to use. Your choice, of course, depends on your **purpose** and how much you think your readers need to know.

Sometimes a short definition is enough to introduce a key term or clarify some technical language that your readers may not know. Short definitions can sometimes be handled by adding a word or two in parentheses after the term, like this:

> If you want your yogurt to yog (thicken), start with a fresh culture.

> Miscommunication occurs when reader and writer do not share the same idea about a word's denotation (direct meaning) or connotation (emotional associations).

If there is no apt synonym, you can add a sentence, using the traditional three-part definition: (1) the *term* to be defined, (2) the *class* to which it belongs, and (3) *specific differences* to distinguish it from other members of its class. This formula may sound dry and academic, but it produces efficient one-sentence definitions. For example:

TERM	CLASS	SPECIFIC DIFFERENCES
A friend	is a person	you know, like, and trust.
Intelligence	is the capacity	to acquire and apply knowledge.

You can leave these single-sentence definitions as they are, or you can expand the third part if you think your readers need more information.

When it comes to controversial, **abstract,** or complex words, you may decide to write an **extended definition.** Such a definition is a kind of explanatory writing that investigates the nature and significance of a term. Writers use extended definitions for one or more of the following reasons.

1. *To explain an abstraction or concept.* An abstraction—like intelligence or compassion or prejudice—is an idea that cannot be directly observed. Its meaning has to be understood indirectly from observable evidence. Ellen Goodman makes the concept of a "workaholic" understandable by describing the actions and behavior of a specific person.

2. *To provide an interpretation of a controversial term.* Any discussion of "family values" or "reverse discrimination" or "the right to life" must include an extended definition of how you are using and applying the phrase.

3. *To increase awareness of a new concept or a poorly understood term.* You might explain the meaning and nature of a term your readers probably don't understand at all, like "hypertext" or "feudalism." Or you might give your readers a new outlook on a familiar word—like "fear" or "wife"—by redefining it for them in a new way, as Judy Brady and Andrew Holleran do in essays in this chapter.

Following Ellen Goodman's lead, Megan Quick decided to describe someone who exemplifies the abstract qualities of "dedication" and "inspiration." She brainstormed a list of points to use in her essay and began to write her first draft.

◆ ORGANIZING A DEFINITION

As you have seen, definitions come in all sizes and serve many different purposes. There is no set formula for writing an extended definition. Because you can use a number of strategies—description, narration, exemplification, comparison and contrast, classification—to develop a definition, you will be able to follow the organizational patterns that govern these techniques. Megan began with the idea of writing an expressive description of Mr. Woods. Her first brainstorming list included a collection of descriptive details and narrative examples. As she worked on her first draft, she discovered that she could limit her discussion to those points that defined Mr. Woods's dedication and showed how he inspired his students. In other words, the definition provided a focus for her thinking and helped her to manage her presentation.

It's always a good idea to center your thoughts and supporting materials on a single controlling idea—a **thesis.** You don't have to state this idea in a thesis sentence, although doing so can be helpful to your readers. What is important is that you let this idea direct your writing. Here are several thesis sentences from the essays in this chapter. Notice how each one makes a definite assertion about the general subject and, at the same time, conveys the writer's point of view.

> In our increasingly urban society, rural Americans have been unable to escape from hillbilly stigma, which is frequently accompanied by labels like "white trash," "redneck," and "hayseed." These negative stereotypes are as unmerciful as they are unfounded. (Rebecca Thomas Kirkendall, "Who's a Hillbilly?")

> But this general panic [about AIDS], this unease, this sense that the world is out of control and too intimately connected, is not *all* the Fear among homosexuals. The Fear among homosexuals is personal, physical, and real. (Andrew Holleran, "The Fear")

> What is so devastating for so many of us in search of our Black fathers is the realization that many of them are utter failures at nurturing us. And now, as many of us are fathers ourselves, we also find ourselves struggling with the identical phenomenon in relation to our own sons. (Michel Marriott, "Father Hunger")

◆ DEVELOPING A DEFINITION

You can develop an extended definition by using any of the strategies discussed in this book. For example, if you wanted to define "sportsmanship," you could *narrate* an incident that illustrates the quality; *describe* how sportsmanship makes people feel and behave; *contrast* a good sport with a sore loser; give *examples* that reveal the nature of good sportsmanship; *classify* competitors into cheaters, arrogant winners, and good sports; or explain the *effects* of good sportsmanship on a team. You could also combine several of these strategies.

The most common methods of defining are the following:

1. *Attributing characteristics.* A true friend is loyal and sensitive, and has a sense of humor.
2. *Providing examples.* A true friend will stay with your children while you go to a party.
3. *Using analogies.* A true friend is a safe port in a storm or a cross between a therapist and a pet who can cook.
4. *Explaining through contrasts.* A true friend is not just an old acquaintance or a jogging partner or a buddy at work.

As she worked on her definition essay, Megan Quick consulted Ellen Goodman's description of a workaholic. She observed that Goodman includes **details** about Phil's job, his physical appearance, and his habits. She also noticed that Goodman shows how Phil's behavior affected others and how other people reacted and related to Phil. Megan used these same strategies in developing her enlightening description of Mr. Woods.

◆ OPENING AND CLOSING A DEFINITION

A good way to begin an extended definition of something is to define its key terms. An example is, "Before we can identify the best living jazz musicians, we must agree on a definition of *jazz.*" You can also open with a three-part, one-sentence definition—"a true friend is someone you can trust and depend on"—and then expand on the specific characteristics mentioned in the last part.

You'll notice that a number of essays in this chapter open with narrative examples. Ellen Goodman and Megan Quick both begin with a specific event: Phil's death, Mr. Woods's arrival. Michel Marriott ("Father Hunger") uses a story about a trip to Cuba to introduce his subject, Rebecca Kirkendall ("Who's a Hillbilly?") narrates an incident from her past, and Judy Brady ("I Want a Wife") combines a classification statement with a brief anecdote about a recently divorced friend. By contrast, Amy Tan ("Mother Tongue") wants her readers to understand the nature of her authority and interest in the topic, so she juxtaposes "I am not a scholar of English or literature" with "I am a writer." Andrew Holleran ("The Fear") plunges right into his topic: "The Fear is of course unseemly—as most fear is."

The **conclusion** of an extended definition often sums up the main characteristics of the term and emphasizes the significance of the definition. That's how many of the essays in this chapter end. Megan Quick, for example, cites Mr. Woods's enthusiasm for music, his interest in his students, and his inspiration—and then closes with an echo of her opening sentence.

Andrew Holleran sums up the essence of his definition of the Fear with this powerful ending:

> The Fear [. . .] feeds on the Imagination. And the moment you know someone who faces this disease daily with composure, calm, humor, and his or her own personality intact, you realize how deforming, how demeaning, how subject to the worst instincts Fear is.

◆ USING THE MODEL

As you have seen, reading and analyzing Ellen Goodman's essay helped Megan Quick in a number of ways. First, she got her topic and basic approach from Goodman: to describe a person she knows who exemplifies certain abstract qualities. Megan also picked up pointers from Goodman's essay on where to look for relevant examples and how to use them to develop her ideas. But she did not follow Goodman in every way. For one thing, Megan's purpose was to hold up Mr. Woods as an admirable example, not to criticize him, as Goodman does with her subject. Megan also decided to conclude with a more conventional summary of her main points, a strategy that Goodman does not employ.

We all know people who seem to represent a certain quality or value. Think of someone whose life defines for you some abstraction, such as ambition, determination, loyalty, enthusiasm, or procrastination. Or perhaps you know somebody who is the perfect example of a perfectionist, a bore, a fanatic, a disciplinarian, a hopeless romantic, a con artist, a deadbeat, or something similar. Talk to other people who know this same person and get their views. Then write a definition essay in which you use this individual as your primary example to illustrate that quality.

◆ ◆ ◆ *Writer's Workshop II* ◆ ◆ ◆
Analyzing a Definition

Working individually or with a small group of classmates, read through Megan Quick's essay "In Tune with His Students" and respond to the following questions.

1. What is Megan's purpose for writing this essay? Does she make her purpose clear in the beginning?
2. Do the examples support Megan's thesis? Which examples are the most effective? Are there any that are incomplete or ineffective? How would you improve them?

3. How does Megan organize her description? Did you find it easy to follow?

4. Do you like the opening and the closing? Would you change them? If so, how?

5. What attitude about Mr. Woods does Megan convey? Does she convince you of her evaluation? Why or why not?

◆ ◆ ◆ *Checklist for Reading and Writing* ◆ ◆ ◆ *Definition Essays*

1. What term or concept is being defined? Does the essay focus clearly on this term or concept?

2. What is the purpose of the definition: to clarify, evaluate, or increase awareness?

3. How is the definition developed? Are there enough details, specific characteristics, examples, analogies, and contrasts?

4. Who is the intended audience? How would the essay be different if written for a different audience? What details and explanations would be added or deleted?

5. Is the organization clear?

6. Does the essay begin and end appropriately and effectively?

◆ ◆ ◆ PREPARING TO READ

Where do you live now: in the city, the suburbs, or the country? What do you like and dislike about where you live? Would you prefer to live somewhere else? Why or why not?

◆ ◆ ◆

Who's a Hillbilly?

REBECCA THOMAS KIRKENDALL

Rebecca Thomas Kirkendall was a doctoral student at the University of Missouri when this essay was first published in *Newsweek* magazine in November 1995. In some ways, her essay is a counterdefinition because it takes issue with the term *hillbilly*. But in attacking the assumptions behind the use of the term, Kirkendall also proposes a more accurate description of what it really means to be part of the rural culture of the Ozarks.

I once dated a boy who called me a hillbilly because my family has lived   1
in the Ozarks in southern Missouri for several generations. I took offense, not realizing that as a foreigner to the United States he was unaware of the insult. He had meant it as a term of endearment. Nonetheless, it rankled. I started thinking about the implications of the term to me, my family, and my community.

While growing up I was often surprised at the way television belittled   2
"country" people. We weren't offended by the self-effacing humor of *The Andy Griffith Show* and *The Beverly Hillbillies* because, after all, Andy and Jed were the heroes of these shows, and through them we could comfortably laugh at ourselves. But as I learned about tolerance and discrimination in school, I wondered why stereotypes of our lifestyle went unexamined. Actors playing "country" people on TV were usually comic foils or objects of ridicule. Every sitcom seemed to have an episode where country cousins, wearing high-water britches, and carrying patched suitcases, visited their city friends. And movies like *Deliverance* portrayed country people as backward and violent.

As a child I laughed at the exaggerated accents and dress, never imag-   3
ining that viewers believed such nonsense. Li'l Abner and the folks on *Hee Haw* were amusing, but we on the farm knew that our work did not lend itself to bare feet, gingham bras, and revealing cutoff jeans.

Although our nation professes a growing commitment to cultural egali-   4
tarianism, we consistently oversimplify and misunderstand our rural culture.
Since the 1960s, minority groups in America have fought for acknowledg-
ment, appreciation, and, above all, respect. But in our increasingly urban society, rural Americans have been unable to escape from the hillbilly stigma,
which is frequently accompanied by labels like "white trash," "redneck," and
"hayseed." These negative stereotypes are as unmerciful as they are
unfounded.

When I graduated from college, I traveled to a nearby city to find work.   5
There I heard wisecracks about the uneducated rural folk who lived a few
hours away. I also took some ribbing about the way I pronounced certain
words, such as "tin" instead of "ten" and "agin" for "again." And my expressed
desire to return to the country someday was usually met with scorn, bewil-
derment, or genuine concern. Co-workers often asked, "But what is there to
do?" Thoreau may have gone to Walden Pond, they argued, but he had no intention of staying there.

With the revival of country music in the early 1980s, hillbillyness was   6
again marketable. Country is now big business. Traditional country symbols—
Minnie Pearl's hat tag and Daisy Mae—have been eclipsed by the commer-
cially successful Nashville Network, Country Music Television, and music
theaters in Branson, Mo. Many "country" Americans turned the negative
stereotype to their advantage and packaged the hillbilly legacy.

Yet with successful commercialization, the authentic elements of Amer-   7
ica's rural culture have been juxtaposed with the stylized. Country and Western bars are now chic. While I worked in the city, I watched with amazement
as my Yuppie friends hurried from their corporate desks to catch the 6:30
line-dancing class at the edge of town. Donning Ralph Lauren jeans and
ankle boots, they drove to the trendiest country bars, sat and danced together,
and poked fun at the local "hicks," who arrived in pickup trucks wearing
Wrangler jeans and roper boots.

Every summer weekend in Missouri the freeways leading out of our   8
cities are clogged with vacationers. Minivans and RVs edge toward a clear
river with a campground and canoe rental, a quiet lake resort, or craft show
in a remote Ozark town. Along these popular vacation routes, the rural hosts
of convenience stores, gift shops, and corner cafés accept condescension along
with personal checks and credit cards. On a canoeing trip not long ago, I recall sitting on the transport bus and listening, heartbroken, as a group of
tourists ridiculed our bus driver. They yelled, "Hey, plowboy, ain't ya got no
terbacker fer us?" They pointed at the young man's sweat-stained overalls as
he, seemingly unaffected by their insults, single-handedly carried their heavy
aluminum canoes to the water's edge. That "plowboy" was one of my high-
school classmates. He greeted the tourists with a smile and tolerated their derision because he knew tourism brings dollars and jobs.

America is ambivalent when it comes to claiming its rural heritage. We   9
may fantasize about Thomas Jefferson's agrarian vision, but there is no mistaking that ours is an increasingly urban culture. Despite their disdain for
farm life—with its manure-caked boots, long hours, and inherent financial
difficulties—urbanites rush to imitate a sanitized version of this lifestyle. And
the individuals who sell this rendition understand that the customer wants
to experience hillbillyness without the embarrassment of being mistaken
for one.

Through it all, we Ozarkians remind ourselves how fortunate we are to   10
live in a region admired for its blue springs, rolling hills, and geological wonders. In spite of the stereotypes, most of us are not uneducated. Nor are we
stupid. We are not white supremacists, and we rarely marry our cousins. Our
reasons for living in the hills are as complex and diverse as our population.
We have a unique sense of community, strong family ties, a beautiful environment, and a quiet place for retirement.

We have criminals and radicals, but they are the exception. Our public-   11
education system produces successful farmers, doctors, business professionals, and educators. Country music is our favorite, but we also like rock and
roll, jazz, blues, and classical. We read Louis L'Amour, Maya Angelou, and
The Wall Street Journal. And in exchange for living here, many of us put up
with a lower standard of living and the occasional gibe from those who per-
sist in calling us "hillbillies."

◆ ◆ ◆

FIRST RESPONSES

Why do people use terms like *hillbilly* or *hick?* Can you think of two
or three well-known labels for urban residents? Are they as unfair and unfounded as *hillbilly?* Why or why not?

TAKING A CLOSER LOOK

Exploring *Who:* Voice and Tone

1. What is Kirkendall's personal agenda in writing about this topic? How
   does she make it clear that she has a personal stake in this discussion?
2. Is the author writing for herself or on behalf of a larger community?
   How would you describe the community she's writing about?
3. Is Kirkendall angry? Is she being defensive? Describe the tone you detect in her writing.

4. How do you respond to the author's survey of attitudes toward rural people? Do you think she is criticizing or challenging you in any way?

Exploring *What:* Content and Meaning

1. What evidence does Kirkendall present to support her claim that rural people are negatively stereotyped? Do you agree with her claim?
2. How have some rural people turned the negative stereotype to their advantage? Does the author approve of this commercialization of the country image?
3. What does Kirkendall mean when she says, "America is ambivalent when it comes to claiming its rural heritage" (para. 9)?
4. ▪️ *Using the Internet.* What do you know about the Ozarks? Visit a Web site on the Internet that gives information about this part of the United States. What does the Web site tell you about the culture and people of this region? Does the presentation of the information confirm or refute what Kirkendall says in her essay?

Exploring *Why:* Purpose

1. Why does the author refer to television shows and movies in the second and third paragraphs of her essay? Do you know the references she makes?
2. Kirkendall refers to "a growing commitment to cultural egalitarianism" in American society. What is "cultural egalitarianism"? Why does the author introduce this idea?
3. What does Kirkendall hope to accomplish with this essay? Does she expect you to alter your attitudes and opinions? Has she succeeded?

Exploring *How:* Style and Strategy

1. Locate the author's use of personal examples to illustrate her points. What is the effect of including these incidents? What other kinds of examples does she use?
2. Kirkendall uses sophisticated words such as *stigma, egalitarianism, eclipsed, legacy, ambivalent, juxtaposed, condescension, derision, inherent, urbanites, geological,* and *supremacists.* How does this vocabulary—along with the references to Thoreau, Louis L'Amour, Maya Angelou, and the *Wall Street Journal*—advance the point of her essay?
3. Reread the last two paragraphs. What is the point of this last section of the essay? Why does Kirkendall include them?

◆ WRITING FROM READING ASSIGNMENT

Sometimes writers, like Rebecca Thomas Kirkendall, think that the accepted definitions do not define a word or term accurately or fairly, so they offer a redefinition that fits their purposes better. In this writing assignment, your goal is to offer a counterdefinition of some word or phrase that you think needs to be clarified or redefined.

A. Begin by identifying a term that you want to write about. You might, like Kirkendall, use a word that carries negative **connotations** you want to challenge and correct. Think of some term like that: *jock, Yuppie, activist, liberal, conservative, feminist, politician, capitalist, socialist,* or *atheist.* Or you could define what people in your community or area are really like (as opposed to what others may think).

B. Consult other people who might have varying points of view about their understanding of the word or phrase. Be sure to ask them if the term carries any negative connotations for them. Then do some brainstorming or freewriting to get your points and ideas down on paper.

C. Try to think of a relevant **anecdote,** then use it to set up your counterdefinition, as Kirkendall does in the opening paragraph of her essay. You could also use a dictionary definition to begin your discussion, pointing out that it gives the basic meaning but doesn't deal with the connotations you propose to focus on. If appropriate, you might consult The Jargon Dictionary (www.info.astrian.net/jargon/) or the WWWebster Dictionary (www.m-w.com/dictionary) to help you get started.

D. Provide examples of people who use the term in a negative or inaccurate way. You might draw on television programs and movies, as Kirkendall does, to illustrate why the word needs to be redefined.

E. After establishing the current use of the term, state the main point and purpose of your essay. Look at paragraph 4 in "Who's a Hillbilly?" to see how Kirkendall presents her thesis.

F. Discuss the problems or consequences of continuing to use the word or phrase inaccurately. Include any evidence you have that some change in usage has already taken place, as Kirkendall does in paragraphs 6 through 8 of her essay.

G. Once you have demonstrated that the word or phrase is being misused and that its misuse is unfair or misleading, present your counterdefinition. Give details, examples, and explanations to make your point. Reread paragraphs 10 and 11 of "Who's a Hillbilly?" for an example.

◆ ◆ ◆ PREPARING TO READ

What tasks does a wife typically perform around the house? What are the typical tasks that a husband does? If both of them are working outside the home, who has the harder job at home?

◆ ◆ ◆

I Want a Wife

JUDY BRADY

Born in 1937, Judy Brady received a B.F.A. in painting from the University of Iowa in 1962. She married in 1960 and is the mother of two daughters. As a freelance writer, Brady has written essays on union organizing, abortion, and the role of women in American society. Motivated by her own struggle with cancer, she edited a collection of articles entitled *1 in 3: Women with Cancer Confront an Epidemic* (1991). The following essay, written after eleven years of marriage and before Brady separated from her husband, first appeared in 1971 in *Ms.* magazine. It has been widely reprinted ever since.

1   I belong to that classification of people known as wives. I am A Wife. And, not altogether incidentally, I am a mother.

2   Not too long ago a male friend of mine appeared on the scene from the Midwest fresh from a recent divorce. He had one child, who is, of course, with his ex-wife. He is obviously looking for another wife. As I thought about him while I was ironing one evening, it suddenly occurred to me that I, too, would like to have a wife. Why do I want a wife?

3   I would like to go back to school so that I can become economically independent, support myself, and, if need be, support those dependent upon me. I want a wife who will work and send me to school. And while I am going to school I want a wife to take care of my children. I want a wife to keep track of the children's doctor and dentist appointments. And to keep track of mine, too. I want a wife to make sure my children eat properly and are kept clean. I want a wife who will wash the children's clothes and keep them mended. I want a wife who is a good nurturant attendant to my children, arranges for their schooling, makes sure that they have an adequate social life with their peers, takes them to the park, the zoo, etc. I want a wife who takes care of the children when they are sick, a wife who arranges to be around when the children need special care, because, of course, I cannot miss classes at school.

My wife must arrange to lose time at work and not lose the job. It may mean a small cut in my wife's income from time to time, but I guess I can tolerate that. Needless to say, my wife will arrange and pay for the care of the children while my wife is working.

I want a wife who will take care of *my* physical needs. I want a wife   4
who will keep my house clean. A wife who will pick up after my children, a wife who will pick up after me. I want a wife who will keep my clothes clean, ironed, mended, replaced when need be, and who will see to it that my personal things are kept in their proper place so that I can find what I need the minute I need it. I want a wife who cooks the meals, a wife who is a *good* cook. I want a wife who will plan the menus, do the necessary grocery shopping, prepare the meals, serve them pleasantly, and then do the cleaning up while I do my studying. I want a wife who will care for me when I am sick and sympathize with my pain and loss of time from school. I want a wife to go along when our family takes a vacation so that someone can continue to care for me and my children when I need a rest and a change of scene.

I want a wife who will not bother me with rambling complaints about   5
a wife's duties. But I want a wife who will listen to me when I feel the need to explain a rather difficult point I have come across in my course of studies. And I want a wife who will type my papers for me when I have written them.

I want a wife who will take care of the details of my social life. When   6
my wife and I are invited out by my friends, I want a wife who will take care of the babysitting arrangements. When I meet people at school that I like and want to entertain, I want a wife who will have the house clean, will prepare a special meal, serve it to me and my friends, and not interrupt when I talk about the things that interest me and my friends. I want a wife who will have arranged that the children are fed and ready for bed before my guests arrive so that the children do not bother us. I want a wife who takes care of the needs of my guests so that they feel comfortable, who makes sure that they have an ashtray, that they are passed the hors d'oeuvres, that they are offered a second helping of the food, that their wine glasses are replenished when necessary, that their coffee is served to them as they like it. And I want a wife who knows that sometimes I need a night out by myself.

I want a wife who is sensitive to my sexual needs, a wife who makes   7
love passionately and eagerly when I feel like it, a wife who makes sure that I am satisfied. And, of course, I want a wife who will not demand sexual attention when I am not in the mood for it. I want a wife who assumes the complete responsibility for birth control, because I do not want more children. I want a wife who will remain sexually faithful to me so that I do not have to clutter up my intellectual life with jealousies. And I want a wife who understands that my sexual needs may entail more than strict adherence to monogamy. I must, after all, be able to relate to people as fully as possible.

If, by chance, I find another person more suitable as a wife than the   8
wife I already have, I want the liberty to replace my present wife with another

one. Naturally, I will expect a fresh, new life; my wife will take the children and be solely responsible for them so that I am left free.

When I am through with school and have acquired a job, I want my   9
wife to quit working and remain at home so that my wife can more fully and completely take care of a wife's duties.

My God, who *wouldn't* want a wife?   10

◆ ◆ ◆

FIRST RESPONSES

Brady wrote this essay in the early 1970s. Is it still relevant today? Have changes in gender roles made Brady's views outdated? Are her points still valid?

TAKING A CLOSER LOOK

Exploring *Who:* Voice and Tone

1. Why does Brady identify herself as a wife and a mother at the beginning of the essay? Is this information important?
2. What assumptions did Brady probably make about her audience (readers of *Ms.* magazine in 1971)? Do you think she can make the same assumptions about you?
3. What evidence is there that the author is being ironic or sarcastic? Look at her use of italics and think about the way she uses these words: *proper* and *pleasantly* (para. 4), *bother* and *necessary* (para. 6), *demand* and *clutter up* (para. 7), *suitable* and *free* (para. 8).
4. Do you think Brady intends to provoke a reaction from her readers? What is your reaction? How do your own experiences (as a husband, wife, child, boyfriend, girlfriend, etc.) affect your responses?

Exploring *What:* Content and Meaning

1. Sum up in one sentence what Brady means by the term *wife*. Does this kind of wife actually exist?
2. Make a list of the specific duties of the wife described in this essay. How many general categories are covered?
3. What does Brady say about the sexual expectations and behavior of husbands? Do you agree with her?
4. Would you want a spouse or partner like the one described in this essay? Do you think Brady really does?

Exploring *Why:* Purpose

1. Is Brady's purpose to explain a wife's duties, to complain about her own situation, to attack or poke fun at men, to call attention to society's treatment of women, or what?
2. Is the author trying to present a realistic and fair definition of a wife? Explain.
3. What part does exaggeration play in this essay? Why would a writer use exaggeration?
4. Brady never uses any pronouns to refer to the wife. Why not?

Exploring *How:* Strategy and Style

1. Why are the words *A Wife* capitalized in the first paragraph?
2. Why does Brady include the story about a male friend who visits her? Is it significant that he is looking for another wife?
3. Give at least two reasons for the frequent repetition of the words "I want a wife."
4. According to what principles does Brady organize the details of her definitions into paragraphs? Why does she end with the point about the wife quitting work and remaining at home (para. 9)?
5. What is the effect of the rhetorical question at the very end? How does this conclusion sum up her main point?

IDEAS FOR WRITING A DEFINITION

1. Write an essay similar to Brady's, defining a word that denotes a social relationship: *husband, friend, lover, mother, father, brother, grandparent, son, daughter, roommate, neighbor, mentor, partner, confidant.* Define the term indirectly by showing what such a person does or should do. You can adopt a serious tone or an ironic one, as Brady does.
2. Go to your local bookstore or card shop, and review the text of greeting cards designed for wives, husbands, or mothers. Using ideas and examples you find, write an essay that defines a wife, a husband, or a mother as viewed by the greeting card industry.
3. ■ *Using the Internet.* Visit the Web site for the National Partnership for Women and Families (www.nationalpartnership.org), and examine some of their articles about work and family. Then write an essay in which you expand on your answers to the questions in the First Responses section: Is the essay still relevant today? Have changes in gender roles made Brady's views outdated? Are her points still valid?

◆ ◆ ◆ PREPARING TO READ

Does your family or close group of friends have a special language all its own? For example, do you cry or break out laughing when you hear words that mean something only within the group or phrases that capture a past experience?

◆ ◆ ◆

Mother Tongue

AMY TAN

Born in Oakland, California, in 1952 to immigrant Chinese parents, Amy Tan has made the experience of being raised in the United States by a Chinese mother the focus of three of her novels: the National Book Award–winning *The Joy Luck Club* (1989), *The Kitchen God's Wife* (1991), and most recently, *The Bonesetter's Daughter* (2001). In each work, Tan struggles to understand and bring to life the gaps of experience created by generational and cultural differences. In "Mother Tongue," first published in 1990, Tan takes up this issue of differences in relation to language.

1   I am not a scholar of English or literature. I cannot give you much more than personal opinions on the English language and its variations in this country or others.

2   I am a writer. And by that definition, I am someone who has always loved language. I am fascinated by language in daily life. I spend a great deal of my time thinking about the power of language—the way it can evoke an emotion, a visual image, a complex idea, or a simple truth. Language is the tool of my trade. And I use them all—all the Englishes I grew up with.

3   Recently, I was made keenly aware of the different Englishes I do use. I was giving a talk to a large group of people, the same talk I had already given to half a dozen other groups. The nature of the talk was about my writing, my life, and my book, *The Joy Luck Club*. The talk was going along well enough, until I remembered one major difference that made the whole talk sound wrong. My mother was in the room. And it was perhaps the first time she had heard me give a lengthy speech, using the kind of English I have never used with her. I was saying things like, "The intersection of memory upon imagination" and "There is an aspect of my fiction that relates to thus-and-thus"—a speech filled with carefully wrought grammatical phrases,

burdened, it suddenly seemed to me, with nominalized forms, past perfect tenses, conditional phrases, all the forms of standard English that I had learned in school and through books, the forms of English I did not use at home with my mother.

Just last week, I was walking down the street with my mother, and I   4
again found myself conscious of the English I was using, and the English I do use with her. We were talking about the price of new and used furniture and I heard myself saying this: "Not waste money that way." My husband was with us as well, and he didn't notice any switch in my English. And then I realized why. It's because over the twenty years we've been together I've often used that same kind of English with him, and sometimes he even uses it with me. It has become our language of intimacy, a different sort of English that relates to family talk, the language I grew up with.

So you'll have some idea of what this family talk I heard sounds like,   5
I'll quote what my mother said during a recent conversation which I videotaped and then transcribed. During this conversation my mother was talking about a political gangster in Shanghai who had the same last name as her family's, Du, and how the gangster in his early years wanted to be adopted by her family, which was rich by comparison. Later, the gangster became more powerful, far richer than my mother's family, and one day showed up at my mother's wedding to pay his respects. Here's what she said in part:

"Du Yusong having business like fruit stand. Like off the street kind.   6
He is Du like Du Zong—but not Tsung-ming Island people. The local people call putong, the river east side, he belong to that side local people. The man want to ask Du Zong father take him in like become own family. Du Zong father wasn't looking down on him, but didn't take seriously, until that man big like become a mafia. Now important person very hard to inviting him. Chinese way, come only to show respect, don't stay for dinner. Respect for making big celebration, he shows up. Mean gives lots of respect. Chinese custom. Chinese social life that way. If too important won't have to stay too long. He come to my wedding. I didn't see. I heard it. I gone to boy's side, they have YMCA dinner. Chinese age I was nineteen."

You should know that my mother's expressive command of English   7
belies how much she actually understands. She reads the *Forbes* report, listens to *Wall Street Week,* converses daily with her stockbroker, reads all of Shirley MacLaine's books with ease—all kinds of things I can't begin to understand. Yet some of my friends tell me they understand 50 percent of what my mother says. Some say they understand 80 to 90 percent. Some say they understand none of it, as if she were speaking pure Chinese. But to me, my mother's English is perfectly clear, perfectly natural. It's my mother's tongue.

Her language, as I hear it, is vivid, direct, full of observation and imagery. This was the language that helped shape the way I saw things, expressed things, made sense of the world.

Lately, I've been giving more thought to the kind of English my mother   8
speaks. Like others, I have described it to people as "broken" or "fractured" English. But I wince when I say that. It has always bothered me that I can think of no way to describe it other than "broken," as if it were damaged and needed to be fixed, as if it lacked a certain wholeness and soundness. I've heard other terms used, "limited English," for example. But they seem just as bad, as if everything is limited, including people's perceptions of the limited English speaker.

I know this for a fact, because when I was growing up, my mother's   9
"limited" English limited *my* perception of her. I was ashamed of her English. I believed that her English reflected the quality of what she had to say. That is, because she expressed them imperfectly her thoughts were imperfect. And I had plenty of empirical evidence to support me: the fact that people in department stores, at banks, and at restaurants did not take her seriously, did not give her good service, pretended not to understand her, or even acted as if they did not hear her.

My mother has long realized the limitations of her English as well.   10
When I was fifteen, she used to have me call people on the phone to pretend I was she. In this guise, I was forced to ask for information or even complain and yell at people who had been rude to her. One time it was a call to her stockbroker in New York. She had cashed out her small portfolio and it just so happened we were going to go to New York the next week, our very first trip outside California. I had to get on the phone and say in an adolescent voice that was not very convincing, "This is Mrs. Tan."

And my mother was standing in the back whispering loudly, "Why he   11
don't send me check, already two weeks late. So mad he lie to me, losing me money."

And then I said in perfect English, "Yes, I'm getting rather concerned.   12
You had agreed to send the check two weeks ago, but it hasn't arrived."

Then she began to talk more loudly. "What he want, I come to New   13
York tell him front of his boss, you cheating me?" And I was trying to calm her down, make her be quiet, while telling the stockbroker, "I can't tolerate any more excuses. If I don't receive the check immediately I am going to have to speak to your manager when I'm in New York next week." And sure enough, the following week there we were in front of this astonished stockbroker, and I was sitting there red-faced and quiet, and my mother, the real Mrs. Tan, was shouting at his boss in her impeccable broken English.

We used a similar routine just five days ago, for a situation that was far   14
less humorous. My mother had gone to the hospital for an appointment, to
find out about a benign brain tumor a CAT scan had revealed a month ago.
She said she had spoken very good English, her best English, no mistakes.
Still, she said, the hospital did not apologize when they said they had lost the
CAT scan and she had come for nothing. She said they did not seem to have
any sympathy when she told them she was anxious to know the exact diagnosis, since her husband and son had both died of brain tumors. She said they
would not give her any more information until the next time and she would
have to make another appointment for that. So she said she would not leave
until the doctor called her daughter. She wouldn't budge. And when the doctor finally called her daughter, me, who spoke in perfect English—lo and
behold—we had assurances the CAT scan would be found, promises that a
conference call on Monday would be held, and apologies for any suffering my
mother had gone through for a most regrettable mistake.

I think my mother's English almost had an effect on limiting my pos-   15
sibilities in life as well. Sociologists and linguists probably will tell you that
a person's developing language skills are more influenced by peers. But I do
think that the language spoken in the family, especially in immigrant families which are more insular, plays a large role in shaping the language of the
child. And I believe that it affected my results on achievement tests, IQ tests,
and the SAT. While my English skills were never judged as poor, compared
to math, English could not be considered my strong suit. In grade school I did
moderately well, getting perhaps Bs, sometimes B-pluses, in English and scoring perhaps in the sixtieth or seventieth percentile on achievement tests. But
those scores were not good enough to override the opinion that my true abilities lay in math and science, because in those areas I achieved As and scored
in the ninetieth percentile or higher.

This was understandable. Math is precise; there is only one correct an-   16
swer. Whereas, for me at least, the answers on English tests were always a
judgment call, a matter of opinion and personal experience. Those tests were
constructed around items like fill-in-the-blank sentence completion, such as
"Even though Tom was _____ Mary thought he was _____."
And the correct answer always seemed to be the most bland combinations
of thoughts, for example, "Even though Tom was shy, Mary thought he was
charming," with the grammatical structure "even though" limiting the correct
answer to some sort of semantic opposites, so you wouldn't get answers like,
"Even though Tom was foolish, Mary thought he was ridiculous." Well, according to my mother, there were very few limitations as to what Tom could
have been and what Mary might have thought of him. So I never did well on
tests like that.

The same was true with word analogies, pairs of words in which you 17
were supposed to find some sort of logical, semantic relationship—for example, "*Sunset* is to *nightfall* as _____ is to _____." And here
you would be presented with a list of four possible pairs, one of which showed
the same kind of relationship: *red* is to *stoplight, bus* is to *arrival, chills* is to
fever, yawn is to *boring*. Well, I could never think that way. I knew what the
tests were asking, but I could not block out of my mind the images already
created by the first pair, "*sunset* is to *nightfall*"—and I would see a burst of
colors against a darkening sky, the moon rising, the lowering of a curtain of
stars. And all the other pairs of words—red, bus, stoplight, boring—just threw
up a mass of confusing images, making it impossible for me to sort out something as logical as saying: "A sunset precedes nightfall" is the same as "a chill
precedes a fever." The only way I would have gotten that answer right would
have been to imagine an associative situation, for example, my being disobedient and staying out past sunset, catching a chill at night, which turns
into feverish pneumonia as punishment, which indeed did happen to me.

I have been thinking about all this lately, about my mother's English, 18
about achievement tests. Because lately I've been asked, as a writer, why
there are not more Asian Americans represented in American literature.
Why are there few Asian Americans enrolled in creative writing programs?
Why do so many Chinese students go into engineering? Well, these are broad
sociological questions I can't begin to answer. But I have noticed in surveys—
in fact, just last week—that Asian students, as a whole, always do significantly
better on math achievement tests than in English. And this makes me think
that there are other Asian-American students whose English spoken in the
home might also be described as "broken" or "limited." And perhaps they
also have teachers who are steering them away from writing and into math
and science, which is what happened to me.

Fortunately, I happen to be rebellious in nature and enjoy the chal- 19
lenge of disproving assumptions made about me. I became an English major
my first year in college, after being enrolled as pre-med. I started writing
nonfiction as a freelancer the week after I was told by my former boss that
writing was my worst skill and I should hone my talents toward account management.

But it wasn't until 1985 that I finally began to write fiction. And at first 20
I wrote using what I thought to be wittily crafted sentences, sentences that
would finally prove I had mastery over the English language. Here's an example from the first draft of a story that later made its way into *The Joy Luck
Club,* but without this line: "That was my mental quandary in its nascent
state." A terrible line, which I can barely pronounce.

Fortunately, for reasons I won't get into today, I later decided I should   21
envision a reader for the stories I would write. And the reader I decided upon
was my mother because these were stories about mothers. So with this reader
in mind—and in fact she did read my early drafts—I began to write stories
using all the Englishes I grew up with: the English I spoke to my mother,
which for lack of a better term might be described as "simple"; the English
she used with me, which for lack of a better term might be described as "broken"; my translation of her Chinese, which could certainly be described as
"watered down"; and what I imagined to be her translation of her Chinese
if she could speak in perfect English, her internal language, and for that I
sought to preserve the essence, but neither an English nor a Chinese structure. I wanted to capture what language ability tests can never reveal: her
intent, her passion, her imagery, the rhythms of her speech, and the nature of
her thoughts.

Apart from what any critic had to say about my writing, I knew I had   22
succeeded where it counted when my mother finished reading my book and
gave me her verdict: "So easy to read."

◆ ◆ ◆

FIRST RESPONSES

How do you feel when around someone whose primary language is not
the same as yours? Have you had an especially positive or negative experience with such a person? What contributed to your reaction?

TAKING A CLOSER LOOK

Exploring *Who:* Voice and Tone

1. In addition to being a novelist, Tan has a master's degree in linguistics.
   Why, then, does she begin the essay by claiming not to be a "scholar of
   English or literature" but instead to be "a writer"?
2. What is the primary "English" Tan uses in this essay? Why?
3. Why does Tan directly address the reader in the first sentence of paragraph 5?
4. How much of the lengthy sample of Tan's mother's English in paragraph 6 are you able to understand? How does this affect your response
   to Tan's point here?

Exploring *What:* Content and Meaning

1. How many Englishes does Tan describe in her essay? Are there examples of each?
2. Were you surprised to discover in paragraph 3 that Tan's mother had never heard her daughter use her public lecture English? What insight into their relationship does this fact provide?
3. How does Tan feel about "family talk"?
4. Why is Tan uncomfortable with the term *broken English?* Does she find a better term for her mother's dialect?
5. ■ *Using the Internet.* The movement to make the United States officially an "English Only" country has raised a number of important issues about the role of language in both our personal and cultural lives. Visit the Web site www.aclu.org/Library.pbp6.html, and compare its arguments with Tan's personal experience of a bilingual United States.

Exploring *Why:* Purpose

1. Why does Tan reveal that as a child she was ashamed of her mother's English? What point about the relationship between language and a person's worth does she wish her readers to confront?
2. What does Tan's personal experience illustrate about the stereotyping of Asians as math and science whizzes? How many different sets of readers might she be trying to reach with this message?
3. What have you learned about being a writer from reading Tan's essay?

Exploring *How:* Style and Strategy

1. Which of the many **anecdotes** about Tan's mother most stands out for you? Why? What point did it help to clarify for you?
2. In paragraph 3, Tan uses two sample sentences to explain the kind of language she uses in her public speeches. She also lists the grammatical features of that speech, for example "nominalized forms." Why didn't she simply use either examples or terms?
3. Why does Tan place the example of her mother's argument with her stockbroker before the conflict with the hospital? Why does Tan include, in paragraph 14, that she spoke "perfect English"?
4. How does this essay prove Tan's initial claim to be "someone who has always loved language"?

IDEAS FOR WRITING A DEFINITION

1. Write an essay defining a word or phrase you came up with in your response to "Preparing to Read." Use anecdotes and examples as Tan does in her essay to illustrate and clarify your definition. Remember that your readers are not just interested in the particular word but also in how it helps them understand your relationship with your family or friends.

2. Have you ever had an experience similar to Tan's with her mother's brain tumor, where someone in a position of authority failed to take you or someone you know seriously? Write an essay defining the characteristic of institutional or human relationships this experience helped you understand. Consider how your insights might help solve the problem.

3. What different "Englishes" do you use? Think about the way your language changes according to the circumstances you are in and the people you are with (friends, parents, teachers, employers, salespeople, etc.). Write an essay in which you define and explain the different forms of English you use.

◆ ◆ ◆ PREPARING TO READ

What kind of relationship do you have with your father or mother? Is he or she warm, loving, and easy to talk to, or do you have a hard time expressing your feelings for each other? Do you get along well, or do you seem to fight all the time? How do you think you might get to know your father or mother better? Do you care to?

◆ ◆ ◆

Father Hunger

MICHEL MARRIOTT

Michel Marriott is a reporter for the *New York Times;* he has also written for *Newsweek* magazine. His areas of interest have included political corruption, street hustlers, youth violence, gang activity, exercise machines, and rap music stars. Most recently, he has written a series of articles about the effects of the Internet on business and the arts. In the following essay, which first appeared in *Essence* magazine in 1990, Marriott explores the meaning of the phrase "father hunger."

1   Once, not too many years ago, I looked up from the scribble on my reporter's pad and stared into the hyperanimated face of Fidel Castro—and I saw my father. As part of a delegation of African-American journalists invited to Cuba in 1986, I counted myself lucky to be among the teeming Caribbeans crammed onto a dusty soccer field just outside a knot of empty shops, crowded flats and stands of sugarcane. Moreover, I felt a stab of surprise that I had somehow stepped, flesh and blood, into my father's dream.

2   Long disenchanted with what he called the "trick bag" of the United States, my father reveled in the sheer bravado of the Cuban revolution, its elevation of the Brown and Black to real power. He often talked, half jokingly, of course, of retiring someday to that island republic and having Uncle Sam send his Social Security checks to Havana.

3   In recognition of the special significance my journey might hold for him, I presented Dad with a gift on my return. To my disappointment, however, he barely accepted the carefully framed photograph I had taken of Castro and inscribed with words of tribute to my father's courage as a freethinker.

Why is it so difficult for us? I asked myself some weeks later when I   4
discovered the picture pitched against a mound of disarray on my father's
desk. After so many years of being buffeted by swirling currents of father-son
tensions, intermittent hostilities and redeeming love, *why,* I mused, *does it
remain so hard for us—two Black men—to, well, just get along?* There had
been times when we had hurled hurtful words at each other like poison-
tipped spears. We had even, in dizzying and terrifying fits of machismo, both
reached for guns, prepared to shoot each other if need be.

Why wasn't it like television, where dads wore suits and ties to the din-   5
ner table and were ever ready to lend an ear or dispense fatherly advice with
a knowing grin? Where was Fred MacMurray in blackface?

The truth is that for millions of Black men, our relationships with our   6
fathers represent lifetimes of unfinished business. Much too often our most
obvious models—from whom we begin to fashion our distinctive sense of
a masculine identity—are marginal to our lives because of our fathers'
physical or emotional absence from home. The issue is not new or exclusive to African-American men. James Herzog, a Harvard University Medical School assistant professor of psychiatry, coined the phrase "father
hunger" to describe the psychological condition young children endure
when long separated from their fathers. English professor Andrew Merton
of the University of New Hampshire wrote in a 1986 article in *New Age*
magazine of many men whose lives have been profoundly shaped and
troubled by failures of intimacy with their fathers. Quoting author Samuel
Osherson, Merton wrote: "The psychological or physical absence of fathers
from their families is one of the great underestimated tragedies of our
times."

What is so devastating for so many of us in search of our Black fathers   7
is the realization that many of them were utter failures at nurturing us. And
now, as many of us are fathers ourselves, we also find ourselves struggling
with the identical phenomenon in relation to our own sons—as if this difficulty were inherent in our Black condition, as if it somehow passes from generation to generation in a recessive gene that we peculiarly carry. But, of
course, it's sociological, not biological.

"The masculine role has clearly restricted our ability to relate to chil-   8
dren," write Joseph H. Pleck and Jack Sawyer of American men in general,
in their 1974 collection *Men and Masculinity.* "Our drive toward getting ahead
means we often find little time or energy for being with children; moreover,
we may project our own strivings for success upon them."

In the case of too many Black men, however, it is more likely that we   9
project upon our sons our fear and profound sense of powerlessness and vulnerability in a society that daily crushes many of us. Countless Black boys, as
a consequence, grow up in a tangle of fatherly love and loathing for what lies
ahead for little Michael, little Jamil.

For example, my father would bristle with indignation whenever he   10
discovered my brother and me, as young boys, watching Saturday-morning
cartoons. "You don't have time for that bullshit," he'd say in a tone so sharp
our child-joy would expire on the spot. "The white man wants you to look at
Bugs Bunny while he's figuring out better ways to beat you. You better learn
some math, read a book."

There'd be no hugs given or "good mornings" spoken. There was al-   11
ways so much harshness, a sternness very much like that I saw years later
captured in Troy Maxson's rage and reason in August Wilson's play *Fences*.
When Troy's teenage son, Cory, asks him why he doesn't like him, Troy responds with fury: "I done give you everything I had to give you. I gave you
your life! Me and your mama worked that out between us. And liking your
black ass wasn't part of the bargain. Don't you try and go through life worrying about if somebody like you or not. You best be making sure they doing
right by you." Similarly, growing up with my father, at the time a factory
worker at a synthetic-rubber manufacturing plant in Louisville, Kentucky,
was like growing up in boot camp, training for the inevitable clashes with
white racism and domination that waited just outside the nest of our segregated neighborhood.

Yet I identified with my father. I marveled at his strength—not merely   12
muscular, since he was never a particularly large man. I was in awe of his ac-
cordionlike ability to expand on demand, to pump up his nerve and face
down anyone who threatened him or his wife or three boys, whether a landlord, a police officer, or a teacher who shirked responsibility. In that way,
among many, I wanted to be like him: smart, tough, the relentless warrior.

James P. Comer, M.D., an African-American professor of child psychi-   13
atry at the Yale University Child Study Center, says that while the concept
of role modeling may sound like a cliché, it is nevertheless "very real" and
necessary. "Kids are here without a road map, and you are like that map to
them," he points out. According to Samuel Osherson in his popular 1986
book *Finding Our Fathers,* the need to "identify with father creates the crucial dilemma for boys. [Father is] often a shadowy figure at best, difficult to
understand." The result can often be a troubling psychological limbo, explains Osherson, in which boys as young as three years old begin pulling
away from their mothers but have no clear male model to identify with.

I've never forgotten the unshed tear in the voice of my best friend when   14
I first asked him about his father, a man I'd never heard him talk about. Until
that afternoon some years ago, my buddy had seemed to be a product of his
mother's labors alone, a bloom from a self-pollinating black orchid.

But there was a man, from whom my friend's features had borrowed   15
heavily. He had never married his mother. My buddy's only contact with the
man was when, as a boy, he occasionally sat in the cluttered back room of the
man's television-repair shop, a place cooled during the Philadelphia sum-

mers by an open door and the warm, breathy air of buzzing electric fans. After being told by his mother that the man in the shop was his father, one day my friend stoked up his nerve and asked the man if this was true.

"You're not any boy of mine," he replied, my friend told me. Wounded   16 deeply, he never returned to the shop. Some years later his father died, a bridge between knowing and not knowing a part of himself forever swept away.

After having dozens of recent conversations with Black men about   17 their relationships with their fathers, a common element emerges, regardless of age: Like a primal impulse, the men who have had injured relations with their fathers are busy trying to heal them. Those who enjoy mutually satisfying, rich and rewarding relationships—if not the exaggerated bliss of *The Cosby Show*—find them invaluable. In an interview with astronaut Colonel Frederick Drew Gregory shortly before he became the first African-American to command a spacecraft in the late 1980s, he spoke with me at length about his father as mentor and role model. It was his father, he said, who inspired him to reach for heights that many, Black and white, would consider unattainable.

James Comer writes lovingly of his late father in his 1988 book *Maggie's*   18 *American Dream: The Life and Times of a Black Family*. Comer, the father of a grown son and daughter, says it is not surprising that many Black men are trying to better understand and appreciate their fathers. "They realize what they have missed," he says. "In some cases there is a struggle for independence that can lead to a difficult relationship," though, he adds, "even bad times can be important once you have reestablished a good relationship." But at any time, Comer emphasizes, "it is important to reestablish the relationship."

Unfortunately that may be more problematic for boys born in the closing years of the twentieth century, since the numbers of African-American   19 families headed by women continue to be substantial. And with alarming regularity, Black fathers are relegating themselves to being ghost dads of sorts: Many are lost to the streets, prisons, to successful careers or to legacies of poor relationships with their own fathers, who had troubles with *their* fathers.

"Imagine what it must be like to have a part of you not there," says   20 Terry M. Williams, author and sociologist at Yale, of boys who don't know or know well their fathers. "You think, *So where can I find it?*" Having the father present in the son's life is key, stresses Williams, even "if his role is not that strong."

Williams, author of the 1989 book *The Cocaine Kids: The Inside Story*   21 *of a Teenage Drug Ring,* in which he chronicles some four years of observing a young crew of cocaine dealers in New York City, says many young men of color perceive themselves as being in a state of war. "They are acting out and trying to find a way to be men, through tough crews and homeboy networks. You can't deny that these are some of the negative sides of not having fathers around."

Williams, who has two sons, suggests that more Black men be more attentive to their roles as fathers and also reach out to be mentors and role models for other boys. Without positive role models, it is obvious that boys may turn to crime or antisocial behavior, says Williams. 22

As my own son nears his teenage years, I worry if our relationship will hold. His mother and I divorced when he was hardly a year old. But I have worked hard through the years to keep our father-son links strong and supportive, despite the hundreds of miles that separate us for most of the year. At the close of every telephone conversation, I tell him I love him. And he is careful to tell me he loves me, something my father has never been able to bring himself to say. 23

I love my father. Some of that love stems from my culture's obligation to honor him because he is my father. Yet another, much larger, part of that love flows from my understanding of him, my empathy with his life and wounds as a proud Black man dangling from a leafless tree of opportunities denied. At 63, my father is a man of enormous talents and, in his own estimation, of humble accomplishments. Many demons still stir in his soul. 24

For the past ten years we have moved, gently, to resolve our conflicts, to settle into roles reassigned to us by time and growth. In the last few years he has let me hug him when I see him now, which is all too infrequently. I, on the other hand, have reined in my juvenile urges to compete with him, to prove in battles of wit and wile that I am as much a man as he is. 25

For the last three years I've pulled out the same card of bright colors and upbeat prose I bought for Father's Day. But each year something prevents me from sending it. Procrastination abounds, moving me to return the card to my top drawer, more determined to actually send it to him the next year. Yet, as I wrote this article in the late summer, a process that forced me to refocus my feelings about Pop, I got out the card, signed it "I love you" and sent it homeward. I hope its arrival, though odd, will signal to him anew my homage to our connections, both involuntary and voluntary, both of the blood and of the heart. 26

I want my father to know that with each morning look into the bathroom mirror, I see a little more of his face peering through mine. Life's journey is circular, it appears. The years don't carry us away from our fathers—they return us to them. 27

If we are lucky, we will have our memories of them. If we are luckier still and work hard for it, we can enjoy with them laughter and tears of recognition, enjoy loving embraces of mutual appreciation and respect. 28

With each day, I feel luckier. 29

FIRST RESPONSES

Do you think the "psychological or physical absence of fathers from their families is one of the great underestimated tragedies of our times"? Why is it difficult for fathers to express their love for their sons?

TAKING A CLOSER LOOK

Exploring *Who:* Voice and Tone

1. In the opening sentence, Marriott reveals that he's a reporter. What other information about himself does he divulge in the essay?
2. Marriott doesn't mention his mother, and he mentions his ex-wife only once. Why doesn't he say more about them? Is this an oversight or an intentional omission?
3. Is Marriott writing only for African American men? Why should other people read this essay and care about the issues it raises?
4. How did your background (race, age, gender) affect the way you responded to the author's ideas and feelings about fatherhood?

Exploring *What:* Content and Meaning

1. What is "father hunger"? Try defining it in several sentences.
2. Where does the author state his thesis? Where does he reinforce and restate his main point?
3. According to Marriott, why do African-American fathers frequently abandon their sons?
4. In paragraph 25, the author talks about his "juvenile urges to compete with" his father. What does he mean? Do you have any experiences or observations that help you understand this idea?
5. ■▯ *Using the Internet.* Find a review of one of the books that Marriott cites in his essay: *Men and Masculinity, Finding Our Fathers, Maggie's American Dream,* or *The Cocaine Kids.* Do any of the reviews touch on the issue of father-son relationships? If so, do they support Marriott's ideas? If not, why do you think they don't mention this topic? You can find links to book reviews at several online bookstores; the BookWire site (www.bookwire.com) includes a list. You could also look at the Web version of *The Quarterly Black Review of Books* (www.qbr.com).

Exploring *Why:* Purpose

1. Why is Marriott "in search of" his father? Was writing this essay a part of that search? See paragraph 26.
2. What does the author say about his own fathering skills? What does his relationship with his own son have to do with his reasons for writing this essay?
3. Reread the last six paragraphs. Notice that in this section, Marriott calls his father "Pop" for the first and only time in the essay. Why does he use that word at this point? Why does he say he feels "luckier" with each day?

Exploring *How:* Strategy and Style

1. Why does Marriott begin with an **anecdote** about Fidel Castro? How does this narrative provide a lead-in to his central idea?
2. Why are the sentences in paragraph 4 in italics?
3. Look at the kinds of evidence Marriott uses to support his thesis; notice how he combines personal experience with expert opinion. Which do you find more persuasive, the quotations from writers and the mention of celebrities or the author's own experiences?
4. Why does the author include the extended example about his best friend (para. 14 through 16)? How did you respond to the father's statement, "You're not any boy of mine"? Do you understand why the father said that?

IDEAS FOR WRITING A DEFINITION

1. Think about all the benefits of a mother's love. Then imagine how your life would have been different if deprived of that love. Write an essay defining "mother hunger."
2. Write an essay defining the distinctive qualities of your family as you were growing up. What were the recurrent themes or persistent issues within your family during this time in your life? Have they changed now that you are older? Why or why not?
3. A number of situation comedies on television depict fathers who are raising children without a mother in the family. Analyze two or three of these sitcoms, and write an essay evaluating how realistically these family situations are being presented. Or explain the appeal of such programs.

◆ ◆ ◆ **PREPARING TO READ**

What is your biggest fear? How do you deal with it? Does it ever make you behave in irrational and unpleasant ways?

◆ ◆ ◆

The Fear

ANDREW HOLLERAN

Andrew Holleran (born in 1934) is the author of three novels about gay life: *Dancer from the Dance* (1978), *Nights in Aruba* (1983), and *The Beauty of Men* (1996). His collection of essays, *Ground Zero* (1988), deals with the public and personal issues surrounding AIDS, and his collection of short stories, *In September, the Light Changes,* was published in 1999. A former resident of New York City, he now lives in Florida. In the following essay, which appeared in a 1989 collection of writers' responses to the AIDS crisis, Holleran examines the anxiety and distrust that grip people who are at risk from infection by the AIDS virus.

The Fear is of course unseemly—as most fear is. People behave at worst   1
with demonic cruelty—at best oddly. Even among those who are good-hearted, the madness breaks out in small ways that bring friendships of long standing to an abrupt end. When the plague began and the television crews of certain TV stations refused to work on interviews with people with AIDS, I wanted to get their names, write them down, publish them on a list of cowards. When the parents in Queens picketed and refused to send their kids to school; when they kicked Ryan White out of class in Indiana; when people called in to ask if it was safe to ride the subway; when Pat Buchanan called for a quarantine of homosexuals; when they burned down the house in Arcadia, Florida, I felt a thrilling disgust, a contempt, an anger at the shrill, stupid, mean panic, the alacrity with which people are converted to lepers and the lepers cast out of the tribe, the fact that if Fear is contemptible, it is most contemptible in people who have no reason to fear.

Even within the homosexual community, however, there was despica-   2
ble behavior: men who would not go to restaurants, hospital rooms, wakes, for fear that any contact with other homosexuals might be lethal. At dinner one night in San Francisco in 1982, a friend said, "There's a crack in the glass," after I'd taken a sip of his lover's wine, and took the glass back to the kitchen

to replace it—a reaction so swift it took me a moment to realize there was no crack in the glass; the problem was my lips' touching it—homosexual lips, from New York: the kiss of death. I was furious then, but the behavior no longer surprises me. AIDS, after all, belongs to the Age of Anxiety. My friend was a germophobe to begin with, who, though homosexual himself, after five years in San Francisco, had come to loathe homosexuals. The idea that they could now kill him, or his lover, fit in. AIDS fed on his free-floating anxiety about the rest of modern life: the fertilizers, pesticides, toxic wastes, additives in food, processing of food, steroids given cattle, salmonella in chickens, killer bees moving up from Brazil, Mediterranean fruit fly, poisoned water, lead in our pipes, radon in our homes, asbestos in our high schools, danger of cigarette smoke, mercury in tuna, auto emissions in the air, Filipinos on the bus, Mexicans sneaking across the border. The society that could make sugar sinister was ready, it would seem, to panic over AIDS, so that when Russia put out the disinformation in its official press that AIDS was the work of a germwarfare laboratory run by the Pentagon, it was only repeating a charge made by homosexuals convinced that AIDS is a right-wing program to eradicate queers.

God only knows what AIDS will turn out to be, years and years from now—perhaps, in 2005, "Sixty Minutes" will reveal it *was* a CIA foul-up. But this general panic, this unease, this sense that the world is out of control and too intimately connected, is not *all* the Fear is among homosexuals. The Fear among homosexuals is personal, physical, and real. It is easy enough to dismiss the idea that the CIA set out to exterminate homosexuals; it is not easy to dismiss the fact that—having lived in New York during the seventies as a gay man—one can reasonably expect to have been infected. "We've all been exposed," a friend said to me in 1981 on the sidewalk one evening before going off to Switzerland to have his blood recycled—when "exposed" was still the word to spare the feelings of those who were, someone finally pointed out, "infected." The idea—that everyone had been swimming in the same sea—made little impression on us at the time; nor did I grasp the implications—because then the plague was still so new, and its victims so (relatively) few, that most homosexuals could still come up with a list of forty to fifty things to distinguish their past, their habits, from those of the men they knew who had it. Now, five years later, that list is in shreds; one by one those distinguishing features or habits have been taken away, and the plague reveals itself as something infinitely larger, more various, more random, than was suspected at the start—as common as the flu—indeed, the thing the doctors are predicting a repeat of: the Spanish influenza following World War I.

Predictions like these, above all, intensify the Fear, to the point that 4 one tenses when a news story comes on the evening news about AIDS—and wonders: What new sadistic detail? What new insoluble problem? One looks away when the word is in the newspaper headline and turns to the comics instead. One hopes the phone will not ring with news of yet another friend diagnosed, because one can always trace a flare-up of the Fear—an AIDS anxiety attack: that period when you are certain you have *It,* and begin making plans for your demise—to some piece of news, or several, that came through the television or the telephone. Sometimes they are so numerous, and all at once, that you are undone—like the man walking down the boardwalk on Fire Island with a friend one evening on their way to dance, who, after a quiet conversation at dinner, suddenly threw himself down on the ground and began screaming: "We're all going to die, we're all going to die!" He did. Sometimes it hits like that. It appears in the midst of the most ordinary circumstances—like the man on that same beach, who in the middle of a cloudless summer afternoon turned to my friend and said: "What is the point of going on?" ("To bear witness," my friend responded.) The Fear is there all the time, but it comes in surges, like electricity—activated, triggered, almost always by specific bad news.

The media are full of bad news, of course—the stories of breakthroughs,   5
of discoveries, of new drugs seem to have subsided now into a sea of disappointment. They do not sound the note of relief and hope and exultation they once did—that dream that one evening you would be brushing your teeth, and your roommate, watching the news in the living room, would shout: "It's over!" and you would run down the hall and hear the Armistice declared. Instead, the media carry the *pronunciamientos* of the Harvard School of Public Health, the World Health Organization, dire beyond our wildest nightmares: What began as a strange disease ten or twelve homosexuals in New York had contracted becomes the Black Death. Of course, journalists, as Schopenhauer said, are professional alarmists, and have only fulfilled their usual role: scaring their readers. They are scaring them so that the readers will protect themselves, of course; they are at the same time inducing despair in those already infected. There's the dilemma: They're all watching the same TV, reading the same newspapers.

After a while, the Fear is so ugly you feel like someone at a dinner party   6
whose fellow guests are being taken outside and shot as you concentrate politely on your salad. There is the school of thought that says the Fear is a form of stress, and stress enhances the virus. Like the man so afraid of muggers he somehow draws them to him, the Fear is said to make itself come true, by those who believe in mind control. As a friend of mine (so fearful of the disease he refused to have sex for four years) said, "I got everything I resisted." So one becomes fearful even of the Fear. The Fear can be so wearing, so depressing, so constant that a friend who learned he had AIDS said, on hearing the diagnosis, "Well, it's a lot better than worrying about it."

He also said, "I wasn't doing anything anyone else wasn't." Which ex-   7
plains the Fear more succinctly than anything else: Tens of thousands were doing the same thing in the seventies. Why, then, should some get sick and not

others? Isn't it logical to expect everyone will, eventually? The Fear is so strong it causes people to change cities, to rewrite their pasts in order to imagine they were doing less than everyone else; because the most unnerving thing about the plague is its location in the Past, the Time allotted to it.

Were AIDS a disease which, once contracted, brought death within 8 forty-eight hours of exposure, it would be a far more easily avoided illness— but because it is not—because it is invisible, unknown, for such a long period of time, because it is something people got before they even knew it existed (with each passing year, the Time Lag gets longer), the Fear of AIDS is limitless. Who has not had sex within the last seven years—once? (The nun in San Francisco who got AIDS from a blood transfusion given her during an operation to set her broken leg, and died, her superiors said, without anger or bitterness.) (The babies who get it in the womb.) There's a memory—of an evening, an incident—to justify every Fear. And nothing exists that will guarantee the fearful that even if they are functioning now, they will not get caught in the future. The phrase that keeps running through the fearful mind is: Everyone was healthy before he got sick. One has to have two programs, two sets of responses, ready at all times: (a) Life, (b) Death. The switch from one category to the other can come at any moment, in the most casual way. At the dentist's, or putting on your sock. Did that shin bruise a little too easily? Is that a new mole? Is the sinus condition that won't go away just a sinus condition? Do you feel a bit woozy standing at the kitchen sink? Do you want to lie down? Is the Fear making you woozy, or the virus? Have you had too many colds this past spring to be just colds? Thus the hyperconsciousness of the body begins. Your body—which you have tended, been proud of—is something you begin to view with suspicion, mistrust. Your body is someone you came to a party with and you'd like to ditch, only you promised to drive him home. Your body is a house—there's a thief inside it who wants to rob you of everything. Your body could be harboring It, even as you go about your business. This keeps you on edge. You stop, for instance, looking in mirrors. Or at your body in the shower—because the skin, all of a sudden, seems as vast as Russia: a huge terrain, a monumental wall, on which tiny handwriting may suddenly appear. The gums, the tongue, the face, the foot, the forearm, the leg: *billions* of cells waiting to go wrong. Because you read that sunburn depresses the immune system, you no longer go out in the sun. You stay in the house—as if already an invalid—you cancel all thoughts of traveling in airplanes because you heard flights can trigger the pneumonia and because you want to be home when it happens, not in some hotel room in Japan or San Diego.

And so the Fear constricts Life. It suffocates, till one evening its prey 9 snaps—gets in the car and drives to the rest stop, or bar, or baths to meet another human being; and has sex. Sometimes has sex; sometimes just talks about the Fear, because a conversation about the danger of sex sometimes replaces sex itself. The Fear is a god to which offerings must be made before sex can commence. Sometimes it refuses the offering. If it does not, it takes its share of the harvest afterward. Sex serves the Fear more slavishly than anything. Even safe sex leads to the question: Why was I even doing something that *required* condoms? The aftermath of sex is fear *and* loathing. AIDS is a national program of aversion therapy. Sex and terror are twins. Death is a hunk, a gorgeous penis. And fear is self-centered, is above all personal, and you vent your terror before you realize how insensitive this is. One day you spill out your fears about the sex you had to a friend who—you realize too late—has had AIDS for a couple of years now. He has lived with his own fear for two years. Your friend merely listens calmly, says what you did does not seem unsafe, and then remarks: "What I'm getting from what you've been saying is that you're still afraid." Of course, you want to reply, *of course* I'm still afraid! "But you have no reason to be," he says, from the height, the eminence of his own fear, digested, lived with, incorporated into his own life by now. "If you don't have it now, you won't." (Your other friend has told you, "The doctors think we're about to see a second wave of cases, the ones who contracted it in 1981.") Going home on the subway, your fear takes the form of superstition: He should never have said that! He himself had said (a remark you've never forgotten) that he was diagnosed just at the point when—after three years of abstinence—he thought he had escaped. It's the Time Lag, of course, the petri dish in which the Fear thrives. Of course, you are afraid; every male homosexual who lived in New York during the seventies is scared shitless. And a bit unstable, withdrawn, and crazy. The tactlessness of venting your fear to a friend who already has been diagnosed is symptomatic of this behavior. People who are afraid are seldom as considerate as those who are unafraid. The ironic thing about my last visit to New York was that the two men I knew who have AIDS were cheerful, calm, gracious, well behaved. Those who did not were nervous wrecks: depressed, irritable, isolated, withdrawn, unwilling to go out at night, in bed by ten under a blanket, with terror and a VCR. The Fear is not fun to live with, though when shared, it can produce occasional, hysterical laughter. The laughter vanishes, however, the moment you leave the apartment building and find yourself alone on the street. Falls right off your face as you slip instantly back into the mood you were in before you went to visit your friend. The Fear breeds depression. The depression breeds anger. (Not to mention the anger of people who have it toward those who don't. Why me? Why should *he* escape?) Friendships come to an end over incidents which would have been jokes before. People withdraw from each other so they don't have to go through the suffering of each other's illness. People behave illogically: One night a friend refuses to eat from a buffet commemorating a dead dancer because so many of the other guests have AIDS ("They shouldn't have served finger food"), but he leaves the wake with a young handsome Brazilian who presumably doesn't, goes home, and has sex. We all have an explanation for our private decisions, our choices of what we will do and what we won't; we all have a rationale for our superstitions. Most of it is superstition, because that is what the Fear produces and always has. Some of it is just muddled thinking, like the nightclub patrons in Miami who said they did not worry about AIDS there because it cost ten dollars to get in. And some of it is perfectly rational, like that which convinces people they should not take the Test because they would rather not live with the knowledge they have antibodies to the virus. (Today, the news announces a home test that will tell you in three minutes if you do, or don't; not much time for counseling!)

The Test is the most concentrated form of the Fear that there is—which   10
is why people are advised not to take it if they think they will have trouble handling the results. Why should we know? The fact is things are happening in our bodies, our blood, all the time we know nothing of, the hole in the dike of our immune systems may appear at any moment, and is always invisible, silent, unadvertised.

When does a person begin to develop cancer? When does a tumor start   11
to grow? When does the wall of the heart begin to weaken? Do you want to know? With AIDS, there is presumably something in hiding, in the brain, the tissues, waiting for some moment to begin its incredibly fast and protean reproduction. It may be waiting—or reproducing—as I type this. This is the Fear that is finally selfish. That is perhaps worse in the imagining than in the reality. This is what makes you think: I must know, I can't bear this, I'll take the Test. So you drive over one hot afternoon to do it, thinking of the letter from a woman whose nephew just died at home of AIDS: "Tony even tested Negative two months before he died." What fun. You feel as if you are driving not toward the county health department but the Day of Judgment. In my right hand, I give you Life, in my left, Death. What will you do, the voice asks, when you find out? How will you live? How do people with AIDS drive the car, fall asleep at night, face the neighbors, deal with solitude? The stupendous cruelty of this disease crashes in upon you. And so you bargain with God. You apologize, and make vows. Ask, How could this have happened? How could I have reached this point? Where did I make the turn that got me on *this* road? Every test you have ever taken, written or oral—the book reports; the thesis examinations; the spelling bees; those afternoons walking home from school as far as you could before turning the page of your test to see the grade, on a corner where no one could see your reaction; the day you got drafted; the day you found out whether you were going to Vietnam—all pale, or come back, in one single concentrated tsunami of terror at this moment.

In eighteenth-century Connecticut, Jonathan Edwards preached a ser-   12
mon called "Sinners in the Hands of an Angry God," which was so terrifying that women in the congregation fainted. Some things never change. The Fear,

like the sermon, feeds on the Imagination. And the moment you know some-one who faces this disease daily with composure, calm, humor, and his or her own personality intact, you realize how deforming, how demeaning, how subject to the worst instincts Fear is.

◆ ◆ ◆

FIRST RESPONSES

If you thought you were at risk for getting AIDS, would you get tested? Do you think it's better to know you have an incurable disease, or would you prefer not to know? Explain your thinking.

TAKING A CLOSER LOOK

Exploring *Who:* Voice and Tone

1. Does Holleran ever say he has AIDS? Why doesn't he reveal this fact?
2. Do you know anyone with AIDS? How might the answer to this question affect your response to the essay?
3. Does the author himself give in to the madness he equates with the Fear? Where do you see evidence of that? How does that perception color your response to the author and his essay?
4. Do you have to be at risk of getting AIDS to understand and appreciate this essay? Point out several passages that illustrate the way fear, of any sort, affects people in general.

Exploring *What:* Content and Meaning

1. Identify and describe several of Holleran's attitudes toward the behavior of various fearful people.
2. Holleran says that "the most unnerving thing" about AIDS is "its location in the Past." What does he mean?
3. How does the Fear constrict life? Have you had any experiences with fear that shed light on this phenomenon? (See the fears Holleran lists in para. 2.)
4. How does fear produce superstitions? Can you cite additional examples that confirm this point?

Exploring *Why:* Purpose

1. Why does the essay focus on the experience of fear rather than on AIDS?
2. What is Holleran's purpose? Do you think he wants to elicit sympathy and understanding for people with AIDS? Does he have a more general purpose?
3. Reread the last sentence. What is the point of this ending? How does it sum up Holleran's main message?
4. What have you learned from reading this essay?

Exploring *How:* Style and Structure

1. Why is the word *fear* sometimes capitalized? What is the difference between "fear" and "the Fear"? Why are other words—Life, Time Lag, the Past, and the Test—capitalized?
2. At first, Holleran writes in the **third person** (talking *about* people and their behavior). In paragraph 4, he begins with the indefinite third-person pronoun *one* ("One looks away[. . .]. One hopes the phone will not ring[. . .].") but then brings in the pronoun *you* ("that period when you are certain you have *It*"), which he uses more frequently as the essay progresses. Why does he use *you*? Does he mean *you* the reader? Could he be referring to himself?
3. Look at Holleran's examples. Which ones are taken from his own experience, and which ones has he gotten from other people? Can you always tell? Is there any reason Holleran would mix the two kinds of examples (personal and hearsay)?
4. Find several examples of **metaphors** and **analogies** in the essay. Which ones catch your attention and make you think?
5. Look at the way Holleran uses parentheses. Does he follow the standard practice of putting parentheses around supplemental material, minor digressions, and afterthoughts? Or does he use parentheses to achieve emphasis?

IDEAS FOR WRITING A DEFINITION

1. Write an essay in which you explore the effects of a powerful emotion, such as love, hate, anger, joy, guilt, or jealousy. Use the techniques that Holleran uses—examples, descriptions, quotations, explanations, and analogies—to show how much an emotion can affect people.

2. Write an essay in which you use examples to define an abstract term like *racism, sexism, discrimination, homophobia, prejudice, intolerance, bigotry,* or *injustice.*

3. ■ *Using the Internet.* Since Andrew Holleran wrote "The Fear" in 1989, many things about the AIDS epidemic have changed: new therapies, better testing, more education, greater support for people with AIDS, changes in insurance coverage, more pubic awareness, for instance. Write an essay entitled "The Hope" in which you define and discuss some of the positive aspects of recent developments in the AIDS crisis. You will find lots of information about AIDS on the Internet to use in your essay. These six Web sites are especially useful: (1) the HIV/AIDS Index Page, prepared by the U.S. Food and Drug Administration (www.fda.gov/oashi/aids/hiv.html); (2) the HIV InfoWeb (www.infoweb.org); (3) the Internet Resource and AIDS Treatment News (www.aids.org); (4) the Gay Men's Health Crisis (GMHC) Web site (www.gmhc.org); (5) the Stops AIDS Project (www.stopaids.org); and (6) the Johns Hopkins University AIDS Service (www.hopkins-aids.edu).

◆ ◆ ◆

◆ FURTHER IDEAS FOR USING DEFINITION

1. Recent research has shown that the birth of a baby causes serious tensions and strains on the new parents' relationship because of the enormous amount of extra work and stress involved in caring for a newborn. Why, then, do you think that most people—including the prospective parents—continue to think of a new baby as a total bundle of joy and often suffer a rude awakening when the baby comes home? Write an essay defining several of the powerful *pronatal influences* in our society, especially influences from the advertising and entertainment industries.

2. For an audience of people from another culture, define *situation comedy, fast food, soap opera, aroma therapy, homecoming weekend,* or another term that labels a cultural phenomenon.

3. COMBINING STRATEGIES. Write an essay that will give your classmates a vivid sense of some place from your past: your high school, your neighborhood, your home town, your favorite hangout. What was valued most there? What were the most important activities? Define the flavor and character of this place by citing examples, describing characteristics, narrating brief stories, explaining qualities, making analogies, and drawing contrasts about particular features and key individuals.

4. COLLABORATIVE WRITING. The purpose of this assignment is to write an article that defines and makes recommendations about a common problem such as procrastination, poor study skills, an eating disorder, self-centeredness, shopping addiction, or the doormat syndrome. Get together with a group of fellow students, and identify a problem that you think is worth writing about. It may help to focus the group's thinking if you assume that you are going to submit this article to your school newspaper or some other student publication. Brainstorm a list of characteristics, examples, and details that define the problem; make another list of recommendations that you can offer to solve the problem. Then write the article, individually or as a group.

5. ■ *Using the Internet.* Choose someone you find especially interesting—an athlete, businessperson, entertainer, or public figure. Through a computer search, locate several online articles or Web pages that give information about that person. (Find substantial articles, not just gossip items.) Using facts and details from these sources, write an essay in which you define the unique traits that have made this person successful. Assume that your audience will be readers of a popular publication like *Parade* or *USA Today.* Be sure to give appropriate credit to your sources.

Strategies for Organizing Ideas and Experience

Division and Classification

♦ ♦ ♦ ♦ ♦

Division and classification writing imposes or reveals order and makes ideas more understandable.

♦ Writers use division and classification to present information in a systematic way.

♦ Meaningful division and classification writing includes a reason or makes a point.

♦ Writers should establish a clear basis for their divisions and make sure their classification system is consistent, complete, significant, and accurate.

The next time you get ready to do your laundry, look on the back of the detergent container. There you will see directions for sorting your clothes according to the temperature of the water that you should use. The directions may read something like this example:

FOR BEST CLEANING RESULTS

Sort clothes and select temperature. Begin filling washer with water.

HOT	WARM	COLD
White cottons	Bright colors	Dark colors
Colorfast pastels	Permanent press	Colors that could bleed
Diapers	Knits	Delicates
Heavily soiled items		Stains like blood and chocolate

Do you follow a procedure like this when you do your laundry? Why do you suppose the detergent makers put directions like these on the back of the box?

As this laundry example shows, separating and arranging things helps us accomplish tasks more efficiently and more effectively. This process of "sorting things out" also helps us clarify our thinking and understand our feelings.

Many writing tasks lend themselves to grouping information into categories. For example, you might write a paper for psychology class on the various ways people cope with the death of a loved one. For a course in economics, you might write about the three basic types of unemployment *(frictional, structural, and cyclical)*. This approach—called **division and classification**—enables you to present a body of information in an orderly way. In the following essay, Lewis Thomas looks at three levels of what he calls "medical technology" in order to advance an argument about the health-care system.

The Technology of Medicine

LEWIS THOMAS

Educated at Princeton University and Harvard Medical School, Lewis Thomas (1913–1993) specialized in pediatrics, public health, and cancer research. He is better known to the public for his witty monthly columns in the *New England Journal of Medicine,* which have been collected in *The Lives of a Cell: Notes of a Biology Watcher* (1974), *The Medusa and the Snail: More Notes of a Biology Watcher* (1979), and *Late Night Thoughts on Listening to Mahler's Ninth Symphony* (1983). In these graceful, informal personal essays, Thomas displayed a rare talent for making scientific matters clear and enjoyable to readers with no special training.

Technology assessment has become a routine exercise for the scientific 1 enterprises on which the country is obliged to spend vast sums for its needs. Brainy committees are continually evaluating the effectiveness and cost of doing various things in space, defense, energy, transportation, and the like, to give advice about prudent investments for the future.

Somehow medicine, for all the $80-odd billion that it is said to cost the 2 nation, has not yet come in for much of this analytical treatment. It seems taken for granted that the technology of medicine simply exists, take it or leave it, and the only major technologic problem which policy-makers are interested in is how to deliver today's kind of health care, with equity, to all the people.

When, as is bound to happen sooner or later, the analysts get around 3 to the technology of medicine itself, they will have to face the problem of measuring the relative cost and effectiveness of all the things that are done in the management of disease. They make their living at this kind of thing, and I wish them well, but I imagine they will have a bewildering time. For one thing, our methods of managing disease are constantly changing—partly under the influence of new bits of information brought in from all corners of biologic science. At the same time, a great many things are done that are not so closely related to science, some not related at all.

In fact, there are three quite different levels of technology in medicine, 4 so unlike each other as to seem altogether different undertakings. Practitioners of medicine and the analysts will be in trouble if they are not kept separate.

1. First of all, there is a large body of what might be termed "nontech- 5 nology," impossible to measure in terms of its capacity to alter either the natural course of disease or its eventual outcome. A great deal of money is spent on this. It is valued highly by the professionals as well as the patients. It consists of what is sometimes called "supportive therapy." It tides patients over through diseases that are not, by and large, understood. It is what is meant by the phrases "caring for" and "standing by." It is indispensable. It is not, however, a technology in any real sense, since it does not involve measures directed at the underlying mechanism of disease.

It includes the large part of any good doctor's time that is taken up 6 with simply providing reassurance, explaining to patients who fear that they have contracted one or another lethal disease that they are, in fact, quite healthy.

It is what physicians used to be engaged in at the bedside of patients   7
with diphtheria, meningitis, poliomyelitis, lobar pneumonia, and all the rest of the infectious diseases that have since come under control.

It is what physicians must now do for patients with intractable cancer,   8
severe rheumatoid arthritis, multiple sclerosis, stroke, and advanced cirrhosis. One can think of at least twenty major diseases that require this kind of supportive medical care because of the absence of an effective technology. I would include a large amount of what is called mental disease, and most varieties of cancer, in this category.

The cost of this nontechnology is very high, and getting higher all the   9
time. It requires not only a great deal of time but also very hard effort and skill on the part of physicians; only the very best of doctors are good at coping with this kind of defeat. It also involves long periods of hospitalization, lots of nursing, lots of involvement of nonmedical professionals in and out of the hospital. It represents, in short, a substantial segment of today's expenditures for health.

2. At the next level up is a kind of technology best termed "halfway   10
technology." This represents the kinds of things that must be done after the fact, in efforts to compensate for the incapacitating effects of certain diseases whose course one is unable to do very much about. It is a technology designed to make up for disease, or to postpone death.

The outstanding examples in recent years are the transplantations of   11
hearts, kidneys, livers, and other organs, and the equally spectacular inventions of artificial organs. In the public mind, this kind of technology has come to seem like the equivalent of the high technologies of the physical sciences. The media tend to present each new procedure as though it represented a breakthrough and therapeutic triumph, instead of the makeshift that it really is.

In fact, this level of technology is, by its nature, at the same time highly   12
sophisticated and profoundly primitive. It is the kind of thing that one must continue to do until there is a genuine understanding of the mechanisms involved in disease. In chronic glomerulonephritis, for example, a much clearer insight will be needed into the events leading to the destruction of glomeruli by the immunologic reactants that now appear to govern this disease, before one will know how to intervene intelligently to prevent the process, or turn it around. But when this level of understanding has been reached, the technology of kidney replacement will not be much needed and should no longer pose the huge problem of logistics, cost, and ethics that it poses today.

An extremely complex and costly technology for the management   13
of coronary heart disease has evolved—involving specialized ambulances and hospital units, all kinds of electronic gadgetry, and whole platoons of new professional personnel—to deal with the end results of coronary

thrombosis. Almost everything offered today for the treatment of heart disease is at this level of technology, with the transplanted and artificial hearts as ultimate examples. When enough has been learned to know what really goes wrong in heart disease, one ought to be in a position to figure out ways to prevent or reverse the process, and when this happens the current elaborate technology will probably be set to one side.

Much of what is done in the treatment of cancer, by surgery, irradiation,   14 and chemotherapy, represents halfway technology—in the sense that these measures are directed at the existence of already established cancer cells, but not at the mechanisms by which cells become neoplastic.

It is a characteristic of this kind of technology that it costs an enormous   15 amount of money and requires a continuing expansion of hospital facilities. There is no end to the need for new, highly trained people to run the enterprise. And there is really no way out of this, at the present state of knowledge. If the installation of specialized coronary-care units can result in the extension of life for only a few patients with coronary disease (and there is no question that this technology is effective in a few cases), it seems to me an inevitable fact of life that as many of these as can be will be put together, and as much money as can be found will be spent. I do not see that anyone has much choice in this. The only thing that can move medicine away from this level of technology is new information, and the only imaginable source of this information is research.

3. The third type of technology is the kind that is so effective that it   16 seems to attract the least public notice; it has come to be taken for granted. This is the genuinely decisive technology of modern medicine, exemplified best by modern methods for immunization against diphtheria, pertussis, and the childhood virus diseases, and the contemporary use of antibiotics and chemotherapy for bacterial infections. The capacity to deal effectively with syphilis and tuberculosis represents a milestone in human endeavor, even though full use of this potential has not yet been made. And there are, of course, other examples: the treatment of endocrinologic disorders with appropriate hormones, the prevention of hemolytic disease of the newborn, the treatment and prevention of various nutritional disorders, and perhaps just around the corner the management of Parkinsonism and sickle-cell anemia. There are other examples, and everyone will have his favorite candidates for the list, but the truth is that there are nothing like as many as the public has been led to believe.

The point to be made about this kind of technology—the real high technology   17 of medicine—is that it comes as the result of a genuine understanding of disease mechanisms, and when it becomes available, it is relatively inexpensive, and relatively easy to deliver.

Offhand, I cannot think of any important human disease for which   18 medicine possesses the outright capacity to prevent or cure where the cost of the technology is itself a major problem. The price is never as high as the cost of managing the same diseases during the earlier stages of no-technology or halfway technology. If a case of typhoid fever had to be managed today by the best methods of 1935, it would run to a staggering expense. At, say, around fifty days of hospitalization, requiring the most demanding kind of nursing care, with the obsessive concern for details of diet that characterized the therapy of that time, with daily laboratory monitoring, and, on occasion, surgical intervention for abdominal catastrophe, I should think $10,000 would be a conservative estimate for the illness, as contrasted with today's cost of a bottle of chioramphenicol and a day or two of fever. The halfway technology that was evolving for poliomyelitis in the early 1950s, just before the emergence of the basic research that made the vaccine possible, provides another illustration of the point. Do you remember Sister Kenny, and the cost of those institutes for rehabilitation, with all those ceremonially applied hot fomentations, and the debates about whether the affected limbs should be totally immobilized or kept in passive motion as frequently as possible, and the masses of statistically tormented data mobilized to support one view or the other? It is the cost of that kind of technology, and its relative effectiveness, that must be compared with the cost and effectiveness of the vaccine.

Pulmonary tuberculosis had similar episodes in its history. There was   19 a sudden enthusiasm for the surgical removal of infected lung tissue in the early 1950s, and elaborate plans were being made for new and expensive installations for major pulmonary surgery in tuberculosis hospitals, and then INH and streptomycin came along and the hospitals themselves were closed up.

It is when physicians are bogged down by their incomplete technolo-   20 gies, by the innumerable things they are obliged to do in medicine when they lack a clear understanding of disease mechanisms, that the deficiencies of the health-care system are most conspicuous. If I were a policy-maker, interested in saving money for health care over the long haul, I would regard it as an act of high prudence to give high priority to a lot more basic research in biologic science. This is the only way to get the full mileage that biology owes to the science of medicine, even though it seems, as used to be said in the days when the phrase still had some meaning, like asking for the moon.

◆ ◆ ◆

◆ ◆ ◆ *Writer's Workshop I* ◆ ◆ ◆
Responding to a Classification

Use the *Who, What, Why,* and *How* questions (p. 3) to explore your own understanding of the ideas and writing strategies used by Lewis Thomas in "The Technology of Medicine." Your instructor may ask you to record these responses in a journal, post them on an electronic bulletin board, or bring them to class to use in small group discussions.

◆ WRITING FROM READING

Freshman Jessica Swigart enjoyed reading "The Technology of Medicine" and thought she would like to write a similar essay. She explored Thomas's ideas and strategies by writing out responses to the *Who*, *What*, *Why*, and *How* questions, and then she wrote the following essay that classifies the kinds of motives that drive ambitious people.

Jessica Swigart
English 1091, Sec. 04
March 10, 2001

Ambition, Good or Bad?

Ambition drives people to do more than they have   1
ever accomplished, discovered, or created before.
Skyscrapers stand tall in the sky, satellites orbit in
space, and technology hums around us because of human
ambition. Much of our modern world would not be here
if some person did not have the ambition to invent and
discover it. The threat of diseases like polio and
smallpox would still be with us today if someone had
not had the ambition to find a cure or a vaccination.
Music and art would be scarce if humans did not
possess the ambition to create.

Not all ambition, however, has served to better   2
society. The evil consequences of ambition had full
reign during Hitler's rise to power as well as in the
atrocities committed against ethnic Albanians in the
Balkans. This dark side of ambition doesn't manifest
itself only in vicious nationalism and ethnic
cleansing; it's also present in everything from
cheating in sports to out-of-control rivalries between
competitors hoping to win fame and glory. Other
manifestations of ambition, such as the desire to
drive the most expensive car on the block or have the
most successful children in school, seem relatively

harmless, yet they still reveal the self-centered, less admirable side of human nature.

Ambition takes many forms, but is it inherently   3
good or harmful? Should ambition be praised in a person? What makes ambition honorable, and what makes it detestable? The worth of an ambition can be found in the underlying motivations fueling the drive to succeed, for motivations color and characterize ambition. There are three motivations by which one can categorize ambition: hunger for recognition or power, personal satisfaction, and love and concern for others.

The motive at the core of the world's ugliest   4
ambition has been a hunger for power and recognition. Hitler, Mussolini, and Milosevec are all leaders who wanted to be served and obeyed by the people they led. Although other examples seem pale by comparison, we can find such destructive ambition in many common situations. Employees, for instance, may snitch on their fellow workers or kowtow to their bosses just to get a more prestigious title. Students may cheat on exams to protect the grade point average in which they have invested so much pride.

Of course, the drive for recognition and power can   5
have favorable consequences. A microbiologist who finds the cure for cancer while in the pursuit of fame and fortune has nonetheless benefited society, regardless of the motives for doing so. On the other hand, how much more would we benefit if people were not motivated by recognition or power? The microbiologist working out of selfish ambition for recognition may hesitate to acknowledge the work of others or refuse to collaborate with peers, thus delaying or subverting an important discovery.

The desire to be recognized and revered is not   6
rare; it presents itself in daily life. Students learn only what will be on the exam. A person buys an impressive home yet has no furniture to put inside it. Ambitions driven by a desire for recognition produce growth and change only on the surface.

Another motivation driving ambition is personal   7
satisfaction. People who crave recognition and power need others to take notice of their works, but people driven by personal satisfaction achieve for the joy of

knowing that they have created something beautiful, have accomplished something difficult, or have done something good. Finishing a college degree for the personal satisfaction of doing it, writing poetry for one's own pleasure, and bicycling across the United States for the mere experience are all outcomes of such motivation. Those who work for personal satisfaction are not tempted to cheat or deceive in their pursuits, for they do not aspire to be recognized or rewarded by others. Artists who create purely for the pleasure of creating fall into this category. Such artists are not concerned solely with achieving greatness or gaining immortality through their works; they delight in satisfying their need to create. To produce art for selfish motives would compromise or destroy the art.

More noble than striving for personal   8
satisfaction, however, is the ambition that is motivated by love and concern, the kind that puts the needs of others above the self. This most admirable ambition is a humble form of ambition; it goes beyond the desires of the individual. Human conditions have improved because people were ambitious and dared to work for what had never been. Because ambitious women struggled to win equal rights, women today can own property, pursue careers, and vote. People with great ambition fought to abolish slavery, get rid of child labor laws, and extend civil rights to everyone--knowing that they may never be recognized or see complete victory in their lifetimes. Such changes would never have come if recognition and power had driven the ambition. The hardships of pursuing these ends would not be endured just for the sake of personal satisfaction. Only genuine love and concern could drive such selfless ambitions.

Ambition is not inherently evil, but the   9
motivations that drive it can be. Although a person may possess all three motivations in setting out on an endeavor, that individual must make a conscious decision to be guided by love and concern. Such a person may never receive recognition and power, but if one's ambition is rooted in love and concern, those rewards will not be missed.

◆ GETTING STARTED ON DIVISION AND CLASSIFICATION WRITING

Dividing and classifying force you to think clearly about a topic. By breaking a subject into its distinct parts, or categories, you can look at it more closely and decide what to say about each part. For example, if you are writing an essay about effective teaching styles, you might begin by dividing the teachers you have had into the "good" ones and the "bad" ones. You could then further break those broad categories into more precise ones: teachers who held your interest, teachers who knew their subject, teachers who made you do busy work, and so forth. As you develop each category, you have to think about the qualities that impressed you, and this thought process leads you to a better understanding of the topic you are writing about. You may end up writing only about the good teachers, but dividing and classifying the examples will help you organize your thinking.

Most things can be classified or divided in more than one way, depending on the reason for making up the groups. In the laundry example, for instance, you are told to sort the clothes according to the temperature of the water. Putting bright colors with knits doesn't make any sense if you don't know the reason—or basis—for the category: *items to be washed in cold water.*

As you begin to divide and classify a topic, try to come up with a sound basis for formulating your categories. For example, if you are writing about friends, you could group them according to how close you are to them, as Phillip Lopate does in "What Friends Are For." You could also group them according to other principles: how long you have known them, what you have in common with them, or how much time you spend with the people in each group. John Holt's three types of discipline are based on the source or origin for each form of control. The important thing is to choose a workable principle and stick with it.

Merely putting facts or ideas into different groups isn't necessarily meaningful. You must consider your **purpose** for using division and classification. Look at these sentences that classify for no apparent reason:

1. There are five kinds of friends in most of our lives.
2. People deal with their spare money in four basic ways.

How could you give a purpose to these ideas? You would have to add a *reason* or declare a *point* for the categories. Here are some revisions that give purpose to these two classifications:

1. a. There are five kinds of friends in most of our lives, and each kind is important in its own way.

      b. Most of us have five kinds of friends, and each one drives us crazy in a special way.

  2. a. People deal with their spare money in four ways that reflect their overall attitudes toward life.

      b. People deal with their spare money in four ways, only one of which is truly constructive.

You should also recognize the difference between useful and useless ways of classifying. Sorting your clothes by brand name probably won't help you get the best cleaning results when doing the laundry. And dividing teachers into those who wear glasses and those who don't is not a very useful way to approach an essay on effective teaching styles. However, classifying teachers into those who lecture, those who use a question-discussion format, and those who run small group workshops might be productive, mainly because such groupings would allow you to discuss the teachers' philosophies, their attitudes toward students, and their effectiveness in the classroom.

◆ ORGANIZING DIVISION AND CLASSIFICATION WRITING

Ideally, your subject will divide naturally into parallel, meaningful categories, and these categories will slip conveniently into well-developed paragraphs of roughly equal length. In reality, that seldom happens. You will probably have to rethink and reorganize the groups or types you first come up with. Here are a couple of important questions to ask about your categories:

1. *Does the basis of the division shift?* If you can see a problem with the following classification system, you already understand this point.

    Types of Teachers

    a. Teachers who lecture

    b. Teachers who lead discussion

    c. Teachers who have a sense of humor

    d. Teachers who run workshops

    e. Teachers who never hold office hours

    Notice that three types of teachers (a, b, and d) are grouped according to the way they run their classes, but two types (c and e) are defined by some other standard. You can see the confusion these shifting groups cause: Can teachers who lecture have a sense of humor? Don't those who use workshops hold office hours?

2. *Are the groups parallel or equal in rank?* The following classification illustrates a problem of rank:

Kinds of Popular Music

a. Easy listening
b. Country and western
c. Rock and roll
d. Ice-T

Although Ice-T does represent a type of popular music distinct from easy listening, country, and rock and roll, the category is not parallel with the others: it is far too small. It should be "rap," with Ice-T used as an example.

After making sure that your categories are logical and consistent, you need to consider how to arrange them. The order in which you first thought of them may not necessarily be the best. Your groups might lend themselves to **chronological order.** In an essay about horror films, for example, you might begin with classic mass-destruction movies (such as *The Blob* and *War of the Worlds*), then move to the supernatural thrillers that came next (*The Exorcist* and *Rosemary's Baby*), and end with the slasher style of more recent movies (*The Texas Chainsaw Massacre* and the *Friday the Thirteenth* series).

A classification of the parts of a machine or process may be arranged spatially: top to bottom, left to right, inside to outside. An essay on types of people, such as gamblers, might be organized by size: from the group with the fewest members to the group with the most. Consider arranging by degree, too: least important to most important, simple to complex, or mildly irritating to totally repulsive. When you organize by degree, you might want to put your strongest category last for **emphasis.**

◆ DEVELOPING DIVISION AND CLASSIFICATION WRITING

Once you have established and organized the categories for your discussion, you need to think about the details that will define and describe the groups, the examples that will support your claims about the groups, and the explanations that will make your purpose clear to your readers. As usual, you can use your favorite invention techniques—brainstorming, freewriting, clustering, questioning—to generate the material you will need to develop and explain your classification system. As you are planning and drafting the content for your essay, you should also address these questions:

1. *Can I handle the subject and its divisions in the number of words that I want?* Entire books have been written on heroes and their qualities and the types that exist. If you want only a 750-word paper, you should probably narrow your categories to "Types of Heroes on Popular TV Shows" or "Barney Fife's Heroic Qualities." On the other hand, if you find that you'll be able to devote fewer than 50 words to each group you've chosen, that is nature's way of telling you to consolidate categories or change topics.

2. *Does my classification cover everything I claim it covers?* If, for instance, you know of teachers who sometimes lecture and sometimes use small groups, you can't pretend these people don't exist simply to make your categories tidy. At least mention exceptions, even if you don't give them as much space as you give the major categories.

3. *Am I presenting stereotypes?* When you write about types of behavior or put people into groups, you run the risk of oversimplifying the material. The best way to avoid this problem is to use plenty of specific examples. You can also point out exceptions and describe variations; such honesty shows that you have been thinking carefully about the topic.

◆ OPENING AND CLOSING DIVISION AND CLASSIFICATION WRITING

Somewhere in the opening you need to let your readers know just what you are dividing and classifying and why: several ways to handle criticism, four kinds of friends, three types of stress, or three levels of intelligence, for example. Here are some strategies for introducing your categories:

1. *Pose a problem.* Simply presenting the problem to be discussed may set an appropriate context for some topics: "Affluent city dwellers are faced with the dilemma of choosing what kind of housing to live in: a rented apartment, a mortgaged condominium, or a single-family house." Then present the information on these options in the body of your paper.
2. *State your purpose.* Indicate the point or value of your classification system: "As a child, I was the victim of baby-sitting blues until I learned to classify the behavior of my sitters and cope with each type differently."

3. *Set a historical context.* Phillip Lopate takes this approach in the first two paragraphs of his essay "What Friends Are For" (p. 306), pointing out that many essayists have written about friendship and that the connection between romantic love and friendship continues to intrigue and puzzle us.

4. *Begin with a pertinent anecdote.* Lee Smith uses this strategy to draw readers into his essay about types of memory (p. 315): "The alarm finally goes off in your head around 3 P.M. Your face flushes and your hands plow through the papers on your desk. You have accidentally stood someone up for lunch. It gets worse. You can't remember who. And still worse: You can't recall where you left your glasses, so you can't look up the name in your appointment book."

The closing of a division and classification essay is a good place to review your categories and draw some final conclusions about the ideas or behaviors you have been describing. That's how Jessica Swigart closes her essay about the motives for ambition: "Although a person may possess all three motivations in setting out on an endeavor, that individual must make a conscious decision to be guided by love and concern. Such a person may never receive recognition and power, but if one's ambition is rooted in love and concern, those rewards will not be missed." You can also look into the future to suggest the longer-term implications of your topic, as Lee Smith does in the last two paragraphs of "What We Now Know about Memory," where he writes about the new class of drugs that may prove to be "the easy, safe, and effective way to freshen old memories."

◆ USING THE MODEL

After reading Lewis Thomas's essay, Jessica Swigart decided that she would also look at the various levels of some topic. Classification is primarily an organizational strategy, so it was natural that Jessica based her discussion on the structure she found in "The Technology of Medicine." Noting that Thomas divides medical technology into three categories, Jessica divided her discussion of ambition into three types. Although Jessica's essay is not as specialized as "The Technology of Medicine," Thomas's interest in the underlying goals of medical practitioners became a key element in Jessica's approach.

You can probably think of some form of human behavior that can be divided into informative and revealing types, such as the way different people walk to class, eat pizza, study for a test, or move on the dance floor. You could consider the ways people approach their work, style their hair, arrange their closets, discipline their children, or shop for groceries. Figure out three or four valid categories into which you can group the people who engage in the behavior, establish a clear basis for grouping them, decide what your purpose is, and write an essay that comments on the foibles and distinctions of human nature.

◆ ◆ ◆ Writer's Workshop II ◆ ◆ ◆
Analyzing a Division and Classification Essay

Working individually or with a small group of classmates, read through Jessica Swigart's essay "Ambition, Good or Bad?" and respond to the following questions:

1. What is Jessica's purpose for writing this essay? Does she make her purpose clear in the beginning?
2. What do you think of Jessica's division of ambition into three types? Is her classification reasonable and useful? Is it complete, or do you think there are other kinds of ambition that she could have discussed?
3. Does Jessica define and explain each type sufficiently? Does she provide enough details and examples to support her judgments about each kind of ambition?
4. Is the conclusion of Jessica's essay satisfactory? Why or why not?

◆ ◆ ◆ Checklist for Reading and Writing ◆ ◆ ◆
Division and Classification Essays

1. What is being divided and classified? What is the basis for the groupings?
2. Who are the intended readers? What purpose do division and classification serve for these readers?
3. Are the categories clearly defined? Do they shift? Do they cover what they claim to cover? Are they parallel?
4. Are the categories clearly arranged? Are the distinctions between groups and subgroups easy to follow?
5. Does the division into groups lead to stereotyping? Are exceptions and variations noted and explained?

◆ ◆ ◆ PREPARING TO READ

Have you ever tried to read a lease agreement, a credit card contract, or an insurance policy? How would you describe the language in these documents? Did you get the feeling that you were not supposed to understand what you were reading?

◆ ◆ ◆

Doublespeak

WILLIAM LUTZ

A professor of English at Rutgers University, William Lutz (born in 1940) has long spoken out against the "conscious use of language as a weapon or tool by those in power." Lutz is the editor of *The Doublespeak Review* and has written extensively on the topic of deceptive and evasive language. His most recent books are *The New Doublespeak: Why No One Knows What Anyone's Saying Anymore* (1996) and *Doublespeak Defined: Cut through the Bull**** and Get the Point* (1999). The following selection is taken from an earlier book, *Doublespeak: How Government, Business, Advertisers, and Others Use Language to Deceive You* (1989).

1 There are no potholes in the streets of Tucson, Arizona, just "pavement deficiencies." The Reagan Administration didn't propose any new taxes, just "revenue enhancement" through new "user's fees." Those aren't bums on the street, just "nongoal oriented members of society." There are no more poor people, just "fiscal underachievers." There was no robbery of an automatic teller machine, just an "unauthorized withdrawal." The patient didn't die because of medical malpractice, it was just a "diagnostic misadventure of a high magnitude." The U.S. Army doesn't kill the enemy anymore, it just "services the target." And the doublespeak goes on.

2 Doublespeak is language that pretends to communicate but really doesn't. It is language that makes the bad seem good, the negative appear positive, the unpleasant appear attractive or at least tolerable. Doublespeak is language that avoids or shifts responsibility, language that is at variance with its real or purported meaning. It is language that conceals or prevents thought; rather than extending thought, doublespeak limits it.

3 Doublespeak is not a matter of subjects and verbs agreeing; it is a matter of words and facts agreeing. Basic to doublespeak is incongruity, the

incongruity between what is said or left unsaid, and what really is. It is the incongruity between the word and the referent, between seem and be, between the essential function of language—communication—and what doublespeak does—mislead, distort, deceive, inflate, circumvent, obfuscate.

How to Spot Doublespeak

How can you spot doublespeak? Most of the time you will recognize   4
doublespeak when you see or hear it. But, if you have any doubts, you can identify doublespeak just by answering these questions: Who is saying what to whom, under what conditions and circumstances, with what intent, and with what results? Answering these questions will usually help you identify as doublespeak language that appears to be legitimate or that at first glance doesn't even appear to be doublespeak.

First Kind of Doublespeak

There are at least four kinds of doublespeak. The first is the euphemism,   5
an inoffensive or positive word or phrase used to avoid a harsh, unpleasant, or distasteful reality. But a euphemism can also be a tactful word or phrase which avoids directly mentioning a painful reality, or it can be an expression used out of concern for the feelings of someone else, or to avoid directly discussing a topic subject to a social or cultural taboo.

When you use a euphemism because of your sensitivity for someone's   6
feelings or out of concern for a recognized social or cultural taboo, it is not doublespeak. For example, you express your condolences that someone has "passed away" because you do not want to say to a grieving person, "I'm sorry your father is dead." When you use the euphemism "passed away," no one is misled. Moreover, the euphemism functions here not just to protect the feelings of another person, but to communicate also your concern for that person's feelings during a period of mourning. When you excuse yourself to go to the "rest room," or you mention that someone is "sleeping with" or "involved with" someone else, you do not mislead anyone about your meaning, but you do respect the social taboos about discussing bodily functions and sex in direct terms. You also indicate your sensitivity to the feelings of your audience, which is usually considered a mark of courtesy and good manners.

However, when a euphemism is used to mislead or deceive, it becomes   7
doublespeak. For example, in 1984 the U.S. State Department announced that it would no longer use the word "killing" in its annual report on the status of human rights in countries around the world. Instead, it would use the phrase "unlawful or arbitrary deprivation of life," which the department claimed was more accurate. Its real purpose for using this phrase was simply

to avoid discussing the embarrassing situation of government-sanctioned killings in countries that are supported by the United States and have been certified by the United States as respecting the human rights of their citizens. This use of a euphemism constitutes doublespeak, since it is designed to mislead, to cover up the unpleasant. Its real intent is at variance with its apparent intent. It is language designed to alter our perception of reality.

The Pentagon, too, avoids discussing unpleasant realities when it refers   8 to bombs and artillery shells that fall on civilian targets as "incontinent ordnance." And in 1977 the Pentagon tried to slip funding for the neutron bomb unnoticed into an appropriations bill by calling it a "radiation enhancement device."

Second Kind of Doublespeak

A second kind of doublespeak is jargon, the specialized language of a   9 trade, profession, or similar group, such as that used by doctors, lawyers, engineers, educators, or car mechanics. Jargon can serve an important and useful function. Within a group, jargon functions as a kind of verbal shorthand that allows members of the group to communicate with each other clearly, efficiently, and quickly. Indeed, it is a mark of membership in the group to be able to use and understand the group's jargon.

But jargon, like the euphemism, can also be doublespeak. It can be—   10 and often is—pretentious, obscure, and esoteric terminology used to give an air of profundity, authority, and prestige to speakers and their subject matter. Jargon as doublespeak often makes the simple appear complex, the ordinary profound, the obvious insightful. In this sense it is used not to express but impress. With such doublespeak, the act of smelling something becomes "organoleptic analysis," glass becomes "fused silicate," a crack in a metal support beam becomes a "discontinuity," conservative economic policies become "distributionally conservative notions."

Lawyers, for example, speak of an "involuntary conversion" of property   11 when discussing the loss or destruction of property through theft, accident, or condemnation. If your house burns down or if your car is stolen, you have suffered an involuntary conversion of your property. When used by lawyers in a legal situation, such jargon is a legitimate use of language, since lawyers can be expected to understand the term.

However, when a member of a specialized group uses its jargon to com-   12 municate with a person outside the group, and uses it knowing that the nonmember does not understand such language, then there is doublespeak. For example, on May 9, 1978, a National Airlines 727 airplane crashed while attempting to land at the Pensacola, Florida, airport. Three of the fifty-two passengers aboard the airplane were killed. As a result of the crash, National made an after-tax insurance benefit of $1.7 million, or an extra 18¢ a share dividend for its stockholders. Now National Airlines had two problems: It did not want to talk about one of its airplanes crashing, and it had to account for the $1.7 million when it issued its annual report to its stockholders. National solved the problem by inserting a footnote in its annual report which explained that the $1.7 million income was due to "the involuntary conversion of a 727." National thus acknowledged the crash of its airplane and the subsequent profit it made from the crash, without once mentioning the accident or the deaths. However, because airline officials knew that most stockholders in the company, and indeed most of the general public, were not familiar with legal jargon, the use of such jargon constituted doublespeak.

Third Kind of Doublespeak

A third kind of doublespeak is gobbledygook or bureaucratese. Basically, such doublespeak is simply a matter of piling on words, of overwhelming the audience with words, the bigger the words and the longer the sentences the better. Alan Greenspan, then chair of President Nixon's Council of Economic Advisors, was quoted in the *Philadelphia Inquirer* in 1974 as having testified before a Senate committee that "It is a tricky problem to find the particular calibration in timing that would be appropriate to stem the acceleration in risk premiums created by falling incomes without prematurely aborting the decline in the inflation-generated risk premiums." 13

Nor has Mr. Greenspan's language changed since then. Speaking to the meeting of the Economic Club of New York in 1988, Mr. Greenspan, now Federal Reserve chair, said, "I guess I should warn you, if I turn out to be particularly clear, you've probably misunderstood what I've said." Mr. Greenspan's doublespeak doesn't seem to have held back his career. 14

Sometimes gobbledygook may sound impressive, but when the quote is later examined in print it doesn't even make sense. During the 1988 presidential campaign, vice-presidential candidate Senator Dan Quayle explained the need for a strategic defense initiative by saying, "Why wouldn't an enhanced deterrent, a more stable peace, a better prospect to denying the ones who enter conflict in the first place to have a reduction of offensive systems and an introduction to defensive capability? I believe this is the route the country will eventually go." 15

The investigation into the Challenger disaster in 1986 revealed the doublespeak of gobbledygook and bureaucratese used by too many involved in the shuttle program. When Jesse Moore, NASA's associate administrator, was asked if the performance of the shuttle program had improved with each launch or if it had remained the same, he answered, "I think our performance in terms of the liftoff performance and in terms of the orbital performance, we knew more about the envelope we were operating under, and we have been pretty accurately staying in that. And so I would say the performance 16 has not by design drastically improved. I think we have been able to characterize the performance more as a function of our launch experience as opposed to it improving as a function of time." While this language may appear to be jargon, a close look will reveal that it is really just gobbledygook laced with jargon. But you really have to wonder if Mr. Moore had any idea what he was saying.

Fourth Kind of Doublespeak

The fourth kind of doublespeak is inflated language that is designed to   17
make the ordinary seem extraordinary; to make everyday things seem impressive; to give an air of importance to people, situations, or things that would not normally be considered important; to make the simple seem complex. Often this kind of doublespeak isn't hard to spot, and it is usually pretty funny. While car mechanics may be called "automotive internists," elevator operators members of the "vertical transportation corps," used cars "pre-owned" or "experienced cars," and black-and-white television sets described as having "non-multicolor capability," you really aren't misled all that much by such language.

However, you may have trouble figuring out that, when Chrysler "ini-   18
tiates a career alternative enhancement program," it is really laying off five thousand workers; or that "negative patient care outcome" means the patient died; or that "rapid oxidation" means a fire in a nuclear power plant.

The doublespeak of inflated language can have serious consequences.   19
In Pentagon doublespeak, "pre-emptive counterattack" means that American forces attacked first; "engaged the enemy on all sides" means American troops were ambushed; "backloading of augmentation personnel" means a retreat by American troops. In the doublespeak of the military, the 1983 invasion of Grenada was conducted not by the U.S. Army, Navy, Air Force, and Marines, but by the "Caribbean Peace Keeping Forces." But then, according to the Pentagon, it wasn't an invasion, it was a "predawn vertical insertion."

◆ ◆ ◆

FIRST RESPONSES

What examples of doublespeak have you come across lately? How do you feel about them after reading Lutz's essay? Jot down any examples of euphemism, jargon, gobbledygook, and inflated language you encounter in the next few days. Pay attention to the language of advertising, the terms used by corporations and politicians, and even some of your textbooks. Bring some examples to discuss with your class.

TAKING A CLOSER LOOK

Exploring *Who:* Voice and Tone

1. How does Lutz feel about doublespeak? Does he feel the same way about each kind of doublespeak? What words and sentences reveal his attitudes?
2. Who uses doublespeak? Is Lutz writing to these people, or does he have a different audience in mind?
3. Do you ever use deceptive language? What kinds do you use: euphemisms, **jargon,** inflated language? Why? After reading this article, will you continue to use such language?
4. What do you think about the examples of inflated language mentioned in the final section of the essay? How do you think Lutz wants you to react to these examples?

Exploring *What:* Content and Meaning

1. According to Lutz, what is doublespeak? What questions help you identify it?
2. How many kinds of doublespeak does Lutz discuss? List them, and give an example of each.
3. What useful functions do euphemisms and jargon serve?
4. ▮▯ *Using the Internet.* Visit the American Newspeak Web site (www.scn.org/news/newspeak/) to look at samples of doublespeak gathered from current news sources. After reading eight to ten examples, answer these questions: Are Lutz's criticisms still valid? Who is using doublespeak today? What kinds are they using? Why do politicians and government agencies use gobbledygook and inflated language?

Exploring *Why:* Purpose

1. Why does Lutz want you to be able to spot doublespeak? What does he want you to do when you spot it?
2. Why does Lutz say that "the doublespeak of inflated language can have serious consequences"? What are those consequences? Do you agree with him?
3. Why does Lutz include the beneficial and harmless uses of euphemism and jargon?
4. Does the language you use *reflect* your character and values, or does the language you use *influence* and *shape* your character and values?

Exploring *How:* Style and Structure

1. Why does Lutz begin with a series of examples? Is that an effective opening?
2. Explain the function of the question that opens paragraph 4.
3. Why does the author use headings?
4. Are the four kinds of doublespeak presented in any particular order? Why does Lutz end with inflated language?
5. How important are the examples in this essay? Would you have understood the author's explanations without them? Which examples did you find most illuminating and interesting?

◆ WRITING FROM READING ASSIGNMENT

William Lutz writes about the way people use language to accomplish certain purposes and communicate with various audiences. Do you use different language with your friends, your boss, your family, and your professors? Your goal in this writing assignment is to examine the way you change your language when you communicate with different audiences.

A. Begin by brainstorming, with help from friends and classmates if you want, for ideas about the various audiences you write and talk to. If you have time, take notes about the conversations you have and writing you do for a week or more. Pay particular attention to how you vary your language from situation to situation. Jot down specific examples to use in developing your essay.

B. Classify the language you use—spoken or written—into three to five distinct types. You might make up a label for each type: shop talk, jock talk, party talk, family talk; or academic writing, e-mail messages, business writing, notes and cards.

C. Decide on a purpose for your division and classification. Why do you alter your language? What do these variations tell you about yourself and your relationships with others? Is this process of tailoring your language to fit your audience harmful? Useful? Beneficial? Necessary? Hypocritical?

D. Develop a section explaining each kind of language you use. Use specific examples, as Lutz does, to illustrate and define the types.

E. Arrange your sections in some **logical order,** perhaps from least formal to most formal or from impersonal to indifferent to casual to intimate. You can point out how each type varies from the others as you go along.

F. Use signals to show when you are moving from one type to the next. You could use headings (as Lutz does) or transitional phrases, such as "The second type of language I use is . . ."

G. Consider an introduction that uses a collection of examples, as Lutz does, to get your readers' attention and set up your categories.

H. One way to close your essay is with a discussion that draws all the kinds together, explaining why you vary your language for each group and what this practice tells you about yourself and your relationships with different audiences.

I. Use the "Checklist for Reading and Writing Division and Classification Essays" (p. 282) when you revise your essay.

◆ ◆ ◆ PREPARING TO READ

Have you ever had a teacher or a coach who insisted that you "do it this way and don't ask why"? How did you respond to this kind of direction? Was it effective?

◆ ◆ ◆

Three Kinds of Discipline

JOHN HOLT

Born in New York City and educated at Yale University, John Holt (1923–1985) taught in public elementary and secondary schools for many years in Colorado and Massachusetts. He later held professorships at Harvard University and the University of California at Berkeley. His numerous books, based on his teaching experiences and concerned with educational reform, include the bestsellers *How Children Fail* (1964), *How Children Learn* (1972), and *Escape from Childhood* (1984). An early advocate of home schooling, Holt founded the magazine *Growing without Schooling* in 1977 as a resource for parents who wanted to pursue that option. The following essay is taken from his 1972 book *Freedom and Beyond*.

A child, in growing up, may meet and learn from three different kinds 1 of discipline. The first and most important is what we might call the Discipline of Nature or of Reality. When he is trying to do something real, if he does the wrong thing or doesn't do the right one, he doesn't get the result he wants. If he doesn't pile one block right on top of another, or tries to build on a slanting surface, his tower falls down. If he hits the wrong key, he hears the wrong note. If he doesn't hit the nail squarely on the head, it bends, and he has to pull it out and start with another. If he doesn't measure properly what he is trying to build, it won't open, close, fit, stand up, fly, float, whistle, or do whatever he wants it to do. If he closes his eyes when he swings, he doesn't hit the ball. A child meets this kind of discipline every time he tries to *do* something, which is why it is so important in school to give children more chances to do things, instead of just reading or listening to someone talk (or pretending to).

This discipline is a good teacher. The learner never has to wait long for 2 his answer, it usually comes quickly, often instantly. Also it is clear, and very often points toward the needed correction; from what happened he can not only see that what he did was wrong, but also why, and what he needs to do instead. Finally, and most important, the giver of the answer, call it Nature, is impersonal, impartial, and indifferent. She does not give opinions, or make judgments: she cannot be wheedled, bullied, or fooled; she does not get angry or disappointed; she does not praise or blame; she does not remember past failures or hold grudges; with her one always gets a fresh start, this time is the one that counts.

The next discipline we might call the Discipline of Culture, of Society, 3 or What People Really Do. Man is a social, cultural animal. Children sense around them this culture, this network of agreements, customs, habits, and rules binding the adults together. They want to understand it and be a part of it. They watch very carefully what people around them are doing and want to do the same. They want to do right, unless they become convinced they can't do right. Thus children rarely misbehave seriously in church, but sit as quietly as they can. The example of all those grownups is contagious. Some mysterious ritual is going on, and children, who like rituals, want to be part of it. In the same way, the little children that I see at concerts or operas, though they may fidget a little, or perhaps take a nap now and then, rarely make any disturbance. With all those grownups sitting there, neither moving nor talking, it is the most natural thing in the world to imitate them. Children who live among adults who are habitually courteous to each other, and to them, will soon learn to be courteous. Children who live surrounded by people who speak a certain way will speak that way, however much we may try to tell them that speaking that way is bad or wrong.

The third discipline is the one most people mean when they speak of 4 discipline—the Discipline of Superior Force, of sergeant to private, of "you do what I tell you or I'll make you wish you had." There is bound to be some of this in a child's life. Living as we do surrounded by things that can hurt children, or that children can hurt, we cannot avoid it. We can't afford to let a small child find out from experience the danger of playing in a busy street, or of fooling with the pots on the top of a stove, or of eating up the pills in the medicine cabinet. So, along with other precautions, we say to him, "Don't play in the street, or touch things on the stove, or go into the medicine cabinet, or I'll punish you." Between him and the danger too great for him to imagine we put a lesser danger, but one he can imagine and maybe therefore wants to avoid. He can have no idea of what it would be like to be hit by a car, but he can imagine being shouted at, or spanked, or sent to his room. He avoids these substitutes for the greater danger until he can understand it and avoid it for its own sake.

But we ought to use this discipline only when it is necessary to protect 5 the life, health, safety, or well-being of people or other living creatures, or to prevent destruction of things that people care about. We ought not to assume too long, as we usually do, that a child cannot understand the real nature of the danger from which we want to protect him. The sooner he avoids the danger, not to escape our punishment, but as a matter of good sense, the better. He can learn that faster than we think. In Mexico, for example, where people drive their cars with a good deal of spirit, I saw many children no older than five or four walking unattended on the streets. They understood about cars; they knew what to do. A child whose life is full of the threat and fear of punishment is locked into babyhood. There is no way for him to grow up, to learn to take responsibility for his life and acts. Most important of all, we should not assume that having to yield to the threat of our superior force is good for the child's character. It is never good for *anyone's* character. To bow to superior force makes us feel impotent and cowardly for not having had the strength or courage to resist. Worse, it makes us resentful and vengeful. We can hardly wait to make someone pay for our humiliation, yield to us as we were once made to yield. No, if we cannot always avoid using the Discipline of Superior Force, we should at least use it as seldom as we can.

There are places where all three disciplines overlap. Any very demanding human activity combines in it the disciplines of Superior Force, of Culture, and of Nature. The novice will be told, "Do it this way, never mind asking why, just do it that way, that is the way we always do it." But it probably *is* just the way they always do it, and usually for the very good reason that it is a way that has been found to work. Think, for example, of ballet training. The student in a class is told to do this exercise, or that; to stand so; to do this or that with his head, arms, shoulders, abdomen, hips, legs, feet. He is constantly corrected. There is no argument. But behind these seemingly autocratic demands by the teacher lie many decades of custom and tradition, and behind that, the necessities of dancing itself. You cannot make the moves of classical ballet unless over many years you have acquired, and renewed every day, the needed strength and suppleness in scores of muscles and joints. Nor can you do the difficult motions, making them look easy, unless you have learned hundreds of easier ones first. Dance teachers may not always agree on all the details of teaching these strengths and skills. But no novice could learn them all by himself. You could not go for a night or two to watch the ballet and then, without any other knowledge at all, teach yourself how to do it.

In the same way, you would be unlikely to learn any complicated and difficult human activity without drawing heavily on the experience of those who know it better. But the point is that the authority of these experts or teachers stems from, grows out of their greater competence and experience, the fact that what they do *works,* not the fact that they happen to be the teacher and as such have the power to kick a student out of the class. And the further point is that children are always and everywhere attracted to that competence, and ready and eager to submit themselves to a discipline that grows out of it.

We hear constantly that children will never do anything unless com-   8
pelled to by bribes or threats. But in their private lives, or in extracurricular
activities in school, in sports, music, drama, art, running a newspaper, and so
on, they often submit themselves willingly and wholeheartedly to very intense disciplines, simply because they want to learn to do a given thing well.
Our Little-Napoleon football coaches, of whom we have too many and hear
far too much, blind us to the fact that millions of children work hard every
year getting better at sports and games without coaches barking and yelling
at them.

FIRST RESPONSES

Do you think children today need more discipline? Of which type? Do
you agree that children don't need teachers and coaches who are "barking
and yelling at them"?

TAKING A CLOSER LOOK

Exploring *Who:* Voice and Tone

1. Holt is writing about the uses of authority. How does he establish his
   own authority as an expert on learning and discipline?
2. Who is Holt's implied audience for this article? Do you think you're
   part of that audience? Why or why not?
3. How would you describe the tone of this writing? Find several phrases
   to support your answer. Is the tone appropriate for the subject matter?

Exploring *What:* Content and Meaning

1. What are the three types of discipline? Summarize each kind in a sentence or two.
2. What are the limitations of the Discipline of Culture? Do you agree
   that children want to understand and be a part of the "network of agreements, customs, habits, and rules" around them (para. 3)?
3. What is Holt's most convincing argument against relying too much on
   the Discipline of Superior Force? Can you think of an additional effect of such overreliance?
4. According to Holt, where does the real authority of experts and teachers come from (para. 7)?

Exploring *Why:* Purpose

1. What argument about discipline is Holt making? What course of action does he want his readers to take?
2. Holt was a strong believer in home schooling. In what ways does this belief relate to and explain his views about discipline?

Exploring *How:* Style and Structure

1. How can you tell that this selection is an excerpt from a book?
2. What's the basis for Holt's division of discipline into three types? Why has he presented them in this particular order? Could they be arranged in a different order?
3. What kinds of examples does Holt use to illustrate each type of discipline? How do the examples differ for each type? Explain how all three kinds of discipline are present in the example of the ballet dancer.

IDEAS FOR WRITING A DIVISION AND CLASSIFICATION PAPER

1. Write an essay about the kinds of discipline you have experienced. You can use Holt's categories or invent your own. Decide who your readers are (for example, teachers at a specific school, future little league coaches, fellow students), and determine what message you want to convey to them.
2. ▣▯ *Using the Internet.* Gather some information on home schooling. For example, look at the Internet Home School (www.internethome-school.com/) or Home School World (www.home-school.com) to get some ideas about curriculum, mission statements, services, and activities. Then write an essay in which you discuss how the types of discipline used by parents in home schooling might differ from those used by teachers in the public schools.
3. Write an essay that investigates an abstract quality (like discipline) by dividing it into types or kinds. Some examples: different kinds of intelligence (or stupidity), different types of courage (or cowardice), different forms of success (or failure), different kinds of goodness (or sinfulness).

◆ ◆ ◆ PREPARING TO READ

Think about the last lie you remember telling. Would you call it a minor lie? What motivated you to tell it?

◆ ◆ ◆

The Ways We Lie

STEPHANIE ERICSSON

Born in 1953, Stephanie Ericsson grew up in San Francisco and began writing in high school. She has written screenplays, worked as an advertising copywriter, and published several books of personal nonfiction. The first two of these books—*Shamefaced: The Road to Recovery* and *Women of AA: Recovering Together* (both 1985)—are based on her experiences with drug and alcohol addiction. After the sudden death of her husband, Ericsson wrote two books about grief and bereavement: *Companion through the Darkness: Inner Dialogues on Grief* (1993) and *Companion into the Dawn: Inner Dialogues on Loving* (1994), a collection of essays. The following selection appeared in the January 1993 edition of the *Utne Reader*, a bimonthly magazine that reprints articles from the "alternative press" on a wide range of social and political topics.

The bank called today and I told them my deposit was in the mail, even 1 though I hadn't written a check yet. It'd been a rough day. The baby I'm pregnant with decided to do aerobics on my lungs for two hours, our three-year-old daughter painted the living-room couch with lipstick, the IRS put me on hold for an hour, and I was late to a business meeting because I was tired.

I told my client the traffic had been bad. When my partner came home, 2 his haggard face told me his day hadn't gone any better than mine, so when he asked, "How was your day?" I said, "Oh, fine," knowing that one more straw might break his back. A friend called and wanted to take me to lunch. I said I was busy. Four lies in the course of a day, none of which I felt the least bit guilty about.

We lie. We all do. We exaggerate, we minimize, we avoid confrontation, 3 we spare people's feelings, we conveniently forget, we keep secrets, we justify lying to the big-guy institutions. Like most people, I indulge in small falsehoods and still think of myself as an honest person. Sure I lie, but it doesn't hurt anything. Or does it?

I once tried going a whole week without telling a lie, and it was para-   4
lyzing. I discovered that telling the truth all the time is nearly impossible. It
means living with some serious consequences: The bank charges me $60 in
overdraft fees, my partner keels over when I tell him about my travails, my
client fires me for telling her I didn't feel like being on time, and my friend
takes it personally when I say I'm not hungry. There must be some merit
to lying.

But if I justify lying, what makes me any different from slick politicians   5
or the corporate robbers who raided the S&L industry? Saying it's okay to
lie one way and not another is hedging. I cannot seem to escape the voice
deep inside me that tells me: When someone lies, someone loses.

What far-reaching consequences will I, or others, pay as a result of my   6
lie? Will someone's trust be destroyed? Will someone else pay *my* penance
because I ducked out? We must consider the *meaning of our actions.* Deception, lies, capital crimes, and misdemeanors all carry meanings. *Webster's*
definition of *lie* is specific: 1: a false statement or action especially made with
the intent to deceive; 2: anything that gives or is meant to give a false
impression.

A definition like this implies that there are many, many ways to tell a   7
lie. Here are just a few.

The White Lie

A man who won't lie to a woman has very little consideration for her
feelings.

—Bergen Evans

The white lie assumes that the truth will cause more damage than a   8
simple, harmless untruth. Telling a friend he looks great when he looks like
hell can be based on a decision that the friend needs a compliment more
than a frank opinion. But, in effect, it is the liar deciding what is best for the
lied to. Ultimately, it is a vote of no confidence. It is an act of subtle arro-
gance for anyone to decide what is best for someone else.

Yet not all circumstances are quite so cut-and-dried. Take, for instance,   9
the sergeant in Vietnam who knew one of his men was killed in action but
listed him as missing so that the man's family would receive indefinite com-
pensation instead of the lump-sum pittance the military gives widows and
children. His intent was honorable. Yet for twenty years this family kept their
hopes alive, unable to move on to a new life.

Facades

> Et tu, Brute?
>
> —Caesar

We all put up facades to one degree or another. When I put on a suit to go to see a client, I feel as though I am putting on another face, obeying the expectation that serious businesspeople wear suits rather than sweatpants. But I'm a writer. Normally, I get up, get the kid off to school, and sit at my computer in my pajamas until four in the afternoon. When I answer the phone, the caller thinks I'm wearing a suit (though the UPS man knows better).

But facades can be destructive because they are used to seduce others into an illusion. For instance, I recently realized that a former friend was a liar. He presented himself with all the right looks and the right words and offered lots of new consciousness theories, fabulous books to read, and fascinating insights. Then I did some business with him, and the time came for him to pay me. He turned out to be all talk and no walk. I heard a plethora of reasonable excuses, including in-depth descriptions of the big break around the corner. In six months of work, I saw less than a hundred bucks. When I confronted him, he raised both eyebrows and tried to convince me that I'd heard him wrong, that he'd made no commitment to me. A simple investigation into his past revealed a crowded graveyard of disenchanted former friends.

Ignoring the Plain Facts

> Well, you must understand that Father Porter is only human. . . .
>
> —A Massachusetts priest

In the '60s, the Catholic Church in Massachusetts began hearing complaints that Father James Porter was sexually molesting children. Rather than relieving him of his duties, the ecclesiastical authorities simply moved him from one parish to another between 1960 and 1967, actually providing him with a fresh supply of unsuspecting families and innocent children to abuse. After treatment in 1967 for pedophilia, he went back to work, this time in Minnesota. The new diocese was aware of Father Porter's obsession with children, but they needed priests and recklessly believed treatment had cured him. More children were abused until he was relieved of his duties a year later. By his own admission, Porter may have abused as many as a hundred children.

Ignoring the facts may not in and of itself be a form of lying, but consider the context of this situation. If a lie is a *false action done with the intent to deceive,* then the Catholic Church's conscious covering for Porter created irreparable consequences. The church became a co-perpetrator with Porter.

Deflecting

> When you have no basis for an argument, abuse the plaintiff.
>
> —Cicero

I've discovered that I can keep anyone from seeing the true me by 14 being selectively blatant. I set a precedent of being up-front about intimate issues, but I never bring up the things I truly want to hide; I just let people assume I'm revealing everything. It's an effective way of hiding.

Any good liar knows that the way to perpetuate an untruth is to deflect 15 attention from it. When Clarence Thomas exploded with accusations that the Senate hearings were a "high-tech lynching," he simply switched the focus from a highly charged subject to a radioactive subject. Rather than defending himself, he took the offensive and accused the country of racism. It was a brilliant maneuver. Racism is now politically incorrect in official circles— unlike sexual harassment, which still rewards those who can get away with it.

Some of the most skillful deflectors are passive-aggressive people who, 16 when accused of inappropriate behavior, refuse to respond to the accusations. This you-don't-exist stance infuriates the accuser, who, understandably, screams something obscene out of frustration. The trap is sprung and the act of deflection successful, because now the passive-aggressive person can indignantly say, "Who can talk to someone as unreasonable as you?" The real issue is forgotten and the sins of the original victim become the focus. Feeling guilty of name-calling, the victim is fully tamed and crawls into a hole, ashamed. I have watched this fighting technique work thousands of times in disputes between men and women, and what I've learned is that the real culprit is not necessarily the one who swears the loudest.

Omission

> The cruelest lies are often told in silence.
>
> —R. L. Stevenson

Omission involves telling most of the truth minus one or two key facts 17 whose absence changes the story completely. You break a pair of glasses that are guaranteed under normal use and get a new pair, without mentioning that the first pair broke during a rowdy game of basketball. Who hasn't tried something like that? But what about omission of information that could make a difference in how a person lives his or her life?

For instance, one day I found out that rabbinical legends tell of another   18
woman in the Garden of Eden before Eve. I was stunned. The omission of the Sumerian goddess Lilith from Genesis—as well as her demonization by ancient misogynists as an embodiment of female evil—felt like spiritual robbery. I felt like I'd just found out my mother was really my stepmother. To take seriously the tradition that Adam was created out of the same mud as his equal counterpart, Lilith, redefines all of Judeo-Christian history.

Some renegade Catholic feminists introduced me to a view of Lilith   19
that had been suppressed during the many centuries when this strong goddess was seen only as a spirit of evil. Lilith was a proud goddess who defied Adam's need to control her, attempted negotiations, and when this failed, said adios and left the Garden of Eden.

This omission of Lilith from the Bible was a patriarchal strategy to keep   20
women weak. Omitting the strong-woman archetype of Lilith from Western religions and starting the story with Eve the Rib has helped keep Christian and Jewish women believing they were the lesser sex for thousands of years.

Stereotypes and Clichés

> Where opinion does not exist, the status quo becomes stereotyped and
> all originality is discouraged.
>
> —Bertrand Russell

Stereotype and cliché serve a purpose as a form of shorthand. Our need   21
for vast amounts of information in nanoseconds has made the stereotype vital to modern communication. Unfortunately, it often shuts down original thinking, giving those hungry for the truth a candy bar of misinformation instead of a balanced meal. The stereotype explains a situation with just enough truth to seem unquestionable.

All the "isms"—racism, sexism, ageism, et al.—are founded on and fu-   22
eled by the stereotype and the cliché, which are lies of exaggeration, omission, and ignorance. They are always dangerous. They take a single tree and make it a landscape. They destroy curiosity. They close minds and separate people. The single mother on welfare is assumed to be cheating. Any black male could tell you how much of his identity is obliterated daily by stereotypes. Fat people, ugly people, beautiful people, old people, large-breasted women, short men, the mentally ill, and the homeless all could tell you how

much more they are like us than we want to think. I once admitted to a group of people that I had a mouth like a truck driver. Much to my surprise, a man stood up and said, "I'm a truck driver, and I never cuss." Needless to say, I was humbled.

Groupthink

> Who is more foolish, the child afraid of the dark, or the man afraid of the light?
>
> —Maurice Freehill

Irving Janis, in *Victims of Group Think,* defines this sort of lie as a psy-   23
chological phenomenon within decision-making groups in which loyalty to the group has become more important than any other value, with the result that dissent and the appraisal of alternatives are suppressed. If you've ever worked on a committee or in a corporation, you've encountered groupthink. It requires a combination of other forms of lying—ignoring facts, selective memory, omission, and denial, to name a few.

The textbook example of groupthink came on December 7, 1941. From   24
as early as the fall of 1941, the warnings came in, one after another, that Japan was preparing for a massive military operation. The Navy command in Hawaii assumed Pearl Harbor was invulnerable—the Japanese weren't stupid enough to attack the United States' most important base. On the other hand, racist stereotypes said the Japanese weren't smart enough to invent a torpedo effective in less than 60 feet of water (the fleet was docked in 30 feet); after all, U.S. technology hadn't been able to do it.

On Friday, December 5, normal weekend leave was granted to all the   25
commanders at Pearl Harbor, even though the Japanese consulate in Hawaii was busy burning papers. Within the tight, good-ole-boy cohesiveness of the U.S. command in Hawaii, the myth of invulnerability stayed well entrenched. No one in the group considered the alternatives. The rest is history.

Out-and-Out Lies

> The only form of lying that is beyond reproach is lying for its own sake.
>
> —Oscar Wilde

Of all the ways to lie, I like this one the best, probably because I get tired   26
of trying to figure out the real meanings behind things. At least I can trust

the bald-faced lie. I once asked my five-year-old nephew, "Who broke the fence?" (I had seen him do it.) He answered, "The murderers." Who could argue?

At least when this sort of lie is told it can be easily confronted. As the person who is lied to, I know where I stand. The bald-faced lie doesn't toy with my perceptions—it argues with them. It doesn't try to refashion reality, it tries to refute it. *Read my lips*. . . . No sleight of hand. No guessing. If this were the only form of lying, there would be no such thing as floating anxiety or the adult-children of alcoholics movement.   27

Dismissal

Pay no attention to that man behind the curtain! I am the Great Oz!
—The Wizard of Oz

Dismissal is perhaps the slipperiest of all lies. Dismissing feelings, perceptions, or even the raw facts of a situation ranks as a kind of lie that can do as much damage to a person as any other kind of lie.   28

The roots of many mental disorders can be traced back to the dismissal of reality. Imagine that a person is told from the time she is a tot that her perceptions are inaccurate. *"Mommy, I'm scared."* "No, you're not, darling." *"I don't like that man next door, he makes me feel icky."* "Johnny, that's a terrible thing to say; of course you like him. You go over there right now and be nice to him."   29

I've often mused over the idea that madness is actually a sane reaction to an insane world. Psychologist R. D. Laing supports this hypothesis in *Sanity, Madness & the Family,* an account of his investigations into families of schizophrenics. The common thread that ran through all of the families he studied was a deliberate, staunch dismissal of the patient's perceptions from a very early age. Each of the patients started out with an accurate grasp of reality, which, through meticulous and methodical dismissal, was demolished until the only reality the patient could trust was catatonia.   30

Dismissal runs the gamut. Mild dismissal can be quite handy for forgiving the foibles of others in our day-to-day lives. Toddlers who have just learned to manipulate their parents' attention sometimes are dismissed out of necessity. Absolute attention from the parents would require so much energy that no one would get to eat dinner. But we must be careful and attentive about how far we take our "necessary" dismissals. Dismissal is a dangerous tool, because it's nothing less than a lie.   31

Delusion

We lie loudest when we lie to ourselves.

—Eric Hoffer

I could write the book on this one. Delusion, a cousin of dismissal, is the   32
tendency to see excuses as facts. It's a powerful lying tool because it filters out
information that contradicts what we want to believe. Alcoholics who believe that the problems in their lives are legitimate reasons for drinking rather
than results of the drinking offer the classic example of deluded thinking.
Delusion uses the mind's ability to see things in myriad ways to support what
it wants to be the truth.

But delusion is also a survival mechanism we all use. If we were to fully   33
contemplate the consequences of our stockpiles of nuclear weapons or global
warming, we could hardly function on a day-to-day level. We don't want
to incorporate that much reality into our lives because to do so would be
paralyzing.

Delusion acts as an adhesive to keep the status quo intact. It shamelessly   34
employs dismissal, omission, and amnesia, among other sorts of lies. Its most
cunning defense is that it cannot see itself.

The liar's punishment . . . is that he cannot believe anyone else.

—George Bernard Shaw

These are only a few of the ways we lie. Or are lied to. As I said earlier,   35
it's not easy to entirely eliminate lies from our lives. No matter how pious we
may try to be, we will still embellish, hedge, and omit to lubricate the daily
machinery of living. But there is a world of difference between telling func-
tional lies and living a lie. Martin Buber once said, "The lie is the spirit
committing treason against itself." Our acceptance of lies becomes a cultural
cancer that eventually shrouds and reorders reality until moral garbage
becomes as invisible to us as water is to a fish.

How much do we tolerate before we become sick and tired of being sick   36
and tired? When will we stand up and declare our *right* to trust? When do we
stop accepting that the real truth is in the fine print? Whose lips do we read
this year when we vote for president? When will we stop being so reticent
about making judgments? When do we stop turning over our personal power
and responsibility to liars?

Maybe if I don't tell the bank the check's in the mail I'll be less toler-   37
ant of the lies told me every day. A country song I once heard said it all for
me: "You've got to stand for something or you'll fall for anything."

◆ ◆ ◆

FIRST RESPONSES

Are there times when lying is justified? Are there times when it's all right for people to lie to you?

TAKING A CLOSER LOOK

Exploring *Who:* Voice and Tone

1. How would you describe the overall tone of this essay? Does the tone change in any sections?
2. How does Ericsson personalize her discussion? Is this approach appropriate for the topic?
3. Do you think you are part of the audience for this essay? Why or why not?

Exploring *What:* Content and Meaning

1. List the ten kinds of lies Ericsson describes, and explain each one in a sentence or two.
2. Why is each kind of lie necessary, according to Ericsson? What is the danger of each kind?
3. The author says that she likes "out-and-out lies" the best (para. 26). Why? Why is "dismissal" (para. 28) "the slipperiest of all lies"?
4. Ericsson ends by quoting a line from a country song: "You've got to stand for something or you'll fall for anything." Explain what that means. How does it relate to lying?

Exploring *Why:* Purpose

1. What is the author's goal in this essay? Does she want to inform her readers, or does she want to bring about some sort of change in them?
2. Is Ericsson defending lying? If not, what is she doing?
3. In paragraph 5, Ericsson says "When someone lies, someone loses." Does the rest of her essay confirm or deny this point? Do you agree with it?

Exploring *How:* Style and Structure

1. Reread the opening paragraphs. What expectations do they create? Do they reflect the type of essay that follows?

2. Each category is introduced with a quotation. Are these quotations effective? Would the essay be better without them?

3. Why does the author present her categories in the order she does? Should any of them be placed somewhere else?

4. Throughout her essay Ericsson uses **rhetorical questions** and **colloquial language.** Look closely at a few examples, and discuss why you think she uses these stylistic devices.

5. Evaluate the author's conclusion (para. 35–37). How does it parallel the introduction? Do you think she should have concluded in a different way?

IDEAS FOR WRITING A DIVISION AND CLASSIFICATION PAPER

1. Using Ericsson's essay as a guide, write an essay that uses classification to examine a human trait or social activity: the ways we . . . spend money, take criticism, make friends, deal with death, handle success (or failure), make decisions, clean house, express affection, manage stress, converse, waste time, maintain health, and so on. (You don't have to come up with ten categories, as Ericsson does; four or five will probably be enough.)

2. Write an essay in which you classify the ways people react to being lied to. Base your essay on personal experience, and include a thesis statement that clearly defends or criticizes these reactions.

3. ◼◻ *Using the Internet.* Write an essay about plagiarism. Are there different kinds of plagiarism? Different motives or causes of it? To get help with this topic, use a search engine to locate Web sites that discuss plagiarism and how to avoid it.

◆ ◆ ◆ **PREPARING TO READ**

List five to ten people you call "friends." Are they all friends to an equal degree? Do you have a flexible meaning for the word *friend?*

◆ ◆ ◆

What Friends Are For

PHILLIP LOPATE

Phillip Lopate (born in 1943) is an acclaimed essayist who has won fellowships from the Guggenheim Foundation and the National Endowment for the Arts. He has edited several essay anthologies, including *The Art of the Personal Essay* (1994) and his latest book, *The Art of John Koch: Painting a New York Life* (2001). The following essay first appeared in *Against Joie de Vivre* (1989), a collection of Lopate's writings.

Is there anything left to say about friendship after so many great es- 1
sayists have picked over the bones of the subject? Aristotle and Cicero, Seneca and Montaigne, Francis Bacon and Samuel Johnson, William Hazlitt, Ralph Waldo Emerson, and Charles Lamb have all taken their cracks at it.

Friendship has been called "love without wings." On the other hand, the 2
Stoic definition of love ("Love is the attempt to form a friendship inspired by beauty") seems to suggest that friendship came first. Certainly a case can be made that the buildup of affection and the yearning for more intimacy, without the release of sexual activity, keeps friends in a state of sweet-sorrowful itchiness that has the romantic quality of a love affair. We know that a falling-out between two old friends can leave a deeper and more perplexing hurt than the ending of a love affair, perhaps because we are more pessimistic about the affair's endurance from the start.

Our first attempted friendships are within the family. It is here we prac- 3
tice the techniques of listening sympathetically and proving that we can be trusted, and learn the sort of kindness we can expect in return.

There is something tainted about these family friendships, however. 4
My sister, in her insecure adolescent phase, told me, "You love me because I'm related to you, but if you were to meet me for the first time at a party, you'd think I was a jerk and not worth being your friend." She had me in a bind: I had no way of testing her hypothesis. I should have argued that even if our bond was not freely chosen, our decision to work on it had been. Still,

we are quick to dismiss the partiality of our family members when they tell us we are talented, cute, or lovable; we must go out into the world and seduce others.

It is just a few short years from the promiscuity of the sandbox to the tormented, possessive feelings of a fifth grader who has just learned that his best and only friend is playing at another classmate's house after school. There may be worse betrayals in store, but probably none is more influential than the sudden fickleness of an elementary school friend who has dropped us for someone more popular after all our careful, patient wooing. Often we lose no time inflicting the same betrayal on someone else, just to ensure that we have got the victimization dynamic right.

What makes friendships in childhood and adolescence so poignant is that we need the chosen comrade to be everything in order to rescue us from the gothic inwardness of family life. Even if we are lucky enough to have several companions, there must be a Best Friend.

I clung to the romance of the Best Friend all through high school, college, and beyond, until my circle of university friends began to disperse. At that point, in my mid-twenties, I also acted out the dark, competitive side of friendship that can exist between two young men fighting for a place in life and love by doing the one unforgivable thing: sleeping with my best friend's girl. I was baffled at first that there was no way to repair the damage. I lost this friendship forever, and came away from that debacle much more aware of the amount of injury that friendship can and cannot sustain. Perhaps I needed to prove to myself that friendship was not an all-permissive resilient bond, like a mother's love, but something quite fragile. Precisely because best friendship promotes such a merging of identities, such seeming boundarylessness, the first major transgression of trust can cause the injured party to feel he is fighting for his violated soul against his darkest enemy. There is not much room to maneuver in a best friendship between unlimited intimacy and unlimited mistrust.

Still, it was not until the age of thirty that I reluctantly abandoned the best friend expectation and took up a more pluralistic model. At present, I cherish a dozen friends for their unique personalities, without asking that any one be my soul-twin. Whether this alteration constitutes a movement toward maturity or toward cowardly pragmatism is not for me to say. It may be that, in refusing to depend so much on any one friend, I am opting for self-protection over intimacy. Or it may be that, as we advance into middle age, the life problem becomes less that of establishing a tight dyadic bond and more one of making our way in a broader world, "society." Indeed, since Americans have so indistinct a notion of society, we often try to put a network of friendships in its place.

If a certain intensity is lost in the pluralistic model of friendship, there is also the gain of being able to experience all of one's potential, half-buried selves, through witnessing all the spectacle of the multiple fates of our friends. As it happens, the harem of friends, so tantalizing a notion, often translates into feeling pulled in a dozen different directions, with the guilty sense of having disappointed everyone a little. It is also a risky, contrived enterprise to try to make one's friends behave in a friendly manner toward each other. If the effort fails, one feels obliged to mediate; if it succeeds too well, one is jealous.

Whether friendship is intrinsically singular and exclusive or plural and   10
democratic is a question that has vexed many commentators. Aristotle distinguished three types of friendship: "friendship based on utility," such as businessmen cultivating each other for benefit; "friendship based on pleasure," like young people interested in partying; and "perfect friendship." The first two categories Aristotle calls "qualified and superficial friendships," because they are founded on circumstances that could easily change. The last, which is based on admiration for another's good character, is more permanent, but also rarer; because good men "are few." Cicero, who wrote perhaps the best treatise on friendship, also insisted that what brings true friends together is "a mutual belief in each other's goodness." This insistence on virtue as a precondition for true friendship may strike us as impossibly demanding: Who, after all, feels himself good nowadays? And yet, if I am honest, I must admit that the friendships of mine that have lasted longest have been with those whose integrity, or humanity, or strength to bear their troubles I continue to admire. Conversely, when I lost respect for someone, however winning he or she otherwise remained, the friendship petered away almost immediately. "Remove respect from friendship," said Cicero, "and you have taken away the most splendid ornament it possesses."

Friendship is a long conversation. I suppose I could imagine a nonver-   11
bal friendship revolving around shared physical work or sport, but for me, good talk is the point of the thing. Indeed, the ability to generate conversation by the hour is the most promising indication, during the uncertain early stages, that a possible friendship will take hold. In the first few conversations there may be an exaggeration of agreement, as both parties angle for adhesive surfaces. But later on, trust builds through the courage to assert disagreement, through the tactful acceptance that differences of opinion will have to remain.

Some view like-mindedness as both the precondition and the product   12
of friendship. Myself, I distrust it. I have one friend who keeps assuming that we see the world eye-to-eye. She is intent on enrolling us in a flattering aristocracy of taste, on the short "we" list against the ignorant "they." Sometimes I do not have the strength to fight her need for consensus with my own stubborn disbelief in the existence of any such inner circle of privileged, cultivated sensibility. Perhaps I have too much invested in a view of myself as

idiosyncratic to be eager to join any coterie, even a coterie of two. What attracts me to friends' conversation is the give and take, not necessarily that we come out at the same point.

"Our tastes and aims and views were identical—and that is where the   13
essence of a friendship must always lie," wrote Cicero. To some extent, perhaps, but then the convergence must be natural, not, as Emerson put it, "a mush of concession. Better be a nettle in the side of your friend than his echo."

Friendship is a school for character, allowing us the chance to study, in   14
great detail and over time, temperaments very different from our own. These charming quirks, these contradictions, these nobilities, these blind spots of our friends we track not out of disinterested curiosity: We must have this information before knowing how far we may relax our guard, how much we may rely on them in crises. The learning curve of friendship involves, to no small extent, filling out this picture of the other's limitations and making peace with the results. Each time I hit up against a friend's inflexibility I am relieved as well as disappointed: I can begin to predict, and arm myself in advance against repeated bruises. I have one friend who is always late, so I bring a book along when I am to meet her. I give her a manuscript to read and she promises to look at it over the weekend. I prepare for a month-long wait.

Though it is often said that with a true friend there is no need to hold   15
anything back ("A friend is a person with whom I may be sincere. Before him I may think aloud," wrote Emerson), I have never found this to be entirely the case. Certain words may be too cruel if they are spoken at the wrong moment—or may fall on deaf ears, for any number of reasons. I also find with all my friends, as they must with me, that some initial resistance, restlessness, some psychic weather must be overcome before that tender ideal attentiveness may be called forth.

I have a good friend, Charlie, who is often very distracted whenever   16
we first get together. If we are sitting in a café, he will look around constantly for the waiter, or be distracted by a pretty woman or the restaurant's cat. It would be foolish for me to broach an important subject at such moments, so I resign myself to waiting the half hour or however long it takes until his jumpiness subsides. Or else I draw this pattern grumpily to his attention. Once he has settled down, however, I can tell Charlie virtually anything, and he me. But the candor cannot be rushed. It must be built up to with the verbal equivalent of limbering exercises.

The friendship scene—a flow of shared confidences, recognitions,   17
humor, advice, speculation, even wisdom—is one of the key elements of modern friendships. Compared to the rest of life, this ability to lavish one's

best energies on an activity utterly divorced from the profit motive and free from the routines of domination and inequality that affect most relations (including, perhaps, the selfsame friendship at other times) seems idyllic. The friendship scene is by its nature not an everyday occurrence. It represents the pinnacle, the fruit of the friendship, potentially ever present but not always arrived at. Both friends' dim yet self-conscious awareness that they are wandering conversationally toward a goal that they have previously accomplished but that may elude them this time around creates a tension, an obligation to communicate as sincerely as possible, like actors in an improvisation exercise struggling to shape their baggy material into some climactic form. This very pressure to achieve "quality" communication may induce a sort of inauthentic epiphany, not unlike what sometimes happens in the last ten minutes of a psychotherapy session. But a truly achieved friendship scene can be among the best experiences life has to offer.

Contemporary urban life, with its tight schedules and crowded appointment books, has helped to shape modern friendship into something requiring a good deal of intentionality and pursuit. You phone a friend and make a date a week or more in advance; then you set aside an evening, as if for a tryst, during which to squeeze in all your news and advice, confession and opinion. Such intimate compression may add a romantic note to modern friendships, but it also places a strain on the meeting to yield a high quality of meaning and satisfaction, closer to art than life. If I see busy or out-of-town friends only once every six months, we must not only catch up on our lives but also convince ourselves within the allotted two hours together that we still share a special affinity, an inner track to each other's psyches, or the next meeting may be put off for years. Surely there must be another, saner rhythm of friendship in rural areas—or maybe not? I think about "the good old days" when friends would go on walking tours through England together, when Edith Wharton would bundle poor Henry James into her motorcar and they'd drive to the south of France for a month. I'm not sure my friendships could sustain the strain of travel for weeks at a time, and the truth of the matter is that I've gotten used to this urban arrangement of serial friendship "dates," where the pleasure of the rendezvous is enhanced by the knowledge that it will only last, at most, six hours. If the two of us don't happen to mesh that day (always a possibility)—well, it's only a few hours. And if it should go beautifully, one needs an escape hatch from exaltation as well as disenchantment. I am capable of only so much intense, exciting communication before I start to fade; I come to these encounters equipped with a six-hour oxygen tank. Is this an evolutionary pattern of modern friendship, or just a personal limitation?

Perhaps because I conceive of the modern friendship scene as a somewhat theatrical enterprise, a one-act play, I tend to be very much affected by   19

     18

the "set." A restaurant, a museum, a walk in the park through the zoo, even accompanying a friend on shopping errands—I prefer public turf where the stimulation of the city can play a backdrop to our dialogue, feeding it with details when inspiration flags.

I have a number of *chez moi* friends who always invite me to come to   20
their homes while evading offers to visit me. What they view as hospitality I see as a need to control the mise-en-scène of friendship. I am expected to fit in where they are most comfortable, while they play lord of the manor, distracted by the props of decor, the pool, the unexpected phone call, the swirl of children, animals, and neighbors. Indeed, *chez moi* friends often tend to keep a sort of open house, so that in going over to see them—for a tête-à-tête, I had assumed—I will suddenly find their other friends and neighbors, whom they have also invited, dropping in all afternoon. There are only so many Sundays I care to spend hanging out with a friend's entourage before I become impatient for a private audience.

Married friends who own their own homes are apt to try to draw me   21
into their domestic fold, whereas single people are often more sensitive about establishing a discreet space for the friendship to occur. Perhaps the married assume that a bachelor like me is desperate for home cooking and a little family life. I have noticed that it is not an easy matter to pry a married friend away from mate and milieu. For married people, especially those with children, the home often becomes the wellspring of all their nurturing feelings, and the single friend is invited to partake in the general flow. Maybe there is also a certain tendency on their part to kill two birds with one stone: They don't see enough of their spouse and kids, and they figure they can visit with you at the same time.

From my standpoint, friendship is a jealous goddess. Whenever a friend   22
of mine marries, I have to fight to overcome the feeling that I am being "replaced" by the spouse. I don't mind sharing a friend with his or her family milieu—in fact I like it, up to a point—but eventually I must get the friend alone, or else, as a bachelor at a distinct power disadvantage, I risk becoming a mere spectator of familial rituals instead of a key player in the drama of friendship.

A person who lives alone usually has more energy to give to friend-   23
ship. The danger is investing too much emotional energy in one's friends. When a single person is going through a romantic dry spell, he or she often tries to extract the missing passion from a circle of friends. This works only up to a point: The frayed nerves of protracted celibacy can lead to hypersensitive imaginings of slights and rejections, and one's platonic friends seem to come particularly into the line of fire.

Today, with the partial decline of the nuclear family and the search for   24
alternatives to it, we also see attempts to substitute the friendship web for

intergenerational family life. Since psychoanalysis has alerted us to regard the family as a mine field of unrequited love, manipulation, and ambivalence, it is only natural that people may look to friendship as a more supportive ground for relation. But in our longing for an unequivocally positive bond, we should beware of sentimentalizing friendship, as saccharine "buddy" movies and certain feminist novels do, and of neutering its problematic aspects. Besides, friendship can never substitute for the true meaning of family: If nothing else, it will never be able to duplicate the family's wild capacity for concentrating neurosis.

In short, friends can't be your family, they can't be your lovers, they   25
can't be your psychiatrists. But they can be your friends, which is plenty.

When I think about the qualities that characterize the best friendships   26
I've known, I can identify five: rapport, affection, need, habit, and forgiveness. Rapport and affection can only take you so far; they may leave you at the formal, outer gate of goodwill, which is still not friendship. A persistent need for the other's company, for the person's interest, approval, opinion, will get you inside the gates, especially when it is reciprocated. In the end, however, there are no substitutes for habit and forgiveness. A friendship may travel for years on cozy habit. But it is a melancholy fact that unless you are a saint you are bound to offend every friend deeply at least once in the course of time. The friends I have kept the longest are those who forgave me time and again for wronging them unintentionally, intentionally, or by the plain catastrophe of my personality. There can be no friendship without forgiveness.

◆ ◆ ◆

FIRST RESPONSES

Do you require "like-mindedness" in your friends? If not, what sort of differences are you comfortable with, and how do you deal with these differences?

TAKING A CLOSER LOOK

Exploring *Who:* Voice and Tone

1. How do the first two paragraphs set the general tone for this essay? How would you describe that tone?
2. Lopate uses "we" and "our" throughout the essay. Why does he use these pronouns? What effect does this usage have on you, the reader?
3. How many of Lopate's personal examples could you identify with?

Exploring *What:* Content and Meaning

1. Make a list of the different kinds of friendships discussed in the essay. Is any kind an exception from the others?
2. What are the functions that friends perform, according to this essay? Are there underlying similarities among the types?
3. What is the "pluralistic model of friendship"? When did Lopate take up the pluralistic model of friends? What did he lose, and what did he gain?
4. What are Aristotle's three types of friendships (para. 10)? What does Lopate think of Aristotle's categories, especially the last one?
5. Which type of friendship makes the most sense to you? Do you think you will change your mind on this point as you grow older?

Exploring *Why:* Purpose

1. Lopate begins by suggesting that there is nothing more to say about friendship. Why does he start this way? What does this opening tell you about his purpose?
2. Lopate writes "personal" essays. In what ways is this essay "personal"? To what extent is he writing to clarify his own feelings and ideas?
3. Is this essay primarily informative or persuasive? Is the author trying to get you to examine your own friendships? If so, does he succeed?
4. Does Lopate give you any new insights or perspectives on the subject? How much did you find yourself agreeing with his analyses?

Exploring *How:* Style and Structure

1. Why does Lopate cite so many other writers in the course of his discussion? How did you respond to all these references?
2. At the end of paragraph 4, Lopate says "we must go out into the world and seduce others"; and at the beginning of the next paragraph, he mentions "the promiscuity of the sandbox." Explain what the words *seduce* and *promiscuity* mean in those sentences. Do you consider them effective word choices?
3. The author uses a lot of personal examples to develop his discussion. Why does he include so many? Which ones did you find most informative and revealing?
4. Lopate uses a number of **similes** and **metaphors** to describe and explain friendship. Find several of each, and comment on their effectiveness.
5. Comment on the conclusion. Does the essay end on a strong point?

IDEAS FOR WRITING A DIVISION AND CLASSIFICATION PAPER

1. There are probably as many kinds of people you dislike as people you like. Write an essay categorizing the types that drive you crazy.

2. ■▯ *Using the Internet.* Locate several sites that are devoted to the same topic (such as libraries, drama, encyclopedias, games, grammar, holidays, magazines, music, poetry, travel, geography, schools, or writing), and examine them closely. Then divide them into groups according to some consistent principle (such as types of information, use of graphics, primary purposes, visual style, or kinds of organization). Write an article directed at Internet users, using your classifications to evaluate and recommend the various sites within a particular topic area.

3. Using plenty of specific examples, write an essay disagreeing with Lopate's statement that "friends can't be your family."

◆ ◆ ◆ PREPARING TO READ

Is it easy for you to memorize facts and details for class? How well do you remember people's names and faces? Do you have any techniques for helping you remember information?

◆ ◆ ◆

What We Now Know about Memory

LEE SMITH

Lee Smith (born in 1937) was educated at Yale University. He began his career in journalism with the Associated Press, then moved to *Newsweek* magazine, where he was a reporter for five years. He has been a writer for *Fortune* magazine since 1977 and has served as that publication's bureau chief in Tokyo and Washington, D.C. He also writes for *Time, New York,* and *Artforum International.* The following article first appeared in the April 1995 edition of *Fortune.*

The alarm finally goes off in your head around 3 P.M. Your face flushes   1
and your hands plow through the papers on your desk. You have accidentally stood someone up for lunch. It gets worse. You can't remember who. And still worse: You can't recall where you left your glasses, so you can't look up the name in your appointment book. This is the afternoon you find yourself at a different place in life. Ten years ago, when you were 40, you would not have—could not have—forgotten anything.

Why do our memories betray us? Is this a precursor of Alzheimer's or   2
some other serious mental disorder? How can some people command a loyal and prodigious memory well into old age? Are there ways to make everyone's memory clear again?

First, reassurance: A momentary loss of memory is most probably not   3
a sign of Alzheimer's, or if so it's a very distant one. People between 65 and 75 face only a 4% chance of suffering from that sad, destructive disease, vs. a frightening 50% chance for those over 85. Yet almost all of us will be tripped up by forgetfulness from time to time as we age. Memory may begin to get a little shaky even in our late 30s, but the decline is so gradual that we don't start to stumble until we're 50ish.

The vanguard of 78 million baby-boomers will be 49 this year, so an   4
ever larger share of the population will be turning desktops upside down.
For many, their anxiety in already difficult careers could rise significantly.
Moderate memory loss may be easily manageable for those who spend their
entire working lives in the same company. In that steady-state universe, new
people arrive and rules change slowly. The 45-year-olds who are downsized
out and working as consultants, on the other hand, suddenly must master the
rosters of half a dozen clients and as many ways of doing business.

Neuroscience, in a timely way, has begun to pay more attention to this   5
condition. Researchers call it AAMI, age-associated memory impairment.
The Charles A. Dana Foundation, named for an early manufacturer of dif-
ferential joints for cars, has given $8.4 million to five major university med-
ical centers to study AAMI. Researchers get the help of powerful instru-
ments like PET (positron emission tomography) scanners that can detect
the chemical changes taking place in the brains of subjects as they perform
such tasks as memorizing vocabulary lists.

Some 450 middle-aged and elderly volunteers visit Johns Hopkins Hos-   6
pital in Baltimore once a year to take a series of memory exams, the results
of which are tracked over decades. The brains of some of these good sports
will be examined after they die to see if their declining scores over the years
relate to physical signs of disease and atrophy.

Much about memory is still baffling. "Despite all the noise we scientists   7
make about memory, it is remarkable how little we know," says Dr. Arnold
Scheibel, director of the UCLA Brain Research Institute. He and his colleagues can be forgiven. The brain has as many as 100 billion neurons, many
with 100,000 or more connections through which they can send signals to
neighboring neurons. The number of potential pathways would be beyond the
ability of the most advanced supercomputers to map.

Some of the predetermined roadways seem bizarre. In early February,   8
for example, researchers discovered that men process language in one part
of their brain, women in several. As for memory, the names of natural things,
such as plants and animals, are apparently stored in one part of the brain; the
names of chairs, machines, and other man-made stuff in another. Nouns seem
to be separated from verbs. (That may explain the resistance of some brains
to neologisms that turn nouns into verbs, such as "Let's dialogue on this" or
"I'll liaise with Helen's team.")

Aspects of memory are scattered throughout the brain, but many re-   9
searchers believe the hippocampus (Greek for "sea horse," the shape of the
tiny organ) has an especially important role. That is where new information
is turned into memory. How memories are made—and fade—is still mysterious. But this much is known. Neuron No. 28, say, fires an electrical signal,
and in the synapse where one of 28's connectors touches a receiver of neuron No. 29, a chemical change takes place that triggers an electrical signal

in 29. That signal gets passed on to neuron No. 30, and on and on. If the connection between 28 and 29 is made often enough, the bond between the two neurons grows stronger. This crucial marriage, the stuff that memory seems to be made of, neuroscientists have dubbed, unpoetically, long-term potentiation, or LTP.

Though memories may be created in the hippocampus, they are stored   10
elsewhere. In TV soap operas the amnesiac is the ingenue who has forgotten she is already married to her fiancé's brother in another city, but is otherwise able to function more or less normally. That doesn't happen often, if ever. Real amnesiacs are people who remember the past but not the present. Their hippocampi have been severely damaged, so they are unable to form new memories, but most old memories remain intact.

Daniel L. Schacter, 42, a Harvard psychology professor, played a round   11
of golf with one such victim. M.T., who was 58, remembered the rules and all the lingo from bogie to wedge. But he couldn't recall where he hit his ball. If Schacter drove first and M.T. followed, M.T. had half a chance of holding on to the image of where his ball went long enough to track it down. But if M.T. drove first and had to wait for Schacter to drive, he had no chance. After M.T. walked off one green, Schacter noted in his journal, "the patient was surprised and confused when told he had not yet putted."

Amnesia can be caused by a virus, a blow to the head, a near drowning   12
or stroke that deprives the brain of oxygen for a time, or a faulty gene that programs parts of the brain to deteriorate early. Stress can play a part as well. Lab animals exposed to low levels of shock they cannot control produce glucosteroids that damage their hippocampi. Marilyn Albert, 51, a researcher at Massachusetts General Hospital, notes that among the elderly she is studying in the Boston area, those who are less educated, are less active physically, and feel less able to influence what happens to them day to day tend to experience greater memory loss than the better educated who regard themselves as more commanding. (This kind of stress is not the same as pressure to finish a job or perform well. Pressure can stir strong emotions that actually help imprint memories more deeply.)

As we age, most of us will experience at least some slowdown in abil-   13
ity to remember. What do we have to fear and how do we avoid it? Laypeople are accustomed to distinguishing between long-term and short-term memory. That oversimplifies the phenomenon. Dr. Murray Grossman, 43, a University of Pennsylvania Medical Center neurologist, has helped develop a model that separates memory into five types. He assigns each a locale, or a possible locale, in the brain and assesses the likelihood of each type's decaying over time. In order of durability, the memory types are as follows:

SEMANTIC. The memory of what words and symbols mean is highly re-   14
silient—even some Alzheimer's patients retain much of their semantic

memory. It's unlikely you'll forget what "Tinkertoy," "prom," and "mess hall" mean even though you haven't used the words in years. Nor do you forget religious symbols and corporate trademarks or what distinguishes a cat from a dog. You can add words to your semantic memory until death.

IMPLICIT. Years ago someone taught you to ride a bike. You may not recall the specific instructions of those wobbly, knee-banging first outings, but you will not forget all that you have learned about bike riding over a lifetime—without even being conscious of learning—from turning corners at high speeds to stopping on a dime. How to swim or drive a car and many other skills that depend on automatic recall of a series of motions don't disappear either. Nor do conditioned responses. Like Pavlov's dogs, once you've learned to salivate at the sound of a bell, you'll do it forever. Nor will you neglect to reach for a handkerchief when you sense a sneeze, or for a dollar bill when you see a doorman. Loss of implicit memory is a sure sign of serious mental deterioration.

REMOTE. This is the kind of memory that wins money on *Jeopardy*. It is data collected over the years from schools, magazines, movies, conversations, wherever. Remote memory appears to diminish with age in normal people, though the decline could be simply a retrieval problem. "It could be interference," says Johns Hopkins neurologist Dr. Barry Gordon, 44. "We have to keep sorting through the constant accumulation of information as we age."

When a 60-year-old hears "war," it has many more associations than Vietnam or the Gulf. And compared with the 30-year-old, the 60-year-old may have to rummage through twice as much data before digging way back to the lessons of a high school history course and finding the names of the five Presidents after Lincoln.

WORKING. Now we enter territory that does erode, at least for most people. This is extremely short-term memory, lasting for no more than a few seconds. It is the brain's boss, telling it what to cling to. In conversation, working memory enables you to hang on to the first part of your companion's sentence while she gets to the end. It also lets you keep several things in mind simultaneously—to riffle through your mail, talk on the phone, and catch the attention of a colleague walking by the door to ask him if he wants to go to lunch—all without losing your place.

For reasons that aren't altogether clear, working memory in many people starts to slow down noticeably between 40 and 50. "Certain environments become more difficult, like the trading floor of a stock exchange, where you have to react very fast to a lot of information," says Richard Mohs, 45, a psychiatry professor at Mount Sinai School of Medicine in New York City. Jetfighter combat is out.

EPISODIC. This is the memory of recent experience—everything from the 20
movie you saw last week and the name of the client with whom you
booked lunch to where you put your glasses—and it too dwindles over
time. This is the form of memory loss, the AAMI, that does, or will,
trouble most people. You remember how to drive your car, but that's
academic because you can't recall where you parked it.

Episodic memory could begin to dwindle in the late 30s, but the 21
downward glide is so gentle that unless you are trying to memorize the
Iliad or pass a bar exam, you probably won't notice for a couple of
decades. At 50, however, you are likely to feel a little anxiety as you
watch the younger people in the office, even the non-techies, learn how
to operate the new computer software much more quickly than you do.

Several years ago a Massachusetts insurance company, observing that
malpractice suits are brought against old doctors more often than young 22
ones, asked researchers to develop tests for identifying physicians at risk.
Dean K. Whitla, 69, a Harvard psychologist, was on a team that examined
1,000 doctors, ages 30 to 80. In one test the subjects were seated in front of
computers and asked to read stories crammed with details, such as street addresses. A few minutes later they took a multiple-choice test.

Ability declined steadily with age, says Whitla. Though some of the 80-
year-olds were as good as the 30s, on average the 80s could remember only 23
half as much as the 30s. But there were also some 80s who on further investigation couldn't match the patients they had seen that day with their complaints. (The insurance company has not yet disclosed whether it plans to act
on the results.)

What's going on up there? Unlike cells elsewhere in the body, neurons
don't divide. They age, and at the rate of 100,000 a day they die, says Dr. 24
Daniel Alkon, 52, chief of the neural science lab at the National Institutes of
Health. By the time someone reaches 65 or 70, he may have lost 20% of his
100 billion. Return to the hippocampus, where episodic memory is first
recorded. Neuron 28 and some of its neighbors may be dead or so feeble
they no longer transmit electrical charges efficiently.

Still, 80 billion remaining neurons is a lot. And even though the brain
cannot grow new ones, the neurons can likely sprout new synapses late into 25
life and thereby form new connections with one another. William Greenough,
50, a researcher at the University of Illinois, supplied lab rats with new balls,
dolls, and other toys to play with daily and changed the chutes and tunnels
in their cages. When he cut open their brains, he counted many more synapses
than in rats that got no toys and no new decor.

It's a good guess that the human brain, too, grows more synapses when
stimulated and challenged. So the brain—even while shrinking—may be able 26
to blaze ever more trails for laying down memory. If the neuron 28 path is no

longer easily passable, the number of alternate routes may be virtually limitless. The trick is to force the brain to make them.

The habits of highly intelligent people offer a clue as to how to do that. 27
By and large, says Harvard's Schacter, the higher people score on the Wechsler Adult Intelligence Scale (100 is the mean), the higher they score on the Wechsler Memory Scale. "Memory depends on processing," he says. "Very smart people process information very deeply." Perhaps they relate a magazine article on memory to a book on artificial intelligence and a play about prison camp survivors. Doing so, they could be laying networks of neuron highways that will make the recollection of the article, book, or play accessible by multiple routes.

With effort, people with average intellects can boost their memories substantially. For example, most people have trouble remembering numbers of more than seven digits or so, a limitation long recognized by telephone companies. But a decade ago, researchers at Carnegie Mellon University trained otherwise undistinguished undergraduates to memorize hundred-digit numbers. Focusing hard on that long string of digits, the students found patterns they could relate to meaningful number series, such as birthdays.

Forgetting names bedevils most people, the more so as they age. So 29
meet Harry Lorayne, 68, a memory coach and theatrical wonder already familiar to many insomniacs. His half-hour TV infomercials with Dick Cavett run at 4 A.M. and other off-price times. Lorayne has also appeared on *The Tonight Show* and memorized the names of as many as 500 people in the audience. His gift is that he can quickly invent a dramatic, often grotesque, image to slap on the face of everyone he encounters. "I meet Mr. Benavena, and I notice he has a big nose," rasps Lorayne in a voice that was trained on New York's Lower East Side. "So I think 'vane,' like weather vane, a nose that's a bent weather vane." Lorayne's Memory Power package of videotapes, audiotapes, and a book sells for $115.

Frank Felberbaum, 58, refers to himself as a corporate memory con- 30
sultant. "Think of bottles of beer falling like bombs," he introduces himself unforgettably. Felberbaum's clients include GE Capital, Condé Nast, and some Marriott hotels. For about $6,000, Felberbaum trains a group of 20 or so executives in a two-day course that instructs them on how to retain such critical data as a range of interest rates and the names of hotel guests.

The methods of Lorayne and Felberbaum are legitimate, say the neu- 31
roscientists. The routines they teach—fastening names and other information to vivid pictures—have been around since the ancient Greeks. Lorayne likes to trace his intellectual roots to Aristotle, who taught that in order to think, we must speculate with images. Matteo Ricci, a 16th-century Jesuit missionary to China, "built" a memory palace in his mind and wandered the halls, storing the dosage for a new medicine in one room, perhaps, and retrieving a Thomistic proof for the existence of God from another.

28

There are modest ways to build, if not a palace, at least a comfortable   32
home for memory. College students may be superior at memorizing not only
because their neurons are young but also because they develop mnemonic
devices to survive exams. That's an easy practice to resume. For example,
memory is WIRES—working, implicit, remote, episodic, and semantic. One
of the clichéd pieces of advice for improving your brain, including memory,
is to marry someone smarter than yourself. If that's inconvenient, at least
hang out with challenging, fast-thinking company. Or study accounting,
zoology or a new language.

Coming someday, perhaps, is a memory pill. Cortex Pharmaceuticals,   33
founded by three neuroscientists from the University of California at Irvine,
claims to have developed a class of drugs called ampakines that revive tired
neurons. Gary Lynch, 52, one of the founders and a prominent LTP researcher, says ampakines heighten the ability of the remaining receptors in
weakened neurons to carry on after some of their synapses have died. "We
know that this works in middle-aged and old rats," says Lynch. "If you give
them ampakines, they will remember in the afternoon where they found food
in the morning."

Cortex President Alan Steigrod, 57, says that preliminary clinical trials   34
on humans in Germany have been encouraging. The company hopes to test
the drugs soon on about 100 Alzheimer's victims in the U.S. Ampakines, or
another series of drugs, may eventually prove to be the easy, safe, and effective way to freshen old memories. Or they may not. A Salk Institute researcher
questions whether they are any more useful than caffeine. And they might
have dangerous side effects. So the Food and Drug Administration could approve ampakines for Alzheimer's sufferers, who don't have much to lose, but
keep them off the market for a long time for those afflicted by normal memory loss. Waiting for the FDA's okay, you could probably learn Chinese.

◆ ◆ ◆

FIRST RESPONSES

Why are the causes of memory disorders still so mysterious? Do you
know people with memory problems? How is their day-to-day existence
affected?

TAKING A CLOSER LOOK

Exploring *Who:* Voice and Tone

1. Is Smith a scientist himself? How can you tell from his writing?
2. Who is the audience for this essay?

3. How does Smith attempt to relate to his readers? What details of language and presentation are used to draw you into the discussion? Do you feel the author is talking down to you at any time?

4. How does reading about this topic make you feel? Does Smith do anything to influence your feelings?

Exploring *What:* Content and Meaning

1. Find the examples Smith uses to illustrate each memory type. How well do these examples help you understand each type? Provide an example of your own for each kind of memory.

2. What is the relationship between intelligence and memory? Why is this relationship important to the research into memory retention for ordinary people?

3. What evidence supports the claim that people with average intelligence can boost their memories substantially?

4. ▇▊ *Using the Internet.* What's a mnemonic device (para. 32)? Does the one that Smith gives (WIRES) seem helpful? Do you know any others? Look on the Internet for Web sites on mnemonics. You'll find that a number of people and groups collect mnemonics as a hobby or as study aids. See, for instance, Amanda's Mnemonics Page (www. frii.com/~geomanda/mnemonics.html) or the Mnemonics Page of the American Medical Student Association (http://uhsweb.edu/rb/mn.htm).

Exploring *Why:* Purpose

1. Is Smith trying to inform, give practical advice, or both?

2. Look at the four questions in paragraph 2. What do these questions reveal about Smith's purpose? Does he answer them all?

3. Why does Smith discuss the causes of amnesia?

Exploring *How:* Style and Structure

1. Why does Smith begin with an anecdote about "you" and "your" memory lapses? Is this **point of view** a good way to open?

2. What principle does the author use to arrange the five memory types?

3. Smith discusses the mechanics of memory before he discusses ways to improve it. Why is this an effective organization?

4. What is the function of the **rhetorical question** in paragraph 13?

5. Why does Smith give the age of every researcher he mentions?

IDEAS FOR WRITING A DIVISION AND CLASSIFICATION PAPER

1. Write an essay that classifies several different types of intelligence. Brainstorm (with help from friends or classmates if you want it) for ideas about the various kinds of "smarts" you see around you. Divide them into types, and discuss their usefulness and relative importance.

2. Return to the Web pages you found on mnemonics (in *What* question 4), and examine them more closely. What are the aims of these sites? How do they sort and present the mnemonics? For an audience of readers who have not viewed these sites, write an essay in which you describe the various sites and discuss their designs and purposes.

3. Write an essay in which you classify the types of stress that college students experience.

◆ ◆ ◆

◆ FURTHER IDEAS FOR USING DIVISION AND CLASSIFICATION

1. ◼▯ *Using the Internet.* What different methods of managing money do you see among your friends and family members? For help in developing this topic, locate some sites on the Internet that give advice and information about managing finances; see what kinds of problems and approaches they mention. Then write an essay classifying several types of money managers. Be sure to give plenty of specific examples to identify each type. You might conclude by offering a few tips of your own for managing money.

2. Perhaps you have had contact with a culture that is "foreign" to you. It may be a culture that is different due to class background, ethnic customs, gender or sexual orientation, religious belief, hierarchy of values, or intellectual persuasion. Write about the categories of differences you see between your culture and the foreign one. If you have not had this experience, interview someone who has—perhaps an exchange student—with the goal of writing about cultural differences.

3. Write an essay in which you divide the topic into humorous categories: ways of putting things off, methods of avoiding work, techniques for ignoring children (or coworkers), bad shopping tips, and so forth.

4. COLLABORATIVE WRITING. Classify and explain the types of stress that distinguish a certain period of life. Get together with a group of classmates to brainstorm lists of the stresses associated with teenagers, the first year of college, marriage, parenthood, retirement. Review the lists and decide which area to write about. Then have each group member gather examples, details, causes, and effects by interviewing at least three people. Assemble your ideas and materials, and write a group report on the topic.

5. COMBINING STRATEGIES. Even the best-integrated person has different selves that come out in different situations. Write an essay telling about your different selves. Describe the environments that bring them out, narrate some experiences that show these selves in action, and explain the effects that these roles have on your life.

CHAPTER 9

Strategies for Examining Connections

Comparison and Contrast

◆ ◆ ◆ ◆ ◆

Comparison and contrast writing purposefully directs a reader's attention to similarities and differences.

◆ Writers use comparison and contrast to clarify, decide, and persuade.

◆ Effective comparison and contrast is organized clearly in either a point-by-point or block-by-block pattern.

◆ Points of comparison or contrast are developed consistently from section to section.

One of the fundamental ways we learn new things is by finding similarities and differences between them and the things we already know. "You'll like Jose," a friend tells you. "He's funny in the same way Ellen is." Here the familiar is used to clarify the unfamiliar. Immediate comparisons of this sort are called **analogies.** Teachers use them frequently, especially to help make abstract or difficult concepts more concrete. A biology professor, for example, might compare the human eye to a camera.

Sometimes analogies are used to persuade. Your English tutor will remind you that practicing the various writing strategies is a lot like standing in the batter's cage for a few hours before a big game: in both cases, the result will be that the skills will be there when you need them the most. The test of an analogy, of course, is its accuracy. Learning to play racquetball is made much easier if a player realizes early in the process that regardless of the seeming similarities, there are significant differences between it and tennis.

More broadly, **comparison and contrast** is a strategy people use on a daily basis to make choices in their lives, to persuade themselves or others, and to help themselves and others select the best of many options. We weigh the pros and cons and consider advantages and disadvantages. What movie should you see, the new hit comedy or the drama based on the novel you just finished reading? Factors that might affect your decision include who the actors are, whether you have seen one of the director's films in the past, and who the people are who have given you the rave and pan reviews.

In general, comparisons seek the likeness between objects or ideas, and contrasts highlight the differences. Although an essay might serve primarily to compare or contrast, the two approaches are quite frequently combined, with a few contrasting points reminding readers of the unique nature of each of the two things being compared or with a striking comparison serving to undercut an overly general or simplistic contrast. In "Day to Night," Maya Angelou contrasts the cotton pickers' early morning hope to their evening despair, with a few significant comparisons to underscore the consistent dignity that defines all their activities.

Day to Night: Picking Cotton

MAYA ANGELOU

Poet, autobiographer, actress—Maya Angelou (born in 1928) has sought and found success in many roles. Raised in rural, segregated Arkansas as well as in urban St. Louis and San Francisco, Angelou found strength, inspiration, and vision in her complex and varied immediate family as well as in the many authors she read so avidly. The first of six volumes of her autobiography, *I Know Why the Caged Bird Sings* (1970), brought her national attention and was made into a television movie in 1979. Angelou's most public role came when President-elect Bill Clinton asked her to compose a poem for his 1992 inauguration. Her reading of *On the Pulse of Morning* was awarded a Grammy. In addition to writing, she has spent the last several years traveling to university campuses lecturing, singing, and inspiring the next generation. A recorded interview with Angelou is available at www.oprah.com/ omagazine/200012/omag_200012_maya.html.

Early in the century, Momma (we soon stopped calling her Grand- 1 mother) sold lunches to the sawmen in the lumberyard (east Stamps) and the seedmen at the cotton gin (west Stamps). Her crisp meat pies and cool lemonade, when joined to her miraculous ability to be in two places at the same time, assured her business success. From being a mobile lunch counter, she set up a stand between the two points of fiscal interest and supplied the workers' needs for a few years. Then she had the Store built in the heart of the Negro area. Over the years it became the lay center of activities in town. On Saturdays, barbers sat their customers in the shade on the porch of the Store, and troubadours on their ceaseless crawlings through the South leaned across its benches and sang their sad songs of The Brazos while they played juice harps and cigar-box guitars.

The formal name of the Store was the Wm. Johnson General Mer- 2 chandise Store. Customers could find food staples, a good variety of colored thread, mash for hogs, corn for chickens, coal oil for lamps, light bulbs for the wealthy, shoestrings, hair dressing, balloons, and flower seeds. Anything not visible had only to be ordered.

Each year I watched the field across from the Store turn caterpillar 3 green, then gradually frosty white. I knew exactly how long it would be be- . fore the big wagons would pull into the front yard and load on the cotton pickers at daybreak to carry them to the remains of slavery's plantations.

During the picking season my grandmother would get out of bed at 4 four o'clock (she never used an alarm clock) and creak down to her knees and chant in a sleep-filled voice, "Our Father, thank you for letting me see this New Day. Thank you that you didn't allow the bed I lay on last night to be my cooling board, nor my blanket my winding sheet. Guide my feet this day along the straight and narrow, and help me to put a bridle on my tongue. Bless this house, and everybody in it. Thank you, in the name of your Son, Jesus Christ, Amen."

Before she had quite arisen, she called our names and issued orders, and 5 pushed her large feet into homemade slippers and across the bare lye-washed wooden floor to light the coal-oil lamp.

The lamplight in the Store gave a soft make-believe feeling to our world 6 which made me want to whisper and walk about on tiptoe. The odors of onions and oranges and kerosene had been mixing all night and wouldn't be disturbed until the wooded slat was removed from the door and the early morning air forced its way in with the bodies of people who had walked miles to reach the pickup place.

"Sister, I'll have two cans of sardines."   7

"I'm gonna work so fast today I'm gonna make you look like you stand-   8
ing still."

"Lemme have a hunk uh cheese and some sody crackers."   9

"Just gimme a coupla them fat peanut paddies." That would be from a   10
picker who was taking his lunch. The greasy brown paper sack was stuck behind the bib of his overalls. He'd use the candy as a snack before the noon
sun called the workers to rest.

In those tender mornings the Store was full of laughing, joking, boast-   11
ing, and bragging. One man was going to pick two hundred pounds of cotton,
and another three hundred. Even the children were promising to bring home
fo' bits and six bits.

The champion picker of the day before was the hero of the day. If he   12
prophesied that the cotton in today's field was going to be sparse and stick
to the bolls like glue, every listener would grunt a hearty agreement.

The sound of the empty cotton sacks dragging over the floor and the   13
murmurs of waking people were sliced by the cash register as we rang up
the five-cent sales.

If the morning sounds and smells were touched with the supernatural,   14
the late afternoon had all the features of the normal Arkansas life. In the
dying sunlight the people dragged, rather than their empty cotton sacks.

Brought back to the Store, the pickers would step out of the backs of   15
trucks and fold down, dirt-disappointed, to the ground. No matter how much
they had picked, it wasn't enough. Their wages wouldn't even get them out
of debt to my grandmother, not to mention the staggering bill that waited on
them at the white commissary downtown.

The sounds of the new morning had been replaced with grumbles about   16
cheating houses, weighted scales, snakes, skimpy cotton, and dusty rows. In
later years I was to confront the stereotyped picture of gay song-singing cotton pickers with such inordinate rage that I was told even by fellow Blacks
that my paranoia was embarrassing. But I had seen the fingers cut by the
mean little cotton bolls, and I had witnessed the backs and shoulders and
arms and legs resisting any further demands.

Some of the workers would leave their sacks at the Store to be picked   17
up the following morning, but a few had to take them home for repairs. I
winced to picture them sewing the coarse material under a coal-oil lamp with
fingers stiffening from the day's work. In too few hours they would have to
walk back to Sister Henderson's Store, get vittles and load, again, onto the
trucks. Then they would face another day of trying to earn enough for the
whole year with the heavy knowledge that they were going to end the season as they started it. Without the money or credit necessary to sustain a
family for three months. In cotton-picking time the late afternoons revealed

the harshness of Black Southern life, which in the early morning had been softened by nature's blessing of grogginess, forgetfulness, and the soft lamplight.

◆ ◆ ◆

◆ ◆ ◆ *Writer's Workshop I* ◆ ◆ ◆ *Responding to Comparison and Contrast*

Use the *Who, What, Why,* and *How* questions (see p. 3) to explore your own understanding of the ideas and the writing strategies employed by Maya Angelou in "Day to Night." Your instructor may ask you to record these responses in a journal, post them on an electronic bulletin board, or bring them to class to use in small group discussions.

◆ WRITING FROM READING

While working her way through the *Who, What, Why,* and *How* questions, student writer Kara Kitner concluded, "The details she [Angelou] focused on in different stages throughout the essay not only made me feel as if I were there, but also created within me the feeling of a childhood memory. When this feeling is contrasted with the reality of the workers' lives, it makes the harshness more startling and lends it more weight." Kara recognized that beneath the most obvious contrast in Angelou's essay—the morning and evening behaviors of the cotton pickers—lay many additional contrasts: Angelou's own childhood idealism versus her adult anger, and the reality of rural poverty against the racist stereotype of the happy cotton picker. Kara decided to brainstorm about her own evolving attitudes toward childhood; she ended by writing "Life: It's All About Choices."

```
Kara Kitner
English 1001
April 23, 1998


                Life: It's All about Choices

    Still lying in bed after I have shut off the alarm    1
that insisted that I get out of bed, I suddenly
remember other mornings much like this one. Well, sort
```

of like this one. On those days, however, it wasn't an alarm that woke me up.

"Rise and shine! It is 7:15--time to get up," my   2
mother would shout.

I would open my eyes at the sound and squint   3
against the morning light. Growing accustomed to the
sudden brightness, my eyes would flit over the contents
of the room: the antique desk my dad had found and
refinished for me, the long lace curtains my mom knew I
would like, and the old wooden dresser I've had since
I was a child. These items were a familiar part of my
everyday life, but while I appreciated their existence
and the thoughtfulness of those who had procured them
for me, I knew I had never actively chosen them for
myself. Finally, I would get up and head for the
shower. On my way, my mom would stop me before she
left for work: "I've got to go--have a good day!"

"You too," I would respond sleepily. Emerging from   4
the bathroom fifteen minutes later, fully awake, I
would begin to hurry to get ready so I would not be
late for school. Rushing in from the parking lot to
the crowded, noisy hallways of the high school, I
would check the clock and always find a few minutes to
talk to friends before the beginning of my formal day,
regularly signaled by the authority of the bell. The
day was divided into eight periods, which included
classes, study hall, lunch, and physical education.
There were specific times to learn, to study, to eat,
and to play. Almost every day the schedule would be
the same, and, again, someone else had chosen it
for me.

After school I would drive down the street to my   5
after-school job, work for about an hour and a half,
and then go home to study. It wasn't too much later
when my mom would arrive, asking me in the same breath
about my day and what I wanted for dinner. If I had
play rehearsal that night, we would decide on
something quickly. Then I'd go back to school, to the
exciting atmosphere exuded by the lights, red velvet
curtains, and hardwood floors of the auditorium. When
rehearsal was over, my friends and I would go for ice
cream or a Coke, but none of us could stay out very
long because we had ten o'clock curfews. Home again, I

would turn on the television and call my boyfriend. We would talk until mom knocked on the door telling me it was time to get off the phone, and soon afterwards I went to bed.

Hearing my roommate leave the apartment for her 6 first class, I am startled from my memory. I am now more aware of my current surroundings. I notice my new desk, which I had to put together myself, along with the papasan chair I had always wanted to buy. Not wanting to be late for class, I quickly get up, take a shower, and throw my hair up into a ponytail, dashing off to class and putting in my backpack the muffins I will eat for breakfast in the hour break between my first two classes. An hour at work is next, and then I walk back home for lunch break--a luxurious two hours.

My day is still scheduled, but it's now completely 7 up to me. With this choice comes more freedom, but also more responsibility. I decide what and when to eat, when to study, when to just relax with friends, even when to take my classes. Every day is what I make it. It is now up to me to make time for all of the events I feel are important in my life.

I walk home from class at the end of the day, 8 considering those high school memories I'd had in the morning and realize the old cliché is true: life is all about choices. Even more importantly, they are now all my choices. During the time I've spent away from home, I have really had to take stock of the values and traditions I was raised with, and decide which of these to carry over into my adult life and which to leave behind. I know that I could skip class tomorrow. No one would check up on me or call my parents. But I will choose to go anyway, because it is something I have made important in my life, something on which I place great value.

◆ GETTING STARTED ON COMPARISON AND CONTRAST

Comparison and contrast is used to *clarify* a point, to *decide* between several options, and to *persuade* you or someone else that one thing might be better than another. Your purpose for turning to this strategy, as well as who your readers might be, should guide you in making early choices about what you will compare or contrast, which points you will base the comparison or contrast on, how you will arrange the essay, and how many illustrations you will use.

Begin by turning your reason for writing into a sentence or question. Maya Angelou, for example, might have started writing "Day to Night" to clarify the reality of the cotton pickers' lives. Kara Kitner, on the other hand, began with the question, "How is my daily life now different from life at home?"

Next it's time to use brainstorming, freewriting, or perhaps clustering to generate answers to your question, points you might compare and contrast to make your point, and examples of your points. Kara brainstormed a list of all the things she heard, saw, and did over the course of her days at home and then did the same for her days now.

After you have generated your options, points, and examples, you'll need to review your reason for writing and decide if research is necessary to supplement your personal experience. The autobiographical nature of both Angelou's and Kara's essays did not require research. Either, however, might have expanded the scope of her essay by surveying others like her or by researching the opinions of professional sociologists or psychologists, as political scientist Andrew Hacker did to support his thesis in "Dividing American Society," which you will see later in the chapter.

When you have generated sufficient material, it's time to decide on a working **thesis,** a sentence that captures the clarification you hope to accomplish or that asserts the decision you would suggest or the position you would persuade your readers to take. With this generalization in mind, you can determine what, exactly, you will need to compare and contrast to accomplish your purpose. Finally, you need to decide the best points upon which to base the comparison and contrast. Angelou wanted to persuade her readers that "In cotton-picking time the late afternoons revealed the harshness of Black Southern life, which in the early morning had been softened by nature's blessing of grogginess, forgetfulness and the soft lamplight." What she wished to contrast was implied in her thesis, and her strong memories of the sights and sounds of her grandmother's store provided her with her points of comparison—the way the workers looked and the things they talked about.

◆ ORGANIZING COMPARISON AND CONTRAST

Once you have determined what you are going to compare or contrast and the points upon which those comparisons or contrasts will be based, you then need to determine how to arrange the essay. You have two primary choices: **point by point** or **block by block.** The material to be covered remains essentially the same, but the pattern variations provide opportunities to fulfill your purpose and meet your readers' needs more precisely. Regardless of which plan you choose, consistency is the key to successful implementation.

Block-by-Block Comparison

Both Angelou and Kara decided on a block-by-block organization. In this pattern, readers are given complete information about one of the things being compared before moving to the next thing. Angelou first writes all about the morning's events and then all about the evening's activities. Kara describes her teen years at home and then brings us up to date on her days at college. Looking closely, however, you'll discover that both have a subplan as well. Within each block or section of their essays are the points that meaningfully connect the things being compared or contrasted. In fact, during her prewriting, Kara produced this outline of Angelou's essay:

DAY	NIGHT
The plentifulness of goods at the store	The lack of goods in the worker's homes
Hope and promise of the new day	Bleakness and despair of the evening
Make-believe world of child— oranges, etc.	Real world of adults—cut fingers, etc.
Workers making purchases	Workers talking about bills
Positive, hopeful discussion of wages	Negative, disillusioned view of wages
"hero of the dawn"	"dirt disappointed" workers
"joking, boasting, and bragging"	"grumbles" and "heavy knowledge"
Dragging cotton sacks	Dragging workers
Daybreak	Dusk

This thoughtful analysis of Angelou's careful structuring provided Kara with a model for paralleling the development of each section of the blocked essay to persuade readers of the accuracy and value of the contrast being described.

In the block method of organization, you can either imply the point of the comparison or contrast, leaving the readers to draw their own conclusions, or direct the readers' attention to the points of comparison. Angelou does the latter in a transitional paragraph between the two sections and again as she develops the parallel points in the second half of her essay. One danger here is that the second block of the comparison may require too much repetition of the material already covered.

Similarities and Differences

A variation on the block-by-block method is to cluster the points of comparison and contrast around similarities and differences. Consider, for example, the proverbial apples and oranges. An advertising executive for the apple industry might organize a fact sheet promoting apples by clustering the similarities between apples and oranges—their nutritional value and availability, for example—and then emphasizing their differences—more varied uses for apples and their lower cost—after that. The purpose, to sell apples, is best served by admitting the comparison but emphasizing the contrasts.

Point-by-Point Comparison

Point-by-point development places responsibility for the comparison or contrast more directly into the hands of the writer. Each major section of the paper covers one point in terms of both or all the things being compared or contrasted. For example, a nutritionist, without the profit motive of the advertising executive, might organize the fact sheet on apples and oranges by drawing conclusions one section at a time about relative cost, nutritional value, availability, and use, covering both apples and oranges under each of these points. For ease of use and consistency, either apples or oranges would be discussed first in each section. Here is an outline of this arrangement:

APPLES VERSUS ORANGES

1. Relative cost
   a. Orange prices remain relatively constant throughout the year.
   b. Apples are least expensive during the fall harvest season.
2. Nutritional value
   a. Oranges contain significant amounts of vitamins A and C and have 62 calories.
   b. Apples offer fiber and have 81 calories.
3. Availability
   a. Oranges are generally available year round.
   b. Apples are best during the fall.
4. Use
   a. Oranges can be used as snacks, & in salads, main dishes, desserts.
   b. Apples can be used as snacks, & in salads, main dishes, desserts.

◆ DEVELOPING COMPARISON AND CONTRAST

After determining what will be compared or contrasted, the points with which to accomplish that, and the best organizing principle, you may want to do additional brainstorming, freewriting, or clustering to ensure the best development of your points. A review of the discussion in Chapter 5 of providing appropriate, relevant, and sufficiently detailed examples might be useful as you generate this additional supporting material. It's also time to reconsider the needs of your readers. Their experience with your topic or level of education might help you select the right **analogy** or comparison to clarify your idea. The extent to which you expect readers to agree or disagree will indicate how many supporting points are needed and the extent to which they will need to be developed. Knowing that most of her readers would be more familiar with the stereotype than with the reality of picking cotton, Angelou provides in-depth descriptions and a wide range of sights and sounds. Kara, on the other hand, assumes her fellow classmates are familiar with college life and so concentrates on her unique behaviors and choices.

One pitfall of comparison and contrast essays can be the overuse of direct transitional phrasing: *but, and, however, on the other hand, in contrast.* The effect is to produce sing-song-like sentences that become annoying to read. Instead, you want to vary your style and allow the ideas themselves to provide the implied comparison or contrast, saving the **transitions** for strategic turning points within and between paragraphs. If you find yourself beginning each new sentence or every few sentences with a transition, it also may indicate that you are not fully developing your individual points. This kind of paragraph reads more like a list than an essay.

◆ OPENING AND CLOSING COMPARISON AND CONTRAST

As with all the strategies, the introductions to comparison and contrast essays are written to provide readers with any background that might be required to understand the points to be developed, to reveal the writer's purpose, to forecast the essay's pattern of development, and to create reader interest.

Angelou chooses to delay her purpose in favor of developing a context for her comparison and contrast. Her own authority for writing about her topic is established in the descriptions of Momma's store; at the same time, readers are drawn into the world through the sensory descriptions that are subsequently used to compare and contrast the cotton pickers. Later, her block-by-block organization allows Angelou a natural spot to state her thesis: at the turning point from the morning section of the essay to the evening section.

Although Kara chose the same block-by-block organization and delayed providing a direct thesis, she decided to emphasize her comparison and contrast strategy in her introduction. Readers are left with the expectation that by the end of the essay they will understand the value of Kara's memories. Wanting to know the unknown is a great reason to keep reading.

Deborah Tannen's "Sex, Lies, and Conversation," a point-by-point essay, begins with an anecdote that recurs throughout her essay. By providing readers with a familiar scene and recognizable people, she prepares doubting readers for her controversial thesis, which appears in paragraph 2, immediately before the actual point-by-point comparisons.

Only two of the essays in this chapter begin with direct theses. Both Denise Noe and Andrew Hacker illustrate why challenging or provocative comparisons might best begin with a straightforward purpose and design. Because readers might easily dismiss Noe's claim for a similarity between rap and country music, she must hit the ground running and immediately convince them of at least one substantial point of comparison. Similarly, Hacker's very topic implies his problem as a writer: many white readers will resist facing the problem of race in America. As a result, he realizes that he must act quickly. In strong, concrete language, within a single, introductory paragraph, he moves readers across the history of slavery to the present and to his central claim that history is itself the foundation of the problem.

Conclusions to comparison and contrast essays depend on the complexity of the material covered, the type of introduction chosen, and the structure of the essay. Only in the most difficult and technical essays will readers require a summary of the points of comparison and contrast. Instead, most essays, such as Kara's, use the conclusion to reveal a delayed thesis or to state directly a previously implied thesis, as Angelou does. Scott Russell Sanders's last paragraph reinforces his central point on gender: where some see a contrast, he sees a comparison. But his final thoughts are questions, leaving readers with a challenge to rethink their preconceptions.

◆ USING THE MODEL

Maya Angelou's interest in writing about the cotton pickers begins with an emotional response to what she believes is a misperception of them. She returns to her own concrete memories to sustain her argument against the stereotype. Although Kara, too, compares past impressions to present understandings, she comes to the conclusion that, in her case, "the old cliché is true: life is all about choices."

We grow up and grow old reacting to and against such commonly held beliefs. Identify some popular perception with which you strongly agree or disagree based on your own experience. Consider whether or not your feelings about the perception have changed as you've grown up. Interview others and record their responses to this same belief, and then write a comparison or contrast essay based on your results.

◆ ◆ ◆ *Writer's Workshop II* ◆ ◆ ◆ *Analyzing Comparison and Contrast*

Working individually or with a small group of classmates, read through Kara Kitner's essay "Life: It's All About Choices," and respond to the following questions.

1. Which of her personal values does Kara hope to emphasize in her essay? Is there sufficient detail to explain what these values are and how they developed?
2. Are Kara's experiences typical? What evidence is there that she thinks they are?
3. What do you think of Kara's parents? Will Kara be a similar kind of parent?
4. Does Kara's conclusion suggest that she hopes to influence her readers in any concrete way? Does she succeed?
5. Why does Kara provide more extensive description of her childhood than of her current routine? Did you need additional information to understand the contrast between the two?

◆ ◆ ◆ *Checklist for Reading and Writing* ◆ ◆ ◆ *Comparison and Contrast Essays*

1. Is a purpose for comparison or contrast made clear through either a direct or implied thesis?
2. Are the things being compared, contrasted, or developed through analogy logically connected to one another?
3. Are the points of comparison useful and sufficient, and are they consistently developed?
4. Is the pattern of development appropriate for the writer's purpose and readers' needs?
5. Are transitions provided where needed but not overused?

◆ ◆ ◆ PREPARING TO READ

Does someone you live with or know make you listen to a type of music that is significantly different from your favorite type of music? What makes the two styles of music so different? Can you find any similarities?

◆ ◆ ◆

Parallel Worlds: The Surprising Similarities (and Differences) of Country-and-Western and Rap

DENISE NOE

Denise Noe seems to have chosen just the right career. Being a journalist allows her to pursue her widely diverse interests, from dinosaurs to the value of technology in the everyday lives of the disabled. Throughout her work, she seeks connections where others may only find differences. The titles of a few of the magazines in which she has been published give some insight into her unusual view of the world: *Gauntlet, Chrysalis, Metis, The Gulf War Anthology, Exquisite Corpse,* and *Nuthouse.* "Parallel Worlds" first appeared in *The Humanist* in the summer of 1995.

In all of popular music today, there are probably no two genres that   1
are more apparently dissimilar than country-and-western and rap: the one rural, white, and southern; the other urban, black, and identified with the two coasts ("New York style" versus "L.A. style"). Yet C&W and rap are surprisingly similar in many ways. In both C&W and rap, for example, lyrics are important. Both types of music tell stories, as do folk songs, and the story is much more than frosting for the rhythm and beat.

The ideologies espoused by these types of music are remarkably   2
similar as well. We frequently stereotype country fans as simple-minded conservatives—"redneck," moralistic super-patriots à la Archie Bunker. But country music often speaks critically of mainstream American platitudes, especially in such highly charged areas as sexual morality, crime, and the Protestant work ethic.

The sexual ethos of C&W and rap are depressingly similar: the men of   3
both genres are champion chauvinists. Country singer Hank Williams, Jr.,

declares he's "Going Hunting Tonight," but he doesn't need a gun since he's hunting the "she-cats" in a singles bar. Male rappers such as Ice-T, Ice Cube, and Snoop Doggy Dogg are stridently misogynist, with "bitches" and "hos" their trademark terms for half of humanity; their enthusiastic depictions of women raped and murdered are terrifying. Indeed, the sexism of rap group NWA (Niggaz with Attitude) reached a real-life nadir when one member of the group beat up a woman he thought "dissed" them—and was praised for his brutality by the other members.

On a happier note, both rap and C&W feature strong female voices as   4
well. Women rappers are strong, confident, and raunchy: "I want a man, not a boy / to approach me / Your lame game really insults me. . . . I've got to sit on my feet to come down to your level," taunt lady rappers Entice and Barbie at Too Short in their duet / duel, "Don't Fight the Feeling." Likewise, Loretta Lynn rose to C&W fame with defiant songs like "Don't Come Home a-Drinkin' with Lovin' on Your Mind" and "Your Squaw Is on the Warpath Tonight."

Country music can be bluntly honest about the realities of sex and   5
money—in sharp contrast to the "family values" rhetoric of the right. "Son of Hickory Hollow's Tramp" by Johnny Darrell salutes a mother who works as a prostitute to support her children. "Fancy" by Bobbie Gentry (and, more recently, Reba McEntire) describes a poverty-stricken woman's use of sex for survival and her rise to wealth on the ancient "gold mine." Both tunes are unapologetic about the pragmatic coping strategies of their heroines.

More startling than the resemblances in their male sexism and "up-   6
pity" women are the parallels between C&W and rap in their treatment of criminality. Country-and-western music is very far from a rigid law-and-order mentality. The criminal's life is celebrated for its excitement and clear-cut rewards—a seemingly promising alternative to the dull grind of day-to-day labor.

"Ain't got no money / Ain't got no job / Let's find a place to rob," sings   7
a jaunty Ricky Van Shelton in "Crime of Passion." In "I Never Picked Cotton," Roy Clark is more subdued but still unrepentant when he says: "I never picked cotton / like my mother did and my sister did and my brother did / And I'll never die young / working in a coal mine like my daddy did." Waylon Jennings' "Good Ole Boys" boast gleefully of having "hot-wired a city truck / turned it over in the mayor's yard."

Similarly, rap songs like "Gangsta, Gangsta" and "Dopeman" by NWA   8
and "Drama" by Ice-T tell of the thrill and easy money offered by a life of crime. "Drama" records the dizzying high of the thief; "Gangsta, Gangsta," the rush of adrenaline experienced by a murderer making a quick getaway. Of course, both C&W and rap songs do express the idea that in the long run crime doesn't pay. The sad narrator of Merle Haggard's "Mama Tried"

"turned 21 in prison / doing life without parole," while the thief of Ice-T's "Drama" is forced to realize that "I wouldn't be here if I'd fed my brain / Got knowledge from schoolbooks / 'stead of street crooks. / Now all I get is penitentiary hard looks."

Though both C&W and rap narrators are often criminals, their atti-   9
tudes toward law enforcement differ radically. The Irish Rovers' "Wasn't That a Party?" ("that little drag race down on Main Street / was just to see if the cops could run") pokes light-hearted fun at the police, while the Bobby Fuller Four's "I Fought the Law and the Law Won" expresses the most common C&W attitude: an acceptance that criminals must be caught, even if you are one. Neither song displays any anger toward the police, who are, after all, just doing their job.

To rappers, on the other hand, cops are the enemy. Two of the most no-   10
torious rap songs are Ice-T's "Cop Killer" and NWA's "Fuck tha Police" (which angrily asserts, "Some police think they have the authority to kill a minority"). Despite ample evidence of police brutality in the inner city, "Fuck tha Police" was almost certainly regarded by nonblack America as a paranoid shriek—until the world witnessed the infamous videotape of several of Los Angeles' finest brutally beating Rodney King while a dozen other "peace officers" nonchalantly looked on.

Interestingly, although the C&W view of law enforcement naturally   11
sits better with the general public (certainly with the police themselves), the fact remains that country-and-western music contains a good deal of crime, violence, and casual sex. Yet it is easily accepted by white Americans while rap arouses alarm and calls for labeling. Why?

I believe there are three major reasons. The first, and simplest, is lan-   12
guage. Rappers say "bitch," "ho," "fuck," and "motherfucker"; C&W artists don't. Country singers may say, "I'm in the mood to speak some French tonight" (Mary Chapin-Carpenter, "How Do") or "There's two kinds of cherries / and two kinds of fairies" (Merle Haggard, "My Own Kind of Hat"), but they avoid the bluntest Anglo-Saxon terms.

A second reason is race. African Americans have a unique history of op-   13
pression in this country, and rap reflects the inner-city African American experience. Then, too, whites expect angry, frightening messages from blacks and listen for them. Many blacks, on the other hand, hope for uplifting messages—and are dismayed when black artists seem to encourage or glorify the drug abuse and violence in their beleaguered communities. Thus, the focus on violence in rap—and the dismissal of same in C&W.

While the differing attitudes toward law enforcement are real enough,   14
much of the difference between violence in country-and-western music and in rap lies not in the songs themselves but in the way they are heard. Thus, when Ice Cube says, "Let the suburbs see a nigga invasion / Point-blank, smoke the Caucasian," many whites interpret that as an incitement to

violence. But when Johnny Cash's disgruntled factory worker in "Oney" crows, "Today's the day old Oney gets his," it's merely a joke. Likewise, when Ice Cube raps, "I've got a shotgun and here's the plot / Taking niggas out with the fire of buckshot" ("Gangsta, Gangsta"), he sends shudders through many African Americans heartbroken by black-on-black violence; but when Johnny Cash sings of an equally nihilistic killing in "Folsom Prison Blues"— "Shot a man in Reno / just to watch him die"—the public taps its feet and hums along. It's just a song, after all.

There is a third—and ironic—reason why rap is so widely attacked: rap   15 is actually closer to mainstream American economic ideology than country-and-western is. While C&W complains about the rough life of honest labor for poor and working-class people, rap ignores it almost entirely. "Work your fingers to the bone and what do you get?" asks Hoyt Axton in a satirical C&W song, then answers sardonically with its title: "Bony Fingers." Likewise, Johnny Paycheck's infamous "Take This Job and Shove It" is a blue-collar man's bitter protest against the rough and repetitive nature of his life's work. Work in C&W is hard and meaningless; it keeps one alive, but leaves the worker with little time or energy left to enjoy life.

Songs by female country singers reinforce this point in a different way;   16 they insist that love (with sex) is more important than affluence. The heroine of Reba McEntire's "Little Rock" says she'll have to "slip [her wedding ring] off," feeling no loyalty to the workaholic husband who "sure likes his money" but neglects his wife's emotional and physical needs. Jeanne Pruett in "Back to Back" lampoons the trappings of wealth and proclaims, "I'd trade this mansion / for a run-down shack / and a man who don't believe in sleeping back to back."

Rap's protagonists, on the other hand, are shrewd, materialistic, and   17 rabidly ambitious—although the means to their success are officially proscribed in our society. Not for them a "life that moves at a slower pace" (Alabama, "Down Home"); unlike the languorous hero of country-and-western, "catching these fish like they're going out of style" (Hank Williams, Jr., "Country State of Mind"), rap singers and rap characters alike are imbued with the great American determination to get ahead.

Rap's protagonists—drug dealers, burglars, armed robbers, and   18 "gangstas"—live in a society where success is "a fistful of jewelry" (Eazy E, "No More ?s"), "Motorola phones, Sony color TVs" (Ice-T, "Drama"), where "without a BMW you're through" (NWA, "A Bitch Iz a Bitch"). In NWA's "Dopeman," sometimes cited as an anti-drug song, the "Dopeman" is the archetypal American entrepreneur: clever, organized, ruthless, and not ruled by impulse—"To be a dopeman you must qualify / Don't get high off your own supply."

The proximity of rap to our success ethic arouses hostility because   19 America is torn by a deep ideological contradiction: we proudly proclaim ourselves a moral (even religious) nation and tout our capitalist economic system. But the reality of a successful capitalist system is that it undermines conventional morality. A glance at the history books shows how our supposedly moral nation heaped rewards upon the aptly named "robber barons": the Rockefellers, Vanderbilts, Carnegies, and Morgans. The crack dealer is a contemporary version of the bootlegger—at least one of whom, Joe Kennedy, Sr., founded America's most famous political dynasty. (Indeed, I would not be surprised if history repeated itself and the son—or daughter—of a drug lord becomes this country's first African American president.)

Capitalism is unparalleled in its ability to create goods and distribute   20
services, but it is, like the hero of "Drama," "blind to what's wrong." The only real criterion of a person's worth becomes how much money she or he has—a successful crook is treated better than a poor, law-abiding failure.

In short, the laid-back anti-materialist of country-and-western can be   21
dismissed with a shrug, but the rapper is attacked for that unforgivable sin: holding a mirror up to unpleasant truths. And one of them is that amoral ambition is as American as apple pie and the Saturday Night Special.

◆ ◆ ◆

FIRST RESPONSES

Is Noe correct in assuming that most of her readers will be surprised by her observations? Has she changed your response to either country-and-western or rap music? Are you interested in paying closer attention to the lyrics now? Why?

TAKING A CLOSER LOOK

Exploring *Who:* Voice and Tone

1. When are Noe's personal political views most directly expressed? Going back, can you find more subtle evidence of her views in early paragraphs?
2. As Noe observes in paragraph 12, many readers will find the strong language of rap difficult to accept, yet as early as paragraph 3, she illustrates her point about rap's sexism with some very explicit lyrics. How did you respond to the examples? Why would Noe make such a risky move?
3. Do a close reading of paragraph 14. How many different "ways of hearing" does the paragraph explore? What does this variety of

perspectives tell you about the care Noe took in writing about the complex problem of race?

4. In paragraph 5, Noe describes country music's opposition to "family values," but she doesn't provide a similar discussion of rap's position on the topic. Why not? What is she assuming about her probable readers here? Is she correct?

Exploring *What:* Content and Meaning

1. List the major "surprising similarities (and differences)" between country-and-western and rap music. Which ones did you already know, and which were new to you? Do you agree with the list? Could you add to it?

2. How familiar were you with the lyrics Noe uses to illustrate her points? Which lyrics did you find most convincing or dramatic? Why?

3. ▇ *Using the Internet.* Use a search engine such as Yahoo to locate a relevant Web site for the styles of music discussed in the essay. Read some of the descriptions of recent songs and artists. How well do Noe's ideas apply to current songs in each style?

4. Did you know that Joseph Kennedy Sr. had been associated with bootlegging? How does Noe hope this information will affect you? Is her purpose to justify crime?

Exploring *Why:* Purpose

1. Which one of the similarities does Noe believe is the most important? Why?

2. Has this essay changed your feelings about issues such as record labeling? How?

3. What is the effect of using Rodney King to justify the accuracy of some of the rap lyrics? Why does Noe place "peace officers" in quotation marks in the same sentence?

4. In the closing paragraphs of the essay, Noe makes some bold claims about American society. What were your responses to these observations? Can you think of other forms of popular culture that might confirm or contradict her claims?

Exploring *How:* Style and Strategy

1. Why does Noe dedicate the first half of the essay to similarities before moving on to differences? For example, try reading paragraph 9 as if it

were the second paragraph of the essay to evaluate the effect of changing its placement.

2. What does Noe mean when she describes women rappers as being
   "raunchy"? What would the country-and-western equivalent be?

3. In paragraph 15, what does Noe mean when she describes her third
   point as being "ironic"? Is this why she lists it third rather than first?

◆ WRITING FROM READING ASSIGNMENT

In "Parallel Worlds," Noe finds similarities where the casual observer
would find only differences. She then digs deep for what she believes are the
more important contrasts. In this writing project, you will identify a misunderstanding you think is caused by a superficial response to similarities and/or
differences.

A. Use a prewriting activity to identify possible topics. Focus on misunderstandings or errors in judgment that might be corrected if the thing
   being misjudged was compared with something that the readers already understand. You might consider different high school cliques,
   types of hobbies, forms of sports, popular heroes, or even other styles
   of music. Be open to all possibilities, however off the wall or startling
   they may seem. Clearly, Noe thought her topic would make a good
   essay in part *because of* its unusual pairing.

B. Now, pick the topic you already know the most about or feel the most
   strongly about. Unless this assignment is a longer paper, you will want
   to limit yourself to comparing only two or three things so that you can
   fully develop your ideas. Noe, for example, didn't add folk music to her
   essay, even though she indicates in her introduction that it has something fundamental in common with country-and-western and rap.

C. Write out a generalization that captures your purpose for writing. Make
   a list of the similarities and differences that will help you to achieve
   that purpose. Review your answer to question 1 in the *What* section to
   get a sense of the kinds and number of comparisons you might want to
   cover.

D. Brainstorm to identify your own storehouse of information about the
   things to be compared. What additional information will you need?
   Noe probably used artists and song titles she was already familiar with,
   but she may have read articles to evaluate the accuracy of her impressions or to identify titles she might add to ensure a responsible discussion of country-and-western and rap. She also may have listened to

CDs or used the Internet to track down the lyrics she needed to illustrate her points more precisely.

E. Review your evaluations of Noe's motives for organizing her paper according to similarities and differences and for ordering her subpoints as she did. Do your purpose and your audience's current attitudes require you to use either the point-by-point or block-by-block pattern? Do you need to arrange the points within the pattern in a particular way? Can you assume that your audience already knows some of what you plan to say, as Noe does in her discussion of family values?

F. Noe chose to introduce her essay with a very direct statement of her topic but developed the implications of her comparisons throughout the essay itself. She saved her underlying social criticism for the conclusion. Decide how and where you will introduce your topic and reveal your purpose. As you plan your comparison or draft the paper, additional insights into the misunderstanding may emerge and provide a generalization like the one Noe uses to conclude your essay.

G. Return to the "Checklist for Reading and Writing Comparison and Contrast Essays" (p. 337) for a final revision of your essay, paying special attention to the need for appropriately used transitions.

◆ ◆ ◆ PREPARING TO READ

What counts most in sports, natural talent or hard work? Which sports were the most popular in your high school? What did people think of those who participated in "minor" sports?

◆ ◆ ◆

Pole Vaulting

WILLIAM FINNEGAN

Born in 1952 in New York, William Finnegan was educated at the University of California, Santa Cruz, and the University of Montana. He is the author of numerous books and articles about poverty, race, and the illegal drug trade in America. Finnegan often lives and works among the people he writes about: *Crossing the Line: A Year in the Land of Apartheid* (1986) depicts his experiences with victims of racial separation in South Africa, and *Cold New World: Growing Up in a Harder Country* (1998) examines the lives of American teenagers and young adults victimized by drugs and violence. Since 1987, he has been a staff writer for *The New Yorker* magazine, where the following reminiscence appeared in August 2000.

Except for the B pole vault, the meet was over. Whoever it was that 1
came to watch track meets at Cleveland High, in the San Fernando Valley, circa 1968 had left the stands. Most of our team was back on the bus. If I had been less absorbed in the vaulting, I might have been outraged by the general indifference.

Brad Bishop, elfin ace of our vaulting squad, was locked in battle with 2
the laughing, dangerous Steve Luce. Luce was, people said, Bishop's only serious rival in the league. He was fast and, I thought, shockingly casual. Two Cleveland girls drifted up, and he actually went over *between jumps* and put his arm around one of them. Luce had long, sun-bleached hair, a wide chest, and a surfer's hipless saunter. He seemed amused to be competing with Bishop, who was six inches shorter, pale and poker-faced, with short dark hair. I was spotting for Bishop—stepping in to catch his pole after jumps. I felt sick with worry that this strange, blithe Luce might win.

I was a freshman at Taft High, and a C vaulter. At a big, athletically 3
competitive California high school like ours, going out for track was like going out for the circus. You needed an act, a specialty, a freakish talent. The

pole vault was an exception. You didn't need to be built like a mastiff (shot put) or a whippet (sprints) or have legs that ended at your armpits (high jump). You could—in theory, anyway—learn vaulting. None of our coaches knew much about it, though. Certainly none of them would have risked his neck demonstrating good technique. So we basically learned from each other. And my exemplar was Bishop.

He was a senior, and so small that he could probably have competed— 4
under the height, weight, and age formula they used—as a C. But most C vaulters were hapless young oafs like me. And so Bishop competed as a B, where he regularly outjumped bigger, stronger, faster guys who lacked his finesse.

Luce lacked it, certainly. He was a classic crash-and-burn artist, relying 5
on raw speed and strength and the wild spring of the big fiberglass poles that had revolutionized vaulting a few years before. Spotting for such vaulters was dodgy, literally—you had to catch the pole, but you also had to watch for the falling body. On jumps that went wrong, they were lucky to land in the pit. Luce was furiously self-destructing on half of his jumps that day, but he was also managing one clean vault at each height. Sometimes he suddenly, appallingly, cleared the bar by a foot or more. When it was raised to eleven-six, only he and Bishop remained in competition.

Bishop's vaults were the antithesis of Luce's mad blasts. In practices, he 6
tinkered endlessly with every aspect of his attack—his "step" (the exact point from which to begin his run), his grip, his acceleration into the box, his plant and pushoff, his quiet, flawless form on the rise, his twist and release. The pole he used was the smallest the school owned. It was barely eleven feet long, but Bishop could send his entire body, in a sort of antigravitational handstand, sailing past the end of the pole as it snapped upright.

It was his elegant combination of coolness and passion that fascinated 7
me. We weren't friends. I knew nothing about his life off the field. He was af-fable, and he could be dryly funny, but he was reserved in a way that made him seem older than even the other seniors. And he was never more reserved than when he was vaulting.

At the Cleveland meet, he wasn't even watching Luce. He was taking 8
his time preparing for his jumps—rocking back and forth at the top of the runway, pole loosely held in one hand, studying the thin, triangular bar set against the sky a hundred feet away. That the rest of the meet was over, that the sun was going down, that whole minutes were passing—none of it seemed to register with him.

The small group of vaulters watching the Bishop-Luce showdown began 9
to swell with new arrivals. I was pleased to see them, but it was also odd. Vaulters were, within the team, not unresented. We were excused from the general fitness drills, and our practices, we were often told, bore an unfortu-nate resemblance to long, lazy bull sessions. It was something about all the

lounging we did on the huge, foam-filled turquoise cushions that served as pits. These were, moreover, the Vietnam War years, when even the high-school track team was riven by Kulturkampf, and the vaulters were suspiciously regarded, often with reason, by the coaches and their more loyal athletes as Thoreau-reading, dope-smoking, John Carlos–loving hippies. Bishop did not belong in this category—he was like a straight arrow from another era. But he was a mainstay of the radical-individualist vaulting clique. And so it was strange, even moving, to see hawkish hurdlers and discus throwers quietly sidling up to find places on the grass near the runway.

Then, abruptly, Luce was out, missing on his third try at eleven-nine. He climbed from the pit looking stricken—the first sign he'd given that he cared if he won or lost. He took his pole from his spotter and, without a word, started toward the Cleveland gym. As he passed Bishop he smiled ruefully and, with a little upsnap of his chin, acknowledged his victory. Bishop nodded once.

Then he went back to work. He had the bar raised to twelve feet, which he cleared. He had it raised to twelve-three. The little pole he was using looked comically unequal to such a height. But Bishop was drawing a new map of the possible. The sun set. The shadows on the field turned a deep blue-green. The arc of watchers alongside the runway continued to grow. It now included our entire team. Even Luce's girls sat and stayed. Our coaches stood off to the side, muttering with the Cleveland coaches. Nobody spoke to Bishop. Two old meet officials who were checking the heights and setting the bar waited quietly beside the vault standards. Bishop stood at the top of the runway rocking and staring at the bar, for minutes on end. When, on his third attempt, he cleared twelve-three, there were shouts. The pole, as I caught it, was quivering like a tuning fork. As he climbed from the pit, Bishop murmured to the meet officials, "Twelve-six."

◆ ◆ ◆

FIRST RESPONSES

Are you glad Bishop beat Luce? Why or why not?

TAKING A CLOSER LOOK

Exploring *Who:* Voice and Tone

1. Was this article written for a general audience? How much do you have to know about athletics—particularly pole vaulting—to follow Finnegan's points and be interested in Bishop's victory?

2. How does the author personalize this account? How much are you aware of his presence at the scene he describes?

3. Why is Finnegan writing about events that took place more than thirty years ago?

Exploring *What:* Content and Organization

1. Finnegan says that "going out for track was like going out for the circus." What does he mean? Do you agree with this view? Is it still true today?

2. Describe the basic differences between Luce and Bishop. Which one does the author seem to prefer? Why?

3. What does Finnegan mean when he says that "the high-school track team was riven by Kulturkampf"?

4. In what ways is Bishop not a typical pole vaulter? In what ways is he not a typical high school athlete?

Exploring *Why:* Purpose

1. ▨⫐ *Using the Internet.* How does this essay differ from a typical sports article? To help you answer this question, log on to a sports site (e.g., www.yahoo.sports.com or www.espn.go.com/main.html) and read a few reports on track and field events.

2. Is the author trying to teach a lesson or convey a message? If so, what would it be?

3. Finnegan says he was part of "the radical-individualist vaulting clique." What does this description reveal about the author and his purpose for writing?

Exploring *How:* Style and Structure

1. In addition to the contrast between Luce and Bishop, what other contrasts does Finnegan develop in this essay? Can you identify three more? How are they interrelated?

2. In the last paragraph, the author uses mostly short, direct sentences; very few of them are more than ten words long. What effect is he trying to create?

3. Do you like the way the essay ends? Is it effective?

IDEAS FOR WRITING COMPARISON AND CONTRAST

1. Write an essay about the contrasting styles of two performers: two athletes, two musicians, two teachers, two talk show hosts, two writers, and so forth. You might, if you want, say which style you prefer and explain why.

2. Sometimes people feel nostalgic about old ways, customs, techniques, or things. Write an essay about something old that you feel nostalgic about that has been replaced with something new. Be sure to tell whether the new thing is an improvement, a decline, or both.

3. Write an essay comparing and contrasting your experience of visiting a particular place as a child and later as an adult—perhaps a family vacation destination, a relative's home, or a grade school classroom. Concentrate on describing the place as well as analyzing any changes in the place and in you.

◆ ◆ ◆ PREPARING TO READ

When you share a personal problem with a friend of the same sex, what kinds of things do you expect him or her to say and do? Does your expectation change when you tell a problem to someone of the opposite sex? Why?

◆ ◆ ◆

Sex, Lies, and Conversation

DEBORAH TANNEN

Deborah Tannen was born in Brooklyn, New York, in 1945. Now a professor of linguistics at Georgetown University, she writes academic and popular articles on how men and women communicate—and fail to communicate—with one another. She is the author of several books on the subject, including *That's Not What I Meant! How Conversational Style Makes or Breaks Relationships* (1986), *You Just Don't Understand: Women and Men in Conversation* (1990), and *I Only Say This Because I Love You: How the Way We Talk Can Make or Break Family Relationships throughout Our Lives* (2001). The following article originally appeared in the *Washington Post* in 1990.

I was addressing a small gathering in a suburban Virginia living room—   1
a women's group that had invited men to join them. Throughout the evening, one man had been particularly talkative, frequently offering ideas and anecdotes, while his wife sat silently beside him on the couch. Toward the end of the evening, I commented that women frequently complain that their husbands don't talk to them. This man quickly concurred. He gestured toward his wife and said, "She's the talker in our family." The room burst into laughter; the man looked puzzled and hurt. "It's true," he explained. "When I come home from work I have nothing to say. If she didn't keep the conversation going, we'd spend the whole evening in silence."

This episode crystallizes the irony that although American men tend to   2
talk more than women in public situations, they often talk less at home. And this pattern is wreaking havoc with marriage.

The pattern was observed by political scientist Andrew Hacker in the   3
late '70s. Sociologist Catherine Kohler Riessman reports in her new book *Divorce Talk* that most of the women she interviewed—but only a few of the men—gave lack of communication as the reason for their divorces. Given

the current divorce rate of nearly 50 percent, that amounts to millions of cases in the United States every year—a virtual epidemic of failed conversation.

In my own research, complaints from women about their husbands   4
most often focused not on tangible inequities such as having given up the chance for a career to accompany a husband to his, or doing far more than their share of daily life-support work like cleaning, cooking, social arrangements, and errands. Instead, they focused on communication: "He doesn't listen to me," "He doesn't talk to me." I found, as Hacker observed years before, that most wives want their husbands to be, first and foremost, conversational partners, but few husbands share this expectation of their wives.

In short, the image that best represents the current crisis is the stereo-   5
typical cartoon scene of a man sitting at the breakfast table with a newspaper held up in front of his face, while a woman glares at the back of it, wanting to talk.

Linguistic Battle of the Sexes

How can women and men have such different impressions of commu-   6
nication in marriage? Why the widespread imbalance in their interests and expectations?

In the April issue of *American Psychologist,* Stanford University's   7
Eleanor Maccoby reports the results of her own and others' research showing that children's development is most influenced by the social structure of peer interactions. Boys and girls tend to play with children of their own gender, and their sex-separate groups have different organizational structures and interactive norms.

I believe these systematic differences in childhood socialization make   8
talk between women and men like cross-cultural communication, heir to all the attraction and pitfalls of that enticing but difficult enterprise. My research on men's and women's conversations uncovered patterns similar to those described for children's groups.

For women, as for girls, intimacy is the fabric of relationships, and talk   9
is the thread from which it is woven. Little girls create and maintain friendships by exchanging secrets; similarly, women regard conversation as the cornerstone of friendship. So a woman expects her husband to be a new and improved version of a best friend. What is important is not the individual subjects that are discussed but the sense of closeness, of a life shared, that emerges when people tell their thoughts, feelings, and impressions.

Bonds between boys can be as intense as girls', but they are based less   10
on talking, more on doing things together. Since they don't assume talk is

the cement that binds a relationship, men don't know what kind of talk women want, and they don't miss it when it isn't there.

Boys' groups are larger, more inclusive, and more hierarchical, so boys must struggle to avoid the subordinate position in the group. This may play a role in women's complaints that men don't listen to them. Some men really don't like to listen, because being the listener makes them feel one-down, like a child listening to adults or an employee to a boss. 11

But often when women tell men, "You aren't listening," and the men protest, "I am," the men are right. The impression of not listening results from misalignments in the mechanics of conversation. The misalignment begins as soon as a man and a woman take physical positions. This became clear when I studied videotapes made by psychologist Bruce Dorval of children and adults talking to their same-sex best friends. I found that at every age, the girls and women faced each other directly, their eyes anchored on each other's faces. At every age, the boys and men sat at angles to each other and looked elsewhere in the room, periodically glancing at each other. They were obviously attuned to each other, often mirroring each other's movements. But the tendency of men to face away can give women the impression they aren't listening even when they are. A young woman in college was frustrated: Whenever she told her boyfriend she wanted to talk to him, he would lie down on the floor, close his eyes, and put his arm over his face. This signaled to her, "He's taking a nap." But he insisted he was listening extra hard. Normally, he looks around the room, so he is easily distracted. Lying down and covering his eyes helped him concentrate on what she was saying. 12

Analogous to the physical alignment that women and men take in conversation is their topical alignment. The girls in my study tended to talk at length about one topic, but the boys tended to jump from topic to topic. The second-grade girls exchanged stories about people they knew. The second-grade boys teased, told jokes, noticed things in the room, and talked about finding games to play. The sixth-grade girls talked about problems with a mutual friend. The sixth-grade boys talked about 55 different topics, none of which extended over more than a few turns. 13

Listening to Body Language

Switching topics is another habit that gives women the impression men aren't listening, especially if they switch to a topic about themselves. But the evidence of the 10th-grade boys in my study indicates otherwise. The 10th-grade boys sprawled across their chairs with bodies parallel and eyes straight ahead, rarely looking at each other. They looked as if they were riding in a car, staring out the windshield. But they were talking about their feelings. 14

One boy was upset because a girl had told him he had a drinking problem, and the other was feeling alienated from all his friends.

Now, when a girl told a friend about a problem, the friend responded 15 by asking probing questions and expressing agreement and understanding. But the boys dismissed each other's problems. Todd assured Richard that his drinking was "no big problem" because "sometimes you're funny when you're off your butt." And when Todd said he felt left out, Richard responded, "Why should you? You know more people than me."

Women perceive such responses as belittling and unsupportive. But the 16 boys seemed satisfied with them. Whereas women reassure each other by implying, "You shouldn't feel bad because I've had similar experiences," men do so by implying, "You shouldn't feel bad because your problems aren't so bad."

There are even simpler reasons for women's impression that men don't 17 listen. Linguist Lynette Hirschman found that women make more listener-noise, such as "mhm," "uhuh," and "yeah," to show "I'm with you." Men, she found, more often give silent attention. Women who expect a stream of listener-noise interpret silent attention as no attention at all.

Women's conversational habits are as frustrating to men as men's are 18 to women. Men who expect silent attention interpret a stream of listener-noise as overreaction or impatience. Also, when women talk to each other in a close, comfortable setting, they often overlap, finish each other's sentences, and anticipate what the other is about to say. This practice, which I call "participatory listenership," is often perceived by men as interruption, intrusion, and lack of attention.

A parallel difference caused a man to complain about his wife, "She 19 just wants to talk about her own point of view. If I show her another view, she gets mad at me." When most women talk to each other, they assume a conversationalist's job is to express agreement and support. But many men see their conversational duty as pointing out the other side of an argument. This is heard as disloyalty by women, and refusal to offer the requisite support. It is not that women don't want to see other points of view, but that they prefer them phrased as suggestions and inquiries rather than as direct challenges.

In his book *Fighting for Life,* Walter Ong points out that men use "ag- 20 onistic" or warlike, oppositional formats to do almost anything; thus discussion becomes debate, and conversation a competitive sport. In contrast, women see conversation as a ritual means of establishing rapport. If Jane tells a problem and June says she has a similar one, they walk away feeling closer to each other. But this attempt at establishing rapport can backfire when used with men. Men take too literally women's ritual "troubles talk," just as women mistake men's ritual challenges for real attack.

The Sounds of Silence

These differences begin to clarify why women and men have such different expectations about communication in marriage. For women, talk creates intimacy. Marriage is an orgy of closeness: you can tell your feelings and thoughts, and still be loved. Their greatest fear is being pushed away. But men live in a hierarchical world, where talk maintains independence and status. They are on guard to protect themselves from being put down and pushed around.

21

This explains the paradox of the talkative man who said of his silent wife, "She's the talker." In the public setting of a guest lecture, he felt challenged to show his intelligence and display his understanding of the lecture. But at home, where he has nothing to prove and no one to defend against, he is free to remain silent. For his wife, being home means she is free from the worry that something she says might offend someone, or spark disagreement, or appear to be showing off; at home she is free to talk.

22

The communication problems that endanger marriage can't be fixed by mechanical engineering. They require a new conceptual framework about the role of talk in human relationships. Many of the psychological explanations that have become second nature may not be helpful, because they tend to blame either women (for not being assertive enough) or men (for not being in touch with their feelings). A sociolinguistic approach by which male-female conversation is seen as cross-cultural communication allows us to understand the problem and forge solutions without blaming either party.

23

Once the problem is understood, improvement comes naturally, as it did to the young woman and her boyfriend who seemed to go to sleep when she wanted to talk. Previously, she had accused him of not listening, and he had refused to change his behavior, since that would be admitting fault. But then she learned about and explained to him the differences in women's and men's habitual ways of aligning themselves in conversation. The next time she told him she wanted to talk, he began, as usual, by lying down and covering his eyes. When the familiar negative reaction bubbled up, she reassured herself that he really was listening. But then he sat up and looked at her. Thrilled, she asked why. He said, "You like me to look at you when we talk, so I'll try to do it." Once he saw their differences as cross-cultural rather than right and wrong, he independently altered his behavior.

24

Women who feel abandoned and deprived when their husbands won't listen to or report daily news may be happy to discover their husbands trying to adapt once they understand the place of small talk in women's relationships. But if their husbands don't adapt, the women may still be comforted that for men, this is not a failure of intimacy. Accepting the difference, the wives may look to their friends or family for that kind of talk. And

25

husbands who can't provide it shouldn't feel their wives have made unreasonable demands. Some couples will still decide to divorce, but at least their decisions will be based on realistic expectations.

In these times of resurgent ethnic conflicts, the world desperately needs   26 cross-cultural understanding. Like charity, successful cross-cultural communication should begin at home.

◆ ◆ ◆

FIRST RESPONSES

Can you remember a specific difficult conversation you had with someone of the opposite sex? How might you have used Tannen's advice to help resolve that conversation more positively?

TAKING A CLOSER LOOK

Exploring *Who:* Voice and Tone

1. How does Tannen achieve a personal voice in the essay while maintaining her professional credibility? Did this voice help to maintain your interest as you read?
2. Clearly, Tannen has done extensive primary research on her topic. Why, then, does she quote several other researchers? Did you recognize the names of these scholars? What other strategies does Tannen use to establish their authority?
3. What evidence is there that Tannen hopes both men and women will be interested in her topic? Did this point of view surprise you?
4. ▮▯ *Using the Internet.* Visit the Web page of the *Washington Post,* where this essay originally appeared. What in the essay reflects that Tannen had the readers of this major national newspaper in mind as she wrote?

Exploring *What:* Content and Meaning

1. Make a point-by-point list of the causes for women's and men's differing feelings about communicating. Now make a list of the behaviors these differences create.
2. Do you recognize yourself in the styles of communication Tannen describes? If not, does that negate her conclusions?

3. Reread the last sentence of paragraph 24. What, exactly, do you think allowed the boyfriend to change his behavior?

Exploring *Why:* Purpose

1. Has Tannen convinced you that this problem is "a virtual epidemic"? Can you identify any marriages where "this pattern is wreaking havoc"?
2. What is Tannen's purpose in describing the cartoon she recalls in paragraph 5 as "stereotypical"? How does her essay change the way you respond to that cartoon?
3. In paragraphs 8 through 11, Tannen traces gender differences to childhood socialization. In what ways is she working with an awareness of the powerful nature of these formative years when she formulates her hopeful suggestions in the closing paragraphs of the essay?
4. In paragraphs 8 and 26, Tannen makes an **analogy** between male/female miscommunication and the problems of cross-cultural communication. What does she mean? Why does she choose this comparison? Does your greater understanding of gender miscommunication also help you better understand cross-cultural problems?

Exploring *How:* Style and Strategy

1. Why does Tannen begin her essay with the anecdote about the husband and wife? What was your response to their predicament? By the time she returns to this couple in paragraph 22, had your response changed? How about your response to the couple in paragraphs 12 and 24?
2. Tannen occasionally uses the jargon of a professional linguist, such as "listener-noise" and "participatory listenership." Did you find this terminology useful or confusing? Why did she choose to use it?
3. Identify the two parallel phrases Tannen uses in paragraph 22. What is the effect of this comparison strategy?

IDEAS FOR WRITING COMPARISON AND CONTRAST

1. Visit a playground. Observe both the boys and girls, playing alone and interacting with one another. Then, focusing on gender or the type of play engaged in, write a brief essay describing one surprising or significant similarity or difference you observe in the children's behaviors.
2. Will either men or women find it easier to adapt to the other gender's communication style? Write an essay comparing and contrasting the

suggestions you would give to women with those you would give to men. Use personal examples as well as ideas from Tannen's essay to support your ideas. Be sure to acknowledge Tannen's ideas through appropriate citations.

3. What other differences might account for miscommunication between friends? Consider, for example, country versus city or suburban childhoods, having blue-collar versus white-collar parents, or being an only child versus growing up in a family of ten. Using personal experience and perhaps interviews with friends or family members, write an essay in which you compare and contrast the ways in which these childhood experiences might shape adult behaviors. Like Tannen, be aware of the realities behind the stereotypes as you write.

◆ ◆ ◆ **PREPARING TO READ**

How old were you when you realized there is a difference between the kind of lives men and women lead? How did you feel about these differences?

◆ ◆ ◆

The Men We Carry in Our Minds

SCOTT RUSSELL SANDERS

In addition to teaching English at Indiana University, Scott Russell Sanders (born in 1945) has had an active career as a freelance journalist, publishing in magazines such as *Audubon,* the *Utne Reader,* and the *Georgia Review.* As a regionalist, he explores everyday life in search of meaningful connections between individual well-being and the common good. His essay collections include *Staying Put: Making a Home in a Restless World* (1994), *Hunting for Hope: A Father's Journey* (1998), and *The Force of Spirit* (2000). Sanders also writes children's books, such as *Crawdad Creek* (1999), which highlights the hidden treasures of animal and plant life from one season to the next. "The Men We Carry in Our Minds" first appeared in *The Paradise of Bombs* in 1987.

"This must be a hard time for women," I say to my friend Anneke. 1
"They have so many paths to choose from, and so many voices calling them."
"I think it's a lot harder for men," she replies. 2
"How do you figure that?" 3
"The women I know feel excited, innocent, like crusaders in a just cause. 4
The men I know are eaten up with guilt."
We are sitting at the kitchen table drinking sassafras tea, our hands 5
wrapped around the mugs because this April morning is cool and drizzly.
"Like a Dutch morning," Anneke told me earlier. She is Dutch herself, a
writer and midwife and peacemaker, with the round face and sad eyes of a
woman in a Vermeer painting who might be waiting for the rain to stop, for
a door to open. She leans over to sniff a sprig of lilac, pale lavender, that rises
from a vase of cobalt blue.
"Women feel such pressure to be everything, do everything," I say. "Ca- 6
reer, kids, art, politics. Have their babies and get back to the office a week
later. It's as if they're trying to overcome a million years' worth of evolution
in one lifetime."

"But we help one another. We don't try to lumber on alone, like so 7
many wounded grizzly bears, the way men do." Anneke sips her tea. I gave
her the mug with owls on it, for wisdom. "And we have this deep-down sense
that we're in the *right*—we've been held back, passed over, used—while men
feel they're in the wrong. Men are the ones who've been discredited, who
have to search their souls."

I search my soul. I discover guilty feelings aplenty—toward the poor, 8
the Vietnamese, Native Americans, the whales, an endless list of debts—a
guilt in each case that is as bright and unambiguous as a neon sign. But toward women I feel something more confused, a snarl of shame, envy, wary
tenderness, and amazement. This muddle troubles me. To hide my unease I
say, "You're right, it's tough being a man these days."

"Don't laugh." Anneke frowns at me, mournful-eyed, through the sas- 9
safras steam. "I wouldn't be a man for anything. It's much easier being the
victim. All the victim has to do is break free. The persecutor has to live with
his past."

How deep is that past? I find myself wondering after Anneke has left. 10
How much of an inheritance do I have to throw off? Is it just the beliefs I
breathed in as a child? Do I have to scour memory back through father and
grandfather? Through St. Paul? Beyond Stonehenge and into the twilit caves?
I'm convinced the past we must contend with is deeper even than speech.
When I think back on my childhood, on how I learned to see men and
women, I have a sense of ancient, dizzying depths. The back roads of Tennessee and Ohio where I grew up were probably closer, in their sexual patterns, to the campsites of Stone Age hunters than to the genderless cities of
the future into which we are rushing.

The first men, besides my father, I remember seeing were black convicts 11
and white guards, in the cottonfield across the road from our farm on the
outskirts of Memphis. I must have been three or four. The prisoners wore
dingy gray-and-black zebra suits, heavy as canvas, sodden with sweat. Hatless,
stooped, they chopped weeds in the fierce heat, row after row, breathing the
acrid dust of boll-weevil poison. The overseers wore dazzling white shirts
and broad shadowy hats. The oiled barrels of their shotguns flashed in the sunlight. Their faces in memory are utterly blank. Of course those men, white and
black, have become for me an emblem of racial hatred. But they have also
come to stand for the twin poles of my early vision of manhood—the brute
toiling animal and the boss.

When I was a boy, the men I knew labored with their bodies. They were 12
marginal farmers, just scraping by, or welders, steelworkers, carpenters; they
swept floors, dug ditches, mined coal, or drove trucks, their forearms ropy
with muscle; they trained horses, stoked furnaces, built tires, stood on assembly lines wrestling parts onto cars and refrigerators. They got up before
light, worked all day long whatever the weather, and when they came home

at night they looked as though somebody had been whipping them. In the evenings and on weekends they worked on their own places, tilling gardens that were lumpy with clay, fixing broken-down cars, hammering on houses that were always too drafty, too leaky, too small.

The bodies of the men I knew were twisted and maimed in ways visi-   13
ble and invisible. The nails of their hands were black and split, the hands tattooed with scars. Some had lost fingers. Heavy lifting had given many of them finicky backs and guts weak from hernias. Racing against conveyor belts had given them ulcers. Their ankles and knees ached from years of standing on concrete. Anyone who had worked for long around machines was hard of hearing. They squinted, and the skin of their faces was creased like the leather of old work gloves. There were times, studying them, when I dreaded growing up. Most of them coughed, from dust or cigarettes, and most of them drank cheap wine or whiskey, so their eyes looked bloodshot and bruised. The fathers of my friends always seemed older than the mothers. Men wore out sooner. Only women lived into old age.

As a boy I also knew another sort of men, who did not sweat and break   14
down like mules. They were soldiers, and so far as I could tell they scarcely worked at all. During my early school years we lived on a military base, an arsenal in Ohio, and every day I saw GIs in the guardshacks, on the stoops of barracks, at the wheels of olive drab Chevrolets. The chief fact of their lives was boredom. Long after I left the Arsenal I came to recognize the sour smell the soldiers gave off as that of souls in limbo. They were all waiting—for wars, for transfers, for leaves, for promotions, for the end of their hitch—like so many braves waiting for the hunt to begin. Unlike the warriors of older tribes, however, they would have no say about when the battle would start or how it would be waged. Their waiting was broken only when they practiced for war. They fired guns at targets, drove tanks across the churned-up fields of the military reservation, set off bombs in the wrecks of old fighter planes. I knew this was all play. But I also felt certain that when the hour for killing arrived, they would kill. When the real shooting started, many of them would die. This was what soldiers were *for*, just as a hammer was for driving nails.

Warriors and toilers: those seemed, in my boyhood vision, to be the   15
chief destinies for men. They weren't the only destinies, as I learned from having a few male teachers, from reading books, and from watching television. But the men on television—the politicians, the astronauts, the generals, the savvy lawyers, the philosophical doctors, the bosses who gave orders to both soldiers and laborers—seemed as remote and unreal to me as the figures in tapestries. I could no more imagine growing up to become one of these cool, potent creatures than I could imagine becoming a prince.

A nearer and more hopeful example was that of my father, who had es-   16
caped from a red-dirt farm to a tire factory, and from the assembly line to the

front office. Eventually he dressed in a white shirt and tie. He carried himself as if he had been born to work with his mind. But his body, remembering the earlier years of slogging work, began to give out on him in his fifties, and it quit on him entirely before he turned sixty-five. Even such a partial escape from man's fate as he had accomplished did not seem possible for most of the boys I knew. They joined the Army, stood in line for jobs in the smoky plants, helped build highways. They were bound to work as their fathers had worked, killing themselves or preparing to kill others.

A scholarship enabled me not only to attend college, a rare enough feat in my circle, but even to study in a university meant for the children of the rich. Here I met for the first time young men who had assumed from birth that they would lead lives of comfort and power. And for the first time I met women who told me that men were guilty of having kept all the joys and privileges of the earth for themselves. I was baffled. What privileges? What joys? I thought about the maimed, dismal lives of most of the men back home. What had they stolen from their wives and daughters? The right to go five days a week, twelve months a year, for thirty or forty years to a steel mill or a coal mine? The right to drop bombs and die in war? The right to feel every leak in the roof, every gap in the fence, every cough in the engine, as a wound they must mend? The right to feel, when the layoff comes or the plant shuts down, not only afraid but ashamed? 17

I was slow to understand the deep grievances of women. This was because, as a boy, I had envied them. Before college, the only people I had ever known who were interested in art or music or literature, the only ones who read books, the only ones who ever seemed to enjoy a sense of ease and grace were the mothers and daughters. Like the menfolk, they fretted about money, they scrimped and made-do. But, when the pay stopped coming in, they were not the ones who had failed. Nor did they have to go to war, and that seemed to me a blessed fact. By comparison with the narrow, ironclad days of fathers, there was an expansiveness, I thought, in the days of mothers. They went to see neighbors, to shop in town, to run errands at school, at the library, at church. No doubt, had I looked harder at their lives, I would have envied them less. It was not my fate to become a woman, so it was easier for me to see the graces. Few of them held jobs outside the home, and those who did filled thankless roles as clerks and waitresses. I didn't see, then, what a prison a house could be, since houses seemed to me brighter, handsomer places than any factory. I did not realize—because such things were never spoken of—how often women suffered from men's bullying. I did learn about the wretchedness of abandoned wives, single mothers, widows; but I also learned about the wretchedness of lone men. Even then I could see how exhausting it was for a mother to cater all day to the needs of young children. But if I had been asked, as a boy, to choose between tending a baby and tending a machine, I think I would have chosen the baby. (Having now tended both, I know I would choose the baby.) 18

So I was baffled when the women at college accused me and my sex of   19
having cornered the world's pleasures. I think something like my bafflement
has been felt by other boys (and by girls as well) who grew up in dirt-poor
farm country, in mining country, in black ghettos, in Hispanic barrios, in the
shadows of factories, in Third World nations—any place where the fate of
men is as grim and bleak as the fate of women. Toilers and warriors. I realize now how ancient these identities are, how deep the tug they exert on
men, the undertow of a thousand generations. The miseries I saw, as a boy,
in the lives of nearly all men I continue to see in the lives of many—the body-
breaking toil, the tedium, the call to be tough, the humiliating powerlessness,
the battle for a living and for territory.

When the women I met at college thought about the joys and privi-   20
leges of men, they did not carry in their minds the sort of men I had known
in my childhood. They thought of their fathers, who were bankers, physicians,
architects, stockbrokers, the big wheels of the big cities. These fathers rode the
train to work or drove cars that cost more than any of my childhood houses.
They were attended from morning to night by female helpers, wives and
nurses and secretaries. They were never laid off, never short of cash at month's
end, never lined up for welfare. These fathers made decisions that mattered.
They ran the world.

The daughters of such men wanted to share in this power, this glory. So   21
did I. They yearned for a say over their future, for jobs worthy of their abilities, for the right to live at peace, unmolested, whole. Yes, I thought, yes yes.
The difference between me and these daughters was that they saw me, because of my sex, as destined from birth to become like their fathers, and
therefore as an enemy to their desires. But I knew better. I wasn't an enemy,
in fact or in feeling. I was an ally. If I had known, then, how to tell them so,
would they have believed me? Would they now?

◆ ◆ ◆

FIRST RESPONSES

What men from your childhood do you carry in your mind? How do
they compare and contrast with the men Sanders carries?

TAKING A CLOSER LOOK

Exploring *Who:* Voice and Tone

1. Describe your impressions of Sanders during the opening conversation he has with his friend Anneke. How do these initial impressions affect your response to his ideas throughout the essay?

2. Explain Sanders's reaction to his college friends and their views of men. How have his views or understanding changed since then?

3. ▣ *Using the Internet.* How does Sanders feel about the differences between his own life and his father's? Visit the Ohio State Web site on early twentieth-century coal mining at www.history.ohio-state.edu/ projects/Lessons_US/Gilded_Age/Coal_Mining/default.htm. What are your responses to these stories and pictures?

4. Does your own experience of gender roles support or contradict Sanders's experiences? How does your experience affect your response to his essay?

Exploring *What:* Content and Meaning

1. What positions on the differences between men and women do Sanders and Anneke take in their talk? By the conclusion, which position does Sanders ultimately seem to be advocating?

2. What two types of men occupied Sander's boyhood? How does he feel about them as he describes them?

3. What does Sanders mean in paragraph 14 when he recalls, "I came to recognize the sour smell the soldiers gave off as that of souls in limbo"?

4. In addition to analyzing gender roles, Sanders addresses issues of class and race differences. How does he see these various categories of human experience as influencing one another? With what effects?

Exploring *Why:* Purpose

1. What clues to his purpose does Sanders reveal in the title of his essay?

2. What is Sanders's reason for including Anneke's line "I think it's a lot harder for men" so early in the essay? What does including this comment tell you about the audience Sanders expected for his essay?

3. At the end of paragraph 10, Sanders contrasts the "sexual patterns" of his youth "to the genderless cities of the future into which we are rushing." What is his tone here?

4. How does paragraph 19 expand Sanders's purpose for writing about this topic?

5. How do you think Sanders would answer the two questions with which he closes his essay? How do you answer them?

Exploring *How:* Style and Strategy

1. How would you describe Sanders's method of comparison and contrast? Are the lives of the men and women of the "backroads

of Tennessee and Ohio" described in the same depth? Why or why not?

2. What personality emerges from Sanders's descriptions of Anneke? Does her dialogue reveal the same personality? If not, what might account for the differences?

3. Paragraph 10 opens with a question. Is that an effective **transition?**

4. Describe the sentence patterns in paragraph 12 and their effects.

5. How does the **simile** that ends paragraph 14 link the two types of men Sanders carries in his mind?

IDEAS FOR WRITING COMPARISON AND CONTRAST

1. Write an essay comparing the traditional childhood experiences and opportunities for males with those for females. You will need to do interviews or research to provide concrete information and a fair perspective about the opposite gender.

2. What are the advantages and disadvantages to living on campus versus living off campus? Write an essay supporting one of the two choices by examining their similarities and differences.

3. Write an essay analyzing significant differences between the daily life of two people who appear on the surface to lead very similar lives—two students in the same major, two employees working the same job, two athletes in the same sport.

◆ ◆ ◆ PREPARING TO READ

Into what racial or ethnic category or categories would you place yourself if given total freedom to choose? Can you remember any specific experiences—at home, with friends, or at school—that led you to this conclusion or that challenged it?

◆ ◆ ◆

Dividing American Society

ANDREW HACKER

Andrew Hacker (born in 1929) is a political scientist who teaches at Queens College in New York and writes regularly on race, family, and health care issues for the influential *New York Review of Books*. Two of Hacker's most recent books—*Two Nations: Black and White, Separate, Hostile, Unequal* (1992), from which the following essay was taken, and *Money: Who Has How Much and Why* (1998)—reflect his lifelong personal and professional efforts to reveal the powerful relationship between economics and social justice.

Race has been an American obsession since the first Europeans sighted "savages" on these shores. In time, those original inhabitants would be subdued or slaughtered, and finally sequestered out of view. But race in America took on a deeper and more disturbing meaning with the importation of Africans as slaves. Bondage would later be condemned as an awful injustice and the nation's shame, even as we have come to acknowledge the stamina and skill it took to survive in a system where humans could be bought and sold and punished like animals. Nor are these antecedents buried away in the past. That Americans of African origin once wore the chains of chattels remains alive in the memory of both races and continues to separate them.   1

Black Americans are Americans, yet they still subsist as aliens in the only land they know. Other groups may remain outside the mainstream—some religious sects, for example—but they do so voluntarily. In contrast, blacks must endure a segregation that is far from freely chosen. So America may be seen as two separate nations. Of course, there are places where the races mingle. Yet in most significant respects, the separation is pervasive and penetrating. As a social and human division, it surpasses all others—even gender—in intensity and subordination.   2

If white Americans regard the United States as their nation, they also   3
see it beset with racial problems they feel are not of their making. Some contrast current conditions with earlier times, when blacks appeared more willing to accept a subordinate status. Most whites will protest that they bear
neither responsibility nor blame for the conditions blacks face. Neither they
nor their forebears ever owned slaves, nor can they see themselves as having held anyone back or down. Most white Americans believe that for at
least the last generation blacks have been given more than a fair chance and
at least equal opportunity, if not outright advantages. Moreover, few white
Americans feel obliged to ponder how membership in the major race gives
them powers and privileges.

America is inherently a "white" country: in character, in structure, in cul-   4
ture. Needless to say, black Americans create lives of their own. Yet, as a people, they face boundaries and constrictions set by the white majority. America's version of *apartheid,* while lacking overt legal sanction, comes closest to
the system even now being reformed in the land of its invention.

That racial tensions cast a pall upon this country can hardly be denied.   5
People now vent feelings of hostility and anger that in the past they repressed.
Race has become a national staple for private conversation and public controversy. So it becomes necessary to ask what in recent decades has brought
the issue and reality of race to the center of the stage[. . .].

To give the names "black" and "white" to races might seem, on its face,   6
quite ludicrous. Clearly, no human beings have skins of either color. Indeed,
very few come even close to those tones. But then "white" and "black" stand
for much more than the shades of epidermal coverings. To start, they refer to
the "Caucasian" and "Negroid" races, whose facial appearances differ as
prominently as their colors.

But more is involved than color or facial features or skeletal structure.   7
The terms also carry cultural connotations. In its basic meaning, "white" denotes European antecedents, while "black" stands for Africa. Since the human
species began in Africa, we can say that black people are those whose ancestors remained on that continent, while whites descend from those who
embarked on migrations to cooler climates. This has led some to the pre-
sumption that the races are at different levels of evolutionary development.
For at least half a dozen centuries, and possibly longer, "white" has implied
a higher civilization based on a superior inheritance.

Europeans who colonized the western hemisphere sought to re-create   8
it in their image, and to transform North and South America into "white"
continents. With conquest comes the power to impose your ways on territo-
ries you have subdued. The treatment of the Native Americans simply rati-
fied that view. (In some places, the native populations remained large enough
to exert a reciprocal influence, as in India and most of Africa. This was not

to be the case in the United States.) Still, something can be learned by looking at how "white" was originally conceived, and the changes it has undergone.

From the colonial period through the Jacksonian era, most white   9
Americans were of English ancestry. Alexis de Tocqueville, during his visit in the 1830s, found he could characterize the country and its people as "Anglo-Americans."

Given the expansion of the population, this epithet could not last. Even   10
so, the Anglo-American model has remained remarkably durable, with most subsequent immigrants adapting to its canons. They not only learned English, the single national language, but also adjusted their lives to the economy and technology associated with that prototype. This does not mean that the majority of white Americans regard themselves as "English" in a literal sense. They can and do identify with other origins. Even so, it could be argued that most contemporary citizens associate themselves to a greater degree with Anglo-American culture than with their actual country of origin.

To say this would seem to resurrect the conception of the melting pot,   11
which argued that immigrants would shed their older identities and assimilate to the new culture they encountered. That view has been challenged in many quarters. Rather than as a cauldron, many commentators today prefer to see America as a mosaic or even a lumpy stew. At best, the pot still contains plenty of unmelted pieces. Hence the renewed emphasis on "ethnicity," with its focus on the country's racial and national and religious diversity[. . .].

With the absorption of increasing numbers of Hispanics and Asians,   12
along with Middle Eastern immigrants, being "white" will cease to carry many of the connotations it did in the past. The future population will reflect a more varied array of national origins rather than races, since—as has been stressed—the new groups cannot be easily assigned to racial classifications.

Nor should we be too quick in proclaiming that America will become   13
"multicultural" as well. True, one can point to exotic neighborhoods, with their parades and festivals, to foreign-language newspapers and television channels, along with calls for new kinds of courses in colleges and schools. It would be more accurate to say that the United States will continue to have a single dominant culture. It doesn't really matter whether it is called "white" or "Western" or European or Anglo-American or by another title. It would be better simply to describe it as a structure of opportunities and institutions that has been willing to use the energies and talents of people from various origins. The reception given to recent immigrants is essentially similar to that accorded to successive waves of Europeans. In neither case have the newcomers been given a very cordial welcome. Indeed, they have often met with mistrust, not to mention violence and hostility. Despite the felicitous words

on the Statue of Liberty, immigrants are allowed entry on the condition that they serve as cheap labor and live unobtrusively. Many will tell you that now, as in the past, they find their religions scorned, their customs ridiculed, and their features caricatured.

Throughout this nation's history, the expectation has been that new-   14
comers will adapt to the models they encounter on their arrival. If that means relinquishing old-country customs, there are signs that many are prepared to do just that, or at least watch as their children assimilate. Perhaps the first instance of the expanded purview of "white" was when the English founders sought the services of two talented Scots—James Madison and Alexander Hamilton—to help found this nation. The process is still going on.

As with "white," being "black" is less one's particular shade of color   15
than physical features and continent of ancestry. Of course, very few Americans are entirely African in origin. As is well known, slave owners and other whites felt free to force themselves on black women. Still, no matter how light their skin tones, if they retained any vestige of African features, they and their descendants continue to be delineated as "black."

The United States, unlike other countries and cultures, no longer uses   16
terms specifying finer gradations. Hence "mestizo" and "mulatto" have disappeared from our parlance, as have "creole" and "quadroon." Nor has this country retained the generic term "colored" for people whose ancestries are obviously mixed. (The last use of an intermediate term was in the 1910 census, in which interviewers identified about 20 percent of the "Negro" group as "Mulattoes.") It has been far from accidental that this country has chosen to reject the idea of a graduated spectrum, and has instead fashioned a rigid bifurcation.

For all practical purposes, "whites" of all classes and ethnicities now   17
prefer to present a common front. Unlike in the past, there are no pronounced distinctions of "purer" versus "lesser" whites, or of those with older claims as against newer arrivals. While immigrants from Colombia and Cyprus may have to work their way up the social ladder, they are still allowed as valid a claim to being "white" as persons of Puritan or Pilgrim stock.

Americans of African ancestry were never given that indulgence. The   18
reason is not that their coloration was too "dark" to allow for absorption into the "white" classification. After all, the swarthiness of some Europeans did not become a barrier to their admission. Had white America really believed in its egalitarian declarations, it would have welcomed former slaves into its midst at the close of the Civil War. Indeed, had that happened, America would not be two racial nations today. This is not to suggest how far blacks themselves would have assimilated, since a lot depends on how far members of a group want to preserve their special heritage. The point is that white America has always had the power to expand its domain. However, in the past

and even now, it has shown a particular reluctance to absorb people of African descent.

How do blacks feel about this bifurcation? Today, most express pride 19 in their African origins, especially those who make a point of calling themselves African-Americans. While, like it or not, a lighter color remains an advantage for women, social advantage is no longer gained by alluding to white elements in one's ancestry. Black Americans are aware that much in the "black" designation represents how whites have defined the term. Still, despite attempts by whites to describe and define them, black Americans have always sought to create their own lives and sustain their sentiments and interests. It started when the first slaves created a culture of their own. Similarly, the drive to replace "colored" with "negro," followed by the move to "Negro," and then on to "black" and "African-American," have all reflected a desire to maintain an autonomous identity.

For most black Americans to be an African-American means literally 20 that in that continent lies the primal origin of your people. The experiences of capture and transportation, of slavery and segregation, never diminished or erased the basic culture and character of tribal ancestries. Yet it is also instructive that blacks from the West Indies and other islands of the Caribbean seek to retain an independent history. Their forebears also originated in Africa and served as slaves, but blacks born in Barbados and Jamaica, or Haiti and Martinique, make clear the British or French connections that distinguish them from others of their race. This emphasis is not intended to render Haitians or Jamaicans "less black" in terms of color. Rather, they wish it known that their antecedents are not exclusively African, but also bear a European imprint.

Black Americans came from the least-known continent, the most exotic, 21 the one remotest from American experience. Among the burdens blacks bear is the stigma of "the savage," the proximity to lesser primates. Hence the question in many minds: Can citizens of African origin find acceptance in a society that is dominantly white, Western, and European?

Even at a time when Americans of European backgrounds are giving 22 less emphasis to their ancestries, it is not as easy for black men and women to assimilate into the American mainstream. Even those who aspire to careers in white institutions, and emulate white demeanor and diction, find that white America lets them only partly past the door.

Arguably, this is because the "Africa" in African-American contrasts 23 with much of the European structure of technology and science, of administrative systems based on linear modes of reasoning. Today, Africa is the least developed and most sorrow-ridden of continents. It has more than its share of malnutrition and debilitating diseases, and at least its share of tribal rancor and bloodshed. It seems always to be petitioning the rest of the world for aid. Since the close of the colonial era, over a generation ago, there have not been many African success stories.

Yet the actual Africa of today is not really the model black Americans 24 have in mind. Of much greater significance is how the continent is construed as a symbol: what it says about the human spirit, what it connotes as a way of life. It is more the Africa of history, before the imperial powers arrived. It is also an Africa of the imagination, of music and dance and stories. This Africa speaks for an ancestral humanity, for an awareness of the self, the bonds of tribe and family and community. If the European heritage imposes the regimens of standardized tests, the African dream inspires discursive storytelling celebrating the soul and the spirit.

But as much as anything, being "black" in America bears the mark of 25 slavery. Even after emancipation, citizens who had been slaves still found themselves consigned to a subordinate status. Put most simply, the ideology that had provided the rationale for slavery by no means disappeared. Blacks continued to be seen as an inferior species, not only unsuited for equality but not even meriting a chance to show their worth. Immigrants only hours off the boat, while subjected to scorn, were allowed to assert their superiority to black Americans.

And in our own time, must it be admitted at the close of the twentieth 26 century, that residues of slavery continue to exist? The answer is obviously yes. The fact that blacks are separated more severely than any other group certainly conveys that message. Indeed, the fear persists that if allowed to come closer they will somehow contaminate the rest of society.

What other Americans know and remember is that blacks alone were 27 brought as chattels to be bought and sold like livestock. As has been noted, textbooks now point out that surviving slavery took a skill and stamina that no other race has been called upon to sustain. Yet this is not what others choose to recall. Rather, there remains an unarticulated suspicion: might there be something about the black race that suited them for slavery? This is not to say anyone argues that human bondage was justified. Still, the facts that slavery existed for so long and was so taken for granted cannot be erased from American minds. This is not the least reason why other Americans— again, without openly saying so—find it not improper that blacks still serve as maids and janitors, occupations seen as involving physical skills rather than mental aptitudes.

The recollections of the past that remain in people's minds continue 28 to shape ideas about the character and capacities of black citizens. Is it possible to erase the stigmas associated with slavery? After all, a very considerable number of black Americans have achieved impressive careers, winning many of the rewards bestowed by white America. Still, there is no way that even the most talented of these men and women will be considered eligible for the honorific of "white." They are, and will remain, accomplished blacks, regarded as role models for their race. But white Americans, who both grant and impose racial memberships, show little inclination toward giving full nationality to the descendants of African slaves[. . .].

Put most simply, none of the presumptions of inferiority associated with   29
Africa and slavery are imposed on other ethnicities. Moreover, as has also been noted, second and subsequent generations of Hispanics and Asians are merging into the "white" category, partly through intermarriage and also by personal achievement and adaptation. Indeed, the very fact that this is happening sheds light on the tensions and disparities separating the two major races.

◆ ◆ ◆

FIRST RESPONSES

What were your reactions to the Rodney King beating and the O. J. Simpson trial? How does either or both relate to Hacker's belief that "the recollections of the past that remain in people's minds continue to shape ideas about the character and capacities of black citizens"?

TAKING A CLOSER LOOK

Exploring *Who:* Voice and Tone

1. How directly does Hacker reveal his personal feelings about race within the first few paragraphs? What were your responses to this point of view? Why would he choose to be so direct so early in the essay?
2. How does Hacker establish his professional credibility on this topic? Did you find his credentials convincing?
3. Where was your understanding of your own racial or ethnic identity reinforced as you read the essay? Where was this understanding brought into question?

Exploring *What:* Content and Meaning

1. ■ *Using the Internet.* Hacker claims that racial division in the United States is "pervasive and penetrating." What does he mean? Does that statement accurately reflect your experience of the relationship between black and white Americans? Visit the Web site of one of the

national African American organizations, such as the NAACP or the Rainbow Coalition, to evaluate how its programs and goals reinforce or challenge Hacker's point of view.

2. What does Hacker think are the predominant attitudes among white Americans toward black Americans? Have you heard people say things that reflect such attitudes? Were they privately or publicly expressed?

3. Why do some people now describe the "melting pot" concept as more accurately being "a mosaic or even a lumpy stew"? Which version makes the most sense to you?

4. According to Hacker, all major immigrant groups, regardless of skin color, have had or now have the potential to become "white." What was required of these groups in the past, and what is required now? Reread paragraph 13 and discuss to what extent Hacker believes this success is positive.

Exploring *Why:* Purpose

1. Golf pro Tiger Woods has often been identified as an African American golfer, even though his mother is Asian American and only his father is African American. How does that support Hacker's view of the complexities of racial categorization?

2. In what ways does our popular culture—movies, television, and music—support Hacker's belief that we live in a culture of "rigid bifurcation"?

3. According to Hacker, what is the primary reason black Americans have not been allowed to assimilate? What is his evidence for this claim?

4. How does the African American's perception of "Africa" compare with its current economic and social realities? Why does Hacker include this contrast (paras. 23 and 24)?

Exploring *How:* Style and Strategy

1. What **paradox** is Hacker exploring when he says in paragraph 1, "Bondage would later be condemned as an awful injustice and the nation's shame, even as we have come to acknowledge the stamina and skill it took to survive in a system where humans could be bought and sold and punished like animals"?

2. What was the effect of Hacker's use of the term *apartheid* in paragraph 4? What associations did it create for you?

3. Hacker uses both point-by-point and block-by-block methods of comparison and contrast. Find examples of each.

IDEAS FOR WRITING COMPARISON AND CONTRAST

1. After interviewing your parents and perhaps other members of your extended family, write an essay comparing and contrasting the ways in which various members of your family consider race or ethnicity in their definitions of who they are and what they can be.

2. Compare and contrast two movies, television series, short stories, or songs that have very similar plots (such as love stories or family tragedies) but whose primary characters belong to different racial or ethnic groups. Concentrate on identifying important similarities and significant differences.

3. Do you and someone you know disagree about something, at least in part, because of a difference in your ages? Compare your positions on the topic, and explain how age helps to create your differences. Music, education, and relationships are possible topics.

◆ ◆ ◆

◆ FURTHER IDEAS FOR USING COMPARISON AND CONTRAST

1. Compare and contrast a job you enjoyed doing to one you considered quitting on a daily basis. What in you and what in the job created the positive and negative feelings? What did you learn about yourself and your work from these experiences?

2. ▇▊ *Using the Internet.* Visit two similar Web sites, such as two museums, two zoos, or two children's museums. When you have finished exploring these two sites, write a comparison and contrast essay analyzing the site's ease of use and any other features you think make such a "visit" interesting and worthwhile.

3. COMBINING STRATEGIES. Write an essay in which you recommend one specific vacation destination over another. Use narration and description to develop this essay in the block pattern. Make your direct recommendations in the introduction and conclusion of the essay. For example, you might write an article for your school newspaper in which you recount two different spring break trips in order to encourage other students to visit your favorite one.

4. COMBINING STRATEGIES. Compare and contrast your process for making an important decision with the way a family member or friend makes such a decision. What are the consequences of the similarities and differences?

5. COLLABORATIVE WRITING/COMBINING STRATEGIES. In small groups, brainstorm a list of the ways in which your concepts of friendship have changed or remained the same since coming to college. After this session, decide which of these changes accurately capture your experience of friendship. Next, freewrite, cluster, or brainstorm examples of childhood, high school, and college friendships. Use these examples to compare and contrast your precollege and college definitions of the term.

CHAPTER 10

Strategies for Interpreting Meaning

Cause and Effect

◆ ◆ ◆ ◆ ◆

Cause and effect writing traces the *why* to reveal the root of a problem or to illuminate the consequence of an action.

◆ Writers use cause and effect to explain both immediate and indirect connections.

◆ Effective cause and effect depends on logical connections and clear, consistent patterns of organization.

Reflection is an essential human act. People want to know *why* and *what if.* It helps us to understand our past and, in turn, to attempt a happier, more successful future. In your personal life, this reflection might involve understanding how you ended up becoming a biology major and how well this choice connects with your future goals. Investigating **causes and effects** is also a basic pursuit in many professional fields, such as marketing and psychology. What will it take to make consumers shift their loyalties from one product to another? Do girls and boys play with different toys because of their genes or the color of the blankets they were placed in at birth?

In all cases, figuring out why things happen takes intellectual effort because your logic can get tangled and some causes and effects are quite subtle. Distance, objectivity, and sustained analysis of your topic, purpose, and audience can help. Glossy ads for Disneyland make it difficult for anyone to arrive at a quick conclusion about the consequences of taking a summer vacation rather than working full time. In addition, it might be comforting to think that failing an examination was the result of staying out too late the night before, but not looking for additional causes can mean continued poor study skills and habits—and more failed exams.

That problems can be solved only by going beyond the obvious and exploring all possibilities fully is illustrated in the following professionally written essay in which Phyllis Rose embraces the effects of expanding consumerism on American small-town life.

Shopping and Other Spiritual Adventures in America Today

PHYLLIS ROSE

Phyllis Rose (born in 1942) has been a professor of English at Wesleyan University since 1969. Although she is best known for the biography *Parallel Lives: Five Victorian Marriages* (1983), she is the author of six other books, ranging from the scholarly *Writing of Women: Essays in a Rennaissance* (1985) to the popular *Jazz Cleopatra: Josephine Baker in Her Time* (1989) and *The Year of Reading Proust* (1997). Rose is also a frequent essayist and reviewer for magazines such as *The Atlantic Monthly* and *Vogue* and was a finalist for the National Book Critics' Circle Citation for Excellence in Reviewing in 1988.

Last year a new Waldbaum's Food Mart opened in the shopping mall on Route 66. It belongs to the new generation of superdupermarkets open twenty-four hours that have computerized checkout. I went to see the place as soon as it opened and I was impressed. There was trail mix in Lucite bins. There was freshly made pasta. There were coffee beans, four kinds of tahini, ten kinds of herb teas, raw shrimp in shells and cooked shelled shrimp, 1 fresh-squeezed orange juice. Every sophistication known to the big city, even goat's cheese covered with ash, was now available in Middletown, Conn. People raced from the warehouse aisle to the bagel bin to the coffee beans to the fresh fish market, exclaiming at all the new things. Many of us felt elevated, graced, complimented by the presence of this food palace in our town.

This is the wonderful egalitarianism of American business. Was it Andy 2
Warhol who said that the nice thing about Coke is, no can is any better or worse than any other? Some people may find it dull to cross the country and find the same chain stores with the same merchandise from coast to coast, but it means that my town is as good as yours, my shopping mall as important as yours, equally filled with wonders.

Imagine what people ate during the winter as little as seventy-five years 3
ago. They ate food that was local, long-lasting, and dull, like acorn squash, turnips, and cabbage. Walk into an American supermarket in February and the world lies before you: grapes, melons, artichokes, fennel, lettuce, peppers, pistachios, dates, even strawberries, to say nothing of ice cream. Have you ever considered what a triumph of civilization it is to be able to buy a pound of chicken livers? If you lived on a farm and had to kill a chicken when you wanted to eat one, you wouldn't ever accumulate a pound of chicken livers.

Another wonder of Middletown is Caldor, the discount department 4
store. Here is man's plenty: tennis racquets, pantyhose, luggage, glassware, records, toothpaste, Timex watches, Cadbury's chocolate, corn poppers, hair dryers, warm-up suits, car wax, light bulbs, television sets. All good quality at low prices with exchanges cheerfully made on defective goods. There are worse rules to live by. I feel good about America whenever I walk into this store, which is almost every mid-winter Sunday afternoon, when life elsewhere has closed down. I go to Caldor the way English people go to pubs: out of sociability. To get away from my house. To widen my horizons. For culture's sake. Caldor provides me too with a welcome sense of seasonal change. When the first outdoor grills and lawn furniture appear there, it's as exciting a sign of spring as the first crocus or robin.

Someone told me about a Soviet emigré who practices English by de- 5
claiming, at random, sentences that catch his fancy. One of his favorites is, "Fifty percent off all items today only." Refugees from Communist countries appreciate our supermarkets and discount department stores for the wonders they are. An Eastern European scientist visiting Middletown wept when she first saw the meat counter at Waldbaum's. On the other hand, before her year in America was up, her pleasure turned sour. She wanted everything she saw. Her approach to consumer goods was insufficiently abstract, too materialistic. We Americans are beyond a simple, possessive materialism. We're used to abundance and the possibility of possessing things. The things, and the possibility of possessing them, will still be there next week, next year. So today we can walk the aisles calmly.

It is a misunderstanding of the American retail store to think we go   6
there necessarily to buy. Some of us shop. There's a difference. Shopping has
many purposes, the least interesting of which is to acquire new articles. We
shop to cheer ourselves up. We shop to practice decision-making. We shop to
be useful and productive members of our class and society. We shop to remind
ourselves how much is available to us. We shop to remind ourselves how
much is to be striven for. We shop to assert our superiority to the material objects that spread themselves before us.

Shopping's function as a form of therapy is widely appreciated. You   7
don't really need, let's say, another sweater. You need the feeling of power
that comes with buying or not buying it. You need the feeling that someone
wants something you have—even if it's just your money. To get the benefit
of shopping, you needn't actually purchase the sweater, any more than you
have to marry every man you flirt with. In fact, window-shopping, like flirt-
ing, can be more rewarding, the same high without the distressing commitment, the material encumbrance. The purest form of shopping is provided
by garage sales. A connoisseur goes out with no goal in mind, open to whatever may come his or her way, secure that it will cost very little. Minimum expense, maximum experience. Perfect shopping.

I try to think of the opposite, a kind of shopping in which the object is   8
all-important, the pleasure of shopping at a minimum. For example, the purchase of blue jeans. I buy new blue jeans as seldom as possible because the
experience is so humiliating. For every pair that looks good on me, fifteen look
grotesque. But even shopping for blue jeans at Bob's Surplus on Main
Street—no frills, bare-bones shopping—is an event in the life of the spirit.
Once again I have to come to terms with the fact that I will never look good
in Levi's. Much as I want to be mainstream, I never will be.

In fact, I'm doubly an oddball, neither Misses nor Junior, but Misses   9
Petite. I look in the mirror, I acknowledge the disparity between myself and
the ideal, I resign myself to making the best of it: I will buy the Lee's Misses
Petite. Shopping is a time of reflection, assessment, spiritual self-discipline.

It is appropriate, I think, that Bob's Surplus has a communal dressing   10
room. I used to shop only in places where I could count on a private dressing room with a mirror inside. My impulse then was to hide my weaknesses.
Now I believe in sharing them. There are other women in the dressing room
at Bob's Surplus trying on blue jeans who look as bad as I do. We take comfort from one another. Sometimes a woman will ask me which of two items
looks better. I always give a definite answer. It's the least I can do. I figure we
are all in this together, and I emerge from the dressing room not only with
a new pair of jeans but with a renewed sense of belonging to a human
community.

When a Solzhenitsyn rants about American materialism, I have to look   11
at my digital Timex and check what year this is. Materialism? Like

conformism, a hot moral issue of the fifties, but not now. How to spread the goods, maybe. Whether the goods are the Good, no. Solzhenitsyn, like the visiting scientist who wept at the beauty of Waldbaum's meat counter but came to covet everything she saw, takes American materialism too materialistically. He doesn't see its spiritual side. Caldor, Waldbaum's, Bob's Surplus—these, perhaps, are our cathedrals.

◆ ◆ ◆

◆ ◆ ◆ *Writer's Workshop I* ◆ ◆ ◆
Responding to Cause and Effect

Use the *Who, What, Why,* and *How* questions (see p. 3) to explore your own understanding of the ideas and the writing strategies employed by Phyllis Rose in "Shopping and Other Spiritual Adventures in America Today." Your instructor may ask you to record these responses in a journal, post them to an electronic discussion list, or bring them to class to compare in small groups.

◆ WRITING FROM READING

After writing his own responses to the *Who, What, Why,* and *How* questions, student writer Ben Erwin chose to work very closely with the Rose model by looking for topics that brought out positives where others might see negatives, or vice versa. After brainstorming about drugs, attending college, and getting married, he decided he was most interested in exploring the too seldom considered negative consequences of parenting.

```
Benjamin Erwin
English 1090
June 7, 2001
```

```
                    Choosing Your Life

     To many, the possibility of having children is        1
simply accepted as an eventual part of their future.
Parenthood is something they look forward to as an
event that will fill their hearts and lives with love
and happiness. Unfortunately, almost no one considers
the multitude of problems, frustrations, and burdens
```

that children will assuredly bring with them. This is not to say that children, by and large, can't enhance your life and serve as a source of both pride and admiration, but the fact remains that many people blindly run headlong into the prospect of having children without giving it the proper consideration. Although kids may look like a lot of fun, especially when they aren't yours, they carry countless disadvantages that most people fail to realize.

First and foremost, children are incredibly 2 expensive. Kids are walking, talking, living, breathing need-machines that require years of tireless effort to ensure their stability. According to the U.S. Agriculture Department, it costs almost a quarter of a million dollars to raise a child from infancy into adulthood. With feeding, clothing, and other expenses, the cumulative cost of raising children is nearly overwhelming. When all these expenditures are fully taken into account, one can quickly realize all the sacrifices that must be made in order to fully care for a child (or, more commonly, children).

These financial demands can't possibly compare with 3 the emotional burden that rearing progeny will surely bring. Children require almost constant attention, a fact that's simply unavoidable. As a parent, your responsibilities will include assuaging fears, mending hurt feelings, teaching right from wrong, as well as a never-ending laundry list of other tasks that you alone have chosen to endure. Despite what many people think, day-care centers, older siblings, and television are not suitable substitutes for parents, and it is you alone who will be responsible for what your child may become as a direct result of your actions. Between the late nights, the various repeated crises, the whining, the crying, and the endless need for understanding that will surely result from their presence, kids can be a tireless and thankless job that will drain both your energy and your patience.

Along with the overwhelming drain on both your 4 mind and your pocketbook, as prospective parents you need to consider the physical work that must go into raising children. To be effective, you have to be available both physically and emotionally for your

children any time they may need you. Not only are you
expected to work in order to care for your offspring,
but you also have the added responsibilities of taking
them to soccer matches and baseball games and losing
sleep when they're convinced something sinister lurks
in the solitude of the dark. Such comforting but
demanding tasks will be required over the roughly
eighteen years that you are legally responsible for
your brood. The amount of work that you'll need to put
into your children borders on the absurd, and just
thinking about it could make you physically exhausted.
With these demands for care and attention on top of a
forty-hour work week, it's a wonder that you ever
thought children were a happy and viable option in the
first place.

So before choosing children that will demand your   5
time, money, and affection, consider your own options.
Contemplate what you could be, or more importantly,
what you want to be. Prospective parents must realize
that some possible career and social options become
moot when children become involved, and that these are
simply sacrifices that you will be forced to make.
First and foremost, you need to choose your most
viable, most fulfilling future. You need to weigh your
own opportunities and choose the life that will
ultimately yield the greatest rewards.

◆ GETTING STARTED ON CAUSE AND EFFECT

Cause and effect writing often starts because of a desire to understand
a problem or the meaning of an event. Ben, for example, wanted to explore
why something that seems so positive on the surface could end up having
negative consequences. Cause and effect can also help a writer persuade the
reader to see an issue from a new point of view, as Phyllis Rose does when
she counters popular criticisms of expanding American commerce.

Prewriting begins with jotting down what the writer already knows,
what prospective readers need to know, and what the writer hopes to know
by the end of the writing project. Is the effect known or the cause, and what,
then, must be uncovered, effects or causes? Rose knew the cause—big-city
products were being sold in her small town—and she wished to explain to
skeptical readers what might be the positive effects of this change.

Focused discovery writing provides writers the opportunity to seek a wide range of appropriate causes and/or effects. The obvious or **immediate causes and effects** should come easily. It's the subtle or **indirect causes and effects** that will take more time and care to discover. A fight with your best friend from high school might seem to explain why you didn't want to see him or her the last time you went home for a weekend. But if you reflect on the situation, you may discover that the alienation had begun long before that fight, a result of the different choices you've made since high school and the new friendships you've each formed. If you find yourself unable to generate in-depth answers or indirect possibilities, because you are too close to the problem or do not have sufficient information, it's time to turn to conversations with others or go to the library.

Having achieved an understanding, you are then ready to shift your attention to your audience and your purpose. The goal of understanding shifts to explanation as you turn your original questions into a thesis or generalization. To narrow the thesis, you will need to sort through the causes and effects identified in your prewriting. Objectively analyzing these causes and effects is essential to this process of selecting which ones are most useful and directly relevant to your readers' understanding. If, for example, you look thoughtfully at your high school friendship and decide to write to your friend to suggest some changes in the relationship, you will need to choose your evidence carefully to explain the changes that have taken place and to anticipate the effects your suggestions will have on your friendship.

◆ ORGANIZING CAUSE AND EFFECT

In modeling his essay after Rose's, Ben chose the same general organizational scheme, which looks like this one:

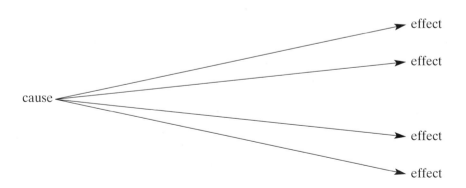

With the context filled in, the two essays look like this:

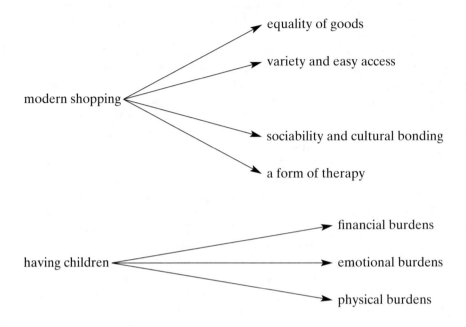

This structure is the same one E. M. Forster uses in his essay "My Wood" (p. 395).

    There are, however, more possibilities for the investigation of causes and effects. For example, you might want to focus on several causes for one effect, reversing Rose's strategy:

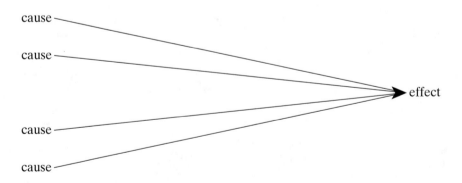

In this case, the effect would be introduced in your opening, and each cause would be developed in sequence in the body of the essay. For example, in the case of tracing the failure of your high school friendship, you can link the present state of things to several causes, each of which could be developed into a paragraph or two. It might be pictured this way:

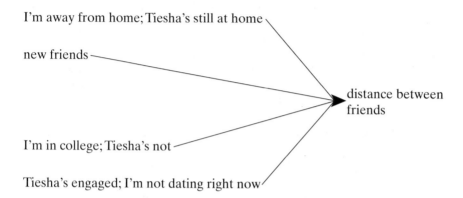

I'm away from home; Tiesha's still at home

new friends

distance between friends

I'm in college; Tiesha's not

Tiesha's engaged; I'm not dating right now

Later in this chapter, you will notice that Stephen King also uses a multiple cause structure to instruct would-be writers ("On Reading and Writing," p. 406). Judith Ortiz Cofer uses a third plan, offering a chain of causes and effects to explore the myths of the Latina woman (p. 412).

◆ DEVELOPING CAUSE AND EFFECT

Having established your major points and the structure of your discussion, you must next determine the order in which you will present your causes and effects. Chronology and order of importance—least to most or most to least—are effective choices for this strategy. Rose, for example, knew that the increased variety of goods was her least important point but would be the effect most familiar to her readers and thus might draw them into her later, more important effects.

Another organizational plan details one primary cause or effect, which is developed extensively in several sections, and then a number of smaller secondary causes, which might be clustered in one or two sections. If you take a chronological approach, take care to check for faulty or unchallenged connections. Simply because one event precedes or follows another does not necessarily prove that a meaningful link exists between the two. If you wake up ill in the night, it might have been those onion rings you ate; then again, it might just be a flu bug you picked up several days earlier.

Transitions will help you communicate your plan to your readers. Notice that in his essay, Ben gives clear indications of a well-thought-out organizational plan: "First and foremost," "These financial demands can't possibly compare with . . .," and "Along with the overwhelming drain . . ." You are never left wondering when a new point is coming or how it relates to the other effects.

Finally, check to ensure that your **tone** fits your purpose and audience and that you have provided sufficient examples to support the cause and effect relationships you claim. As Ben reviewed his first draft, he realized he had gotten caught up in his own strong feelings about the topic, which led him to the controversial position that having children was a "mistake." He realized that this conclusion could alienate many readers before they had the chance to consider his reasons for choosing to have children rather than just falling into parenthood. He also found that he needed to show as well as tell if he were to reach these idealistic readers, so he brainstormed additional concrete evidence for prospective parents, such as the creative "losing sleep because they're convinced something lurks in the solitude of the dark."

◆ OPENING AND CLOSING CAUSE AND EFFECT

Rose begins her essay with a long and very detailed listing of all the new foods that the Waldbaum Food Mart has brought to her small town. Her purpose is to capture the audience's interest through describing her childlike wonder at the experience: "Many of us felt elevated, graced, complimented by the presence of this food palace in our town." Rose delays the possible negative effects, the ones upon which her reader might focus, until paragraph 2. Her strategy worked with Ben, who was skeptical about her topic but said in his prewriting that he was drawn into the essay by its "succinct nature and frankness," which reflected Rose's "honesty and unapologetic opinions." When finishing his own essay, however, Ben decided on a more straightforward introduction, setting up his readers' assumptions about parenting and his understanding of their views, but then challenging them to reconsider. Each introduction displays the writer's control of the topics and understanding of the audience's needs and attitudes.

Rose and Ben also chose different tactics to close their essays. Like her introduction, Rose's conclusion is vividly concrete, with specific references to Solzhenitsyn's dislike of American materialism and to the "beauty of Waldbaum's meat counter," tying the closing and opening of the essay. In the final paragraph, however, Rose is more explicit in her purpose, criticizing those who don't see the "spiritual side" of consumerism that she hopes she has shown in her essay. Ben closes his essay with a call to his readers to take his views of parenting's true effects as a warning and therefore to "weigh" their options more thoughtfully. Cause and effect, in its revelation of new insights and logical relationships, lends itself to both forms of issue reevaluation by readers.

◆ USING THE MODEL

Ben used Rose's essay as a model for approaching a topic. Each creatively undermines common assumptions about the world around us. Like Ben, you too may decide to copy the structure of the model but select a topic that has nothing to do with the effects of materialism. For example, you might write about several effects of global warming. In such a case, you would not mention Rose's essay at all. You may decide, however, to use the model essays provided here in a more direct way. If you have strong feelings about the negative effects of chain stores on your community's economy and identity, you could provide examples to counter Rose's optimism. On the other hand, if you agree with Rose, you might search for additional activities or institutions that link people across the country and contribute to our common national identity.

◆ ◆ ◆ Writer's Workshop II ◆ ◆ ◆
Analyzing Cause and Effect

Working individually or with a small group of classmates, read through Ben Erwin's essay "Choosing Your Life" and respond to the following questions.

1. What tone of voice does Ben assume in this essay? Is it effective?
2. Has he accurately captured any of your assumptions about what having children would be like? Which insights were new to you?
3. Which were Ben's most effective and least effective examples? Why?
4. What does Ben hope to accomplish with his essay? Will reading this essay affect your future plans?
5. What is your favorite sentence in the essay? Why?

◆ ◆ ◆ Checklist for Reading and Writing ◆ ◆ ◆
Cause and Effect Essays

1. Is there a clear thesis that reveals the exact cause and effect relationship under consideration?
2. Is the essay's purpose appropriate for its intended audience?

3. Are all causal connections logical, and is that logic sufficiently explained?

4. Is there an evident pattern of development that is consistently followed, avoiding confusing shifts between causes and effects?

5. Are transitions provided to assist readers in seeing and following the cause and effect connections?

6. Are all appropriate causes and effects, both immediate and indirect, included and fully developed? If there is a chain of causes and effects, are all links included?

◆ ◆ ◆ PREPARING TO READ

What were your favorite toys when you were a child? Why? Were there toys you would have liked but were discouraged from playing with by your family or friends?

◆ ◆ ◆

Why Boys Don't Play with Dolls

KATHA POLLITT

Poet and essayist Katha Pollitt was born in New York City in 1949. Her writing has been described as "lucid, gutsy, funny, and just." Her very first book of poetry, *Antarctic Traveller* (1982), brought her wide recognition, including the National Book Critics Circle Award. A number of her essays, which first appeared in *The New Yorker*, the *New York Times*, and *The Nation*, have been published in the collections *Reasonable Creatures: Essays on Women and Feminism* (1994) and *Subject to Debate: Sense and Dissents on Women, Politics, and Culture* (2001). With sharp humor and insight, Pollitt grapples with many of our most challenging problems: abortion, the media, surrogate motherhood. "Why Boys Don't Play with Dolls" was written in 1995 for the *New York Times Magazine*.

It's twenty-eight years since the founding of NOW, and boys still like 1
trucks and girls still like dolls. Increasingly, we are told that the source of these robust preferences must lie outside society—in prenatal hormonal influences, brain chemistry, genes—and that feminism has reached its natural limits. What else could possibly explain the love of preschool girls for party dresses or the desire of toddler boys to own more guns than Mark from Michigan.

True, recent studies claim to show small cognitive differences between 2
the sexes: he gets around by orienting himself in space, she does it by remembering landmarks. Time will tell if any deserve the hoopla with which each is invariably greeted, over the protests of the researchers themselves. But even if the results hold up (and the history of such research is not encouraging), we don't need studies of sex-differentiated brain activity in reading, say, to understand why boys and girls still seem so unalike.

The feminist movement has done much for some women, and some- 3
thing for every woman, but it has hardly turned America into a playground

free of sex roles. It hasn't even got women to stop dieting or men to stop interrupting them.

Instead of looking at kids to "prove" that differences in behavior by   4
sex are innate, we can look at the ways we raise kids as an index to how unfinished the feminist revolution really is, and how tentatively it is embraced even by adults who fully expect their daughters to enter previously male-dominated professions and their sons to change diapers.

I'm at a children's birthday party. "I'm sorry," one mom silently mouths   5
to the mother of the birthday girl, who has just torn open her present—Tropical Splash Barbie. Now, you can love Barbie or you can hate Barbie, and there are feminists in both camps. But *apologize* for Barbie? Inflict Barbie, against your own convictions, on the child of a friend you know will be none too pleased?

Every mother in that room had spent years becoming a person who   6
had to be taken seriously, not least by herself. Even the most attractive, I'm willing to bet, had suffered over her body's failure to fit the impossible American ideal. Given all that, it seems crazy to transmit Barbie to the next generation. Yet to reject her is to say that what Barbie represents—being sexy, thin, stylish—is unimportant, which is obviously not true, and children know it's not true.

Women's looks matter terribly in this society, and so Barbie, however   7
ambivalently, must be passed along. After all, there are worse toys. The Cut and Style Barbie styling head, for example, a grotesque object intended to encourage "hair play." The grown-ups who give that probably apologize, too.

How happy would most parents be to have a child who flouted sex con-   8
ventions? I know a lot of women, feminists, who complain in a comical, eyeball-rolling way about their sons' passion for sports: the ruined weekends, obnoxious coaches, macho values. But they would not think of discouraging their sons from participating in this activity they find so foolish. Or do they? Their husbands are sports fans, too, and they like their husbands a lot.

Could it be that even sports-resistant moms see athletics as part of man-   9
liness? That if their sons wanted to spend the weekend writing up their diaries, or reading, or baking, they'd find it disturbing? Too antisocial? Too lonely? Too gay?

Theories of innate differences in behavior are appealing. They let par-   1(
ents off the hook—no small recommendation in a culture that holds moms, and sometimes even dads, responsible for their children's every misstep on the road to bliss and success.

They allow grown-ups to take the path of least resistance to the dom-   11
inant culture, which always requires less psychic effort, even if it means more actual work: just ask the working mother who comes home exhausted and nonetheless finds it easier to pick up her son's socks than make him do it

himself. They let families buy for their children, without too much guilt, the unbelievably sexist junk that the kids, who have been watching commercials since birth, understandably crave.

But the thing the theories do most of all is tell adults that the *adult* 12 world—in which moms and dads still play by many of the old rules even as they question and fidget and chafe against them—is the way it's supposed to be. A girl with a doll and a boy with a truck "explain" why men are from Mars and women are from Venus, why wives do housework and husbands just don't understand.

The paradox is that the world of rigid and hierarchical sex roles evoked 13 by determinist theories is already passing away. Three-year-olds may indeed insist that doctors are male and nurses female, even if their own mother is a physician. Six-year-olds know better. These days, something like half of all medical students are female, and male applications to nursing school are inching upward. When tomorrow's three-year-olds play doctor, who's to say how they'll assign the roles?

With sex roles, as in every area of life, people aspire to what is possible, 14 and conform to what is necessary. But these are not fixed, especially today. Biological determinism may reassure some adults about their present, but it is feminism, the ideology of flexible and converging sex roles, that fits our children's future. And the kids, somehow, know this.

That's why, if you look carefully, you'll find that for every kid who fits 15 a stereotype, there's another who's breaking one down. Sometimes it's the same kid—the boy who skateboards *and* takes cooking in his afterschool program; the girl who collects stuffed animals *and* A-pluses in science.

Feminists are often accused of imposing their "agenda" on children. 16 Isn't that what adults always do, consciously and unconsciously? Kids aren't born religious, or polite, or kind, or able to remember where they put their sneakers. Inculcating these behaviors, and the values behind them, is a tremendous amount of work, involving many adults. We don't have a choice, really, about whether we should give our children messages about what it means to be male and female—they're bombarded with them from morning till night.

The question, as always, is what do we want those messages to be? 17

◆ ◆ ◆

FIRST RESPONSES

How would you feel about your daughter playing with a toy bulldozer? Would you let your son play with a Tropical Splash Barbie? Can both boys and girls play with stuffed animals? Why or why not?

TAKING A CLOSER LOOK

Exploring *Who:* Voice and Tone

1. Reread paragraph 1. By the end of the paragraph, do you know whether Pollitt is a liberal or a conservative? What is the effect of her strategy?
2. Find several examples of phrases that reveal Pollitt's explicitly feminist perspective. Did her tone of voice reinforce your views of feminists or challenge them? Did that affect your openness to her ideas?
3. Describe the group of people Pollitt seems most interested in reaching with this essay. How does paragraph 16 help answer this question?
4. Is Pollitt discouraged by traditional gender roles continuing three decades after the National Organization for Women (NOW) was founded? Where does she place her hope? Do you share any of her feelings?

Exploring *What:* Content and Meaning

1. What has science concretely proven about the influence of genetics on gender behavior? Does Pollitt dispute this research? Why or why not?
2. Pollitt locates one of the primary causes for the continuation of traditional gender roles in "adults who fully expect their daughters to enter previously male-dominated professions and their sons to change diapers." Did this claim surprise you? What proof does she offer? Can you add other causes or think of additional examples to support her viewpoint?
3. Why does Pollitt think that a boy's love of sports is a sign of a "sex convention"? Has Title IX, which mandates equal opportunity in school athletics, had any effect on this traditional division of interests? How does popular culture, such as the television sitcom, reinforce or challenge the norm?
4. What does Pollitt mean when she says, "Theories of innate differences in behavior are appealing. They let parents off the hook."?

Exploring *Why:* Purpose

1. Pollitt writes, "The feminist movement has done much for some women, and something for every woman." Name some changes she might have been thinking of when writing this sentence.
2. ◼▯ *Using the Internet.* When you watch younger children at play or see commercials for children's toys, what similarities and what differences do you see between now and when you were a child? Use a search en-

gine to find an Internet site for children's toys (company sites, such as Disney, or organizations that evaluate the quality of toys, for example), and note the extent to which gender is part of the presentation. Do you think gender considerations have become more important in the toy business than they used to be?

3. Exactly what changes does Pollitt hope to encourage? Has she affected your attitudes toward parenting?

4. Why are children changing their habits despite their parents' attitudes?

Exploring *How:* Style and Strategy

1. Outline Pollitt's chain of causes and effects. Why did she choose this in-depth approach rather than offer a wider variety of causes for gender differences? What explains the order of her points?

2. What is the effect of saying that boys' liking trucks and girls' playing with dolls are "robust preferences"?

3. Why does Pollitt use the word *hoopla* to describe the opposition's viewpoint in paragraph 2?

4. What is Pollitt's intention when she uses questions in paragraph 5? How is it different from her use of a question as the conclusion to her essay?

◆ WRITING FROM READING ASSIGNMENT

Katha Pollitt took what she saw as a superficial response to the problem of gender-role preferences in children and uncovered several sites of responsibility in a surprising place: parents who themselves have struggled to lead nontraditional lives. By doing so, she hoped to contradict her opposition and to encourage genuine change for children.

In this writing assignment, your goal is to dig beneath the surface to trace not only the *immediate* but also the *indirect* and interrelated causes for a current problem. One place to look is your campus: the lack of a day-care center, a parking crisis, a refusal to fund a new student group, or trouble getting the courses needed to graduate. You might also write about a problem in your family if understanding the nature of the problem would be valuable to your readers in some way. If formal research is allowed or required, you might consider writing about a problem in your local community, such as an increase in sexual assaults.

A. Brainstorming is a productive way to discover the best topic for this assignment. Don't stop at the first problem that comes to mind, but remember that unless you will be doing formal research, the topic must be one you know well enough to discuss in some depth. If nothing comes to mind, review past issues of your campus newspaper or chat with family and friends to identify possibilities. You might also glance through the readings in this book for inspiration.

B. Once you've decided what to write about, you'll want to list all the causes that you and others have thought of so far, even the ones you don't necessarily see as primary or correct. Again, conversations with others and research might be useful to extend the possibilities.

C. Clustering the points on your list will help you start the process of see-ing connections among the causes: immediate or easily observable causes in one group, indirect or less easily seen in another. Next, clus-ter around the indirect causes, trying to identify where those causes might originate. Pollitt's search for causes led her to where children learn their gender roles, which led her to the parents, which led her to the social pressures the parents themselves face.

D. Like Pollitt, you now will need to select the few most important causes for the problem to allow you the space to develop each one fully. Con-sider which lines of analysis are least familiar, even surprising, to your readers and most likely to influence their thinking on the problem. A new perspective can sometimes move those with set opinions to re-consider their views.

E. A sketch outline of your chain of causes will let you know how fully pre-pared you are to begin your draft. If the chain reveals a need for more examples or explanations, return to brainstorming or research to fill in the gaps.

F. Before you begin the draft, you might also review Pollitt's organiza-tion. Do you want to introduce the essay as she does, with causes that inaccurately or inadequately account for the problem? Will you begin with the most immediate causes to trace your way back or vice versa? Your readers' familiarity with the problem and their attitudes toward it will help you make these decisions.

G. In your conclusion, consider using Pollitt's technique of placing the next step in the hands of your readers: What will they or can they do with the insights you have provided them?

H. Focus your first-stage revisions on the logic of your connections and the adequacy of your supporting examples and analysis. Before the last round of editing, consider how clearly you have guided the readers through the logical connections. Are there appropriate transitional words and phrases?

◆ ◆ ◆ PREPARING TO READ

Have you ever made a decision to do something and then been totally unprepared for the consequences of the choice? What made you expect different results, and how did you handle the consequences you faced?

◆ ◆ ◆

My Wood

E. M. FORSTER

A prolific essayist, fiction writer, and social critic, E. M. Forster (1879–1970) was born in London and earned two undergraduate degrees and a master's degree from Cambridge University. He is highly regarded for both originality of voice and subtlety of style. His novels about early twentieth-century British culture, especially the transition from youth to adulthood, have been rediscovered by a modern audience through their film adaptations, including *A Room with a View* (1908), *Howards End* (1910), *A Passage to India* (1924), and *Maurice* (written in 1913, published in 1971). He also published a book of short stories, *The Celestial Omnibus* (1911), and several collections of essays, including *Abinger Harvest* (1936), from which the following selection is taken.

A few years ago I wrote a book which dealt in part with the difficulties   1
of the English in India. Feeling that they would have had no difficulties in India themselves, the Americans read the book freely. The more they read it the better it made them feel, and a check to the author was the result. I bought a wood with the check. It is not a large wood—it contains scarcely any trees, and it is intersected, blast it, by a public footpath. Still, it is the first property that I have owned, so it is right that other people should participate in my shame, and should ask themselves, in accents that will vary in horror, this very important question: What is the effect of property upon the character? Don't let's touch economics; the effect of private ownership upon the community as a whole is another question—a more important question, perhaps, but another one. Let's keep to psychology. If you own things, what's their effect on you? What's the effect on me of my wood?

In the first place, it makes me feel heavy. Property does have this effect.   2
Property produces men of weight, and it was a man of weight who failed to get into the Kingdom of Heaven. He was not wicked, that unfortunate

millionaire in the parable, he was only stout; he stuck out in front, not to mention behind, and as he wedged himself this way and that in the crystalline entrance and bruised his well-fed flanks, he saw beneath him a comparatively slim camel passing through the eye of a needle and being woven into the robe of God. The Gospels all through couple stoutness and slowness. They point out what is perfectly obvious, yet seldom realized: that if you have a lot of things you cannot move about a lot, that furniture requires dusting, dusters require servants, servants require insurance stamps, and the whole tangle of them makes you think twice before you accept an invitation to dinner or go for a bathe in the Jordan. Sometimes the Gospels proceed further and say with Tolstoy that property is sinful; they approach the difficult ground of asceticism here, where I cannot follow them. But as to the immediate effects of property on people, they just show straightforward logic. It produces men of weight. Men of weight cannot, by definition, move like the lightning from the East unto the West, and the ascent of a fourteen-stone bishop into a pulpit is thus the exact antithesis of the coming of the Son of Man. My wood makes me feel heavy.

In the second place, it makes me feel it ought to be larger.   3

The other day I heard a twig snap in it. I was annoyed at first, for I   4 thought that someone was blackberrying, and depreciating the value of the undergrowth. On coming nearer, I saw it was not a man who had trodden on the twig and snapped it, but a bird, and I felt pleased. My bird. The bird was not equally pleased. Ignoring the relation between us, it took flight as soon as it saw the shape of my face, and flew straight over the boundary hedge into a field, the property of Mrs. Henessy, where it sat down with a loud squawk. It had become Mrs. Henessy's bird. Something seemed grossly amiss here, something that would not have occurred had the wood been larger. I could not afford to buy Mrs. Henessy out, I dared not murder her, and limitations of this sort beset me on every side [. . .].

In the third place, property makes its owner feel that he ought to do   5 something to it. Yet he isn't sure what. A restlessness comes over him, a vague sense that he has a personality to express—the same sense which, without any vagueness, leads the artist to an act of creation. Sometimes I think I will cut down such trees as remain in the wood, at other times I want to fill up the gaps between them with new trees. Both impulses are pretentious and empty. They are not honest movements toward money-making or beauty. They spring from a foolish desire to express myself and from an inability to enjoy what I have got. Creation, property, enjoyment form a sinister trinity in the human mind. Creation and enjoyment are both very, very good, yet they are often unattainable without a material basis, and at such moments property pushes itself in as a substitute, saying, "Accept me instead—I'm good enough for all three." It is not enough. It is, as Shakespeare said of lust, "The expense of spirit in a waste of shame"; it is "Before, a joy proposed; behind, a dream."

Yet we don't know how to shun it. It is forced on us by our economic system as the alternative to starvation. It is also forced on us by an internal defect in the soul, by the feeling that in property may lie the germs of self-development and of exquisite or heroic deeds. Our life on earth is, and ought to be, material and carnal. But we have not yet learned to manage our materialism and carnality properly; they are still entangled with the desire for ownership, where (in the words of Dante) "Possession is one with loss."

And this brings us to our fourth and final point: the blackberries.　　6

Blackberries are not plentiful in this meager grove, but they are easily　　7
seen from the public footpath which traverses it, and all too easily gathered. Foxgloves, too—people will pull up the foxgloves, and ladies of an educational tendency even grub for toadstools to show them on the Monday in class. Other ladies, less educated, roll down the bracken in the arms of their gentlemen friends. There is paper, there are tins. Pray, does my wood belong to me or doesn't it? And, if it does, should I not own it best by allowing no one else to walk there? There is a wood near Lyme Regis, also cursed by a public footpath, where the owner has not hesitated on this point. He had built high stone walls each side of the path, and has spanned it by bridges, so that the public circulate like termites while he gorges on the blackberries unseen. He really does own his wood, this able chap [. . .]. And perhaps I shall come to this in time. I shall wall in and fence out until I really taste the sweets of property. Enormously stout, endlessly avaricious, pseudo-creative, intensely selfish, I shall weave upon my forehead the quadruple crown of possession until those nasty Bolshies come and take it off again and thrust me aside into the outer darkness.

◆ ◆ ◆

FIRST RESPONSES

What's the most important thing you own? Why is it important to you? Has it affected you the way Forster's wood affected him?

TAKING A CLOSER LOOK

Exploring *Who:* Voice and Tone

1. What is the tone of this essay? Is it formal or informal? How does the author achieve that tone?

2. What expectations does Forster have about his readers? Does he want you to sympathize with him, criticize him, or what?

3. Is Forster's style of humor familiar to you? How would you describe it? How does his humor influence your response to the essay's main point?

Exploring *What:* Content and Meaning

1. What are the four effects of owning property?
2. Explain what Forster means when he says his property makes him "feel heavy."
3. What character traits most disturb Forster? Why?
4. In paragraph 1, the author says, "Don't let's touch on economics." Does he keep to this plan? What economic factors come up in the discussion?

Exploring *Why:* Purpose

1. Why does Forster want to share these experiences and reactions with others? What insights does he want to reveal?
2. Forster buys his property by using the royalties from a book about England's problems with India. Explain the **irony** in this fact. Does it help explain why Forster wrote this essay? (To help answer this question, you might see what you can find out about Forster's novel *A Passage to India.*)

Exploring *How:* Style and Structure

1. Why does Forster refer to so many other writers in this essay?
2. ■▯ *Using the Internet.* The author uses a number of **allusions** in this essay. Look up the following allusions: the wealthy man in the parable (para. 2), Shakespeare and Dante (para. 5), Bolshies (para. 7). How does each allusion support Forster's point? You can probably find the information you need by searching an online reference site such as www.encyclopedia.com or www.britannica.com.
3. Forster doesn't end with an explicit statement about the effects of owning property. Write a new conclusion for this essay in which you spell out the message. What is the effect of this new ending? Is it an improvement over Forster's?

IDEAS FOR WRITING CAUSE AND EFFECT

1. Write an essay in which you answer Forster's question, "If you own things, what's their effect on you?" You can use almost any belonging

on the "cause" side: my house, my computer, my wardrobe, my sound system, my partner, my new baby, my gold medal. Try to come up with at least four effects, as Forster does.

2. Why do people want to own property? Write an essay in which you explore the causes or reasons for owning something.

3. Write an essay developing a short list of reasons why your readers should or should not do something that is a common human activity, such as shop, watch television, listen to music, have pets, exercise. Focus on the effects the activity has on individuals as well as on society as a whole.

◆ ◆ ◆ PREPARING TO READ

Have you ever been in a difficult situation and really needed help, but for some reason you were unable to ask for or accept assistance? What explains your behavior? Would you act differently now?

◆ ◆ ◆

The Greenland Viking Mystery

KATHY A. SVITIL

Kathy A. Svitil writes for *Discover* magazine, a Disney publication that brings recent scientific research and insights to a popular audience. Svitil's interests encompass the past, present, and future, from the disappearance of the dinosaurs to our current struggles with global warming and how robotics will shape our lives in days to come. "The Greenland Viking Mystery," which first appeared in June 1997, calls on the wonders of modern technology to help explain the disappearance of two separate groups of Icelandic colonists in the Middle Ages.

To the Norse men and women living in Iceland in the tenth century, an   1
island called Greenland must have sounded like Eden. At the time, the North Atlantic was in the throes of a warm spell, and parts of southern Greenland were actually green and fertile, at least by Icelandic standards. Enticed by the promise of truly greener pastures, a group of Norse Icelanders established two settlements on Greenland—the Eastern, as archeologists call it, on the southern tip of the island; and the Western, along the southwest coast near the modern capital of Nuuk. The settlers built farms and large stone churches, raised animals, hunted seals and walrus, traded with Europe, and struggled to survive.

Survive they did, for centuries, even as the temperatures chilled at the   2
end of the thirteenth century with the onset of a prolonged European cooling trend often called the little ice age. Then, mysteriously, the Norse Greenlanders—some 5,000 to 6,000 strong at their peak—disappeared. The Western Settlement succumbed first, sometime in the mid-1300s; Eastern settlers hung on longer, until the mid-fifteenth century. Almost ever since the settlers' demise, historians and archeologists have speculated about what happened to them. Were they killed by invaders from arctic Canada? Were they carried off by Basque pirates? Or did they starve to death in the bitter cold?

Now a diverse body of research is shedding new light on those final   3
desperate years. Pirates and war weren't the agents of doom, according to the
emerging view. Rather, an unlikely combination of changing climate and ethnocentrism probably brought down the Norse colonies in Greenland.

The Norse colonists couldn't have had a better start. Both the Eastern   4
and Western settlements were ideally placed—located on inner fjords miles
from the sea, nestled up against the ice sheet and sheltered from fierce winds.
A persistent high-pressure zone over the ice cap made for warm summers on
the fjords by deflecting coastal storms out to sea. From archeological excavations, researchers know that the Greenlanders subsisted on a diet of harp
and harbor seal (and sometimes caribou), which were hunted in the summer
on the outer fjords near the ocean, along with food from cows, sheep, and
goats. The domestic animals pastured year-round along the inner fjords that
produced grasses during the brief summer growing season. Despite their
closeness to the sea, the Greenlanders, for unknown reasons, apparently
didn't fish.

A model of that economy, created by archeologist Thomas McGovern   5
of the City University of New York and his colleagues, indicates that the summer growth of fodder for those domestic animals—and, in turn, the survival
of the Greenlanders—was critically linked to climate change. "The model
showed that the kind of climate change that would be most damaging would
not be the once-every-500-years very bad year," McGovern says, or even a
record-breaking cold winter. "The most difficult thing for them to cope with
would be a string of especially cold summers."

That conclusion is supported by the findings of Lisa Barlow, a paleo-   6
climatologist at the University of Colorado in Boulder who has analyzed
cores from the Greenland ice sheet. To measure temperature change, Barlow
looked at the ratio of deuterium (a heavy isotope of hydrogen) to normal hydrogen in sections of the ice core covering the last 700 years. Ocean-borne
water molecules made up of normal hydrogen evaporate at slightly lower
temperatures than do water molecules made with the heavier deuterium.
But as the temperature goes up, more heavy hydrogen evaporates, eventually precipitating out over Greenland.

Barlow managed to trace the fluctuations of the two forms of hydrogen   7
and found that the fourteenth century suffered four periods with summer
temperatures cooler than average. The longest cold spell lasted for about
twenty grim years, from 1343 to 1362, give or take a year—the same period
during which the Western Settlement is believed to have collapsed. (In one
historical account, a seafaring Norwegian priest finds the Western Settlement
eerily abandoned sometime before 1361.)

"In a cool summer the settlement is not going to get as much grass   8
growth as it needs to get through the winter," Barlow says. "If that consistently
happened for a number of years, then they probably reached a breaking

point. When you are dealing with a colony that was living at a subsistence level anyway, it wouldn't take much to put them over the edge."

Did the Norse in the Western Settlement all die, or could some have evacuated? "It would be nice to think that there were survivors" who fled to the Eastern Settlement or perhaps to Europe, says McGovern. "But the problem is that there is absolutely no evidence of that. In many parts of Europe at that time you could have a few boatloads of people show up and disappear into the population, but I think a formal abandonment of the Greenland colony would have been sufficiently newsworthy that it would have ended up in the annals of Iceland and the continent." 9

And yet it seems that the Europeans were totally unaware of the fate of the Greenland settlements. In the late thirteenth and early fourteenth centuries, vast amounts of sea ice began to clog navigation lanes, making travel to and from Greenland difficult even during the summer. "As late as the 1600s the Pope was still appointing bishops to Greenland, who of course never left Rome," says McGovern. "As far as he was concerned, Greenland was then still a functioning part of Christendom." 10

McGovern suspects a bleaker fate. "As far as we can tell, they starved to death." Excavations have turned up many expensive portable items, like crucifixes, that would probably have been removed by the settlers in an evacuation. And had the colony's population gradually diminished, McGovern says, the wood in many of the farms—a valuable commodity in a place with few trees—would have been scavenged by the remaining settlers. Such was not the case. "At least one of the farms we've examined shows evidence of a tough winter," McGovern says. "We find the bones of a number of cows—about the same number that lived in the barn—and mixed in with them are a bunch of ptarmigan feet, also famine food. Mixed in with that are the bones of one of the big hunting dogs." Cut marks on the bones suggest the dogs were butchered; even the cow hooves were eaten. "It looks as though they ate the cows and then ate the dogs. It looks like hard times." 11

Other evidence supports this grim scenario. Entomologist Peter Skidmore of the University of Sheffield in England uncovered an orderly succession of fossil flies in a Western Settlement farmhouse. In the lower layers he found warm-temperature houseflies; in the layers above, cold-tolerant, indoor carrion-eaters that might have moved in when the homestead could no longer be kept warm; and in the final layer, outdoor flies. At that point, the roof of the farmhouse had probably caved in. 12

This was no Jamestown: the Norse toughed it out for generations under steadily worsening conditions. The Greenlanders became more isolated from Europe. Yet they apparently clung steadfastly to a European way of life, shunning contact with the Thule Inuit peoples who began immigrating to the island from northern Canada in A.D. 1100. "There is indication on the Thule side of interest in the Norse and their technology. Inuit excavations contain 13 quite a lot of material," McGovern says. The Norse, on the other hand, suspiciously avoided contact with the Thule. "You don't have this kind of barrier between cultures for so long without someone working very hard to maintain it."

The Norse could have learned from the Thule. After all, there was food   14
to be had, even in winter—under the ice. "What has kept the Inuit communities alive through the winters, all through history, has been hunting through the ice or at the ice edge for ring seals," McGovern says. "They have developed this complex hunting technology—harpoons and all sorts of other gadgets—that allows them to do this successfully." But the Norse never learned to use harpoons, and their animal-bone collections are strikingly absent of ring seals. "Out of several thousand bones, there are two or three ring seal bones," says McGovern.

"They didn't adopt harpoons, they didn't adopt skin clothing, and they   15
didn't adopt skin boats," says McGovern. "The extinction of the Norse in Greenland, aided certainly as it was by climatic change, possibly could have been avoided if they had picked up more of those arctic adaptations from the Inuit. You could argue that these folks managed to maintain ethnic purity at the expense of survival."

◆ ◆ ◆

FIRST RESPONSES

Can you imagine yourself in the situation these Norse colonists faced? Why or why not?

TAKING A CLOSER LOOK

Exploring *Who:* Voice and Tone

1. How would you describe Svitil's role in this essay? Do you know her personal opinions about this mystery or her views about the researchers' explanations?

2. How many different types of professional researchers does Svitil call on to develop her topic? Reread some of their quotations. Describe the feelings these researchers reveal about their work and their topic.

3. Is your background in science sufficient to understand the evidence Svitil provides? How easily did you follow her explanations for the disappearance?

Exploring *What:* Content and Meaning

1. What has been the predominant theory used to explain why the colonists starved to death? What kinds of evidence support it?
2. What is the more recent theory of what caused the crisis? What new evidence supports it?
3. Are scientists equally certain about both theories? What were your responses to the two theories?
4. How have scientists disproved other speculations about the extinction?

Exploring *Why:* Purpose

1. What is "ethnocentrism"?
2. Why was the Greenland situation "no Jamestown"? Why does Svitil use this historical reference to make her point?
3. What is meant by "ethnic purity" in the last paragraph? Can you think of other past or current problems that can be explained by the same cause?

Exploring *How:* Style and Strategy

1. Svitil's thesis does not appear until paragraph 3. Why?
2. In how many different ways does Svitil attempt to draw in readers who might love a good "mystery" but don't usually read about science?
3. ■ *Using the Internet.* How much did Svitil assume you already knew about Greenland's history and climate? Visit the Web site of the National Tourist Board of Greenland (www.greenland-guide.dk/gt/default.htm#Facts), and use the links to answer any questions or pursue any interests that the essay might have raised for you.
4. Go through the whole essay reading just the first sentence of each paragraph that doesn't begin with a quotation. How much of her topic does Svitil outline through these lead sentences?

IDEAS FOR WRITING CAUSE AND EFFECT

1. Is there a prejudice or preconception that especially bothers you? Write an essay explaining why people might think in this way and why you are offended by it.

2. What is currently the most popular daytime show among your friends or on campus? Write an essay explaining what causes the show to appeal to this particular group of people. You might interview people to gather supporting evidence.

3. Review the "Preparing to Read" discovery writing that you did for this essay. If you want, discuss your responses with other members of your class. Then write an essay tracing the causes for a difficult situation you have found yourself in, one from which you learned something about how to avoid a similar problem or difficulty in the future.

◆ ◆ ◆ PREPARING TO READ

Who was your favorite author when you were a child? Your least favorite? What did you learn from these writers about what makes writing interesting?

◆ ◆ ◆

On Reading and Writing

STEPHEN KING

Born in Portland, Maine, in 1947 and still a Maine resident, Stephen King gave up a high school teaching job at the age of twenty-six when the novel *Carrie* (1974) launched his highly successful fiction career. With sales in the millions and almost thirty novels still in print, including *The Shining* (1977), *Pet Sematary* (1983), *The Green Mile* (1996), and *Black House* (2001), King regularly shares his insights into the writer's craft. In 1986, in "Everything You Need to Know About Writing Successfully—in Ten Minutes," he reduced his advice to twelve rules, including "Ask yourself frequently, 'Am I having fun?' The answer needn't always be yes. But if it's always no, it's time for a new project or a new career." This same core wisdom appears in the following essay taken from *On Writing: A Memoir of the Craft* (2000).

If you want to be a writer, you must do two things above all others: read a lot and write a lot. There's no way around these two things that I'm aware of, no shortcut.   1

I'm a slow reader, but I usually get through seventy or eighty books a year, mostly fiction. I don't read in order to study the craft; I read because I like to read. It's what I do at night, kicked back in my blue chair. Similarly, I don't read fiction to study the art of fiction, but simply because I like stories. Yet there is a learning process going on. Every book you pick up has its own lesson or lessons, and quite often the bad books have more to teach than the good ones.   2

When I was in the eighth grade, I happened upon a paperback novel by Murray Leinster, a science fiction pulp writer who did most of his work during the forties and fifties, when magazines like *Amazing Stories* paid a penny a word. I had read other books by Mr. Leinster, enough to know that the quality of his writing was uneven. This particular tale, which was about mining in the asteroid belt, was one of his less successful efforts. Only that's too   3 kind. It was terrible, actually, a story populated by paper-thin characters and driven by outlandish plot developments. Worst of all (or so it seemed to me at the time), Leinster had fallen in love with the word *zestful.* Characters watched the approach of ore-bearing asteroids with *zestful smiles.* Characters sat down to supper aboard their mining ship with *zestful anticipation.* Near the end of the book, the hero swept the large-breasted, blonde heroine into a *zestful embrace.* For me, it was the literary equivalent of a smallpox vaccination: I have never, so far as I know, used the word *zestful* in a novel or a story. God willing, I never will.

Asteroid Miners (which wasn't the title, but that's close enough) was 4 an important book in my life as a reader. Almost everyone can remember losing his or her virginity, and most writers can remember the first book he/she put down thinking: *I can do better than this. Hell, I* am *doing better than this!* What could be more encouraging to the struggling writer than to realize his/her work is unquestionably better than that of someone who actually got paid for his/her stuff?

One learns most clearly what not to do by reading bad prose—one 5 novel like *Asteroid Miners* (or *Valley of the Dolls, Flowers in the Attic,* and *The Bridges of Madison County,* to name just a few) is worth a semester at a good writing school, even with the superstar guest lecturers thrown in.

Good writing, on the other hand, teaches the learning writer about 6 style, graceful narration, plot development, the creation of believable characters, and truth-telling. A novel like *The Grapes of Wrath* may fill a new writer with feelings of despair and good old-fashioned jealousy—"I'll never be able to write anything that good, not if I live to be a thousand"—but such feelings can also serve as a spur, goading the writer to work harder and aim higher. Being swept away by a combination of great story and great writing—of being flattened, in fact—is part of every writer's necessary formation. You cannot hope to sweep someone else away by the force of your writing until it has been done to you.

So we read to experience the mediocre and the outright rotten; such ex- 7 perience helps us to recognize those things when they begin to creep into our own work, and to steer clear of them. We also read in order to measure ourselves against the good and the great, to get a sense of all that can be done. And we read in order to experience different styles.

You may find yourself adopting a style you find particularly exciting, and 8 there's nothing wrong with that. When I read Ray Bradbury as a kid, I wrote like Ray Bradbury—everything green and wondrous and seen through a lens smeared with the grease of nostalgia. When I read James M. Cain, everything I wrote came out clipped and stripped and hardboiled. When I read Lovecraft, my prose became luxurious and Byzantine. I wrote stories in my teenage years where all these styles merged, creating a kind of hilarious stew. This sort of stylistic blending is a necessary part of developing one's own style, but it doesn't occur in a vacuum. You have to read widely, constantly refining (and redefining) your own work as you do so. It's hard for me to believe that people who read very little (or not at all in some cases) should presume to write and expect people to like what they have written, but I know it's true. If I had a nickel for every person who ever told me he/she wanted to become a writer but "didn't have time to read," I could buy myself a pretty good steak dinner. Can I be blunt on this subject? If you don't have time to read, you don't have the time (or the tools) to write. Simple as that.

Reading is the creative center of a writer's life. I take a book with me   9
everywhere I go, and find there are all sorts of opportunities to dip in. The trick is to teach yourself to read in small sips as well as in long swallows. Waiting rooms were made for books—of course! But so are theater lobbies before the show, long and boring checkout lines, and everyone's favorite, the john. You can even read while you're driving, thanks to the audiobook revolution. Of the books I read each year, anywhere from six to a dozen are on tape. As for all the wonderful radio you will be missing, come on—how many times can you listen to Deep Purple sing "Highway Star"?

Reading at meals is considered rude in polite society, but if you expect   10
to succeed as a writer, rudeness should be the second-to-least of your concerns. The least of all should be polite society and what it expects. If you intend to write as truthfully as you can, your days as a member of polite society are numbered, anyway.

Where else can you read? There's always the treadmill, or whatever   11
you use down at the local health club to get aerobic. I try to spend an hour doing that every day, and I think I'd go mad without a good novel to keep me company. Most exercise facilities (at home as well as outside it) are now equipped with TVs, but TV—while working out or anywhere else—really is about the last thing an aspiring writer needs. If you feel you must have the news analyst blowhards on CNN while you exercise, or the stock market blowhards on MSNBC, or the sports blowhards on ESPN, it's time for you to question how serious you really are about becoming a writer. You must be prepared to do some serious turning inward toward the life of the imagination, and that means, I'm afraid, that Geraldo, Keith Obermann, and Jay Leno must go. Reading takes time, and the glass teat takes too much of it.

Once weaned from the ephemeral craving for TV, most people will find   12
they enjoy the time they spend reading. I'd like to suggest that turning off that endlessly quacking box is apt to improve the quality of your life as well as the quality of your writing. And how much of a sacrifice are we talking about here? How many *Frasier* and *ER* reruns does it take to make one American life complete? How many Richard Simmons infomercials? How many whiteboy/fatboy Beltway insiders on CNN? Oh man, don't get me started. Jerry-Springer-Dr.-Dre-Judge-Judy-Jerry-Falwell-Donny-and-Marie, I rest my case.

When my son Owen was seven or so, he fell in love with Bruce Spring-   13
steen's E Street Band, particularly with Clarence Clemons, the band's burly
sax player. Owen decided he wanted to learn to play like Clarence. My wife
and I were amused and delighted by this ambition. We were also hopeful, as
any parent would be, that our kid would turn out to be talented, perhaps
even some sort of prodigy. We got Owen a tenor saxophone for Christmas and
lessons with Gordon Bowie, one of the local music men. Then we crossed
our fingers and hoped for the best.

Seven months later I suggested to my wife that it was time to discon-   14
tinue the sax lessons, if Owen concurred. Owen did, and with palpable
relief—he hadn't wanted to say it himself, especially not after asking for the
sax in the first place, but seven months had been long enough for him to realize that, while he might love Clarence Clemons's big sound, the saxophone
was simply not for him—God had not given him that particular talent.

I knew, not because Owen stopped practicing, but because he was prac-   15
ticing only during the periods Mr. Bowie had set for him: half an hour after
school four days a week, plus an hour on the weekends. Owen mastered the
scales and the notes—nothing wrong with his memory, his lungs, or his eye-
hand coordination—but we never heard him taking off, surprising himself
with something new, blissing himself out. And as soon as his practice time
was over, it was back into the case with the horn, and there it stayed until the
next lesson or practice-time. What this suggested to me was that when it came
to the sax and my son, there was never going to be any real play-time; it was
all going to be rehearsal. That's no good. If there's no joy in it, it's just no
good. It's best to go on to some other area, where the deposits of talent may
be richer and the fun quotient higher.

Talent renders the whole idea of rehearsal meaningless; when you find   16
something at which you are talented, you do it (whatever *it* is) until your fingers bleed or your eyes are ready to fall out of your head. Even when no one
is listening (or reading, or watching), every outing is a bravura performance,
because you as the creator are happy. Perhaps even ecstatic. That goes for
reading and writing as well as for playing a musical instrument, hitting a baseball, or running the four-forty. The sort of strenuous reading and writing program I advocate—four to six hours a day, every day—will not seem strenuous if you really enjoy doing these things and have an aptitude for them; in
fact, you may be following such a program already. If you feel you need permission to do all the reading and writing your little heart desires, however,
consider it hereby granted by yours truly.

The real importance of reading is that it creates an ease and intimacy   17
with the process of writing; one comes to the country of the writer with one's
papers and identification pretty much in order. Constant reading will pull
you into a place (a mind-set, if you like the phrase) where you can write

eagerly and without self-consciousness. It also offers you a constantly grow-ing knowledge of what has been done and what hasn't, what is trite and what is fresh, what works and what just lies there dying (or dead) on the page. The more you read, the less apt you are to make a fool of yourself with your pen or word processor.

◆ ◆ ◆

FIRST RESPONSES

What activity—for example, a job or a hobby—makes you feel joyful? Does that feeling affect your level of commitment to the activity?

TAKING A CLOSER LOOK

Exploring *Who:* Voice and Tone

1. Make a list of all the words and phrases you can think of to describe the persona King uses in this essay, especially his attitudes toward himself, his topic, and his readers.
2. Were you surprised to hear that King is a "slow reader"? Why does he include this detail so early in his essay?
3. Reread the last four sentences in paragraph 8. What tone of voice is King using here? Was it a risky choice?
4. Why did King include the last sentence in paragraph 16? What is your response to it?

Exploring *What:* Content and Meaning

1. What was wrong with Leinster's novel? Why does King remember it so vividly?
2. Why does King include the fact that Leinster was paid "a penny a word"?
3. ■▯ *Using the Internet.* What did the good novelists teach King? Specif-ically, how did *The Grapes of Wrath* author, John Steinbeck, and the authors Bradbury, Cain, and Lovecraft influence King's career and writ-ing style? Visit http://dir.yahoo.com/arts/humanities/literature/authors/ and look for a writer you've read and enjoyed; browse the sites to gather information about influences on that writer's career. Do any of that writer's experiences seem similar to King's?

4. What does King mean when he says that "rudeness should be the second-to-least of your concerns" as a writer (para. 10)? What's the least concern?

5. What was the point of King's **anecdote** about his son? Do you agree with his point?

Exploring *Why:* Purpose

1. King states, "Reading is the creative center of a writer's life." Did he convince you of that? What was his most effective point or illustration?

2. King makes some sharp attacks on television. Closely examine his language at the end of paragraph 11 and the start of paragraph 12, and discuss what it reflects about King's purpose for writing this essay.

3. The last sentence of the essay seems both a threat and a promise. Is that an effective combination? Why?

Exploring *How:* Style and Strategy

1. Examine and discuss the variation in sentence types in paragraph 2.

2. King uses a number of **analogies** and **metaphors** in the essay, such as suggesting that reading *Asteroid Miners* was the equivalent of getting "a smallpox vaccination" (para. 3). Identify as many of these comparisons as you can, and discuss what each means and what each contributes to the success of the essay.

3. What purpose does paragraph 7 serve?

IDEAS FOR WRITING CAUSE AND EFFECT

1. Write an essay tracing the most significant influences on your decision to pursue your current career path. Consider narrating specific experiences that illustrate these influences.

2. Write an essay identifying the sources of your greatest strengths and challenges as a writer. Consider specific classes you took, assignments you wrote, and the teachers you had.

3. What experiences—with teachers, librarians, family, friends—shaped the kind of reader you are and the kind of reading you most enjoy?

◆ ◆ ◆ PREPARING TO READ

Were you ever embarrassed by your family, by having to be seen with them, by something one of them did? What caused those feelings at the time? How do you feel about the experience now?

◆ ◆ ◆

The Myth of the Latin Woman: I Just Met a Girl Named Maria

JUDITH ORTIZ COFER

Judith Ortiz Cofer was born in Puerto Rico in 1952 but has lived most of her life in the United States. Most of her books, including *Silent Dancing: A Partial Remembrance of a Puerto Rican Childhood* (1990) and *The Year of Our Revolution: Selected and New Stories and Poems* (1998), mix poetry, folktales, and stories to bring to life her native Puerto Rico and the U.S. barrios, or neighborhoods, to which many Puerto Ricans emigrate. In *The Latin Deli* (1993), Cofer wrote, "I was born a white girl in Puerto Rico but became a brown girl when I came to live in the United States." The challenge of living between two cultures is the focus of her essay "The Myth of the Latin Woman."

On a bus trip to London from Oxford University where I was earning   1
some graduate credits one summer, a young man, obviously fresh from a pub, spotted me and as if struck by inspiration went down on his knees in the aisle. With both hands over this heart he broke into an Irish tenor's rendition of "Maria" from *West Side Story*. My politely amused fellow passengers gave his lovely voice the round of gentle applause it deserved. Though I was not quite as amused, I managed my version of an English smile: no show of teeth, no extreme contortions of the facial muscles—I was at this time of my life practicing reserve and cool. Oh, that British control, how I coveted it. But Maria had followed me to London, reminding me of a prime fact of my life: you can leave the Island, master the English language, and travel as far as you can, but if you are a Latina, especially one like me who so obviously belongs to Rita Moreno's gene pool, the Island travels with you.

This is sometimes a very good thing—it may win you that extra minute   2
of someone's attention. But with some people, the same things can make *you* an island—not so much a tropical paradise as an Alcatraz, a place nobody

wants to visit. As a Puerto Rican girl growing up in the United States and wanting like most children to "belong," I resented the stereotype that my Hispanic appearance called forth from many people I met.

Our family lived in a large urban center in New Jersey during the six- 3
ties, where life was designed as a microcosm of my parent's casas on the is-
land. We spoke in Spanish, we ate Puerto Rican food bought at the bodega, and we practiced strict Catholicism complete with Saturday confession and Sunday mass at a church where our parents were accommodated into a one-hour Spanish mass slot, performed by a Chinese priest trained as a mission-ary for Latin America.

As a girl I was kept under strict surveillance, since virtue and modesty 4
were, by cultural equation, the same as family honor. As a teenager I was in-structed on how to behave as a proper señorita. But it was a conflicting mes-sage girls got, since the Puerto Rican mothers also encouraged their daugh-ters to look and act like women and to dress in clothes our Anglo friends and their mothers found too "mature" for our age. It was, and is, cultural, yet I often felt humiliated when I appeared at an American friend's party wear-ing a dress more suitable to a semiformal than to a playroom birthday cele-bration. At Puerto Rican festivities, neither the music nor the colors we wore could be too loud. I still experience a vague sense of letdown when I'm in-vited to a "party" and it turns out to be a marathon conversation in hushed tones rather than a fiesta with salsa, laughter, and dancing—the kind of cel-ebration I remember from my childhood.

I remember Career Day in our high school, when teachers told us to 5
come dressed as if for a job interview. It quickly became obvious that to the barrio girls, "dressing up" sometimes meant wearing ornate jewelry and cloth-ing that would be more appropriate (by mainstream standards) for the com-pany Christmas party than as daily office attire. That morning I had agonized in front of my closet, trying to figure out what a "career girl" would wear be-cause, essentially, except for Marlo Thomas on TV, I had no models on which to base my decision. I knew how to dress for school: at the Catholic school I attended we all wore uniforms; I knew how to dress for Sunday mass, and knew what dresses to wear for parties at my relatives' homes. Though I do not recall the precise details of my Career Day outfit, it must have been a com-posite of the above choices. But I remember a comment my friend (an Italian-American) made in later years that coalesced my impressions of that day. She said that at the business school she was attending the Puerto Rican girls always stood out for wearing "everything at once." She meant, of course, too much jewelry, too many accessories. On that day at school, we were sim-ply made the negative models by the nuns who were themselves not credi-ble fashion experts to any of us. But it was painfully obvious to me that to the others, in their tailored skirts and silk blouses, we must have seemed "hope-less" and "vulgar." Though I now know that most adolescents feel out of step

much of the time, I also know that for the Puerto Rican girls of my generation that sense was intensified. The way our teachers and classmates looked at us that day in school was just a taste of the culture clash that awaited us in the real world, where prospective employers and men on the street would often misinterpret our tight skirts and jingling bracelets as a come-on.

Mixed cultural signals have perpetuated certain stereotypes—for example, that of the Hispanic woman as the "Hot Tamale" or sexual firebrand. It is a one-dimensional view that the media have found easy to promote. In their special vocabulary, advertisers have designated not only the foods but also the women of Latin America. From conversations in my house I recall hearing about the harassment that Puerto Rican women endured in factories where the "boss men" talked to them as if sexual innuendo was all they understood and, worse, often gave them the choice of submitting to advances or being fired. 6

It is custom, however, not chromosomes, that leads us to choose scarlet over pale pink. As young girls, we were influenced in our decisions about clothes and color by the women—older sisters and mothers—who had grown up on a tropical island where the natural environment was a riot of primary colors, where showing your skin was one way to keep cool as well as to look sexy. Most important of all, on the island, women perhaps felt freer to dress and move more provocatively, since, in most cases, they were protected by the traditions, mores, and laws of a Spanish/Catholic system of morality and machismo whose main rule was: *You may look at my sister, but if you touch her I will kill you.* The extended family and church structure could provide a young woman with a circle of safety in her small pueblo on the island; if a man "wronged" a girl, everyone would close in to save her family honor. 7

This is what I have gleaned from my discussions as an adult with older Puerto Rican women. They have told me about dressing in their best party clothes on Saturday nights and going to the town's plaza to promenade with their girlfriends in front of the boys they liked. The males were thus given an opportunity to admire the women and to express their admiration in the form of *piropos:* erotically charged street poems they composed on the spot. I have been subjected to a few piropos while visiting the island, and they can be outrageous, although custom dictates that they must never cross into obscenity. This ritual, as I understand it, also entails a show of studied indifference on the woman's part; if she is "decent," she must not acknowledge the man's impassioned words. So I do understand how things can be lost in translation. When a Puerto Rican girl dressed in her idea of what is attractive meets a man from the mainstream culture who has been trained to react to certain types of clothing as a sexual signal, a clash is likely to take place. The line I first heard based on the aspect of the myth happened when the boy who took me to my first formal dance leaned over to plant a sloppy over-eager kiss painfully on my mouth, and when I didn't respond with sufficient 8 passion said in a resentful tone: "I thought you Latin girls were supposed to mature early"—my first instance of being thought of as a fruit or vegetable— I was supposed to *ripen,* not just grow into womanhood like other girls.

It is surprising to some of my professional friends that some people, 9 including those who should know better, still put others "in their place." Though rarer, these incidents are still commonplace in my life. It happened to me most recently during a stay at a very classy metropolitan hotel favored by young professional couples for their weddings. Late one evening after the theater, as I walked toward my room with my new colleague (a woman with whom I was coordinating an arts program), a middle-aged man in a tuxedo, a young girl in satin and lace on his arm, stepped directly into our path. With his champagne glass extended toward me, he exclaimed, "Evita!"

Our way blocked, my companion and I listened as the man half-recited, 10 half-bellowed "Don't Cry for Me, Argentina." When he finished, the young girl said: "How about a round of applause for my daddy?" We complied hoping this would bring the silly spectacle to a close. I was becoming aware that our little group was attracting the attention of the other guests. "Daddy" must have perceived this too, and he once more barred the way as we tried to walk past him. He began to shout-sing a ditty to the tune of "La Bamba"— except the lyrics were about a girl named Maria whose exploits all rhymed with her name and gonorrhea. The girl kept saying "Oh, Daddy" and looking at me with pleading eyes. She wanted me to laugh along with the others. My companion and I stood silently waiting for the man to end his offensive song. When he finished, I looked not at him but at his daughter. I advised her calmly never to ask her father what he had done in the army. Then I walked between them and to my room. My friend complimented me on my cool handling of the situation. I confessed to her that I really had wanted to push the jerk into the swimming pool. I knew this same man—probably a corporate executive, well educated, even worldly by most standards—would not have been likely to regale a white woman with a dirty song in public. He would perhaps have checked his impulse by assuming that she could be somebody's wife or mother, or at least *somebody* who might take offense. But to him, I was just an Evita or a Maria: merely a character in his cartoon-populated universe.

Because of my education and my proficiency with the English language, 11 I have acquired many mechanisms for dealing with the anger I experience. This was not true for my parents, nor is it true for the many Latin women working at menial jobs who must put up with stereotypes about our ethnic group such as "They make good domestics." This is another facet of the myth of the Latin woman in the United States. Its origin is simple to deduce. Work as domestics, waitressing, and factory jobs are all that's available to women with little English and few skills. The myth of the Hispanic menial has been sustained by the same media phenomenon that made "Mammy" from *Gone with the Wind* America's idea of the black woman for generations; Maria, the housemaid or counter girl, is now indelibly etched into the national psyche. The big and the little screens have presented us with the picture of the funny Hispanic maid, mispronouncing words and cooking up a spicy storm in a shiny California kitchen.

This media-engendered image of the Latina in the United States has   12
been documented by feminist Hispanic scholars, who claim that such portrayals are partially responsible for the denial of opportunities for upward mobility among Latinas in the professions. I have a Chicana friend working on a Ph.D. in philosophy at a major university. She says her doctor still shakes his head in puzzled amazement at all the "big words" she uses. Since I do not wear my diplomas around my neck for all to see, I too have on occasion been sent to that "kitchen," where some think I obviously belong.

One such incident that has stayed with me, though I recognize it as a   13
minor offense, happened on the day of my first public poetry reading. It took place in Miami in a boat-restaurant where we were having lunch before the event. I was nervous and excited as I walked in with my notebook in my hand. An older woman motioned me to her table. Thinking (foolish me) that she wanted me to autograph a copy of my brand new slender volume of verse, I went over. She ordered a cup of coffee from me, assuming that I was the waitress. Easy enough to mistake my poems for menus, I suppose. I know that it wasn't an intentional act of cruelty, yet of all the good things that happened that day, I remember that scene most clearly, because it reminded me of what I had to overcome before anyone would take me seriously. In retrospect I understand that my anger gave my reading fire, that I have almost always taken doubts in my abilities as a challenge—and that the result is, most times, a feeling of satisfaction at having won a convert, when I see the cold, appraising eyes warm to my words, the body language change, the smile that indicates that I have opened some avenue for communication. That day I read to that woman and her lowered eyes told me that she was embarrassed at her little *faux pas,* and when I willed her to look up at me, it was my victory, and she graciously allowed me to punish her with my full attention. We shook hands at the end of the reading, and I never saw her again. She has probably forgotten the whole thing but maybe not.

Yet I am one of the lucky ones. My parents made it possible for me to   14
acquire a stronger footing in the mainstream culture by giving me the chance at an education. And books and art have saved me from the harsher forms of ethnic and racial prejudice that many of my Hispanic *compañeras* have had to endure. I travel a lot around the United States, reading from my books of poetry and my novel, and the reception I most often receive is one of positive interest by people who want to know more about my culture. There are, however, thousands of Latinas without the privilege of an education or the

entree into society that I have. For them life is a struggle against the misconceptions perpetuated by the myth of the Latina as whore, domestic, or criminal. We cannot change this by legislating the way people look at us. The transformation, as I see it, has to occur at a much more individual level. My personal goal in my public life is to try to replace the old pervasive stereotypes and myths about Latinas with a much more interesting set of realities. Every time I give a reading, I hope the stories I tell, the dreams and fears I examine in my work, can achieve some universal truth which will get my audience past the particulars of my skin color, my accent, or my clothes.

I once wrote a poem in which I called us Latinas "God's brown   15 daughters." This poem is really a prayer of sorts, offered upward, but also, through the human-to-human channel of art, outward. It is a prayer for communication, and for respect. In it, Latin women pray "in Spanish to an Anglo God / with a Jewish heritage," and they are "fervently hoping / that if not omnipotent, / at least He be bilingual."

◆ ◆ ◆

FIRST RESPONSES

Are there myths—about farm people, red-haired people, or tall people, for example—that have led to misunderstandings about you?

TAKING A CLOSER LOOK

Exploring *Who:* Voice and Tone

1. What aspect of her identity does Cofer choose to reveal in the first sentence of the essay? Why? How is this choice further explained at the end of the essay in paragraph 14?

2. The word *Daddy* is used three times in paragraph 10. How does its tone change?

3. In paragraph 11, Cofer tells us she has "acquired many mechanisms for dealing with the anger" in her life. How many ways of coping can you find in this essay?

4. ▣ *Using the Internet.* Visit the official Web site of MANA: The National Latina Organization (www.hermana.org/) to learn more about issues of importance to Hispanic American women. How does Cofer's essay support the need for the types of projects undertaken by this group?

Exploring *What:* Content and Meaning

1. Have you seen advertisements that support Cofer's claims about the "Hot Tamale" stereotype? What other images of Latina women have you noticed on television?
2. What caused the problems Cofer and her friends faced on Career Day? Can you remember any similar confusions about appropriate behavior in a new situation?
3. Why are Latina women "freer to dress and move more provocatively" in Puerto Rico? How does Cofer explain the reactions of American men to this behavior?
4. What "myth of the Latin woman" led to Cofer's traumatic experience at her "first formal dance"? Can you name other kinds of myths that create problems for young men and women on such occasions?

Exploring *Why:* Purpose

1. What does Cofer mean when she says, "It is custom, however, not chromosomes, that leads us to choose scarlet over pale pink," in paragraph 7?
2. Both of the public male assaults on Cofer result in part from the man's experience with popular culture: *West Side Story, Evita, La Bamba.* What was responsible for the experience with the woman at the poetry reading? Can you speculate about the gender differences revealed here?
3. Why does Cofer speak to the daughter, not the father, at the conclusion of the hotel experience?
4. How does Cofer expand her topic by including a reference to "Mammy" from *Gone with the Wind*?
5. Did you identify with Cofer or with the woman at the poetry reading? Why? How does the way Cofer handled her anger about being mistaken for a waitress connect to her purpose for writing this essay?

Exploring *How:* Style and Strategy

1. Cofer cites several myths as the cause for mainstream American responses to Latina women. How many additional strategies of development does she use to support this thesis?
2. How did you respond to the opening anecdote about the young British singer? Would you have applauded? Why did Cofer begin with this story?

3. How did Cofer's "island" **metaphor** in paragraph 2 prepare you for the rest of her essay?

4. Why do the first five paragraphs focus on Cofer's personal experiences? How does the decision to take this approach relate to the author's analysis of her readers?

IDEAS FOR WRITING CAUSE AND EFFECT

1. One of Cofer's reactions to stereotypical thinking was to take any "doubts in my abilities as a challenge." Write an essay about a negative experience you turned into a positive one. What in your past enabled you to turn bad into good?

2. Write an essay based on your responses to the second part of question 2 under "Exploring *What*" concerning confusion about appropriate behavior in a new situation. Consider what caused your confusion as well as the effects the experience had on you.

3. Have you ever hidden something about yourself because you feared the reactions you might get? Write an essay explaining what caused your fears and the effects of your decision not to reveal the truth.

◆ ◆ ◆

◆ FURTHER IDEAS FOR USING CAUSE AND EFFECT

1. What are the major challenges being experienced by your generation? Select one that you feel strongly about, and write an essay explaining what created the challenge and what immediate and indirect effects it is having on you and the people around you.

2. Discuss the effects of television portrayals of some group (men, women, parents, police officers, teenagers, doctors, etc.).

3. ■ *Using the Internet.* Does playing video games shape values and personality? Is it an addiction, or does it teach meaningful lessons and important skills? Brainstorm your own thinking on the topic, and then gather other ideas by using a search engine to browse sites on the Internet—those where video games are advertised and played as well as those where other points of view might be provided, such as sites created by parent-teacher associations.

4. COLLABORATIVE WRITING. With a small group of classmates, discuss the following questions about your daily life: Why do you dress the way you do, eat the foods you do, and hope to live in a certain kind of neighborhood or house? What values do these habits or goals reflect? Next choose one or two of the values you identified during the discussion. Write an essay connecting the habits to the values and explaining the influences that created them.

5. COMBINING STRATEGIES. Write an essay narrating a major change in your life, such as a move to a new place, a friendship with someone very different from you, or a marriage. Concentrate on how well or ill prepared you were to make the change as well as how the change affected your life.

6. COMBINING STRATEGIES. Is there a special relationship you had with someone—a parent, a child, an aunt, a teacher, a coach—that significantly affected the person you are? Write an essay about the development of that effect by describing or narrating important interactions you had with this person.

Strategies for Influencing Opinion

Argument

◆ ◆ ◆ ◆ ◆

> **Argumentation seeks to persuade readers to think and act in agreement with the writer's opinion.**
>
> ◆ Arguments are organized according to the nature of the writer's material and purpose: point-by-point *for,* point-by-point *against,* point-by-point *refutation,* or *problem-solution.*
>
> ◆ Writers use strategies of all kinds to develop their points of argument: cause and effect, comparison and contrast, logical reasoning, description, narration, definition, and classification.

Persuasion is one of the most powerful uses of the written word. Think of a time when you chose to express yourself in a letter rather than having a conversation. We usually choose to express ourselves in writing when we want a chance to present our side of an issue carefully, with plenty of thought and control over what we have to say, with no unplanned interruptions from the other side. We also have a record of our thinking and proof of what we said, which is a major improvement over our slips of memory in recalling conversations, especially heated ones.

While these letters usually have an audience of one, the written **arguments** you compose in college and thereafter have a larger readership. The purpose is the same: to persuade others to consider your opinion on an issue and perhaps take some action. Cookbook author Laurel Robertson used her forum to convince readers that regular breadbaking is worth the trouble. Student writer Sean Stangland, spurred to thoughts about human values by reading Robertson's essay, defended the source of his own ethical development—films. Notice that in neither case does the everyday connotation of *argument* apply: a negative, confrontational, emotional tone is absent from both essays.

Bake Your Bread at Home

LAUREL ROBERTSON

Laurel Robertson became famous with her first down-to-earth vegetarian cookbook, *Laurel's Kitchen,* published in 1976. Her sensible advice about vegetarian cooking and nutrition is carried in "Notes from Laurel's Kitchen," a column published in more than twenty newspapers across the country. In *The Laurel's Kitchen Bread Book* (1984), Robertson combines recipes and detailed directions with brief essays on the art and science of breadbaking. This selection is an excerpt from one of those thought-provoking essays.

Watch a four-year-old burst in the door after a long morning with his buddies, still exultant, talking nonstop, but exhausted, too, from the sustained stress of it all. Watch him fall with instinctive good sense on a pile of playdough, and pull, push, pummel and squeeze until finally all the tension has flowed out through his fingertips and he is at peace. Watch him, and wonder why on earth grownups shouldn't have access to the same very healing, very basic kind of activity. And in fact, they can. For kneading bread dough, forming it into coffee-cake wreaths or cottage loaves or long baguettes affords exactly this kind of satisfaction.

Good breadbaking is much more, though, than just a good outlet. At certain critical junctures, you really have got to block out extraneous goings-on and attend meticulously to small details. Far from being onerous, these more exacting phases of the baking process can also be the most calming—precisely because they do require such powerful concentration. And the very fact that so much of oneself is called upon, in the way of artistry and resourcefulness, makes the whole business that much more gratifying—enhances the quality of life overall.

That breadbaking—as well as gardening, spinning, beekeeping, and animal husbandry—is in fact creative and exacting is often overlooked. Instead, they are regarded as "subsistence skills"—what you have to deal with to scratch out a bare living, reeling, as you do, from the endless labor entailed. You can hardly blame our parents and grandparents for having set firmly behind them so rigorous and chancy a way of life, and for thinking a bit daft those of us who cast a rueful glance backwards. For it was with full, trusting, and grateful consent that people began to buy what they needed, use "convenience foods," and adopt a full complement of helpful household machines. Hardly a voice was raised in protest when our traditionally home-centered, small-scale system of food production gave way, little by little, to what has been called "the corporate cornucopia."

Today, though, there is good reason to question whether our present food system can be sustained—so profoundly dependent on petroleum is it, and so flagrantly wasteful of other resources as well. Good reason, too, to seek out more direct ways of meeting our food needs, and to breathe a little easier when you find them. This ease of mind is yet another source of satisfaction that comes of being a competent whole grains baker. Revival of what is, yes, a subsistence skill, means you know yourself able to turn just about any flour or grain that might come your way into something that will nourish and even delight. Knowing this, you feel that much less vulnerable to circumstance. It's a subtle change, but it goes deep.

Reinstate breadbaking as a home-based activity, and you begin to change the home, too. Once you have established a regular baking pattern and the people who live with you *know* that on, say, Tuesday evenings and Saturday mornings there will be fresh bread, and good smells, and you there, too, manifestly enjoying yourself, there begins to be more reason for *them* to be there as well. The place starts to exert its own gentle tug, a strong counterforce to the thousand-and-one pulls that would draw them out and away.

The creature comfort of a warm kitchen and people to chat with accounts only in part for this magnetic force. It's the baking itself: the artistry, the science, the occasional riddle of it. People of all ages, but particularly children, seem to draw immense satisfaction from hanging around a place where work is taken as seriously as we've come to take baking. We observed this when we first began the kitchen research that preceded *Laurel's Kitchen,* and had a chance to reaffirm it just last year, when we constructed the oven where our beloved "desem" bread is baked.

Building the oven, which extended along the top of an enormous fireplace as part of a large new kitchen, was a formidable undertaking. It drew in an architect, bricklayers, carpenters, a blacksmith, and several master bakers. It also drew in every toddler in the vicinity. At every opportunity, there they'd be, watching unblinking as each brick was laid in place and each fitting was forged. My own son was among them and for months afterward, once the oven was working he would watch twice weekly with equal fascination as the bread itself came out of the oven—loaf after round, brown loaf, sliding out on a wooden paddle we learned to call a "peel," caught in leather-gauntleted hands and then pitched onto racks to cool. Back in his room later, he would re-enact the entire sequence, molding loaves out of clay, using a spatula and my old driving gloves to unload the "oven" he'd built out of wooden blocks.

Now, at four, Ramesh proudly brings in firewood for the baking—and he's not likely to stop there. He is as crazy about the desem bread as we are, and he's well aware how much care goes into its making. To him, a kitchen is a place where unquestionably important things go on, and where everyone has a contribution to make. I'm profoundly glad he feels that way. 8

Much of what gives traditional communities their special character and form has to do with the way they go about meeting basic life needs. In the past, to get crops harvested, wheat ground, or a well dug and maintained, people had to come together in respectful cooperation, suspending for the moment any private grievances they might be nursing. Often, they even managed to get some fun out of what they were doing—enough, even, to lay some of those grievances to rest. It was in the course of carrying out all that work—the "bread labor" of which Leo Tolstoy was so enamored—that the essential values of a particular society got hammered out and then transmitted to the young people growing up and working in its midst. 9

Until quite recently, this has been true for families as well as communities. Just about everything people ate, wore, slept under, and sat on was produced at home. Everyone took part in the producing and everyone knew he or she was needed. It was in work carried out together that relationships deepened and values were handed on. Kitchens, gardens, woodshops—workshops of any sort that aren't dominated by machines too loud to talk over—are ideal places to exchange confidences as well as acquire skills. There's no more effective situation to impart "the way we do things here" than in the throes of a specific job—no better place to show by example the patience to see out a task, or the good humor and ingenuity to set things right when they go awry. 10

In today's world, the home tends not to be as productive a place as it once was. We take jobs elsewhere, earn money, buy things, and bring them home to use. If we want our families to benefit from work undertaken together, we have deliberately to set up situations where that can happen. A great many families are doing just that today, in a variety of ways. Bread-baking maybe, or a vegetable garden, the tasks assigned by age and skill. One 11 family of friends maintains a cottage-scale spinning and weaving industry using wool from their goats. The proceeds from what they sell go into a college savings fund.

Still another friend, a single mother and full-time librarian, missing the 12 fine, fresh milk of her native Scotland and feeling vaguely that something was missing in her admittedly hectic life, decided that what she and her teenaged daughter needed more than anything . . . was a cow. Skeptical friends like me have been chastened to observe that she may have been right. Having the common, and thoroughly endearing focal point of a soft-eyed Jersey cow, knowing that she's got to be milked no matter who's overslept or who has a cold, having to arrange for grain, and hay, and visits from the vet, actually has not stressed the relationship of mother and daughter to the breaking point or sent either of them into exhaustion. Rather, it seems to have compelled them to stay in closer touch than they would have otherwise, and they both find the outdoor work, the contact with the animal herself, to be a perfect restorative. Not for everyone, a cow, but it does illustrate the principle and makes a twice-weekly baking seem small potatoes by comparison!

◆ ◆ ◆

◆ ◆ ◆ *Writer's Workshop I* ◆ ◆ ◆
Responding to an Argument

Use the *Who, What, Why,* and *How* questions (see p. 3) to explore your own understanding of the ideas and writing strategies employed by Laurel Robertson in "Bake Your Bread at Home." Your instructor may ask you to record these responses in a journal, post them to an electronic bulletin board, or bring them to class to use in small group discussions.

◆ WRITING FROM READING

Student writer Sean Stangland was caught up in the idea of how "the essential values of a particular society got hammered out and then transmitted to the young people growing up and working in its midst" when he read Robertson's essay. He began to think about how knowledge, wisdom, and values had been imparted to him. He realized that this process, for him, did not come from sharing work with his family, but from his absorption in movies. Sean brainstormed a list of films that had affected him in different ways and wrote some notes about each one. These notes became the following essay.

Sean Stangland
English 101
February 2, 1999

                    The Educational Value of Film

        Picture this: The young boy pulls the drawer open,   1
looking for his favorite compact disc. He searches for
a while and finally finds it; there are a lot of CDs in
there. He reaches up to press the button marked
OPEN/CLOSE, and the CD tray shoots out with a mechanical
whir. The CD is placed carefully in the tray, and the
button is pressed again, sending the shiny disc of
music into the player. He cues up track seven, his
very favorite selection.

        The piece is called "Eine Kleine Nachtmusik,"   2
which, when translated from German, means "A Little
Night Music." It is one of Wolfgang Amadeus Mozart's
most famous pieces of music. The child has no
background in German, nor do his parents force a love
for classical music upon him. This child loves the
movies, in fact, and the CD that contains this
particular version of "Eine Kleine Nachtmusik" is the
second volume of the soundtrack of *Amadeus,* the 1984
Academy Award winning film about the famed composer.

        That kid was me. At age seven or eight, I had   3
earned an appreciation for classical music and even
had enough knowledge to tell someone what three words
in German could translate to. At this young age, I was
spellbound by Milos Forman's movie that told a tragic
story about one of the world's most heralded
composers, a child prodigy whose playful nature and
immature lifestyle led him to a young death. On the
surface, *Amadeus* appeared to be a stuffy costume
drama, something that no one but the haughtiest of
critics would want to watch. In reality, *Amadeus* is a
grand teaching tool, a work of art so wonderful that
it can open the eyes of even a seven-year-old.

        My sisters and I used to watch Forman's movie two   4
or three times a week. We marveled at the period
costumes, the grand scale of the Austrian opera

houses, and the sheer power of Mozart's music. In a time when most elementary school kids were listening to Michael Jackson and watching *Diff'rent Strokes,* the Stangland kids were absorbed in the music of a man who had died two hundred years ago. *Amadeus* is the prime example of how the movies are an educational tool, a way of conveying ideas and facts that will captivate and excite viewers everywhere.

As I got older and watched *Amadeus* more and more, 5 I took an active interest in Mozart's life. The encyclopedia had plenty of information to offer, but it also gave me a new perspective on the film. The incredible story and music of Mozart became more real, more tangible to me. I also discovered that the film's opposition between Mozart and fellow composer Antonio Salieri was pretty much an imaginative fiction on the part of the filmmakers. I learned my first lesson about "creative license."

Films based on historical fact are almost always a 6 valid teaching tool, whether the film is accurate or not. When I first saw *Braveheart,* Mel Gibson's epic about Scottish freedom fighter William Wallace, I immediately went home and looked up his name in the *World Book.* It turns out that Gibson and writer Randall Wallace took a lot of license and created most of the story off the tops of their heads. Very little is known about the real William Wallace, but Gibson's film will serve as a historical document for all. The movie is full of passion, courage, and life, even though it's all wrong. Still, the film conveyed the horror of the battlefield and the frustration that Scotland's people must have felt being under the constant rule of the English King.

Of course, some movies are dead on in their 7 historical accounts, like Milos Forman's *The People vs. Larry Flynt.* This movie about a pornographer's struggle against society and the Reverend Jerry Falwell was very accurate. The writers, Scott Alexander and Larry Karaszewski, went so far as to include the statement that Flynt's lawyer, Alan Isaacman, made to the Supreme Court--with no Hollywood alterations. The film teaches a lot about the way our country works, a lot about freedom of expression in the United States, and a fair amount about the rules of libel and obscenity.

But such films are not the only ones with value. Any movie can be of value, even something as sophomoric and silly as John Landis's *Three Amigos!*, starring Martin Short, Chevy Chase, and Steve Martin as a band of would-be heroes in Mexico. How can a film so stupid have value? Well, at one point, the villain, El Guapo (Alfonso Arau), proclaims that he has a "plethora of piñatas." "A plethora?" his sidekick asks. When El Guapo explains that "plethora" means "many," the viewer has learned a new word. Somehow, that word has stuck with me forever since the first time I saw that silly little film.   8

In fact, any time I hear an unfamiliar word in a movie, I want to find out what it means. Nothing bothers me more than not knowing what the characters are talking about in a movie. This attention to language and how it is used has benefited me today. I truly believe that I would not be a good writer were it not for my continued focus on film dialogue. I remember the way that a sentence is structured, and try to imitate that structure in my writing. Learning new words and new techniques has improved all of my scholastic abilities.   9

But most of all, films have taught me about people, about the way the world works. A great film can portray humanity at its finest, like *The Shawshank Redemption* (directed by Frank Darabont). The hope and love inside all humans have never been more powerfully conveyed than in this film about the friendship between two inmates at a Maine prison. *The Shawshank Redemption* examines how humanity, at its best, never gives up hope, never stops trying. Even in the worst of times, when life is hardest, the human spirit can go on, and I'd like to think that that's in all of us (especially in me).   10

Another such film is Steven Spielberg's *Schindler's List*, arguably the most powerful movie ever made. This story of a factory owner who defied Nazi Germany and worked tirelessly to save the lives of over a thousand   11

Jews during World War II portrays the human race at both its best and its worst. Even in the face of the most terrible event in history, Oskar Schindler (Liam Neeson) was able to conquer tyranny and save lives that would have surely been lost without his help. *Schindler's List* is more a documentary than a movie; it is an honest, well-researched account of history and humanity.

So I think that everyone should sit down and enjoy   12 a great movie with frequency. Parents should encourage their children to learn more about the people and events depicted in what they watch, and adults should never underestimate a child's ability to learn and to think. Films, like books, capture the raw emotion and experience of life and tell a story. Every story we take in, every line of dialogue we soak up, every powerful image that our eyes witness represents another memory, another lesson. The more we are exposed to, the more we will know about our world and our existence. The movies are more than a diversion, more than light entertainment; they are pieces of our lives.

◆ GETTING STARTED ON AN ARGUMENT

Because the whole point of an argument is to persuade, your starting point must be a belief, opinion, or idea that you hold strongly enough to want others to share it, and usually even to act on it. This point is your **thesis.** Your paper will be more effective if your idea is controversial, but it doesn't have to be controversial in the usual sense, like the arguments for and against gun control. Both Laurel Robertson and Sean Stangland argue for activities that few people would come to harsh words over. For each one, however, there is another side that gives the topic some dynamic tension: Robertson may be facing an audience who thinks that the time and effort involved in baking bread weekly are just not worthwhile; Sean may address readers who believe that immersing themselves (or their children) in movies is harmful or at least frivolous. Once you have decided on your main point, ask yourself, "What is the point of view on the other side?" Even if you never directly refer to the opposite point of view, the question will help you firm up your own.

One way to think of an idea for an argumentative essay is to look at your own life, the way Sean did when he read the breadbaking piece. He asked himself what had transmitted knowledge and values in his past, since it wasn't weekly breadbaking with the family. Follow yourself through a normal week as though you were viewing a documentary about yourself. Your activities each day, from the most obvious to the smallest detail, reflect your beliefs about what is important and how your values are prioritized. One of these beliefs and values is probably worth supporting in a persuasive piece of writing. For example, what goods and services do you pay for rather than making them or doing them yourself and vice versa? Why?

Sean started by making a list of films off the top of his head. Then he made notes on what he had learned from each of them. As he wrote, he remembered more titles that would support his points; for example, thinking about the made-up elements of *Amadeus* brought to mind other films that had varying levels of historical accuracy and what he learned from that. When you start out with an idea, you don't need to have all your points firmly in mind to consider it a good topic for argument. You will discover more points as you play around with the idea, both on paper and in your mind, as you go about your business. You might discuss your idea with other people, either with those who you know have a different point of view or with those who agree with you. If Sean had gotten stuck in the prewriting phase, he could have talked with his sisters, who obviously shared his love of movies, or his parents, who must have had their own reasons for letting their children become entranced by the silver screen.

◆ ORGANIZING AN ARGUMENT

Most arguments, no matter what the topic is, involve one or more points, subarguments that build up to prove the main idea. When you scribble down your ideas on your subject as they come into your mind, as you talk to other people, and as you do research, the ideas begin to congregate in groups that belong together logically. On your notes, use arrows and lassos to show which jottings seem to hang together. Sometimes you need to take a new piece of paper to reorganize your notes in a visibly sensible form. Laurel Robertson probably sat down while her bread was rising and listed all the benefits she could think of for baking your own bread. As she wrote, she probably noticed two clusters of ideas: one about how the activity benefits an individual and another about how it benefits a household or family. She used this **clustering** as a basis for organization. The micro to macro structure—from small to large concerns—is a common way to structure ideas. And in fact, the continuation of Robertson's chapter, which we do not print here, takes up the political implications of domestic self-sufficiency.

Within each of the two clusters, individual and family, Robertson still had to decide an order for her subarguments. This part of her organization is more subtle, but if you look closely, you can see that in both sections she works from fairly concrete points to larger, more abstract ideas:

INDIVIDUAL BENEFITS

Concrete: tension release of
   pounding dough
Abstract: lack of dependence on
   "the corporate cornucopia"

FAMILY BENEFITS

Concrete: human attraction of
   a warm, busy kitchen
Abstract: transmittal of values

You too can look at your notes and see whether you can organize them along some range, such as small to big, concrete to abstract, trivial to important, or personal to global.

You will see the point-by-point organization that you see in Robertson's piece in other forms within this chapter. For example, while Robertson writes a series of points *for* a social activity, Jeanne Heaton provides a series of points *against* another one ("Tuning in Trouble"). Edward Koch ("Death and Justice") and Lindsy Van Gelder ("Marriage as a Restricted Club") define their points by envisioning what people on the other side would say and by talking back to them, organizing according to counterargument or **refutation.** Finally, Sue Ferguson ("The Wired Teen") and Jonathan Alter ("The Death Penalty on Trial") develop points on *both* sides of their issues to explain the pros and cons of a controversial topic; they then propose points of remedy, in a **problem-solution** structure. These four approaches constitute the primary ways to organize an argument essay:

- ◆ point-by-point *for*
- ◆ point-by-point *against*
- ◆ point-by-point *refutation*
- ◆ *problem-solution*

The student writer, Sean Stangland, also uses a point-by-point organization to defend movies as teaching tools. His structure, however, proceeds film by film rather than benefit by benefit. An outline of his essay would include the headings *Amadeus, Braveheart, The People vs. Larry Flynt, Three Amigos!, The Shawshank Redemption,* and *Schindler's List.* Under each heading, he discusses the film's educational role in his life. This structure gives the essay a loose, conversational feel.

◆ DEVELOPING AN ARGUMENT

To be convincing, each point within your argument needs to be developed. Laurel Robertson has some complex and abstract ideas, which she usually develops in paragraphs of around 150 words, mostly following **cause-and-effect** reasoning. Look at paragraph 3, for example. The point is that breadbaking, properly done, is not just a physical outlet for tension. After making this claim, Robertson anticipates the reader's question, "Why?" Well, pounding out the dough, which she describes as the physical release in paragraph 2, is not all there is. Several aspects of the process require mental focus and concentration, which calm by blocking out "extraneous goings-on." The cause-and-effect reasoning is that concentration leads to calm. The next **development** of the topic is also cause and effect: putting a great deal of oneself into a project leads to gratification, which leads to enhanced quality of life. Most readers can follow these lines of reasoning and agree. Robertson assumes knowledge of breadbaking on the part of her readers. Otherwise, she would have to provide specific details about which parts of baking require concentration and artistry.

Sean Stangland, on the other hand, does not assume that his readers have seen the films he discusses. Therefore, in his development he needs to give the relevant details and show how they contributed to his education. Each film is described briefly; the inclusion of writers' and directors' names helps establish Sean's credibility as a serious film fan. The main development tactic he uses is **exemplification,** with his own learning experiences from each film serving as arguments. By analogy, readers are encouraged to believe that all children would gather knowledge about history, creative license, public affairs, language, and human values from watching movies.

◆ OPENING AND CLOSING AN ARGUMENT

Both pieces we are analyzing here open with a *scene* to place the topic in a context. Robertson puts us in the kitchen with a group of enthusiasts; Sean opens with a peek at a seven-year-old choosing his favorite CD, unexpectedly a classical composition by Mozart. These openings give the readers immediate visual images. One of our colleagues in composition says, "The first sentence should put a picture in the reader's mind." These openings do so. Robertson moves easily to her thesis in the next paragraph: "the very fact that so much of oneself is called upon, in the way of artistry and resourcefulness, makes the whole business that much more gratifying—enhances the quality of life overall." Sean develops his opening scene fully before coming to his thesis statement in paragraph 4: "The movies are an educational tool, a way of conveying ideas and facts that will captivate and excite viewers everywhere." He can get away with this delayed thesis because his first example is the "prime example" and begins to develop the argument in a clear direction before the thesis is stated.

Robertson closes her argument similarly, with a "prime example." Her conclusion takes a step back from the activity of breadbaking to emphasize a broader point: the restorative nature of home production. In the same way, many experienced writers use the conclusion to suggest the larger implications or applications of the thesis. Sean's conclusion is much more traditional. He restates the main point and touches upon each of his arguments, in a summary. He also includes a conventional *call to action* by encouraging everyone to "sit down and enjoy a great movie with frequency."

◆ USING THE MODEL

Laurel Robertson and Sean Stangland both suggest ways of passing along knowledge and values that most people don't usually consider when they think about education. The fact that the two writers chose topics so remote from each other is proof that following a model does not result in a cookie-cutter similarity. It's hard to imagine Robertson tuning in *Die Hard* while waiting for her dough to rise, and Sean probably enjoys without guilt his mass-produced Ding-Dongs during a movie. Yet Sean's chain of thought began when he considered how he received knowledge and values in his own life, a consideration that came from reading "Bake Your Bread at Home." Ask yourself where, outside of school, your own education took place. Was there an unusual or unexpected site of learning? Could you encourage others to think of this site as educational, as an essay topic?

◆ ◆ ◆ *Writer's Workshop II* ◆ ◆ ◆
Analyzing an Argument

Working individually or with a group of classmates, read through Sean Stangland's essay "The Educational Value of Film," and respond to the following questions.

1. Imagine how the essay would be different if Sean had organized it benefit by benefit instead of film by film. Make a scratch outline of how the essay would look. Would any changes in order be called for? For example, how would he arrange the topics along some range like small to large, minor to major, or concrete to abstract? Would the benefit-by-benefit structure be an improvement?

2. Did the title of the essay catch your interest? Did it capture the tone of the piece? Make up a title that would be more effective.

3. Were there enough examples to convince you of the main point? Did the essay make you think about examples from your own movie-watching experience? What tactics other than exemplification could you use to develop the thesis that films are learning tools? Review the previous chapter titles in this book to get ideas.

4. Sean's essay does not deal with arguments on the other side; that is, it does not include *refutation*. What are some points against frequent movie watching or against films as educational? If you were Sean, how would you argue back against these points? Where in the essay would you put your refutation?

◆ ◆ ◆ Checklist for Reading and Writing ◆ ◆ ◆ Argument Essays

1. Is the main point of the argument clear? Where is it stated? How directly is it stated?

2. Is there an identifiable plan of organization: point-by-point *for,* point-by-point *against,* or point-by-point *refutation*? Does the essay instead establish a problem and then argue for a solution (*problem-solution* structure)?

3. Is the argument convincing? What contributes to either agreement or disagreement with the author's main point? Have any important arguments been omitted? Have serious counterarguments been refuted?

4. What strategies were used to develop the points? What other strategies could be used?

5. Who is the intended audience for this essay? Are the tone and approach appropriate for this audience?

◆ ◆ ◆ PREPARING TO READ

Many single people complain that the social world in the United States seems to be designed for couples. Have you ever noticed this arrangement? As you go about your business for the next couple of days, pay attention to places where coupledom seems to be the norm. Make lists of places where it seems all right to be alone or in same-sex pairs or groups and where it seems customary to be in traditional male-female couples.

◆ ◆ ◆

Marriage as a Restricted Club

LINDSY VAN GELDER

Lindsy Van Gelder (born 1944) is an old hand at writing about controversial topics for various audiences: she has contributed to *Esquire, Rolling Stone,* the *Village Voice, Redbook,* and *Ms.,* where the following selection originally appeared. The daughter of a railroad freight agent and a receptionist, Van Gelder has worked as a UPI reporter, a TV news commentator, and a professor of journalism. In 1996, she published *The Girls Next Door,* and she has recently written for several online publications, including *Salon.com.* Her articles and essays often make use of her personal experience to illuminate larger public issues.

Several years ago, I stopped going to weddings. In fact, I no longer cel- 1
ebrate the wedding anniversaries or engagements of friends, relatives, or anyone else, although I might wish them lifelong joy in their relationships. My explanation is that the next wedding I attend will be my own—to the woman I've loved and lived with for nearly six years.

Although I've been legally married to a man myself (and come close to 2
marrying two others), I've come, in these last six years with Pamela, to see heterosexual marriage as very much a restricted club. (Nor is this likely to change in the near future, if one can judge by the recent clobbering of what was actually a rather tame proposal to recognize "domestic partnerships" in San Francisco.) Regardless of the *reason* people marry—whether to save on real estate taxes or qualify for married student housing or simply to express love— lesbians and gay men can't obtain the same results should they desire to do so. It seems apparent to me that few friends of Pamela's and mine would even join a club that excluded blacks, Jews, or women, much less assume that

they could expect their black, Jewish, or female friends to toast their new status with champagne. But probably no other stand of principle we've ever made in our lives has been so misunderstood, or caused so much bad feeling on both sides.

Several people have reacted with surprise to our views, it never having occurred to them that gay people can't legally marry. (Why on earth did they think that none of us had bothered?) The most common reaction, however, is acute embarrassment, followed by a denial of our main point—that the about-to-be-wed person is embarking on a privileged status. (One friend of Pamela's insisted that lesbians are "lucky" not to have to agonize over whether or not to get married.) So wrapped in gauze is the institution of marriage, so ingrained the expectation that brides and grooms can enjoy the world's delighted approval, that it's hard for me not to feel put on the defensive for being so mean-spirited, eccentric, and/or politically rigid as to boycott such a happy event.

Another question we've fielded more than once (usually from our most radical friends, both gay and straight) is why we'd want to get married in the first place. In fact, I have mixed feelings about registering my personal life with the state, but—and this seems to me to be the essence of radical politics—I'd prefer to be the one making the choice. And while feminists in recent years have rightly focused on puncturing the Schlaflyite myth of the legally protected homemaker, it's also true that marriage does confer some very real dollars-and-cents benefits. One example of inequity is our inability to file joint tax returns, although many couples, both gay and straight, go through periods when one partner in the relationship is unemployed or makes considerably less money than the other. At one time in our relationship, Pamela—who is a musician—was between bands and earning next to nothing. I was making a little over $37,000 a year as a newspaper reporter, a salary that put me in the 42 percent tax bracket—about $300 a week taken out of my paycheck. If we had been married, we could have filed a joint tax return and each paid taxes on half my salary, in the 25 or 30 percent bracket. The difference would have been nearly $100 a week in our pockets.

Around the same time, Pamela suffered a months'-long illness which would have been covered by my health insurance if she were my spouse. We were luckier than many; we could afford it. But on top of the worry and expense involved (and despite the fact that intellectually we believe in the ideal of free medical care for everyone), we found it almost impossible to avoid internalizing a sense of personal failure—the knowledge that *because of who we are, we can't take care of each other.* I've heard of other gay people whose lovers were deported because they couldn't marry them and enable them to become citizens; still others who were barred from intensive-care units where their lovers lay stricken because they weren't "immediate family."

I would never begrudge a straight friend who got married to save a   6
lover from deportation or staggering medical bills, but the truth is that I no
longer sympathize with most of the less tangible justifications. This includes
the oft-heard "for the sake of the children" argument, since (like many gay
people, especially women) I *have* children, and I resent the implication that
some families are more "legitimate" than others. (It's important to safeguard
one's children's rights to their father's property, but a legal contract will do
the same thing as marriage.)

But the single most painful and infuriating rationale for marriage, as far   7
as I'm concerned, is the one that goes: "We wanted to stand up and show the
world that we've made a *genuine* commitment." When one is gay, such sentiments are labeled "flaunting." My lover and I almost never find ourselves
in public settings outside the gay ghetto where we are (a) perceived to be a
couple at all (people constantly ask us if we're sisters, although we look nothing like each other), and (b) valued as such. Usually we're forced to choose
between being invisible and being despised. "Making a genuine commitment" in this milieu is like walking a highwire without a net—with most of
the audience not even watching and a fair segment rooting for you to fall. A
disproportionate number of gay couples do.

I think it's difficult for even my closest, most feminist straight women   8
friends to empathize with the intensity of my desire to be recognized as
Pamela's partner. (In fact, it may be harder for feminists to understand than
for others; I know that when I was straight, I often resented being viewed as
one half of a couple. My struggle was for an independent identity, not the
cojoined one I now crave.) But we are simply not considered *authentic,* and
the reminders are constant. Recently at a party, a man I'd known for years
spied me across the room and came over to me, arms outstretched, big happy-
to-see-you grin on his face. Pamela had a gig that night and wasn't at the
party; my friend's wife was there but in another room, and I hadn't seen her
yet. "How's M———?" I asked the man. "Oh, she's fine," he replied, continuing to smile pleasantly. "Are you and Pam still together?"

Our sex life itself is against the law in many states, of course, and like   9
all lesbians and gay men, we are without many other rights, both large and
small. (In Virginia, for instance, it's technically against the law for us to buy
liquor.) But as a gay couple, we are also most likely to be labeled and dis-
criminated against in those very settings that, for most heterosexual Americans, constitute the most relaxed and personal parts of life. Virtually every tiny
public act of togetherness—from holding hands on the street to renting a
hotel room to dancing—requires us constantly to risk humiliation (I think,
for example, of the two California women who were recently thrown out of
a restaurant that had special romantic tables for couples), sexual harassment
(it's astonishing how many men can't resist coming on to a lesbian couple),

and even physical assault. A great deal of energy goes into just expecting possible trouble. It's a process which, after six years, has become second nature for me—but occasionally, when I'm in Provincetown or someplace else with a large lesbian population, I experience the *absence* of it as a feeling of virtual weightlessness.

What does all this have to do with my friends' weddings? Obviously, I   10
can't expect my friends to live my life. But I do think that lines are being drawn in this "profamily" Reagan era, and I have no choice about what side I'm placed on. My straight friends do, and at the very least, I expect them to acknowledge that. I certainly expect them to understand why I don't want to be among the rice-throwers and well-wishers at their weddings; beyond that, I would hope that they would commit themselves to fighting for my rights— preferably in personally visible ways, like marching in gay pride parades. But I also wish they wouldn't get married, period. And if that sounds hard-nosed, I hope I'm only proving my point—that not being able to marry isn't a minor issue.

Not that my life would likely be changed as the result of any individ-   11
ual straight person's symbolic refusal to marry. (Nor, for that matter, do all gay couples want to be wed.) But it's a political reality that heterosexual live-together couples are among our best tactical allies. The movement to repeal state sodomy laws has profited from the desire of straight people to keep the government out of *their* bedrooms. Similarly, it was a heterosexual New York woman who went to court several years ago to fight her landlord's demand that she either marry her live-in boyfriend or face eviction for violating a lease clause prohibiting "unrelated" tenants—and whose struggle led to the recent passage of a state rent law that had ramifications for thousands of gay couples, including Pamela and me.

The right wing has seized on "homosexual marriage" as its bottom-line   12
scare phrase in much the same way that "Would you want your sister to marry one?" was brandished twenty-five years ago. *They* see marriage as their turf. And so when I see feminists crossing into that territory of respectability and "sinlessness," I feel my buffer zone slipping away. I feel as though my friends are taking off their armbands, leaving me exposed.

◆ ◆ ◆

FIRST RESPONSES

Do you have any strong opinions that your close friends do not share? Do you identify with Van Gelder's reactions to such a disagreement? Are there ever times that your strong opinions set you apart in public, such as asking that your companions eat at a restaurant that serves some vegetarian choices or refusing to go into a strip club for a drink? What is this experience like? What is it like to be in the group that does not hold a strong opinion when one individual among you does?

TAKING A CLOSER LOOK

Exploring *Who:* Voice and Tone

1. What personal experiences does Van Gelder draw on in her argument? How might the essay be different if she did not identify herself as a lesbian in paragraph 1?
2. How do you think that Van Gelder's straight friends reacted when they read this essay? Did Van Gelder do anything to help them accept her arguments?
3. Was the essay successful in changing your attitude toward heterosexual marriage? Will it have any repercussions in your behavior? Why or why not?
4. Do you think you were able to read the essay objectively, or did your preconceived ideas lead you to agree or disagree from the beginning?

Exploring *What:* Content and Meaning

1. What benefits does marriage confer on heterosexual couples?
2. What social, psychological, and legal drawbacks does Van Gelder find in being in a lesbian couple?
3. What image is Van Gelder trying *not* to project in her argument? Why does she want to avoid this image?
4. Van Gelder refers to the question, "Would you want your sister to marry one?" from "twenty-five years ago." What does she mean? What is the question's relationship to the topic of this essay?
5. What are the "armbands" that the marrying friends seem to be taking off (para. 12)?

Exploring *Why:* Purpose

1. ▇▊ *Using the Internet.* If this essay had a call to action, what would it be? Could more than one call to action be possible? Use the Internet to explore the topic of same-sex marriage. Try to find out what actions, if any, are being taken by advocates and opponents.
2. What are Van Gelder's reasons for wanting to marry? Which reason is most compelling for her? Which reason is most convincing to you?

3. This essay appeared in *Ms.* magazine. If Van Gelder had wanted to write an essay with the same purpose for *Esquire, Newsweek,* or *USA Today,* how might it be different?

Exploring *How:* Style and Strategy

1. What is the **analogy** used to support the thesis in paragraph 2? What similarity is the basis of the analogy?
2. "Several years ago, I stopped going to weddings." How does this short opening sentence serve to grab your attention?
3. Find examples of the following development techniques: statistics, examples, comparison/contrast, and logical reasoning. Which technique is used most often in the essay?
4. The writer uses "I" and "we" and contractions (*can't, it's, we've*), usually signs of informality. Why do you think she chose this informal level? In what situation do you think she would have chosen a more formal style? An even less formal style?

◆ WRITING FROM READING ASSIGNMENT

"Marriage as a Restricted Club" explains why the author refuses to celebrate weddings and anniversaries, even among her friends. In this writing assignment, you will write about some principle you hold strongly enough to deny yourself a pleasure or to set you apart from your group of friends. For example, you may be a vegetarian among meat-eaters or someone who declines to celebrate Christmas because you think it's too commercialized. Perhaps you take the letter of the law very seriously and refuse to engage in even minor infractions, or you may be more scrupulously honest or hardworking or religious or studious than your friends are. You may be more cautious with money or more generous in your spending than the norm, or you may be more accepting or limiting about choosing members of your social group. (If you cannot think of a way you are set apart by your principles, ask your friends for ideas. You may finally have to write about someone else instead of yourself, in which case you will have to interview the other person extensively.)

A. Begin by writing a sentence expressing the principle (or set of related principles) you hold strongly.
B. Brainstorm about various situations when acting on your principle made your difference from other people obvious. Do additional

freewriting about each situation so that you will be able to develop it with details if you decide to use it in your essay.

C. List as many reasons as you can, explaining why you stick to your principle. As you make the list, some of the reasons will go together or overlap. Draw lines and lassos to show which ones belong together. Put a star by the reason you consider most important.

D. Van Gelder explains many drawbacks to being different. List the drawbacks you have noticed related to your own difference. Van Gelder discusses social, psychological, and legal drawbacks, and you may find some structure like that for your list. If possible, connect the drawbacks to the situations you brainstormed in step B.

E. Van Gelder also provides the advantages that come to people who are in the mainstream. What benefits are enjoyed by those who don't hold your principle strongly? What benefits would you get if you compromised your principle? Jot down these ideas and connect them to concrete situations from step B as well.

F. You now have several sheets of prewriting material, including reasons, situations, drawbacks, and advantages and their interrelationships. The next step is to organize them into a point-by-point structure. For example, you could decide on a paragraph that describes one of the drawbacks of your different stance, compares and contrasts it with the advantages of the mainstream stance, gives an example from your experience to develop the point, and explains the reason why you stick to your principle. Put together four or five of these "packages" of points and related evidence, and write the body paragraphs from the "packages."

G. Choose an order for the paragraphs you have written. As noted earlier, you can usually organize them along some range of values: least to most important, concrete to abstract, personal to political.

H. Begin your essay with a short, arresting sentence that forces your readers to ask, "Why?" as Van Gelder does.

I. Close your essay by reflecting on how you feel when you see your friends ignoring the principle you hold dear. Review Van Gelder's closing for an example.

◆ ◆ ◆

◆ FURTHER IDEAS FOR USING ARGUMENT

1. Argue for the value of some particular domestic activity, as Laurel Robertson does in "Bake Your Bread at Home." Then, explain how the world of work prevents or hinders people from engaging in this activity. Suggest a solution to the dilemma if you can.

2. COLLABORATIVE WRITING. Work with a small group of students to investigate the stance your college has regarding diversity. Are undergraduates required to take a course in multiculturalism? Are there policies and programs to increase ethnic diversity among students and faculty? After completing your investigation, develop a collaborative essay that takes a position on diversity at your school. Do you support the current policies? Do new policies needs to be established?

3. COMBINING STRATEGIES. Narrate an experience that practically single-handedly led you to take a side on some issue. For example, a car accident might convince you that seat belt laws are justified. Looking for an apartment in a predominantly white community, when you are African American, might persuade you that racist stereotypes are alive and thriving. Unexpectedly losing your job might give you a different point of view of unemployment.

4. COMBINING STRATEGIES. Write an essay refuting the myths about some topic. You might choose a public issue like welfare, a workplace topic like flex time, a social science subject like unemployment, or a psychological topic like schizophrenia. Or you might enjoy writing a humorous essay like "Three Myths About Computer Nerds." This essay will require that you collect and *classify* beliefs about your subject; then you will *argue* that each general classification is a myth. You can model your essay on David Cole's "Five Myths about Immigration" in Chapter 12 (p. 499).

◆ **DEBATE: HOW IS THE INTERNET AFFECTING YOUNG PEOPLE?**

Innocent humans lured into an alternative reality more enchanting than the real world: the story used to be a staple of science fiction. But now the story is true, say many commentators on the social impact of Internet communication. Unmonitored communication and courtship with virtual strangers over the Web are a source of alarm to some observers, yet welcome opportunities to most participants. Web culture has no doubt touched you in some way—good, bad, or in between.

Today, teenagers are the group commonly believed to be most affected by the Internet's presence in their lives. In this section, you will read three very different points of view about teenagers and the Web.

◆ ◆ ◆ **PREPARING TO READ**

Why do you use the Internet? How important is e-mail to you? What is your opinion of people whose social lives are mainly online?

◆ ◆ ◆

Young Cyber Addicts

AMY WU

A graduate of New York University, Amy Wu has written articles on technology and business for *Newsweek, U.S. News & World Report, Billboard,* and the *New York Times.* The following essay appeared in *Minutes of the Lead Pencil Club: Pulling the Plug on the Electronic Revolution,* a 1996 collection of "letters, essays, cartoons, and commentary on how and why to live contraption-free in a computer-crazed world."

The phenomena of sending letters to all of my high school friends with the touch of a button, and joining the "rec.music.Dylan" for diehard Dylan fans, transformed me into a shameless cyber addict in my freshman year. Like the hundreds of other bleary-eyed addicts I made my nightly trek to the computer lab, where a queue-shaped waiting line was already formed, my fingers itching to touch the keyboard and my mind already set on chatting 1 with my online boyfriend R2D2. For weeks I forfeited sunshine for a fluorescent terminal. A whole new world was opening up before me until my "A" average in anthropology drifted to a mediocre "B."

The Internet is becoming young America's latest addiction, especially   2
on college campuses. The "Just Say No" to sex, drugs, and alcohol may soon pertain to e-mail and surfing the information superhighway. Soon CA (Cyber addicts Anonymous) may be added to AA. Blame it on the free e-mail accounts and easy access most colleges offer.

A cyber addict is as easy to distinguish as a swaggering alcoholic. They   3
sit before a screen for hours laughing, talking, and smiling at a screen, hopelessly lost in their own world. They proudly tell you that yes they do spend four hours a day in cyberspace, that yes they have a fruitful social life where they chat with friends with names like KillBarney, that yes they procrastinate on major papers so they can keep up with their e-mail correspondence.

When asked what they would do if the school took away their most   4
prized possession, they gasp and turn pale with the possibility. "If I didn't have access I'd have to get a life," a junior said with a nervous laugh. For others it would be more of an inconvenience than a total loss. "I wouldn't freak, some people would just freak," a freshman said. Others say that they would just buy a modem. All they have to do is log on to the school's system, still free of cost.

The temptation of entering cyberspace is great for many young people.   5
It's a cheap and quick alternative to snail mail (the kind with a stamp). The "Talk" channel bears an uncanny resemblance to the telephone. Logging onto the Net allows you to chat with as many as thirty people at the same time. There are hundreds of newsgroups where the latest movies can be debated, where the psychology of body art can be dissected, and where Camille Paglia and Rush Limbaugh can be bashed. Instant friends from as far away as Australia and Africa are made through the "soc.penpals." Love at first byte is even a possibility. My girlfriend and a cyber friend went out to a cafe after meeting each other online. Unfortunately conversation over cappuccino didn't make them compatible, and they never e-mailed each other again.

The Internet is a channel for the curious. With the click of a mouse   6
the Dead Sea scrolls can be viewed, the President's health care plan will appear, and letters to editors or to cyberzines can be written. For a generation accustomed to fast music, fast food, and quick results, the Internet is a perfect match—it's easy, it's fast, it's fun, it's free. It is also addictive and as dangerous as it is educational.

There are stories of young people who have disappeared into the com-   7
puter, who become so addicted that they cybersurf for nine or ten hours and continue into the night. There are always one or two of these hopeless addicts in the lab. They have glazed expressions on their faces and if you wave to them they think you're a figment of virtual reality instead of reality.

The Dead Sea scrolls aren't addictive, but mudding—a Dungeons and Dragons type game—and checking how many e-mail messages you've received is. One young woman tearfully told me how she became addicted. "Oh I was bad," she said. "I wouldn't count the hours, I would just be there." She and her channel friends would chat about everything from Nine Inch Nails's newest album to rumors of Kurt Cobain's ghost. Her addiction reminded me of my addicted roommate who begged me to hold her computer card for a week after she had done poorly on a mid-term because she spent the previous night on the Internet. Needless to say the week didn't last. Another young woman, whose grades plummeted from 3.3 to 2.5 after getting hooked on the Internet, tried to explain. "I didn't stop studying," she said, "you just like get addicted to it. You're so into the conversation you don't want to get off and study, you just study less." It's a typical response from a cyber addict. 8

These young people are drawn into a world where they are connected to the world but sadly disconnected to their environment. Many have lost friends and a social life which includes going to the movies or out for pizza. Some haven't talked on the phone and written a letter for a year. Many have given up school activities, student government, and sports. Earlier this year my suitemate's boyfriend even called my room and told me to tell her to get off the computer so he could talk to her. "Get off the computer!" I screamed. "Don't bother me!" she shot back. The boyfriend was despondent and inconsolable and threatened to throw her computer out the window. Many addicts lock themselves in coffin-styled dorm rooms and spend sunny days sitting under a fluorescent light staring at a screen for hours until that glazed expression is achieved. 9

If only colleges charged Internet use per hour, if only accounts were given out on the basis of need, if only hours were limited, then maybe horror stories about young people who have failed classes because of too much e-mail, who have disappeared in the mudding world, who haven't spoken to a human being in a week, who haven't felt the sun in days, and are proud of all the above, wouldn't exist. 10

As seemingly great as free access on the information superhighway may seem to prospective students and parents, the dangers and damage it can cause outweigh the positives. "I know some people who had to cut down because they developed carpal tunnel syndrome," one young woman said. She stared at her own atrophying wrists, the result of one too many hours chatting with the "Mystery Theater 3000," smiled sweetly, and said she had to finish e-mailing Darth Vader, her new online boyfriend. It was just another sad story from a young cyber addict. 11

FIRST RESPONSES

Would you like to be a cyber addict's college roommate? Why or why not?

TAKING A CLOSER LOOK

Exploring *Who:* Voice and Tone

1. How old is the writer of this piece? How do you know?
2. What is Wu's attitude toward young cyber addicts? Point out some sentences that reveal her attitude.
3. Wu evidently overcame her freshman-year Web addiction. In this essay, why doesn't she reveal how she recovered from it?

Exploring *What:* Content and Meaning

1. Define the Internet jargon Wu uses: *cyberzine, modem, byte, cyberspace.* What do these terms add to the essay?
2. What kind of evidence does Wu provide in support of her thesis? Do you find this evidence persuasive? What other evidence would help persuade you?
3. Reread paragraph 5. Wu suggests that compatibility online is different from compatibility in person. Why might that be?
4. What is the solution to cyber addiction among college students, according to Wu? Using this solution, where would control over Internet access lie? What do you think of this solution?

Exploring *Why:* Purpose

1. By the time you are finished reading paragraph 2, you're probably aware of Wu's purpose, although it is not directly stated. What clues you in?
2. What kind of topics do people discuss and research on the Internet, according to Wu? What impression of the Net user do you get from these topics?
3. What activities are young cyber addicts neglecting? Why did Wu choose these particular activities to mention? Are there other activities cyber addicts might be missing that would *not* fit Wu's argument?

1. Trace the **analogy** between cyber addictions and other addictions throughout the essay. Are there any weaknesses to the analogy between cyber addiction and drug addiction?
2. Identify a sentence using **parallel structure** in paragraph 4. Find at least two other sentences in the essay that use parallel structure in a series.
3. List at least ten instances of strong language used to influence the reader's point of view—for example, "coffin-styled" in paragraph 9 and "uncanny" and "instant friends" in paragraph 5. What words could be used to impart a positive rather than negative view in the same phrases?
4. Wu's essay relates a series of loosely connected observations. How could you make this essay more formally structured? Make an outline of the structure you suggest.

We're Teen, We're Queer, and We've Got E-mail

STEVE SILBERMAN

Steve Silberman is a contributing editor for *Wired,* an online magazine. He has written more than eight hundred articles and columns for a variety of Internet publications, including *The Netizen, HotWired, Packet, Synapse,* and *Wired News.* Silberman is also the author of *Skeleton Key: A Dictionary for Deadheads* (1994) and one of the editors of Allen Ginsberg's photo collection *Snapshot Poetics.* He wrote the liner notes for the Jerry Garcia Band album *How Sweet It Is* and for David Crosby and Graham Nash's *Another Stoney Evening.* The following article appeared on *Wired* in 1994.

There's a light on in the Nerd Nook: JohnTeen Ø is composing e-mail   1
into the night. The Nerd Nook is what John's mother calls her 16-year-old's bedroom—it's more cramped than the bridge of the Enterprise, with a Roland CM-322 that makes "You've got mail" thunder like the voice of God.

John's favorite short story is "The Metamorphosis." Sure, Kafka's fable   2
of waking up to discover you've morphed into something that makes everyone tweak speaks to every teenager. But John especially has had moments of feeling insectoid—like during one school choir trip, when, he says, the

teacher booking rooms felt it necessary to inform the other students' parents of John's "orientation." When they balked at their kids sharing a room with him, John was doubled up with another teacher—a fate nearly as alienating as Gregor Samsa's.

The choir trip fiasco was but one chapter in the continuing online jour- 3
nal that has made JohnTeen Ø—or as his parents and classmates know him, John Erwin—one of the most articulate voices in America Online's Gay and Lesbian Community Forum.

> From: JohnTeen Ø   4
>
> My high school career has been a sudden and drastic spell of turbulence and change that has influenced every aspect of life. Once I was an automaton, obeying external, societal, and parental expectations like a dog, oblivious of who I was or what I wanted. I was the token child every parent wants—student body president, color guard, recipient of the general excellence award, and outstanding music student of the year. I conformed to society's paradigm, and I was rewarded. Yet I was miserable. Everything I did was a diversion from thinking about myself. Finally, last summer, my subconsciousness felt comfortable enough to be able to connect myself with who I really am, and I began to understand what it is to be gay.

JohnTeen Ø is a new kind of gay kid, a 16-year-old not only out, but al- 5
ready at home in the online convergence of activists that Tom Rielly, the cofounder of Digital Queers, calls the "Queer Global Village." Just 10 years ago, most queer teens hid behind a self-imposed don't-ask-don't-tell policy until they shipped out to Oberlin or San Francisco, but the Net has given even closeted kids a place to conspire. Though the Erwins' house is in an unincorporated area of Santa Clara County in California, with goats and llamas foraging in the backyard, John's access to AOL's gay and lesbian forum enables him to follow dispatches from queer activists worldwide, hone his writing, flirt, try disposable identities, and battle bigots—all from his home screen.

John's ambitions to recast national policy before the principal of Menlo 6
School even palms him a diploma (John's mother refers to him as her "little mini-activist") are not unrealistic. Like the ur-narrative of every video game, the saga of gay teens online is one of metamorphosis, of "little mini" nerds becoming warriors in a hidden Stronghold of Power. For young queers, the Magic Ring is the bond of community.

John's posts have the confidence and urgency of one who speaks for   7
many who must keep silent:

> The struggle for equal rights has always taken place on the frontier of
> the legal wilderness where liberty meets power. Liberty has claimed
> much of that wilderness now, but the frontier always lies ahead of
> us. . . . The frontier of liberty may have expanded far beyond where it
> began, but for those without rights, it always seems on the horizon, just
> beyond their reach.

And the messages that stream back into John's box are mostly from   8
kids his own age, many marooned far from urban centers for gay and lesbian youth. Such is Christopher Rempel, a witty, soft-spoken Ace of Base
fan from (as he puts it) "redneck farmer hell." Christopher borrowed the
principal's modem to jack into a beekeepers BBS and gopher his way to the
Queer Resources Directory, a multimeg collection of text files, news items,
and services listings.

> My name is Christopher and I am 15 years old. I came to terms that
> I was gay last summer and, aside from some depression, I'm OK. I am
> *not* in denial about being gay. I would like to write to someone that
> I can talk to about issues I can't talk about with my friends. I don't play
> sports very much, but I make it up in my knowledge of computers. I
> am interested in anybody with an open mind and big aspirations for
> the future.

A decade ago, the only queer info available to most teens was in a few   9
dour psychology texts under the nose of the school librarian. Now libraries
of files await them in the AOL forum and elsewhere—the Queer Resources
Directory alone contains hundreds—and teens can join mailing lists like
Queercampus and GayNet, or tap resources like the Bridges Project, a re-
ferral service that tells teens not only how to get in touch with queer youth
groups, but how to jump-start one themselves.

Kali is an 18-year-old lesbian at a university in Colorado. Her name   10
means "fierce" in Swahili. Growing up in California, Kali was the leader of
a young women's chapter of the Church of Jesus Christ of Latter-day Saints.
She was also the "Girl Saved by E-mail," whose story ran last spring on CNN.
After mood swings plummeted her into a profound depression, Kali—like too
many gay teens—considered suicide. Her access to GayNet at school gave her
a place to air those feelings, and a phone call from someone she knew online
saved her life. Kali is now a regular contributor to Sappho, a women's board

she most appreciates because there she is accepted as an equal. "They forgive me for being young," Kali laughs, "though women come out later than guys, so there aren't a lot of teen lesbians. But it's a high of connection. We joke that we're posting to 500 of our closest friends."

"The wonderful thing about online services is that they are an intrinsi-   11
cally decentralized resource," says Tom Rielly, who has solicited the hardware and imparted the skills to get dozens of queer organizations jacked in. "Kids can challenge what adults have to say and make the news. One of the best examples of teen organizing in the last year was teens working with the Massachusetts legislature to pass a law requiring gay and lesbian education in the high schools. If teen organizers are successful somewhere now, everyone's gonna hear about it. This is the most powerful tool queer youth have ever had."

Another power that teenagers are now wielding online is their anger.   12
"Teens are starting to throw their weight around," says Quirk, the leader of the AOL forum. (Quirk maintains a gender-neutral identity online, to be an equal-opportunity sounding board for young lesbians and gay men.) "They're complaining. It used to be, 'Ick—I think I'm gay, I'll sneak around the forum and see they're doing.' With this second wave of activism, it's like, 'There's gay stuff here, but it's not right for me.' These kids are computer literate, and they're using the anger of youth to create a space for themselves."

The powers that be at AOL, however, have not yet seen fit to allow that   13
space to be named by its users—the creation of chat rooms called "gay teen" anything is banned. "AOL has found that the word 'gay' with the word 'youth' or 'teen' in a room name becomes a lightning rod for predators," says Quirk. "I've been in teen conferences where adult cruising so overwhelmed any kind of conversation about being in high school and 'What kind of music do you like?' that I was furious. Until I can figure out a way to provide a safe space for them, I'm not going to put them at risk."

Quirk and AOL are in a tight place. Pedophilia has become the trendy   14
bludgeon with which to trash cyberspace in the dailies, and concerned parents invoke the P-word to justify limiting teens' access to gay forums. At the same time, however, postings in the teens-only folder of the Gay and Community Forum flame not only the invasion of teen turf by adults trolling for sex, but also the adults claiming to "protect" them by limiting their access to one another.

One anonymous 17-year-old poster on AOL dissed the notion that   15
queer teens are helpless victims of online "predators":

There are procedures for dealing with perverts, which most teens (in contrast with most of the adults we've encountered) are familiar with. Flooding e-mail boxes of annoying perverts, 'IGNORE'-ing them in chat rooms, and shutting off our Instant Messages are all very effective methods. We are not defenseless, nor innocent.

The issue is further complicated by the fact that the intermingling of old　16
and young people online is good for teens. The online connection allows them to open dialogs with mentors like Deacon Maccubbin, co-owner of Lambda Rising bookstore in Washington, D.C. As "DeaconMac," Maccubbin has been talking with gay kids on CompuServe and AOL for eight years. One of the young people DeaconMac corresponded with online, years ago, was Tom Rielly. "Deacon was the first openly gay man I'd ever had a convesation with, and he had a very clear idea of what his role was. He was nurturing and mentoring; he sent me articles; and he didn't come on to me," says Rielly. "I'll never forget it as long as I live."

In the past, teens often had to wait until they were old enough to get　17
into a bar to meet other gay people—or hang around outside until someone noticed them. Online interaction gives teens a chance to unmask themselves in a safe place, in a venue where individuals make themselves known by the acuity of their thought and expression, rather than by their physical appearance.

When JohnTeen Ø logged his first post in the gay AOL forum, he expressed　18
outrage that the concerns of queer teens—who are at a disproportionately high risk for suicide—were being shunted aside by adult organizations. His post was spotted by Sarah Gregory, a 26-year-old anarchist law student who helped get the National Gay and Lesbian Task Force wired up. "I really wanted to hit this kid between the eyes with the fact that a national organization saw what he was saying and cared that gay youth were killing themselves," Gregory recalls. A correspondence and friendship began that would have been unlikely offline—for, as Gregory says, "I don't notice 16-year-old boys in the real world."

Gregory explains: "I remember one particularly graphic letter I sent　19
John in response to his questions. I wrote a huge disclaimer before and after it. But then I remembered how desperately I wanted to be talked to as an adult, and a sexual being, when I was 14. Thinking back, that's the point where John stopped sounding so formal, so much like a well-bred teenager talking to an authority figure, and became my friend. It's also the last time he talked about suicide. It scared me how easily his vulnerability could have been exploited, but I'd do it again in a heartbeat."

"I didn't even listen to music," moans John recalling his nerdhood, when　20
the only thing he logged for was shareware. Now the background thrash for his late-night e-mail sessions is Pansy Division. "To keep myself in the closet, I surrounded myself with people I'd never find attractive. I had two different parts of my life: the normal part, where I worked hard in school and got good

grades, and this other part, where I was interested in guys but didn't do anything about it." For many kids, writing to John or to other posters is where a
more authentic life begins:

> Dear JohnTeen:
>
> I am so frustrated with life and all of its blind turns. Am I gay? What
> will happen if I tell friends and my mom? . . . (I still don't 100% know
> that I am gay only that I am not heterosexual SO WHAT AM I) I really
> want to fit somewhere and also to love someone (at this point I don't
> care who). . . . Please EMAIL back and enlighten me. You have been
> very inspirational to me. I have no idea how you gained the courage
> to come out. Thanks, James

But John Erwin must guard against JohnTeen Ø becoming a full-time   21
gig: he not only has the frontiers of liberty to defend and his peers to "en-
lighten," but like any 16-year-old, he needs space to mess up, be a normal
teenage cockroach, and figure out who he is. And he'd like to find someone
to love. Does he have anyone in mind? "Yes!" he grins, pulling out his year-
book and leafing to a photo of a handsome boy who says he's straight.

Is John's dream guy online?   22

"No. I wish," John says. "If he was online, I could tell him how I feel."   23

◆ ◆ ◆

FIRST RESPONSES

How do you think your response to the essay was affected by whether
you are gay, lesbian, or straight? Do you think most readers are able to see
past the gay issue?

TAKING A CLOSER LOOK

Exploring *Who:* Voice and Tone

1. What words and phrases in paragraph 1 establish the audience? Who
   might be confused by paragraph 1?
2. How does Silberman feel about homosexuality? How soon was his attitude clear to you as you read?

Exploring *What:* Content and Meaning

1. ▣▯ *Using the Internet.* What happens in Kafka's short story "The Metamorphosis"? If you don't know, look up the story in the library or on the Internet.
2. Why does every teenager feel "morphed into something that makes everyone tweak" (para. 2)? Why does John in particular feel this way?
3. Explain the references in paragraph 6. Why are they appropriate In this context?
4. What is the major advantage of Internet access for gay teens? What is the main disadvantage? How do teens deal with the disadvantage?

Exploring *Why:* Purpose

1. According to Silberman, how has the Internet created "a new kind of gay kid" (para. 5)? How is the new kind an improvement over the old kind?
2. Given that Silberman wants to emphasize the positive aspects of the Internet for gay teens, why does he even bring up the issue of adult predators (paras. 13–16)? Why would any writer bring up a strong counter-argument?

Exploring *How:* Style and Strategy

1. Imagine the essay without the examples of real e-mails. How would it be different?
2. In what way does Silberman most often support his arguments? Is this type of evidence convincing to you?
3. Does Silberman try to persuade nongays to his point of view? How can you tell? Why did he choose the audience he appealed to?
4. Among the stories Silberman provides, which one most impressed you, positively or negatively? Why do you think you responded strongly to this story?
5. In the closing vignette, John talks about his "dream guy." Explain whether or not this closing effectively concludes the essay.

The Wired Teen

SUE FERGUSON

Author and researcher Sue Ferguson is the chief of research and the managing editor for the University and College Guide at *Maclean's*, a weekly newsmagazine published in Toronto, Canada. The following article appeared in the May 2000 issue of *Maclean's*.

The boy at the center of Canada's latest teen hacker drama was almost too perfect a stereotype. Just one month after police in Montreal arrested accused cyber-vandal Mafiaboy, another Montreal computer whiz kid known as Jon pleaded guilty last week to playing havoc with data systems at NASA, Harvard, and the Massachusetts Institute of Technology. The 17-year-old former boy scout revealed in court that since quitting school two years ago, he had spent up to 15 hours a day on the Internet on his home computer.   1

Jon, who was sentenced to 240 hours of community work, fuels a popular image: the teenage loner who takes refuge in cyberspace, unable to resist the allure of the Net's nefarious subcultures. But is he representative of Canada's teen Internet users? The answer, according to a new survey on young people and the Internet, is emphatically, no. In fact, the study found that kids aged 12 to 17 who regularly go online are pretty normal—they hold a broad range of interests, play sports, listen to the radio, read magazines and value friendships. As well, they say they use the Net for relatively harmless purposes like chatting with other kids, getting the scoop on their favorite celebrities and doing their homework.   2

Parents should breathe a sigh of relief at that profile—since chances are their teen spends a lot of spare time surfing the Web. According to the survey, designed by Northstar Research Partners for Youth Culture Inc., a Toronto-based media and research firm, a full 85 per cent of Canada's teenagers are wired, three-quarters of them at home. That's a hefty figure—about double the proportion of Canadian households that use the Internet. On average, says the poll—entitled "Youth Culture's report on the Net generation"—boys go online for more than 10 hours a week, girls for 8 hours.   3

But far from isolating kids in a cyber-netherworld, the Net has become a tool for expanding and enhancing most young people's social connections. Instant messaging services like icq (for "I seek you," found at www.icq.com) allow users to get around the limitations of both telephone and e-mail with a chat room–like format in which numerous people congregate. Emma McDermott, an outgoing 14-year-old with a penchant for acting,   4 got wired as a Christmas gift last year. "Of course, the first month you're hooked," says the Toronto student. "I was in the chat rooms, like, three hours a day. It's craziness." While the novelty wore off, Emma still spends about 20 hours a week online, most of it on icq.

Instant messaging programs differ from chat-room Web sites in that 5 users exercise more control over who they communicate with by creating personalized chat lists. While many teens enjoy chatting with strangers, a surprising number simply want to talk to their friends. Three-quarters of Emma's icq list covers people she knows. As for meeting new people, she believes the Internet is a great equalizer: "Everyone's on the same level and no one can be cooler than the next person."

That does not stop parents from worrying about what sorts of sites their 6 children may happen upon. A full 73 per cent of parents of teenagers believe the Internet should be more heavily monitored. Intriguingly, so do 51 per cent of teens—though monitored not by their parents, but by someone Out There. Marilyn Tiller, a Halifax mother of three, says she trusts her children to be responsible and talks to them about her concerns. Still, she installed the program Cyber Patrol, which blocks access to offensive sites. "I've been mindful of media since they were infants," she says. "Kids can become desensitized to violence or pornography."

Vancouver couple Judith Ince and Richard McMahon prefer simply to 7 try to help their kids Paul, 16, Laura, 14, and Allison, 12, learn to make smart decisions for themselves. "I think that values are really what's going to protect them more than any censorship," says McMahon. In any case, Ince adds, "you can get pornography at the 7-Eleven, violent videos at Blockbuster or on TV. If my kids do find that stuff on the Net—and it wouldn't surprise me if they have—then they're going to be able to cope with it." And they probably have: according to the survey, 56 per cent of teens said they knew people who visit sites their parents would disapprove of.

Yet many teens, it appears, do manage to cope easily. When Allison accidentally clicks on an offensive site, she simply closes it. "Then I go back 8 and block it out," she says, using a function in her Microsoft Windows software. And if someone mistakenly admits an undesirable person into an icq chat? Adam Ing, a Toronto 12-year-old, says: "I just hit Ignore." Clicking Ignore lets Adam block intruders' comments—a simple but effective form of online shunning.

Moreover, the image of teens wandering aimlessly around the Web, 9 tripping onto sinister sites and bumping into shady characters, may be misleading. Outside of socializing through e-mail, icq and chat rooms, the Youth Culture survey found that doing homework is the single most popular reason teens identify for going online. In this, they are remarkably similar to their parents, most of whom cite research as their primary activity.

The Internet also offers young people a chance to express themselves   10
in an uncensored environment. "It gives teens a voice," observes Patrick
Thoburn, director of Internet strategy at Youth Culture. "It is the only
medium to do that." Many teen sites involve kids in submitting poetry, writing book or movie reviews, or commenting about issues such as school uniforms, the Columbine shootings or their favorite TV show. And some, like
Adam Ing, take this a step further by constructing their own home pages, a
skill he picked up at summer camp.

This creative, two-way relationship with the Net may be behind one   11
of the survey's most surprising findings: teens who use it are about as likely
to click on the Net as they are to flick on the TV. While they tend to perceive television as relaxing, they also complain it can be a waste of time.
Young people think of the Net, on the other hand, as a trend-setting medium
that offers plenty of amusement. "The Net is more interactive," says Emma
McDermott. "You can't talk at the TV and expect it to respond."

But teens are not simply dupes of Internet hype. Allison McMahon   12
thinks the content is "sometimes repetitive." And the sheer volume of information leads to frustrations, especially when researching a homework
topic. Allison's brother Paul prefers to go to the library because "the information on the Net isn't always reliable."

Similarly, teens have not abandoned more traditional media. Emma   13
loves to read books and teen magazines. The Net, she says, "shows you enough
to entice you, but then you have to buy something. With a magazine, it's right
there, it's colorful, you can flip it, you can touch it." She also cuts pictures out
for her bedroom walls and school agenda. That way, she says, "you can share
it with your friends."

To Sean Saraq, Youth Culture's 35-year-old director of consumer in-   14
telligence, teens are not intimidated by the Net, as adults may be. Kids relate
to the Web "not as technology, but as an appliance," he says. Moreover, his
colleague Thoburn, 31, believes young people's identification with the Net is
not just a phase they will outgrow. Rather, it represents a true generational
shift. With the teen population—largely the "echo" children of the baby
boomers—increasing 10 per cent faster than Canadians overall, businesses
face a challenge. Currently, television swallows up 40 per cent of the ap-
proximately $11 billion Canadian companies spend on advertising. Only a
fraction of a per cent, Saraq estimates, makes it to the Net. If advertisers
want to reach teens—and they do—they need to radically rethink their habits,
he says.

The same goes for purchases online. Teens browse the Net to find out   15
information about products, but only about 10 per cent have actually pur-
chased something. Teens don't buy much online for a variety of reasons, the
survey shows, including lack of access to a credit card, fears about giving out
confidential information over the Net and a simple preference for shopping

in person. "It's just a lot easier going to the mall," says Tom Clarke, a Toronto 12-year-old. "You go with all your friends. You're not just sitting at home." Kids, it seems, are still kids—on and off the Net.

◆ ◆ ◆

FIRST RESPONSES

Does Ferguson's point of view fit your own perceptions of teens in cyberspace? Why or why not?

TAKING A CLOSER LOOK

Exploring *Who:* Voice and Tone

1. How would you describe Ferguson's tone? List four adjectives that reflect the writer's emotional stance.
2. What features of the article make the writer seem credible?

Exploring *What:* Content and Meaning

1. What research is much of the article based upon? Are you willing to accept the results of this research as valid? Why or why not?
2. Is there a meaningful difference between the amount of time boys spend on the Net and the amount girls spend? If so, what might account for the difference?
3. In paragraph 5, Ferguson calls the Internet "a great equalizer." What does that mean? Is it true in your experience?

Exploring *Why:* Purpose

1. Who is the main intended audience for this report? How old are the readers? What are some of their worries?
2. What evidence does Ferguson use to soothe parents' anxieties about teen use of the Net?

Exploring *How:* Style and Strategy

1. In paragraph 1, what elements of the **anecdote** are shocking or surprising? How is the anecdote used in paragraph 2? Did you expect it to be followed up this way?

2. Reread paragraph 4. Compare the language Ferguson uses to describe Internet use with the language Wu uses in "Young Cyber Addicts" for the same phenomena.

3. What is the writer's basis for concluding that "Kids, it seems, are still kids"? Why is this statement reassuring? What does the comment "Kids will be kids" usually mean?

IDEAS FOR WRITING ABOUT THE TEENS ONLINE CONTROVERSY

1. Wu uses the addiction analogy to condemn Internet overuse. Argue against some other activity using an analogy to addiction: studying, working, dating, gardening, quilting, worrying. Take either a serious or a humorous approach.

2. Compare Wu's point of view with Silberman's on whether the Internet provides connection or disconnection with the rest of life. Argue one way or the other using your own experience. You might also interview others or gather additional evidence from the Internet.

3. What would happen if the Net were gone from your own life? Acquire evidence by staying away from the Web for two or three days and keeping notes about your experience. See which of the three views represented in this section are confirmed by your responses to Internet withdrawal.

4. Many people worry about children younger than teens gaining access to unsavory Internet sites. Write a problem-and-solution essay about dealing with children's exposure to the Internet.

5. ■▯ *Using the Internet.* Think about whether Silberman's assertions might apply to other groups of teenagers who communicate with each other over the Net. Argue that the Internet has benefited or harmed some other specific group. Make several visits to chat rooms frequented by this group to gather specifics to support your argument.

6. Most people agree that the Web is a useful research tool. Write an essay about the pros and cons of collecting information from the Web.

7. In 1998, R. Kraut and colleagues published a study of the psychological effects of Internet use (R. Kraut, et al., "Internet Paradox: A Social Technology That Reduces Social Involvement and Psychological Well-Being?" *American Psychologist* 53:1017–1031). Read the article, and write an essay that integrates the research findings there with the assertions of the three writers in this section.

◆ DEBATE: ARE TV TALK SHOWS HARMFUL?

Have you ever turned off a television show because you found it too stupid, disgusting, or distressing to watch? The downhill slide of good taste in popular culture is a perennial worry of media watchers. Do the violence and ugliness on TV reflect our culture, or is our culture affected by them, becoming more violent and ugly through exposure to the media? Who benefits from popular media, and who is harmed? How can we explain the fact that everyone disparages TV fare, yet advertisers concur that everyone is watching the lowest forms of entertainment?

Critics frequently target daytime talk shows as circus rings for the worst antics of humanity. In this section, you will read two writers' analyses of talk shows in our culture.

◆ ◆ ◆ PREPARING TO READ

How much do you watch talk shows on television? What attracts you to them? Why do you think they're so popular?

◆ ◆ ◆

Tuning in Trouble: Talk TV's Destructive Impact on Mental Health

JEANNE A. HEATON

Jeanne A. Heaton is a psychologist and a professor of guidance and counseling at Ohio University. The following is an excerpt from her 1995 book of the same title. Heaton sees the proliferation of nationally syndicated daytime talk shows (more than twenty at last count) as a threat to the soundness of the audience's worldview.

In 1967, *The Phil Donahue Show* aired in Dayton, Ohio, as a new daytime talk alternative. Donahue did not offer the customary "women's fare." On Monday of his first week he interviewed atheist Madalyn Murray O'Hair. Tuesday he featured single men talking about what they looked for in women. Wednesday he showed a film of a baby being born from the obstetrician's point of view. Thursday he sat in a coffin and interviewed a funeral director. And on Friday he held up "Little Brother," an anatomically correct doll without his diaper. When Donahue asked viewers to call in response, phone lines jammed.

For eighteen years daytime talk *was* Donahue. His early guests reflected   2
the issues of the time and included Ralph Nader on consumer rights, Bella Abzug on feminism, and Jerry Rubin on free speech. Never before had such socially and personally relevant issues been discussed in such a democratic way with daytime women viewers. But his most revolutionary contribution was in making the audience an integral part of the show's format. The women watching Donahue finally had a place in the conversation, and they were determined to be heard. The show provided useful information and dialogue that had largely been unavailable to house-bound women, affording them the opportunity to voice their opinions about everything from politics to sex—and even the politics of sex.

No real competition emerged until 1985, when *The Oprah Winfrey*   3
Show went national. Her appeal for more intimacy was a ratings winner. She did the same topics Donahue had done but with a more therapeutic tone. Donahue seemed driven to uncover and explore. Winfrey came to share and understand. In 1987, Winfrey's show surpassed Donahue's by being ranked among the top twenty syndicated shows. Phil and Oprah made it easier for those who followed; their successors were able to move much more quickly to the top.

At their best, the shows "treated the opinions of women of all classes,   4
races, and educational levels as if they mattered," says Naomi Wolf in her book *Fire with Fire:* "That daily act of listening, whatever its shortcomings, made for a revolution in what women were willing to ask for; the shows daily conditioned otherwise unheard women into the belief that they were entitled to a voice." Both Donahue and Winfrey deserve enormous credit for providing a platform for the voices of so many who needed to be heard, and for raising the nation's consciousness on many important topics, including domestic violence, child abuse, and other crucial problems. But those pioneering days are over. As the number of shows increased and the ratings wars intensified, the manner in which issues are presented has changed. Shows now encourage conflict, name-calling, and fights. Producers set up underhanded tricks and secret revelations. Hosts instruct guests to reveal all. The more dramatic and bizarre the problems the better.

While more air time is given to the problems that women face, the top-   5
ics are presented in ways that are not likely to yield change. The very same stereotypes that have plagued both women and men for centuries are in full force. Instead of encouraging changes in sex roles, the shows actually solidify them. Women viewers are given a constant supply of the worst images of men, all the way from garden-variety liars, cheats, and con artists to rapists and murderers.

If there is a man for every offense, there is certainly a woman for every   6
trauma. Most women on talk TV are perpetual victims presented as having
so little power that not only do they have to contend with real dangers such
as sexual or physical abuse, but they are also overcome by bad hair, big thighs,
and beautiful but predatory "other" women. The women of talk are almost
always upset and in need. The bonding that occurs invariably centers around
complaints about men or the worst stereotypes about women. In order to be
a part of the "sisterhood," women are required to be angry with men and
dissatisfied with themselves. We need look no further than at some of the
program titles to recognize the message. Shows about men bring us a steady
stream of stalkers, adulterers, chauvinistic sons, abusive fathers, and men who
won't commit to women.

The shows provide a forum for women to complain, confront, and ca-   7
jole, but because there is never any change as a result of the letting loose, this
supports the mistaken notion that women's complaints have "no weight,"
that the only power women have is to complain, and that they cannot effect
real changes. By bringing on offensive male guests who do nothing but ver-
ify the grounds for complaint, the shows are reinforcing some self-defeating
propositions. The idea that women should direct their energies toward men
rather than look for solutions in themselves is portrayed daily. And even
when the audience chastises such behavior, nothing changes, because only arguments and justifications follow.

On *The Jenny Jones Show* a woman was introduced as someone who no   8
longer had sex with her husband because she saw him with a stripper. Viewers got to hear how the stripper "put her boobs in his face" and then kissed
him. The husband predictably defended his actions: "At least I didn't tongue
her." The next few minutes proceeded with insult upon insult, to which the
audience "oohed" and "aahed" and applauded. To top it all off, viewers were
informed that the offense in question occurred at the husband's birthday
party, which his wife arranged, *stripper and all.* Then in the last few minutes
a psychologist pointed out the couple weren't wearing rings and didn't seem
committed. She suggested that their fighting might be related to some other
problem. Her comments seemed reasonable enough until she suggested that
the wife might really be trying to get her husband to rape her. That comment
called up some of the most absurd and destructive ideas imaginable about
male and female relationships—yet there was no explanation or discussion.

It is not that women and men don't find lots of ways to disappoint each   9
other, or that some women and some men don't act and think like the women
and men on the shows. The problem is talk TV's fixation on gender war, with
endless portrayals of vicious acts, overboard retaliations, and outrageous justifications. As a result, viewers are pumped full of the ugliest, nastiest news
from the front.

When issues affecting people of color are dealt with, the stereotypes   10
about gender are layered on top of the stereotypes about race. Since most of

the shows revolve around issues related to sex, violence, and relationships, they tend to feature people of color who reflect stereotypical images—in a steady stream of guests who have children out of wedlock, live on welfare, fight viciously, and have complicated unsolvable problems. While there are less than flattering depictions of white people on these shows, white viewers have the luxury of belonging to the dominant group, and therefore are more often presented in the media in positive ways.

On a *Ricki Lake* show about women who sleep with their friends' boyfriends, the majority of the guests were African American and Hispanic women who put on a flamboyant display of screaming and fighting. The profanity was so bad that many of the words had to be deleted. The segment had to be stopped because one guest yanked another's wig off. For many white viewers these are the images that form their beliefs about "minority" populations.

The shows set themselves up as reliable sources of information about what's really going on in the nation. And they often cover what sounds like common problems with work, love, and sex, but the information presented is skewed and confusing. Work problems become "fatal office feuds" and "back-stabbing coworkers." Problems concerning love, sex, or romance become "marriage with a fourteen-year-old," "women in love with the men who shoot them," or "man-stealing sisters." TV talk shows suggest that "marrying a rapist" or having a "defiant teen" are catastrophes about to happen to everyone.

Day in and day out, the shows parade all the myriad traumas, betrayals, and afflictions that could possibly befall us. They suggest that certain issues are more common than they actually are, and embellish the symptoms and outcomes. In actuality, relatively few people are likely to be abducted as children, join a Satanic cult in adolescence, fall in love with serial rapists, marry their cousins, hate their own race, or get sex changes in midlife, but when presented over and over again the suggestion is that they are quite likely to occur.

With their incessant focus on individual problems, television talk shows are a major contributor to the recent trend of elevating personal concerns to the level of personal rights and then affording those "rights" more attention than their accompanying responsibilities. Guests are brought on who have committed villainous acts (most often against other guests). The host and audience gratuitously "confront" the offenders about their wrongdoing and responsibilities. The alleged offenders almost always refute their accountability with revelations that they too were "victimized." On *Sally Jessy Raphael,* a man appeared with roses for the daughter he had sexually molested. He then revealed that he had been molested when he was five, and summed it up with "I'm on this show too! I need help, I'll go through therapy."

His sudden turnabout was not unusual. Viewers rarely see guests admit   15
error early in the show, but a reversal often occurs with just a few minutes
remaining. This works well for the shows because they need the conflict to
move steadily to a crescendo before the final "go to therapy" resolution.
But before that viewers are treated to lots of conflict and a heavy dose of
pseudo-psychological explanations that are really nothing more than excuses, and often lame ones at that. The guests present their problems, the
hosts encourage them to do so with concerned questions and occasional self-
disclosures, and the audience frequently get in on the act with their own tes-
timonies. Anything and everything goes.

The reigning motto is "Secrets keep you sick." On a *Jerry Springer* show   16
about confronting secrets, a husband revealed to his wife that he had been
having an affair. Not only was the unsuspecting wife humiliated and speechless, but Springer upped the ante by bringing out the mistress, who kissed
the husband and informed the wife that she loved them both. Conflict predictably ensued, and viewers were told this was a good idea because now the
problem was out in the open. When Ricki Lake did a similar show, a man explained to his very surprised roommate that he had "finally" informed the
roommate's mother that her son was gay, a secret the roommate had been
hiding from his family.

Referring to these premeditated catastrophes as simply "disclosures"   17
softens their edges and affords them a kind of legitimacy they do not deserve. On a program about bigamy, Sally Jessy Raphael invited two women
who had been married to the same man at the same time to appear on the
show. The man was also on, via satellite and in disguise. His nineteen-year-
old daughter by one of the wives sat on the stage while these women and
her father tore each other apart. Sally and the audience encouraged the fight
with "oohs" and "aahs" and rounds of applause at the ever-increasing accusations. A "relationship therapist" was brought on to do the postmortem.
Her most notable warning was that all this turmoil could turn the daughter
"to women," presumably meaning that she could become a lesbian. The
scenario was almost too absurd for words, but it was just one more show
like so many others: founded on stereotypes and capped off with clichés.
From the "catfight" to the "no-good father" to archaic explanations of
homosexuality—cheap thrills and bad advice are dressed up like information and expertise.

These scenarios are often legitimized by the use of pseudo-   18
psychological explanations, otherwise known as psychobabble. This is regularly used as a "disclaimer," or as a prelude to nasty revelations, or as a new
and more sophisticated way of reinforcing old stereotypes: "men are cognitive, not emotional," or "abused women draw abusive men to them." This
not only leaves viewers with nothing more than platitudes to explain problems and clichés to resolve them, but it fails to offer guests with enormous

conflicts and long histories of resentment and betrayals practical methods for changing their circumstances. The "four steps to get rid of your anger" may sound easy enough to implement, but what this kind of ready-made solution fails to acknowledge is that not all anger is the same, and certainly not everyone's anger needs the same treatment. Sometimes anger is a signal to people that they are being hurt, exploited, or taken advantage of, and it can motivate change.

Rather than encouraging discussion, exploration, or further under-   19
standing, psychobabble shuts it off. With only a phrase or two, we can believe that we understand all the related "issues." Guests confess that they are "codependents" or "enablers." Hosts encourage "healing," "empowerment," and "reclaiming of the inner spirit." In turn, viewers can nod knowingly without really knowing at all.

Talk TV initially had great potential as a vehicle for disseminating ac-   20
curate information and as a forum for public debate, although it would be hard to know it from what currently remains. Because most of these talk shows have come to rely on sensational entertainment as the means of increasing ratings, their potential has been lost. We are left with cheap shots, cheap thrills, and sound-bite stereotypes. Taken on its own, this combination is troubling enough, but when considered against the original opportunity for positive outcomes, what talk TV delivers is truly disturbing.

FIRST RESPONSES

Have you witnessed any of the negative effects Heaton warns of among people you know, including yourself? If so, describe the effects. If not, why not?

TAKING A CLOSER LOOK

Exploring *Who:* Voice and Tone

1. What is the tone of the essay; that is, what emotion does the writer convey?
2. What can you infer about Heaton's attitude toward television?
3. What tone do you usually hear when people discuss daytime TV talk shows?

Exploring *What:* Content and Meaning

1. According to Heaton, what were the positive contributions of TV talk shows such as *Oprah* and *Phil Donahue*?
2. List Heaton's main points against daytime TV talk shows.
3. What stereotypes does the writer accuse today's talk shows of reinforcing? Do you see this reinforcement when you watch such shows?
4. What is the difference between "psychobabble" and psychological explanations? Why do talk shows lean toward psychobabble? Why is that damaging to audiences?
5. What danger lies in overestimating the frequency of common problems (paras. 12 and 13)? Do you know people who overestimate the risk of getting robbed, experiencing violence, or being cheated? What is the source of their overestimation?

Exploring *Why:* Purpose

1. Was this essay written to persuade fans of daytime TV talk shows? What evidence did you see to decide your answer?
2. If the author had included a direct call to action, what might it be?
3. Was the point suggested by the title—that daytime TV talk shows destroy mental health—proven in this selection?
4. What do you know about the author? How does her profession affect her goals and intentions in writing about talk shows?

Exploring *How:* Style and Strategy

1. Given the title, were you surprised by the first three paragraphs? How do these three paragraphs affect the way you read the rest of the piece?
2. What are the two main types of supporting evidence used? What other types of evidence would be persuasive?
3. Identify two or three places where Heaton uses strong, emotional language. If her editor asked her to tone down her word choice, how could she defend its vividness?
4. If you were writing a critique of a daytime TV talk show you recently watched, which of Heaton's main points would you follow? What points would you add and develop that are not covered in Heaton's essay?

In Defense of Talk Shows

BARBARA EHRENREICH

Born in Butte, Montana, in 1941, Barbara Ehrenreich earned a doctorate in biology and taught for several years at the university level before turning to writing full time. An outspoken feminist and political activist, Ehrenreich has published eleven books, including *Blood Rites: Origins and History of the Passions of War* (1997) and *Nickel and Dimed: On (Not) Getting By in America* (2001). She is a frequent contributor to *Harper's Magazine, The New Republic, The Nation, The Progressive,* and the *New York Times Magazine.* The following essay first appeared in *Time* magazine in 1995.

Up until now, the targets of Bill (*The Book of Virtues*) Bennett's crusades have at least been plausible sources of evil. But the latest victim of his wrath—TV talk shows of the *Sally Jessy Raphael* variety—are in a whole different category from drugs and gangsta rap. As anyone who actually watched them knows, the talk shows are one of the most excruciatingly moralistic forums the culture has to offer. Disturbing and sometimes disgusting, yes, but their very business is to preach the middle-class virtues of responsibility, reason and self-control.   1

Take the case of Susan, recently featured on *Montel Williams* as an example of a woman being stalked by her ex-boyfriend. Turns out Susan is also stalking the boyfriend and—here's the sexual frisson—has slept with him only days ago. In fact Susan is neck deep in trouble without any help from the boyfriend: she's serving a yearlong stretch of home incarceration for assaulting another woman, and home is the tiny trailer she shares with her nine-year-old daughter.   2

But no one is applauding this life spun out of control. Montel scolds Susan roundly for neglecting her daughter and failing to confront her role in the mutual stalking. A therapist lectures her about this unhealthy "obsessive kind of love." The studio audience jeers at her every evasion. By the end Susan has lost her cocky charm and dissolved into tears of shame.   3

The plot is always the same. People with problems—"husband says she looks like a cow," "pressured to lose her virginity or else," "mate wants more sex than I do"—are introduced to rational methods of problem solving. People with moral failing—"boy crazy," "dresses like a tramp," "a hundred sex partners"—are introduced to external standards of morality. The preaching—delivered alternately by the studio audience, the host and the ever-present guest therapist—is relentless. "This is wrong to do this," Sally Jessy tells a cheating husband. "Feel bad?" Geraldo asks the girl who stole   4 her best friend's boyfriend, "Any sense of remorse?" The expectation is that the sinner, so hectored, will see her way to reform. And indeed, a Sally Jessy update found "boy crazy," who'd been a guest only weeks ago, now dressed in schoolgirlish plaid and claiming her "attitude [had] changed"—thanks to the rough-and-ready therapy dispensed on the show.

All right, the subjects are often lurid and even bizarre. But there's no part of the entertainment spectacle, from *Hard Copy* to *Jade,* that doesn't trade in the lurid and bizarre. At least in the talk shows, the moral is always loud and clear: Respect yourself, listen to others, stop beating on your wife. In fact it's hard to see how The Bill Bennett Show, if there were to be such a thing, could deliver a more pointed sermon. Or would he prefer to see the feckless Susan, for example, tarred and feathered by the studio audience instead of being merely booed and shamed? 5

There is something morally repulsive about the talks, but it's not anything Bennett or his co-crusader Senator Joseph Lieberman has seen fit to mention. Watch for a few hours, and you get the claustrophobic sense of lives that have never seen light of some external judgment, of people who have never before been listened to, and certainly never been taken seriously if they were. "What kind of people would let themselves be humiliated like this?" is often asked, sniffily, by the shows' detractors. And the answer, for the most part, is people who are so needy—of social support, of education, of material resources and self-esteem—that they mistake being the center of attention for being actually loved and respected. 6

What the talks are about, in large part, is poverty and the distortions it visits on the human spirit. You'll never find investment bankers bickering on *Rolonda,* or the host of *Gabrielle* recommending therapy to sobbing professors. With few exceptions the guests are drawn from trailer parks and tenements, from bleak streets and narrow, crowded rooms. Listen long enough, and you hear references to unpaid bills, to welfare, to 12-hour workdays and double shifts. And this is the real shame of the talks: that they take lives bent out of shape by poverty and hold them up as entertaining exhibits. An announcement appearing between segments of *Montel* says it all: the show is looking for "pregnant women who sell their bodies to make ends meet." 7

This is class exploitation, pure and simple. What next—"homeless people so hungry they eat their own scabs"? Or would the next step be to pay people outright to submit to public humiliation? For $50 would you confess to adultery in your wife's presence? For $500 would you reveal your thirteen-year-old's girlish secrets on *Ricki Lake*? If you were poor enough, you might. 8

It is easy enough for those who can afford spacious homes and private therapy to sneer at their financial inferiors and label their pathetic moments of stardom vulgar. But if I had a talk show, it would feature a whole differ- 9 ent cast of characters and category of crimes than you'll ever find on the talks: "CEOs who rake in millions while their employees get downsized" would be an obvious theme, along with "Senators who voted for welfare and Medicaid cuts"—and, if he'll agree to appear, "well-fed Republicans who dithered about talk shows while trailer-park residents slipped into madness and despair."

◆ ◆ ◆

FIRST RESPONSES

Do you find that people "sneer at their financial inferiors"? Think of an example. Can you also think of an example showing that people can be sympathetic to their financial inferiors?

TAKING A CLOSER LOOK

Exploring *Who:* Voice and Tone

1. List three words that describe the emotional tone of the essay.
2. What stance does the title suggest? That is, how do people sound when they defend something?
3. How does Ehrenreich sustain an analogy between talk shows and religious revivals? How does this analogy support her tone?

Exploring *What:* Content and Meaning

1. What are some targets of Bill Bennett's crusades, other than TV talk shows? Why are these targets "plausible sources of evil" (para. 1)?
2. What virtues are taught on talk shows, according to Ehrenreich?
3. What are "external standards of morality" (para. 4)?
4. Why is Ehrenreich sympathetic to the people who appear on talk shows?
5. Do you agree with the last sentence of paragraph 8? Why or why not?
6. What is "class exploitation" (para. 8)? What are some other examples of it?

Exploring *Why:* Purpose

1. Does the essay defend talk shows, as the title says? What is another title the essay could be given?
2. What does Ehrenreich want the reader to see about talk show guests? Have you ever thought about them in these terms before?
3. ▨ *Using the Internet.* Do some research to see what other topics Ehrenreich has written about recently. You can find information on her writing at www.well.com/user/srhodes/ehrenreich.html and at http://Inf.uoregon.edu/notable/ehrenreich.html. Does "In Defense of Talk Shows" fit in with her other topics? Is there a common purpose across her writings?

Exploring *How:* Style and Strategy

1. Reread the example in paragraph 2. What picture does it put in your mind? Add some more details you envision to the scene.
2. List the verbs and verbals (words made from verbs) in paragraph 3. What do they have in common?
3. What is humorous about "investment bankers bickering" and "sobbing professors" on daytime talk shows (para. 7)?
4. How many times does Ehrenreich use direct quotations from talk shows? Are they necessary?
5. Who is the "well-fed Republican" in the last line? Why is this ending appropriate for the piece?

IDEAS FOR WRITING ABOUT TALK SHOWS

1. ▨ *Using the Internet.* Defend your favorite TV talk show. To gather specific information and help develop your arguments, consult the show's Web page (most of them have one), or look at The Talkshow Page (www.eden.com/~johnny/letstalk.html), which has links to all the major talk shows.
2. Defend some other type of TV show that often comes under negative criticism (sitcoms, soap operas, sports coverage, reality TV, music TV, shopping TV, etc.).
3. How are the very rich portrayed on television? Write a critique of the treatment of the upper class in a defined type of TV show.

4. Choose some other form of media, communication, or art that once served a positive purpose or had promise (e.g., cartoons, music videos, performance art, rap music, call-in radio, TV courtroom shows, comedy clubs, reality TV, Internet chat rooms). Argue that it exploits a class or type of person, either as topic or audience (or both).

5. Look up Bill Bennett's point of view on TV talk shows around 1995, the target of Ehrenreich's defense. Write an essay that evenhandedly analyzes Ehrenreich's and Bill Bennett's arguments.

6. Would you allow your child to watch daytime TV talk shows? Write an essay persuading parents to ban a certain type of TV show from their children's viewing.

7. Heaton believes that the problems paraded on TV talk shows are actually rare, while Ehrenreich believes that the same problems are common to a certain class of people. How might you find out which writer is accurate? Choose one of the problems (or a set of related problems) and do some research to discover the facts about its frequency and class distribution, then argue for either Heaton's or Ehrenreich's point of view.

◆ DEBATE: SHOULD THE DEATH PENALTY BE ABOLISHED?

In 1972, the U.S. Supreme Court declared executions unconstitutional. Four years later, the Court approved their resumption. Between 1977 and 2001, 695 prisoners were put to death in the United States, most of them in the 1990s as the pace of executions increased, with a record number of 98 in 1999. As of January 2002, there were more than 3,700 inmates on death row in the United States.

The use of death as a punishment is one of America's most divisive issues. It raises difficult ethical, practical, and legal questions: Is it the most effective way to deal with convicted murderers? Is it fair to those who died to let their murderers go on living? Does it deter violent crime? Can innocent persons be executed by mistake? Is the possible execution of the innocent a necessary price to pay for the security of society? Can the death penalty be administered fairly? Although recent DNA evidence has cast doubt on the fairness and justice of executing criminals, opinion polls still show that most Americans favor some form of capital punishment, especially for vicious murders.

❖ ❖ ❖ PREPARING TO READ

Does your state sanction capital punishment? If you had to vote in a referendum to legalize or outlaw the death penalty in your state, how would you vote? What reasons would you give for your decision?

◆ ◆ ◆

Death and Justice

EDWARD I. KOCH

Edward Koch was born in the Bronx in 1924. He attended City College of New York, served in World War II, and received a law degree from New York University in 1948. Koch is best known for being the three-term mayor of New York City from 1978 to 1989. Prior to being mayor, he served for nine years in the U.S. Congress and for two years on the New York City Council. Koch is the author of twelve books, including *Mayor* (1984), *Citizen Koch* (1992), and *I'm Not Done Yet: Remaining Relevant* (2000). He has also acted as the presiding judge on *The People's Court.* The following article appeared in the April 1985 issue of the *New Republic* magazine.

Last December [1984] a man named Robert Lee Willie, who had been   1
convicted of raping and murdering an 18-year-old woman, was executed in the Louisiana state prison. In a statement issued several minutes before his death, Mr. Willie said: "Killing people is wrong. . . . It makes no difference whether it's citizens, countries, or governments. Killing is wrong." Two weeks later in South Carolina, an admitted killer named Joseph Carl Shaw was put to death for murdering two teenagers. In an appeal to the governor for clemency, Mr. Shaw wrote: "Killing is wrong when I did it. Killing is wrong when you do it. I hope you have the courage and moral strength to stop the killing."

It is a curiosity of modern life that we find ourselves being lectured on   2
morality by cold-blooded killers. Mr. Willie previously had been convicted of aggravated rape, aggravated kidnapping, and the murders of a Louisiana deputy and a man from Missouri. Mr. Shaw committed another murder a week before the two for which he was executed, and admitted mutilating the body of the 14-year-old girl he killed. I can't help wondering what prompted these murderers to speak out against killing as they entered the death-house door. Did their newfound reverence for life stem from the realization that they were about to lose their own?

Life is indeed precious, and I believe the death penalty helps to affirm   3
this fact. Had the death penalty been a real possibility in the minds of these murderers, they might well have stayed their hand. They might have shown moral awareness before their victims died, and not after. Consider the tragic death of Rosa Velez, who happened to be home when a man named Luis Vera burglarized her apartment in Brooklyn. "Yeah, I shot her," Vera admitted. "She knew me, and I knew I wouldn't go to the chair."

During my 22 years in public service, I have heard the pros and cons of   4
capital punishment expressed with special intensity. As a district leader, councilman, congressman, and mayor, I have represented constituencies generally thought of as liberal. Because I support the death penalty for heinous crimes of murder, I have sometimes been the subject of emotional and outraged attacks by voters who find my position reprehensible or worse. I have listened to their ideas. I have weighed their objections carefully. I still support the death penalty. The reasons I maintained my position can be best understood by examining the arguments most frequently heard in opposition.

1. *The death penalty is "barbaric."* Sometimes opponents of capital   5
punishment horrify with tales of lingering death on the gallows, of faulty electric chairs, or of agony in the gas chamber. Partly in response to such protests, several states such as North Carolina and Texas switched to execu-

tion by lethal injection. The condemned person is put to death painlessly, without ropes, voltage, bullets, or gas. Did this answer the objections of death penalty opponents? Of course not. On June 22, 1984, *The New York Times* published an editorial that sarcastically attacked the new "hygienic" method of death by injection, and stated that "execution can never be made humane through science." So it's not the method that really troubles opponents. It's the death itself they consider barbaric.

Admittedly, capital punishment is not a pleasant topic. However, one 6 does not have to like the death penalty in order to support it any more than one must like radical surgery, radiation, or chemotherapy in order to find necessary these attempts at curing cancer. Ultimately we may learn how to cure cancer with a simple pill. Unfortunately, that day has not yet arrived. Today we are faced with the choice of letting the cancer spread or trying to cure it with the methods available, methods that one day will almost certainly be considered barbaric. But to give up and do nothing would be far more barbaric and would certainly delay the discovery of an eventual cure. The analogy between cancer and murder is imperfect, because murder is not the "disease" we are trying to cure. The disease is injustice. We may not like the death penalty, but it must be available to punish crimes of cold-blooded murder, cases in which any other form of punishment would be inadequate and, therefore, unjust. If we create a society in which injustice is not tolerated, incidents of murder—the most flagrant form of injustice—will diminish.

2. *No other major democracy uses the death penalty.* No other major 7 democracy—in fact, few other countries of any description—are plagued by a murder rate such as that in the United States. Fewer and fewer Americans can remember the days when unlocked doors were the norm and murder was a rare and terrible offense. In America the murder rate climbed 122 percent between 1963 and 1980. During that same period, the murder rate in New York City increased by almost 400 percent, and the statistics are even worse in many other cities. A study at M.I.T. showed that based on 1970 homicide rates a person who lived in a large American city ran a greater risk of being murdered than an American soldier in World War II ran of being killed in combat. It is not surprising that the laws of each country differ according to differing conditions and traditions. If other countries had our murder problem, the cry for capital punishment would be just as loud as it is here. And I daresay that any other major democracy where 75 percent of the people supported the death penalty would soon enact it into law.

3. *An innocent person might be executed by mistake.* Consider the work 8 of Adam Bedau, one of the most implacable foes of capital punishment in this country. According to Mr. Bedau, it is "false sentimentality to argue that the death penalty should be abolished because of the abstract possibility that an innocent person might be executed." He cites a study of the 7,000 executions in this country from 1893 to 1971, and concludes that the record fails to show

that such cases occur. The main point, however, is this. If government functioned only when the possibility of error didn't exist, government wouldn't function at all. Human life deserves special protection, and one of the best ways to guarantee that protection is to assure that convicted murderers do not kill again. Only the death penalty can accomplish this end. In a recent case in New Jersey, a man named Richard Biegenwald was freed from prison after serving 18 years for murder; since his release he has been convicted of committing four murders. A prisoner named Lemuel Smith, who, while serving four life sentences for murder (plus two life sentences for kidnapping and robbery) in New York's Green Haven Prison, lured a woman corrections officer into the chaplain's office and strangled her. He then mutilated and dismembered her body. An additional life sentence for Smith is meaningless. Because New York has no death penalty statute, Smith has effectively been given a license to kill.

But the problem of multiple murder is not confined to the nation's penitentiaries. In 1981, 91 police officers were killed in the line of duty in this country. Seven percent of those arrested in the cases that have been solved had a previous arrest for murder. In New York City in 1976 and 1977, 85 persons arrested for homicide had a previous arrest for murder. Six of these individuals had two previous arrests for murder, and one had four previous murder arrests. During those two years the New York police were arresting for murder persons with a previous arrest for murder on the average of one every 8.5 days. This is not surprising when we learn that in 1975, for example, the median time served in Massachusetts for homicide was less than two-and-a-half years. In 1976 a study sponsored by the Twentieth Century Fund found that the average time served in the United States for first-degree murder is ten years. The median time served may be considerably lower.   9

4. *Capital punishment cheapens the value of human life.* On the contrary, it can be easily demonstrated that the death penalty strengthens the value of human life. If the penalty for rape were lowered, clearly it would signal a lessened regard for the victims' suffering, humiliation, and personal integrity. It would cheapen their horrible experience, and expose them to an increased danger of recurrence. When we lower the penalty for murder, it signals a lessened regard for the value of the victim's life. Some critics of capital punishment, such as columnist Jimmy Breslin, have suggested that a life sentence is actually a harsher penalty for murder than death. This is sophistic nonsense. A few killers may decide not to appeal a death sentence, but the overwhelming majority make every effort to stay alive. It is by exacting the highest penalty for the taking of human life that we affirm the highest value of human life.   10

5. *The death penalty is applied in a discriminatory manner.* This factor no longer seems to be the problem it once was. The appeals process for a condemned prisoner is lengthy and painstaking. Every effort is made to see that the verdict and sentence were fairly arrived at. However, assertions of   11

discrimination are not an argument for ending the death penalty but for extending it. It is not justice to exclude everyone from the penalty of the law if a few are found to be so favored. Justice requires that the law be applied equally to all.

6. *Thou shalt not kill.* The Bible is our greatest source of moral inspi-   12
ration. Opponents of the death penalty frequently cite the sixth of the Ten Commandments in an attempt to prove that capital punishment is divinely proscribed. In the original Hebrew, however, the Sixth Commandment reads, "Thou Shalt Not Commit Murder," and the Torah specifies capital punishment for a variety of offenses. The biblical viewpoint has been upheld by philosophers throughout history. The greatest thinkers of the 19th century— Kant, Locke, Hobbes, Rousseau, Montesquieu, and Mill—agreed that natural law properly authorizes the sovereign to take life in order to vindicate justice. Only Jeremy Bentham was ambivalent. Washington, Jefferson, and Franklin endorsed it. Abraham Lincoln authorized executions for deserters in wartime. Alexis de Tocqueville, who expressed profound respect for American institutions, believed that the death penalty was indispensable to the support of social order. The United States Constitution, widely admired as one of the seminal achievements in the history of humanity, condemns cruel and inhuman punishment, but does not condemn capital punishment.

7. *The death penalty is state-sanctioned murder.* This is the defense with   13
which Messrs. Willie and Shaw hoped to soften the resolve of those who sentenced them to death. By saying in effect, "You're no better than I am," the murderer seeks to bring his accusers down to his own level. It is also a popular argument among opponents of capital punishment, but a transparently false one. Simply put, the state has rights that the private individual does not. In a democracy, those rights are given to the state by the electorate. The execution of a lawfully condemned killer is no more an act of murder than is legal imprisonment an act of kidnapping. If an individual forces a neighbor to pay him money under threat of punishment, it's called extortion. If the state does it, it's called taxation. Rights and responsibilities surrendered by the individual are what give the state its power to govern. This contract is the foundation of civilization itself.

Everyone wants his or her rights, and will defend them jealously. Not   14
everyone, however, wants responsibilities, especially the painful responsibilities that come with law enforcement. Twenty-one years ago a woman named Kitty Genovese was assaulted and murdered on a street in New York. Dozens of neighbors heard her cries for help but did nothing to assist her. They didn't even call the police. In such a climate the criminal understandably grows bolder. In the presence of moral cowardice, he lectures us on our supposed failings and tries to equate his crimes with our quest for justice.

The death of anyone—even a convicted killer—diminishes us all. But   15
we are diminished even more by a justice system that fails to function. It is an illusion to let ourselves believe that doing away with capital punishment

removes the murderer's deed from our conscience. The rights of society are paramount. When we protect guilty lives, we give up innocent lives in exchange. When opponents of capital punishment say to the state: "I will not let you kill in my name," they are also saying to murderers: "You can kill in your *own* name as long as I have an excuse for not getting involved."

It is hard to imagine anything worse than being murdered while neighbors do nothing. But something worse exists. When those same neighbors shrink back from justly punishing the murderer, the victim dies twice.   16

◆ ◆ ◆

FIRST RESPONSES

After reading Koch's essay, would you change your vote in the referendum on the death penalty?

TAKING A CLOSER LOOK

Exploring *Who:* Voice and Tone

1. Why does Koch take the point-by-point refutation approach in this essay? What response is he anticipating with this approach?
2. Why does Koch include the information about himself in paragraph 4? How do these points influence your reactions to his argument?
3. How would you describe the author's tone in this essay? Does he seem to be lecturing his readers at any point? How do you respond to this tone of voice?

Exploring *What:* Content and Meaning

1. What sentence clearly expresses Koch's thesis?
2. Which of Koch's refutations are most convincing? Which are least convincing?
3. How does the author deal with the biblical injunction "Thou shalt not kill"? Did you find his reasoning persuasive?
4. What does the author mean when he says that "the state has rights that the private individual does not" (para. 13)? Do you agree with this view?
5. 🖥️ *Using the Internet.* Use a search engine to find information about recent capital cases in which DNA evidence has played a central role. How might familiarity with such cases force Koch to revise his arguments?

Exploring *Why:* Purpose

1. Why does Koch support the death penalty?
2. According to the author, how does the death penalty affirm that life is precious?
3. In paragraphs 14 and 15, Koch suggests that opponents of capital punishment are being irresponsible. Can you explain his reasoning on this point? Do you concur?

Exploring *How:* Style and Structure

1. Koch begins his essay with an extended example. Is that an effective opening? How does he use that example later in his essay?
2. Koch uses statistics and examples to support his arguments. Which of these types of evidence is more compelling? Explain your answer.
3. The author appeals to reason, character, and emotion. Find at least one example of each kind of appeal. Which ones are most effective? Why?
4. In paragraph 6, Koch compares murder and the death penalty to cancer. Is this **analogy** persuasive?

Forgiving the Unforgivable

CLAUDIA DREIFUS

Claudia Dreifus (born in 1944) has won several awards for her investigative reporting. Her 1978 story about the murder of a young American in Chile, which appeared in *Mother Jones,* was named Best Feature Article of the Year by the American Society of Journalists; her article "How Rural Women Are Saving Their Families' Farms," published in *Glamour,* received the American Values Award. Today, Dreifus is considered one of the leading interviewers in American journalism. Since the 1980s, more than 300 of her interviews have appeared in publications ranging from *TV Guide* and the *New York Times* to *Playboy* and *The Nation.* The following article comes from the July–August 2001 issue of *My Generation* magazine.

The white clapboard house that Robert "Renny" Cushing Jr. shares   1
with his wife, Kristie Conrad, and their three girls, looks like all the others

in the pretty New Hampshire village of Hampton—toys on the lawn, a barbecue and swing set in the back, a basketball hoop and two jaunty plastic flamingos planted in the ground. "This is it," Cushing says quietly as we step through the front door and into a small, white-painted, wood-paneled vestibule. "This is where it happened." He's talking about the murder of his father, Robert Cushing Sr., a retired elementary-school teacher and father of seven, who was shot in the chest, in this hallway, 13 years ago.

"After my father was killed, it seemed real important not to lose this   2 house," Cushing explains. He is a slim man with a long melancholy face and a strong New England accent. "My Dad and my grandfather built it. The killer may have taken my dad from us, but he wasn't going to take my roots, too. Staying here was one way of regaining control over my life. Besides, with time, the house has become something else. The floors that were once stained with my father's blood are also where my daughters learned how to walk."

The brutal murder of Robert Cushing Sr. could have turned his son   3 into someone obsessed with retribution; instead, it set him on the road to becoming one of the country's most articulate spokesmen against capital punishment, a practice that he believes to be "state-sanctioned, ritualized murder." As executive director of the 5,000-member Murder Victims' Families for Reconciliation, he now spends 12 hours a day counseling and supporting others who've experienced a homicide in their families. He also serves, he says, as the voice of victims within the anti–death penalty movement. "There's this myth out there that the families of victims need another killing for their healing," Cushing explains over coffee in his bright kitchen. A huge cat sleeps in a rocking chair, and his daughter Grace, 3, hums a "Barney" song in the next room. "The truth is, a lot of people are horrified by the very idea of an execution," he adds. "We know firsthand what violent death means, and we don't want to see society do it."

For years, a seriously disturbed Hampton police officer, Robert   4 McLaughlin Sr., had harbored an obsession with the Cushings. As a teenager, McLaughlin had shot his best friend to death, engaged in an armed robbery, and spent time at a reform school. After changing his name he had somehow managed to get onto the police force, where, Cushing believes, his badge protected him for 18 years.

As for Renny and his younger brothers, they were activists, '60s types   5 who had stayed in the village where they'd grown up, agitating for social change. In 1975, when an elderly neighbor claimed that Officer McLaughlin had manhandled and falsely arrested her, the Cushing brothers circulated a petition asking the town fathers to investigate. Nothing came of it, except that McLaughlin started keeping a paranoid eye on the Cushings. There was a lot to watch. In the late 1970s, Renny helped found the Clamshell Alliance, an activist organization opposed to the development of a nuclear-power station in the nearby town of Seabrook. McLaughlin would observe him leading demonstrations against the plant, and return to the police station to grumble: "Those Cushings have no respect for authority!"

By the spring of 1988, Cushing was a member of the state's House of Representatives. And although they had long forgotten about him, McLaughlin was still obsessively interested in the Cushings. Sometime in the 1980s, McLaughlin and his second wife, Susan, rented an apartment that faced directly into Robert Sr.'s backyard. The Cushings had no idea who their new neighbor was, but McLaughlin was watching them and stoking his grudge. One day he announced to his wife that he was going to teach the lawless clan next door a lesson—he was going to kill a Cushing.   6

At 10 P.M. on June 1, 1988, with Susan standing guard, McLaughlin rang the Cushings' doorbell and fired two blasts from a stolen shotgun at the first person to appear—Robert Cushing Sr. The McLaughlins fled into the protective darkness, leaving all of Hampton mystified by the terrifying event.   7

When a killing like this happens, it creates a circle of victimization that extends beyond the murdered person to the family and out into the community. "It's not just that you terribly miss the murdered person, which you do," Cushing tells me. "It's also that you feel like the world has gone out of control. There were three months where we had no idea who had done it. It was the worst—not knowing. For the victims to start to recover, you have to have some answers—and some justice."   8

But what kind of justice? Cushing had to confront that question publicly when he drove to a local store for groceries soon after the McLaughlins' arrest. A neighbor offered sympathy and then said, "I hope they fry those people, so your family can get some peace." Cushing was horrified that someone who knew him and his position on the death penalty could think he would change his beliefs as a result of what had happened.   9

The break in the case had come three months after the killing. McLaughlin began to fall apart, telling people he'd "whacked" the guy next door. He and his wife were arrested and put on trial in a lengthy, bizarre proceeding during which they often changed stories and strategies. What made it particularly difficult for Cushing was that his beliefs came under fierce scrutiny. "My opposition to nuclear power became an issue," he says. "The victims always get put on trial."   10

One day during a pretrial hearing, Cushing saw a young man at the courthouse. He was Robert McLaughlin Jr., the accused killer's son from a previous marriage. Watching him, Cushing felt "there was almost a black hole between the two of us that could suck us both down—we might both lose our fathers to this horrible act." He adds, "Advocates of the death penalty were telling me that I should want for Robert McLaughlin Jr. to have to visit the death house and wait for his father to be strapped down and poisoned. I realized then that I don't like the death penalty because it creates more victims."   11

In the end, both McLaughlins were sentenced to life imprisonment   12
without parole. The Cushing family finally felt safe, and able to move forward. "Prosecutors say that they often go for the death penalty because
victims' families need it for closure," Cushing says. "But a lot of families
are like mine, and they are appalled by it. I know of one woman who was
re-traumatized when she was invited to attend the execution of her relative's
killer. She couldn't understand why anyone thought she'd want to see that."

Life is never the same after a murder. The best survivors can do is try   13
to incorporate their burden and search for a way to honor the victim. Cushing began by moving his young family into his parents' house. His mother
couldn't bear to live there, and he eventually bought the place. He and his
wife renovated it, and their three girls, two of them born after the murder,
filled the home with a karma that was new, bright, optimistic.

Cushing found his opportunity to oppose the death penalty in 1998,   14
when, in the wake of several grisly homicides, the New Hampshire legislature
began considering a law to expand the grounds for capital punishment. Some
officials, including the Democratic governor, Jeanne Shaheen, were calling for
tougher death-penalty laws. As Cushing, also a Democrat, watched this stampede, he thought it reprehensible. Knowing that time and again studies had
shown capital punishment to be no deterrent to murder, he thought expanding the death penalty was a cynical political trick designed to allay legitimate public anxiety.

In an audacious move, he sponsored a bill to abolish the death penalty.   15
To give weight to his action, he went on the House floor and told his story.
"As one victim," he told his fellow legislators, "I favor abolition . . . not so
much because I want murderers to live as because, if the state kills them,
that forever forecloses the possibility that those of us who are victims might
figure out how to forgive. We've lost enough already. Don't take that option
for healing away, please." After Renny Cushing finished his speech, which
one legislator called one of the most emotional she'd ever heard, the Shaheen
proposal, which had been expected to pass easily, was voted down. But Cushing had opposed a governor from his own party on an issue with great popular support, and he was a Democrat in a traditionally Republican district.
Not surprisingly, he was voted out in the 1998 elections.

By then he was on fire about capital punishment. In the 10 years since   16
his father's murder, the national rate of executions had accelerated from 11
to 85 per year. In Cushing's mind, politicians were just ducking the hard work
of making the criminal justice system more effective. So during the 1998 election campaign, when he heard that a group of homicide survivors called Murder Victims' Families for Reconciliation (MVFR) was searching for a new
executive director, he went for the job. Working for MVFR was so important
to him that, Cushing says, "Even if I'd been re-elected, I would have resigned
my seat to take the job."

MVFR was founded 25 years ago by murder survivors who abhor cap-   17
ital punishment and consider themselves a bridge between the abolitionist
movement and the victims' rights community. Operating out of a small basement office in Cambridge, Massachusetts, with a staff of three, its membership list includes Samuel R. Sheppard—son of Dr. Sam Sheppard, whose
trial for the murder of his wife inspired two TV series and the movie *The
Fugitive*—and board member Bud Welch, whose daughter, Julie Marie, was
killed in the Oklahoma City bombing. Last spring, Welch had to relive his
tragedy when relatives of the bombing victims were granted the right to
watch Timothy McVeigh's execution. "Maybe this is some way for the people who are still carrying around a lot of revenge to vent," Welch said
somberly.

As executive director, Cushing travels the country speaking out against   18
capital punishment, publishes a newsletter, and counsels victims' families, as
well as the families of the condemned, about how to survive their trauma.
He's very good at his job. When the man who murdered former Congressman
Allard Lowenstein was unexpectedly freed by a New York judge last year,
Cushing immediately visited his son, MVFR member Thomas Lowenstein.
"He just showed up and comforted me," says Lowenstein. "He's lived through
the difficulties of the criminal justice system himself and has a lot of insights
on how you keep your values intact despite it." Lowenstein says both men
count on humor to get through the bad times. "He's got just enough nuttiness
not to take himself too seriously."

Cushing's achievements are substantial. He used the testimony of his   19
members to defeat two bills that would have imposed capital punishment in
Massachusetts. Across the country he has supported victims' families during
trials, hearings, and executions—most recently in Nebraska, where MVFR
helped two murder survivors, both Quakers, who had opposed the death
penalty for the killer of their relative and were refused a hearing because of
their position. "There's this assumption that if you don't want more killing,
you didn't really love the murdered person," says Cushing, who is a tireless
advocate for better victim-compensation laws. "We think that victims would
be much better off with counseling, financial assistance—which they often
need for funerals and medical expenses, legal help—than with an invitation
to an execution."

Listening to this passionate, persuasive man, one can't help but feel   20
that he's a better person than most of us. He brushes that idea aside. "I'm
doing this for myself, as well as others," he says firmly. "I didn't choose to be
a murder survivor; the situation chose me. I can, however, have some effect
on how I define the rest of my life. And this is my way of honoring my father's
memory."

◆ ◆ ◆

FIRST RESPONSES

Do you think you could forgive a person who killed someone you love? Does Renny Cushing's story help you to see the value of forgiveness?

TAKING A CLOSER LOOK

Exploring *Who:* Voice and Tone

1. How does Dreifus present Renny Cushing to her readers? Is she neutral, sympathetic, critical?
2. What is your response to Cushing and his views?
3. In the last paragraph, the author says, "Listening to this passionate, persuasive man, one can't help but feel that he's a better person than most of us." Why does she use "one" and not "I" in that sentence? Why does she say "most of us" rather than "most people"? Is there an inconsistency in the use of those two pronouns (*one* and *us*)?

Exploring *What:* Content and Meaning

1. Why did Robert McLaughlin kill Renny Cushing's father? What effect did seeing the accused killer's son have on Cushing? What did it make him realize about the death penalty?
2. Why does Cushing want murderers to live?
3. Cushing says that families of victims "know firsthand what violent death means, and we don't want to see society do it." How do you think Edward Koch would respond to this view?
4. According to Cushing, the increase in the number of executions is because politicians are "ducking the hard work of making the criminal justice system more effective" (para. 16). What does he mean?
5. What does Cushing think victims need more than "an invitation to an execution"?

Exploring *Why:* Purpose

1. What is Dreifus's purpose for writing this article? Is it primarily informative or persuasive?
2. To what extent is Dreifus's purpose the same as Cushing's? Explain.
3. In paragraph 3, the author includes this sentence: "A huge cat sleeps in a rocking chair, and his daughter Grace, 3, hums a "Barney" song in the next room." Why does she include these details? How do they contribute to the purpose of her article?

Exploring *How:* Style and Structure

1. Why does Dreifus begin with a description of the Cushings' house? What surprise element does she use in her opening?
2. The author quotes extensively from Cushing and others. What is the effect of these direct quotations? In what ways does the final quotation sum up the main point of the whole article?
3. Dreifus includes a number of examples of Cushing's actions and achievements. What do they illustrate about his character and beliefs? Which ones did you find most effective?

The Death Penalty on Trial

JONATHAN ALTER

Born in Chicago, Illinois, in 1957, Jonathan Alter received his B.A. in history from Harvard University in 1979. After working as a freelance reporter and editor at several publications, he joined the staff of *Newsweek* in 1983, where he moved to media critic in 1984, senior writer in 1987, and senior editor in 1991. Alter has covered the past four presidential campaigns and frequently interviewed Bill Clinton and other world leaders. In recent years, he has written extensively about the crisis of at-risk children in the United States. The following article appeared in June 2000 as part of *Newsweek*'s coverage of the Bush-Gore election campaign.

He stood at the threshold of the execution chamber in Huntsville, Texas, 18 minutes from death by lethal injection, when official word finally came that the needle wouldn't be needed that day. The rumors of a 30-day reprieve were true. Ricky McGinn, a 43-year-old mechanic found guilty of raping and killing his 12-year-old stepdaughter, will get his chance to prove his innocence with advanced DNA testing that hadn't been available at the time of his 1994 conviction. The double cheeseburger, French fries and Dr. Pepper he requested for dinner last Thursday night won't be his last meal after all.

Another galvanizing moment in the long-running debate over capital punishment: last week Gov. George W. Bush granted his first stay of execution in five years in office not because of deep doubts about McGinn's guilt; it was hard to find anyone outside McGinn's family willing to bet he was truly innocent. The doubts that concerned Bush were the ones spreading across the country about the fairness of a system with life-and-death stakes. "These death-penalty cases stir emotions," Bush told *Newsweek* in an exclusive interview about the decision. Imagine the emotions that would have been stirred had McGinn been executed, then proved innocent after death by DNA. So, Bush figured, why take the gamble?

"Whether McGinn is guilty or innocent, this case has helped establish 3 that all inmates eligible for DNA testing should get it," says Barry Scheck, the noted DNA legal expert and coauthor of *Actual Innocence*. "It's just common sense and decency."

Even as Bush made the decent decision, the McGinn case illustrated 4 why capital punishment in Texas is in the cross hairs this political season. For starters, McGinn's lawyer, like lawyers in too many capital cases, was no Clarence Darrow. Twice reprimanded by the state bar in unrelated cases (and handling five other capital appeals simultaneously), he didn't even begin focusing on the DNA tests that could save his client until this spring. Because Texas provides only $2,500 for investigators and expert witnesses in death-penalty appeals (enough for one day's work, if that), it took an unpaid investigator from out of state, Tina Church, to get the ball rolling.

After *Newsweek* shone a light on the then obscure case, Scheck and 5 the A-team of the Texas defense bar joined the appeal with a well-crafted brief to the trial court. When the local judge surprised observers by recommending that the testing be done, it caught Bush's attention. The hard-line higher state court and board of pardons both said no to the DNA tests— with no public explanation. This time, though, the eyes of the nation were on Texas, and Bush stepped in.

But what about the hundreds of other capital cases that unfold far from 6 the glare of a presidential campaign? As science sprints ahead of the law, assembly-line executions are making even supporters of the death penalty increasingly uneasy. McGinn's execution would have been the fifth in two weeks in Texas, the 132d on Bush's watch. Is that pace too fast? We now know that prosecutorial mistakes are not as rare as once assumed, competent counsel not as common. Since the Supreme Court allowed reinstatement of the death penalty in 1976, 87 death-row inmates have been freed from prison. With little money available to dig up new evidence and appeals courts usually unwilling to review claims of innocence (they are more likely to entertain possible procedural trial-court errors), it's impossible to know just how many other prisoners are living the ultimate nightmare.

So for the first time in a generation, the death penalty is in the dock— 7 on the defensive at home and especially abroad for being too arbitrary and too prone to error. The recent news has prompted even many conservative hard-liners to rethink their position. "There seems to be growing awareness that the death penalty is just another government program that doesn't work very well," says Stephen Bright of the Southern Center for Human Rights.

When Gov. George Ryan of Illinois, a pro-death-penalty Republican, 8 imposed a moratorium on capital punishment in January after 13 wrongly convicted men were released from Illinois's death row, it looked like a one-day event. Instead, the decision has resonated as one of the most important national stories of the year. The big question it raises, still unanswered: how can the 37 other states that allow the death penalty be so sure that their systems don't resemble the one in Illinois?

In that sense, the latest debate on the death penalty seems to be turning less on moral questions than on practical ones. While Roman Catholicism and other faiths have become increasingly outspoken in their opposition to capital punishment (even Pat Robertson is now against it), the new wave of doubts seems more hardheaded than softhearted, more about justice than faith.   9

The death penalty in America is far from dead. All it takes to know that is a glimpse of a grieving family, yearning for closure and worried about maximum sentences that aren't so long. According to the new *Newsweek* Poll, 73 percent still support capital punishment in at least some cases, down only slightly in five years. Heinous crimes still provoke calls for the strongest penalties. It's understandable, for instance, how the families victimized by the recent shooting at a New York Wendy's, which left five dead, would want the death penalty. And the realists are right: the vast majority of those on death row are guilty as hell.   10

But is a "vast majority" good enough when the issue is life or death? After years when politicians bragged about streamlining the process to speed up executions, the momentum is now moving the opposite way. The homicide rate is down 30 percent nationally in five years, draining some of the intensity from the pro-death-penalty argument. And fairness is increasingly important to the public. Although only two states—Illinois and New York—currently give inmates the right to have their DNA tested, 95 percent of Americans want that right guaranteed, according to the *Newsweek* Poll. Close to 90 percent even support the idea of federal guarantees of DNA testing (contained in the bipartisan Leahy-Smith Innocence Protection bill), though Bush and Gore, newly conscious of the issue, both prefer state remedies.   11

The explanation for the public mood may be that cases of injustice keep coming, and not just on recent episodes of the "The Practice" that (with Scheck as a script adviser) uncannily anticipated the McGinn case. In the last week alone Bush pardoned A. B. Butler after he served 17 years in prison for a sexual assault he didn't commit, and Virginia Gov. James Gilmore ordered new testing that will likely free Earl Washington, also after 17 years behind bars. All told, more than 70 inmates have been exonerated by DNA evidence since 1982, including eight on death row.   12

Death-penalty advocates often point out that no one has been proved innocent after execution. But the DNA evidence that could establish such innocence has frequently been lost by prosecutors with no incentive to keep it. In a recent Virginia case, a court actually prevented posthumous examination of DNA evidence. On the defense side, lawyers and investigators concentrate their scarce resources on cases where lives can be spared.   13

And while DNA answers some questions, it raises others: if so many inmates are exonerated in rape and rape-murder cases where DNA is obtainable, how about the vast majority of murders, where there is no DNA? Might not the rate of error be comparable?

Politics, for once, seems to be in the background, largely because views of the death penalty don't break down strictly along party lines. Ryan of Illinois is a Republican; Gray Davis, the hard-line governor of California, a Democrat. The Republican-controlled New Hampshire Legislature recently voted to abolish the death penalty; the Democratic governor vetoed the bill. Perhaps the best way to understand how the politics of the death penalty is shifting is to view it as a tale of two Rickys:

In January 1992, Arkansas Gov. Bill Clinton interrupted his presidential campaign to return home to preside over the execution of Ricky Ray Rector, a black man convicted of killing a police officer. Rector had lobotomized himself with a bullet to his head; he was so incapacitated that he asked that the pie served at his last meal be saved for "later." By not preventing the execution of a mentally impaired man, Clinton was sending a strong message to voters: the era of soft-on-crime Democrats was over. Even now, Al Gore doesn't dare step out front on death-penalty issues.

Ricky McGinn's case presented a different opportunity for Bush. While the decision to grant a stay was largely based on common sense and the merits of the case, it was convenient, too. In 1999, *Talk* magazine caught Bush making fun of Karla Faye Tucker, the first woman executed in Texas since the Civil War. Earlier this year, at a campaign debate sponsored by CNN, the cameras showed the governor chuckling over the case of Calvin Burdine, whose lawyer fell asleep at his trial. In going the extra mile for McGinn over the objections of the appeals court and parole board, Bush looked prudent and blunted some of the criticism of how he vetoed a bill establishing a public defenders' office in Texas and made it harder for death-row inmates to challenge the system.

That system has scheduled 19 more Texas executions between now and Election Day. Gary Graham, slated to die June 22, was convicted on the basis of one sketchy eyewitness account when he was 17. The absence of multiple witnesses would make him ineligible for execution in the Bible ("At the mouth of one witness he shall not be put to death"—Deuteronomy 17:6); and Graham's age at the time he was convicted of the crime in 1981 would make him too young to be executed in all but four other nations in the world.

Americans might not realize how upset the rest of the world has become over the death penalty. All of our major allies except Japan (with a half-dozen executions a year) have abolished the practice. Only China, Iran, Saudi Arabia, and Congo execute more than the United States. A draft version of the European Union's Bill of Rights published last week bars EU countries from extraditing a suspected criminal to a country with a death penalty. (If approved, this could wreak havoc with international law enforcement.) Admission to the EU is now contingent on ending capital punishment, which will force Turkey to abolish its once harsh death-penalty system.

The execution of juvenile offenders is a particular sore spot abroad. 20 The United States has 73 men on death row for crimes committed when they were too young to drink or vote (mostly age 17); 16 have been executed, including eight in Texas. That's more than the rest of the world combined.

So far, opposition abroad has had little effect at home. What changed 21 the climate in the United States was a series of cases in Illinois. The story traces back to the convictions of four black men, two of whom were condemned to die, for the 1978 murders of a white couple in the Chicago suburb of Ford Heights. In the early 1980s, Rob Warden and Margaret Roberts, the editors of a crusading legal publication called *The Chicago Lawyer*, turned up evidence that the four might be innocent. The state's case fell apart in 1996, after DNA evidence showed that none of the so-called Ford Heights Four could have raped the woman victim. It was only one case, but it had a searing effect in Illinois for this reason: three other men confessed to the crime and were convicted of it. The original four were unquestionably innocent—and two of them had nearly been executed.

By then other Illinois capital cases were falling apart. Some of the key 22 legwork in unraveling bum convictions came from Northwestern University journalism students. Late in 1998 their school hosted a conference on wrongful convictions. The event produced a stunning photo op: 30 people who'd been freed from death rows across the country, all gathered on one Chicago stage.

But it was another Illinois case, early in 1999, that really began to tip 23 public opinion. A new crop of Northwestern students helped prove the innocence of Anthony Porter, who at one point had been just two days shy of lethal injection for a pair of 1982 murders. Once again, the issue in Illinois wasn't the morality of death sentences, but the dangerously sloppy way in which they were handed out. Once again a confession from another man helped erase doubt that the man convicted of the crime, who has an IQ of 51, had committed it.

By last fall the list of men freed from death row in Illinois had grown 24 to 11. That's when the *Chicago Tribune* published a lavishly researched series explaining why so many capital cases were suspect. The *Tribune*'s digging found that almost half of the 285 death-penalty convictions in Illinois involved one of four shaky components: defense attorneys who were later suspended or disbarred, jailhouse snitches eager to shorten their own sentences, questionable "hair analysis" evidence, or black defendants convicted by all-white juries. What's more, in the weeks after those stories appeared, two more men were freed from death row. That pushed the total to 13—one more than the number of inmates Illinois had executed since reinstating the death penalty in 1977.

The Porter case and the *Tribune* series were enough for Governor   25
Ryan. On Jan. 31, he declared a moratorium on Illinois executions, and appointed a commission to see whether the legal process for handling capital
cases in Illinois can be fixed. Unless he gets a guarantee that the system can
be made perfect, Ryan told *Newsweek* last week, "there probably won't be
any more deaths," at least while he's governor. "I believe there are cases
where the death penalty is appropriate," Ryan said. "But we've got to make
sure we have the right person. Every governor who holds this power has the
same fear I do."

But few are acting on it. In the wake of the Illinois decision, only Ne-   26
braska, Maryland, Oregon, and New Hampshire are reviewing their systems.
The governors of the other states that allow the death penalty apparently
think it works adequately. If they want to revisit the issue, they might consider
the following factors:

Race. The role of race and the death penalty is often misunderstood. On   27
one level, there's the charge of institutional racism: 98 percent of prosecutors
are white, and, according to the NAACP Legal Defense Fund, they are much
more likely to ask for the death penalty for a black-on-white crime than when
blacks are the victims. Blacks convicted of major violent offenses are more
likely than white convicts to end up on death row. But once they get there,
blacks are less likely than white death-row inmates to be executed because
authorities are on the defensive about seeming to target African-Americans.
The result is both discrimination and reverse discrimination—with deadly
consequences.

The risk of errors. The more people on death row, the greater chance   28
of mistakes. There are common elements to cases where terrible errors have
been made: when police and prosecutors are pressured by the community
to "solve" a notorious murder; when there's no DNA evidence or reliable
eyewitnesses; when the crime is especially heinous and draws large amounts
of pretrial publicity; when defense attorneys have limited resources. If authorities were particularly vigilant when these issues were at play, they might
identify problematic cases earlier.

Deterrence. Often the first argument of death-penalty supporters. But   29
studies of the subject are all over the lot, with no evidence ever established
of a deterrent effect. When parole was more common, the argument carried
more logic. But nowadays first-degree murderers can look forward to life
without parole if caught, which should in theory deter them as much as the
death penalty. It's hard to imagine a criminal's thinking: "Well, since I might
get the death penalty for this crime, I won't do it. But if it was only life in
prison, I'd go ahead."

Inadequate counsel. Beyond the incompetent lawyers who populate   30
any court-appointed system, Congress and the Clinton administration
have put the nation's 3,600 death-row inmates in an agonizing Catch-22.

According to the American Bar Association Death Penalty Representation Project, in a state like California, about one third of death-row inmates must wait for years to be assigned lawyers to handle their state direct appeals. And at the post-conviction level in some states, inmates don't have access to lawyers at all. The catch is that the 1996 Anti-Terrorism and Effective Death Penalty Act has a statute of limitations requiring that inmates file federal habeas corpus petitions (requests for federal court review) within one year after the end of their direct state appeal. In other words, because they have no lawyer after their direct appeals, inmates often helplessly watch the clock run out on their chance for federal review. This cuts down on frivolous appeals—but also on ones that could reveal gross injustice.

Fact-finding. Most states aren't as lucky as Illinois. They don't have re-   31
porters and investigators digging into the details of old cases. As the death penalty becomes routine and less newsworthy, the odds against real investigation grow even worse. And even when fresh evidence does surface, most states place high barriers against its use after a trial. This has been standard in the legal system for generations, but it makes little sense when an inmate's life is at stake.

Standards of guilt. In most jurisdictions, the judge instructs the jury to   32
look for "guilt beyond a reasonable doubt." But is that the right standard for capital cases? Maybe a second standard like "residual doubt" would help, whereby if any juror harbors any doubt whatsoever, the conviction would stand but the death penalty would be ruled out. The same double threshold might apply to cases invoking single eyewitnesses and key testimony by jailhouse snitches with incentives to lie.

Cost. Unless executions are dramatically speeded up (unlikely after so   33
many mistakes), the death penalty will remain far more expensive than life without parole. The difference is in the up-front prosecution costs, which are at least four times greater than in cases where death is not sought. California spends an extra $90 million on its capital cases beyond the normal costs of the system. Even subtracting pro bono defense, the system is no bargain for taxpayers.

Whether you're for or against the death penalty, it's hard to argue that   34
it doesn't need a fresh look. From America's earliest days, when Benjamin Franklin helped develop the notion of degrees of culpability for murder, this country has been willing to reassess its assumptions about justice. If we're going to keep the death penalty, the public seems to be saying, let's be damn sure we're doing it right. DNA testing will help. So will other fixes. But if, over time, we can't do it right, then we must ask ourselves if it's worth doing at all.

◆ ◆ ◆

FIRST RESPONSES

Do you agree that the death penalty needs "a fresh look"? What needs to be reconsidered? What will that fresh look accomplish?

TAKING A CLOSER LOOK

Exploring *Who:* Voice and Tone

1. Does this article present an objective discussion of the death penalty debate? Where does Alter reveal his own opinions about the issues?
2. There are a number of references to *Newsweek* in the article: "Bush told *Newsweek*," "After *Newsweek* shone a light," "According to the new *Newsweek* Poll." What is the point of these citations? How do they affect your response to the article?

Exploring *What:* Content and Meaning

1. ▆ *Using the Internet.* Why does the article focus on the Ricky McGinn case? What happened to him after the article was written? You can find the answer to that question on the Internet. Does the outcome of his case change the point of the article?
2. According to Alter, why is the death penalty "on the defensive"?
3. What did Governor George Ryan of Illinois do that was so unusual and important? Why did he do what he did?
4. What point does Alter make about world opinion on capital punishment (paras. 19–21)? Do you think the opinion of other countries is important?
5. Explain what the author means when he says there is "both discrimination and reverse discrimination" in applying the death penalty (para. 27).

Exploring *Why:* Purpose

1. The author says that "the new wave of doubts [about the death penalty] seems more hardheaded than softhearted, more about justice than faith" (para. 9). What does he mean? What does this observation imply about the article's purpose?
2. Why does Alter suggest that the governors of other states might want to "revisit the issue" (para. 26)? What is his goal in giving them a list of factors to consider?

Exploring *How:* Style and Structure

1. Alter cites a lot of statistics. Does he use them logically and convincingly? Which uses of statistics did you find most persuasive?
2. Where does the author appeal to your reason and good judgment? Where does he appeal to your emotions? Find examples of each. Are these valid appeals? Are they effective?
3. Why does the author quote the Bible in paragraph 18?
4. Find five examples of **rhetorical questions.** Explain how each one functions.

IDEAS FOR WRITING ABOUT THE DEATH PENALTY

1. Using the point-by-point refutation format, respond to the seven arguments Edward Koch makes in his essay "Death and Justice." Begin each point of refutation by summarizing Koch's position, and then present your reply to that position.
2. ▮📄 *Using the Internet.* Visit the Web site for Murder Victims' Families for Reconciliation (www.mvfr.org). Then write a letter to the organization, supporting or objecting to their work. Be sure to give reasons and explanations for your views.
3. The film *Dead Man Walking* (1995) focuses on capital punishment. Check out a video of *Dead Man Walking* from the library or a local video store, and take notes on its treatment of the death penalty debate. Is it for or against capital punishment, or does it present a balanced view? Write a review of the film in which you evaluate its handling of the issues.
4. ▮📄 *Using the Internet.* Write an essay in which you argue for the best way to punish people convicted of capital crimes. Be sure to address possible objections to your views. If you need to, gather more information at the Death Penalty Information Center at www.deathpenaltyinfo.org/.

◆◆◆◆◆◆◆◆ C H A P T E R   12 ◆◆◆◆◆◆◆◆

Further Readings

Two Thematic Clusters

◆ ◆ ◆ ◆ ◆

◆ ON IMMIGRATION

What would it feel like to leave your home and settle in a foreign country? How would you feel about leaving your friends and relatives, knowing you might not see them again? What would motivate you to make such a move? Thousands of people resettle in new countries every year. Some are driven by hope, others by economic hardships or political oppression, many by a combination of forces and conditions. They all must figure out how to adapt to the beliefs and customs of their new homeland while holding on to their own heritage and cultural identity.

Although the United States has been shaped by successive waves of immigrants, Americans have often seen immigration as a problem. A hundred years ago, at the peak of the last great wave of immigration, people feared that the new immigrants would never fit in, that they were bringing alien values, that they would harm the economy, that they would never learn English. Today, the grandchildren of those immigrants are expressing similar fears.

The articles in this section examine some of the current issues surrounding immigration and immigrants in this country. In "Life and Hard Times on the Mexican Border," Luis Alberto Urrea describes the plight of "undocumented workers" who are seeking a new life in the United States. In "Two Ways to Belong in America," Bharati Mukherjee explains the differences between herself, who chose to become a U.S. citizen, and her sister, who remained a resident alien (an immigrant who lives in the country legally but chooses not to apply for citizenship). And in "Five Myths about Immigration," David Cole refutes the principal misconceptions many Americans have about immigrants.

Life and Hard Times on the Mexican Border

LUIS ALBERTO URREA

Born in 1955 in Tijuana to a Mexican father and an American mother, Luis Alberto Urrea grew up in San Diego and attended the University of California. After a brief career as a movie extra, he worked with an organization that provides food, clothing, and medical supplies to the poor of northern Mexico. Urrea now teaches writing at the University of Illinois at Chicago. He has written a novel and several collections of poetry, but he is best known for the series of autobiographical books—*Across the Wire* (1993), *Sleeping Children* (1996), and *Nobody's Son* (1998)—that dramatize the lives and struggles of Mexicans living just south of the U.S. border.

1   At night, the Border Patrol helicopters swoop and churn in the air all along the line. You can sit in the Mexican hills and watch them herd humans on the dusty slopes across the valley. They look like science fiction crafts, their hard-focused lights raking the ground as they fly.

2   Borderlands locals are so jaded by the sight of nightly people-hunting that it doesn't even register in their minds. But take a stranger to the border, and she will *see* the spectacle: monstrous Dodge trucks speeding into and out of the landscape; uniformed men patrolling with flashlights, guns, and dogs; spotlights; running figures; lines of people hurried onto buses by armed guards; and the endless clatter of the helicopters with their harsh white beams. A Dutch woman once told me it seemed altogether "un-American."

3   But the Mexicans keep on coming—and the Guatemalans, the Salvadorans, the Panamanians, the Colombians. The seven-mile stretch of Interstate 5 nearest the Mexican border is, at times, so congested with Latin American pedestrians that it resembles a town square.

4   They stick to the center island. Running down the length of the island is a cement wall. If the "illegals" (currently, "undocumented workers"; formerly, "wetbacks") are walking north and a Border Patrol vehicle happens along, they simply hop over the wall and trot south. The officer will have to drive up to the 805 interchange, or Dairy Mart Road, swing over the overpasses, then drive south. Depending on where this pursuit begins, his detour could entail five to ten miles of driving. When the officer finally reaches the group, they hop over the wall and trot north. Furthermore, because freeway arrests would endanger traffic, the Border Patrol has effectively thrown up its hands in surrender.

5   It seems jolly on the page. But imagine poverty, violence, natural disasters, or political fear driving you away from everything you know. Imagine

how bad things get to make you leave behind your family, your friends, your lovers; your home, as humble as it might be; your church, say. Let's take it further—you've said good-bye to the graveyard, the dog, the goat, the mountains where you first hunted, your grade school, your state, your favorite spot on the river where you fished and took time to think.

Then you come hundreds—or thousands—of miles across territory utterly unknown to you. (Chances are, you have never traveled farther than a hundred miles in your life.) You have walked, run, hidden in the backs of trucks, spent part of your precious money on bus fare. There is no AAA or Travelers Aid Society available to you. Various features of your journey north might include police corruption; violence in the forms of beatings, rape, murder, torture, road accidents; theft; incarceration. Additionally, you might experience loneliness, fear, exhaustion, sorrow, cold, heat, diarrhea, thirst, hunger. There is no medical attention available to you. There isn't even Kotex. 6

Weeks or months later, you arrive in Tijuana. Along with other immigrants, you gravitate to the bad parts of town because there is nowhere for you to go in the glittery sections where the *gringos* flock. You stay in a run-down little hotel in the red-light district, or behind the bus terminal. Or you find your way to the garbage dumps, where you throw together a small cardboard nest and claim a few feet of dirt for yourself. The garbage-pickers working this dump might allow you to squat, or they might come and rob you or burn you out for breaking some local rule you cannot possibly know beforehand. Sometimes the dump is controlled by a syndicate, and goon squads might come to you within a day. They want money, and if you can't pay, you must leave or suffer the consequences. 7

In town, you face endless victimization if you aren't streetwise. The police come after you, street thugs come after you, petty criminals come after you; strangers try your door at night as you sleep. Many shady men offer to guide you across the border, and each one wants all your money now, and promises to meet you at a prearranged spot. Some of your fellow travelers end their journeys right here—relieved of their savings and left to wait on a dark corner until they realize they are going nowhere. 8

If you are not Mexican, and can't pass as *tijuanense*, a local, the tough guys find you out. Salvadorans and Guatemalans are routinely beaten up and robbed. Sometimes they are disfigured. Indians—Chinantecas, Mixtecas, Guasaves, Zapotecas, Mayas—are insulted and pushed around; often they are lucky—they are merely ignored. They use this to their advantage. Often they don't dream of crossing into the United States: a Mexican tribal person would never be able to blend in, and they know it. To them, the garbage dumps and street vending and begging in Tijuana are a vast improvement over their former lives. As Doña Paula, a Chinanteca friend of mine who lives at the Tijuana garbage dump, told me, "This is the garbage dump. Take all you need. There's plenty here for *everyone!*" 9

If you are a woman, the men come after you. You lock yourself in your room, and when you must leave it to use the pestilential public bathroom at the end of your floor, you hurry, and you check every corner. Sometimes the lights are out in the toilet room. Sometimes men listen at the door. They call you "good-looking" and "bitch" and "*mamacita*", and they make kissing sounds at you when you pass. 10

You're in the worst part of town, but you can comfort yourself—at least there are no death squads here. There are no torturers here, or bandit land barons riding into your house. This is the last barrier, you think, between you and the United States—*los Yunaites Estaites*. 11

You still face police corruption, violence, jail. You now also have a wide variety of new options available to you: drugs, prostitution, white slavery, crime. Tijuana is not easy on newcomers. It is a city that has always thrived on taking advantage of a sucker. And the innocent are the ultimate suckers in the Borderlands. 12

◆ ◆ ◆

Two Ways to Belong in America

BHARATI MUKHERJEE

Born in India in 1940, Bharati Mukherjee was educated in Calcutta by Irish nuns and later went to school in England and Switzerland. After attending the Writer's Workshop at the University of Iowa in 1961, she moved to Canada, where she taught at McGill University. Now a naturalized U.S. citizen, she teaches at Skidmore College. Her novels—*Tiger's Daughter* (1972), *Jasmine* (1989), and *Leave It to Me* (1997)—depict Indian women confronting the disparity between Indian and American cultures. Her story collections—*Darkness* (1975) and *The Middleman and Other Stories* (1988)—also focus on the immigrant experience. Mukherjee wrote the following article in response to proposals (eventually defeated) to deny government benefits, such as Social Security, to resident aliens; it appeared in the *New York Times* in 1996.

This is a tale of two sisters from Calcutta, Mira and Bharati, who have   1
lived in the United States for some 35 years, but who find themselves on different sides in the current debate over the status of immigrants. I am an American citizen and she is not. I am moved that thousands of long-term residents are finally taking the oath of citizenship. She is not.

Mira arrived in Detroit in 1960 to study child psychology and pre-school   2
education. I followed her a year later to study creative writing at the University of Iowa. When we left India, we were almost identical in appearance and attitude. We dressed alike, in saris; we expressed identical views on politics, social issues, love, and marriage in the same Calcutta convent-school accent. We would endure our two years in America, secure our degrees, then return to India to marry the grooms of our father's choosing.

Instead, Mira married an Indian student in 1962 who was getting his   3
business administration degree at Wayne State University. They soon acquired the labor certifications necessary for the green card of hassle-free residence and employment.

Mira still lives in Detroit, works in the Southfield, Michigan, school sys-   4
tem, and has become nationally recognized for her contributions in the fields of pre-school education and parent-teacher relationships. After 36 years as a legal immigrant in this country, she clings passionately to her Indian citizenship and hopes to go home to India when she retires.

In Iowa City in 1963, I married a fellow student, an American of Cana-   5
dian parentage. Because of the accident of his North Dakota birth, I bypassed labor-certification requirements and the race-related "quota" system that favored the applicant's country of origin over his or her merit. I was prepared for (and even welcomed) the emotional strain that came with marrying

outside my ethnic community. In 33 years of marriage, we have lived in every part of North America. By choosing a husband who was not my father's selection, I was opting for fluidity, self-invention, blue jeans and T-shirts, and renouncing 3,000 years (at least) of caste-observant, "pure culture" marriage in the Mukherjee family. My books have often been read as unapologetic (and in some quarters overenthusiastic) texts for cultural and psychological "mongrelization." It's a word I celebrate.

Mira and I have stayed sisterly close by phone. In our regular Sunday   6
morning conversations, we are unguardedly affectionate. I am her only blood relative on this continent. We expect to see each other through the looming crises of aging and ill health without being asked. Long before Vice President Gore's "Citizenship U.S.A." drive, we'd had our polite arguments over the ethics of retaining an overseas citizenship while expecting the permanent protection and economic benefits that come with living and working in America.

Like well-raised sisters, we never said what was really on our minds,   7
but we probably pitied one another. She, for the lack of structure in my life, the erasure of Indianness, the absence of an unvarying daily core. I, for the narrowness of her perspective, her uninvolvement with the mythic depths or the superficial pop culture of this society. But, now, with the scapegoating of "aliens" (documented or illegal) on the increase, and the targeting of long-term legal immigrants like Mira for new scrutiny and new self-consciousness, she and I find ourselves unable to maintain the same polite discretion. We were always unacknowledged adversaries, and we are now, more than ever, sisters.

"I feel used," Mira raged on the phone the other night. "I feel manip-   8
ulated and discarded. This is such an unfair way to treat a person who was invited to stay and work here because of her talent. My employer went to the I.N.S. and petitioned for the labor certification. For over 30 years, I've invested my creativity and professional skills into the improvement of *this* country's pre-school system. I've obeyed all the rules, I've paid my taxes, I love my work, I love my students, I love the friends I've made. How dare America now change its rules in midstream? If America wants to make new rules curtailing benefits of legal immigrants, they should apply only to immigrants who arrive after those rules are already in place."

To my ears, it sounded like the description of a long-enduring, com-   9
fortable yet loveless marriage, without risk or recklessness. Have we the right to demand, and to expect, that we be loved? (That, to me, is the subtext of the arguments by immigration advocates.) My sister is an expatriate, professionally generous and creative, socially courteous and gracious, and that's as far as her Americanization can go. She is here to maintain an identity, not to transform it.

I asked her if she would follow the example of others who have de-   10
cided to become citizens because of the anti-immigration bills in Congress.

And here, she surprised me. "If America wants to play the manipulative game, I'll play it, too," she snapped. "I'll become a U.S. citizen for now, then change back to Indian when I'm ready to go home. I feel some kind of irrational attachment to India that I don't to America. Until all this hysteria against legal immigrants, I was totally happy. Having my green card meant I could visit any place in the world I wanted to and then come back to a job that's satisfying and that I do very well."

In one family, from two sisters alike as peas in a pod, there could not be a wider divergence of immigrant experience. America spoke to me— I married it—I embraced the demotion from expatriate aristocrat to immigrant nobody, surrendering those thousands of years of "pure culture," the saris, the delightfully accented English. She retained them all. Which of us is the freak?   11

Mira's voice, I realize, is the voice not just of the immigrant South Asian community but of an immigrant community of the millions who have stayed rooted in one job, one city, one house, one ancestral culture, one cuisine, for the entirety of their productive years. She speaks for greater numbers than I possibly can. Only the fluency of her English and the anger, rather than fear, born of confidence from her education, differentiate her from the seamstresses, the domestics, the technicians, the shop owners, the millions of hardworking but effectively silenced documented immigrants as well as their less fortunate "illegal" brothers and sisters.   12

Nearly 20 years ago, when I was living in my husband's ancestral homeland of Canada, I was always well-employed but never allowed to feel part of the local Quebec or larger Canadian society. Then, through a Green Paper that invited a national referendum on the unwanted side effects of "nontraditional" immigration, the Government officially turned against its immigrant communities, particularly those from South Asia.   13

I felt then the same sense of betrayal that Mira feels now. I will never forget the pain of that sudden turning, and the casual racist outbursts the Green Paper elicited. That sense of betrayal had its desired effect and drove me, and thousands like me, from the country.   14

Mira and I differ, however, in the ways in which we hope to interact with the country that we have chosen to live in. She is happier to live in America as expatriate Indian than as an immigrant American. I need to feel like a part of the community I have adopted (as I tried to feel in Canada as well). I need to put roots down, to vote and make the difference that I can. The price that the immigrant willingly pays, and that the exile avoids, is the trauma of self-transformation.   15

◆ ◆ ◆

Five Myths about Immigration

DAVID COLE

David Cole (born 1928) is a graduate of Yale University and Yale Law School and a professor of constitutional law at Georgetown University. He frequently writes articles both for general audiences in newspapers such as the *New York Times* and the *Washington Post* and for legal experts in journals such as *Legal Times* and the *Stanford Law Review*. His most recent book is *No Equal Justice: Race and Class in the American Criminal Justice System* (1999). The following essay appeared in *The Nation* in the fall of 1994.

For a brief period in the mid-nineteenth century, a new political move-   1
ment captured the passions of the American public. Fittingly labeled the "Know-Nothings," their unifying theme was nativism. They liked to call themselves "Native Americans," although they had no sympathy for people we call Native Americans today. And they pinned every problem in American society on immigrants. As one Know-Nothing wrote in 1856: "Four-fifths of the beggary and three-fifths of the crime spring from our foreign population; more than half the public charities, more than half the prisons and almshouses, more than half the police and the cost of administering criminal justice are for foreigners."

At the time, the greatest influx of immigrants was from Ireland, where   2
the potato famine had struck, and Germany, which was in political and economic turmoil. Anti-alien and anti-Catholic sentiments were the order of the day, especially in New York and Massachusetts, which received the brunt of the wave of immigrants, many of whom were dirt-poor and uneducated. Politicians were quick to exploit the sentiment: There's nothing like a scapegoat to forge an alliance.

I am especially sensitive to this history: My forebears were among those   3
dirt-poor Irish Catholics who arrived in the 1860s. Fortunately for them, and me, the Know-Nothing movement fizzled within fifteen years. But its pilot light kept burning, and is turned up whenever the American public begins to feel vulnerable and in need of an enemy.

Although they go by different names today, the Know-Nothings have   4
returned. As in the 1850s, the movement is strongest where immigrants are most concentrated: California and Florida. The objects of prejudice are of course no longer Irish Catholics and Germans; 140 years later "they" have become "us." The new "they"—because it seems "we" must always have a "they"—are Latin Americans (most recently, Cubans), Haitians, and Arab-Americans, among others.

But just as in the 1850s, passion, misinformation, and short-sighted fear   5
often substitute for reason, fairness, and human dignity in today's immigration debates. In the interest of advancing beyond know-nothingism, let's look
at five current myths that distort public debate and government policy relating to immigrants.

◆ *America is being overrun with immigrants.* In one sense, of course, this   6
is true, but in that sense it has been true since Christopher Columbus arrived. Except for the real Native Americans, we are a nation of immigrants.

It is not true, however, that the first-generation immigrant share of our   7
population is growing. As of 1990, foreign-born people made up only 8 percent of the population, as compared with a figure of about 15 percent from
1870 to 1920. Between 70 and 80 percent of those who immigrate every year
are refugees or immediate relatives of U.S. citizens.

Much of the anti-immigrant fervor is directed against the undocu-   8
mented, but they make up only 13 percent of all immigrants residing in the
United States, and only 1 percent of the American population. Contrary to
popular belief, most such aliens do not cross the border illegally but enter
legally and remain after their student or visitor visa expires. Thus, building a
wall at the border, no matter how high, will not solve the problem.

◆ *Immigrants take jobs from U.S. citizens.* There is virtually no evidence   9
to support this view, probably the most wide-spread misunderstanding about
immigrants. As documented by a 1994 ACLU Immigrants' Rights Project report, numerous studies have found that immigrants actually create more jobs
than they fill. The jobs immigrants take are of course easier to see, but immigrants are often highly productive, run their own businesses, and employ
both immigrants and citizens. One study found that Mexican immigration to
Los Angeles County between 1970 and 1980 was responsible for 78,000 new
jobs. Governor Mario Cuomo reports that immigrants own more than 40,000
companies in New York, which provide thousands of jobs and $3.5 billion to
the state's economy every year.

◆ *Immigrants are a drain on society's resources.* This claim fuels many   10
of the recent efforts to cut off government benefits to immigrants. However,
most studies have found that immigrants are a net benefit to the economy because, as a 1994 Urban Institute report concludes, "immigrants generate significantly more in taxes paid than they cost in services received." The Council of Economic Advisers similarly found in 1986 that "immigrants have a
favorable effect on the overall standard of living."

Anti-immigrant advocates often cite studies purportedly showing the   11
contrary, but these generally focus only on taxes and services at the local or
state level. What they fail to explain is that because most taxes go to the federal government, such studies would also show a net loss when applied to
U.S. citizens. At most, such figures suggest that some redistribution of federal
and state monies may be appropriate; they say nothing unique about the
costs of immigrants.

Some subgroups of immigrants plainly impose a net cost in the short   12
run, principally those who have most recently arrived and have not yet "made
it." California, for example, bears substantial costs for its disproportionately
large undocumented population, largely because it has on average the poor-
est and least educated immigrants. But that has been true of every wave of
immigrants that has ever reached our shores; it was as true of the Irish in the
1850s, for example, as it is of Salvadorans today. From a long-term perspective, the economic advantages of immigration are undeniable.

Some have suggested that we might save money and diminish incentives   13
to immigrate illegally if we denied undocumented aliens public services. In
fact, undocumented immigrants are already ineligible for most social programs, with the exception of education for schoolchildren, which is constitutionally required, and benefits directly related to health and safety, such as
emergency medical care and nutritional assistance to poor women, infants,
and children. To deny such basic care to people in need, apart from being in-
humanly callous, would probably cost us more in the long run by exacerbat-
ing health problems that we would eventually have to address.

◆ *Aliens refuse to assimilate, and are depriving us of our cultural and po-*   14
litical unity. This claim has been made about every new group of immigrants
to arrive on U.S. shores. Supreme Court Justice Stephen Field wrote in 1884
that the Chinese "have remained among us a separate people, retaining their
original peculiarities of dress, manners, habits, and modes of living, which are
as marked as their complexion and language." Five years later, he upheld the
racially based exclusion of Chinese immigrants. Similar claims have been
made over different periods of our history about Catholics, Jews, Italians,
Eastern Europeans, and Latin Americans.

In most instances, such claims are simply not true; "American culture"   15
has been created, defined, and revised by persons who for the most part are
descended from immigrants once seen as anti-assimilationist. Descendants of
the Irish Catholics, for example, a group once decried as separatist and alien,
have become Presidents, senators, and representatives (and all of these in
one family, in the case of the Kennedys). Our society exerts tremendous pressure to conform, and cultural separatism rarely survives a generation. But
more important, even if this claim were true, is this a legitimate rationale
for limiting immigration in a society built on the values of pluralism and
tolerance?

◆ *Noncitizen immigrants are not entitled to constitutional rights.* Our   16
government has long declined to treat immigrants as full human beings, and
nowhere is that more clear than in the realm of constitutional rights. Although the Constitution literally extends the fundamental protections in the
Bill of Rights to all people, limiting to citizens only the right to vote and run
for federal office, the federal government acts as if this were not the case.

In 1893 the executive branch successfully defended a statute that   17
required Chinese laborers to establish their prior residence here by the

testimony of "at least one credible white witness." The Supreme Court ruled that this law was constitutional because it was reasonable for Congress to presume that nonwhite witnesses could not be trusted.

The federal government is not much more enlightened today. In a pend-   18
ing case I'm handling in the Court of Appeals for the Ninth Circuit, the Clinton Administration has argued that permanent resident aliens lawfully living here should be extended no more First Amendment rights than aliens applying for first-time admission from abroad—that is, none. Under this view, students at a public university who are citizens may express themselves freely, but students who are not citizens can be deported for saying exactly what their classmates are constitutionally entitled to say.

Growing up, I was always taught that we will be judged by how we treat   19
others. If we are collectively judged by how we have treated immigrants—those who appear today to be "other" but will in a generation be "us"—we are not in very good shape.

◆ ◆ ◆

IDEAS FOR WRITING ABOUT IMMIGRATION

1. Interview an immigrant or an immigrant's child about his or her experience in the United States. Write about some aspect of this experience—for example, the impact of immigration on family dynamics—and indicate whether stereotypes or myths came into play.

2. *Using the Internet.* Use a search engine to research how some other country deals with regulating immigration and obtaining citizenship. Look, for example, at Canada: An Immigration Index (www. canada-ny.org/immigration/html), which provides help for people who are interested in moving to Canada. Write an essay arguing for the strength or weakness of this other system compared with the U.S. system.

3. Write an imaginary letter in which Mira, the author's sister, responds to Bharati's essay. Try to make clear Mira's views about assimilation.

4. Write an essay about moving to a different country or a very different community. Did the move turn out as you expected? What problems did you encounter? What benefits or positive experiences did you have?

◆ ON SPORTS

What role do sports play in your life? Which sports do you play? Which ones do you enjoy watching? Even if you don't play or watch sports, you still hear about them and read about them. Whole magazines and sections of the daily newspaper are devoted to sports; at least three television networks cover nothing but sports. Are sports merely entertainment? Are they primarily big business? Or are they part of the fabric of life for most Americans?

The readings in this section look at the place of sports in our culture and in our everyday lives. Katha Pollitt suggests that we get rid of sports—a satiric proposal that allows her to detail the negative consequences of sports in American society. Ian Frazier presents the story of a young Native American woman whose athletic ability inspires her community. Finally, Thad Williamson examines the effects of corporate sponsorship on college athletics.

Let's Get Rid of Sports

KATHA POLLITT

Katha Pollitt was born in New York City in 1949. Her writing has been described as "lucid, gutsy, funny, and just." A number of her essays, which first appeared in *The New Yorker*, the *New York Times*, and *The Nation*, have been published in two collections: *Reasonable Creatures: Essays on Women and Feminism* (1994) and *Subject to Debate: Sense and Dissents on Women, Politics, and Culture* (2001). In her regular column for *The Nation*, Pollitt grapples with many of society's most challenging problems: abortion, the media, and surrogate motherhood. The following article was written for that column in the summer of 1995.

There ought to be a rule that bold proposals for the social and politi- 1
cal betterment of mankind be accompanied by explanations of how these ideas will be brought to reality and why, if they're so brilliant and beneficial as all that, they haven't already been implemented. I figure this requirement would put most pundits out of business within weeks, which would be all to the good. Imagine, for example, if the many who facilely advocate adoption over abortion actually had to explain how it would work: where the millions of would-be parents would come from; how women with unplanned pregnancies, who overwhelmingly reject adoption no matter how desperate their circumstances, will be brought to embrace it; how mass adoption will sit with current notions of genetic determinism, father's rights, cultural and racial identity. Are Tennessee Baptists really prepared to see their grandchildren shipped off to be raised by New York Jews—or vice versa? To spell out what it would really involve is to make clear what a crackpot idea it is—which is, of course, why its advocates tend to move right along to the next "thought experiment," like orphanages over A.F.D.C.

But why criticize the right alone? Our own pages are full of visionary 2
schemes. Let's tell Clinton to abolish the C.I.A.! Let's permit noncitizens to vote! Let's raise children to be noncompetitive! Missing is a serious discussion of what organized interests are served by the status quo, how those interests are to be defeated and by whom. Lots of good ideas have no constituency in a position to bring them about: Think of all those Op-Ed articles that crop up every four years advocating the abolition of the Electoral College.

Well, I'm no better than the next pundit, so here's my big idea: Let's 3
get rid of sports. Baseball, basketball, football, boxing—especially boxing—tennis, gymnastics, Little League, high school, college, professional, Olympic, the whole schmear. Away with them!

Fans say athletics promote values, and so they do—the wrong values,   4
like the childish confusion of physical prowess with "character" that is such
a salient feature of the O.J. Simpson trial. Sports pervert education, draining
dollars from academic programs and fostering anti-intellectualism. They skew
the priorities of the young, especially the poor, black young, by offering them
the illusory hope of wealth and fame. Sports scholarships, often touted as
a poor kid's only chance, just mean less money available to other poor kids,
like girls, and ones with O.K. grades and no trophies. Besides, without the
will-o'-the-wisp incentive of a scholarship, physically gifted kids might not be
so ready to blow off their schoolwork. Why not give scholarships for art or
music instead?

Although women are becoming more involved in sports, it's still a male   5
world, which actively encourages and protects the worst forms of male privilege and jerkiness. Athletes are disproportionately represented in reported
campus sex crimes, and the pros' reputation for violence, against women
or otherwise, is legendary. Without sports, we never would have heard of
Ty Cobb, O.J. Simpson, Mike Tyson, Billy Martin, Darryl Strawberry.

Being a sports fan is even worse than being an actual athlete, since in-   6
stead of getting all that exercise, one simply watches TV, punches the chair
and curses. But for both fans and players, sports are about creating a world
from which women are absent. Men who follow sports, which means most
men, have a realm of conversation that allows them to bond across classes ef-
fortlessly but superficially. Lefty sports advocates like to tout this cross-class
appeal as a virtue—How about those Knicks?—but, even setting aside the
fact that it's based on the exclusion of women, why would a leftist think it's
good for class divisions to be smoothed over?

Sports fandom trains the young in group identification, passivity, spec-   7
tatorship and celebrity-worship. I know men whose entire lives are mediated
through sports, like my cousin who brings a little TV to family gatherings to
catch The Game, or my writing student whose efforts at autobiography con-
sisted entirely of play-by-play of long-ago Little League tournaments. Maybe
once, sports functioned as a family, communal activity—the whole town out
at the ballpark for a good time. Now it's just another form of isolation: every
man in his own living room, staring at the screen. Women who object to
pornography should be even more upset about sports. After all, whatever
else porn may do, it does encourage sexual interest, which is why couples
rent those videos. But sports are basically a way for men to avoid the claims
of other people. That's one of several reasons why David ("Fatherless America") Blankenhorn's idea of promoting fatherhood by getting athletes to en-
dorse it is such a joke: A guy who spends half the year on the road with the
team pitches family life to men who are watching him expressly because he
symbolizes the footloose and fancy-free life.

But what about the game, you cry, the thwack of ball against bat, the arc   8
of football on its way to touchdown, the swish of ball into net? O.K., let's

keep sports—but let's have only women play. Women can thwack and throw and swish too, after all. Turning sports over to women would change their meaning—you can't have bimbo cheerleaders if the athletes are women too—and, instead of promoting the worst qualities of men, they'd counteract the worst qualities of women, like defining themselves through men and wearing three-inch fake fingernails.

I know what you're thinking: Sports is a billion-dollar industry, deeply   9 woven into the fabric of American life, avidly followed by millions who would go berserk if deprived. Besides, all-female football wouldn't be football. Right. Forget the whole thing. I don't know what came over me. And the next time a pundit comes up with a big idea—Let's bring back shame! Let's not let parents divorce!—you can probably forget that too.

SuAnne Marie Big Crow

IAN FRAZIER

Journalist Ian Frazier (born in 1951, in Cleveland, Ohio) writes frequently for both the *Atlantic Monthly* and *The New Yorker*. In his most recent book, *On The Rez* (2000), Frazier explores the modern-day lives and
culture of the Oglala Sioux Indians of Pine Ridge, South Dakota. The following excerpt from that book relates one of the stories about SuAnne Big
Crow, the most admired Oglala basketball player of all time.

Pine Ridge had a winter basketball league for girls aged seven to eleven,   1
and SuAnne later recalled that she played her first organized game in that
league when she was in kindergarten. She had gone with her sisters to a tournament in Rushville when a sudden snowstorm kept some of the players
away. The coach, finding himself short-handed, put SuAnne in the game. "It
was funny," SuAnne told a basketball magazine, "because all I really knew
how to do was play defense, so that's all I did. I not only took the ball away
from our opponents, but also from my own teammates!" A coach who
watched her play then said, "If you ever saw the movie *Star Wars*—well, you
remember the Ewoks? Well, SuAnne was so much smaller than the other
kids, she looked like one of those little Ewoks out there runnin' around."

In the West, girls' basketball is a bigger deal than it is elsewhere. High   2
school girls' basketball games in states like South Dakota and Montana draw
full-house crowds, and newspapers and college recruiters give nearly the
same attention to star players who are girls as they do to stars who are boys.
There were many good players on the girls' teams at Pine Ridge High School
and at the Red Cloud School when SuAnne was little. SuAnne idolized a
star for the Pine Ridge Lady Thorpes named Lolly Steele, who set many
records at the school. On a national level, SuAnne's hero was Earvin "Magic"
Johnson, of the Los Angeles Lakers pro team. Women's professional basketball did not exist in those years, but men's pro games were reaching a level
of popularity to challenge baseball and football. SuAnne had big posters of
Magic Johnson on her bedroom walls.

She spent endless hours practicing basketball. When she was in the fifth   3
grade she heard somewhere that to improve your dribbling you should
bounce a basketball a thousand times a day with each hand. She followed
this daily exercise faithfully on the cement floor of the patio; her mother and
sisters got tired of the sound. For variety, she would shoot layups against
the gutter and the drainpipe, until they came loose from the house and had
to be repaired. She knew that no girl in an official game had ever dunked a
basketball—that is, had leaped as high as the rim and stuffed the ball through
the hoop from above—and she wanted to be the first in history to do it. To

get the feel, she persuaded a younger boy cousin to kneel on all fours under the basket. With a running start, and a leap using the boy's back as a springboard, she could dunk the ball.

Charles Zimiga, who would coach SuAnne in basketball during her   4 high school years, remembered the first time he saw her. He was on the cross-county track on the old golf course coaching the high school boys' cross-country team—a team that later won the state championship—when SueAnne came running by. She was in the seventh grade at the time. She practiced cross-country every fall, and ran in amateur meets, and sometimes placed high enough to be invited to tournaments in Boston and California. "The fluidness of her running amazed me, and the strength she had," Zimiga said. "I stood watching her go by and she stopped right in front of me—I'm a high school coach, remember, and she's just a young little girl—and she said, 'What're you lookin' at?' I said 'A runner.' She would've been a top cross-country runner, but in high school it never did work out, because the season conflicted with basketball. I had heard about her before, but that day on the golf course was the first time I really noticed her."

SuAnne went to elementary school in Wolf Creek, because of her fam-   5 ily's connections there. Zimiga and others wanted her to come to Pine Ridge High School so she could play on the basketball team, and finally they persuaded Chick to let her transfer when she was in junior high. By the time SuAnne was in eighth grade, she had grown to five feet, five inches tall ("but she played six foot," Zimiga said); she was long-limbed, well-muscled, and quick. She had high cheekbones, a prominent, arched upper lip that lined up with the basket when she aimed the ball, and short hair that she wore in no particular style. She could have played every game for the varsity when she was in eighth grade, but Coach Zimiga, who took over girls' varsity basketball that year, wanted to keep peace among older players who had waited for their chance to be on the team. He kept SuAnne on the junior varsity during the regular season. The varsity team had a good year, and when it advanced to the district playoffs, Zimiga brought SuAnne up from the JVs for the play-off games. Several times she got into foul trouble; the referees rule strictly in tournament games, and SuAnne was used to a more headlong style of play. She and her cousin Doni De Cory, a 5′ 10″ junior, combined for many long-break baskets, with Doni throwing downcourt passes to SuAnne on the scoring end. In the district play-off against the team from Red Cloud, SuAnne scored thirty-one points. In the regional play-off game, Pine Ridge beat a good Todd County team, but in the state tournament they lost all three games and finished eighth.

Some people who live in the cities and towns near reservations treat   6 their Indian neighbors decently; some don't. In cities like Denver and Minneapolis and Rapid City, police have been known to harass Indian teenagers and rough up Indian drunks and needlessly stop and search Indian cars. Local banks whose deposits include millions in tribal funds sometimes charge Indians higher loan interest rates than they charge whites. Gift shops near reservations sell junky caricature Indian pictures and dolls, and until not long ago, beer coolers had signs on them that said, INDIAN POWER. In a big discount store in a reservation border town, a white clerk observes a lot of Indians waiting at the checkout and remarks, "Oh, they're Indians—they're used to standing in line." Some people in South Dakota hate Indians, unapologetically, and will tell you why; in their voices you can hear a particular American meanness that is centuries old.

When teams from Pine Ridge play non-Indian teams, the question of race is always there. When Pine Ridge is the visiting team, usually their hosts are courteous, and the players and fans have a good time. But Pine Ridge coaches know that occasionally at away games their kids will be insulted, their fans will not feel welcome, the host gym will be dense with hostility, and the referees will call fouls on Indian players every chance they get. Sometimes in a game between Indian and non-Indian teams, the difference in race becomes an important and distracting part of the event.   7

One place where Pine Ridge teams used to get harassed regularly was in the high school gymnasium in Lead, South Dakota. Lead is a town of about 3,200 northwest of the reservation, in the Black Hills. It is laid out among the mines that are its main industry, and low, wooded mountains hedge it round. The brick high school building is set into a hillside. The school's only gym in those days was small, with tiers of gray-painted concrete on which the spectator benches descended from just below the steel-beamed roof to the very edge of the basketball court—an arrangement that greatly magnified the interior noise.   8

In the fall of 1988, the Pine Ridge Lady Thorpes went to Lead to play a basketball game. SuAnne was a full member of the team by then. She was a freshman, fourteen years old. Getting ready in the locker room, the Pine Ridge girls could hear the din from the fans. They were yelling fake-Indian war cries, a "woo-woo-woo" sound. The usual plan for the pre-game warm-up was for the visiting team to run onto the court in a line, take a lap or two around the floor, shoot some baskets, and then go to their bench at courtside. After that, the home team would come out and do the same, and then the game would begin. Usually the Thorpes lined up for their entry more or less according to height, which meant that senior Doni De Cory, one of the tallest, went first. As the team waited in the hallway leading from the locker room, the heckling got louder. The Lead fans were yelling epithets like "squaw" and "gut-eater." Some were waving food stamps, a reference to the reservation's receiving federal aid. Others yelled, "Where's the cheese?"—the joke being that if Indians were lining up, it must be to get commodity cheese. The Lead high school band had joined in, with fake-Indian drumming and a fake-Indian tune. Doni De Cory looked out the door and told her teammates,   9

"I can't handle this." SuAnne quickly offered to go first in her place. She was so eager that Doni became suspicious. "Don't embarrass us," Doni told her. SuAnne said, "I won't. I won't embarrass you." Doni gave her the ball, and SuAnne stood first in line.

She came running onto the court dribbling the basketball, with her 10 teammates running behind. On the court, the noise was deafeningly loud. SuAnne went right down the middle; but instead of running a full lap, she suddenly stopped when she got to center court. Her teammates were taken by surprise, and some bumped into one another. Coach Zimiga at the rear of the line did not know why they had stopped. SuAnne turned to Doni De Cory and tossed her the ball. Then she stepped into the jump-ball circle at center court, in front of the Lead fans. She unbuttoned her warm-up jacket, took it off, draped it over her shoulders, and began to do the Lakota shawl dance. SuAnne knew all the traditional dances—she had competed in many pow-wows as a little girl—and the dance she chose is a young woman's dance, graceful and modest and show-offy all at the same time. "I couldn't believe it—she was powwowin', like, 'get down!' " Doni De Cory recalled. "And then she started to sing." SuAnne began to sing in Lakota, swaying back and forth in the jump-ball circle, doing the shawl dance, using her warm-up jacket for a shawl. The crowd went completely silent. "All that stuff the Lead fans were yelling—it was like she *reversed* it somehow," a teammate said. In the sudden quiet, all you could hear was her Lakota song. SuAnne stood up, dropped her jacket, took the ball from Doni De Cory, and ran a lap around the court dribbling expertly and fast. The fans began to cheer and applaud. She sprinted to the basket, went up in the air, and laid the ball through the hoop, with the fans cheering loudly now. Of course, Pine Ridge went on to win the game.

◆ ◆ ◆

Bad as They Wanna Be

THAD WILLIAMSON

Thad Williamson grew up in Chapel Hill, North Carolina, where he acquired a passion for college basketball. He remains a loyal follower of Atlantic Coast Conference basketball and writes a column for *InsideCarolina* (http://northcarolina.theinsiders.com/), an independent magazine and Web site devoted to University of North Carolina sports. Williamson also contributes regularly to *Dollars & Sense, Cross Currents*, and *Tikkun*. The following essay was published in *The Nation* in August 1998.

For the thoughtful fan of college sports, it's getting harder to check   1
your critical intelligence at the door and simply enjoy the game. The appeal of college athletics has long rested on their "amateur" status, the notion that the kids play mostly for the love of the game, without the pressures and influences that suffuse professional sports. These days, however, it's increasingly clear that big-time college athletics—in particular, men's basketball and football—are as wrapped in commercial values as the pros, and the system is rapidly spinning out of control.

In college arenas the best seats are now routinely reserved not for stu-   2
dents and die-hard fans but for big-money boosters and private donors to the universities. The arenas themselves are being turned into prime advertising venues: Georgia Tech's revamped Alexander Memorial Coliseum, for example, goes so far as to place the McDonald's trademark "M" on the floor. Meanwhile, the NCAA's lucrative television contracts—an eight-year, $1.7 billion deal with CBS for broadcast rights to the Men's Division I basketball tournament and similar deals in football—are changing the fabric of the game, as top competition is slotted for prime-time viewing hours and games are steadily lengthened by TV timeouts.

Even the University of North Carolina (UNC), which to this day   3
bans all corporate advertising inside arenas, has largely succumbed to the trend. In the eighties UNC used some $34 million in private funds to build a 21,500-seat basketball arena, in the process setting a precedent of entitlement for major boosters. Not only did they win rights to the best seats in the arena, they are also allowed to pass on those seats to their progeny. More recently, university officials convinced the state highway board to authorize $1.2 million for a special road to allow top-dollar Tar Heels donors a convenient exit from home games.

There's more. Last summer the university signed a five-year, $11 mil-   4
lion contract to use Nike-provided gear in all practices (for all sports) and to

wear the familiar swoosh. No faculty members or students were directly involved in the negotiations, and no serious questions were raised about Nike's
notorious labor practices abroad. Subsequently, concerned UNC students
and faculty generated considerable public debate about the deal, but UNC
plans to remain on the take.

Indeed, shoe companies like Adidas and Nike are now prime players   5
in the college game. Most major Division I football and basketball coaches
receive lucrative payments from the companies in exchange for outfitting
their teams with the appropriate logo—and in some cases, such as the University of California, Berkeley, for encouraging their players to buy additional Nike gear. The sneaker sellers also operate most of the major summer
camps for elite high school athletes, where schoolboy stars show their wares
to college coaches (many of whom are themselves on Nike's or Reebok's
payroll) in hopes of landing a top-flight scholarship. While the hottest
prospects are showered with expenses-paid travel and free athletic gear, the
companies develop relationships with future stars that might culminate in
endorsement contracts. In his fine book *The Last Shot,* Darcy Frey likened
the atmosphere at Nike's annual high school summer camp to a meat market, where the mostly black kids are herded around like cattle while the overwhelmingly white coaches and corporate sponsors look on.

Nowhere are the priorities of the new corporate order of college sports   6
clearer than in the treatment of athletes—though you'd never know it from
the popular image of those athletes as coddled superstars. In *He Got Game,*
Spike Lee depicts the campus as a pleasure dome for young men treated to
unlimited cars, women, and material perks for four blissfully hedonistic years.
The truth is often far less alluring. "It's not as glamorous as people think," cautions Sheray Gaffney, a former reserve fullback for the football powerhouse
Florida State Seminoles. "If you're in the program, it's not glamorous at all."

One reason for this is the so-called grant-in-aid system that character-   7
izes all athletic scholarships in the NCAA. Originally established in 1956,
grant-in-aid was intended to level the playing field by providing a fixed set
of benefits to college athletes. Schools were allowed to offer scholarships of
one to four years and were bound to honor them even if the athlete quit the
team altogether. In 1973, however, the NCAA abruptly shifted course and
mandated that the grants be limited to a one-year, annually renewable grant.
The purpose of this change was to enable schools—in actuality, coaches—to
keep tabs on each player's performance from year to year, and to cut off the
scholarships of those whom the coach considered dispensable.

"Colleges changed the rule so they could run off the athletes who   8
weren't good enough," explains Walter Byers, who oversaw the growth of
college athletics while serving as NCAA executive director from 1951 to
1987. Back in the fifties Byers coined the term "student-athlete," a romantic
idea that the NCAA continues to use in its promotional literature. These

days, he is one of the NCAA's leading critics. "Once the colleges gave coaches the power to control those grants," he says, "that was a perversion that permanently changed the way things were done. It used to be that at least athletes could get an education if they couldn't play for the team."

Indeed, under the new system athletes do as the coaches say or risk being kicked out. Coach Rick Majerus of Utah, whose team reached the NCAA basketball finals this year, recently "released" Jordie McTavish saying he just wasn't good enough. A year ago, Coach Bobby Cremins of Georgia Tech asked freshman point guard Kevin Morris to leave for the same reason. More often than direct dismissals, coaches pressure players to leave on their own. Indiana's Bobby Knight, seeking to clean house after a disappointing 1996–97 season, drove starting point guard Neil Reed out of town with one year of eligibility remaining. Reed left, but not before accusing Knight of physical and emotional abuse.   9

Given the pressures to stay in the good graces of coaches—players know that missing even one session in the weight room risks incurring the coach's wrath—it's no wonder that graduation rates for Division I football and basketball players in the NCAA hover at roughly 50 percent, a figure that exaggerates the amount of learning that actually takes place. Instead of promoting a balance between sports and academics, the system forces athletes to pour every ounce of energy into the game, with little recognition that the vast majority of players are in a vocational dead end. A sad rite of passage for most college athletes is the existential realization that they will never make it to the pros. "What was astonishing was the number of scars that [the program] left on athletes that came to the surface behind closed doors," recalls Gaffney. "It was painful to see athletes crying in distress because they see their dreams slowly fading away. All of a sudden at age twenty, twenty-one, they are required to make a complete transition."   10

True, college sports still represent a way out for poor or working-class athletes. Some find jobs in coaching, pro leagues overseas, or business. Others succeed in getting an education. But the inequities are glaring. While generating an enormous revenue stream for their universities through ticket sales, merchandising, advertising, and TV deals, athletes are forbidden from sharing in any of the gains. "When these commercial activities came along," notes Byers, "the overseers and supervisors made sure that the benefits went to them, not the athletes." College coaches routinely earn six-figure salaries, sign endorsement deals with corporations, and jump from school to school for more lucrative contracts. The athletes, meanwhile, are the focus of scandal and media outrage if they so much as accept money for an extra trip home. Under the grant-in-aid rule, athletes may not use their talent or name recognition to earn money while in school except under tightly defined conditions.   11

In Byers's view, the "gobs of money" now flowing to the universities make a return to the amateur ideal impossible. What is possible, he believes,   12 is scrapping the current grant-in-aid system, which leads not only to the rampant exploitation of athletes but, he argues, violates antitrust laws because colleges essentially operate as a cartel, setting a national limit on what a whole class of students can earn. He would require athletes to apply for financial aid like any other student but would remove all restrictions on how they could earn money while in college.

Rick Telander, a *Sports Illustrated* writer and author of *The Hundred Yard Lie,* an exposé of college football, proposes a more radical solution: namely, severing big-time college football programs from the schools that lend them their name. In Telander's view, an NFL-subsidized "age-group professional league" could be established in which universities would own and operate teams, using university facilities and traditional school colors. Players need not be students but would earn a year of tuition for each year played, redeemable at any time, during or after their playing careers. College basketball would also benefit from the creation of an NBA-backed age-group league. Such leagues could offer gifted players with no interest in academics a credible alternative to college, and a second chance to earn an education should their professional dreams fade.   13

Of course, given the entrenched institutional support for the status quo, none of this can happen without a sustained demand from the public, including students, coaches not yet corrupted, and athletes themselves. In the meantime, students and faculty can make their voices heard by continuing—and expanding—their campaigns challenging the corporate sponsorship of university athletic departments. Over the past year campus activists at Duke and other universities have successfully pushed administrators to adopt rules requiring that all campus sweatshirts and athletic gear be produced in compliance with labor and human rights standards. These same activists should insist that corporate advertising be banned from all arenas; that universities cap athletic budgets for football and basketball and put an end to the "arms race" for bigger facilities and more amenities; and that the influence of big-money donors be limited so that students and fans can continue to attend athletic events at reasonable prices. Activists might also find unexpected common ground with coaches and fans concerned about how the integrity of the game has been subordinated to television, or how corporations are colonizing and poisoning the high school recruiting scene.   14

Speaking for myself, probably only death will cure my love affair with North Carolina basketball, and no doubt there are millions of people who feel the same way about their own teams. But loving the game need not mean having a romantic view of how college sports are organized. College sports are far too visible in American society to be simply thrown to the wolves. Ultimately, the only productive route forward is to insist that those who love the game also fight to change it.   15

◆ ◆ ◆

IDEAS FOR WRITING ABOUT SPORTS

1. Write about the role sports has played in your life. For example, did participating in sports affect your ability to form close friendships? Did a coach or fellow player significantly shape your career plans or cause a shift in your personal values? Has being a loyal fan cost you socially or affected other parts of your life negatively?

2. Choose a sports figure who you believe acts as a positive or negative role model. Argue for your choice by using examples, reasons, and explanations.

3. Write about the violence associated with a particular sport. Analyze the causes and effects of the violence and suggest possible solutions.

4. ▣▯ *Using the Internet.* Write about some recent trend in sports, such as snowboarding, skateboarding, street luge, inline skating, motocross, BMX, or sport climbing. Find information on the Internet about this trend and its popularity.

Using and Documenting Sources

◆ ◆ ◆ ◆ ◆

Many kinds of writing involve the use of secondary source materials. In your college classes, you will often be asked to write research papers for which you read a number of sources, combine and organize this accumulated information, and present your findings in a clear and coherent form. One important difference between writing a paper using your own ideas and writing a paper incorporating research involves acknowledging your sources. This appendix reviews the Modern Language Association (MLA) style for citing sources, integrating sources, using quotations, incorporating quotations, avoiding plagiarism, and documenting sources. It also includes a sample student research paper in MLA style.

◆ CITING SOURCES

The main purpose of documentation—citing sources used in a research paper—is to give credit for ideas, information, and actual phrasing that you borrow from other writers. You cite sources in order to be honest and to lend authority to your own writing. You also include citations to enable your readers to find more extensive information than your paper furnishes, in case they become fascinated with your subject and want to read some of your sources in full.

We are all unsure occasionally about when a citation is necessary. We can say with authority that you must include a citation for:

1. All direct quotations
2. All indirect quotations

3. All major ideas that are not your own
4. All essential facts, information, and statistics that are not common knowledge, especially anything controversial

The last category is the one that causes confusion. In general, the sort of information available in an encyclopedia does not need a citation. But statements interpreting, analyzing, or speculating on such information should be documented. If you write that President Warren G. Harding died in office, you do not need a citation because that is a widely known and undisputed fact. If you write that Harding's administration was one of the most corrupt in our history, most people would not feel the need for a citation because authorities agree that the Harding scandals were flagrant and abundant, and you would therefore find the same idea repeated in several different sources. But if you write that Harding was sexually intimate with a young woman in the White House cloakroom, you should cite your source. Because such information is not widely known and is also debatable, you need to identify your source so that your readers can judge the reliability of the claim. They also might want further enlightenment on the matter, and your citation will lead them to a more complete discussion. It's probably better to have too many citations than to have your readers question your integrity by having too few.

◆ INTEGRATING SOURCES

Whether you are quoting directly or simply paraphrasing someone else's ideas and observations, you should always give credit in the text of your paper to the person from whom you are borrowing. Most academic documentation styles require you to cite all sources *within* the paper. Many people who do researched writing make no attempt to work in direct quotations or provide complete citations in the first draft because pausing to do so interrupts the flow of their ideas. They just jot down the name of the person who has provided the information or idea; they go back later to fill in page numbers and integrate exact quotations.

Using the "Hamburger" Model

Think of each use of a source as a hamburger, with its two buns and a burger. The top bun is your introduction of the source, telling your reader that material from some authority is coming up, who or what the source is, and what the person's credentials are, if you know them. The burger is the information from the source, quoted or paraphrased. The bottom bun is the *parenthetical documentation,* which tells your reader that your use of the source is over and gives the page number for the source of that particular material.

The hamburger model is crucial because your reader needs to know where your own ideas stop and others' begin and end. The following example from student Bob Harmon illustrates the hamburger approach to documentation:

> Behavior research has clearly shown that different types of music have different effects on different people. Music can increase or decrease anxiety, but its use in business to improve morale is questionable. In the *Journal of Marketing,* researcher John Milliman points out that past decisions to use music in the marketplace have been based on folklore or intuition rather than on empirical results (88). His study focused primarily on the experimental manipulations of no music, slow music, and fast music. The results indicate music does control the speed with which subjects move through a store. Slow music results in subjects spending more time, and fast music means less time spent (Milliman 86–91). If music does affect the speed with which people move through a store, does it affect their perceptions of time? If fast music is used for music-on-hold, it may decrease people's sense of how long they are on hold; and slow music may expand the perceived length of time. Here again, proper selection is critical.

In this example, you see the student's transition from a preceding paragraph, his use of a paraphrase of the thesis of Milliman's article, then his summary of Milliman's research, and then his own application of the research. You never confuse which is which, because the hamburger system of source citation makes clear where all the ideas come from.

◆ USING QUOTATIONS

You quote sources to support your ideas, not to state them for you. Using a lot of direct quotations suggests that you have few ideas of your own. So quote directly only when (1) the material is authoritative and convincing evidence in support of your point, (2) the statement is especially well phrased, or (3) the idea is controversial and you want to assure your readers that you are not slanting or misinterpreting the source. You would probably quote an observation as well put as this one:

> Charles Darwin concluded that language ability is "an instinctive tendency to acquire an art."

There is no need, however, for the direct quotation in the following sentence:

> The ICC, in an effort to aid the rail industry, has asked for a "federal study of the need and means for preserving a national passenger service" (Weber 10).

You could phrase that just as well yourself:

> The ICC has requested federal help to determine whether the rail industry needs assistance and how it could be preserved (Weber 10).

Remember, though, that even after you put the statement into your own words, you still have to indicate (in a parenthetical citation) where you got the point.

Quoting Quotations

Sometimes in your reading you will come across a quotation that says precisely what you've been looking for and says it well. If the quotation is complete enough to serve your purpose, and if you honestly don't think you would benefit from tracking down the original, don't bother. Instead, include that quotation in the usual way. Notice, however, that your parenthetical citation will include "qtd. in" before the source and page number:

> Oscar Wilde once said about education, "It is well to remember from time to time that nothing that is worth knowing can be taught" (qtd. in Pinker 19).

◆ INCORPORATING QUOTATIONS

If you want your research paper to read smoothly as you shift from your own voice to the author of the quotation, you must take care when incorporating quotations into your writing. You'll need to have a ready supply of introductory phrases for sliding the quotations in gracefully, phrases like "As Le Seure discovered," "Professor Weber notes," and "According to Dr. Carter." These attributions help your readers evaluate the source material as they read it and distinguish source material from your remarks about it.

Notice that the more famous the person, the less likely we are to use Mr., Miss, Mrs., or Ms. in front of the name. "Mr. Shakespeare" sounds quite amusing. If the person has a title, you can use it or not, as you think appropriate: Dr. Pauling or Pauling, Senator Boxer or Boxer, President Wilson or Wilson. What is important is to be consistent.

Using Lead-Ins

Don't drop in quotations without preparing your readers. Provide clear lead-ins, usually including the author's name, to connect the quotation to your text:

> Many fluent native speakers of English will claim they don't understand grammar. As Professor David Crystal points out, "Millions of people believe they are failures at grammar, say that they have forgotten it, or deny they know any grammar at all—in each case using their grammar convincingly to make their point" (191).

For variety, you may want to place the connecting phrase in the middle every so often, this way:

> The fundamental purpose of language is to communicate intelligibly. "But if thought corrupts language," warns George Orwell, "language can also corrupt thought" (38).

You don't always have to quote full sentences from your sources. You can quote only the telling phrases or key ideas of your authority, as done in this example:

> Barbara Strang remarks that worrying about split infinitives is "one of the most tiresome pastimes" invented by 19th-century grammarians (95).

or in these examples:

> The play's effectiveness lies, as E. M. W. Tillyard points out, in "the utter artlessness of the language" (34).
>
> The self-portraits of Frida Kahlo are bold and personal. Art critic Hayden Herrera describes them as "autobiography in paint" (xii).

But do introduce your quotations. Identifying the source before presenting the borrowed material helps your readers know which ideas are yours and which come from sources.

Matching the Grammar

When you incorporate a quotation into your own sentence, you are responsible for making sure that the entire sentence makes sense. You must adjust the way your sentence is worded so that the grammar comes out right. Read your quotations over carefully to be sure they don't end up like this one:

> When children are born, their first reactions are "those stimuli which constitute their environment."

"Reactions" are not "stimuli." The sentence should read this way:

> When children are born, their first reactions are to "those stimuli which constitute their environment."

What a difference a word makes: the difference here between sense and nonsense. Take particular care when you are adding someone else's words to your own; you get the blame if the words in the quotation do not make sense, because they *did* make sense before you lifted them out of context.

Using Special Punctuation: Ellipsis Dots and Brackets

When you write a documented paper, you may need to use *ellipsis dots* and *brackets* to condense quotations and blend them in smoothly with your text.

To shorten a quoted passage, use ellipsis dots (three periods with spaces between) to show your readers that you've omitted some words. To distinguish between your ellipsis points and the spaced periods that sometimes appear in written works, put square brackets around any ellipsis dots that you add:

> "The time has come [. . .] for us to examine ourselves," declares James Baldwin, "but we can only do this if we are willing to free ourselves from the myth of America and try to find out what is really happening here" (18).

Ellipsis dots are not needed if the omission occurs at the beginning or end of the sentence you are quoting. But if *your* sentence ends with quoted words that are not the end of the original quoted sentence, then use ellipsis dots:

> Thoreau insisted that he received only one or two letters in his life "that were worth the postage" and commented summarily that "to a philosopher all news, as it is called, is gossip [. . .]."

That fourth dot is the period. If you include documentation, such as a page number, add the period after the parentheses:

> "is gossip [. . .]" (27).

Use *brackets* to add words of your own to clarify the meaning or make the grammar match:

> In her memoir, Jessica Mitford confirms that "In those days [the early 1940s] until postwar repression set in, the [Communist] Party was a strange mixture of openness and secrecy" (67).

Handling Long Quotations

If you quote more than four typed lines of prose or more than three lines of poetry, set the quotation off by indenting it one inch or ten spaces. Introduce the quotation, usually with a complete sentence followed by a colon; begin the indented quotation on the next line; double-space the quotation and do not use quotation marks (the indention signals that the material is quoted).

> In 1892, George Bernard Shaw wrote to the editor of the London *Chronicle,* denouncing a columnist who had complained about split infinitives:
>
> > If you do not immediately suppress the person who takes it upon himself to lay down the law almost every day in your columns on the subject of literary composition, I will give up the *Chronicle* [. . .]. I ask you, Sir, to put this man out [. . .] without interfering with his perfect freedom of choice between "to suddenly go," "to go suddenly" and "suddenly to go." Set him adrift and try an intelligent Newfoundland dog in his place. (qtd. in Crystal 195)

Notice that in an indented quotation, the page number is cited in parentheses *after* the period. The quotation marks within the indented material indicate that Shaw punctuated those phrases in that way.

◆ AVOIDING PLAGIARISM

Plagiarism means using somebody else's writing without giving proper credit. You can avoid this dishonesty by using a moderate amount of care in taking notes. Put quotation marks around any material—however brief—that you copy verbatim into your notes or onto note cards. As you're leafing through your note cards and grouping them into categories, circle the quotation marks in red so you can't miss them or highlight the quoted material as a reminder.

You must also avoid the author's phrasing if you decide not to quote directly but to paraphrase. You naturally tend to write an idea down using the same language as your source, perhaps changing or omitting a few words. This close paraphrasing is still plagiarism. To avoid it, read the passage first, and then look away from the original as you put the idea down in your own words. You are less likely to fall into the original phrasing that way, but double-check after completing the paragraph.

Writing an Acceptable Paraphrase

Sometimes, of course, you must do fairly close paraphrasing of important ideas. Because plagiarism can often be accidental, we will give a couple of examples to show exactly what unintentional plagiarism looks like. Here is a passage from *The Language Instinct* by Steven Pinker. Assume that you want to use this idea to make a point in your paper.

> Language is not a cultural artifact that we learn the way we learn to tell time or how the federal government works. Instead, it is a distinct piece of the biological makeup of our brains. Language is a complex, specialized skill, which develops in the child spontaneously, without conscious effort or formal instruction.

If you incorporate this material into your paper in the following way, you have plagiarized:

> (wrong)   Humans do not learn language the way we learn to tell time or how the federal government works. Language is a part of the biological makeup of our brains, a complex skill that a child develops spontaneously, without conscious effort or formal instruction (Pinker 18).

The source citation suggests that this plagiarism probably resulted from ignorance rather than deception, but it is plagiarism nonetheless. Changing a few words or rearranging the phrases is not enough. Here is another version, somewhat less blatant but still plagiarism:

> (wrong)   Humans do not learn language in the way we learn to count or understand how a steam engine works. Language is part of

> our physical makeup, a complex, specialized skill that
> develops automatically, without conscious effort or formal
> instruction (Pinker 18).

There are still two phrases that are distinctly Pinker's: "a complex, specialized skill" and "without conscious effort or formal instruction." It is quite all
right to use those phrases, but *only if you put them in quotation marks.* You
should also acknowledge your source in the text of your paper whenever
possible, like this:

> (right)   According to linguist Steven Pinker, humans do not learn
>   language in the way we learn to count or understand how a
>   steam engine works. Language is part of our physical makeup,
>   "a complex, specialized skill" that develops automatically,
>   "without conscious effort or formal instruction" (18).

Notice, by the way, that the phrase "in the way we learn" and the words
"makeup" and "develops" do not have quotation marks around them, even
though they appear in the original. These words are so common and so frequently used that quotation marks are unnecessary. Here is another accept-
able paraphrase in which none of the original phrasing is used:

> (right)   Linguist Steven Pinker claims that human beings do not learn
>   language in the way that we learn to count or understand how
>   a steam engine works. Language is a part of our physical
>   makeup; it's a sophisticated skill that children acquire
>   automatically and effortlessly without explicit training (18).

◆ DOCUMENTING SOURCES USING MLA STYLE

The documentation style of the MLA—used in English, foreign lan-
guages, and some other humanities—requires that source citations be given
in the text of the paper rather than in footnotes or endnotes. This in-text style
of documentation involves parenthetical references.

Keep in mind that the purpose of documentation is two-fold:

1. To give credit to your sources
2. To allow your readers to find your sources in case they want further
   information on the subject

If you are ever in doubt about documentation form (if you are citing something so unusual that you can't find a similar entry in the samples here), use

your common sense and give credit the way you think it logically should be done. Be as consistent as possible with other citations.

Throughout this section, titles of books and periodicals are underlined (a printer's mark to indicate words to be set in italic type). If you have italic lettering on a computer, you can use italics instead of underlining, as long as your instructor approves.

A. Usually, you will introduce the cited material by mentioning the name of the author in your lead-in and giving the page number (or numbers) at the end in parentheses, as in this example:

> Edmund Wilson tells us that the author of Uncle Tom's Cabin felt "the book had been written by God" (5).

B. Your readers can identify this source by consulting your Works Cited at the end of your paper (see items H through K). The entry for the source cited above would appear like this one:

> Wilson, Edmund. Patriotic Gore: Studies in the Literature of the American Civil War. New York: Oxford UP, 1966.

C. If you do not mention the author in your lead-in, include his or her last name in parentheses along with the page number, like this:

> One of the great all-time best-sellers, Uncle Tom's Cabin sold over 300,000 copies in America and more than 2 million copies world wide (Wilson 3).

D. If you have to quote indirectly—something from another source not available to you—use "qtd. in" (for "quoted in") in your parenthetical reference. This example refers to a book written by Donald Johanson and Maitland Edey:

> Richard Leakey's wife, Maeve, told the paleoanthropologist David Johanson, "We heard all about your bones on the radio last night" (qtd. in Johanson and Edey 162).

E. If you are using a source written or edited by more than three people, use only the name of the first person listed, followed by "et al." (meaning "and others") in your lead-in:

> Blair et al. observe that the fine arts were almost ignored by colonial writers (21).

F. If you refer to more than one work by the same author, include a shortened title in the parenthetical reference:

> (Gould, Mismeasure 138).

G. If the author's name is not given, use a shortened title instead. Be sure to use at least the first word of the full title to send the reader to the proper alphabetized entry on your Works Cited page. The following is a reference to a newspaper article entitled "Environmental Group Calls DuPont's Ads Deceptive":

> The Friends of the Earth claimed that, despite DuPont's television ads about caring for the environment, the company is the "single largest corporate polluter in the United States" ("Environmental Group" F3).

H. On a separate page at the end of the paper, alphabetize your Works Cited list for all sources mentioned in your paper. Use *hanging indention;* that is, after the first line of each entry, indent the other lines five spaces.

I. Omit any mention of *page* or *pages* or *line* or *lines*. Do not even include abbreviations for these terms. Use numbers alone:

> Kinsley, Michael. "Continental Divide" Time 7 Jul. 1997: 89–91.

J. Shorten publishers' names: for example, use Prentice instead of Prentice Hall or Norton instead of W. W. Norton and Co. or Oxford UP instead of Oxford University Press or U of Illinois P instead of University of Illinois Press. See sample entries 1 through 13.

K. Use *lowercase* roman numerals (ii, xiv) for citing page numbers from a preface, introduction, or table of contents; use roman numerals in names of monarchs (Elizabeth II).

L. Use raised note numbers for *informational notes* only (that is, notes containing material pertinent to your discussion but not precisely to the point). Include these content notes at the end of your paper just before your Works Cited page, and use the heading Notes.

M. Abbreviate months and titles of magazines as shown in the sample entries.

◆ SAMPLE ENTRIES FOR A WORKS CITED LIST

The following models will help you write Works Cited entries for most of the sources you will use. If you use a source not illustrated in these examples, consult the more extensive list of sample entries found in the *MLA Handbook for Writers of Research Papers,* 5th ed., or ask your instructor for guidance.

Books

1. Book by one author

   Chused, Richard H. <u>Private Acts in Public Places: A Social History of Divorce.</u> Philadelphia: U of Pennsylvania P, 1994.

2. Two more books by the same author

   Gould, Stephen Jay. <u>The Mismeasure of Man.</u> New York: Norton, 1981.

   ---. <u>The Panda's Thumb: More Reflections in Natural History.</u> New York: Norton, 1980.

   [Give the author's name in the first entry only. Thereafter, use three hyphens in place of the author's name, followed by a period and the title.]

3. Book by two or three authors

   Anderson, Terry, and Donald Leal. <u>Free Market Environmentalism.</u> Boulder: Westview, 1991.

   McCrum, William, William Cran, and Robert MacNeil. <u>The Story of English.</u> New York: Viking, 1986.

4. Books by more than three authors

   Medhurst, Martin J., et al. <u>Cold War Rhetoric: Strategy, Metaphor, and Ideology.</u> New York: Greenwood, 1990.

   [The phrase *et al.* is an abbreviation for *et alii,* meaning "and others."]

5. Book by an unknown author

   <u>Literacy of Older Adults in America: Results from the National Adult Literacy Survey.</u> Washington: Center for Educ. Statistics, 1987.

6. Book with an editor

   Gallegos, Bee, ed. <u>English: Our Official Language?</u> New York: Wilson, 1994.

   [For a book with two or more editors, use "eds."]

7. Book with an author and an editor

   Whorf, Benjamin. <u>Language, Thought, and Reality: Selected Writings of Benjamin Lee Whorf.</u> Ed. J. B. Carroll. Cambridge: MIT P, 1956.

8. Book by a group or corporate author

   National Research Council. <u>The Social Impact of AIDS in the United States.</u> New York: National Academy P, 1993.

   [When a corporation, organization, or group is listed as the author on the title page, cite it as you would a person.]

9. Work in a collection or anthology

> Gordon, Mary. "The Parable of the Cave." The Writer on Her Work. Ed. Janet Sternburg. New York: Norton, 1980. 27–32.

10. Work reprinted in a collection or anthology

> Sage, George H. "Sport in American Society: Its Pervasiveness and Its Study." Sport and American Society. 3rd ed. Reading: Addison-Wesley, 1980. 4–15. Rpt. in Physical Activity and the Social Sciences. Ed. W. N. Widmeyer. 5th ed. Ithaca: Movement, 1983. 42–52.

> [First give complete data for the earlier publication; then add "Rpt. in" and give the reprinted source.]

11. Multivolume work

> Blom, Eric, ed. Grove's Dictionary of Music and Musicians. 5th ed. 10 vols. New York: St. Martin's, 1961.

12. Reprinted (republished) book

> Jespersen, Otto. Growth and Structure of the English Language. 1938. Chicago: U of Chicago P, 1980.

13. Later (second or subsequent) edition

> Gibaldi, Joseph. MLA Handbook for Writers of Research Papers. 5th ed. New York: MLA, 1999.

14. Book in translation

> Grmek, Mirko D. History of AIDS: Emergence and Origin of a Modern Pandemic. Trans. Russell C. Maulitz and Jacalyn Duffin. Princeton: Princeton UP, 1990.

Newspapers

15. Signed newspaper article

> Krebs, Emilie. "Sewer Backups Called No Problem." Pantagraph [Bloomington] 20 Nov. 1985: A3.

> [If the city is not part of the name of a local newspaper, give the city in brackets, not underlined, after the newspaper's name.]

> Weiner, Jon. "Vendetta: The Government's Secret War Against John Lennon." Chicago Tribune 5 Aug. 1984, sec 3:1.

> [Note the difference between "A3" in the first example and "sec. 3:1" in the second. Both refer to section and page, but each newspaper indicates the section in a different way. Give the section designation and page number exactly as they appear in the publication.]

16. Unsigned newspaper article

    "No Power Line-Cancer Link Found." Chicago Tribune 3 Jul. 1997,
    final ed., sec. 1: 5.

    [If an edition is specified on the paper's masthead, name the edition
    (late ed., natl ed., final ed.) after the date and before the page ref-
    erence. Different editions of the same issue of a newspaper contain
    different material.]

17. Letter to the editor

    Kessler, Ralph. "Orwell Defended." Letter. New York Times Book
    Review 15 Dec. 1985: 26.

18. Editorial

    "From Good News to Bad." Editorial. Washington Post 16 Jul.
    1984: 10.

Magazines and Journals

19. Article from a monthly or bimonthly magazine

    Lawren, Bill. "1990's Designer Beasts." Omni Nov.–Dec. 1985: 56–61.

    Rosenbaum, Dan, and David Sparrow. "Speed Demons: Widebody
    Rackets." World Tennis Aug. 1989: 48–49.

20. Article from a weekly or biweekly magazine (signed and unsigned)

    Coghlan, Andy. "Warring Parents Harm Children as Much as
    Divorce." New Scientist 15 Jun. 1991: 24.

    "Warning: 'Love' for Sale." Newsweek 11 Nov. 1985: 39.

21. Article from a journal with continuous pagination throughout the whole
    volume

    Potvin, Raymond, and Che-Fu Lee. "Multistage Path Models of Ado-
    lescent Alcohol and Drug Use." Journal of Studies on Alcohol
    41 (1980): 531–42.

22. Article from a journal that paginates each issue separately or that uses
    only issue numbers

    Holtug, Nils. "Altering Humans: The Case For and Against Human
    Gene Therapy." Cambridge Quarterly of Healthcare Ethics 6.2
    (Spring 1997): 157–60.

    [This notation means volume 6, issue 2.]

Other Sources

23. Book review

> Emery, Robert. Rev. of The Divorce Revolution: The Unexpected Social and Economic Consequences for Women and Children in America by Lenore Weitzman. American Scientist 74 (1986): 662–63.

24. Personal interview or letter

> Ehrenreich, Barbara. Personal interview. 12 Feb. 1995.

> Vidal, Gore. Letter to the author. 2 Jun. 1984.

25. Anonymous pamphlet

> How to Help a Friend with a Drinking Problem. American College Health Assn., 1984.

26. Article from a reference work (signed and unsigned)

> "Psychopharmacology." The Columbia Encyclopedia. 5th ed. 1993.

> Van Doren, Carl. "Samuel Langhorne Clemens." The Dictionary of American Biography. 1958 ed.

> [Treat a dictionary entry or an encyclopedia article like an entry from an anthology, but do not cite the editor of the reference work.]

27. Government publication

> United States Dept. of Labor, Bureau of Statistics. Dictionary of Occupational Titles. 4th ed. Washington: GPO, 1977.

> [GPO stands for Government Printing Office.]

28. Film or videotape

> Citizen Kane. Dir. Orson Welles. Perf. Orson Welles, Joseph Cotton, Dorothy Comingore, and Agnes Moorehead. RKO, 1941. 50th Anniversary Special Edition videorecording: Turner Home Entertainment, 1991.

29. Lecture

> Albee, Edward. "A Dream or a Nightmare?" Illinois State University Fine Arts Lecture. Normal, IL. 18 Mar. 1979.

For any other sources (such as televised shows, performances, advertisements, recordings, works of art), include enough information to permit an interested reader to locate your original source. Be sure to arrange this information in a logical fashion, duplicating as much as possible the order and punctuation of the entries above. To be safe, consult your instructor for suggestions about documenting unusual material.

Electronic Sources

If you use material from a computer database or online source, you need to indicate that you read it in electronic form. In general, follow the style for citing print sources, modifying them as appropriate to the electronic source. Include both the date of electronic publication (if available) and the date you accessed the source. In addition, include the Uniform Resource Locator (URL) in angle brackets. If a URL must be divided between two lines, MLA style requires that you break it only after a slash and not introduce a hyphen at the break. For more detailed information about citing electronic sources, consult *The MLA Handbook for Writers of Research Papers*, 5th ed. (1999) or the MLA's Web site (http://www.mla.org).

30. Article in an online reference book or encyclopedia

> Daniel, Ralph Thomas. "The History of Western Music." Britannica Online: Macropaedia. 1995. Online Encyclopedia Britannica. 14 June 1995. ⟨http//www.eb.com:180/cgi-bin/g:DocF=macro/5004/45/O.html⟩.

31. Article in an online magazine

> Yeoman, Barry. "Into the Closet: Can Therapy Make Gay People Straight?" Salon.com 22 May 2000. 23 May 2000. ⟨http://www.salon.com/health/feature/2000/05/22/exgay/html⟩.

32. Article from an online full-text database

> To cite online material without a URL that you get from a service to which your library subscribes, complete the citation by giving the name of the database (underlined), the library, and the date of access.

> Viviano, Frank. "The New Mafia Order." Mother Jones May–Jun. 1995: 44–56. InfoTrac Expanded Academic Index ASAP. Eastern Ill. U Lib. 17 Jul. 1995.

33. Article from a commercial online service

> Howell, Vicki, and Bob Carlton. "Growing up Tough: New Generation Fights for Its Life: Inner-City Youths Live by Rule of Vengeance." Birmingham News. 29 Aug. 1993: 1A+. Lexis-Nexis. Eastern Ill. U Lib. 26 Apr. 1997.

> [Lexis-Nexis is both the database and the name of the online service.]

34. Material accessed on a CD-ROM

> Shakespeare. Editions and Adaptations of Shakespeare. Interactive multimedia. Cambridge, UK: Chadwick-Healey, 1995. CD-ROM. Alexandria: Electronic Book Technologies, 1995.

> "Silly." The Oxford English Dictionary. 2nd ed. CD-ROM. Oxford: Oxford UP, 1992.

35. Web site

> Cummings, Shelly. "Genetic Testing and the Insurance Industry."
> <u>Electronic Genetics Newsletter</u> 18 Mar. 1996 17:442. 23 Dec.
> 1997. ⟨http://www.westpub.com/Educate/mathsci/insure.htm⟩.

36. Message posted to a discussion list

> Morris, Richard. "Teaching Cause-Effect Thinking." Online posting.
> 10 Aug. 2001. Writing Discussion List. 15 Aug. 2001. ⟨news:
> comp.edu.writing.instruction⟩.

> [Include a title or description of the posting, the date of the posting,
> the name of the discussion forum, the date of access, and the
> URL or e-mail address of the list's moderator or supervisor in angle
> brackets.]

◆ SAMPLE STUDENT RESEARCH PAPER

The following documented essay was written by Jessie Everts, a student at Iowa State University. Primarily a cause-and-effect analysis, the essay also includes definition, classification, comparison, and exemplification. Jessie follows the conventions of MLA documentation style. The annotations call your attention to certain features of this style. To make room for the annotations, the essay has been reproduced in a narrower format than you will have on a standard (8½-by-11 inch) sheet of paper.

Everts 1

Jessie Everts
Professor Day
Psychology 102
8 April 2001

Stop in the Name of Love:
Fear of Intimacy and Its Causes

Give your paper a title that suggests not only the topic but also your point of view or main idea.

Some people shiver with delight when a loved one touches them; others shiver with terror. Some welcome an evening alone with their significant other; others want to invite several friends along. Some people have dreams of their wedding day; others call them nightmares.

Fear of intimacy is a troubling condition, both for those who endure it, and for those who try to understand and help its victims. There is no single definition of this problem--it shows up in many ways. As author Eric Berne explains, some people have trouble sharing feelings, while others feel uneasy or panicky in romantic scenarios--and may even avoid affectionate physical contact altogether (32). Experts on interpersonal relations stress the need for love, acceptance, commitment, and intimacy as the keys to happiness and fulfillment. How, then, do we explain people who shun love, who shrink away from commitment and serious relationships?

The 32 is the exact page number on which the information in the sentence originally appeared.

Everts 2

Your last name and page number are typed one-half inch from top of each page.

Very little research has been done on "fear of intimacy" or "fear of commitment," mainly because they are not officially recognized diseases or phobias. There are no approved measurement tools, no defined populations, no treatments or therapies for these conditions (Stein et al. 33). Yet a large number of people avoid intimate relationships. Psychologists and counselors need to better understand this condition in order to help these individuals to cope and recover.

Until recently, fears about relationships have been explained by "attachment theory." "Attachment theory," says G. Scott Acton of the Langley Porter Psychiatric Institute, "is meant to describe and explain people's enduring patterns of relationships from birth to death." It was first studied in nonhuman animals, then in human infants, and later in human adults (Acton 1). Developed by John Bowlby of the Tavistock Clinic in London, attachment theory examines the relationships people form as infants with the protective figures in their lives. According to Bowlby, patterns of responses to the presence and absence of a guardian are termed "attachment style" and become an essential part of our psychological makeup (18). As Marjory Roberts

Wherever possible, give the credentials and titles of the people you quote.

Everts 3

explains in *Psychology Today*, "Infants talk baby talk, cooing and gurgling to their parents. When mom and dad leave, babies cry and carry on until their return. Grown-ups in love are not so different" (22). Thus, babies who consistently show signs of distress when separated from their mothers but recover when the mothers return are said to have a secure, healthy attachment style.

Researchers have applied this attachment theory to adult relationships. In two recent studies, psychologist Phillip Shaver and research associate Cindy Hazan found that "the kind of attachment people form with their parents during childhood could affect their romantic relationships and beliefs about love they form as adults" (511). Based on their findings, they divided people into three groups: "securely attached" people, who believe it's easy to get close to others; "avoidant" people, who feel uneasy when others get too close to them; and "anxious/ambivalent" people, who want a level of closeness that many partners don't seem willing to give (522). Thus, fear of intimacy is a reflection of poor attachment formation in childhood.

Rather than trying to explain the causes of the fear of intimacy, some researchers have looked at the

Notice that the quotation marks close the sentence. The parenthetical citation then appears, followed by the period to close the whole thing.

Everts 4

behavior itself. Their observations
vary. Anne Schaef, for example,
believes that individuals who fear
intimacy attempt to avoid it by
entering into what she calls
"pseudo-relationships"--ones that are
superficial and lack true closeness
(24). A pseudo-relationship provides
a feeling of security and normalcy,
while protecting the fearful
individual from true intimacy. Berne
also describes false types of
relationships that can result when
one partner fears intimacy (203). He
says they take the form of "games"--
patterns of interactions that have a
concealed motive. According to
Berne, people regulate or invent
emotions to achieve an ulterior
purpose, to maintain distance, or to
avoid self-disclosure. These games
substitute for close relationships
and distract fearful individuals
from admitting their problem with
intimacy (210-11).

  If fear of intimacy inspires
ingenious ways of avoiding it, then
how can people overcome this fear?
They can start by breaking down
their defenses. People develop their
defenses and negative beliefs in
childhood in order to protect
themselves against emotional pain
and, later, against anxiety about
death. According to Robert Firestone
and Joyce Catlett, coauthors of Fear
of Intimacy, a core defense that

When you give the name of the person or author you're using and you place a parenthetical citation at the end of the same sentence put only the page number in the parentheses.

This citation shows that the information in the last two sentences came from pages 210–11 of Berne's book. Provide just the pages you use.

Everts 5

often leads to the downfall of a
partnership is the "fantasy bond"
(164-66). This is an illusion of a
connection to another person,
developed first with the mother or
primary parent figure. People often
try to re-create it in their adult
relationships by selecting a partner
who fits their model, someone they
can relate to in the same way they
related to their parent. But they
usually distort their perception to
make the partner more like the
parent than he or she really is. If
all else fails, they try to provoke
their partner into the behavior they
seek.

A secondary defense that helps
preserve the fantasy bond, according
to Firestone and Catlett, is "the
voice" (7). All people tend to
carry on a kind of internal
dialogue with themselves as
though another person were talking:
reprimanding them, denouncing
them, divulging negative information
about others, and so on. In intimate
relationships both individuals may
be listening to the demands of
their respective voices. These
demands, unfortunately, only create
more defensiveness, since both
partners may use rationalizations
promoted by "the voice" to ward off
loving responses and justify their
distancing behavior (Firestone and
Catlett 227-30).

Notice that there is
no punctuation
between the
author's name and
the page number,
just a space.

Everts 6

A technique developed by Dr.
Firestone to reverse the process and
allow greater intimacy is "voice
therapy" (228-29). By bringing
hidden negative thoughts to the
conscious level, this procedure
helps each individual to identify
the "voice attacks" that are
creating conflict and distance in
their relationship (245-47).
Partners who can identify specific
self-criticisms as well as
judgmental and hostile thoughts
about each other are able to relate
more openly. Professor Firestone
explains the process:

> Clients discuss their
> spontaneous insights and
> their reactions to
> verbalizing the voice. They
> then attempt to understand
> the relationship between
> their voice attacks and
> their self-destructive
> behavior patterns. They
> subsequently develop insight
> into the limitations they
> impose on themselves in
> everyday life functions.
> (246)

If you use more
than four typed lines
of direct quotation
from a source,
indent all the lines
ten spaces (or one
inch) from the left
margin. Don't use
quotation marks
around the indented
material.

The period follows
the quotation in this
block form.

Changing old patterns often
produces anxiety, so part of the
treatment process is to learn to
tolerate anxiety and work through
it. The goal is to sustain the

changes and ultimately to increase
intimacy.

People always have choices to
make about intimacy--from the
partners they choose to the way they
interact with them each day.
Recognizing patterns of behavior,
tolerating anxieties, and working
together on relationships will help
them to overcome their fears of
intimacy. Learning how best to treat
and communicate with one another
will help everyone to enjoy loving,
lasting relationships.

Everts 8

Works Cited

Acton, G. Scott. "Attachment
  Theory." Great Ideas in
  Personality. 15 Apr. 2001.
  ⟨http://www.personalityresearch.
  org/attachment.html⟩.
Berne, Eric. Games People Play: The
  Psychology of Human Relationships.
  New York: Grove, 1964.
Bowlby, John. The Making and
  Breaking of Affectional Bonds.
  London: Tavistock, 1979.
Firestone, Robert W., and Joyce
  Catlett. Fear of Intimacy.
  Washington: APA, 1999.
Roberts, Majory. "Baby Love."
  Psychology Today Mar. 1987: 22.
  InfoTrac Expanded Academic Index
  ASAP. Iowa State Univ. Lib.,
  Ames. 19 Apr. 2001.
Schaef, Anne Wilson. Escape from
  Intimacy: The Pseudo-Relationship
  Addictions. New York:
  HarperCollins, 1989.
Shaver, Phillip, and Cindy Hazan.
  "Romantic Love Conceptualized as
  an Attachment Process." Journal
  of Personality and Social
  Psychology 52 (1987): 511-24.
  OCLS FirstSearch. Iowa State
  Univ. Lib., Ames. 19 Apr. 2001.
Stein, Henry, et al. "What Do Adult
  Attachment Scales Measure?"
  Bulletin of the Menninger Clinic
  62 (1998): 33-82.

The Works Cited
form for a book
gives the city of
publication, the
publisher's name,
and the copyright
date, but no page
numbers.

The Roberts article
appeared in print in
Psychology Today
but was accessed
online through
InfoTrac database.

With multiple
authors, reverse the
order of only the
first author's name.

In the Works Cited
listing for a printed
article, give the
number for the
whole span of the
article, even if you
used material from
only one or a few
pages. This article
spanned pages
33–82.

Glossary

◆ ◆ ◆ ◆ ◆

Abstract words: language that refers to ideas, conditions, and qualities that cannot be observed directly through the five senses. Words such as *beauty, love, joy, wealth, cruelty, power,* and *justice* are abstract. In his essay (p. 258), Andrew Holleran explores the abstract term *fear,* offering a series of concrete examples and incidents to make the meaning clearer. *Also see* Concrete words.

Active reading: *See* Engaged reading.

Allusion: a passing reference to a familiar person, place, or object in history, myth, or literature. Writers use allusions to enrich or illuminate their ideas. For instance, in his essay about African-American men, Michel Marriott makes an allusion to lynching when he describes his father as "a proud Black man dangling from a leafless tree of opportunities denied" (p. 255). And when Jessica Mitford writes "Alas, Poor Yorick!" (p. 199), she's alluding to the skull of an old friend that Shakespeare's Hamlet discovers in the graveyard.

Analogy: a comparison that uses a familiar or concrete item to explain an abstract or unfamiliar concept. For example, a geologist might compare the structure of the earth's crust to the layers of an onion or a nature writer might describe the effect of pollution on the environment by comparing it to cancer in the human body. See the introduction to Chapter 9.

Anecdote: a brief story about an amusing or interesting event, usually told to illustrate an idea or support a point. Writers also use anecdotes to begin essays, as Rebecca Kirkendall does in "Who's a Hillbilly?" (p. 234) or Deborah Tannen does in "Sex, Lies, and Conversation" (p. 351).

Antonym: a word that has the opposite meaning of another word. For example, *wet* is an antonym of *dry, coarse* is an antonym of *smooth,* and *cowardly* is an antonym of *brave.*

Argumentation: a type of writing in which the author tries to influence the reader's thinking on a controversial topic. See the introduction to Chapter 11.

Audience: the readers for whom a piece of writing is intended. Many essays are aimed at a general audience, but a writer can focus on a specific group of readers. For example, Anne Lamott directs her essay "Shitty First Drafts" (p. 140) to writers and would-be writers, and Bud Herron addresses cat owners in "Cat Bathing as a Martial Art" (p. 178).

Block-by-block pattern: an organizational pattern used in comparison and contrast writing. In this method, a writer presents, in a block, all the important points about the first item to be compared and then presents, in another block, the corresponding points about the second item to be compared. See the introduction to Chapter 9.

Brainstorming: a method for generating ideas for writing. In brainstorming, a writer jots down a list of as many details and ideas on a topic as possible without stopping to evaluate or organize them. See Chapter 2.

Cause and effect: the rhetorical strategy that allows a writer to interpret the meaning of events by focusing on reasons and/or consequences. See the introduction to Chapter 10.

Causes: the reasons or explanations for why something happens. Causes can be *immediate* or *indirect.* See the introduction to Chapter 10.

Chronological order: the arrangement of events according to time—that is, in the sequence in which they happened.

Classification: the process of sorting items or ideas into meaningful groups or categories. See the introduction to Chapter 8.

Cliché: a phrase or expression that has lost its originality or force through overuse. To illustrate, novelist and teacher Janet Burroway writes: "Clichés are *the last word* in bad writing, and it's *a crying shame* to see all you *bright young things* spoiling your *deathless prose* with phrases *as old as the hills.* You must *keep your nose to the grindstone,* because the *sweet smell of success* only comes to those who *march to the tune of a different drummer.*"

Clustering: a method of exploring a topic and generating material in which a writer groups ideas visually by putting the main point or topic in the center of a page, circling it, and surrounding it with words or phrases that identify the major points to be discussed. The writer creates new clusters by circling these points and surrounding them with additional words and phrases. See Chapter 2.

Coherence: the logical flow of ideas in a piece of writing. A writer achieves coherence by having a clear thesis and by making sure that all the supporting details relate to that thesis. Coherence within paragraphs is established with a clear topic sentence and maintained with transitions, pronoun reference, parallelism, and intentional repetition. *Also see* Unity.

Colloquial language: conversational words and expressions that are sometimes used in writing to add color and authenticity. Mike Royko (p. 44), Judy Brady (p. 239), Stephanie Ericsson (p. 296), and Stephen King (p. 406) all use colloquial language to good effect in their writing. *Also see* Informal writing.

Comparison and contrast: a strategy of writing in which an author points out the similarities and differences between two or more subjects. See the introduction to Chapter 9.

Conclusion: the sentences and paragraphs that bring an essay to its close. In the conclusion, a writer may restate the thesis, sum up complex and important ideas, emphasize the topic's significance, make a generalization, offer a solution to a problem, or encourage the reader to take some action. Whatever the strategy, a conclusion should end the essay in a firm and definite way.

Concrete words: language that refers to real objects that can be seen, heard, tasted, touched, or smelled. Words like *tree, desk, car, orange, Chicago, Roseanne,* or *jogging* are concrete. Concrete examples make abstractions easier to understand, as in "Contentment is a well-fed cat asleep in the sun." *Also see* Abstract words.

Connotation and denotation: terms used to describe the different kinds of meaning that words convey. **Denotation** refers to the most specific or direct meaning of a word, the dictionary definition. **Connotations** are the feelings or associations that attach themselves to words. For example, *assertive* and *pushy* share a similar denotation—both mean "strong" or "forceful"— but their differing connotations suggest different attitudes: an assertive person is admirable; a pushy person is offensive.

Controlling idea: *See* Thesis.

Conventions: customs or generally accepted practices. The conventions of writing an essay require a title, a subject, a thesis, a pattern of organization, transitions, and paragraph breaks.

Definition: a method of explaining a word or term so that the reader understands what the writer means. Writers use a variety of methods for defining words and terms; see the introduction to Chapter 7.

Denotation: *See* Connotation and denotation.

Description: writing that uses sensory details to create a word picture for the reader. See the introduction to Chapter 4.

Details: specific pieces of information (examples, incidents, dates, statistics, descriptions, and the like) that explain and support the general ideas in a piece of writing.

Development: the techniques and materials that a writer uses to expand and build on a general idea or topic.

Dialogue: speech or conversation recorded in writing. Dialogue, which is commonly found in narrative writing, reveals character and adds life and authenticity to an essay.

Diction: choice of words in writing or speaking.

Discovery: the first stage in the writing process. It may include finding a topic, exploring the topic, determining purpose and audience, probing ideas, reading and doing research, and planning and organizing material. Discovery usually involves writing and is aided considerably by putting preliminary thoughts and plans in writing. See the introduction to Chapter 3.

Division: the process of breaking a large subject into its components or parts. Division is often used in combination with classification. See the introduction to Chapter 8.

Dominant impression: the main idea or feeling that a writer wants to convey in an extended description: that a teacher is competent and well liked, for example, or that an event is terrifying. See the introduction to Chapter 4.

Drafting: the stage in the writing process during which the writer puts ideas into complete sentences, connects them, and organizes them into a meaningful sequence.

Editing: the last stage in the writing process, during which the writer focuses on the details of mechanics and correctness.

Effects: the results or outcomes of certain events. Effects can be *immediate* or *indirect*. Writers often combine causes and effects in explaining why something happens. See the introduction to Chapter 10.

Ellipsis: an omission of words that is signaled by three equally spaced dots.

Emphasis: the placement of words and ideas in key positions to give them stress and importance. A writer can emphasize a word or idea by putting it at the beginning or end of a paragraph or essay. Emphasis can also be achieved by using repetition, parallelism, and figurative language to call attention to an idea or term.

Engaged reading: the process of getting involved with the reading material. An engaged reader surveys the text, makes predictions, asks questions, writes notes and responses in the margins or in a notebook, rereads difficult passages, and spends time afterward summarizing and reflecting.

Essay: a short prose work on a limited topic. Essays can take many forms, but they usually focus on a central theme or thesis and often convey the writer's personal ideas about the topic.

Euphemism: an inoffensive or polite term used in place of language that readers or listeners might find distasteful, unpleasant, or otherwise objectionable; *passed on* is a euphemism for *died*.

Evidence: *See* Supporting material.

Examples: specific cases or instances used to illustrate or explain a general concept. See the introduction to Chapter 5.

Exemplification: the strategy of development in which a writer uses particular instances to support a general idea or thesis. See the introduction to Chapter 5.

Extended definition: a lengthy exploration of a controversial term or an abstract concept, developed by using one or more of the rhetorical strategies discussed in this book.

Figurative language: words that create images or convey symbolic meaning beyond the literal level. Diane Ackerman, for example, uses figurative language to depict the coming of autumn: "Keen-eyed as leopards, we stand still and squint hard, looking for signs of movement. Early-morning frost sits heavily on the grass, and turns barbed wire into a string of stars. On a distant hill, a small square of yellow appears to be a lighted stage. At last the truth dawns on us: Fall is staggering in, right on schedule. . . ." (See "Why Leaves Turn Color in the Fall," p. 194.)

Figures of speech: deliberate departures from the ordinary, literal use of words to provide fresh perceptions and create lasting impressions. *See* Metaphor, Paradox, Personification, *and* Simile.

First person: the use of *I, me, we,* and *us* in speech and writing to express a personal view or present a firsthand report. *Also see* Point of view.

Flashback: a narrative device that presents material that occurred prior to the opening scene. Various flashback methods—recollections of characters, narration by characters or the narrator, dream sequences, reveries—can be used.

Focus: the narrowing of a topic to a specific aspect or set of features.

Freewriting: a procedure for exploring a topic that involves writing without stopping for a set period of time. See Chapter 2.

General and specific: a way of referring to the level of abstraction in words. A *general* word names a group or a class; a *specific* word refers to an individual member of a group or class. The word *nature* is general, the word *flower* is more specific, and the word *orchid* is even more specific.

Generalization: a broad assertion or conclusion based on specific observations. The value of a generalization is determined by the number and quality of the specific instances.

Illustration: the use of examples, or a single long example, to support or explain an idea. See the introduction to Chapter 5.

Image: a description that appeals to a reader's senses of sight, smell, sound, touch, or taste. Images add interest and clarify meaning. See the introduction to Chapter 4.

Immediate causes and effects: the reasons and consequences that are the most obvious; also called *direct* or *proximate* causes and effects. See the introduction to Chapter 10.

Indirect causes and effects: the reasons and consequences that are not easily perceived. Indirect causes are also called *remote* or *underlying* causes; indirect effects may also be called *long-term* effects. See the introduction to Chapter 10.

Inference: a conclusion drawn by a reader from the hints and suggestions provided by the writer. Writers sometimes express ideas indirectly rather than stating them outright; readers must use their own experience and knowledge to read between the lines and make inferences to gather the full meaning of a selection.

Informal writing: the familiar, everyday level of usage, which includes contractions and perhaps slang but requires standard grammar and punctuation. Dereck Williamson (p. 188) uses an informal style to entertain and engage his readers while telling them how to hang wallpaper.

Introduction: the beginning or opening of an essay, which usually presents the topic, arouses interest, and prepares the reader for the development of the thesis.

Irony: the use of words to express the opposite of what is stated. Writers use irony to expose unpleasant truths or to poke fun at human weakness.

Jargon: the specialized or technical language of a trade, profession, or similar group. To readers outside the group, however, jargon can be inaccessible and meaningless.

Journalistic style: the kind of writing found in newspapers and popular magazines. It normally employs informal diction with relatively simple sentences and unusually short paragraphs. Many of the selections in this book first appeared as columns and articles in magazines or newspapers.

Logical order: the arrangement of points and ideas according to some reasonable principle or scheme (e.g., from least important to most important).

Main idea: *See* Thesis.

Metaphor: a figure of speech in which a word or phrase that ordinarily refers to one thing is applied to something else, thus making an implied comparison. For example, Mark Twain writes of "the language of this water" and says the river "turned to blood" ("Two Views of the Mississippi," p. 89). Similarly, Phillip Lopate says "Friendship is a long conversation" (p. 308), and Bill Scott Russell Sanders writes of "what a prison a house could be" (p. 362).

An **extended metaphor** may serve as a controlling image for a whole work, as indicated in this opening sentence from Sue Hubbell's essay about truck stops: "In the early morning there is a city of the mind that stretches from coast to coast, from border to border. Its cross streets are the interstate highways[. . .]. Its citizens are all-night divers, the truckers, and the waitresses at the stops" (p. 134).

A **dead metaphor** is an implied comparison that has become so familiar that we accept it as literal: the arm of a chair, the leg of a table, the hands of a clock. A **mixed metaphor** runs two metaphors together in an illogical way: "the wheels of justice are coming apart at the seams."

Modes: *See* Rhetorical strategies.

Narration: writing that recounts an event or series of interrelated events; presentation of a story to illustrate an idea or make a point. See the introduction to Chapter 3.

Objective and subjective: terms that refer to the way a writer handles a subject. Objective writing presents the facts without including the writer's own feelings and attitudes. Subjective writing, on the other hand, reveals the author's personal opinions and emotions.

Onomatopoeia: the use of words that suggest or echo the sounds they are describing; *hiss, plop,* and *sizzle* are examples.

Order: the sequence in which the information or ideas in an essay are presented. *Also see* Chronological order *and* Logical order.

Parable: an illustrative story that teaches a lesson or points out a moral. In Christian countries, the most famous parables are those told by Jesus, the best known of which is that of the Prodigal Son.

Paradox: a seeming contradiction that may nonetheless be true. Examples are "Less is more" and "The simplest writing is usually the hardest to do."

Paragraph: a series of two or more related sentences. Paragraphs are units of meaning; they signal a division or shift in thought. In newspapers and magazines, paragraph divisions occur frequently, primarily to break up the narrow columns of print and make the articles easier to read.

Parallelism: the presentation of two or more equally important ideas in similar grammatical form. Writers use parallelism to organize their ideas and give them force, as William Lutz does in this sequence of parallel sentences: "Doublespeak is language that pretends to communicate but really doesn't. It is language that makes the bad seem good, the negative appear positive, the unpleasant appear attractive or at least tolerable. Doublespeak is language that avoids or shifts responsibility, language that is at variance with its real or purported meaning" (p. 283).

Patterns of organization: *See* Rhetorical strategies.

Person: *See* Point of view.

Personification: a figure of speech in which an inanimate object or an abstract concept is given human qualities; for example, "Hunger sat shivering on the road" or "Flowers danced on the lawn." In "Two Views of the Mississippi" (p. 89), Mark Twain refers to the "river's face" and describes the river as a subtle and dangerous enemy.

Persuasion: writing that attempts to move readers to action or to influence them to agree with a position or belief.

Point-by-point pattern: an organizational pattern used in comparison and contrast writing. In this method (also called the *alternating method*), the writer moves back and forth between two subjects, focusing on particular features of each in turn: the first point or feature of subject A is followed by the first point or feature of subject B, and so on. See the introduction to Chapter 9.

Point of view: the angle or perspective from which a story or topic is presented. Personal essays often take a first-person (or "I") point of view and sometimes address the reader as "you" (second person). The more formal third person ("he," "she," "it," "one," "they") is used to create distance and suggest objectivity.

Previewing: the first step in engaged reading in which the reader prepares to read by looking over the text and making preliminary judgments and predictions about what to expect.

Prewriting: the process that writers use to prepare for the actual writing stage by gathering information, considering audience and purpose, developing a provisional thesis, and mapping out a tentative plan.

Problem-solution: a strategy for analyzing and developing an argument in which the writer identifies a problem within the topic and offers a solution (or solutions) to it. See the introduction to Chapter 11.

Process writing: a rhetorical strategy in which a writer explains the step-by-step procedure for doing something. See the introduction to Chapter 6.

Purpose: the writer's reasons for writing; what the writer wants to accomplish in an essay.

Refutation: in argumentation, the process of acknowledging and responding to opposing views. See the introduction to Chapter 11.

Revising: the stage in the writing process during which the author makes changes in focus, organization, development and style to make the writing more effective. See Chapter 2.

Rhetorical question: a question that a writer or speaker asks to emphasize or introduce a point and usually goes on to answer. Lee Smith uses a series of rhetorical questions to launch his discussion of memory: "Why do our memories betray us? Is this a precursor of Alzheimer's or some other serious mental disorder? How can some people command a loyal and prodigious memory well into old age? Are there ways to make everyone's memory clear again?" (p. 315).

Rhetorical strategies: patterns for presenting and developing ideas in writing. Some of these patterns relate to basic ways of thinking (classification, cause and effect, problem-solution), whereas others reflect the most common means for presenting material (narration, comparison and contrast, process) or developing ideas (exemplification, definition, description) in writing.

Sarcasm: obviously insincere and biting irony, often used to express strong disapproval.

Satire: writing that uses wit and irony to attack and expose human folly, weakness, and stupidity. Judy Brady (p. 239) and Katha Pollitt (p. 505) use satire to question human behavior and criticize contemporary values.

Sexist language: words and phrases that stereotype or ignore members of either gender. For example, the sentence "A doctor must finish his residency before he can begin to practice" suggests that only men are doctors. Writing in the plural will avoid this exclusion: "Doctors must finish their residencies before they can begin to practice." The terms *mailman, stewardess, manpower,* and *mothering* are also sexist; the gender-neutral terms *mail carrier, flight attendant, workforce,* and *parenting* are preferred.

Simile: a figure of speech in which two essentially unlike things are compared, usually in a phrase introduced by *like* or *as*. For example, in "Shitty First Drafts," Anne Lamott uses several similes to make the point that few writers know what they want to say before they begin to write: "[Writers] do not type a few stiff warm-up sentences and then find themselves bounding along *like* huskies across the snow [. . .]. We all often feel *like* we are pulling teeth, even those writers whose prose ends up being the most natural and fluid. The right words and sentences just do not come pouring out *like* ticker tape most of the time" (p. 141).

Slang: the informal language of a given group or locale, often characterized by racy, colorful expressions and short-lived usage.

Specific: *See* General and specific.

Structure: the general plan, framework, or pattern of a piece of writing.

Style: individuality of expression, achieved in writing through selection and arrangement of words, sentences, and punctuation.

Subject: what a piece of writing is about.

Subjective: *See* Objective and subjective.

Supporting material: facts, figures, details, examples, reasoning, expert testimony, personal experiences, and the like, which are used to develop and explain the general ideas in a piece of writing.

Symbol: a concrete or material object that suggests or represents an abstract idea, quality, or concept. For example, the lion is a symbol of courage, a voyage or journey can symbolize life, water suggests spirituality, and dryness stands for the absence of spirituality. In E. B. White's "Once More to the Lake" (p. 114), the lake comes to symbolize the author's awareness of his own mortality.

Synonym: a word that means the same or nearly the same as another word. *Sad* is a synonym of *unhappy*. *Also see* Antonym.

Thesis: the main point or proposition that a writer develops and supports in an essay. The thesis is often stated early, usually in the first paragraph, to give the reader a clear indication of the essay's main idea.

Third person: the point of view in which a writer uses *he, she, it, one,* and *they* to give the reader a less limited and more seemingly objective account than a first-person view would provide. *Also see* Point of view.

Title: the heading that a writer gives to an article or essay. The title usually catches the reader's attention and indicates what the selection is about.

Tone: the attitude that a writer conveys toward the subject matter. Tone can be serious or humorous, critical or sympathetic, affectionate or hostile, sarcastic or soothing, passionate or detached—or any of numerous other attitudes.

Topic sentence: the sentence in which the main idea of a paragraph is stated. Writers often state the topic sentence first and develop the rest of the paragraph in support of this main idea. Sometimes a writer will build up to the topic sentence and place it at the end of a paragraph.

Transitions: words and expressions such as *for example, on the other hand, next,* or *to illustrate* that help the reader to see the connections between points and ideas. Pronouns, repeated words and phrases, and parallel structure also help to link sentences or paragraphs and to point out relationships within them.

Understatement: a type of irony that deliberately represents a point or idea as less than it is so as to stress its importance or seriousness.

Unity: the fitting together of all elements in a piece of writing; sticking to the point. *Also see* Coherence.

Usage: the way a word or phrase is normally spoken or written.

Voice: the expression of a writer's personality in his or her writing; an author's distinctive style or manner of writing.

Writing process: the series of steps that most writers follow in producing a piece of writing. The five major stages in the writing process are finding a topic and generating ideas (discovering), focusing on a main idea and mapping out an approach (organizing), preparing a rough draft (drafting), reworking and improving the draft (revising), and proofreading and correcting errors (editing).

Acknowledgments

Diane Ackerman, "Why the Leaves Turn Color in the Fall" from *A Natural History of the Senses*. Copyright © 1990 by Diane Ackerman. Used by permission of Random House, Inc.

Jonathan Alter, "The Death Penalty," from *Newsweek,* June 12, 2000. Copyright © 2000 Newsweek, Inc. All right reserved. Reprinted by permission.

Maya Angelou, "From Day to Night: Picking Cotton" [Editors' title.] from *I Know Why the Caged Bird Sings*. Copyright © 1969 and renewed 1997 by Maya Angelou. Reprinted with the permission of Random House, Inc.

Judy Brady, "I Want a Wife" from *Ms.* (December 31, 1971). Copyright © 1970 by Judy Brady. Reprinted with the permission of the author.

Judith Ortiz Cofer, "The Myth of the Latin Woman: I Just Met a Girl Named Maria" from *The Latin Deli*. Copyright © 1993 by The University of Georgia Press. Reprinted with the permission.

David Cole, "Five Myths about Immigration" from *The Nation* (October 17, 1994). Reprinted with the permission.

Joan Didion, "Marrying Absurd" from *Slouching Toward Bethlehem*. Copyright © 1966, 1968, renewed 1996 by Joan Didion. Reprinted by permission of Farrar, Straus and Giroux, LLC.

Claudia Dreifus, "Forgiving the Unforgivable," from *My Generation,* No. 3, July–August 2001, pp. 56–59. Reprinted with permission from Claudia Dreifus.

Barbara Ehrenreich, "In Defense of Talk Shows." From *Time,* December 4, 1995. Copyright © 1995 Time Inc. Reprinted by permission.

Stephanie Ericsson, "The Ways We Lie." Copyright © 1992 by Stephanie Ericsson. Originally published in the *Utne Reader*. Permission granted by Rhoda Weyr Agency, NY. Stephanie Ericsson is also the author of *Companion Through the Darkness: Inner Dialogues on Grief,* published by HarperCollins.

Sue Ferguson, "The Wired Teen." From *MacLean's Magazine,* May 29, 2000, p. 38. Copyright © 2000 by MacLean's Magazine. Reprinted by permission.

William Finnegan, "Pole Vaulting." Reprinted by permission of International Creative Management, Inc. Copyright © 2000 by William Finnegan. First appeared in *The New Yorker,* August 21–28, 2000 issue.

E.M. Forster, "My Wood" from *Abinger Harvest.* Copyright © 1936 and renewed 1964 by Edward Morgan Forster. Reprinted with the permission of Harcourt, Inc. and Edward Arnold Publishers.

Anne Frank, from *The Diary of Anne Frank: The Critical Edition* by Anne Frank, copyright © 1986 by Anne Frank-Fonds, Basel/Switzerland, for all texts of Anne Frank. Used by permission of Doubleday, a division of Random House, Inc.

Ian Frazier, "Street Scene: Minor Heroism in a Major Metropolitan Area" from *The Atlantic Monthly* (February 1995). Copyright © 1995 by Ian Frazier. Reprinted with the permission of The Wylie Agency.

Ian Frazier, "SuAnne Marie Big Crow" [Editors' title] excerpt from *On the Rez* by Ian Frazier. Copyright © 2000 by Ian Frazier. Reprinted by permission of Farrar, Straus and Giroux, LLC.

Emilie Gallant, "White Breast Flats" from Beth Brant (ed.), *A Gathering of Spirit: A Collection by North American Indian Women.* Copyright © 1984 by Firebrand Books, Milford, Connecticut.

Henry Louis Gates Jr., "In the Kitchen" from *Colored People: A Memoir.* Copyright © 1994 by Henry Louis Gates Jr. Reprinted with the permission of Alfred A. Knopf, a division of Random House, Inc.

Malcolm Gladwell, "The Trouble with French Fries." Reprinted with permission from the author. Originally appeared in *The New Yorker,* March 5, 2001, pp. 52–57. An archive of stories written by Malcolm Gladwell is available at www.gladwell.com.

Ellen Goodman, "The Company Man" from *Close to Home.* Copyright © 1979 by The Washington Post Company. Reprinted with the permission of Simon & Schuster.

Andrew Hacker, "Dividing American Society" from *Two Nations: Black and White, Separate, Hostile, Unequal.* Copyright © 1992 by Andrew Hacker. Reprinted with the permission of Scribner, a division of Simon & Schuster, Inc.

Jeanne Heaton, "Tuning in Trouble: Talk TV's Destructive Impact on Mental Health" from *Ms.* (September/October 1995). Originally published in *Tuning in Trouble: Talk TV's Destructive Impact on Mental Health.* Copyright © 1995 by Jossey-Bass, Inc. Reprinted with the permission of John Wiley & Sons, Inc.

Howard Herron, "Cat Bathing as a Martial Art." Copyright © 1983 by Howard Herron. Reprinted by permission of the author.

Andrew Holleran, "The Fear" from John Preston (ed.), *Personal Dispatches: Writers Confront AIDS.* Copyright © 1989 by John Preston. Reprinted with the permission of St. Martin's Press, LLC.

John Holt, "Three Kinds of Discipline" is reprinted by permission from *Freedom and Beyond* by John Holt. Copyright © 1995, 1972 by Holt Associates. Published by Boynton/Cook, a subsidiary of Reed Elsevier, Inc., Portsmouth, NH.

Denise Noe, "Parallel Worlds: The Surprising Similarities (and Differences) of Country-Western and Rap" from *The Humanist* (July–August 1995). Copyright © 1995 by Denise Noe. Reprinted with the permission of the author.

George Orwell, "Shooting an Elephant" from *Shooting an Elephant and Other Essays.* Copyright 1950 by Sonia Brownell Orwell and renewed 1978 by Sonia Pitt-Rivers. Reprinted with the permission of Harcourt, Inc. and Bill Hamilton as the Literary Executor of the Estate of the late Sonia Brownell Orwell.

Katha Pollitt, "Why Boys Don't Play with Dolls" from *The New York Times* (October 8, 1995). Copyright © 1995 by The New York Times Company. Reprinted by permission. All rights reserved.

Katha Pollitt, "Let's Get Rid of Sports" [Editors' title] from "Subject to Debate" in *The Nation* (July 17–24, 1995). Reprinted with permission from the author.

Laurel Robertson, "Bake Your Bread at Home" [Editors' title] from Laurel Robertson with Carol Flinders and Bronwen Godfrey, *The Laurel's Kitchen Bread Book.* Copyright © 1984 by The Blue Mountain Center for Meditation, Inc. Reprinted with permission of Random House, Inc.

Phyllis Rose, "Shopping and Other Spiritual Adventures in America Today" from *Never Say Good-Bye* by Phyllis Rose. Copyright © 1991 by Phyllis Rose. Reprinted with the author's permission.

Mike Royko, "Jackie's Debut: A Unique Day" from *Slats Grobnik and Some Other Friends.* Copyright © 1973 by Mike Royko. Reprinted with the permission of Sterling Lord Literistic, Inc.

Scott Russell Sanders, "The Men We Carry in Our Minds." Copyright © 1984 by Scott Russell Sanders; first appeared in *Milkweed Chronicle;* reprinted by permission of the author and the author's agent, The Virginia Kidd Agency, Inc.

Steve Silberman, "We're Teen, We're Queer, and We've Got E-mail." This article originally appeared in *Wired,* November 1994, pp. 76–80. Reprinted with permission from Steve Silberman.

Lee Smith, "What We Now Know about Memory" [Editors' title. Originally titled "Memory: Why You're Losing It, How to Save It."] from *Fortune* (April 17, 1995). Reprinted with the permission from Fortune Magazine.

Gary Soto, from *A Summer Life,* pp. 5–8. © 1990. Reprinted by permission from University Press of New England and the author.

Brent Staples, "Just Walk On By: A Black Man Ponders His Ability to Alter Public Space" from *Ms.* (September 1986). Copyright © 1986 by Brent Staples. Reprinted with the permission of the author.

Kathy A. Svitil, "The Greenland Viking Mystery" from *Discover* (July 1997). Copyright *Discover Magazine.* Reprinted by permission from Kathy Svitil.

Amy Tan, "Mother Tongue." Copyright © 1990 by Amy Tan. First appeared in *The Threepenny Review.* Reprinted by permission of the author and the Sandra Dijkstra Literary Agency.

Deborah Tannen, "Gender Gap in Cyberspace" from *Newsweek* (May 16, 1994). This article is based in part on material from *You Just Don't Understand* (Ballantine, 1990). Copyright © 1994 by Deborah Tannen. Reprinted with the permission of the author.

Deborah Tannen, "Sex, Lies and Conversation" from *The Washington Post* (June 14, 1990). This article is based in part on material from *You Just Don't Understand* (Ballantine, 1990). Copyright © 1990 by Deborah Tannen. Reprinted with the permission of the author.

Lewis Thomas, "The Technology of Medicine." Copyright © 1971 by The Massachusetts Medical Society, from *The Lives of a Cell,* by Lewis Thomas. Used by permission of Viking Penguin, a division of Penguin Putnam, Inc.

Sallie Tisdale, "A Weight That Women Carry" from *Harper's* (March 1993). Copyright © 1993 by *Harper's Magazine.* All rights reserved. Reprinted from the March issue by special permission.

Luis Alberto Urrea, "Life and Hard Times on the Mexican Border," from *Across the Wire: Life & Hard Times.* Copyright © 1993 by Luis Alberto Urrea. Used by permission of Doubleday, a division of Random House, Inc.

Lindsy Van Gelder, "Marriage as a Restricted Club" from *Ms. Magazine* (February 1984). Copyright © 1984 by Lindsy Van Gelder. Reprinted with the permission of the author.

Alice Walker, "In Search of Our Mothers' Gardens" from *In Search of Our Mothers' Gardens: Womanist Prose,* copyright © 1974 by Alice Walker, reprinted by permission of Harcourt, Inc.

E. B. White, "Once More to the Lake" from *One Man's Meat.* Copyright © 1941 by E. B. White. Reprinted with the permission of Tilbury House, Publishers, Gardiner, Maine.

Dereck Williamson, "Wall Covering" from *The Complete Book of Pitfalls: A Victim's Guide to Repairs, Maintenance, and Repairing the Maintenance.* Copyright © 1971 by Dereck Williamson. Reprinted with the permission of the author.

Thad Williamson, "Bad as They Wanna Be." Reprinted with permission from the August 10, 1998 issue of *The Nation.*

Amy Wu, "Young Cyber Addicts." From *Minutes of the Lead Pencil Club: Pulling the Plug on the Electronic Revolution,* edited by Bill Henderson, pp. 91–96. Copyright © by Pushcart Press. Reprinted by permission.

Index